Man and Society

VOLUME TWO

MAN AND SOCIETY

*A Critical Examination of
Some Important Social and Political Theories from
Machiavelli to Marx*

VOLUME TWO

JOHN PLAMENATZ
*Fellow of Nuffield College
Oxford*

LONGMANS

LONGMANS, GREEN AND CO LTD
48 Grosvenor Street, London W1
*Associated companies, branches and representatives
throughout the world*

*Printed in Great Britain by
Northumberland Press Limited
Gateshead*

To My Father

PREFACE

THIS book is not a history of political thought; it is, as its title implies, a critical examination of a number of important theories. It is not concerned to argue for some interpretations of these theories against others but to examine assumptions, ideas and attitudes.

The book is an expansion of lectures given at various times at three universities, Columbia, Harvard and Oxford. It is hoped that it will prove useful to students of social and political theory whose interest in the subject is more philosophical than historical; and the author has had in mind students in the United States as much as in Britain. He has aimed at lucidity but is aware that some parts of the book make difficult reading.

The most difficult part of all, which treats of Hegel, has been read by Professor H. L. A. Hart and Sir Isaiah Berlin, by Professor Herbert Deane of Columbia University, and by Mr William Weinstein and Mr John Torrance of Nuffield College, and the author is grateful to them for valuable comments and criticisms. He thanks Mr. Alan Ryan of Balliol College for making the index. He also thanks his wife for reading the book in manuscript and suggesting improvements of grammar and style.

July 1961   J.P.

CONTENTS

CHAP.   PAGE

Preface   vi

Introduction   ix

1. BENTHAM AND HIS SCHOOL   I

2. THE EARLY SOCIALISTS, FRENCH AND
    ENGLISH   37

3. THE SOCIAL AND POLITICAL PHILOSOPHY OF
    HEGEL I   129

4. THE SOCIAL AND POLITICAL PHILOSOPHY OF
    HEGEL II   216

5. MARXISM I   269

6. MARXISM II   351

7. THE BELIEF IN PROGRESS   409

Index   459

INTRODUCTION

THE artist ploughs his own furrow; the scholar, even in the privacy of his study, cultivates a common field. He is responsible to others for what he does; he feels the need to explain his purpose, to justify his efforts.

There are many things well worth doing not attempted in this book. It is not a history of social and political thought; it does not enquire how one thinker influenced another, and compares them only to make clearer what they said. It scarcely looks at the circumstances in which this or that theory was produced. And it quite neglects several important thinkers. Althusius will get into the index only because he is mentioned on this page, and so too will Vico, who has been greatly and rightly admired. Grotius and Kant are mentioned only in passing. If my purpose had been to produce a history, however brief, of political thought from Machiavelli to Marx, this neglect or scanty treatment would have been without excuse.

Every thinker, even the most abstract, is deeply influenced by the circumstances of his day. To understand why Machiavelli or Hobbes or Rousseau wrote as he did, we must know something of social and political conditions in their day and country and of the controversies then to the fore. But this does not, I hope, mean that whoever discusses their theories must also discuss these conditions and controversies. Is there to be no division of labour? These conditions and controversies have often been described, and the writer who is primarily concerned with arguments and ideas need not discuss them except to make something clear which might otherwise be misunderstood. He must use his judgement: at times he may need to make a considerable digression, and at other times a passing reference or mere hint will be enough.

Those who say that to understand a theory we must understand the conditions in which it was produced sometimes put their case too strongly. They speak as if, to understand what a man is saying, we must know why he is saying it. But this is not true. We need understand only the sense in which he is using words. To understand Hobbes, we need not know what his purpose was in writing *Leviathan* or how he felt about the rival claims of Royalists and Parliamentarians; but we do need to know what he understood by such words as *law*, *right*, *liberty*, *covenant*, and *obligation*. And though it is true that even Hobbes, so 'rare' at definitions, does not always use a word in the sense which he defines, we are more likely to get the sense in which he does use it by a close study of his argument than by looking at the condition of England or at political controversies in his day.

A*

These are, of course, well worth looking at on their own account. Nevertheless, we can go a long way in understanding Hobbes' argument and yet know very little about them.

No doubt, Hobbes is a special case. We can get more of his meaning by merely reading what he wrote than we can, say, of Machiavelli's or Montesquieu's or Burke's. It is a matter of degree. But, even in their case, we learn more about their arguments by weighing them over and over again than by extending our knowledge of the circumstances in which they wrote. Hobbes was not less a child of his times than they were. If we want to know why he wrote as he did, or why an argument such as his was produced and found exciting, we have to look at what was happening when he wrote; he was no more independent of his times than was Machiavelli or Burke. Of every really great thinker we can say that, compared with lesser men, he is idiosyncratic; he is, for a time, more liable than they are to be misunderstood because he has more to say that is unfamiliar. He uses the common language but uses it differently. But this is not more true of Hobbes than of Machiavelli. Hobbes belongs as completely to his age as Machiavelli does to his; and if, in order to understand him, we need take less notice of the circumstances in which he wrote, this is because his style and method are different. To understand the argument of *Leviathan* is one thing; to understand the age in which alone it could have been written is another. I do not deny that the second understanding may contribute to the first; I merely doubt whether the contribution is anything like as great as it is sometimes made out to be. Of course, it is of absorbing interest to see a great thinker in the setting of his age. How society and politics are related to political and social theory is as well worth studying as theory itself. Who would deny it? But that is another matter.

Students of society and government make use of ideas and assumptions inherited from the past. In this book I have not been concerned to trace the origins and evolution of these ideas, but rather to examine them critically by considering some of the most familiar and most famous theories which contain them. I have chosen these theories, rather than others, precisely because they are familiar, and because, between them, they contain most of the important ideas and assumptions still used or made, whether by students of society and politics or by persons engaged in political controversies. All these theories, in one way or another, are inadequate; they fail to explain satisfactorily what they set out to explain. They are also – though this is less important – 'out-of-fashion': by which, I am sorry to say, I mean no more than this, that sociologists and political scientists in many places (though not in all) now believe that they have less to learn from them than from one another.

These ideas and assumptions ought to be examined critically; and where can they be so examined to better advantage than in the context of well-known, long discussed and, in some cases, still influential theories? It is sometimes objected that the questions raised by, say, Hobbes or Locke are no longer relevant. But if we discuss social and political matters, we must still speak, as they did, of *law*, of *rights*, of *obligation* and of *consent*. By seeing how they used these words and what arguments they constructed, we learn to use them ourselves. By seeing where their explanations are inadequate, we learn something about what they sought to explain. To treat *right* as absence of obligation (which is what Hobbes did) may do for some purposes, but not for others. By examining critically the argument of *Leviathan* and *De Cive*, we learn why this is so. It may be true, as Locke said, that the authority of governments rests in some sense on the consent of the governed; but perhaps it cannot do so unless consent is understood in a sense different from his. By seeing where his argument goes wrong, we are better placed to construct another to take its place. If we do not get from Hobbes or Locke answers to the questions we now put, we do, by examining their theories, learn to put our own questions more clearly. And I take Hobbes and Locke for examples deliberately because they are among the most abstract of political theorists. Machiavelli, Bodin, Montesquieu, Hume, Burke, Hegel and Marx all take larger account than they do of history and of the machinery of government.

The great advantage of these old theories is that they are both rich in content and familiar. If our purpose is to examine ideas used to explain society and government, these theories provide them abundantly, vigorously and attractively. They are a fertile field for the exercise we have in mind. Everyone agrees that students of society and government need to look carefully at the assumptions they make and the ideas they use; that they, owing to the nature of their subject, are especially liable to be the dupes of words. Yet there are now many who question the use of a close study of theories produced long ago in circumstances widely different from our own. It is therefore a point worth making, that these ideas are nowhere better or more economically studied than in these old theories. Nowhere *better* because of the richness and variety they present, and nowhere *more economically* because they have been sifted again and again and we can get down quickly to essentials.

In some circles where the study of these theories is depreciated, there is nevertheless a keen interest taken in the ideas and assumptions used or made by the sociologist or the political scientist. There are sociologists and political scientists who put themselves to great trouble to define the terms they use and to state their assumptions. They do not always do it well. They wish to be lucid, precise and realistic; they aim at explaining the facts and are in search of a vocabulary adequate to their purpose. It is impossible not to sympathize with them. Yet, for all their efforts, they are often more obscure, or looser in their arguments, or more incoherent than the makers of the old theories which they neglect on the ground that they are irrelevant. A close study of these theories might be a good discipline for them.

Or the social scientist, though he does not know it, repeats what has been said as well, or better, long ago. Ideas very like his own have been used long before his time, and yet he thinks them new because he has coined new words to express them. It is sad to read a book for which it is claimed that it breaks new ground, and to find it thin and stale.

Not for a moment do I suggest that these old theories provide the social scientist with all that he is looking for. They are not a stock of ideas sufficient for his purposes. They are inadequate for all kinds of reasons, some of which are discussed in this book. I suggest only that the study of them is still amply rewarding, and to no one more so than to the student of society who feels that he lacks the ideas needed to explain what he studies. Of course, he will not find the ideas he wants ready made in these theories, but he will become more adept in the handling of ideas and a better judge of their uses. He will be more discriminating, more scrupulous, and perhaps also more severe with himself and his contemporaries. Bentham said that his purpose in writing *A Fragment on Government* was to teach the student 'to place more confidence in his own strength, and less in the infallibility of great names – to help him to emancipate his judgement from the shackles of authority'. An admirable purpose. But today, in some intellectual circles, the authority of great names is less oppressive than is fashion, which is an even worse guide. If we neither neglect great names nor defer to them, but seek, to the best of our ability, to take their measure, we are then better placed to take our own.

It is said that, in the past, it was difficult, if not impossible, to study the facts, social and political, whereas now it is much less difficult. There are vastly greater records than there were, more easily accessible; there are methods now used to get at the facts which could not have been used in earlier periods; it is easier than it was to test hypotheses, and we are more sophisticated in the making and testing of them. The social sciences may have no spectacular achievements to their credit, but then it is not to be expected that they should. It is admitted that they differ greatly from the natural sciences, that there are difficulties peculiar to them, that their conclusions are less precise and more open to question. Such is their nature that, though they call for no less imagination, no less intelligence, no smaller talents from their devotees than other sciences, they afford lesser opportunities; and we are not to expect from them hypotheses as precise, as impressive, as revolutionary and as widely acclaimed as those of, say, Copernicus or Newton or Darwin or Pasteur. And yet it is claimed for them that they do now deserve to be called *sciences* because those who practise them are seriously concerned to construct theories to explain the facts, and are self-critical and open-minded. As much as the natural scientists, they are imbued with the scientific spirit, even though their methods are more uncertain and their results looser and less well established. The social scientist is much more apt than the natural scientist to talk nonsense and to make a fool of himself. This is one of the hazards of his occupation. Yet his occupation is science.

But the occupation of the great social and political theorists of the past was not science. They did not study the facts or did so only at random; they did not construct hypotheses and test them. They deduced their conclusions from axioms *a priori* and from definitions, or they relied on what they chose to consider the common sense of mankind. They were not scientific but speculative. What is more, their aim was often less to explain than to justify or to condemn. That they seldom distinguished between their aims is only one proof the more that they were not scientists. And so it is sometimes held that their theories are much more impediments than helps to the social scientist, who need not rate his own achievements high to feel that, as compared with them, he is moving in the right direction, given that the object of the journey is to extend knowledge. Hence the need often felt by the social scientist to turn his back on these old and famous theories.

There is nothing arrogant about this attitude, with which it is easy to sympathize.[1] But there can be no real turning of the back on these old theories, whose ideas and assumptions still permeate our thinking about society and government, whether we know it or not. We are not free of them as the natural scientists are of the essences and entelechies of mediaeval and Aristotelian philosophy. We have still to come to terms with these thinkers of the past, to make up our minds about them, if we are to learn to think more clearly than they did.

Moreover, these theories were by no means entirely speculative, nor was their function always primarily to justify or to condemn. They were also, to a greater or a lesser extent, attempts to explain the facts; to explain what the social scientist aims at explaining. To examine them, as is still sometimes done, merely in order to establish how far they are internally consistent, is not an exercise of much use to the social scientist. Nor does it matter to him just which, among several different interpretations of a well-known doctrine, is the nearest to being correct. The enquiry perhaps most useful to him is an enquiry into the adequacy and relevance of these theories. How far do they provide a satisfactory explanation of what they seek to explain? How far are their assumptions and ideas useful for purposes of explanation?

---

[1] There is more that is arrogant about the disparagement of the social sciences still common in England than about the claims made for them in the United States.

Granted that the theories are in many ways inadequate or irrelevant, just why are they so? This book attempts, among other things, to answer these questions; and never more so than when it treats, sometimes at considerable length, of three among the more recent and still widely influential theories, those of Rousseau, Hegel and Marx.

The expositor and critic is bound to give what he honestly believes to be a fair interpretation of the doctrines he discusses. But, if his purpose is not to offer an interpretation which he believes to be an improvement on others, or to pronounce in favour of one among several current versions, he is not bound to argue the case for his interpretation. Since I have been concerned much more to examine the adequacy and relevance of assumptions, ideas and arguments than to establish that Machiavelli or Hume or Marx meant this rather than that, I have refrained from defending my interpretations, except where it has seemed to me that they might strike the reader as unusual or not plausible.

Again, I have not considered every aspect of the most important theories; I have considered only those aspects which raised most sharply the issues I wanted to discuss. For example, I have not considered what Montesquieu has to say about religion and its social functions, though in fact he has a great deal to say about it and says it in the most interesting way. The points I wanted to make about religion, and its place in society, I have tried to make in discussing certain beliefs of Machiavelli and of Marx. It may well be that to someone whose field of study is the sociology of religion, Montesquieu has more to offer than either Machiavelli or Marx. Certainly, he treats of religion more elaborately and with greater subtlety than they do. But it seemed to me that their simpler and perhaps cruder treatment served my purposes better.

These theories are more than attempts to explain society and government, and more also than apologies for or attacks upon the established order. They are philosophies of life; and philosophies of this kind are often dismissed as useless or pernicious on the ground that they claim to be more than they really are.

They throve, it is said, before the scientific study of man, of society and of government had properly begun; they pretended to a knowledge they did not possess. But now that men are beginning to see how to get this knowledge, how to study themselves and society to good purpose, they can do without these pretentious theories. When these theories are not, in the Marxian sense, *ideologies* (when their function is not to defend or challenge the interests of some class or group), they are merely personal statements. They express what somebody feels about man and man's condition in the world. Taken for what they are they may be interesting, but they must not be taken for more.

Certainly, the makers of these theories had illusions about them, and often claimed a knowledge they did not possess. I have already said in their defence that they took some account of the facts and made some attempt to explain them, and I do not suppose that the persons who call their theories 'ideologies' or 'fantasies' or 'mere personal statements' mean to deny this. I believe that these theorists took larger account of the facts and were more seriously concerned to explain them than their critics imply, but that is not what I now want to argue. Nor do I want to argue that the element of class or group *ideology* in these theories is smaller than Marxists have supposed. I want rather to insist that these theories, even when they are not attempts to explain the facts and do not serve to defend or challenge class or group interests, are more than mere personal statements; and that to call them so is grossly misleading. They do more than express personal preferences, even though preferences which many share.

Some of these theories are integral parts of a cosmology, of a sometimes elaborate theory about the universe and man's place in it; others are not. Hegel affirms that reality is an infinite Mind or Spirit seeking self-realization, an activity or process passing from level to level, and which is manifest, at its highest levels, in communities of finite selves; that is to say, in communities of men. His social and political theory is rooted in a philosophy which purports to explain everything; or alternatively (and this alternative is perhaps nearer the truth) his philosophy is an attempt to apply to all things ideas which make sense only when applied to human activities and social institutions. Others, as for example the Utilitarians, are more modest. The Utilitarians, for the most part, do not seek to improve upon or to add to the explanations of the physical and biological offered by science; with rare exceptions they say nothing about divine or immanent purposes. They confine themselves to explaining man and his social behaviour. They take man as they think he is, as a creature of desires who seeks to satisfy them as abundantly as he can at the least cost to himself. They seek to explain his behaviour and all social institutions on this and a few other assumptions about man and his environment; and in support of their assumptions they appeal above all to what they take to be the common sense of mankind. Yet they, too, are concerned to do much more than explain the facts; they too seek to criticize and to persuade. They too have a philosophy of life which is something more than an explanation (however inadequate) of how men live.

All these theories, no matter how 'pretentious' or 'modest' they may be, are elaborate philosophies which contain a large element which is not science or conceptual analysis or ideology in the Marxian sense. They are what I venture to call, for want of a better word, practical philosophies or philosophies of man; they are forms of self-expression of which it is lamentably inadequate to say that they are mere personal statements. They are neither mere exercises in psychology, statements about how men feel and think and behave, nor mere excursions into morals. They involve much more than the laying down of ultimate rules (as, for example, the 'greatest happiness' principle or the principle of 'self-realization') or even the construction of elaborate hierarchies of rules.

There is always a close connection between a philosopher's conception of what man is, what is peculiar to him, how he is placed in the world, and his doctrines about how man should behave, what he should strive for, and how society should be constituted. The connection is there, multiple and close, whether the philosopher is a Rousseau or a Hegel, who does not agree with Hume that there is no deriving an *ought* from an *is*, or whether he is Hume himself. For Hume, though he believes that no rule of conduct follows logically from any description of man and his condition in the world, offers to show how man, being the sort of creature he is, comes to accept certain rules. Man and the human condition are, in some respects, everywhere the same, and therefore there are some rules which are everywhere accepted. They are not the only rules which men accept, and are not always in keeping with the other rules. Indeed, these other rules are sometimes preferred to them. Nevertheless, there are some rules which men everywhere accept, or would accept if they understood themselves and their condition; therefore, we have only to understand what man is and how he is placed in the world to know what those rules are. This way of thinking is not confined to the natural law philosophers and Idealists; it is common to them and to the Utilitarians, and (as we shall see) there is a large dose of it even in Marxism.

In this book I am as much concerned to discuss these theories as *philosophies of life* as I am to examine critically the assumptions they make and the ideas they use in the attempt to explain the facts. And, here again, I confine myself almost entirely to what my authors have to say, attending hardly at all to the origins of their theories or the circumstances in which they were produced. I have already said enough, I hope, to show that this neglect does not come of a failure to appreciate the importance of what I have not tried to do. I have learnt much from many scholars, but the attempt to tread in all their footsteps would be absurd.

Man, as Machiavelli sees him, is self-assertive. He lives, not to seek God's favour or to serve some larger than human purpose, but to satisfy himself; he seeks security and something more, he seeks to make himself felt. He seeks reputation, to make his mark, to create some image of himself which is impressive to others. The stronger he is, the more he is willing to risk security for reputation. Man is both self-preserving and self-assertive; but Machiavelli sympathizes more with the second than the first of these needs. He values above all the two qualities which enable a man to assert himself: courage and intelligence. These are not just preferences which Machiavelli happens to have; they are rooted in his conception of what it is to be a man. Hobbes also sees man as self-assertive but sees him even more as in search of security in a world of self-seeking men; and he puts a high value on prudence and consistency of purpose. Organized society is a discipline which the prudent accept and the imprudent must be forced to submit to. Rousseau sees man as the victim of society, as a creature who has lost his integrity. Society derives from his needs, develops his faculties, and yet is oppressive to him. As a rational and moral being, man is at once the creature and the victim of society, and can be cured of the ills it produces in him only in a reformed society. Bentham sees man as a subject of desires who, unlike other animals, can compare and foresee; he sees him as a competitor and collaborator with other men in the procuring of what satisfies his desires. The proper function of rules and institutions is to ensure that competition and collaboration are as effective as possible; that they help and do not impede men in their efforts to satisfy their desires. Hegel sees man as a creature who becomes rational and moral in the process of coming to understand and master an environment; he sees him transformed and elevated by his own activities. He sees him as changing from age to age, and the course of this change as 'implicit' in his nature, in his capacity to reason and to will. Marx sees man as a creature whose image of himself and the world is a product of what he does to satisfy his basic needs; and yet he also sees him as a creature who comes in the end to know himself and the world, understanding his condition and accepting it, and who thereby attains freedom.

We have here six very different philosophies, even though there are elements common to several of them. And, though we can say of each of them that it was 'the product of its age', though we can give reasons for its appearing when and where it did, we cannot say of any one of them that it is obsolete or irrelevant. They are ways of looking at man and society which are of perennial interest; we can find traces of them in philosophies much older than the ones which now seem to us to give fullest expression to them. Man and his social condition do change from age to age but they also remain the same; and the different philosophies which men have produced reflect not only how they and their condition have changed but also the diversity of their reactions to what has not changed. Professor Whitehead once said that all later philosophies are footnotes to Plato. This may be extravagant but is not absurd, and is least extravagant when applied to Plato's views about man and society. Plato's theory of knowledge and Aristotle's logic have been superseded in a sense in which their political philosophies have not. This is not because epistemology and logic have made progress since their time as the study of man and society has not; it is because political philosophy has always aimed at something more than explanation. One explanation of what is involved in having knowledge or in reasoning may be an improvement on another. But with philosophy, in the sense in which I am now using the word, it is a different matter.

Today, in the social as in other studies, two kinds of enquiry find favour: the aim of one is to explain the facts, and when its methods are (or are held to be) adequate to its aim, it is called science; and the aim of the other is to examine the ideas and methods used in explanation and in other forms of discourse, and when those ideas and methods are of wide application, it is sometimes called analytical philosophy. The theories expounded and criticized in this book, though by no means unscientific and unphilosophical in these two senses, are also more than science and analytical philosophy. Moreover (as I have said already, though in different words) as science and analytical philosophy they are often grossly inadequate. Therefore, since science and this kind of philosophy are in favour, these theories, which are often indifferent specimens of both, are in disfavour. And even when it is conceded that there is a large element in them which is neither the one nor the other, this element is written off as an aberration, due to a failure to understand what is the proper business of science or philosophy.

The suggestion is that these theories aim at extending knowledge but do not know how it is to be extended, or that they confuse other things with the extension of knowledge. They have several purposes but fail to distinguish between them, or have purposes so vague that they are not really purposes at all. They aim at explaining the facts or at elucidating ideas or at defining rights and obligations or at persuasion; and move from one aim to the next without knowing that they have done so. They are uncertain of purpose. The present-day critic, coming upon this confusion and trained to make the distinctions these theories too often fail to make, easily concludes that, if they have some purpose beyond explanation, elucidation, definition or persuasion, beyond the purposes familiar to him (and which he does not quarrel with provided the man who has them knows what he is doing), that purpose is illusory, rooted in misunderstanding. By all means let a political writer explain or analyse or persuade, but let him know what he is doing. For, if he does not know what he is doing, he will aim at the impossible or will delude himself into believing he is contributing to knowledge when he is not or will unconsciously seek to pass off his peculiar preferences as eternal truths.

I have already conceded that most of the great political and social thinkers of the past failed to make certain distinctions now commonly made, and that they were under illusions about their theories. Yet it is a mistake to conclude that, to the extent that they aimed at more than explanation, analysis or persuasion, their efforts were pointless or useless. Their theories have another function besides these, and a function which is not less important than they are.

Sophisticated man has a need to 'place' himself in the world, to come to terms intellectually and emotionally with himself and his environment, to take his own and the world's measure. This need is not met by science. It is not enough for him to have only the knowledge which the sciences and ordinary experience provide. Or perhaps I should say, to avoid misunderstanding, it is not enough for him to have only knowledge; for I do not wish to suggest that what he needs and science and ordinary experience cannot provide is knowledge in the same sense as what they provide is so but merely comes to him from another source. Nor is it enough for him to have this knowledge together with a moral code and a set of preferences. He needs a conception of the world and man's place in it which is not merely scientific, a conception to which his moral code and preferences are closely related. I have here in mind something more than the assumptions on which science and everyday experience themselves rest, assumptions which cannot be verified because they must first be accepted before it makes sense to speak of verification. This need is not felt by all men; and it is felt by some much more strongly than by others; but it is a persistent need. It is a need which can be met for some only by religion, but which for others can be met in other ways (unless any system of beliefs which meets it is to be called a religion). The theories examined in this book are systems of belief of this kind; or, rather, this is one aspect of them, and a very important aspect of some of them.

It would be profoundly misleading to speak of this aspect of them as if it were no more than a statement of preferences or a laying down of rules or a defining of goals. If it were only that, it would be possible to reduce it to a list; and this is not possible. A hostile or perverse critic may say that, as far as he can see, there is nothing more to it than that and a whole lot of verbiage besides, which to him means nothing. If he says this, there may be no arguing with him, beyond pointing out that it is perhaps a kind of verbiage in which he himself indulges when, momentarily, he forgets his opinions about it. When Rousseau or Hegel or Marx tells us what is involved in being a man, he is not, when what he says cannot be verified, either expressing preferences or laying down rules; he is not putting 'imperatives' in the indicative mood; he is not prescribing or persuading under the illusion that he is describing. He is not doing that or else talking nonsense. It might be said that he is telling his reader how he feels about man and the human predicament; or, more adequately and more fairly, that he is expressing some of the feelings that man has about himself and his condition. But he is not describing those feelings or just giving vent to them; he is *expressing* them, and the point to notice is that this expression takes the form of a theory about man and his condition. It could not take any other form. Thus, if it is an expression of feeling, the feeling requires systematic and conceptual expression. Only a self-conscious and rational creature could have such feelings about itself and its condition; and the theories which express these feelings, far from being statements of preference or rules of conduct passed off as if they were something different from what they really are, serve only to give 'meaning' to these statements and rules. Not that they are needed to make the statements and rules intelligible, to make it clear what the preferences are or what is involved in conforming to the rules; nor yet to justify the preferences or rules by pointing to their consequences. They give 'meaning' to them, not by explaining or justifying them, but by expressing an attitude to man and the human condition to which they are 'appropriate'; so that, even when we do not share the attitude, we understand how it is that those who do share it have those preferences and accept those rules. We do not infer the rules from the attitude, nor do we establish, in the manner of the scientist, a constant connection between the attitude and the rules and preferences; our understanding is different in kind from that of the scientist or the logician. It is neither an understanding of how things happen nor that some things follow from others; and yet it is an intellectual enterprise, a rational experience.

Man, being self-conscious and rational, has theories about himself and his social condition which profoundly affect his behaviour; theories which have not been, are not, and never will be merely scientific. They will always be more than explanations of how he behaves and how institutions (which are conventional modes of behaviour) function. And they will always be more than statements of preference or assertions of principle and attempts to justify them; they will be more than 'personal statements' and more than exercises in persuasion. I do not say that there cannot be theories about man and society which are merely scientific, nor yet that any social theory which is more than merely scientific must have this particular more to it; I say only that the need for this more is enduring, and is in no way weakened by the spread of the scientific spirit.

But, it may be asked, granted that this is so, is not the study of these old theories, insofar as they do not attempt to explain the facts or do not examine the ideas used in explanation, of merely historic interest? They may once have been persuasive but are not so today when the issues which inspired them are dead; and, to the extent that they do not seek to persuade but express what you have called attitudes to man and the human condition, our attitudes are no longer theirs. These theories, in this aspect of them, speak for their contemporaries and not for us; they belong to the past and the study of them is mere history.

To this there are two answers. Issues and attitudes change less than they seem to, for the language used to express them changes more than they do. These theories are products of their age but are also ageless; their diversity shows not only how epochs and countries differ from one another but also the variety of man's attitudes to himself and his condition. It has been said that all men (or is it all thinking men?) are either Platonists or Aristotelians; which, though not literally true, makes a point worth making. So too, in similar style, we can say that in all ages there are Machiavellians and Marxists and Utilitarians, and even men who, like poor Rousseau, despair of the future of mankind while protesting that man is naturally good.

Secondly, man is an object of thought to himself and would not have the capacities peculiar to his kind unless he were such an object. His being a person, his sense of his own identity, his feeling that he has a place in the world, depend on memory, his own and other men's, for he has rational intercourse with them and belongs to enduring communities. Man is more than just the product of his past; he is the product of memory. The past 'lives on' in him, and he would not be what he is unless it did so. Thus, for him, as for no other creature, to lose his past, to lose his memory, is to lose himself, to lose his identity. History is more than the record of how man became what he is; it is involved in man's present conception of what he is, it is the largest element in his self-knowledge.

Man, being rational and capable of self-knowledge, puts to himself two sorts of questions, and science answers only one of them. The sort of question which science answers he puts both of himself and of what is external to him; but the sort which science does not answer he puts only of himself or of creatures whom he believes to be in his own condition. And these questions which science does not answer are also not answered by an analytical philosophy. They are questions which have no final answers; for the answers to them differ from age to age and, perhaps even more, from person to person. These questions which science cannot answer are often put in the same form as the questions which science can answer. We may ask, 'What is man?' meaning 'What sort of creature is man?' and look for answers to the biologist, the psychologist, and the social scientist. Or we can put the question which Pascal tried to answer in the *Pensées*, which is a different question altogether, though put in the same words. Pascal believed in God; but the need to put this question does not arise from this belief. An atheist may put it and find an answer which satisfies him, and yet remain an atheist. But the answer, whatever it is, is not a mere set of rules. The question, 'What is man?', as Pascal put it, a question which science cannot answer, is not to be reduced to the question, 'How ought man to behave?'

Political and social theories of the kind discussed in this book are not the only theories, nor even the most important, which attempt answers to this sort of question; and of course they also put questions of other sorts. But this is an important element in them, and still as much worth studying as any other. The putting and answering of questions of this sort is an activity not less rational and not less difficult than scientific enquiry, and neither more nor less useful. These theories have helped to form sophisticated man's image of himself. No doubt, in primitive and illiterate communities men make do without them; but then they also make do without science. To ask, as some have done, 'What is the use of these theories?' is as pointless as to put the same question of science.

Chapter 1

BENTHAM AND HIS SCHOOL

I

OF the many doctrines put forward by the Utilitarians I shall discuss only three: Bentham's theory of morals, his account of sovereignty, and the argument which he and James Mill used in favour of representative democracy. Bentham's account of morality, though in some ways very like Hume's, is also, as I shall try to show, in other ways quite unlike it. I want to make clearer than I have done before how they differ, and to criticize Bentham's views more sympathetically (and I hope also more adequately) than I did in my book *The English Utilitarians*. Bentham's account of supreme power has received less attention than it deserves; it makes many things clear that Hobbes confused. The Utilitarian argument for democracy, which does not rest on the doctrine of the rights of man, gains certain advantages thereby; but it also has difficulties peculiar to itself because it starts from the assumption that every man is apt to be the best judge of his own interests. The classical economists also made this assumption when they argued for *laissez faire*. I want to consider both the advantages and the difficulties of the Utilitarian argument.

I. BENTHAM'S THEORY OF MORALS

In his theory of morals, Bentham is engaged in two quite different activities without seeing clearly the difference between them. He tries to establish the meanings of such moral terms as *good, right*, and *duty*; he defines them entirely in terms of the desires which move men to action and the consequences of those actions. But he also puts forward rules for the attainment of what he says is alone desired for its own sake, namely pleasure. In putting forward these rules he uses such words as *right, good*, and *duty*; but he does not use them in the senses he has defined. His definitions make these words merely descriptive, whereas he uses them for other than descriptive purposes. Hence the considerable ambiguity of his doctrines.

There is another source of confusion in his moral theory. He sometimes speaks as if the rules he puts forward, and above all the greatest happiness principle, followed logically from his definitions of *right* and *good*. At other times, he does not seek to derive the greatest happiness principle logically from his definitions, but tries to show that, man being the sort of creature he is, the greatest happiness principle is universally accepted when it is properly understood. This second line of argument has received less notice than it deserves, and neglect of it has led some critics of Bentham into error.

Let us first consider what Bentham says about moral terms when he explains how we use them.

If we want to understand what morality is, we must, according to Bentham, begin by seeing that men desire only pleasure and are averse only to pain. 'Take away pleasures and pains,' he says in his *Springs of Action,* '[and] not only happiness, but justice and duty and obligation . . . are so many empty words.'[1] Bentham sometimes speaks as if 'good' meant just pleasant, though more often as if it meant either desired for its own sake or universally desired. He usually defines a right action as the action which, under the circumstances, is conducive to the greatest amount of pleasure, or to the greatest excess of pleasure over pain. Bentham's theory therefore requires, not only that pleasures should be measurable, but that pleasure should be commensurable with pain. Yet, when Bentham says that an action is right, he is not just saying that it conduces to the greatest possible amount of pleasure. He is also saying that we ought to do it because it conduces to the greatest pleasure. When he uses the word *right* in this way he is no longer using it only descriptively; he is advocating a course of action. But, though he uses the word *right* in two different ways, to say that an action is of a certain type and to tell us what we ought to do, he never distinguishes between the two uses.

Bentham sometimes speaks as if duty were merely liability to punishment, or, more widely, liability to unpleasant consequences. 'That is my duty to do', he says in the *Fragment on Government,*[2] 'which I am liable to be punished, according to law, if I do not do: this is the original, ordinary, and proper sense of the word duty.' Elsewhere he broadens the notion of duty to cover any action backed by what he calls a sanction, and by a sanction he usually means any unpleasant consequences to be feared by the person who is considering what to do. There are, he says, four kinds of sanctions: natural, legal, religious, and moral.[3] A natural sanction is an unpleasant consequence which is not due to the reaction of some other intelligent being. If I knock my head against the wall, I shall hurt myself, and that is a reason for

---

[1] *Works*, Vol. I, p. 211.

[2] *Fragment on Government* (F. C. Montague edition), p. 234.

[3] Bentham admits that people can be encouraged to act by hope of pleasant consequences as well as discouraged by fear of unpleasant consequences; that there are 'positive' sanctions as well as 'negative' ones. But he does not take the first into account when he is explaining duty; for when a man has a duty, he is said to be obliged, and we do not ordinarily speak of people being obliged to do something when they act from hope of benefit to themselves.

keeping my head away from the wall. Thus, it might be said that it is my duty not to knock my head against the wall. There is no need to explain what Bentham means by a legal sanction. By a religious sanction he means a punishment to be expected at the hands of God, and by a moral sanction 'various mortifications resulting from the ill-will of persons uncertain and variable',[1] or, in other words, the blame or other unwelcome reactions of the people you come into contact with. These reactions are not arbitrary; there are habits of praise and blame.

Though Bentham includes natural sanctions along with the others in his list, we can in practice ignore them when we are considering his account of what duty is. Duty, as he explains it, is liability to punishment, and a natural sanction is clearly not a punishment even in the widest ordinary use of that term. Nor is arbitrary ill-will punishment. Before there can be punishment, there must be some rule of conduct which people are required to obey; and the punishment must consist, not in the fact that a breach of the rule leads to unpleasant consequences, but in people's behaving to the supposed breaker of the rule in ways likely to discourage the breach of it. Their reaction to him is not punishment, even in the wide sense, unless they react as they do because they believe that he has broken the rule. This is the interpretation fairest to Bentham. He says that the original and proper sense of the word *duty* makes it a man's duty to do what he is liable to be punished, according to law, for not doing. This defines only legal duty; but Bentham clearly supposes that the other notions of duty are, as it were, extensions of this primary notion. There are duties wherever there are rules which people are required to obey, and are liable to punishment for not obeying.

This account of right action and duty is suspect because it leads us immediately into paradox. If the rightness of an action *consists* in its conduciveness to the greatest amount of pleasure possible in the circumstances, and if duty *consists* in liability to punishment for not doing what is required of us, then clearly it may be our duty *not* to do what is right. Bentham was in fact very far from believing that the rules which people are liable to punishment for disobeying (which therefore impose duties by his definition) always make for the greatest happiness. It was precisely because he did not believe this that he wanted to reform the law. Yet it never occurred to him that, if we accept his account of duty and right action, it must sometimes (perhaps even often) be our duty to do what is wrong and to refrain from doing what is right. He took it for granted that it is always our duty to do right and to avoid wrong. Just as he used *rightness* in two senses, to mean conduciveness to pleasure and also to tell us what we ought to do, so he used *duty* in two senses, to mean liability to punishment and also to

[1] Op. cit., p. 234, note.

tell us what to do.[1] In other words, though he defined *rightness* and *duty* as if they meant different things, he often used them as if they were synonyms; but the sense in which he used them, when he used them as synonyms, he never defined. Hence the considerable obscurity of his theory of morals.

Bentham wanted to keep all 'empty' or, as he sometimes put it, all 'metaphysical' notions out of his account of morals. He would not have it that the rightness of an action or the goodness of a motive or condition is some inherent quality not given in sensation but directly apprehended by reason; nor would he allow that there is some special 'moral sense' which perceives the moral qualities. Also, he would not admit that moral judgements are no more than expressions of feeling. He wanted to show that there are objective moral standards. Speaking of theories other than his own, he says: 'The various systems that have been formed concerning the standard of right and wrong, may all be reduced to the principle of sympathy and antipathy. One account may serve for all of them. They consist all of them in so many contrivances for avoiding the obligation of appealing to some external standard, and for prevailing upon the reader to accept the author's sentiment or opinion as a reason for itself.'[2] He includes in this general condemnation just as much the moralists who speak of a Law of Nature or a Law of Reason as those who speak of a moral sense. If the moral law is directly apprehended by reason, one man's reason may judge differently from another's; there is no means of deciding the issue between them, and one man's judgement is as good or as bad as another's. It helps nothing to say that reason is the same in all men, if the judgements they make differ, and if there is no agreed method for deciding who is right. Now, from the nature of the case, there can be no such method, it being supposed that reason in every man directly apprehends right and wrong. The appeal to so-called rational intuition is therefore at bottom the same as the appeal to taste or feeling.

Bentham believed that he was providing what he called an external standard by equating goodness with pleasure (or if not with pleasure, with desiredness) and rightness with conduciveness to the greatest amount of pleasure possible in the circumstances. Everybody, he thought, knows what pleasure is, and wants to have it; while statements about conduciveness to pleasure can be verified. If two people disagree about what action is right, they can argue the matter out rationally; each can produce evidence that the action he favours is the

---

1 Thus, in a well-known passage from the *Fragment on Government* (p. 154, note), Bentham, speaking of Hume, says that he learnt from him 'that the obligation to minister to general happiness was an obligation paramount to and inclusive of every other.'

2 *An Introduction to the Principles of Morals and Legislation*, Oxford, 1876, p. 17.

more conducive to pleasure, and the one who produces the stronger evidence is likely to convince the other.

Bentham failed to notice that his definitions of *good* and *right* altogether neglect what makes them properly moral terms, and therefore persuasive in argument. If to call something good is only to say it is pleasant or desired for its own sake,[1] then no one who is told that it is *good* will be moved by the statement, unless he himself finds it pleasant or desires it; and in that case he scarcely needs to be told. If *it is good* means merely *it gives pleasure to someone* or *someone desires it for its own*, then it always makes sense to ask, Why should anyone who is not to get the pleasure or who does not desire it strive to bring it about? Similarly, if *this action is right* means *it conduces to the greatest amount of pleasure possible under the circumstances*, it always makes sense to ask, Why should anyone who is not to get the pleasure, or who can get more pleasure some other way, do it? Bentham insists that we should aim at the good, no matter whose it is or who desires it, and that we should do what is right even when we could get more pleasure by not doing it. But these rules no more derive logically from his definitions of *right* and *good* than the laws of nature, as they were traditionally conceived, derive logically from the humanity of man, from the capacities peculiar to the species *homo sapiens*.

Bentham wanted to explain what we are doing when we make moral judgements without recourse to what he called *metaphysics*, without postulating the existence of any qualities not given in sense-experience, any qualities apprehended by reason 'intuitively' or perceived by a special moral sense. He also wanted to provide an external standard of morality involving no appeal to our feelings. If he had had only the first object in view, he might have been content to follow Hume; he might have been willing to say that moral judgements are merely expressions of feeling, of approval and disapproval, whose function is to encourage some kinds of behaviour and to discourage others.

Hume's moral theory is purely explanatory. Its purpose is only to tell us what is involved in the making of moral judgements and how we come to make them as we do; its purpose is emphatically not to improve our behaviour. The primary function of moral judgements, Hume tells us, is to influence behaviour in the ways that make for happiness. We need not know this when we make moral judgements, for we may make them as we do because we have been taught to do so. Yet, if we enquire how men first came to make these judgements, we soon see that there is no satisfactory explanation except that experience taught them what kinds of behaviour ordinarily increase happiness and what kinds ordinarily diminish it. Since men

---

[1] It is true that Bentham (and other Utilitarians) sometimes mean by good *universally desired*; but this implies only that nothing is good unless it is the kind of thing that everyone desires.

desire happiness for themselves and also sympathize with this desire in others, they come to approve of the types of behaviour which increase it and to disapprove of the types which diminish it. Thus, for Hume, the rules of morality are ordinarily also rules of utility; they help to ensure that, in the pursuit of happiness, we get in each other's way as little as possible. But Hume does not make the morality of an action consist in its utility, its tendency to promote happiness. Its morality consists in how we feel about it, or rather in how we feel about the motives that inspire it. Thus Hume's theory allows us to say that an action is moral even when it is not an action of a type which is ordinarily useful. For that type of action, though it first came to be approved of because it was useful, may now have ceased to be useful and still be approved of, from habit or for some other reason. Hume's theory does not treat morality and utility as the same thing, but merely asserts that the primary function of expressions of approval and disapproval is to encourage useful behaviour and to discourage harmful behaviour. Though Hume does not, as some philosophers now do, treat moral judgements as disguised imperatives, he does say that they ordinarily serve to control behaviour, and that this explains how men have come to make them.

Bentham cannot follow Hume because he wants to do something that Hume cared little about; he wants to change people's habits of approval and disapproval. He wants to do more than explain what moral judgments are and how we come to make them as we do; he also wants to reform our moral standards. He cannot do this merely by defining *goodness*, *rightness*, and *duty*, as he does define them; because from these definitions nothing follows about how people ought to behave. His definitions reduce these moral terms to mere descriptive epithets. Before he can achieve his purpose, he must get people to accept a fundamental principle which logically has nothing to do with his definitions, though Bentham clearly thinks otherwise. This principle is what he calls the *greatest happiness principle*, or the rule which requires us always so to act as to create the greatest happiness possible in the circumstances.

Though this rule does not follow logically from Bentham's definitions, it is not altogether surprising that he thought it did; for if we accept the definitions, we are disposed to accept the rule. And this for a simple reason. True, if *good* means merely pleasant or desired for its own sake, it does not follow that we ought to aim at what is good. But then *good* does not mean pleasant or desired for its own sake. To say that something is good is to say, or at least to imply, that we ought to aim at it. That is ordinary usage, and by defining the word contrary to that usage, we do not ensure that we use it in the way we define it. Bentham defines the word *good* in his own way, and his definition is incorrect, because it purports to tell us, not just how he intends to use the word, but how it is ordinarily used; and then, having defined it incorrectly, he goes on to use it correctly, as indeed he can hardly avoid doing. He tells us that *good* means pleasant or desired for its own sake,[1] which is not true; and then goes on to use the word to tell us what we ought to aim at, which is to make a proper use of it. If, then, we accept his definition, we are disposed to agree that pleasure or what is desired for its own sake (which are, of course, for him the same) is what we ought always to aim at. In the same way, Bentham tells us, falsely, that *right* means conducive to the greatest amount of pleasure possible in the circumstances, and then makes a proper use of the word to urge a line of conduct on us. Once again, if we accept the definition, we are disposed to accept the conclusion, that we ought always to do what conduces to the greatest possible pleasure, even though the conclusion does not follow logically from the definition. There are few more effective methods of persuasion than first to define a word incorrectly and then to go to use it correctly, provided of course that the definition is plausible. And the method is the more effective for being used, as Bentham used it, unconsciously.

I have said that Bentham, apart from trying to derive his greatest happiness principle from his definitions of moral terms, also produced arguments to show that, since man is the sort of creature he is, egoistic and rational, he always accepts the greatest happiness principle when he understands it properly. I want now to discuss these arguments.

Sometimes, especially when he is deliberately laying down his basic principles, Bentham speaks as though we never desire anything except pleasure and to avoid pain. But more often (and more plausibly), in the actual course of his arguments, he says that we desire *for its own sake* nothing except pleasure and the avoidance of pain. I shall assume that the second is his true position; and, for the sake of simplicity, I shall take desire for pleasure to include aversion to pain.

Believing that nothing but pleasure is desired for its own sake, Bentham thought he could persuade everyone that the greatest happiness principle is the one rule which is universally acceptable. Given that, whatever people may desire, they desire it either for the pleasure in it or for the pleasure it will bring, and given that the intensity of their desire varies with the amount of pleasure they expect, you have (thinks Bentham) only to convince them that some things are more pleasant than others or are likely to bring more pleasure to get them to desire those things. If, for instance, they approve of one line of conduct rather than another, and this habit of approval stands in the way of their getting as much happiness as they could get, you have only to point this out to them, and they will cease to approve of that

---

[1] Good does sometimes mean 'desired' or 'desired for oneself', as when we say of a man that 'he is out for his own good'. But this is not to use the word as a moral term.

line of conduct. They only came in the first place to approve it because they believed that it promoted happiness. They may have been mistaken from the beginning, or that mode of behaviour, once a means to happiness, may now have become an obstacle to it, without their seeing that it has. They may still be attached to it from habit, and it may be difficult to break the habit, because the breaking of a habit often involves considerable pain. Nevertheless, to break the habit, to get them to cease approving of this mode of behaviour, all you have to do (however difficult it may be) is to persuade them that it never did, or no longer does, promote happiness. This is the way to reform both moral standards and the laws.

The only rule that is always accepted when it is properly understood is the greatest happiness principle. Indeed, Bentham seems to have believed that it always is accepted, though not always explicitly, by everyone. He speaks as if his problem were not really to persuade people to accept a principle entirely new to them but to get them to see it clearly and to see its implications. He says, in his *Theory of Legislation*: 'It is not the principle of utility which is new; on the contrary, that principle is necessarily as old as the human race. All the truth there is in morality, all the good there is in the laws, emanate from it; but utility has often been followed by instinct, while it has been combated by argument.'[1] What is needed, in the sphere of morals, is not to give people new ideas so much as to help them bring the ideas they already have into good order. Because they do not see clearly that the original function of moral rules was to promote happiness, they treat many of these rules as absolute. If they do promote happiness, the mistake is not dangerous; but if they do not, it is. The only rule which is absolute is the greatest happiness principle, because it is the only rule which always of necessity promotes happiness.

We have been so busy criticizing Bentham for the clumsy way in which he tries to derive moral rules from statements of fact, for not seeing that to say that something is universally desired or is alone desired for its own sake is still not to say or to imply that we ought always to aim at it, that we have almost entirely neglected this quite different line of reasoning. The fault, no doubt, is partly Bentham's own. He often mixes up different arguments so much that it is difficult to see that they are different. Yet we must admit that he does say that the greatest happiness principle is the only rule which we can expect people always to accept and to prefer to any other rule which conflicts with it when they clearly understand both rules. There is no question here of deriving moral rules logically from statements of fact. Bentham merely tells us that men, given that they desire only pleasure for its own sake, will always accept the greatest happiness principle,

---

[1] *Theory of Legislation*, C. K. Ogden, edit., p. 67.

and will always prefer it to any rule which conflicts with it provided they see clearly the practical consequences of following the two rules. Bentham does not put his position in exactly these words, but they are words which do, I think, put the gist of it without distorting it.

When Bentham says that we desire nothing for its own sake except pleasure, the pleasure he has in mind is nearly always our own. Much of the time, though not all of it, he is a psychological egoist; he holds that it is his own pleasure and not somebody else's that a man desires for its own sake. There may be nothing logically absurd about holding that, though we desire only pleasure for its own sake, we can desire other people's pleasure in that way (that is, for its own sake) as well as our own; but this is a position which few philosophers have taken. Those who have said that only pleasure is desired for its own sake have usually gone on to say that, when we desire other people's pleasure, it is as a means to our own. This is certainly what Bentham believed, at least while he bore in mind his own assertion that pleasure alone is desired for its own sake. Only when he forgot this assertion did he sometimes speak as if we could desire other people's pleasure without any thought of our own.

It has been argued that psychological egoism is incompatible with the greatest happiness principle. If egoism is true, I can accept the greatest happiness principle while the behaviour making for my own happiness also makes for the happiness of other people; but as soon as there is a divergence between what makes for my happiness and what makes for theirs, the greatest happiness principle is unacceptable to me. It is often said that I *ought* implies *I can*. But the word *ought* can be used in such a way that this does not hold. If, for example, *I ought to do this* means only that there is a rule which I ordinarily accept requiring me to do it, or if it means that this is a kind of action generally approved, then it does make sense to say that I ought to do it even though I cannot. No doubt, if I cannot do it, it is no use my saying to myself that I ought to; and no doubt, too, I am not likely to go on saying it if I am convinced that I cannot do it. But that is beside the point. The social function of the rule is to control behaviour, and I can accept it even though it is sometimes impossible for me to obey it. I can desire that there should be such a rule which everyone, including myself, is required to obey. My acceptance of the rule may be merely this desire and the behaviour inspired by it; namely, my appealing to the rule on appropriate occasions when I consider other people's actions or my own. The appeal, of course, will be in vain whenever I see that I have, on the whole, more to gain than to lose by ignoring it. Yet it is still my interest that there should be such a rule generally obeyed, and I therefore accept it. I cannot invoke it against others unless I am prepared to have them invoke it against me; and if I live in a society where the rule is generally respected, 1 shall soon acquire the habit of invoking it against myself, often effectively, though sometimes in vain.

There is, of course, a rule which it is more my interest should be generally accepted than the greatest happiness principle; and that is the rule that everyone should act so as to increase *my* happiness. But, alas, I am not the only egoist in the world; other people are as exclusively concerned with their happiness as I am with mine. They will not accept the rule which is ideally in my best interest. The most I can hope for is that they will accept the greatest happiness principle. I cannot, of course, hope that they will act on it when it is clearly their interest not to do so; but I can hope that, in a world where the principle is generally accepted, it often will be their interest to act upon it. Among the pleasures that count most with most people is the pleasure of a good reputation, and a good reputation is only to be had by obeying the rules, legal and moral, which are generally accepted. Though it matters enormously to me how other people behave, I cannot control their behaviour in my own exclusive interest, simply because I have not the power to do so. I need the help of others to control it; and I cannot get that help unless I appeal to a common interest. That is why, however selfish men may be, social rules always serve some common interest.

This common interest need not be universal; it may be the interest of a class or profession. No one was more willing to admit this than Bentham. Yet there is at least one interest common to all mankind. It is everyone's interest that other people should recognize that his happiness matters as much to him as theirs to them; that he too should count for one, and that no one should count for more than he does. The rule that serves this universal interest is the greatest happiness principle, which is therefore the universally accepted rule. When we appeal to it, we can expect all mankind to accept the standard we appeal to. Though it may be the interest of some group or class to put forward claims incompatible with the greatest happiness principle, it will never be their interest to repudiate that principle; because they need it to protect themselves against the claims of others. They will take the principle for granted, or else will try to prove that the claims they make on their own behalf are compatible with it. Therefore it will always be possible to appeal to the principle against them.

This argument, as far as it goes, is, I think, sound. There is nothing illogical about holding both that men desire nothing for its own sake except their own pleasure and that the greatest happiness principle is the ultimate moral rule, in the sense of the only rule which is always and everywhere accepted when it is properly understood. It is a mistake to argue, as I have done in the past, that egoistic hedonism and Utilitarianism are mutually exclusive doctrines. They may be false or inadequate, but they are not inconsistent with one another.

Yet I am no more inclined than I was to accept either egoism or Utilitarianism, because the arguments against them seem to me as strong as ever they seemed. These arguments have frequently been put, and I propose to say very little about them. Egoism and hedonism (of which Bentham's Utilitarianism is one variety) both rest on rather simple mistakes. When a man gets what he wants, it is often said that he has satisfied himself. Even if what he wants is something for someone else, he is said to have satisfied *himself* when he succeeds in his purpose. It is easy to pass from this use of language to the conclusion that the object of all desire is self-satisfaction. But the conclusion is absurd. A man is not satisfied until he has attained the object of his desire; and to say that he is satisfied is only another way of saying that he has attained his object. Similarly, when a man gets what he wants, it is often said that he has pleased himself. This is just another way of saying that he is satisfied or else it refers to some feeling he has when he gets what he wants, some pleasant feeling which accompanies success. In either case, it is improper to say that his object is pleasure. His object is pleasure only when he wants to procure for himself or for someone else an experience because he believes it to be pleasant.

Bentham took it for granted that the notion of pleasure is simple, and that everyone would understand him when he said that we desire only pleasure for its own sake. But it is not clear whether he thought of pleasure as a feeling about the experiences called pleasant or as a quality inherent in them. His friend and disciple James Mill, who in his *Analysis of the Human Mind* went further into these matters than Bentham did, sometimes spoke as if pleasure were a simple quality, varying in intensity but not in kind, inhering in pleasant sensations; sometimes as if the pleasantness of a sensation consisted merely in our desire to continue having it; and perhaps also sometimes (though rarely) as if pleasure were a separate feeling annexed to the experiences called pleasant, as if we first had an experience and then felt pleased with it. Both Bentham and James Mill, though they say that we desire nothing for its own sake except our own pleasure, and sometimes even that we desire nothing at all except our own pleasure, also say that we can come to desire the means to something as intensely as the thing itself, and can even continue to desire the means when we have forgotten the end. If we can do his, it follows that we can desire for their own sake other things besides our own pleasure, including among these things the pleasures of other people.

But I shall pursue these objections no further. I mention them only to show how confused were the ideas about pleasure and the means to it of two philosophers who were nonetheless always very certain that nothing is desired for its own sake except pleasure. Nor shall I trouble to consider Bentham's felicific calculus, his elaborate scheme for estimating amounts of pleasure, which assumes that the intensity of a pleasure can be set against its duration, its duration against the likeli-hood of its being enjoyed, and so on, as if these and other properties were all amenable to a single standard of measurement, and could be multiplied together to get a quantity of happiness, as length, breadth and height are multiplied to get a volume. Suffice it to say that the felicific calculus is useless, not only because we cannot in practice get the required information, but also because the operations it consists of are logically absurd.

It is, however, possible to substitute for the greatest happiness prin-ciple another rule which does not require us to make meaningless calculations. Instead of saying, 'Act so as to produce the largest amount of pleasure possible in the circumstances', we can say, 'Act so as to ensure, as far as you can, that people get what they want, according to their own preferences.' Of course, I have put this rule very roughly; it needs to be qualified in several ways. We need not always take into account everyone likely to be affected by our actions; we are rightly much more concerned to satisfy some people, our friends and relations, than others. Bentham thought so too, and argued that in the long run the general happiness is better promoted if our benevolence is mostly confined to persons close to us, whose wants we know. Again, we must not give people what they want if by doing so we are likely to harm either them or other people. But this qualification does not detract from our principle, if we hold that they are harmed when something happens to them which they would rather did not happen. By not giving them what they want now we may ensure that, in the long run, more of their desires are satisfied.

Bentham would no doubt say that this rule is at bottom the same as his greatest happiness principle; that it is only a looser way of saying what he wanted to say more precisely. In his eyes, 'Give people as great a sum of pleasures as possible' and 'Give them what they want in the order of their preferences' are equivalent rules. But they are equivalent only if it is true that what men desire is always pleasure, or other things for the sake of pleasure, and if the strength of their desires varies with the amount of pleasure they expect. Since neither of these things is true, the two rules are not equivalent. The first rule really makes no sense because 'a sum of pleasures' (as Bentham defines it) is a logically absurd notion; whereas the second rule does make sense. Bentham accepted both rules, the second as much as the first; and indeed often used the second in place of the first precisely because he believed that the two were equivalent. That is one reason among others why, in spite of his greatest happiness principle, he often spoke the most admirable sense.

This second rule, the rule which does make sense, requires us to help people get what *they* want and not what *we* think is good for them. Nothing could be more in the spirit of Bentham's philosophy. It is not our business to try to make other people better than they are or to try to bring into existence some social order which seems to us the most just or the best suited to the dignity of man. We can discover what we ought to do only by finding out what it is that people in fact want. We must look to their desires and not to any conceptions we may have of a perfected human nature or of rights that belong to men in virtue of their humanity. The Utilitarian argument is that, in any case, these conceptions first emerged because they were useful, because they helped men to control one another's behaviour to prevent their getting too much in each other's way as they strove to satisfy their desires. Ideals and conventions arose out of the need to reconcile desires, and we must see to it that what originally served this need does not now impede it.

This is not to say that we must care nothing for what people are like in themselves; that we must accept all their wants, without venturing to praise or blame them. Some of their wants are frustrating to other people or to themselves; some types of character are harmful and others are helpful. But we must judge characters and wants by their consequences; we must condemn or praise them for the evil or good effects of the actions they inspire.[1] There is nothing ultimately good or evil except people's getting what they want or their failing to get it. We cannot help having our own preferences, being more attracted by some people than by others; but we ought not to interfere with other people except to discourage harmful behaviour or to encourage useful behaviour. It matters what people do rather than what they are; and it matters what they are only to the extent that their being one sort of person rather than another makes them dangerous or helpful. This is the core of Benthamism.

Benthamism is optimistic and liberal and also inadequate; inadequate not because of its liberalism and optimism but in spite of them. It is liberal because it invites us to take men as they are, and to aim at giving them what they want and not what we think is good for them; because it forbids our using any notion of duty to God or any conception of human nature or society made perfect as an excuse for bending other people to our will. It is optimistic because it takes for granted that we can, by reforming our laws and institutions, go a long way towards making it easier for people to get what they want.

Bentham's liberalism is, in one way, an improvement on Locke's. It has no truck with the doctrine of natural rights; it does not require us to believe that no government is legitimate unless it rests on the consent of the governed, or that property is inalienable except with the consent of its possessor. It is less rigid than the liberalism of Locke.

---

[1] That is, for the pain and frustration or the pleasure and opportunity resulting from those actions.

In general, and quite apart from Locke's version of it, it seems to me that the doctrine of natural rights is either so broad as to amount to little more than the rule, *Act so as to help other people get what they want and not what you think is good for them*, or else leads to conclusions which even the liberal does not in practice always find acceptable. The fundamental rule of the Utilitarians, amended as I have suggested it should be, seems to me preferable to the doctrine of natural rights, because it says what that doctrine has to say more simply and clearly without using difficult and misleading ideas. True, the amended rule is no longer the greatest happiness principle; yet it deserves to be called Utilitarian because both Bentham and James Mill accepted it, even though they did so under the mistaken belief that it was equivalent to the greatest happiness principle.

Bentham's optimism seems to me naïve and facile. No doubt, if human wants were limited and unchanging, it would be possible, by taking thought, to make continual progress towards satisfying them completely. Even though we could never ensure that they were always satisfied, we could presumably get indefinitely closer towards satisfying them all. But wants are not unchanging; and by our endeavours to satisfy the wants we have, we create new wants. That does not make it irrational for us to try to satisfy our wants; nor does it invalidate the fundamental rule I have just discussed. It merely makes optimism irrelevant. Certainly, it would be absurd to say, *Don't let us bother about our present wants because, in satisfying them, we shall only create new wants.* It is our nature to try to satisfy the wants we have; and if we have them and do nothing about them, we only make ourselves miserable. Pessimism and quietism are as much out of place here as optimism.

The inadequacy of Bentham's philosophy is that it treats happiness as Hobbes treated felicity; as if it consisted in successfully satisfying one desire after another. But men have not only desires; they have ideals as well, and we cannot go far towards explaining their desires except in relation to these ideals. What men want depends largely on what they think is worth having, on the kinds of reputation they aspire to, on what they need to believe about themselves in order to have self-respect. These things will vary greatly from community to community, from age to age, from person to person. Man in society is as much a creature of ambitions as of desires; he has a scheme of life. It may be a vague scheme, it may change as he grows older, but it is always there. Whatever it is, however admirable or base, it can never be explained merely as a train or succession of desires. Social man is a moral and aesthetic animal; he is not just a creature of appetites, whose superior reason enables him to foresee what he is likely to want better than other animals, and to take more elaborate precautions to get it. He is a member of a community who is ordinarily much more concerned about how he stands in that community than about pursuing happiness as Bentham understood it. Man is spectator and judge as well as actor, and what he wants to do depends largely on the part he sees himself playing among other men. He is, as the Idealists put it, 'his own end'; with this proviso, that the phrase is not to be taken literally, as the Idealists would have us take it, but metaphorically. It matters enormously to man what he is like, both in his own eyes and in other people's. If that were not so, he would not be the tragic, pathetic, and sometimes absurd animal that he is.

Bentham treats man much as the economists treat him, as a competitor and collaborator with other men for the satisfaction of one desire after another; with this difference, that Bentham imagines that he has explained all that there is to man, whereas the economists usually admit that they are interested in only a part of his life.

Yet, inadequate though Bentham's conception of man as a social and moral being is, his fundamental rule, that we should aim rather at helping people get what they want than at making them the sort of people we think they should be, may still be acceptable.

II. SUPREME POWER

In the seventeenth century, it had been the fashion to defend absolute power. Hobbes' doctrine of sovereignty, unlike some other parts of his political theory, had been widely attractive. In the eighteenth century, at least in England and France (the two countries whose political writers had the greatest influence in the European world generally), it was much more the virtues of limited government that were extolled. Bolingbroke, Montesquieu, Hume, and Burke, each in his own way, were champions of limited monarchy. They were also admirers of the British constitution. Rousseau had claimed for the assembly of the people an authority in some ways more absolute than Hobbes had claimed for the sovereign, but the *Social Contract* was avowedly the description of an ideal state and made no claims on behalf of existing governments.

Bentham was the first to attack the fashionable arguments in favour of the separation of powers. In the course of this attack, which he made in his *Fragment on Government*, he produced a theory of sovereignty different from Hobbes' theory and in many ways more plausible. He freely admitted that political power is always limited and always shared. His account of sovereignty is emphatically not an argument for unconditional obedience; on the contrary, it is combined with a plea for watchful criticism of government and resistance when resistance is for the public good.

As an expounder and critic of political ideas, Bentham is usually little more than a disciple of either Hobbes or Hume, less formidable than the first and less subtle than the second. He is stronger as a critic of institutions than of ideas. His account of supreme power is, I think, the one important exception to this general verdict upon him; for he gets it neither from Hobbes nor Hume. He rejects, even more completely than Hobbes, the traditional theory of natural law, and also the doctrine of the separation of powers, and yet produces a conception of supreme power very different from Hobbes' conception of it. Bentham makes distinctions that Hobbes never made, and which need to be made to avoid confusion of thought.

Continental exponents of natural law had long insisted that a monarch can be absolute and yet not have unlimited authority. They had repudiated or ignored the argument of Hobbes that the positive law of the sovereign necessarily contains the natural law; or alternatively, that it is the duty of the subject always to act on the assumption that it does contain it. Hobbes had denied that the subject can be guilty of sin when he obeys a command of his sovereign which is contrary to natural law; for it belongs to the sovereign alone to define that law. Pufendorf, who had a liking for absolute monarchy, nevertheless contradicted Hobbes, saying that a man may sin even when he obeys his lawful sovereign. Yet Pufendorf was reluctant to advise disobedience; he equivocated and in the end almost enjoined complete obedience. Other jurists were bolder than he was: the subject, they said, must refuse obedience, even to an absolute ruler, if he cannot conscientiously do otherwise. The absoluteness of absolute human authority consists, they said, not in its always being the subject's duty to obey whatever that authority may command, but in there being no conventional or statutory limits to it. The ruler's authority is always limited by his duty to respect the natural law and by his subjects' duty to prefer God's law to all human law. Human authority is absolute as long as it is not limited in any other way.

Hobbes wanted to show that men, when they institute a sovereign, leave themselves without rights against him; because the only rights they then have are legal rights, which are grants from the sovereign. At the same time, since his whole theory turned on the argument that men set up the sovereign in the first place for the sake of security, he could not really lay on them an absolute duty of obedience; he had to admit that the subject may disobey when the sovereign seeks to destroy him. Yet, in spite of this admission, which he could not avoid, Hobbes' purpose, when he called the sovereign's power *absolute*, was to do more than say that it is not limited by law, and that therefore the subject has no legal redress; he also wanted to say that, because the subject has no legal redress against the sovereign, he can never have the right to disobey the sovereign, except when the sovereign seeks to destroy him. Hobbes wanted to treat legality and morality as if they were the same, and yet could not avoid sometimes using arguments which mean nothing unless they are different.

Bentham's theory of supreme power, though it completely rejects the traditional conception of natural law, is not open to this objection; it treats supremacy entirely as a political and legal matter. For Bentham, as for Hobbes, there is no law, properly so called, except what the ruler commands. But Bentham does not conclude that the subject has no right to resist the ruler, or has it only when the ruler seeks to destroy him. Bentham's account of morality may be defective, but it does at least enable him to distinguish moral from legal rules. Indeed, he makes this distinction, not only more clearly than Hobbes, but more clearly even than Locke and Pufendorf. He holds that moral rules are not, properly speaking, any kind of law. Law, as he defines it, consists of whatever rules are in fact enforced by those in authority. The rules enforced by mere public opinion are not laws. He distinguishes laws, properly so called, from other rules by the nature of the sanctions attached to them. But he does not, on that account, suppose that rules which are not laws are therefore less effective or inferior. They serve, alongside the laws, to hold society together; and they serve also to limit the power of governments. Whether law is to be preferred to conventional morality or the other way about depends on circumstances. The proper function of both moral rules and laws is to promote happiness, and when the two conflict, the one to be preferred is the one that promotes happiness best. The supreme rule is always so to act as to increase happiness as much as possible. There is not for Bentham, as there was for Hobbes, a direct connection between absolute authority and the duty of obedience. The duty of subjects to their rulers depends on how they govern; only if they govern the better for having absolute power is the duty to obey them thereby increased.

By supreme power Bentham means legislative authority not limited by any express convention. 'Grant', he says, 'that there are certain bounds to the authority of the legislature: – Of what use is it to say so, when those bounds are what nobody has ever attempted to mark out to any useful purpose; that is, in any such manner whereby it might be known beforehand what description a law must be of to fall within, and what to fall beyond them?'[1] Bentham wrote the *Fragment on Government* before the American constitution was made; and he gives, as examples of countries where the powers of the legislature are limited by 'express convention', the German Empire, the Dutch Provinces, the Swiss Cantons, and the Achaean League. He does not suppose that, in every developed state, there *must* be a supreme legislature; but he does, I think, take it for granted that there will be one unless there are special reasons why there should not be.

[1] *Fragment on Government*, pp. 218-9.

Hobbes' sovereign of necessity wields, either directly or through subordinates, every kind of authority, legislative, executive, and judicial; he is lawmaker, governor, and judge, all in one. Though Hobbes argues that the legislative is the supreme political power, he does not think it enough that the sovereign should be merely the supreme legislator; or rather, he speaks as if the legislative power, being supreme, carried with it the judicial and executive powers. Bentham does not follow his example. Though he, too, treats the legislative power as supreme, he never speaks as if its being supreme meant that whoever possesses it also has the executive and judicial powers. The executive and judicial powers are exercised according to rules which the sovereign may alter, but this does not of itself make the sovereign's authority more than merely legislative; it does not even require that those who have the highest executive and judicial powers should be responsible to the legislature. Because they exercise their powers within limits prescribed by the legislature, they do not therefore exercise them as agents of the legislature. Bentham never suggests, as Hobbes does, what is patently false: that whoever has the right to make laws regulating the executive and judicial powers virtually exercises those powers through subordinates.

According to Bentham's account of the matter, there can be a supreme power even though the highest legislative, executive and judicial powers are in separate hands, even though the executive and the judges are not appointed by or responsible to the legislature. But this does not mean that there can be a supreme power, in Bentham's sense, where there is a separation of powers, as Montesquieu understood it. Montesquieu never asserted the legally unlimited right of the legislature to make law; he never distinguished, as Bentham did, between moral and legal right. The idea of sovereignty, as we find it in Bentham, is entirely absent from his works, just as entirely as the idea of sovereignty as we find it in Hobbes. Montesquieu never attributed to the legislature the right to decide how the executive and judicial powers should be organized. He said nothing which suggests that he included in the legislative power the right to make constitutional laws, the right to decide how the community shall be governed. He neither attributed nor denied this right to the supreme legislature. On this matter, where Bentham is explicit, Montesquieu is silent. True, Bentham does not say that it is always desirable that the legislature should have this right (which it must have if it is to be supreme or sovereign in his sense); he is ready to admit that there may be circumstances where it neither has it nor ought to have it, as for example in a federal state. But he does speak as if, except where there are special reasons which make it impossible or undesirable, the legislature probably ought to have this right. Certainly, he sees no threat to liberty in the legally unlimited right to make law.

Though Montesquieu is silent where Bentham is explicit, there are grounds for believing that, had he not been silent, he would have disagreed with Bentham. He did not look upon governments as deliberately set up to achieve definite ends. He thought of them as more or less well adjusted to the communities in which they maintain order; he saw them as the unwilled and unforeseen products of human activities, products which men become attached to from habit. He saw the form of government, or the distribution of power among those possessing it, as a system imperfectly understood by those who govern and understood almost not at all by the vast majority of their subjects. The rules regulating the exercise of authority or, as we might put it, the constitutional rules, were conventional and supported by venerable traditions; and he thought of the separation of powers, where it existed, as resting on custom. He had not in mind a system where the authority of each branch of government is defined by a written constitution which the legislature may not alter nor yet one in which the right of the legislature to make laws is held to include the right to lay down the legal limits of the authority of the other branches. He believed that in practice those who govern have little power to change the structure of government, and said nothing to suggest that he regretted this; he probably took it for granted that, where that structure establishes a separation of powers, the legislature cannot, and ought not to be able to, decide how and within what limits the other two powers are exercised. He believed that it is a condition of liberty, not only that the legislative, executive, and judicial powers should be in separate hands, but also that those who exercise the legislative power should not be able to use it to curtail the authority of the other two powers.

Bentham differs from both Hobbes and Montesquieu. He sees that legally unlimited legislative power is not incompatible with a separation of powers, whereas Hobbes says explicitly that it is incompatible, while Montesquieu, though he neither asserts nor denies the incompatibility, seems to take it for granted.

Supreme legislative authority, though without limit in law, is always, according to Bentham, limited in two ways, morally and in fact. It is not true that subjects ought to obey any law which the supreme legislature may choose to make, nor is it true that all its laws are in fact habitually obeyed. Therefore, to say that a legislature is supreme is merely to make a negative statement about it: it is to say that no one has a legal right to set aside or to alter or disobey its laws. It is not to say that it has, in any sense which can deprive subjects of the moral right to resist it, an unlimited right to make what laws it pleases. It has no moral right to legislate as it pleases because it has a moral duty to legislate for the public good; and it has a legal right to do so, only in the sense that all persons within the territory in which its law runs are *legally* obliged to accept whatever laws it makes as valid laws. The legislature also has a moral right to make law, but that right is limited by the nature of the end it ought to pursue. It is supreme only because there are no definite conventions or laws which it has to conform to, no rules which it is someone's legal duty to see that it follows. In that sense, and that sense only, its authority is unlimited. But there is still a right of resistance, which is not confined (as it is with Hobbes) to persons who happen to be in mortal danger from their sovereign, nor justified (as it is with Locke) by an appeal to a higher kind of law. Any subject may resist when, ' according to the best calculations he is able to make, the probable mischiefs of resistance (speaking with respect to the community in general) appear less . . . than the probable mischiefs of submission '.[1]

Just as Bentham is aware that supreme power does not imply a right to govern as one pleases, so he knows that it does not require that all power should belong to one person or assembly. He admits that the supreme governor's power must, except where it is limited by express convention, be indefinite. How, then, he goes on to ask, can we distinguish between a free and a despotic government? To Hobbes, this distinction could mean nothing; but to Bentham it is important. Does the despot have greater power than a free government? Bentham does not think so: 'The distinction turns upon circumstances of a vastly different complexion: – on the manner in which that whole mass of power . . . is, in a free state, *distributed* among several ranks of persons that are sharers in it: – on the source whence their titles are derived: – on the frequent and easy changes of condition between governors and governed: . . . on the liberty of the press . . . . on the liberty of public association '.[2] These are all limitations on the power of the supreme legislature and yet take nothing away from its supremacy. Supremacy, thus conceived, does not exclude the division of power; it excludes only the kind of separation of powers that leaves to no person or body of persons the legally unlimited right to make laws. It excludes the separation of powers as the makers of the American constitution established it, and also, I think, as Montesquieu imagined it.

The British Parliament is legally supreme or sovereign, and yet Britain enjoys a freedom which depends on something more than the limits set to power by popular morality and public opinion; for these limits exist even where there is despotism. Freedom depends, says Bentham, on how the 'whole mass of power' is 'distributed among several ranks of persons that are sharers in it', 'on the frequent and easy changes of condition between governors and governed', 'on the liberty of the press', and so on. In other words, it depends on how power is organized. Parliament is supreme, and yet has no monopoly

[1] *Fragment on Government*, p. 215.
[2] Ibid., pp. 216-7.

of power. It is limited, in all kinds of ways, by the other institutions of State. Bentham therefore agrees with Montesquieu that to preserve freedom adequately power must be limited by power, and not just by common morality and public opinion. But he goes further than Montesquieu; he sees that this limitation of power by power need not exclude legal supremacy. Sovereign decisions may be of no effect, not only because they too grossly offend ordinary morals, but because the executive or the courts would not enforce them, even though legally obliged to do so. The supreme legislature's power is limited partly by what people will put up with and partly by the kind of co-operation it can rely on from the other branches of government.

It is the great merit of Bentham's *Fragment on Government* that it makes this clearer than it was ever made before. Bentham does not, as some theorists have done, assume that in every well-regulated State there must be a supreme legislature; nor does he treat supremacy as monopoly of power. Above all, his account of sovereignty or legislative supremacy is quite distinct from his doctrine of political obligation. We cannot, from his definition of supreme power, predict when he will think it right for subjects to obey or disobey their rulers. Here he improves on Hobbes and anticipates Austin.

III. THE UTILITARIAN ARGUMENT FOR DEMOCRACY

Arguments for democracy have been mostly of two kinds: they have, for the most part, assumed either that all men have certain fundamental rights, or else that every man follows his own 'interest', which he prefers to other people's and of which he is usually the best judge. The first argument assumes an equality of rights, the second assumes a certain kind of natural equality or similarity. These two arguments do not exclude one another; it is possible, without inconsistency, to use both. For convenience sake, I shall call the first liberal and the second utilitarian.

Neither of the assumptions on which these arguments rest implies that democracy is the only rightful form of government, or even that it is the best. Of course, if man's fundamental rights include the right not to be governed except with his consent, and if the notion of consent is not emasculated until it is left almost without content, then it does follow that democracy is the only rightful form of of government. But it is possible to assert a natural right to freedom without including this right in it. As I tried to show, when I was discussing Locke's theory, it does not follow, because every man, in the absence of all government, would have the right to do what he pleases short of doing harm to others, that he cannot rightfully be governed except with his own consent. If there is a natural right to freedom, and if government in fact serves to secure that right, then a man ought to obey government whether or not he has consented to do so. By deriving man's right not to be governed except with his own consent from his natural freedom, Locke (and others who thought like him) made a false inference.

Having made the false inference, they then usually avoided the conclusion that only democracy is rightful by emasculating the notion of consent. They neglected to consider what consent must be if government by consent is to be distinguishable from tyranny. We have already seen the consequences of this neglect for Locke's theory; and Locke was by no means the most negligent. On the Continent, there were philosophers and jurists who found it possible to combine a preference for absolute monarchy with the doctrine that man is by nature free and therefore cannot be justly governed except with his consent. They did this by taking such liberties with the notion of consent as to reduce it to insignificance.

The Utilitarians did not believe in natural rights. Yet there is a right entailed both by the *greatest happiness principle* and by the rule which I said might be substituted for it; and that is the right of every man that his happiness or his wants should not count for less than anyone else's. This is the right to equality, which is as fundamental to the Utilitarian philosophy as natural rights are to Locke's; though fundamental in a different sense. The Utilitarian argument for democracy does not proceed merely from this right; it proceeds from it together with certain assumptions about human nature: that every man prefers his own interest to other people's, and that he is usually the best judge of his own interest. Before I consider the Utilitarian argument for democracy, I want to say a few words about *natural* equality and inequality; meaning thereby, not an equality of rights, but of abilities. This is the kind of equality which the Utilitarians assert when they say that every man is usually the best judge of his own interest. It is a kind of equality in wisdom. The claim is not that men are equally wise in all respects, but that they are so in some respect which happens to be relevant.

There was nothing new about their asserting this kind of equality. Hobbes asserted it long before the Utilitarians, and so did other people, many of them believers in absolute monarchy. It never occurred to these people that by asserting this kind of natural equality they might be logically committed to preferring democracy to other forms of government; just as it usually did not occur to people who preferred monarchy to democracy that they might be committed to denying this equality. Indeed, I would hazard the generalization that in the Christian era before the eighteenth century the case against democracy did not rest primarily on the belief that men are unequal, either in virtue or wisdom. I do not suggest that obvious natural inequalities were denied, but only that they were usually ignored, presumably on the ground that they were irrelevant. This is one conspicuous difference between Plato and Aristotle and most of the great political thinkers of the Christian era until quite recent times. Plato argues repeatedly from natural to political inequalities, and so does Aristotle; though Aristotle is also more inclined than Plato to argue from some kinds of natural to some kinds of political equality, as, for example, when he says that all citizens should take part in electing the magistrates because they are on the whole fairly good judges of ability.

How different Plato is from Hobbes! It is unlikely that Hobbes really wanted to deny the obvious: that men differ greatly in intelligence, courage, and virtue. Though he explained the virtues as refined forms of egoism, and said that all men are egoists, he never for a moment suggested that all men are equally endowed with virtue. But, for the purposes of his political theory, he assumed that men are pretty much of a muchness, the sovereign being ordinarily no wiser and no more foolish, no better and no worse, than the great mass of his subjects. There is no question of justifying absolute power, as Aristotle justified monarchy, by the superior wisdom and virtue of its possessor. For anything that Hobbes says to the contrary, there might be innumerable persons as fit to have that power as the person (or assembly) who actually has it. It is merely the paramount interest of everybody that only one person or assembly should have it. Absolute government is best, not because the wisest ought to rule or are likely to rule, but because it is everybody's interest that supreme authority should not be divided. This was by no means an opinion peculiar to Hobbes; it was shared by most believers in absolute monarchy, and even by many who believed in the divine right of kings.

Until the eighteenth century, people were more directly concerned with political than social questions; they wanted to justify or condemn forms of government rather than this or that social order. But when they did consider the division of society into classes, they were seldom inclined to justify it on the ground of the natural superiority of the privileged classes. The social teaching of the Christian Churches, though often strongly conservative, was not flattering to the rich, the educated, and the powerful. It taught that if men were without sin they would live like brothers, without property or power among them. All the institutions making for inequality were supposed to be consequences of Adam's Fall, serving to protect men from one another's evil passions. Hierarchy was necessary to hold society together, and every man ought therefore to accept patiently his lot in life. But this acceptance was by no means held to carry with it respect or admiration for the great of this world or belief in their natural superiority. Though it was commonly admitted that there are great natural inequalities between men, it was also commonly held that they have little or nothing to do with differences in power or wealth or worldly esteem.

This Christian tradition was still powerful in the seventeenth century and is nowhere better expressed than in Pascal's *Pensées*. Pascal treats social inequalities as effects of selfishness, force, and chance. They are accepted, as most things are by men, from habit and for the sake of peace. It is absurd, Pascal thinks, to contest privilege on the ground that the possessor does not deserve it. 'How wise it is', he says, 'to distinguish men by their outward rather than their inner qualities! Who shall pass first of us two? Who shall give way to the other? The less able? But I am as able as he is, and we must fight it out. But he has four servants, and I have only one. It is for me to give way, and I am a fool if I contest it. Thus there is peace between us, which is the greatest good.'[1]

I do not suggest that this attitude was universal but only that it was common. For reasons not far to seek, champions of aristocracy were more inclined than champions of monarchy to justify social inequalities as effects of natural differences of ability. The privileged classes were never quite rigid castes; it was always possible to rise and to fall in the social hierarchy. That the privileged, in spite of conspicuous examples to the contrary, on the whole deserved their privileges was a not uncommon opinion, at least among the upper classes, before the French Revolution. It was also argued that among these classes natural abilities were strengthened by education. There was room for only a few on the upper levels of society, and those who got there mostly deserved to do so. If getting there enabled them to cultivate their talents, thus artificially widening natural differences of ability, so much the better for society whose leaders they were. And yet, in spite of arguments like these, which Burke magnified but did not invent, it never became fashionable before the eighteenth century to justify political and social privileges on the ground that their possessors were abler and better than other people.

The ardour for equality of rights which led to revolution in France and to reform in England was not born of men's at last discovering that they were by nature less unequal than they had hitherto supposed, or that social distinctions bore too little relation to differences of character and talent. It came from the decay of a religion which had taught contempt for worldly distinctions; it came from an increasing determination to make the best of life in this world; it came, above all, from the belief that men could by their own efforts change and improve their political and social environment. It is this belief, this faith, which sets thinkers like the Encyclopaedists in France and the

---

[1] *Pensées*, Edition de la Pléiade, p. 902.

Philosophical Radicals in England apart from the great majority of political and social theorists before them. They were egalitarians because they were optimists. But their optimism did not consist in their asserting human equality in a sense denied before them; in their saying that all men have certain inalienable rights, or that one man's happiness must count for as much as another's, or that every man is apt to be a better judge than other people of his own interest. All this had been said long before they said it. Their optimism consisted in their belief that a great deal could be done, here and now, to improve the lot of all classes in society.

Bentham believed in two kinds of equality long before he became a democrat; he believed that one man's happiness must count for as much as another's, which is an equality of right, and that every man is apt to be the best judge of his own interest, which is a sort of natural equality. He was also, from the beginning of his career, a radical, a severe critic of existing institutions eager to make great changes. In the *Fragment on Government*, which he wrote when he was a young man, he says that the 'motto of the good citizen' is 'to obey punctually, to censure freely', and that censure, 'though ill-founded', serves to promote every useful reform. He was as critical of the political system as of other aspects of social life. Yet it was a long time before it was borne in upon him that that system could be improved by increasing the electorate. Revolutionary France roused neither his enthusiasm nor his anger; he felt for it the benevolent curiosity not unmixed with contempt that radical Englishmen often feel for foreign countries in the throes of revolution.

Bentham always believed that government ought to interfere as little as possible with its subjects; that its essential role is negative. Given that every man pursues his own interest and is likely to be a better judge of it than other people, it follows, so Bentham thought, that the first duty of government is to ensure that men get in each other's way as little as possible. It is not the business of government to procure happiness for its subjects so much as to remove hindrances to their getting it for themselves. In other words, its function is to keep the peace between them by maintaining laws giving elbow-room to them all. Government should seek to affect a man's behaviour, not primarily for his benefit, but for the benefit of others. It forbids certain kinds of behaviour and requires or encourages other kinds by attaching sanctions to them; by giving pain to people who do what it forbids or who fail to do what it requires, and by giving pleasure to people who do what it seeks to encourage. Its aim ought to be to promote happiness by indirect means, by removing obstacles to it. Thus the principle of its conduct is, or should be, economy. For practical reasons, the sanctions it uses have to be much more often punishments (or inflictions of pain) than rewards (or bestowals of pleasure). Therefore its chief concern ought to be to get people to behave as it requires at the cost of inflicting as little pain as possible on them.

Until he was well over forty Bentham was more eager to advise governments how they should act than to discover what conditions must hold before they were likely to take his advice. It was only when he found them uninterested in the reforms and schemes he advocated that it was brought home to him that governments are often indifferent to the good of the governed. He had begun by taking it more or less for granted that governments normally do care for the public good; that it is their own interest, as well as the interest of their subjects, that they should govern efficiently. He took this for granted without assuming that governments are better or wiser than the general run of their subjects; just as Hobbes had supposed that the sovereign, even though in no way superior to his subjects, normally has a selfish interest in maintaining the public good.

It is always the common interest that there should be government; people are always better off with some government than with none. This Bentham never doubted. But in middle life he came to believe much more strongly than he had done hitherto that it mattered greatly that they should have one form of government rather than another. We must not, he thought, assume that a form of government which has lasted for a long time is likely to be the best suited to the people; we must not assume it, because the interests of rulers and ruled, though they always coincide to some extent, can also greatly diverge. Every man always desires his own greatest happiness, and does not cease to do so when he rules over others. The actual end of every government is therefore the greatest happiness of the governors, whereas its proper end is *the greatest happiness of the greatest number,* Bentham's formula for the public good. Since the actual and the proper ends do not, unfortunately, always coincide, we must, wherever conditions allow, try to establish a form of government likely to ensure that they do coincide. This form of government is representative democracy, the only kind of democracy possible in any but the simplest societies. Given that every man is apt to be the best judge of his own interests, the people generally will choose representatives keen to promote the public interest, which is merely a sum of individual interests. The representatives will be keen to promote the public interest because they know that, unless they promote it, they risk losing power.

When Bentham decided to move in any direction, he usually went a long way. He wanted much more than manhood suffrage; he wanted votes for women, annual parliaments, and the secret ballot; he wanted to get rid eventually of the monarchy, the House of Lords, and the Established Church. Members of Parliament should be mere delegates of their electors; the Prime Minister should be chosen by Parliament and should hold office for four years; civil servants should be appointed by competitive examination, and should be invited to put in tenders for doing their work as economically as possible. Since government is a necessary evil, governors should be watched and every device used to ensure that they do their duties. Though Bentham never became an anarchist, his suspicion of government deepened as he grew older. As his reputation and self-confidence grew, so did his mistrust of the men who, having power, were not willing to take the good advice he gave them. He became, in the end, as fervent a radical as Tom Paine without ever ceasing to regard the doctrine of the rights of man as so much nonsense. Liberty, he thought, is nothing in itself, and is valuable only as a means to happiness. Let people alone as much as possible, for then each man will seek his own happiness, of which he is apt to be the best judge. That is the rule of liberty. If decisions have to be made that concern all, then those who make them ought, wherever possible, to be responsible to all, or else they will prefer their own to the public interest, when the two conflict. That is the case for democracy. And equality is merely the rule that no man's happiness is to be preferred to another's unless it is greater or the cost of producing it is less.

James Mill, in an article on 'Government' published in the *Encyclopaedia Britannica* in 1820, puts essentially the same case for democracy, except that he lays more stress on government as a device for protecting men from one another. Since labour is needed to procure most of the means to happiness, it matters greatly that every man should get his proper share of these means. Labour, generally speaking, is troublesome, and trouble is a kind of pain. Most people, more often than not, are averse from labour. They undertake it, not for its own sake, but for what it brings; it is an effort that they would rather not make but which they do make because their desire for what it brings is stronger than their desire to avoid it. If a man gets less by his labour than that labour produces, he suffers more pain than is needed to create the pleasures he gets; or, alternatively, he gets less pleasure than the pain he has undergone produces. A man's proper share of the means to happiness produced by labour is therefore the produce of his own labour or its equivalent. If he gets less than his share, someone else gets more. The general happiness is best promoted, says James Mill, by 'assuring to every man the greatest possible quantity of the produce of his own labour'. I do not think that this conclusion follows; but I shall not contest it, as the Utilitarian case for democracy does not really depend on it.

The strong, says Mill, will always try to get more than their proper share; they will always, if left to themselves, try to deprive the weak of the produce of their labour. Therefore men must unite and delegate to a few the power needed to protect them all. Government is essentially a device for protecting the produce of every man's labour from

the greed of other men; or, in other words, a device for the protection
of property.

But government itself makes some men much more powerful than
others; it makes it possible for the rulers to plunder the very people
they are supposed to protect. How is this plunder to be prevented? Men
are so made, Mill tells us, that they always try, if they can, to make
the persons and properties of other people subservient to their pleasures. Their lust for power is insatiable. Those who have power will
always abuse it unless they are restrained; and they can be effectively
restrained only if they get power from the people over whom they
exercise it. Just as government is the device that prevents the exploitation of the weak by the strong among private persons, so representative
democracy is the device that prevents the exploitation of the governed
by their rulers. James Mill did not want representative democracy
because he thought it would lead to a redistribution of property in
favour of the poor; he wanted it only to prevent misgovernment. In
his day there were great inequalities among the classes unrepresented
or under-represented in Parliament. He did not condemn these inequalities. He wanted no more than to prevent the classes that dominated Parliament from using it in their own interest to the detriment
of other classes. Like most of his contemporaries who favoured parliamentary reform, he took it for granted that there was no serious
divergence of interest among the classes for whom he claimed the vote.
He even believed that the manual workers, if they got the vote, would
follow the lead of the new middle class; and he approved of their
doing so because he thought it in the common interest.

Mill did not suppose that men always are good judges of their own
interests; he admitted that quite often they are not. But he thought
this an effect of lack of education, and therefore curable. A narrow
ruling class, no matter how able, will always prefer its own interests
to the public good, whenever the two conflict. Ignorance is curable,
selfishness is not. Education cannot make a monarch or a privileged
class prefer the public good to their own, and it must often happen
that the good of one man or one class diverges from the public good.
Only democracy can be improved indefinitely by education. It is therefore ideally the best form of government, even though it may not suit
all peoples at all times. It can be said for it that it is the form best
suited to human nature, in the sense that, where conditions are favourable, it comes nearer than other forms to creating a harmony of
interests among creatures by nature self-regarding. Men can be made
fit for democracy, and, when they are fit for it, they are likely to be
happier than they would otherwise be.

This is a more modest argument for democracy than the argument
of Tom Paine. If Paine is right in thinking that no government is
legitimate unless it has the consent of the governed, it follows that

democracy alone is legitimate, everywhere and always. This drastic conclusion can be avoided only by cheating; by passing something off as consent which is really not consent. Bentham and James Mill had no need to cheat in this way; they could freely admit that some people's good is better pursued by others than by themselves. This is always true of children, and often also of whole classes of adults, if they are so ignorant as to have more to lose by choosing their governments than by submitting quietly to irresponsible rulers, even though these rulers prefer their own to the public interest when the two conflict.

The Utilitarian argument for representative democracy has, I think, a good deal to be said for it. I have tried to say some of it. But there is one part of it that I find puzzling. How, exactly, are we to understand the assertion, that every man is apt to be the best judge of his own interest? There is a sense in which it is obviously true. But is it the sense relevant to the Utilitarian argument? The classical economists also rested their rule of *laissez faire* on the assumption that every man is the best judge of his own interest. What did they understand by it? That a man is apt to know better than other people what he now wants? Or that he knows better the general pattern of his wants, how frequently they recur and which are the most pressing? In other words, that he is the best judge of his own needs, defined in terms of his own actual and probable desires? For many practical purposes we can accept these assumptions.

True, there quite often are people who know more about a man's needs than he does himself; but they are usually close relatives and friends, and not the government and its agents. We can take it as broadly true, at least where social conditions are stable, that men are ordinarily better judges than their governments of their own personal needs. In this sense, which is (unless I am mistaken) the sense both of the classical economists and of Bentham and James Mill, the presumption is that every man is the best judge of his own interest.

But is this sense relevant when we are comparing the merits of different forms of government? Governments do not provide directly for their subjects' personal needs; they do not stand to them as parents do to their children, considering the problems of each in turn and doing what they can to help. They deal with whole groups of people at a time, trying to promote and reconcile group interests. A man's being the best judge of his own interests, in the sense I have already discussed, does not necessarily make him even a passable judge of what policies are likely to reconcile the interests of the group he belongs to with the interests of innumerable other groups; or of whom he can trust to do this work of reconciliation; or of what institutions and political methods are best suited to getting it done. Presumably, people in the countries we call *backward* know their personal interests as well as we know ours; they know as much about their desires and preferences, actual and probable, as we do; they know as well as we do what they need to make them happy. I do not see that we have any good reason for denying this. When we deny, as we sometimes do, that they are fit for democracy, we are not saying that they know less than we do what they need to make them happy. We are saying only that they do not know what to do to ensure that their rulers promote the common interest, which includes their own. They do not know how to work the institutions whose function is to make it the interest of their rulers to meet their demands as far as possible. That every man is apt to be the best judge of his own needs is not enough to justify even *laissez faire*, let alone democracy.

If the proper end of government is taken to be to help people get what they need to make them happy, and if they are the best judges of their needs, they must of course be consulted about those needs. But can we discover people's needs by the simple process of counting their votes at elections? Is this not a very clumsy method? Is it not better to ask them, separately and in greater detail, what they need, and then, having got the answers, to set about using limited resources efficiently so as to give them as much as possible of what they need? Is not the *questionnaire* an incomparably better method for this purpose than the general election? If we assume only that each person is the best judge of what he needs to make him happy, we cannot go on to conclude that the policy he votes for is the best suited to give him what he needs, or that the party he favours is the most able or willing to provide it. We cannot argue from such a premise that the policy or party which gets the most votes is the one most likely to give the people as much as possible of what they need to make them happy.

Why, then, should a government's being responsible to the people make it more likely that it acts in the common interest? Where rulers are elected by their subjects, they have a powerful motive for pleasing them. They are likely to take great care not to do what makes the people angry or disgusted or suspicious. But if the people do not know what must be done to enable as many as possible of them to satisfy their needs, there is no ground for believing that the selfish rulers of a community of selfish men will promote the common interest the better for being responsible to their subjects.

I do not say that a logically sound case for representative democracy could not be made on somewhat the same lines as Bentham and James Mill make it.[1] But it would need to be more elaborately and carefully

---

[1] This case, though logically sound, is not necessarily the best case. It is possible to justify democracy on different assumptions from these, and assumptions more generally acceptable. But arguments for democracy of a broadly Utilitarian type have been popular among intellectuals, especially in English-speaking countries. It is therefore worthwhile considering what would be a logically sound argument of this type. Bentham and James Mill would prob-

argued than they argue their case, and it would reach a more modest conclusion. It would start from different assumptions and arrive at different conclusions; it would be a different argument from theirs. But it would also be in some important respects similar. It would accept one of the basic assumptions of Utilitarianism: that the business of government is to help people get what they ask for and not what their rulers think is good for them.

This amended argument would dispense altogether with the idea that the proper business of government is to make people happy. It would dispense with much more than the obviously untenable conception of happiness as a sum of pleasures; it would dispense with every conception of happiness. For we can hardly ever, when we are comparing whole communities, have good grounds for believing that one is happier than another. Nor yet for believing, of any one community, that people inside it are more or less happy at one time than another. We can hazard a guess, but it will be so uncertain as scarcely to be worth using as a basis for policy. The conditions making for happiness vary from community to community, from person to person; and they also vary with time in ways which are seldom predictable.

No doubt, we have good reason to believe that some conditions nearly always make for unhappiness, and ought therefore to be avoided. Certain minimal needs for food and shelter must be satisfied, certain brutal methods must be used as little as possible. These needs are common to all mankind and these methods are resented everywhere. We also have reason to believe that people are usually made unhappy when their conditions of life change quickly and in unexpected ways. But the minimal needs that must be satisfied in any society, however poor, are modest indeed. Though the standard of living of the Indian peasant, who is not actually starving, is much lower than that of the English working man, we have little reason to believe that he is less happy. He may even, as his standard of living rises, grow more unhappy; for his idea of what is due to him may change, and he may come to suffer more than he used to do from the knowledge that he lacks many things that other people have. Though we admit that starvation makes for unhappiness, we need not agree that material progress makes for happiness. It may be that democracy encourages people to make greater demands on government than they used to do, it may be that it inflates their ideas of what society owes them. If that is so, we can say that it encourages material progress by perpetually adding to the needs

ably accept the argument but not my comments on it.

Let me say, at this point, that intellectuals do not always value things for the reasons they give for valuing them. They prefer some arguments to others because they look simpler or less sentimental. The English-speaking peoples, even the intellectuals among them, do not really value democracy primarily on utilitarian grounds, even though, more than other peoples, they have a taste for Utilitarian or quasi-Utilitarian arguments for it.

which have to be satisfied to avoid unhappiness; but we cannot say that it makes people happier.

The Utilitarians assumed that the more a man gets what he wants, the happier he is. They also sometimes spoke as if it followed from this that, the more a man wants, the happier he is, provided he gets what he wants. To increase his happiness, he must not only get what he wants; he must also multiply his wants along with his capacity to satisfy them. Material progress is good because it both adds to our wants and to our power to satisfy them. We can, I think, demolish this argument without even troubling to question the notion that happiness is merely the successful pursuit of one satisfaction after another; or, as Benham would put it, of one pleasure after another. Why should we take it for granted that material progress adds to our wants and to our capacity to satisfy them? It may give us wants we did not have before merely by depriving us of other wants. It may do little more than multiply in us wants which are difficult to satisfy. Instead of wanting to talk or sit in the sun or sing or dance or take a walk, we may want to go to the cinema or to drive a car or to wear expensive clothes. We may not have more varied or stronger desires; we may have only desires which cost more to satisfy. We may lead as dull or duller lives; the advanced industrial society, though it enormously increases the variety of human occupations, does not therefore ensure that each occupation is less monotonous, or make it easier for a man to choose his occupation or to pass from one to another if he feels he has made a bad choice.

In building up our case for representative democracy, we say nothing about happiness. We do not deny that people make their demands on the government largely in the hope of being the happier for getting what they ask for. We neither deny nor assert it; we merely assume that the proper business of government is to satisfy, as far as may be, the demands made upon it by its subjects, whether or not the satisfaction of these demands increases their happiness.

This assumption needs to be qualified. In its endeavours to satisfy the demands made upon it at any particular time, the government may so act as to make it impossible or much more difficult for it to satisfy future demands. We must therefore qualify our initial assumption, saying that the proper business of government is to satisfy the people's actual and their probable future demands. Government must look ahead, and yet not too far ahead. The further ahead it looks, the more uncertain its predictions about future demands.

Government, in looking ahead, is not acting contrary to the people's will; for no people, however democratic, expect their government to take notice only of their present demands. They expect it to take reasonable precautions on their behalf. They expect more than just to be warned about the harmful consequences of their getting what they ask for; they also expect their demands to be disregarded in their own interest. That is to say, they will blame a government for the harm done to them by its acceding to their demands. This attitude to government seems to me quite reasonable. Sometimes, disrespectfully, it is called capricious; I prefer, more respectfully, to call it feminine, because it is so much like the attitude many sensible women take to their menfolk. They expect to be taken seriously, and they are perfectly well aware of their power. There is nothing servile in their attitude; it is merely a demand that the people whose business it is to look after certain of their interests should use intelligence on their behalf. A trustee, even when he is chosen by the persons for whom he acts, does not carry out his trust effectively if he undertakes to satisfy *all* their demands. When he is chosen by them, the extent to which he can disregard their wishes depends on how far he is able to persuade them after the event that he has acted in their interest.

At this point we must make another assumption: that government must not be able to decide what demands shall be made upon it. Inevitably, however democratic it is, it will have a large influence on public opinion. But it ought to exercise this influence in competition with others, so that the demands made upon it are not demands which it has decided shall be made. In other words, what is required of government must arise out of negotiations and discussions which those who govern do not control, even though necessarily they take a large part in them.

Our first principle, that the business of government is to meet the demands made upon it by its subjects, would be accepted by Bentham and James Mill. They might think, as I do, that it needs to be qualified, but they would accept it. It would seem to them to follow from the greatest happiness principle together with certain other assumptions; we can disagree with them here and still agree that the proper business of government is to meet the demands made upon it by its subjects.

Our second principle, that government must not be able to decide what demands shall be made upon it, was never actually asserted by the Utilitarians. Yet, clearly, it must be asserted if there is to be a sound case for representative government. If all that matters is that the people's demands should be met by the government, then it does not matter how the people come to make the demands which they do make. If those who govern can decide what the people shall demand of them, there is no need for them to be responsible to the people. Our second principle, though it is not put forward by the Utilitarians, would probably be accepted by most of them. But they would accept it more in spite of their Utilitarianism than because of it. For, though they said that freedom is valuable only because it makes for happiness, they were in fact more liberal than they knew. They probably cared for freedom for its own sake, though they did not admit it. That is why they were so ready to believe, without producing good evidence for it, that men must be free if they are to be happy. At least, I suspect that it was so; for where we find people who say that only happiness is desirable for its own sake then go on to take it for granted, sometimes even against the evidence, that freedom is a means to it, there is reason to suspect that they value for its own sake what they say they value only as a means. Utilitarianism need not, logically, be a liberal doctrine, but most of the Utilitarians were in fact liberals.

On these two principles we can build up a case for representative democracy. We can say that it is the form of government best suited to countries where there has been great material progress; that is to say, to countries where needs which are difficult to satisfy have greatly multiplied. To put the same point differently, it is the form of government best suited to countries which have become industrial and literate. In such countries government is extraordinarily active. The work it does or which is done on its behalf or under its control is a large proportion of all the work done in the country. The people expect the government to do much more than just maintain law and order. They do not accept institutions as they find them, asking little more of government than that it should preserve them. They belong to a type of society which stimulates ambitions and ideals not to be satisfied while the social order remains unchanged. In a society of that kind, government, whether or not it is democratic, is likely to be immensely enterprising. But it may be enterprising without doing what its subjects want it to do. To ensure that it does what they want, it must either be able to decide what they want by controlling their opinions and feelings, or it must be responsible to them. Our second assumption forbids the first of these alternatives, and we are left only with the second.

It is, in any case, easier to control overt demands than desires. A government in a position to decide what its subjects demand of it is not necessarily in a position to decide what they really want it to do. But I have purposely neglected this point, though it may be important, because I am not sure how important it is. People are very suggestible, and are nowhere more suggestible than in countries where government has always been authoritarian. I would not therefore like to say that, where a government decides what its subjects openly demand of it and then does what they demand, it is much further from doing what they really want it to do than it would be if it were genuinely democratic. That is why I put forward my second assumption as one which needs to be made if we are to have a sound case for representative democracy.

Where representative democracy has lasted for any length of time, there soon arise all kinds of bodies, not controlled by government or by one another, acting as intermediaries between the people and their rulers. The function of these bodies is to formulate popular demands and to put pressure on the government to meet them. This formulation of demands is a creative process, because many of the demands made by these bodies would never have been thought of but for them. As Rousseau only half understood, it is by being organized that the people acquire a political will. These bodies have leaders who are not in the government but whose business is to watch closely some part or other of what the government does. They learn by experience what can be got out of the government, and they also learn something of the difficulties that face the government. They help to multiply and to give precision to popular demands, thus enabling the government to know what the people want it to do for them; and they also teach their clients, the people, to be moderate and realistic, understanding that there are many demands being made on government and only limited means for satisfying them. Representative government enlarges and gives precision to popular demands on government and also evolves methods of satisfying these demands which come to be accepted as substantially just.

Representative democracy, by its very operation, disposes people to accept our second principle and to attach importance to it. Where government is in fact not able to decide what demands its subjects shall make upon it, where these demands are largely the product of discussions and negotiations between bodies and persons independent both of the government and of one another, it comes to be generally accepted that government ought not to be able to decide what these demands shall be. Representative government strengthens the principles used to justify it in the sense that it creates conditions which make people feel more strongly about them than they otherwise would. Yet they are not principles accepted only where there is representative government. Everywhere where there exists a strong tradition that government exists for the benefit of the governed, our second principle is likely to be accepted as soon as it is formulated. Hume, Locke, Burke, and Montesquieu would probably all have accepted it, though none of them was a democrat. They did not need to formulate the principle because in their day much less was demanded of government than is demanded today, and also because government's power to influence opinion was much less. It is only when government greatly extends its activities that, in countries with a liberal tradition, a need is felt to put forward this second principle. It is not right that government should be able to decide what its subjects want; its proper business is to help them get what they want.

This principle is not challenged even in countries which are not democratic but whose rulers pride themselves on being 'progressive'. In the Soviet Union, it is the rulers who decide what popular demands shall be made upon them. They have forced what they call progress on the people, and have perhaps in time succeeded in making the people like it. No age has been as successful as ours in devising methods enabling governments to get their subjects to demand, and even to want, what those in authority have decided to give them. Yet the governments who use these methods successfully do not admit that they use them. They too claim to be responsive to the people's will and not to be in a position to decide what it shall be. We can therefore say that, in countries which are already industrial and literate or else are fast becoming so, our two principles are in fact widely accepted, in the letter if not in the spirit. And there soon will be no other countries but these.

We have seen Bentham arguing that the greatest happiness principle is the one which everyone is disposed to accept when he understands it. He thought this must be so because man is the sort of creature he is. Instead of appealing, as Bentham did, to psychology, we appeal to history; we say that recent developments all over the world are disposing more and more people to accept the two principles on which we rest our argument for representative democracy.

This argument, though it makes no use of the greatest happiness principle, does make use of the rule which I said the Utilitarians were as willing to accept as the greatest happiness principle, believing mistakenly that it is equivalent to it: the rule, *Act so as to ensure, as far as you can, that people get what they want, according to their own preferences.* It is for this reason, and also because it makes no use of such notions as natural right and natural law, that I have ventured to call this argument Utilitarian.

Chapter 2

THE EARLY SOCIALISTS, FRENCH AND ENGLISH

I

I. THEIR PREDOMINANT INTERESTS

THE French economist, Bastiat, writing before the world had heard of Marx, called the socialists 'grandchildren of Rousseau'. Presumably Bastiat had in mind the early French socialists rather than the English ones, for his remark seems to apply more readily to them. Not that the French socialists thought of themselves as being descended, morally and intellectually, from Rousseau. Many of them, as we shall see, spoke contemptuously of what seemed important to him and cherished hopes which he would have thought absurd. Yet the early socialists, English and French, held two beliefs which we associate more with Rousseau than with anyone else because he was by far the most eloquent exponent of them: the belief that man in his wretchedness is the victim of society, and the belief that freedom is impossible except in a community of equals. No doubt, most of the great political thinkers before Rousseau had proclaimed a belief in equality, in one form or another; but equality, as they conceived of it, consisted in all men's having natural rights, prior to government, rights held to be realized in existing society or to require only an extension of the franchise for their realization. They did not hold, as Rousseau did, that equality, and therefore freedom as well, is impossible except in communities profoundly different, socially as much as politically, from any that existed.

Society is evil, irrational, and corrupting because it allows of great inequalities unconnected with differences of ability or merit. This is one of the two recurrent themes of Rousseau's philosophy; and the other is that freedom is grounded in an equality consisting in much more than everyone's enjoying the sort of rights which had interested Locke or the Levellers. These are themes as central to socialism as to the philosophy of Rousseau. The early socialists were indeed, in a limited but important sense, though most of them did not know it, 'grandchildren of Rousseau'. For Rousseau was the most revolutionary of all critics of the established order. Revolutionary, not in calling for its destruction by force – for that he never did – but in expressing a horror of it so profound and persuasive as to make it seem hateful to many who might otherwise have resigned themselves to it, as Christians had long been taught to do. And yet his disgust with the world was in many ways in the Christian tradition, though his message was to his own and to succeeding generations, to men who (like himself) mostly could not find in their hopes of the next world compensation for their anxieties in this one. Like the early Christians, he made the world distasteful to men but, unlike them, he did so without reconciling them to their lot and without giving them hopes for the future. He was a great disturber of souls, an enthusiast who was also a pessimist.

1. Their Difference from Rousseau

(i) It is here that the early socialists differ the most obviously from him. They were all hopeful men; they all believed in progress, as he did not. They also differed from him in other ways, which I propose to discuss because they serve to bring out sharply some of the essentials of nineteenth-century socialism. The early socialists nearly all believed in the salutary effects of the extension of knowledge; they were most of them either suspicious of the State or uninterested in it; there was little or nothing Stoic or ascetic about their creeds; and several of them were ardent feminists. Bastiat might just as truly have called them 'grand-children of Hume and the Encyclopaedists', for they had at least as much in common with them as with Rousseau. And yet it is natural that he should have been more struck by their community with Rousseau. He himself, as a disciple of the classical economists, was a 'grandchild' of the Encyclopaedists, just as he was a critic of the socialists; he was therefore less impressed by what he had in common with them than by what made them seem so different. If they had not seen man as the victim of society, if they had not condemned inequalities rooted in the social system which the economists took for granted, they would not have been socialists. This was obvious to Bastiat. What was not obvious to him was that they could hardly have been socialists unless they had been hopeful of the future, and that their hopes rested on convictions and arguments which they held in common with the philosophers of the previous century with whom Rousseau had quarrelled, not only because he was temperamentally unsuited to them, but because his whole attitude to life was different.

Admittedly, the vision of man as at once the maker and the victim of society, whose institutions arise out of his efforts and yet are imperfectly understood and scarcely controlled by him, is less elaborate, less profound, less deeply felt in the early socialists than in Rousseau. We can scarcely find in their writings, as we can in Hegel's and in Marx's, the conception of *alienation*; and it is this conception, perhaps more than any other common to these two thinkers, which brings them closest in thought and feeling to Rousseau. The sense in which, for the early socialists, man is the victim of society is relatively simple. Man has a variety of illusions about himself and his environment which prevent his attaining happiness; he is a victim of ignorance. He sees the world and himself as different from what they really are, and, because he is thus mistaken, he behaves from motives which would not be so strong in him if he knew the truth, motives which bring misery to himself and to others. As seen by the early socialists (and by Condorcet) mankind has suffered from an ignorance which has been, until recently, inevitable, because it takes time for men to accumulate and to organize the knowledge required to give them a true picture of the world. To begin with, they scarcely know how to correct their mistakes; they are incapable of distinguishing knowledge from fantasy. In order to have scientific or solid and systematic knowledge, they must come to understand and to criticize the methods whereby they accumulate what they take to be knowledge; they must learn to be philosophical, to doubt and to test assumptions hitherto unchallenged. While they are ignorant, they do not understand and cannot control the social effects of their own activities. They create, without knowing how they do it, an environment in which, being the sort of creatures they are, it is only natural that they should act as they do. In this sense, they are the victims of a social order which they and their ancestors have made without having desired to make it. Within that social order there arises a variety of what Bentham would call ' sinister interests ', so that it becomes the advantage of certain privileged groups to perpetuate a system which is harmful to the community as a whole.

Now, it is possible to believe all this – and many of the early socialists believed it – without having any conception (even though by another name) of what Hegel and Marx understood by *alienation*. To make my point clearer, let me compare this conception with the difference between the state of nature and the social state as Hobbes imagined it. In the state of nature man is more suspicious, more treacherous, more aggressive than in the social state; he, too, can be said to be a victim of his environment. He is in a situation in which he is impelled to behave in ways which make others, and himself also, insecure and unhappy. In the social state, he is no longer impelled to act in these ways; he can afford behaviour which reconciles his own permanent interest with other people's. Passions which were strong in him in the state of nature are much weaker in the social state, and other passions which were weak are much stronger. But man, essentially, remains always the same. His nature is not transformed by the social discipline to which he is subjected. This is what Hobbes usually gives us to understand, though there are times when his words suggest that he knows better.

Of course, for Hobbes, man is not the victim of society; it is society which is the saviour of man. Nor does Hobbes envisage a long process whereby man acquires the knowledge enabling him to create the environment which makes for his happiness in the place of the one which leads to misery. The state of nature, the wretched state, is the condition into which man is born before he has used his reason to get out of it; it is not, as is the society of which man is the victim in the eyes of the socialist, itself the outcome of a long process of evolution. There are no illusions and no sinister interests in the state of nature to stand between mankind and the enlightenment which is to bring happiness. Two centuries of speculation and scholarship separate the early socialists from Hobbes; they belong to different intellectual worlds. Yet the socialists come scarcely closer than he does to believing that man, if he is to escape misery and find happiness, must himself be profoundly changed in the process which transforms his environment. There is in Rousseau a conception, rich though confused, of *alienated* man, of man deeply disturbed, psychologically and morally, by the pressure of society on him, of man 'outside himself' (*hors de lui-même*) driven by his environment to seek satisfaction where it is not to be had; there is this same conception in Hegel and in Marx, together with the idea of man made whole again, 'restored to himself', gradually and painfully, by his own endeavours to become master of himself and his environment. These are the conceptions lacking, except for occasional hints, in the writings of the early socialists, and it is largely this which makes the idea of progress so much more shallow and less exciting in their writings than in those of Hegel or Marx.

Similarly, in deploring the ill effects of inequality, the early socialists merely see men as driven to crime and violence by poverty and ignorance. Because men are situated as they are, they are exposed to great temptations. The difference between them in their degradation and as they would be in the just society is seen almost entirely as a difference between external situations. Change their situation and they will behave differently, not so much because this change will lead eventually to a psychological and moral transformation, as because what once seemed worth doing will no longer seem so. The early socialists do not follow Rousseau in seeing man as deeply corrupted by excessive poverty or excessive wealth; they see him rather as deprived of opportunities which he otherwise would have or as exposed to temptations from which he would otherwise be free. They do not see him in the grip of contrary passions produced in him by his environment; they do not see him driven by these passions into courses which create frustration and self-disgust because they infringe principles which are themselves products of social life. They do not see man as half accepting and half rejecting these principles; they do not see him at war with himself, an unwilling hypocrite, a creature impelled by desires which make him what he does not want to be. Or, if they do see him in this way, it is only fitfully and almost unconsciously, as persons unaware of what their own thoughts imply. Teach the poor what they do not know, give them what they do not have, and the evil effects of poverty and ignorance will quickly vanish. This is the gist of what Owen, Saint-Simon, Fourier and Proudhon all tell us, and they were the most influential socialists before Marx. But Marx, though less impressive as an observer of the psychology of social man than either Rousseau or Hegel, says more than this, no doubt because of what he has learnt from Hegel: he imagines a long and difficult advance towards equality, an advance in which man, as he gradually transforms society, also transforms himself, both intellectually and at a deeper level than the intellect.

The conception of man as at war with himself, as in need of internal peace, is also Christian, and can perhaps be found in other religions. Mankind did not need to wait for Rousseau to become aware of the spiritual conflict expressed by St Paul to the Romans in the words: 'For the good which I would I do not: but the evil which I would not, that I do.' But Christianity does not see this conflict as an effect of man's social environment; it does not see natural man as innocent, un-rational and unmoral, and becoming rational and moral only as he becomes social; it does not see him as creating by activities whose remoter consequences are unforeseen by him both the moral rules which bind him inwardly and the excessive and disorderly passions which move him to break the rules; nor does it imagine a worldly, a social order, in which man would be free of this conflict. Rousseau was deeply affected by Christian thought, and was also caught up in moral crises of which Christianity takes large account although it offers only a theological explanation of them. But the explanation which Rousseau attempted was sociological and psychological.

2. *Their Interest in History*

Though most of the early socialists were not, in any serious sense, historians, they had what may be called a sense of history. They were believers in progress and they knew that progress in the past had been slow. They knew that the society which they hoped to transform had been different in the past from what it was in their time, and they were aware that the pace of change was increasing. They were there-fore very conscious, as for example Hobbes and Locke had not been, of having a place in history. There is little evidence that either Hobbes or Locke thought of their doctrines as being products of an age, as being conceivable and persuasive only in a period which was unique because it was a particular stage in an unceasing course of social change, a course whose every stage differed from the one before it. But the socialists believed that their doctrines had come in the fullness of time, as incidents in a long process of social evolution which was at once economic, political and intellectual. History had prepared their audience for them, and they expected to be listened to because they were convinced that their message was timely.

Of all the early socialists, Saint-Simon was the most interested in history. As much as Hegel or Marx, he had what is called a 'philosophy of history', which we shall examine later; he had a fairly well defined and elaborate theory about how European society had changed since the eleventh century, and he claimed to be able to use this theory to predict, in broad outline, the course of future change. Actually, his interest in the future was limited; he was mostly concerned with the immediate future. But he did claim to base his predictions, not merely on observations of the present and the recent past, but on a number of general propositions about the course of history over a period of eight hundred years. And, though he had little to say about events outside that period and outside Europe, he believed that he had discovered a law of change which applied to all societies and all epochs.[1]

Fourier's 'philosophy of history' is much less interesting than Saint-Simon's. Saint-Simon was deeply excited by history; he was no exact scholar, but he was bold and perceptive. His account of the course of change in the West from the eleventh to the nineteenth centuries is brilliant and suggestive; or, rather, his various though broadly similar accounts are so, for he quite often changed his mind about details. Moreover, his conception of the course of history is closely connected with his views about how society should be transformed. With Fourier it is quite different. To understand why he wanted society transformed in the way he did, there is really no need to know anything about the pattern of social change as he imagined it. He had a passion for tidy elaboration. Where Saint-Simon confines himself almost entirely to describing in considerable detail only two stages of social evolution and how the earlier passes into the later one, giving only the vaguest indication of what any other stage might be like, Fourier asserts that mankind must pass through thirty-six different periods, though he offers

[1] I do not believe that he ever succeeded in formulating this law clearly enough to make it worth while discussing it; he never got even as far as Marx did in the Preface to his *Critique of Political Economy*. He believed, presumably, that any society similar to western Europe in the eleventh century would develop more or less as western Europe had done; and he also believed, presumably, that mediaeval Europe had developed out of an older type of society much as any other society would have developed. But he never described this older type nor attempted to show how mediaeval Europe arose out of it. In practice, he was interested only in how mediaeval Europe had developed into the Europe of his day.

to describe only the first eight, the others being so far in the future that we cannot imagine them. The West, as he knows it, is in the fifth period, which he calls 'civilization'. Indeed, the West has been, he thinks, in the third phase of the fifth period for nearly one hundred years, though it shows signs of having passed, in some respects, into the fourth and last phase of that period, and even into the sixth period; for a society can, he tells us, be more advanced in some respects than others. The period he is most concerned with, the period he describes in loving detail as being the best that we can now imagine and foresee, is the eighth, which he calls *harmonism* or *composite association*. It is the period when the social order ceases to frustrate man, when it is in keeping with his natural passions, allowing them full and harmless expression. But Fourier, though he deals with the past with a tidiness and self-confidence which never desert him, deals with it scantily and with little insight. It is not his brief survey of the past, it is his condemnation of the present and his detailed hopes for the future that reveal what he knows of human nature and the influence upon it of the social environment. And yet it would be misleading to say that he lacks a sense of history. He gives little evidence of having understood the past or how the present has emerged out of it, but he is very much aware that the present, which he condemns, and the future, which he foresees and approves of, are products of a long course of gradual change. He is aware also, though less certainly, that the times must be ripe if ideas like his own are to catch on.[1]

Proudhon can hardly be said to have a philosophy of history; he has no developed theory about what causes society to evolve and he puts forward no set pattern of social change. Sometimes he speaks as if progress were inevitable and sometimes as if it were not. Since man is rational, he can come to see that, in the long run, equality is the only rule acceptable to all creatures like himself. Man, being free and rational, is faced with problems which he is able to solve, and by solving them he changes his situation and enlarges his understanding. Progress is therefore possible, and to the extent that it happens, it brings men closer to the society of equals, but it is not inevitable. This is, I believe, the gist of Proudhon's doctrine of progress as it is expounded in *De La Justice dans la Révolution et l'Église*, published in 1858, a work which, in the opinion of many, is his greatest. It is probable that when he was younger he believed that progress was inevitable

---

[1] I say 'less certainly' because Fourier once said that his discoveries might have been made two thousand years earlier and mankind have been spared much suffering. This is a curious statement for a man to make who insists that progress is made by stages and that the passage from stage to stage is *necessary*. Even if we allow, as Fourier does, that some sides of social life are well in advance of others, this *necessity* implies that every side of it must pass through every stage. Whether this was clear to Fourier, I do not know.

C

and that later he changed his mind. It is difficult with a writer so much given to paradox, so much excited by ideas and with so little intellectual discipline, to be quite sure of his meaning. But, whatever his views about progress, it is certain that he believed that it was only in his time that the workers were acquiring the capacity to understand and carry out proposals such as his. For all his confusions and paradoxes, Proudhon was as much steeped in history as Marx, and as much aware that the times must be ripe for them if social theories calling for great changes are to be well received.

Of the four most famous socialists before Marx, Owen was perhaps the least interested in history; and yet even he was aware that he lived in an age unlike any other before it and that he therefore had unprecedented opportunities. He believed that hitherto men had been educated on false principles, and that it could hardly have been otherwise, for they were ignorant and prejudiced. Only recently had they become enlightened enough to receive the truth offered to them by Owen. As he put it, ' the time is *now* arrived when the public mind of this country and the general state of the world call imperatively for the introduction of this all-pervading principle, not only in theory, but in practice. Nor can any human power now impede its progress.'[1] The ' all-pervading' principle is that ' any general character, from the best to the worst . . . may be given to any community . . . by the application of proper means, which means are to a great extent at the command . . . of those who have influence in the affairs of men.'[2] Nobody believed more firmly than Owen that there had been and would be progress, that it had been slower in the past and would be quicker in the future because the obstacles to it were breaking down, and that he was himself in the van of progress, because he had a message peculiarly suited to the times. And this belief was shared by most of the early socialists in France and England, even those among them least interested in history.

Marx and Engels called the early socialists Utopian. If they meant by this that the early socialists took no account of the state of society at the time they wrote, of what Marxists like to call ' the objective conditions', the charge they make is grossly exaggerated. No doubt, the early socialists were too sanguine, too little impressed by the difficulties that stood in their way. But they most of them thought they had good reason to believe that, society and the intellectual climate having become what they were, they would find a ready audience for their doctrines, an audience made ready for them by the ' march of events'. Some of them, indeed, gave only a little thought to the matter, but others gave a great deal. For example, Owen comes much closer to being a Utopian, in this particular sense, than does Saint-Simon. Owen is content to say little more than that progress has now reached the point when the world, or at least the small part of it known to him, is ready to accept and to apply the great principle preached by him. He produces no arguments to support this assertion, any more than he produces evidence to support the principle about which he makes it. And he says, time and again, that whoever understands his principle cannot but accept it and be moved to act upon it; he takes little notice of the fact that men may have interests which close their minds to the principle, or which move them not to apply it even when they have understood and accepted it. But Saint-Simon does produce arguments tending to show that his doctrines are likely to be accepted by the class to whom they are addressed because they are in line with the 'true' interests of that class; he claims that his insight into the course of social change has taught him what those interests are and how they can be promoted. He produces what he takes to be good evidence that this class are already so placed in society that they have power enough to do what he urges upon them. His arguments, no doubt, were not as sound as he thought them, but then neither were Marx's when he discussed the 'true' interests and future destiny of the proletariat. But that is not to my present point, which is merely that Saint-Simon's attitude to the *industriels*, the class whose cause he espoused, was essentially the same as Marx's to the proletariat. He, too, thought that he was taking large and sufficient account of the 'objective conditions'. We may therefore say that, in at least one sense, he was no more Utopian than Marx. I shall say more later of the mistakes made by the early socialists about the success likely to attend their efforts, and how their mistakes compare with Marx's.

3. *Their Dislike of the State*

The early socialists were almost all of one mind in predicting that, as a result of the reforms they advocated, the use of force to maintain order would greatly diminish. Society had hitherto enabled a small privileged class to exploit the rest of the community; it had been divided into rich and poor, and the rich had needed to defend their property. Though this exploitation and this division could now be shown to be necessary at a particular stage of social evolution, though they could now be justified retrospectively as essential parts of a process leading to a desirable end, they had had to be maintained by force. They were practices and institutions made necessary by the ignorance of mankind, and therefore capable of rational justification. While that ignorance lasted, while they were justifiable, they had to be maintained by force, because the ignorant could not otherwise be induced to accept them; but as soon as the ignorance was dispelled, they ceased to be justifiable. If the unprivileged and the poor had been enlightened enough to understand their necessity, they would already have ceased to be necessary. Seen as elements in a necessary process, exploitation and inequality can be justified rationally, but by the time that most men are capable of appreciating these reasons the need for exploitation and inequality has disappeared. Force to maintain order is necessary and therefore reasonable only while reason in most men is still defective because not sufficiently educated. In the societies of the future, as imagined by the socialists, men will see that the rules they are expected to obey, whether customary or deliberately made, are in the common interest, and they will therefore want to obey them. They will be societies where, for the first time, every man's interest will be in keeping with the common interest, and everyone will be enlightened enough to see that it is so. Temptations to disobey the rules, though they will occur, will do so much less frequently than they do now, and will ordinarily be much weaker. Therefore the mere pressure of public opinion will be enough to maintain social discipline.

We need not suppose that even the most sanguine of the early socialists believed that in the future society of equals (and each of them conceived of it in his own way[1]) nobody would ever be unreasonable or violent. The use of force to maintain order ceases to be necessary, not where everyone is always reasonable and pacific, but where there is so little to be gained and so much to be lost, even in the short run, by violence that whoever is violent, as soon as he begins to cool down, sees that he has made a mistake. His anger and the violence it leads to isolate him morally, and this isolation must be painful to him unless he is an *enemy of society*; that is to say, unless he has been so treated by society as to reject the values it upholds. But this, in the just society as the socialists imagined it, never happens; no man is an enemy of society. And the painful moral isolation ceases as soon as the offender sees the error of his ways. There may be some violence, and therefore a need for those directly exposed to it to use force to defend themselves; but there is no need for the use of organized force, no need for the infliction of punishment by a regular process in the name of the community. This is an extreme position which only some of the socialists took up fully, though many of them were attracted by it.

---

1 Saint-Simon attacked the dogma of equality as Rousseau preached it; he did not want all men taking part in the making of the laws, he welcomed hierarchy and was willing to tolerate considerable inequalities of wealth. As much can be said of his disciples, except that they went further than he did in condemning private inheritance. It would be misleading to say that Saint-Simon and his disciples wanted a society of equals, since they did not want what was ordinarily understood by that term. But they did believe in equality of opportunity, preaching the doctrine, *from each according to his ability and to each according to his work*.

Rousseau also believed that in his ideal society, which he thought of as a community of equals, rules would be in the common interest and citizens would ordinarily see that they were so. He also believed that, where there is equality, there are no enemies of society. And yet he did not say that in the society of equals there would be no need of organized force to maintain social discipline. Why was Rousseau so much less hopeful than Saint-Simon or Fourier?

No doubt, Rousseau did not believe that citizens can discover the common interest merely by getting at the facts and reflecting upon them, nor did he believe that they will come to desire it merely by getting to know it. He believed that citizens acquire knowledge of the common interest and the desire to promote it by taking an active part in managing the affairs of the community. If I have understood his doctrine of the general will rightly, Rousseau did not believe that the common interest can be discovered by a mere process of calculation, by finding out how best to reconcile particular interests. He believed rather that a common interest and particular interests in keeping with it both emerge in the process of men's living together as equals, which they can do only if they all take part in the making of law. That the common interest can be discovered by experts was not admitted by Rousseau precisely because he did not see it as something which can be determined by anyone who knows the facts and whose logic is sound. Nor did he allow that it can emerge from the mere interplay of particular interests, as some of the classical economists thought. Nobody was further than he was from believing in a natural harmony of interests. There is no harmony of interests until men have acquired notions of justice and the desire to be just, until they have become moral persons so that even their particular interests are the interests of moral persons. But, we may ask, could not Rousseau have insisted on all this (and therefore on much that the early socialists took no notice of) and yet have allowed that in the just society there would be no need of organized force to maintain social discipline?

Certainly, if he had allowed it, he would not have been guilty of inconsistency. Why, then, did he not allow it? Was it merely that he was less hopeful than the socialists, less inclined to believe that, in the just society, the passions moving men to injustice would be much weaker than they were in his day? This would, I think, be too simple an explanation. Rousseau did believe that the motives to injustice would be weaker in a society of equals, but it was not only because he differed from the socialists about the extent to which they would be weakened that he never imagined the just society without organized force. In Rousseau's just society man is free and also just because he has an internal censor who agrees with the external judge. His freedom does not consist in the absence of passions moving him to break the law; it consists in his wanting to be law-abiding because he sees that the law is just, even though his passions sometimes tempt him to break the law. Admittedly, the more just a man is, the weaker in him the passions making for injustice. As I said in an earlier chapter, Rousseau does not see the just man as a moral hero gaining one hard victory after another over his evil passions. But neither does he see him as giving free play to all his passions because they are all either harmless or good; he sees him as a moral or self-disciplined person, and he sees this self-discipline as intimately bound up with a law imposed by all upon each. Where there is no internal censor there is no moral freedom, which is the only kind of freedom that a social being can achieve fully even in ideal conditions (the conditions described in the *Social Contract*); and there is no internal censor where there is no external judge. What is wrong ought to be *punishable*, not because these two terms are synonymous, but because where men are not liable to punishment the sense of wrong is weakened in them. Discipline is needed because men's unjust passions are strong. That is true. But it is also true that discipline weakens those passions. To be happy, man needs a discipline which he is convinced is just, and can have it only in a society so constructed that the internal censor agrees with the external judge. This is an idea not dreamt of in the philosophies of the early socialists.

The doctrine that in society rationally organized government gives place to administration will always be associated with Saint-Simon. If he was not the first to expound it, he invented the formula which gives neatest expression to it. Government gives way to administration; the prime function of those who control society ceases to be the maintenance of order by the organized use of force and becomes the management of the community's resources to ensure that they are used to the best advantage of the community. And the work of management is to be done by experts, by the persons who have proved their ability to undertake it. To begin with, Saint-Simon accepted the parliamentary system, though without noticeable enthusiasm and without pressing for extensions of the franchise. But, eventually, he came to reject political democracy and the parliamentary system on the ground that they attribute to the people a competence which they lack. The people generally do not decide who is to practise medicine or be an engineer; it is important to them that doctors and engineers should be competent but they are unable to judge of their competence. Of this they are aware, and therefore do not claim the right to make these decisions. The management of the community's resources is no less a matter for experts than medicine or engineering. The people will come in time to know this and will not want to undertake what they are incompetent to do; they will not want to damage themselves.

In *L'Organisateur* Saint-Simon describes how he thinks this management should be constituted; it is not the only scheme of its kind which he put forward but it serves as well as any to illustrate his conception of what management is and how it should be carried on. He puts forward a plan of administration by three chambers, of which the first, the chamber of invention, is to consist of artists and engineers whose function is to make plans and to explain them, the second, the chamber of examination, is to consist of scientists who examine the plans made by the first chamber and who also control education, while the third, the chamber of deputies, is to consist of the heads of business enterprises and will alone approve and put into execution plans proposed by the first chamber and examined by the second. It is not made clear how these three chambers are to be recruited, but, since they are chambers of experts and Saint-Simon is contemptuous of political democracy as the French revolutionaries conceived of it, it is clear that they are not to be elected by the people generally. The name of the third chamber, the *Chamber of Deputies*, does however suggest that Saint-Simon thought it might be elected by much the same persons as elected the lower chamber under the restored monarchy. That electorate was narrow and consisted for the most part of the better-to-do members of what Saint-Simon called the industrial class. In that class he included everyone who worked and whose work was useful to society; he included in it both entrepreneurs and wage-labourers, as well as scientists and artists. But he insisted that the natural leaders of that class were the entrepreneurs, and especially the more substantial among them, the 'captains of industry'. Saint-Simon thought them the men best suited to control an 'industrial society'; his complaint against them was not that they lacked capacity but that they were too diffident. He thought it his mission in life to persuade them to take over the over-all control of production, which was precisely what he meant by the administration of society as distinct from its government.

The 'industrial society' (whose prophet he thought he was) would be a society of equals, and yet it would be hierarchical. The ablest would rule, and everyone would be rewarded according to the contribution he made to the community. True equality consists, according to Saint-Simon, not in everyone's taking an equal part in the management of common affairs (which, in any case, is impossible as well as undesirable), nor in everyone's getting the same income no matter how little useful the work he does, but in everyone's having the chance to contribute as much as he is by nature capable of doing and being rewarded according to his contribution. If every man's position in society depends on his usefulness to it, and if all men are sufficiently educated to see that it is so, then hierarchy is acceptable to all and there can be effective authority with almost no use of force. Saint-Simon does not forbid the use of organized force or even predict its complete disappearance; he is content to say that the longer 'industrial society' endures the less the need for such force, and that those who apply it perform only a subordinate function.

Of the early socialists only Saint-Simon pays much attention to the problem of political (or, as he might prefer to put it, *administrative*) organization on a large scale. The others, for the most part, confine themselves to explaining how the small communities they advocate should be run (either taking the established political system for granted or else passing severe judgements upon it without troubling to say how it should be reformed), or they wish for and foretell the disappearance of the 'bureaucratic state', or they accept it and lay new functions upon it, demanding only that it be made democratic.

Fourier's ideal community, the phalanx, is to consist of about 1,600 persons; it is to be so organized that everyone will want to do what it is in the common interest that he should do, and so there will be no coercion. There will be officials to organize the work of the community, and Fourier foresees that they will be elected. Though each phalanx will be largely self-sufficing, it cannot be so entirely; there will be movement of persons and goods from phalanx to phalanx. Fourier does not see mankind in the future divided into innumerable small communities shut off from one another. And, certainly, there is no reason for supposing that co-operative production, even by groups of only about 1,600 persons, makes administration on a large scale less necessary than the productive system of France as Fourier knew it. Yet Fourier, who goes minutely into the organization of the phalanx, touches but lightly upon problems insoluble inside it; indeed, he is scarcely aware that there are such problems. He does not suggest that there will be no need for administration outside the phalanx when all men shall have become members of a phalanx, but he thinks it enough that there should be a loose federal structure which leaves almost intact the autonomy of the small community in which alone he delights.

Owen and Thompson also produced schemes for co-operative production, and they both took it for granted that these co-operatives would be run democratically by their members. The prime function of these communities would be, not to keep the peace, but to organize labour efficiently and to distribute its fruits justly; it would be, in the language of Saint-Simon, *administration* rather than *government*. Owen supposed that the communities would be formed by persuading workers to join them, getting well-to-do men of goodwill to put up the money needed to launch them, and even by enlisting the government's support. Thompson, much less inclined to believe in the goodwill of the rich and the powerful, expected the workers to provide most of the money needed to found the communities and hoped that the trade unions might take the initiative in founding them. Owen was not much interested in strictly political questions. Presumably he accepted the parliamentary system as he found it in his own country; at least he did not attack it, and seems to have believed that some form of nation-wide government would always be needed to see to the defence of the country and to look after its external affairs, and might eventually carry out certain economic functions, but he never made it clear what those functions would be.

Thompson, as might be expected of a disciple of Bentham, was a more convinced democrat. He favoured a system of provincial, state and national legislatures elected by the people grouped in communes. Every law voted by a higher legislature must also receive the assent of a majority of the legislatures inside the region subject to it. Thompson proposed many other devices to ensure that laws would, as far as possible, be acceptable to the persons required to obey them; he advocated the referendum and the recall. He also favoured the popular election of all officials, including judges. But Thompson, despite his much greater interest in government and his much stronger devotion to democracy, was no more interested than Owen in the control of production and exchange outside the co-operatives. Neither of them thought in terms of a national economy to be managed to the greatest advantage of a vast community numbering millions of souls. Therefore they never put the question first raised by Saint-Simon: What is the structure of authority appropriate to a vast economy centrally controlled, an economy whose resources are used as efficiently as possible to satisfy the wants of millions of persons most of whom are strangers to one another? This question meant no more to them than to Fourier, even though they accepted industrialism much more whole-heartedly than he did, and refrained, as he did not, from disparaging the parliamentary type of democracy dear to the radicals.

Louis Blanc wanted the State to control all the banks, the factories, the railways, the insurance companies, and the larger commercial enterprises, and he also wanted manhood suffrage. Small businesses should remain in private hands. Like the social-democrats in the West today, he called for an economy divided into a 'public' and a 'private sector' over which the State should exercise an over-all control. But he never really went into the question of how the State should manage the economy and the public sector, and how this management could be reconciled with effective democracy. He also neglected the question put by Saint-Simon: What is the structure of authority appropriate to a large-scale economy centrally controlled?

Proudhon is much the most difficult to understand of all the early socialists. M. Bouglé, speaking of one of the earlier of his works, called it 'l'examen de conscience hâtif et comme fiévreux d'un autodidacte qui a trop d'idées'.[1] This could be said almost as truly of his later

---

[1] C. Bouglé, *La Sociologie de Proudhon*, Paris, 1911, p. 86.

works, including even the best of them, *De la Justice dans la Révolution et l'Église*. Proudhon sees the course of history as a slow process whereby men acquire an ever deeper understanding of justice and of other 'eternal' ideas. If anyone could grasp these ideas intuitively, he could show men how to get peace and absolute justice. But all men are children of their times, and the wisest are only a little wiser than their own generation; and so mankind have to come slowly and painfully by the knowledge which brings peace and justice. This peace and this justice, when men come to possess them fully, will not be an order maintained by force or rules made by a government and applied, albeit impartially, to its subjects. There will be neither organized force nor laws made by a central authority controlling the lives of millions of persons, an authority whose very size ensures that it can never be truly responsible to those required to accept its decisions. In the place of legislation Proudhon puts contract or agreement. Guided by common principles of justice, individuals will form groups by mutual agreement, and neither individuals nor groups will be bound by anything except by the principles of justice and agreements freely made. There will be no authority above the contracting parties to enforce their contracts, to decide how they are to be understood, or to set limits on them. This, at least, is how I interpret a passage from Proudhon, which seems to put his position more clearly than many others.[1]

Proudhon does not explain what is to happen when some contracts are found to be incompatible with others, or when a contract made by two individuals or groups is deemed by third parties to be injurious to them, or when the parties to a contract disagree about how it is to be interpreted and cannot agree on an arbitrator. Does he imagine that such things will not happen in a society where certain necessarily rather abstract principles of justice are shared by everyone? It seems not to have occurred to him that in every society, even when there are bitter disputes inside it, there are many principles of justice shared in common.

The system whereby contract takes the place of law Proudhon called 'mutualist', and admitted that it could work well only on a small scale. He therefore favoured loose federations of small communities or associations. But he never undertook to show how these federations can hold together if the associations inside them differ strongly on matters of policy. Yet he did not deplore the increasing division of labour or the use of machinery on a large scale; he did not want to confine men to methods of production which make it easy and

---

[1] 'Justice commutative, règne des contrats, régime économique ou industriel . . . autant de synonymes de l'idée qui, par son avènement, doit abolir les vieux systèmes de justice distributive, de règne des lois, en termes plus concrets, de régime féodal, gouvernemental ou militaire: l'avenir de l'humanité est dans cette substitution.' *Idée générale de la Révolution*, p. 115.

natural for them to form small and almost self-sufficing communities. He was blind where Rousseau's vision was clear; he did not see that it is impossible to have a highly industrial society of small communities loosely federated.

Sometimes the Marxian doctrine of the *withering away* of the State is traced back to Saint-Simon and to the distinction he made between government and administration. Certainly, Engels also made this distinction and understood it in part as Saint-Simon had done. The formula is that the *government of persons* will give way to the *administration of things*; and this is taken to mean that there will be some form of social control of production but no force used by a hierarchy of officials to maintain obedience to the law. Yet the Marxian doctrine of the withering away of the State is more than another way of saying what had already been said by Saint-Simon. It is also a prediction that in the classless society there will be no bureaucracy, no elaborate and highly centralized administration. There is implicit in it Proudhon's promise that in the society of equals contract will take the place of legislation. The 'withering away' of the State implies more than the disappearance of organized force; it also carries with it the suggestion that there will be no law as we know it, no rules made to control the actions of millions of persons by sovereign legislatures, no professional courts to settle disputes about how the rules apply to particular cases, no vast executive hierarchy to carry out policies made by a handful of leaders on behalf of an immense community. But all this, though quite in the spirit of Proudhon, is not at all in the spirit of Saint-Simon.

Clearly, we cannot say that the early socialists neglected political questions. We have seen that two of the most important of them, Saint-Simon and Proudhon, had a great deal to say about government in the ordinary broad sense of the word and not only in the narrow sense peculiar to the socialists who distinguished it from administration. They reflected about government, its uses in the contemporary world and its place in the better world predicted by them. We have seen that some of them paid large attention to it, and yet their theories are not, for the most part, impressive.[1] They were misled by their hopes and by their fears. Because they disliked the use of force to maintain order, they easily persuaded themselves that force would no longer be needed when all men were educated and production was rationally organized. It seemed to them that they had plenty of evidence that force was used in the present, and had been used in the

---

[1] I say *for the most part* because in some ways they *are* impressive. Saint-Simon was perhaps the first to see the need for economic planning on a large scale in an industrial society, and this planning, which he called administration as as distinguished from government, differed in kind as well as in scale from ordinary business management. Proudhon was a shrewd critic of parliamentary democracy.

past, by the idle rich, the privileged, and the secure to keep the ignorant, the exploited and the insecure subservient to them, and so they concluded that in a society without ignorance, exploitation and insecurity there would be no need for organized force. But, even if we suppose that all the facts they pointed to in support of their argument were well established (and they mostly were), the conclusion they wanted to reach does not follow. For these are not the only relevant facts. It may be true that where there is no organized force there cannot be unearned privilege and regular exploitation of the poor by the rich, but it does not follow that where there is no privilege and no exploitation there is no need for force. They were so intent on showing that the force they abominated served purposes which it could not serve in a society of equals that they never stopped to enquire what other purposes it served.

Some of the early socialists went much further than to condemn force; they were suspicious of all authority. They disliked the modern State as much for being an elaborate and immensely powerful hierarchy, a vast administrative machine, as for being an organ of force and an instrument in the hands of the wealthy and privileged. They wanted to preserve the individual from the hazards, the waste and the injustice of a competitive economy *and* from the pressure of a gigantic, monstrous, many tentacled State. They persuaded themselves that this monster owed its being to poverty, exploitation, and inequality; that the same causes which had made force necessary had also allowed bureaucracy to flourish. It seems not to have occurred to them that in mediaeval Europe (not to speak of other parts of the world), where the governmental machine had been much smaller and simpler than in the western Europe of their day, there had been as much inequality and perhaps more oppression. They favoured small communities where there would be little or no officialdom, where such administration as might be needed would be done in their spare time by men always under the eye of their fellows. They deluded themselves into believing that the most important decisions affecting men's lives could be taken within these communities, even in a region as technically advanced and as socially mobile as western Europe in the first part of the nineteenth century. With this belief to sustain them, they felt themselves justified in sparing but little attention for the administrative structure which they did not deny would need to be superimposed on the communities they described more fully, and often in loving detail.

That the political theories of the early socialists who produced anything deserving the name of political theory were unrealistic can hardly be denied. But we must, when we consider Marx's accusation against them that they were Utopian, make a distinction which Marx did not make. What is it that is unrealistic about their theories? Is it their accounts of how the society of equals would be organized, or is it their beliefs about how it would come into being? These accounts we have already discussed and have conceded that they are unrealistic. But this is not what Marx had in mind when he called the early socialists Utopian. He was not concerned so much with the shortcomings of this side of their theories as with the inadequacy of their views about how society could be changed. True, he refrained from the elaborate descriptions in which they delighted, but his conception of an equalitarian society, though he gave only the briefest and broadest indications, owed much to those descriptions. He followed the example they set in predicting the disappearance of the State both as an organ of force and as a centralized administrative hierarchy. If, then, Marx and Engels were less Utopian than the early socialists, it must be because they had more realistic ideas about how society could be transformed.[1] I shall come back to this question later in another connection.

---

[1] There is also a third sense in which wholesale reformers may be called Utopian. We may not trouble to criticize them on the ground that their visions of the ideal society are unrealistic. We may think it wasted labour to object to these visions on specific grounds; we may object more generally that it is unreasonable to prepare schemes for the future because men, being limited by the ideas of their own time, cannot predict what the future will be like, since those who come after them will have ideas different from theirs. Marx and Engels, when they called the more speculative of the early socialists Utopian, also had this objection in mind. Now, it might be held that this is an objection which would come better from such a man as Burke than from them. If what is to come after cannot be foreseen, is not the revolutionary, the man who wants society completely transformed, merely destructive? He aims at putting an end to what exists without knowing what will take its place. What reason can he have for believing that the unknowable future will be better than the past?

But it is to do less than justice to Marx and Engels to turn the tables on them in this way. True, they sometimes speak as if, the moral values of each age being peculiar to it, it can make no sense to say that one age is better than another, and sometimes also as if it were impossible to predict what our successors will think desirable. And yet, in spite of this, they are believers in moral progress; believers in more than the extension of human knowledge and power. They believe that the course of history is a gradual progress to a type of society whose moral values will be in keeping with the ambitions and opportunities which men will have inside it. They also believe that we can already know what the basic values of that society will be; that we can know that it will be a society of equals. At the same time, by calling the early socialists Utopian, they imply that we cannot know how that society will be organized. This position, so far, is not unreasonable. But, given this position, it is unreasonable to predict the withering away of the State, if this means the disappearance of bureaucracy. For, if we do not know how the society of equals will be organized, how can we know that it will dispense with bureaucracy? Can we know it, because bureaucracy is incompatible with equality? But how can we know that future generations will not know how to reconcile bureaucracy with equality?

4. Their 'Materialism'

Rousseau condemned society for multiplying men's wants indefinitely. He was no ascetic and did not preach austerity; he did not think it good for men's souls that their desires should be frustrated or the flesh mortified. That society was best which produced in men no desires which they could not satisfy. Society, as he knew it, was evil because it caused men to want so much that they could not get and so much that did not satisfy when they got it. That was one reason why he preached the simple life.

Another reason connected with this first was that he disliked the social and political effects of an extensive division of labour. The more numerous men's wants, the greater the division of labour needed to produce what satisfies them, and the greater the division of labour, the larger the number of persons on whose labour each man depends. But Rousseau thought that a political community could not be truly independent unless it was economically self-supporting, or at least not dependent on foreigners except for what its citizens could easily do without. More important still, he believed that a large community could not be truly democratic. Therefore, where there is an extensive division of labour, a community large enough to be self-supporting is too large to be democratic; it is too large to allow all its members to take an active part in the making of law. It cannot be a true society of equals because it is divided into two parts, of which the smaller makes the laws and the larger is required to obey them without having helped to make them. Moreover, production for and dependence on distant markets makes producers and consumers dependent on middlemen who grow rich at their expense. Economic and political inequalities reinforce one another. This reason for disliking the multiplication of wants goes, in Rousseau's mind, with the belief that where there are great inequalities, men come to have insatiable ambitions and implacable resentments. They have wants which stand in the way of their getting happiness; they are moved by an obsessive need to preserve and to enhance the marks of their superiority. They do not want what really satisfies them, but what they imagine gives them worth in the eyes of others. Rousseau did not use the word *competitive*, which belongs to a later period when the influence of the classical economists affected all types of social theory; but he certainly hated what later came to be known as the competitive spirit. He was not an economist; he did not have in mind the competition of entrepreneurs for the market or of workers for jobs. The competition he deplored was the ceaseless striving to get ahead of others and to appear important to them; and, though he was no economist and had only the vaguest ideas about the functioning of the economy which Adam

Smith was to describe, he did claim to see a close connection between its size and complexity and this striving.

The early socialists condemned both the sort of competition which offended Rousseau and the sort described by the economists. But they did not follow Rousseau in deploring the multiplication of wants. On the contrary, like Mandeville and Hume, like Bentham and the Utilitarians, like most of the Encyclopaedists, they welcomed it and took it for a mark of progress. The more men's wants multiply, the greater the need for peaceful collaboration between them and the greater the cohesion of society, provided, of course, that wants do not increase faster than the ability to satisfy them. What was wrong with industrial society was not that it multiplied men's wants, for it also multiplied the wherewithal to satisfy them; what was wrong was that it was so organized that it gave the largest rewards to idlers and the smallest to the industrious who could not afford to purchase the fruits of their industry. It was also wasteful, producing more than was needed to satisfy some wants and too little to satisfy others; its economy was blindly competitive and liable to sudden and disastrous crises. The remedy was to organize production more rationally and to distribute what was produced more justly.

Saint-Simon was perhaps the most whole-hearted exponent of these views. Of the major French socialists, he was the farthest removed in spirit from Rousseau. The same cause which multiplies men's wants not only increases their capacity to satisfy those wants but also enhances the social importance of a class enlightened enough to know how to organize production rationally and how to distribute its fruits justly. The cause is the progress of science and technology and the class are the leaders of industry. It seemed obviously desirable to Saint-Simon that production should increase as rapidly as possible so long as it increased smoothly and was aimed at satisfying the wants of all classes. Saint-Simon had much the same conception of happiness as Bentham had. The more we want, provided we can get what we want, the happier we are. The workers, the most numerous and the poorest class, have more unsatisfied wants than the other classes, and therefore it is the prime duty of society to satisfy their wants.

Proudhon had not the same enthusiasm as Saint Simon for increasing production; he was more concerned to ensure that the worker got the full product of his labour and to decrease the authority of man over man. He cared more for equality and freedom than for productivity. Nevertheless, he welcomed the use of machinery and the wealth it brought. He was always the friend of the small man against the powerful and the rich, and shared more of Rousseau's likes and dislikes than any of the other socialists. But he did not preach the simple life or condemn the technical progress which made life complicated. Nor did most of the other socialists, English and French. When

Owen (in the report known as *Mr. Owen's Plan*) explained that the widespread distress in England after the Napoleonic wars was due to a great increase in machine production, stimulated by the needs of a country at war and followed by an abrupt falling off of demand with the coming of peace, he took care to add that to destroy this machinery would be absurd. He wanted an England continually growing in wealth, and we may assume that Thompson, a good Utilitarian, also wanted it. Hodgskin's quarrel with the capitalist economy was not that it multiplied men's wants and complicated their lives beyond the point compatible with freedom and equality; it was merely that it deprived the worker of the product of his labour. Hodgskin believed in progress, and thought of it (after the fashion of his day, which was the fashion of almost everyone except Rousseau) as both material and moral. The natural increase of population, leading to an extended division of labour and to the accumulation of knowledge and technical improvements, makes for progress. It is true that some of the early socialists disliked factory production, but they disliked it because it made work monotonous and degrading and not because a rapid increase in wealth multiplies wants and produces a type of society in which men cannot be equal and free.

There is one important, though only partial, exception to the general statement I have made. Fourier certainly shared some of the fears which moved Rousseau to extol the simple life. Fourier believed that in industrial society there are three kinds of waste: there are idlers who in a properly constituted society would be producers, there is inefficiency, and there are things produced in abundance giving little or no pleasure. It was the first two kinds of waste, more than the third, that Fourier attacked. But he did also attack the third kind, saying that in industrial society the rich accumulate luxuries which add nothing to their happiness while the poor envy them their lot. Thus we have society divided into two classes, neither of them truly satisfied, of which the poorer envy the richer largely because they have illusions about them. This is an argument very much in the style of Rousseau. So also is Fourier's attack on commerce. Widely felt emotions, he tells us, are rarely mistaken, and in most countries traders have been despised. He approves Christ's rebuke to the merchants driven from the temple: '*You have made of my house a den of thieves.*' He concedes that the ancients went perhaps too far in their contempt for traders, but that is a better fault than to exalt them, as is done in industrial society. For there the merchant and the banker call the tune. They are the middlemen, the controllers of the market, the speculators who levy tribute on consumer and producer, and who create disorder by their manoeuvres to increase their profits. Fourier sees free competition in industrial society leading inevitably to a kind of mercantile feudalism, to the dependence of the producer (both the manual worker

and the manager) on the merchant and the banker, the real masters
of society. These are arguments quite in the spirit of Rousseau, though
they are clearer and better worked out than anything on similar
topics from Rousseau's pen. The phalanx is an economy organized to
do without the middleman, the manipulator of the market and creator
of insecurity, the man more interested in making profits than in seeing
that needs are met; the phalanx excludes him but welcomes the honest
owner of property who, by joining the phalanx, thereby proves that he
wants his property used to good effect. The phalanx also excludes the
factory and includes only the workshop, because the factory makes the
producer a mere tender of machines, taking all pride and pleasure out
of his work, because it is unhealthy, and because the goods it produces
are shoddy.

Yet Fourier did not follow Rousseau in praising the simple life. Nor
did he attack the economy of his day because it extended the division
of labour too far and made life too complicated to allow of genuine
democracy. His reasons for keeping the phalanx small had nothing to
do with the conviction that men can be equal and free only when they
can all take a direct part in making the laws they are required to
obey. Fourier was an ardent hedonist. He believed that in the phalanx
all men's pleasures, physical and mental, would be more varied and
more exquisite than the pleasures of the rich in contemporary France.
He was not himself a voluptuary; he was too poor and also too much
a man with a mission for that. But the men and women living in his
phalansteries were to enjoy life abundantly, uninhibited by the scruples
which now spoil the pleasures of civilized man.

In 1848, in a debate in the Constituent Assembly as to whether the
droit au travail (the right of the worker against the State that it should
provide work for him when he is unemployed) should be included in
the constitution, Tocqueville asked: 'What then is socialism?' and
answered his own question in these words: 'It is a vigorous, im-
moderate appeal to the material passions. It wants the rehabilitation
of the flesh and unlimited consumption.' Tocqueville was seldom
grossly inaccurate, even in his attacks upon what he detested. The
socialists did not preach the virtues of poverty; they wanted the poor
to live abundantly, as the rich lived. They wanted wealth to grow fast,
believing that the faster it grew the happier men would be, provided
only that wealth were justly distributed. What Tocqueville forgot is that
the Encyclopaedists in France and the Utilitarians in England had
appealed no less vigorously to the same passions, with only this difference, that their appeal, though addressed formally to all men, was
directed in practice almost entirely to the educated classes, while the
socialists directed their appeal either to the poor or to the consciences
of the rich on behalf of the poor.

Durkheim makes this materialism, this assumption that the multiplication of wants is desirable so long as they can be satisfied, one of the two distinguishing marks of nineteenth-century socialism as compared with older equalitarian and communist doctrines; the other is the desire for some form of social control of production. Plato, he says, was not concerned to increase wealth or to rationalize production; he wanted the rulers to own all things in common because he believed that this was a condition of their being whole-heartedly devoted to the good of the State. Sir Thomas More was concerned with the individual rather than the State, and his Utopia is so organized as to make its citizens virtuous and contented. Though in Utopia everyone works and no one goes hungry, it is not thought desirable that wealth should increase indefinitely, and the Utopians do not ask themselves how production should be controlled in order to be more efficient. Durkheim sees the same indifference to the increase of wealth and the social control of production even in eighteenth-century writers who attacked the established system of property before 1789, even in such writers as Mably and Morelly. If they wanted private property abolished, it was because they thought it corrupted morals; it was not in order to make easier the rational control of production nor to satisfy material wants more abundantly.

Durkheim is substantially right, though he makes the contrast rather too sharply. More's Utopians do not aim at increasing wealth indefinitely; they aim rather at reducing the labour needed to produce the necessaries of life so as to leave as much time as possible for the cultivation of the mind. Nevertheless, the Utopians live commodiously and the aged and the sick are provided for. And there is social control of production; the phylarch or head bailiff, elected annually by every group of thirty families, allots work and sees to it that it is done properly. Everyone who has not earned exemption from manual labour by proving himself worthy of promotion to the order of scholars must be trained for husbandry and must engage in it, and must also learn and follow a useful trade. In Utopia there is elaborate direction of labour and therefore also planned production. But all this is not done to make production more efficient, as Adam Smith or Saint-Simon or Owen would have understood efficiency; it is not done to ensure that available resources are used to produce the greatest possible quantity of goods and services; it is done to enable the Utopians to live healthy and virtuous lives. So too Morelly does not confine himself to proposing common ownership on the ground that private property is corrupting; he also proposes the direction of labour, public works to absorb unemployment, and the closing down of unprofitable industries. He wants to ensure that production as a whole satisfies all needs and that no one is overworked. The communist economy described in *La Code de la Nature*, which is only one (and the most extreme) of several projects prepared by Morelly during the course of his life, involves just as much social control of production as the schemes of Saint-Simon, Fourier and Owen. But Morelly never says or even implies that the indefinite increase of wealth is desirable, and his conception of efficient production is not the same as that of the economists and nineteenth-century socialists. It matters to him that the idle should not exploit the industrious, that all who can should work, that no one should be unprovided for, that the vices born of inequality should disappear; but it does not matter to him that production should be so organized as to make men much wealthier than they are. Though he approves of lavish spending on public monuments and festivals, he expects the citizens to live modestly. The communists of the eighteenth century mostly favoured sober living; it was much more Voltaire, Mandeville, and Montesquieu, and after them the Encyclopaedists and Utilitarians, who took the accumulation of wealth for a mark of progress and who approved of high living. It was not till the nineteenth century that the champions of the poor, the preachers of equality, the scourges of the idle rich, came to be materialists, in the sense in which Tocqueville used the word when he applied it to them.

5. Their Feminism

Several of the early socialists were ardent feminists. It was indeed to this part of their doctrine (and to an aspect of it likely to shock the bourgeois) that Tocqueville referred when, in the speech from which I quote, he used the phrase 'the rehabilitation of the flesh'. That phrase was invented by Enfantin, who after Saint-Simon's death proclaimed himself one of his disciples; it expressed Enfantin's belief in easy divorce and dislike of the chastity and the continence preached by the Church. Fourier, though he thought easy divorce unsuited to the social system of the period in which he lived, a period which he called civilization, predicted it for the period next after it, and even foresaw the eventual disappearance of marriage. He said of the civilized[1] that they demand unlimited freedom for trade, where crime and trickery cry out for restraint by law, but wish to deprive of all freedom the one passion, love, which must be free if men are to be happy and good.

Attacks on the sanctity of marriage have in themselves nothing to do with feminism; they had been made in the eighteenth century by

---

[1] This term has for Fourier a historical reference; it refers to people living in the fifth period of social evolution, the period he calls civilization. It also has, for him, a pejorative sense because the social order of the fifth period is, he thinks, irrational and destined to pass away, and indeed in some respects is already passing away. The civilized are, in the eyes of Fourier, absurd and also by way of being backward.

men whose object had not been to improve the position of women. It is only when existing forms of marriage and conventions of sexual morality are thought to lay a much heavier burden on women than on men that the attack on them deserves to be called feminism. But Fourier and the disciples of Saint-Simon did so regard them. They believed that men had made chattels and servants of women, and that nothing proved this better than the way that women were given in marriage and the wifely duties laid upon them by custom and by law. Some of the disciples of Saint-Simon, to mark their sense of women's equality with men, called God both the Father and the Mother of mankind, and sent a mission to the East to welcome the Woman Messiah, whose coming they expected, of all unlikely places, in Constantinople. Their feminism was as absurd as it was sincere.

Fourier thought it one of the great advantages of the communal living which he preached that it would free women from drudgery in the kitchen and the nursery. The small family living in the small house cannot but deprive the married woman of the opportunity to cultivate her mind, tying her to the home and to menial duties. Fourier even put it forward as a general thesis that social progress can be measured by the extent to which women have moved towards liberty, and decadence by the extent to which they have been deprived of it. Such statements are probably not meant to be taken literally. Fourier no doubt believed that there are other forms of progress besides the emancipation of women, and he certainly had no warrant for holding that progress is never made in any direction without also being made in this.[1] But the statement, though palpably false if taken literally, does show how strongly Fourier believed in the emancipation of women.

The disciples of Saint-Simon were not democrats, and were therefore not moved by their feminism to demand political rights for women. Fourier's hopes were confined to the community of the future, the phalanx, where the occupations open to men would also be open to women, who would presumably take part in choosing what officials might be needed; he was not concerned to extend the franchise in merely civilized communities. The most fervent advocate of political rights for women was Thompson, whose *Appeal of One Half of the Human Race, Women, against the Pretensions of the other Half, Men, to restrain them in Political and then in Civil and Domestic Slavery* appeared in 1825. Thompson's book was directed against James Mill who, in his article on 'Government' in the *Encyclopaedia Britannica* of 1824, had said that the interests of women were included in those of their menfolk, their husbands or fathers, and so, without actually

---

[1] Fourier did not deny that the ancient Greeks made great progress in several directions between the Homeric and the classical periods. But women enjoyed greater freedom in the first of these periods than in the second, and there is no reason to believe that Fourier did not know this.

denying the vote to women, had implied that it was not important that they should have it. How, asks Thompson, can Mill, who admits that man is a selfish creature seeking to make others subservient to his will, assume that women's interests are included in those of men? Even children's interests are not included in those of their fathers, or else it would never have been necessary to pass such a law as the Factory Act. The reason for not giving the vote to children is not that their interests are included in their fathers'; it is that they do not know how to use the vote to protect their interests, that they do not know how to use the vote rationally. But Mill does not suppose (what Thompson takes to be obviously false) that women cannot use the vote rationally. Nobody's interest is included entire in anyone else's, and if we tie one person to dependence on another, we enable that other to exploit him, and so create a situation making for a greater divergence of interest. And, in any case, it would not be enough to have men, even though they were unselfish, look after women's interests, for women's abilities, like men's, are developed by their having to care for their own and the common interest.

Proudhon was conspicuously not a feminist. Not that he believed in the inferiority of women to men. But he wanted to preserve the family, and therefore resisted any claims made on behalf of women which seemed to him to weaken that institution. He, who wanted to loosen all other social ties, wanted to keep family ties as strong as ever. The child learns to be sociable and just inside the family, where he is under parental discipline, where he is controlled and punished by those who love him. Proudhon believed that the best type of family, the type best suited for the training of the young, exists only where monogamy is the rule and divorce is rare. Women are not inferior to but different from men, and they are happiest and most useful as wives and mothers; they are the creators and preservers of the family, of the most tightly knit and important of social groups, because it is inside it that the child becomes a social and a moral being. But, admirable though the family is, larger social groups must not be families writ large; for the family is by nature hierarchic and under paternal authority, while all larger social groups ought to consist only of equals, of men who are not under authority but are bound only by agreements voluntarily made and by a moral law whose sanction is the individual's own conscience. The family is unique; it prepares man by love and coercive discipline for the larger society in which he is eventually to achieve justice without coercive discipline. The discipline of the family will always be needed to educate the child into a rational and sociable adult; it will still be needed when grown men shall have become capable of society without coercive discipline. And to Proudhon it seemed to go without saying, or rather without needing to be proved, that the head of the small monogamous family must be the husband and the father, even though the wife and the mother is the centre of it and exercises the deeper moral influence.

Marx called Proudhon a *petit bourgeois* writer, and Marxists have ever since followed this example. There is nothing *petit bourgeois* about Proudhon's anarchism or his dislike of nationalism, Jacobinism and Bonapartism; the *petit bourgeois* does not want to destroy the State power, even though he resents bureaucratic interference with his small business. He does not want the State to tell him what to do with his own, but he does want it to protect him both from the propertyless and from the wealthy. In France, in Proudhon's day, the *petit bourgeois*, when he feared disorder, was inclined to Bonapartism, and when he feared the wealthy, to Jacobinism, both of which Proudhon despised. But Proudhon's defence of the small family, whose natural head he took to be the father, would certainly have been very much to the taste of the lesser bourgeoisie and also of the peasants, whom Marxists have often assimilated to that class.[1] It is, however, possible to insist upon the need to preserve that type of family without treating the father as any more its natural head than the mother.

It is not his wanting to preserve the small family which makes Proudhon conspicuously not a feminist; it is rather his defence of paternal authority, and – even more important – his failure to take into account the possibility that, though woman's capacities may be different from man's, she needs to have the same civil and political rights as man if she is to make the best of them. Proudhon believed that men and women excel in different ways, that men have in larger measure the qualities making for social superiority outside the family – such qualities as physical strength, power of reasoning, and consistency of purpose – while women are more intuitive, have more grace and delicacy of mind and a greater capacity for love. He admitted that the qualities in which they excel are as admirable and as useful to society as any, but he thought them qualities better suited to family life than to conspicuous achievement outside it.

Proudhon may be right. Certainly, many men, and perhaps also many women, would agree with him that the two sexes differ greatly and even that they differ much as he said they do. There is nothing new about his views as to how men and women differ. But it is im-

---

1 The *bourgeois*, great or small, is, as his name implies, a town-dweller. The point of calling the peasant a *petit bourgeois* is that he is supposed to share many of the political and social attitudes of the artisan and the shopkeeper, the *petit bourgeois* in the strict sense. The supposition is largely correct when made about the French peasants in the last century, except that they were much more inclined to Bonapartism than to Jacobinism. It is much further from the truth when made about peasants in Russia and other Slav lands in this century.

portant to notice that a man or woman might share these views and yet be an ardent feminist. There are two kinds of feminism. We may hold, with Mary Wollstonecraft, that, while women can do all that men can, they have been unjustly deprived by men of the opportunity to do any but menial tasks; or we may hold that women, being by nature different from men, will not, except rarely, want to engage in most of the occupations traditionally reserved for men, but that this is no reason for not giving them the same civil and political rights as men. The socialists who were also feminists did not distinguish between these two kinds of feminism, and therefore did not consciously adhere to either in preference to the other. But I suspect that Enfantin and Fourier were both feminists of the second kind; they probably agreed with Proudhon that women differ greatly from men. They certainly did not want to make men out of women; but they thought that women could not make the best of their capacities unless they were given the same freedom as men; unless they were removed from the tutelage of the other sex. Enfantin and Fourier did not believe in strict monogamy and the close family circle; but it is possible to believe in them without denying that women should have the same rights as men. It is possible to put a high value on chastity and monogamy, to admit that the two sexes differ greatly, mentally and morally as well as physically, and yet to make a strong case for their both having the same civil and political rights. It is possible to insist strongly on natural difference and no less strongly on social equality.

Women feminists have been more inclined to the first kind of feminism than to the second. This is certainly true of Mary Wollstonecraft, whose *Vindication of the Rights of Women* appeared in 1792, of the English suffragettes before 1914, and perhaps also of Flora Tristan, who was a socialist as well as a feminist. Mary Wollstonecraft and the suffragettes insisted that women are as good as men in all the ways in which men have claimed to be superior; they argued that if women have not in the past excelled in these ways it is because they have been kept down by men; they looked forward to women playing as great a part as men in every sphere hitherto reserved for men. They denied to men every superiority except greater physical strength. They have been accused of a lack of proper pride in their sex, of being envious of the male, of suffering from an acute sense of inferiority unconsciously revealed by the kind of argument they use to show that women are as good as men, arguments tending to prove, not that women's peculiar qualities are as valuable as men's, but that women, given the chance, could do all that men do equally well. This kind of feminism, so its critics say, may in the long run prove burdensome to women, making them competitors with men in spheres where masculine values prevail and where women are therefore likely to be at disadvantage.

This criticism, for what it is worth, cannot be justly made of the socialists who were also feminists, for they were mostly feminists of the second kind; they did not want to make women more like men but to give them as good a chance as men to make the best of whatever gifts nature had endowed them with. This is especially true of the French socialists, perhaps because theirs is the country where women have been most appreciated for being what they are.

II. SAINT-SIMON'S ACCOUNT OF SOCIAL CHANGE. WERE THE EARLY SOCIALISTS UTOPIAN?

I have considered what is common to Rousseau and to the early socialists and also where they differ from him. This comparison serves to draw attention to the ways in which criticism of the established order changed as a result of the French and the industrial revolutions. The early socialists were all radicals of the post-revolutionary epoch, familiar with the hopes raised by the revolution and the disillusionments which followed it. They had lived through immense changes; they had witnessed what had been until then the boldest of all attempts to reconstruct a great society. They were used to change and expected more of it. For all that they deprecated violence, they were revolutionaries in a sense in which Rousseau never was; they aspired to a decisive influence on the course of change. Rousseau had predicted the revolution but had never sought to hasten its coming, or to advise men what they should do when it came. If he was a prophet, he was so rather in the style of the Old Testament; he saw evils all around him and foretold calamity. He saw no connection between the course of events which he deplored and the just society which he described but whose coming he never really hoped for.[1] And he lived before the age of factory production, of which the economists and early socialists took so large account.

---

[1] Goethe says somewhere that with Voltaire one world ends and with Rousseau another begins. This is true in the sense that Rousseau gave birth to ideas only half understood in his own day, and destined to be more fully understood in a society very different from the one he knew, whereas Voltaire came closer than any other man to being the epitome of his age. Yet Voltaire, very much at home in the society which he dominated intellectually, had not the same forebodings about the future. He was, on the whole, a cheerful pessimist, while Rousseau, who was almost never cheerful, dared not hope in the future even though he believed in the providence of God and quarrelled with Voltaire for denying it.

Marx, though he claimed to be a scientific socialist in some sense in which the early socialists were not scientific, admitted his debt to them. He had, he believed, superseded them, but he had also taken up elements of their theories into his own. If not always a just, he was, on the whole, a generous critic of the early socialists; that is to say, generous to most of them except to Proudhon, who was, in any case, more a contemporary than a precursor. What he learnt from the French socialists was, of course, different from what he learnt from the English, for their interests were by no means the same. Though the early socialists were believers in progress, though they were aware that a long process of change had been needed to make society as they knew it, though they held or hoped that it had at last become (or was soon to be) propitious to socialism, they for the most part produced no theories about the course of history. And those of them that did so were French, which is not surprising. For the French had had a great revolution, and it was only natural that they should speculate about it and its causes. Of these philosophies of history (or theories about the course of history) only one, Saint-Simon's, need detain us, not only because Marx owed more to it than to any other, but also because it is much the most interesting in itself; it is more perceptive and suggestive than Fourier's account of the first eight of the thirty-six periods which he allotted to human history, and more of a piece and clearer than Proudhon's far-ranging reflections on the great revolution and the destiny of man. Saint-Simon and Proudhon, because of their extensive interest in history, had more developed ideas than the others about social classes, their rise and decay, and their changing roles. If they were not the most class-conscious of socialists, they were certainly the socialists who, except for Marx, produced the boldest and the most ingenious theories about classes. But the most arresting psychologist among the early socialists was certainly Fourier; he made what he believed to be an exhaustive analysis of the human passions, and sought to show how they are frustrated in the commercial and industrial society of his day and can be given a free and harmless outlet in the phalanx, the only fully rational society because the only one fully adapted to human nature.

As philosophers of history, as speculators about social classes and their historic roles, as social psychologists, the French socialists have more to offer than the English ones. But as economists, and more particularly as critics of classical economics, it is the English socialists who excel. The only one of the major French socialists to attempt a sustained criticism of the classical economists was Proudhon, and he was nowhere near as acute a critic as either Hodgskin or Thompson. If I may hazard a generalization, I should say that the French socialists were broader in their interests and more imaginative, while the English were more lucid and more rigorous. Owen, no doubt, was both narrow and vague, as business men are apt to be when they take to social theory in middle age; he was much more popular than Thompson or Hodgskin, and made a much greater impression on his contemporaries, but to the student of theory he is perhaps the least interesting of the three.

1. Saint-Simon on the Course of Social Change

It is in the eighth and ninth letters of *L'Organisateur*[1] that Saint-Simon describes in broad outline the course of social evolution which transformed feudal society into the industrial society which he urges the industrialists, supported by the scientists and artists, to take over.

What Saint-Simon calls the feudal and theological system of the Middle Ages was born, he tells us, in and after the fourth century of our era, with the triumph of Christianity and the irruption of the barbarians into the Roman Empire. This system was fully mature by the eleventh century, but as soon as it reached maturity the seed of its destruction appeared inside it – the enfranchised commune. Before the appearance of the commune, the craftsman had been the mere servant or creature of the feudal lord, as much dependent on him as the serf who was tied to the soil. With the appearance of the commune, the craftsman became an independent producer. Hitherto the wealthy and the powerful had not been producers of wealth, they had not been engaged in industry, they had not been what Saint-Simon calls *industriels*; they had been feudal lords and churchmen. The emergence of the commune made it possible for the producer of wealth, the *industriel*, to grow wealthy and in the course of time to acquire social influence and power.

But the feudal lords and the men in Holy Orders were not, until the feudal and theological system was in decay, parasites; they performed useful functions. The feudal lords maintained order and protected their dependents from attack, the Church maintained the cultural and moral unity which every society needs. Saint-Simon even says that the

---

[1] It has been said that *L'Organisateur* was written for Saint-Simon by Comte. But it was published as coming from the pen of Saint-Simon, and the ideas in it are probably his. Where, as in the third part of *Le Catéchisme des Industriels*, the part called *Système de Politique Positive*, Comte interprets the master's thought very freely and neglects a part of it which seems important to the master, the work appears under the name of Comte, who is styled a pupil of Henri Saint-Simon. – But these problems of attribution are not our concern.

feudal system was natural to a society where the principal means to national prosperity was war.[1]

At about the time that the communes emerged, science was introduced into Europe by the Arabs. The feudal lords required (this is Saint-Simon's account of the matter and is not necessarily true) passive obedience, while the spiritual power demanded complete submission to its teachings. But industrial power is of its nature less arbitrary than military power; the man who directs the labour of others in order to create wealth does not demand passive obedience of his subordinates. He is a man whose skill and experience are greater than theirs, and whose authority over them rests largely on a superiority as evident to them as to him. So, too, masters of science do not demand blind submission of their students; they offer them truths which they support with evidence. The authority of the scientist depends as much (and indeed more) on acknowledged ability as that of the leader of industry; it depends on his ability to offer explanations which satisfy the critical intelligence of his hearers. Thus the spirit of the old society was quite contrary to the spirit of the new classes growing up inside it, the new society centred in the chartered towns and in the universities founded in them.

Conflict between the old and the new was inevitable but could not break out openly while the emergent classes were still weak. The craftsmen in the towns who had obtained charters from kings and feudal lords did not look upon themselves as the enemies of those who had enfranchised them, nor did the universities look upon themselves as enemies of the Church. They did not, and could not, see themselves as the beginnings of a new social order destined to replace the old; they had no conception of themselves as involved in a necessary historical process. For generations they accepted the superiority of the established authorities, of the territorial magnates and the Church. But, inevitably, they acquired interests and attitudes incompatible with the old order.

It was not until the sixteenth century that the old society was openly challenged by the new society to which it had given birth. Luther and the other reformers successfully attacked the authority of the Pope and thereby weakened irretrievably the Church which had until then dominated society intellectually, and weakened it so much that,

[1] This, surely, is an absurdity which serves to obscure what is valuable in Saint-Simon's thought. All wealth, as he knew, is created by labour, whereas war destroys wealth. War may enable some nations to plunder others, but it impoverishes the plundered much more than it enriches the plunderer. It is nonsense to say that in a feudal society war is a means to national prosperity whereas in an industrial society the means to it is work. The important point which Saint-Simon makes is that in the first type of society wealth and power belong to a military caste and a church while in the second they belong to producers of wealth.

even in the countries that remained Catholic, the Church, from being a rival of the monarch, became his subsidiary ally. The struggle against the spiritual power occupied the sixteenth and the seventeenth centuries, and then came the struggle against the temporal feudal power. The commons[1] were too weak to challenge both the monarch and the nobles: and so in England they allied themselves with the nobles against the monarch, while in France they allied themselves with the monarch against the nobles. To contemporaries in these two countries (which Saint-Simon regarded as the most advanced), the main conflict seemed to be in each case between the monarch and the nobility, with the commons playing a minor part, but the historically important conflict in France as well as in England was between the commons and one part or other of the old temporal power.

At this point of his narrative, Saint-Simon assesses the importance of three great events: the discovery of America and of the route to India, the invention of printing, and the theories of Copernicus and Galileo. Unless there had been a large increase in trade and considerable scientific progress in the Middle Ages, the journeys of the great navigators would have been impossible, but they in their turn encouraged trade and stimulated enquiry; the tight little world dominated by the feudal lords and the Church was suddenly and greatly enlarged. The invention of printing ensured that the discoveries of scientists and their speculations could reach many more minds than before; it multiplied the impact of mind on mind and so made intellectual activity much greater than before. The theories of Copernicus and Galileo, offering simpler and clearer explanations better supported by the facts, were fatal to the anthropomorphic theology of the Church; they could not be accommodated to that theology and therefore, as they were more widely accepted, inevitably undermined the authority of the old spiritual power.

By the eighteenth century the commons had become strong enough to challenge the entire old order, and science had developed so much, had acquired so great a prestige, that the Protestant attack on the spiritual authority of the papacy could be expanded into a general attack on every attempt to impose beliefs by coercive methods. It was then that the claim was made for complete freedom of private judge-

---

[1] The word *commons* is used here in the same sense as Saint-Simon used the French word *communes*; it refers to the townsmen, the third estate of the *ancien régime*; it therefore excludes the gentry, whose representatives sat in the English House of Commons. The English gentry are equivalent to what the French would call *la petite noblesse*. It would be absurd in a summary of this kind to stop to criticize the many doubtful or misleading statements which Saint-Simon makes; our purpose is not to enquire into the truth of his account of social and political evolution in western Europe but to consider what kind of account it is, what factors are treated as the most important in explaining social change.

THE EARLY SOCIALISTS, FRENCH AND ENGLISH   71

ment. 'Thus', we are told, 'the eighteenth century carried the attack
on the two powers [the temporal and the spiritual] to its ultimate
limits, and completed the ruin of the old system in its parts and as a
whole.'[1]

Unfortunately, in France, Louis XIV, having humbled the nobility,
abandoned the alliance with the commons and sought the friendship
of the defeated power. This mistake, which was continued by his
successors, led in the end to the French Revolution. Saint-Simon, when
he says this, is not suggesting that, if the three Louis had not made
this mistake, the old monarchy could have lasted indefinitely. The old
régime was bound to have come to an end, but if the French kings had
continued their alliance with the commons, with the rising industrial
class, it would have ended without violence. The French revolution
destroyed the monarchy, an institution still popular in France and
well adapted to lead the country through the last stages of transition
to the full industrial society. The destruction of the monarchy was
therefore also a mistake, though the last three kings were to blame
for creating the situation which caused the mistake to be made. The
monarchy, still having an important function to perform, was re-
established. It is interesting to notice that in speaking of the French
monarchy Saint-Simon passes a judgement which brings to mind one
of the fundamental doctrines of Marx. He says: 'The royal power
was soon reconstituted, because it was in France at once the head and
the heart of the old system, and could only disappear with it, and a
system can only disappear to the extent that another already exists
entirely formed and ready to take its place immediately.'[2]

It is only now, looking back on the past, that we can properly understand it; it is only now that historians have accumulated the facts
which enable us to discern a necessary course of social evolution. The
commons had no sense of the process in which they were involved; the
kings who needed money and invited the commons to meetings of the
estates to vote taxes did not know that they were strengthening the
class destined to destroy the old system. The scientists who put forward
the hypotheses incompatible with theology did not know that they
were the agents of a vast cultural revolution. The commons in pro-

---

[1] *Oeuvres de Saint-Simon et d'Enfantin*, Paris 1869, Vol 20, p. 104.
[2] Ibid., Vol. 20, pp. 105-6. – The second half of this sentence illustrates something else which Saint-Simon shares with Marx: a difficulty in finding words
to express his meaning exactly when what he means is at all complicated. His
actual words suggest that the old system survives entire until the new system
is entirely formed. But Saint-Simon has already shown the old system in
process of disappearing as the new system emerges. What he really means is
that the old form of government cannot disappear until the new system is
completely formed, which suggests that what completes the forming of the
new system is the emergence of a class willing and able to take over the
direction of society; but this is not what he says.

moting their interests and making the most of their opportunities did not know that they were gradually transforming the social order.

The expansion of industry and the progress of science have changed the nature of authority. In industrial society everyone makes a contribution, everyone is a collaborator, and everyone understands that he is engaged in an elaborate enterprise with others. Hierarchy is grounded in differences of ability obvious to everyone, and social discipline need no longer be military in character, consisting of arbitrary command and unquestioning obedience. In the old society, those who produced no wealth received the greater part of it; it was therefore necessarily a society of masters and servants. Already, in many industrial enterprises, order results from force of habit and a sense of the common interest, and so it will be eventually in society as a whole. Already, those who are not scientists have learnt to trust those who are; they believe, without being able to prove it, that the earth is round, that it revolves round the sun, and more besides. But they are not credulous, for the beliefs they accept are subject to verification by persons competent to verify them. Even the scientist outside the sphere of his own competence accepts things on trust, just as the layman does. Thus it is that science and industry bring into being a new kind of hierarchy, a new kind of authority, not known before, a hierarchy and an authority based on proved ability and tested knowledge. Culturally and morally the people have been weaned away from the old system of authority, temporal and spiritual, and so they 'no longer need to be governed, that is to say commanded. It is enough for the maintenance of order that matters of common interest should be administered.'[1] The people are already mature enough to do without government, and yet they are still governed. The parliamentary régime and full liberty of conscience are the furthest concessions that the old system can make to the new forces arising in its midst without completely disappearing. The new system, industrially and intellectually, is fully developed; it pervades society but does not yet dominate it. By this Saint-Simon means that the industrial class have not yet taken over control of society; they still do not administer matters of common concern; they have not yet stepped fully into their inheritance. Saint-Simon conceives it to be his mission to persuade them to do it and to persuade the monarch to help them do it. That is why so many of his open letters are addressed 'to the King and to men of industry' or to 'MM les députés who are men of industry (industriels).'[2]

In the tenth letter of L'Organisateur Saint-Simon considers the situation since 1814. He expects a smooth transition from the parliamentary régime to the sort of administration he has in mind. The

[1] Ibid., Vol. 20, p. 144.
[2] But not the letters which make up L'Organisateur; they are addressed by the author to his compatriots.

leaders of industry already form a large part of the electorate, they have only to vote members of their own class into the chamber quite to alter its character. They have only to take the opportunities open to them, and this they are bound to do in the end. They will then set up an administration along the lines suggested by Saint-Simon in the sixth letter, whose contents we have already touched upon.

Saint-Simon protests that there is nothing Utopian about the scheme proposed in the sixth letter; it may seem new, and indeed is new, but it is something for which history has prepared the way. 'It is not I who have formed the constitutional project whose basic principles I have expounded; it is the mass of the European population who have laboured to shape it during the eight centuries which have preceded this one.'[1] The author invites his readers to enquire whether his account of the broad course of events since the eleventh century is accurate and whether his project fits in with it, for this is the only valid line of criticism.

Saint-Simon was not as successful as he had hoped to be in persuading the leaders of industry to take over the direction of society. This lack of success moved him to sharper criticism of the French Revolution and of the ideas associated with it, ideas which were, he thought, turning men's minds away from essentials. During the period of transition from a feudal to an industrial social order two groups had appeared, the lawyers and the metaphysicians, who now stood in the way of progress. Originally their functions had been useful; the lawyers had served the royal power against the feudal nobles by undermining their privileges, and the metaphysicians had loosened the hold of theology on men's minds. There cannot be an abrupt transition from one system, be it social or intellectual, to another; there is necessarily a long course of change leading from the one to the other, and in this intervening period there emerge institutions, attitudes of mind, and social groups which will disappear as soon as the new system is fully established. Liberalism is such an attitude; it is the philosophy of the lawyers and metaphysicians who played so prominent a part in demolishing the old system and in making the French Revolution. This philosophy has acquired an immense prestige, but it is at bottom negative. The ideas of liberty and equality, as proclaimed by the liberals, effectively challenged the privileges enjoyed by classes who, as the old system decayed, ceased to be useful to society; that was their true and important historical function. But as ideals to be realized in the new society they are useless and even harmful.

It is absurd to consider every citizen competent in political matters, which are more difficult to understand than, say, chemistry, where the authority of experts is undisputed. It is only because politics is not a

[1] Ibid., Vol. 20, pp. 179-80.

science that this assumption of universal competence can pass muster; its absurdity will be fully apparent when the study of society and administration has become scientific. Saint-Simon even accuses the lawyers and metaphysicians, whom he calls a bastard class born of the decay of the feudal system, of wanting to become a privileged order. They made the revolution in the name of all Frenchmen but now want to dominate the France which has emerged from the revolution. These negative conceptions of equality and liberty now stand in the way of the positive principle suited to the new industrial society: *from* everyone according to his capacity and *to* everyone according to his contribution. This is the true principle of equality, which gives to every man rewards and authority in proportion to his ability and willingness to serve the community. And so Saint-Simon, during the last years of his life, thought it his mission to combat the false ideals of the liberals and democrats as well as to persuade the leaders of industry to take charge of society; or rather, he saw these two things as parts of the same mission.

I have argued, in discussing Hegel's philosophy of history, that, though it treats history as a necessary course of change, it does not explain how any one stage in that course leads to the one after it; it gives us an account of a variety of stages and seeks to explain how in the later stages the essential nature of Spirit is more adequately realized than in the earlier, but it does not show how the earlier stages change into the later ones. This criticism cannot be made of Saint-Simon; he does offer an account of how feudal society evolves into industrial society. No doubt, his account is far from satisfactory, but it is an attempt to do something which Hegel never attempted. If we were to describe a child's condition, physical and mental, at various stages of its growth, explaining how at each stage it was closer to maturity than at the stage before it, we should be using Hegel's method, but if we tried to explain how it had passed from each stage to the next, we should be using the method of Saint-Simon and of Marx.

Saint-Simon's account is open to two kinds of criticism: we can object to his interpretation of the facts, or we can object to the concepts he uses and the assumptions he makes. It is, of course, the second kind of criticism, rather than the first, which interests the social and political theorist, and I shall confine myself to it.

There is no harm in speaking of periods of transition. If, like Saint-Simon, we consider the social and political order in western Europe as it was in the eleventh century and as it is in our own, we can treat the intervening centuries as a period of transition. Our purpose is then to explain how one social and political order was transformed into another, and since that is our purpose, whatever falls in time between the two belongs properly to the period of transition; but if our purpose had been to explain how the social and political order of the ninth century was transformed into that of the sixteenth, then the eleventh century would have been transitional. True, the social and political order is always changing; it changed not only during the eleventh century but in every year of that century. Nevertheless, since social change is always gradual (though sometimes much more rapid than at other times), we can, if we take a relatively short period, speak of the social order during that period as if it were unchanging. Indeed, we not only can but must; it is a condition of our explaining a course of constant change that we should select points along it and show what happened between them. But the points are not really points, they are periods of time and there was change while they lasted. We ignore this change and attend only to what remained the same during each period, since our purpose is to explain the great changes which occurred between the periods and not the small changes within them. It would be absurd to criticize Saint-Simon for treating the eight hundred years separating the eleventh and the nineteenth century as a period of transition, if he had had no other purpose than to explain how the social order at the beginning of that period was transformed into the social order at the end of it.

But he did have another purpose; he wanted to show that, since the eleventh century, there had been social disintegration as well as social change. He spoke of the social order of the eleventh century, as he spoke of the future fully industrial society, as if it were a social order in some sense in which there was no social order in, say, the sixteenth or the seventeenth century. In the sixteenth century there were philosophy and religion and government and production just as there had been in the eleventh; there were many kinds of institutions, theories and attitudes of mind. In both centuries men engaged in different kinds of activity, which reacted upon one another. These kinds were just as characteristic of the age in the sixteenth century as they had been in the eleventh. But the institutions and beliefs of the eleventh century constituted – so thought Saint-Simon – a social and moral order in some sense in which those of the sixteenth century did not.

What could this sense be? Did the socially important beliefs, the beliefs about man's place in the world, about right behaviour, about what was worth having and doing, which people held in the eleventh century, form a coherent whole? Were they consistent with one another? Were these beliefs in keeping with existing institutions? Saint-Simon evidently thought that they were. And he believed that, in the sixteenth century, socially important beliefs were much less consistent with one another and much less in keeping with established institutions. No doubt, they could not have been completely inconsistent with one another or completely out of keeping with institutions, or else there would have been no stability and no peace, no society. But the degree of consistency and compatibility was much smaller in the six-

D

teenth than in the eleventh century. Saint-Simon's disciple, Bazard, in lectures which were later published under the title of *The Exposition of the Doctrine of Saint-Simon*, used the terms *organic* and *critical* to mark this distinction between periods when the degree of this consistency and compatibility is high and periods when it is low. Ancient Greece, before the time of Socrates, had passed through an *organic* period and so had western Europe in the Middle Ages. Europe was now at the end of a *critical* period and on the threshold of an *organic* one, when industrial society would be fully mature. So Bazard told his listeners in the lecture-room in the rue Taranne.

But, we may ask, why did Saint-Simon and Bazard believe that the Middle Ages were an *organic* period, in this peculiar sense? What was the evidence which satisfied them? I am not asking whether what they took for facts really were facts; I am asking only what kind of facts they thought would establish their conclusion. In the Middle Ages there existed a single Church to which everyone in the West belonged, a Church whose doctrines no one questioned. At least Saint-Simon and Bazard believed that it was so, and we can, for our purpose, suppose that they were right. But can we conclude, as they do, that where there is a Church teaching unquestioned doctrine, socially important beliefs are mutually consistent and in keeping with established institutions? Can we come to this conclusion even if we suppose that Church to be the most powerful of social organizations, dominating all the others?

It seems to me that we cannot; it seems to me that a society dominated by such a Church is no more likely than any other to be *organic*. What reason have we for thinking that the beliefs which constitute orthodoxy, the beliefs placed by the powerful Church out of reach of open criticism, are consistent with one another? No doubt, they are held to be mutually consistent by the body which propagates them. But an orthodox set of beliefs is not put together by impeccable logicians who know all the relevant facts; nor is there a process of natural attraction among beliefs ensuring that they never come together to form an orthodox corpus of doctrine unless they are consistent with one another. An orthodox system of doctrines building up over a long period of time in a large and variegated society is most unlikely to contain only mutually consistent beliefs and beliefs in keeping with established institutions. True, beliefs which have important practical consequences are continually being adapted to one another and to existing institutions; but this happens in all societies, and as much in those where there is no orthodoxy as in those where there is. In all societies there are factors making for greater consistency and compatibility and factors making for less, but there is no reason to believe that the first kind are stronger where society is dominated by a powerful Church or party propagating an orthodox body of doctrines than where it is not. Therefore, the mere fact that there was a Church

in the West whose authority was virtually undisputed in the eleventh
century, while in the sixteenth there was not, is not good evidence that
the earlier period was any nearer being *organic* than the later. It may
have been or it may not. Neither Saint-Simon nor Bazard produced
evidence which would help to settle the question.

The distinction between *organic* and *critical* periods, or *organic*
and *critical* societies (for these terms can be applied as readily to
societies as to periods), is not so much improper as useless for Saint-
Simon's purpose, which is to explain the course of social evolution.
Admittedly, socially important beliefs can be mutually consistent or
inconsistent, and beliefs can be compatible or incompatible with
institutions; they can serve to maintain them or to destroy them. How
beliefs and institutions affect one another must always be of absorbing
interest to the student of society. And these inconsistencies and in-
compatibilities are, no doubt, much greater at some times and places
than at others. But, unless there is a discernible alternation, a flux and
reflux as of the tides, a period when consistency and compatibility
decrease following regularly on a period when they increase, the distinction between the *organic* and the *critical*, as Saint-Simon and
Bazard make it, does not provide us with a pattern of social change.
And even this is not enough. Each *organic* period must differ from
the one before it, the beliefs reaching a high point of consistency with
one another and of compatibility with institutions being no longer
what they were when harmony was last attained. Otherwise, there is
no point in speaking of a social order which gradually disintegrates
and gives way to another building up inside it; there is no point in
treating history as Saint-Simon treated it and Marx was to treat it
after him. Saint-Simon believed that there is a discernible alternation
or rhythm, and also that he had produced evidence to support his
claim. Unfortunately, he was mistaken. He predicted that, in the
mature industrial society, there would be mutually consistent beliefs
compatible with established institutions; he predicted that industrial
society would be what Bazard was to call *organic*. But industrial society,
as he described it, would not be dominated intellectually by a dogmatic Church; authority inside it, administrative and intellectual,
would be different in kind from the authority known to mediaeval
Europe. The universal acceptance of that authority, if ever it happened,
might be evidence that society was *organic*; that it was a social and
moral order in a special sense in which not every society is one. But the
unquestioned authority of the Church in the Middle Ages is no more
evidence that mediaeval society was *organic* than the unquestioned
authority of the Communist Party is evidence that Soviet Society is
so.

Saint-Simon offers us another criterion besides the two I have discussed (which are the mutual consistency of socially important beliefs

and the compatibility of these beliefs with established institutions) for distinguishing the two types of society which Bazard calls *organic* and *critical*. Industrial society, to be fully mature, must have *a positive purpose*; it must aim at increasing production, especially for the benefit of the poor. This requirement, that the new industrial society should have *a positive purpose*, was insisted upon even more strongly by Saint-Simon's disciples than by the master himself. In the third part of *Le Catéchisme des Industriels*, written by Comte while he was still attached to Saint-Simon, we are told that ' any social system . . . aims at directing all particular forces towards some general goal. For there is no society except where there operates a combined general action.'[1] The whole tenour of Comte's argument makes it clear that he considers that a society is not properly a social and moral order unless ' all particular forces' are directed to a 'general goal', unless its leaders have a common purpose which is generally accepted and to which all private purposes are subordinate. A society lacking such a purpose is in a state of moral disorder. Saint-Simon and Comte preached the need for such a common purpose to men living in a society which (in their opinion) was in a state of moral disorder; and they found mediaeval society superior to their own in at least one respect, in having a common purpose.

Clearly, by a common purpose Saint-Simon means something more than common notions of justice maintained by a government enjoying the confidence of its subjects. In one of the letters which make up that part of his writings entitled *Du Système Industriel*, Saint-Simon says that ' society does not live on *negative* ideas, but on *positive* ideas. It is today in an extreme moral disorder, selfishness is spreading at an astonishing rate, and everything tends to isolate man from man (*tout tend à l'isolement*).'[2] The *negative* ideas which Saint-Simon had in mind were the ideas of the French Revolution; and he called them negative partly because he thought that they had been used to attack the privileges of the nobles and the Church, and partly because, in his opinion, they did nothing to strengthen men's devotion to the community and their sense of belonging to it. They served only to remove obstacles in the way of each man's pursuing his own ends. If (what was in fact far from being the case) all Frenchmen had accepted wholeheartedly the doctrine of the rights of man and had supported a government willing and able to maintain them, France would still have lacked a common purpose, as Saint-Simon understood it. To have a common purpose, men must do more than share certain notions of justice; they must be engaged in some common enterprise. In other words, in order to have a common purpose in Saint-Simon's sense, they

1 *Oeuvres de Saint-Simon et d'Enfantin*, Vol. 38, p. 45.
2 Ibid., Vol, p. 51 (my italics).

must be agreed about something more than the rules which have to be enforced if each man is to pursue his private ends with as little interference as possible from others.

There is no need for us to quarrel with Saint-Simon and Comte for giving this meaning to the expression *a common purpose*. But we can object to their saying that, where there is no common purpose in this sense, there is *moral disorder*. No doubt, if the expressions *having a common purpose* and *belonging to a moral order*, as they use them, were equivalent, we could not object. But they are not equivalent. Moral disorder is something which, in their opinion, results from lack of a common purpose. Now, we can reasonably doubt whether this assertion is true; we have the right to expect those who make it to produce arguments to support it. What is moral disorder, if it is not lack of a purpose common to the whole community and taking precedence over other purposes? Presumably, it is either serious disagreement about what is right or desirable or it is adherence to values which are seriously incompatible. What reason is there for believing that there will be moral disorder in this sense where there is not a common purpose in the sense understood by Saint-Simon?

No doubt, in all societies there are many common purposes; there are purposes shared by smaller or larger numbers of persons. No doubt, too, it is as much by working together for the attainment of common purposes as by learning not to interfere with one another in the pursuit of private ends that men acquire a common and a self-consistent code of morals – to the extent that they do acquire one. But these are not the common purposes which Saint-Simon has in mind; for these purposes are limited, though there are many of them and everyone shares in some. There can be an immense number of such purposes, varying in extent and importance, even in a society where there is no common purpose in the sense of Saint-Simon; even where there is no purpose, shared by the whole community, taking precedence over all other purposes.

Why, if there is to be moral order, if there are to be no serious disagreements about the right and the desirable, no adherence to values which are seriously incompatible, need there be a pre-eminent purpose shared by everyone? Where has there ever been such a purpose, except in time of war? Certainly, we cannot assume that, where there are rulers able to mobilize the resources and the labour of a community for some vast enterprise to which they attribute supreme importance, the people generally share their purpose. We cannot assume that they willingly participate in it or that they sympathize with it. They may have many motives for doing what is required of them by their rulers. Moreover, even where there is widespread sympathy for the supreme purpose, as there often is in time of war, there may still subsist other purposes, private or shared by smaller groups, which conflict with the supreme purpose and yet are no less important to those who have them. A vast enterprise may affect the persons involved in it (even when they are involved willingly, as the majority of Englishmen were in the endeavour to defeat Hitler's Germany) in ways unforeseen and unnoticed by either the directors of the enterprise or those they direct; it may, even where there is genuine and widespread enthusiasm for the enterprise, increase moral disorder, if by moral disorder is meant serious disagreement about moral values or adherence to values which are seriously incompatible. When do nations come closer to having a common and supreme purpose than in time of war? And when are they more liable to moral disorder?

No doubt, the mature industrial society, if it were as Saint-Simon conceived of it, would have a purpose common to all its members, and a purpose important to them; and it would also be a true moral order, with no serious disagreements or inconsistent moral values. It would be organic in both the senses we have discussed; it would be what Saint-Simon meant by a moral order and would have what he understood by a common purpose. In such a society there would be no need for coercion, and the authority of all having authority would be the fruit of a competence universally recognized. But, if there were such a society, it would be the first society to be organic in both of these senses in time of peace. It may be that there have been primitive societies which were organic in the first sense, in which there were neither serious disagreements nor seriously inconsistent moral values, but primitive societies do not have common purposes except in time of war. But there is no more evidence that mediaeval society was organic in the second sense than there is that it was so in the first.

No doubt, there were small communities in the Middle Ages which were organic in both senses for perhaps years at a time: religious houses whose members were devoted to a common faith and a common way of life. And it may be that there were more such communities in the twelfth century than when Saint-Simon was alive. But that is nothing to Saint-Simon's purpose. He had in mind, not religious houses or other closed communities, but mediaeval western society taken generally. In what way were western Europeans in the twelfth century nearer to having a common purpose than their descendants in the eighteenth or early nineteenth? Even if we suppose (what is probably untrue) that they were Christians who understood the teachings of their Church, who shared the same conception of God, who aspired to the same heaven, this is not enough to give them a common purpose in Saint-Simon's sense. The Church, merely by endeavouring to assist every Christian to deserve heaven, no more serves a common purpose than the State does by affording to every citizen secure possession of what he owns. In the society condemned by Saint-Simon for being in moral disorder, men were perhaps as much attached to their property as their ancestors had been to God and to hopes of an after-life. The State, by maintaining the law, assists all men to preserve their property, which all men desire to do, but that is not enough to ensure that it serves a common purpose. To have a common purpose men must do more than pursue similar private ends and be assisted by Church or State in doing so. This is how we have to interpret the sense in which Saint-Simon speaks of a common purpose if his attack on the individualism of the French revolutionaries and of the liberals who came after them is not to be pointless. That being so, we have also to conclude that mediaeval Europe lacked a common purpose as much as the Europe familiar to Saint-Simon, who (though he believes otherwise) gives one only example of an organic society: namely, the mature industrial society whose coming he foretells, and to which, because it does not exist, he can, within limits, attribute what qualities he pleases.

Saint-Simon believed that there ordinarily is, and that there ought always to be, a close connection between the social order and the form of government. He also believed that a form of government can survive the social order out of which it arises and to which it is adapted. He sometimes spoke as if the form of government were the last thing to disappear as one social order gives way to another. These are beliefs which we can find also in the writings of Marx. Saint-Simon tells us that the industrial class has been growing in wealth and social influence for centuries, and that it ought now to 'direct' society or, as he also puts it, to 'administer' its affairs. There was a time when the feudal nobles were the wealthiest class and the common people lived mostly on their estates and in their protection, and it was therefore inevitable and natural that they should govern.[1] But they have since lost their social importance, and it is now natural and inevitable that the socially predominant class, the leaders of industry, should become the 'directing' class. As Comte puts it: 'the political order is, and can only be, the expression of the civil order, which means, in other words, that the socially preponderant forces necessarily end by becoming the directing forces.'[2] Presumably, it is *natural* that the leaders of industry should 'direct' society because, human nature being what it is, those

---

[1] Neither Saint-Simon nor his disciples (who follow him here) had any notion of how this argument looks when it is applied to the feudal lords. Their social superiority resulted from their political functions, from the protection they afforded to their dependents, from the justice dispensed by them or in their name. They did not govern or 'direct' society because they were wealthy or had a high social position; they were wealthy and had that position because they governed. It is odd to say of them that they ought to have governed, or that it was *natural* they should do so, because they were wealthy and socially predominant. Their case differed completely from that of the leaders of industry, who had acquired great wealth and influence in a society in which they exercised no political functions.

[2] Ibid., Vol. 38, p. 96.

who have some forms of power (e.g., wealth and managerial skill) ordinarily aspire to, and are well placed to obtain, forms which they do not yet have (e.g., political power); and they ought to 'direct' society because, society being what it is, they are the most likely to 'direct' it for the common good.

There is no need, at this stage, to contest the claims made by Saint-Simon on behalf of the leaders of industry, who were so much immersed in their own affairs that they never aspired to the role which he reserved for them. Nor need we enquire what warrant there is for assuming (as Saint-Simon does) that it is the social order which determines what class shall control society and by what methods. It is doubtful whether it is proper to make so sharp a distinction between social predominance and political power. But these are matters best left to a later stage, when we come to discuss the political theories of Marx and Engels. For the moment it is enough to point to the absurdity of Saint-Simon speaking of the form of government in France after 1815 as if it were the last important survival from a social order which had been in its prime some six centuries earlier. He called it a relic of the feudal system, though the form of government in France had changed since the high Middle Ages just as drastically as the relative importance of the social classes or the system of production. Indeed, Saint-Simon knew this, for it was too obvious to be ignored even by an intellectual enamoured of his own theories; he knew it and often admitted it, at least implicitly. The feudal nobles had been exalted and powerful in their prime by virtue of the services they had done, and these services, if they are examined, are seen to be political; the nobles in the Middle Ages governed. Since that time, they had ceased to perform these services, they had ceased to govern. The kings of France had gradually taken over the functions of the nobles; and France had acquired a centralized monarchy. Saint-Simon, far from denying this, tried to explain how it had happened. It was therefore absurd of him to speak of France's government in the eighteen-twenties as if it were a survival from the Middle Ages, a remnant of feudalism.

Though Saint-Simon distinguished between the social and political order, and spoke of the second as if it were determined by the first, he never said anything to suggest that he was, in the same sense as Marx, an economic determinist. The event which he sees as the conception of the new industrial order in the womb of the old feudal society is not a technical invention or a change in a method or pattern of production, a shift of labour and resources from one to another line of production; it is the enfranchisement of the communes, or the grant of rights by the nobles to the craftsmen. He also attaches importance to the introduction into mediaeval Europe of sciences cultivated by the Arabs. As science flourishes, theology decays; but science is not, in the eyes of Saint-Simon, the handmaid of industry. The technical invention which Saint-Simon singles out as being the most important of all is the printing press, which makes knowledge spread much more quickly and therefore arouses curiosity in many more minds. Science makes possible all kinds of technical improvements; Saint-Simon is well aware that it does so, but that is not what strikes him most forcibly. He is more impressed by how science affects man's conception of the world and of his place in it. Durkheim says that Saint-Simon treats the accumulation of knowledge as the prime cause of social change. Saint-Simon is not unambiguous, but the weight of evidence favours Durkheim's hypothesis. Comte, in his section of *Le Catéchisme des Industriels*, which he wrote while still an avowed pupil of Saint-Simon, distinguishes between the theological, metaphysical and positive stages in the evolution of mankind; these are distinctions turning entirely upon the character of what men take for knowledge, upon how they look upon the world and themselves.

2. *Their Illusions*

Among the early socialists only Saint-Simon (assisted by Comte) and Bazard[1] have philosophies of history sufficiently developed and *plausible*[2] to be worth comparing with Marxism. Just as Marx's view of his own age is intimately bound up with his conception of the past and his hopes for the future, so too is Saint-Simon's. Just as Marx's advice to the proletariat is the fruit of a wisdom derived from much thinking about the past, so too is Saint-Simon's advice to the leaders of industry. Just as Marx treats political history as essentially the record of a struggle for influence and power between classes, some of which are growing stronger and others weaker through the operation of causes of which they are unconscious, so too does Saint-Simon. Just as Marx assumes that the proletariat (unlike other classes whose action has transformed society in the past) must be enlightened about its historic role in order to perform it, so Saint-Simon makes the same assumption about the leaders of industry. In all these ways Marx stands closer to Saint-Simon than to any other of the early socialists.

[1] Bazard's account of the course of social evolution is substantially like Saint-Simon's. Bazard put himself forward as an interpreter of Saint-Simon, and not as an original thinker, though he was, in fact, a very free interpreter. But the differences between their two accounts, interesting though they are in themselves, do not raise important issues for us, since we are more concerned to examine the concepts they use to explain the course of events than their actual explanations.

[2] I intend no disparagement by this word. Saint-Simon and Bazard were excited by the past and perceptive about it. The historian, while rejecting their theories, might be impressed by them, as he would not be, I suspect, by Fourier's tidy division of the past and the future into periods and phases.

Though Proudhon had no philosophy of history, no conception as definite and elaborate as Saint-Simon's or Marx's of a course of social evolution lasting many centuries, he did philosophize about the past and the present; he took as passionate and as enduring an interest in history, and was as much steeped in it, as either of them. And it deserves notice that he too ascribed historic roles to social classes and fashioned his advice to them accordingly. Saint-Simon directed his message to the leaders of industry, looking upon them as spokesmen for all who earned a living by producing wealth; Marx directed his to the urban proletariat; and Proudhon his to all who made a living in a small way, whether they worked for others or were their own masters. With all three of them, there is a close connection between their views about history and the direction of their political efforts; there is also an extensive interest in social classes, their rivalries, their opportunities and their destinies.

Several of the other socialists took as active a part in politics as they did. Both Owen and Thompson did so, and were by no means lacking in realism. They understood the importance of the trade unions and tried, with considerable success, to win them over to their views. They collaborated with the workers and came closer to gaining their confidence than ever Marx did. They were not without shrewdness. Nor were the schemes they produced fantasies unrelated to existing conditions. Both the reports prepared by Owen, the first at the request of a committee chaired by the Archbishop of Canterbury in 1816, the one which came to be known as *Mr Owen's Plan*, and the later *Report to the County of Lanark* (1821) are quite sensible schemes. They were sympathetically received by the bodies, consisting of practical men, to whom they were addressed. These reports proposed the setting up of communities which (though more modest) were just as truly socialist as the ones which Owen set up years later at New Harmony and Queenwood, when he had become more obstinate and reckless. Owen's schemes for co-operation were by no means as unpractical as his theories about human nature were simple-minded. If he is open to the charge of lack of realism, it is less his schemes than his theories which make him so. They were not in themselves unworkable, and it was not unreasonable to hope that they might be adopted. Thompson, less simple-minded than Owen as a theorist, was not more unpractical. And as much can be said of Louis Blanc; his proposals were moderate enough, and he was not unreasonable in hoping that some of them might be adopted, though, as a matter of fact, they were not. The national workshops established soon after the February revolution differed in important respects from the ones he had proposed before the revolution, and moreover there were prominent persons who did what they could to bring them into disrepute. Of all the proposals made by the early socialists in England and France, we can say that they were not adopted or that, if they were, they did not work; but this, as I hope to show in a moment, does not in itself bear out the Marxist charge that the early socialists were Utopians.

If we compare Saint-Simon and Proudhon with Owen and Louis Blanc, we see that the first two, whose interest in philosophy and history was much the greater, had a deeper understanding of society and their own age, while the last two made the more timely and the more practical proposals. The leaders of industry, so assiduously courted by Saint-Simon, took no notice of him, and the workers, though they warmed to Proudhon when he defended them after the June days or when he attacked the bureaucratic state, were not much interested in his proposal for a *Banque du Peuple*. Proudhon's very considerable influence was almost entirely negative; the workers shared little more than his dislikes and suspicions. He was, at times, very much their spokesman, closer to them perhaps than any other socialist. He spoke for them as Cobbett spoke for the village labourers in England. But he gave them no practical advice which they were inclined to take. He was, at times, as popular with the French workers as Owen with the English ones, but he never had the same power to move them to attempt what he advocated. And he never had the ear of ruling circles to the extent that Owen still had it when he produced *Mr Owen's Plan*. Nor did he make practical proposals which aroused even the same degree of interest as those of Louis Blanc, either among the workers or among the more radical sections of the middle class parties. Clearly, Owen and Louis Blanc had proposals to make which attracted wide attention among men active in politics, and just as clearly Saint-Simon and Proudhon, whose judgements about the past and whose criticisms of the present cut so much deeper, whose views about society and government were so much fresher and more perceptive, had not.

What then was it about the early socialists that was Utopian or unrealistic? Was it their theories about how the society of equals would be organized? Or was it their beliefs about how it would come into being? I have conceded that their theories were to a large extent unrealistic, but this, I suggest, was not the real point of Marx's criticism when he called them Utopian. Having only the vaguest ideas himself about the society of equals, he was not much interested in the shortcomings of this part of their theories; he was not concerned to show that a large economy could not be managed as Saint-Simon proposed that it should be or that a community organized in the manner of Fourier's phalanx would soon break down. His own ideas about the future, vague though they were, owed more than a little to the speculations of the early socialists. His real objection to them was that their beliefs about how society could be transformed were based on illusions. I do not want to reject this verdict so much as to qualify it, and I also want to examine one of the assumptions on which it rests. For it often happens that a conclusion which is right or partly right rests on arguments and assumptions which are mistaken.

We have seen that Saint-Simon based his political tactics on a theory of social evolution which he believed gave him a deeper insight than others had into the realities of the situation. He was aware that his ideas might seem bizarre to others but that, he thought, was only because they had not seen, as he had, how the present had emerged from the past. He was as firmly convinced as ever Marx was that he saw deeply into the forces moulding his own age, and that he was therefore well equipped to enlighten the class to whom he addressed his message about their true interests. No more than Marx did he appeal to 'eternal' principles of justice or to unchanging human nature. And the claims which he made for himself, openly or tacitly, were not altogether unjustified. He did have a deeper insight, in many ways, than his contemporaries, and he did owe it in large part to his excursions into history. And yet he was also what Marx accused him of being when he called him Utopian; he was unrealistic. Many things which other people did not see were clear to him, but others more obvious escaped his notice. Even in his day a man had to shut his eyes to much that was going on around him to be as convinced as he was that the 'leaders of industry' were trusted by the workers or cared much for their good. Why should he have supposed that he could interest them in running the nation's economy principally for the benefit of 'the poorest and the most numerous class', whose welfare he had so much at heart? He failed to notice a divergence of class interests which was already obvious to several of the classical economists (and more especially to Adam Smith and Ricardo) as well as to Sismondi. It was a much grosser error of judgement on his part to suppose that he could induce the leaders of industry to manage the nation's economy for the common good than it was on Owen's part that he could find men of good will to put up the money to finance his schemes. If Saint-Simon had not been blinded by his hopes, it might have occurred to him that businessmen in the highly competitive economy of his day were too much engrossed in making profits and avoiding ruin to lend an ear to such proposals as his; that they were even less disposed by the nature of their occupations to accept responsibility for the welfare of the poor than the servants of the Crown had been under the old monarchy. It is easy to see how blind to some realities Saint-Simon was, even if we compare him with some of his contemporaries.[1] To a

---

1 Perhaps Saint-Simon, born a nobleman, remained all his life influenced, though unconsciously, by attitudes typical of his class. To the eighteenth-century nobleman the most striking social cleavage was the one separating his own class from the rest of society. The *industriels* all belonged to the unprivileged orders, and in the eyes of Saint-Simon were workers on whom

man like Marx, in whose eyes the divergence of interest between capitalists and wage-earners was the essential feature of the age, he must have seemed in some ways very simple-minded.

It would not be difficult to make a case against each of the early socialists, showing that, in one way or another, his hopes were unreasonable; that the methods he used or advocated to induce governments and private citizens to try out his schemes were unlikely to succeed. This is not surprising. The understanding of the early socialists, both of government and of production, was limited; they lived at a time when the social studies were scantier and less cautious (though not perhaps more confused) than they are now. They were often and widely mistaken, both in their explanations and their forecasts. And it may be that Marx and Engels, though they too made serious mistakes, had a deeper understanding of society and fewer illusions than their precursors. This claim is still made on their behalf, even by some of their more severe critics, and I shall not contest it, partly because I suspect that it may be true and partly because it does not affect my argument.

Marx and Engels did not confine themselves to pointing out the various mistakes made by the socialists whom they called *Utopian*; they did not merely say that it was simple-minded of Saint-Simon to believe that he could persuade the leaders of industry to take his advice, that it was unlikely that communities of the types advocated by Owen or Fourier could operate successfully in the existing social environment. If that were all they had said, we should have to agree with them in principle, even though we might insist that some of the early schemes and proposals were much nearer being realistic than others. But Marx and Engels were not really concerned to make a separate case against each of the Utopian socialists, showing just why his proposals, made at the time they were made, were unrealistic; they set much greater store by a general argument directed against them all, a blanket condemnation. It is this general argument which seems to me mistaken.

The error of the Utopian socialists generally, according to Marx and Engels, was that they supposed that it was possible to transform society by appealing to the privileged classes. But the privileged classes owe their privileges to society's being what it is; it is therefore their interest that it should not change in any way which destroys or greatly reduces their privileges. Classes cannot be persuaded to do what is against their class interests, and they will not allow it to be done by

the drones, his own class, were parasites. According to André Lichtenberger (see his *Le Socialisme et la Révolution Française*) it was in about 1793 that the old social division of France into the privileged and the unprivileged became politically less important than the division into the rich and the poor. Saint-Simon was already thirty-three years old in 1793.

others unless they are too weak to prevent it. Therefore, since the transformations desired by the socialists involved the destruction of privileges, they should have aimed at persuading, not the privileged, but the unprivileged. There is only one really effective method for putting an end to exploitation, and that is to enlighten the exploited and to encourage them to organize themselves until they are strong enough to put an end to the system against the will of the exploiters. The early socialists were *Utopian*, in the eyes of Marx and Engels, not so much because of the many mistakes they made in sizing up the situations in which they acted, but because they believed that it was possible to reconcile the interests of the propertied and working classes by appealing to a sense of justice common to all classes.

In a later chapter, where I deal with Marxism at considerable length, I examine more closely the Marxian conception of a class interest and also enquire what could be meant by saying that the interests of two classes are *irreconcilable*. I shall not anticipate here what I say there, for these are difficult matters and cannot be discussed briefly. Suffice it to say, for the moment, that the mistakes made by the early socialists are not in themselves good evidence that Marx and Engels are right when they say that it is wasted labour appealing to privileged classes to transform society. Yet many people have supposed otherwise; they have been inclined to accept the charge brought by Marx against the early socialists because they have been impressed by their lack of realism. The early socialists had many illusions, they tried to persuade the unpersuadable. This is a widely accepted verdict on them. The first part of it, that they had many illusions, is true; as it nearly always is true of those who have great hopes and are active in their service. It is a judgement which applies as truly to Lenin as to Owen. And the second part of the verdict, properly qualified, is also true. The 'leaders of industry' cared nothing for Saint-Simon's arguments, and even the prominent men who listened to Owen or Louis Blanc were disposed to go only a little way in taking their advice. The appeals of the early socialists, to the extent that they were addressed to the powerful and the rich, did mostly fall on deaf ears. But from this judgement on the early socialists (which in any case needs to be qualified) to the general conclusion reached by Marx, there is a long leap and one made in the dark.

The early socialists appealed to the workers as much as to the propertied class, and had as many illusions about them. Owen appealed to both classes and got a considerable response from both. If he failed to achieve what he hoped to achieve with their help, it was not really because the class interests of the privileged stood in his way. The experiments at New Harmony and Queenwood did not fail because governments took steps against them or because of the hostility they aroused; they failed because they were badly run, and so too did the

Orbiston community founded on his principles. The National Equitable Labour Exchange, which he set up in Gray's Inn Road in 1832 for selling goods at prices varying with the time needed to produce them, failed because the goods were priced either too high or too low as compared with ordinary market prices. Of all Owen's schemes only the Grand National Consolidated Trade Union frightened the propertied and the government, and perhaps inspired the action taken against the Tolpuddle martyrs, but its collapse was due more to internal weakness than to pressure from outside. If we read accounts of the experiments promoted by the early socialists and their disciples, we nearly always find that their failure was due primarily to bad organization or lack of discipline and not to the hostility they provoked.

Now this, it may be objected, does not really meet the Marxian argument, which holds that the experiments of the early socialists failed not so much because they provoked the government and the propertied classes into taking action against them as because they were made in an unpropitious environment. Take, for example, Owen's National Equitable Labour Exchange; it did not fail because of hostile action taken against it but because it was an experiment made in a market economy. The surrounding system doomed it to failure without anyone's needing to take action to ensure that it failed, and even without anyone's noticing that, if it did succeed, it might eventually destroy the system. The social system prevents, as it were automatically, the success of experiments which threaten it, even though the classes whose interest it is to preserve the system do not feel themselves threatened by the experiments and take no action hostile to them.

This explanation is ingenious, but what reason is there for believing that it is true? As anyone who looks at the experiments tried or inspired by the early socialists can see, there were many reasons other than this to explain their failure. Are we then entitled to say that, if they had not failed for these other and more obvious reasons, they would have failed for this one? What is the evidence to support this conclusion? Much the more numerous and the more weighty reasons, the ones which thrust themselves upon us as we read the accounts (most of them written by persons with strongly socialist sympathies and often deeply influenced by Marxism), have no logical connection with this reason, which is usually brought in to the rear of them, as if to set the seal of Wisdom upon them. But the evidence to support it is weak indeed. Did the National Equitable Labour Exchange fail because it was tried in the midst of a market economy? Very probably it did. But what does that prove? That the market economy dooms to failure every experiment whose success would destroy the system on which the privileges of the propertied classes rest? This is a tremendous conclusion to draw from this piece of evidence and a few others like it.

It is also a conclusion which contradicts other parts of the Marxian theory. For Marx holds, as Saint-Simon does, that in every social system (except the last) there emerge the forces destined to destroy it. What, then, are these forces? They are practices and institutions which prove to be, in the long run, incompatible with the system in which they first appear and are tolerated. These practices and institutions arise, presumably, because some sections of the community believe them to be in their interest. The feudal lords who enfranchised the commons did so, either because they thought they had something to gain by so doing or because demands were made on them which they saw no good reason for refusing. The trade unions threatened the interests of the propertied classes rather more obviously than did the National Equitable Labour Exchange, and were also, though in a different way, out of keeping with a free market economy. Parliament, dominated by the propertied classes, first made *combinations* illegal and then allowed them. Were the workers already too formidable for Parliament to dare to deny them the right to combine? This is not the verdict of the historians. But the workers became, as Marx saw, a much more formidable class for being allowed to combine. Those who pressed for the repeal of the Combination Laws appealed to ideas of justice very widely held in England. We need not call them 'eternal' ideas; they have been denied or neglected or unheard of in some countries. In the early nineteenth century they formed part of a culture favourable to the predominance of a small section of the community, and yet it was possible to appeal to these ideas to persuade that section to allow practices which eventually helped to transform the social order.

Law and morality, even in a society of unequals, even when they serve to support the claims of the privileged, also often allow practices which, sometimes quickly, sometimes slowly, subvert the society which tolerates them. A conception of justice or liberty or property which, far from being eternal, was perhaps unknown several centuries ago and which in the past has made easier the enrichment of some at the expense of others, may come to be used to justify innovations fatal to a supremacy which rests on wealth. Very probably the innovations will modify the conceptions originally used to justify them, and the old social order be subverted all the more quickly. When a social class rises in importance and challenges the supremacy of another, the legal and moral conceptions favourable to the established order do usually change; but that does not touch my present argument, which is that the old conceptions could be used to justify practices subversive of the old order. We can say this without assuming that there is, in any sense in which Marx would deny it, an 'eternal' justice, and without denying that, where there is social inequality, current ideas of what is just usually support the pretensions of the rich and the powerful. There is evidence in plenty that the privileged are apt to resist proposals which they believe are against their interests, but there is also evidence that they sometimes take the initiative in making reforms raising the status and improving the lot of the unprivileged. The privileged accept for generations conditions of which in the end they come to be ashamed, though they do not suffer from them. Is it always fear of revolution which causes them to change their minds?

Certainly, the better organized and the more enlightened the poor, the more persuadable the rich. It is a fair criticism of several of the early socialists, though by no means of all of them, that they devoted too many of their efforts to persuading the rich and the powerful and too few to persuading the poor. It applies to Saint-Simon and to Fourier. But if a general charge is to be brought against the early socialists, it is not that they tried to persuade the unpersuadable, seeking to transform society without the massive and organized support of the workers; it is rather that they believed that society could be transformed according to a recipe prepared beforehand. To say this is not to repeat against them what Burke said against the French revolutionaries, for he condemned every attempt to make large reforms. Nor is it to condemn the making of plans in advance, nor the description in detail of ideal societies. It is sometimes desirable to make large changes quickly, and it is certainly wise to prepare a plan beforehand, provided we do not adhere to it rigidly as we try to execute it. For all plans are (or ought to be) provisional; they are based on limited knowledge, and ought to change as knowledge increases. Moreover, the changes in group attitudes and interests which create a need for large reforms are not effects of any one man's criticism of the established order or vision of a just society; they arise, in so far as their causes are intellectual, from the impact of many theories on many minds. Western Europe has changed enormously in the last four or five generations, and one of the important causes of this change is the preaching of socialist doctrines, but none of the doctrines foretold the course of this change. The socialists helped to formulate the ideals which have guided the reformers and the concepts they have used to state their problems and to find solutions of them; they have transformed both the language of politics and the aspirations of mankind, but they have not produced plans which men could follow, even in broad outline, in the attempt to realize these aspirations.[1]

I would not say that it is virtually impossible to transform a large society more or less according to a plan not much changed in the course of execution. Certainly, it has not been done in the West or in

[1] The greatest and most rapid deliberate transformations of society have been made by disciples of Marx, who refrained from producing an ideal model of post-revolutionary society. But, in spite of Marx's reticence in this respect, he did say enough about socialism and the dictatorship of the proletariat to warrant our saying that none of the societies created by his disciples is *socialist* or *proletarian*, as Marx understood those terms, or shows any sign of becoming so.

the Soviet Union, no doubt because they are parts of the world where there has been *unprecedented* change. The reformers in the West and the revolutionaries in Russia were *pioneers*; they were moving in directions in which no one had moved before them. Russia as she now is was no more foretold and desired by the Bolsheviks in 1917 than the West as it now is was foretold and desired by the radicals and socialists of the nineteenth century. But it may be that reformers active in countries which, when compared with certain other countries, are backward (according to standards accepted by the reformers) can produce beforehand a vast and intricate scheme of transformation and adhere to it, at least in broad outline. They, however, are not taking for their model an ideal society unlike any that exists; they are following along a road already trodden before them, they are aiming at something similar to what already exists outside their own country. They will want to avoid, no doubt, the 'mistakes' of their precursors, but they will have a fairly clear and detailed idea of their goal and of how it can be achieved. They are not engaged in exploration but only in catching up others who, in their opinion, are in advance of them.

Marx and Engels have themselves been called Utopian. But this sort of *tu quoque*, though tempting, is not really justified. They produced no plan of an ideal community, as Saint-Simon, Owen and Fourier did, who believed that the time had come already to put it into practice.[1] Those who call Marx and Engels Utopian mean to suggest that they were so in the same sense as they accused the early socialists of being so, and the suggestion is false. Yet they may have been, though in a different way, as unrealistic as the men whose lack of realism was so obvious to them. For, though they produced no model of an ideal community, they did express some general, mostly negative, opinions about what society would be like after the proletarian revolution – opinions largely inspired by the early socialists; and they also held strongly to certain beliefs about how bourgeois society would come to an end. And, surely, a man is lacking in realism if he holds these opinions together with these beliefs. If the proletarians are to organize politically in order to capture the State from the bourgeois, why should the State wither away? Within a very numerous class politically organized, there is necessarily a structure of authority; there are leaders accustomed to power and eager to keep and enlarge it. Those who gain control of a great community, no matter what their class origins or class support, have an interest in maintaining that control. Moreover, if, already before the collapse of bourgeois society, the average size of the unit of production has grown rapidly, and

---

[1] I take it that no man is Utopian, in Marx's sense, unless he produces an ideal model and mistakenly believes that it can be realized immediately or in the near future. The author of *Utopia* was therefore not Utopian in this sense, and neither was Plato or Rousseau.

every part of a vast economy has become more closely dependent on the other parts, then the workers, when they take control, must either maintain a numerous and centralized bureaucracy or else must revert (at enormous material sacrifice) to a much simpler system where units of production are smaller and there is much less need for the entire economy to be controlled from the centre. Is a man more lacking in realism who holds, with Proudhon, that the workers must boycott the State and must abandon their capitalist employers to start ventures of their own, or one who, with Marx, holds that when the workers have captured the State and have taken control of a vast and closely knit economy, bureaucracy (that is to say, a centralized administration remote from the ordinary citizen and taking important decisions which affect him nearly) will quickly disappear? Is not the second man as fantastic as the first, as much the victim of illusion? The revolutions of the past, which both Marx and Proudhon called *bourgeois*, had strengthened the State, as they both noticed. Why then should the proletarian revolution destroy it or set in motion a process which would cause it to disappear?

3. *Their Dislike of Violence*

We have seen that most of the early socialists believed that, in the ideal communities they described, there would be no need for organized force. We have seen why they held this belief, and why Rousseau did not hold it of his ideal community. In this matter, Marx and Engels agreed with them and not with Rousseau; for the 'withering away' of the State implies the disappearance of organized force. And yet, in spite of this agreement, Marx and Engels did not dislike and distrust force as the early socialists did; they were not pacific by temperament. Their doctrine is altogether more combative and angry.

The early socialists were not revolutionaries; they deprecated the use of force against established authority, even when they strongly disapproved of that authority. Saint-Simon and his disciples, Fourier, Victor Considérant, Owen, Thompson, Bray, Cabet, Leroux, Louis Blanc, and Proudhon: they all hoped to achieve their objects by peaceful means. Of the English and French socialists who were important before the rise of Marxism, only the Blanquists believed that the established system must be destroyed by violence and were willing to resort to violence to destroy it.[1]

---

[1] The Blanquists were, I suppose, *socialists*, though they were in practice concerned only to destroy what they believed to be evil without troubling themselves about what would take its place. Still, they were opposed to forms of property which they believed allowed the idle to exploit the industrious, and they did look forward to a type of society where the workers would organize production and exploitation would cease.

It might be said that this objection to violence was an effect of misplaced optimism; that it was connected with those aspects of their
teaching which moved Marx to call the early socialists Utopian. But
this judgement would not apply to them all, for by no means all of
them were optimists. Saint-Simon and Fourier preached mostly to the
propertied and educated classes, expecting to convince them by argument, and took little notice of how widely the interests of the propertied
and the propertyless diverged. Owen, at one time highly respected in
governing circles, never lost faith in his own powers of universal persuasion. These three pioneers were incorrigible optimists. But others,
like Leroux and Louis Blanc, though they said (and no doubt believed)
that it was in the *true* or long-term interest of both capitalists and
workers that society should be greatly changed, were well aware of
how deeply the rich feared the poor and the poor hated the rich. They
wanted to make great reforms precisely in order to avoid revolution.
Cabet, whose influence on the French workers was at one time very
great indeed, said that, if he held a revolution in his fist, he would keep
that fist shut, even if it meant his having to die in exile. He knew that
there was danger of revolution in France; he knew how angry and how
ready for violence the workers were in Paris and in other towns. But he
also believed that the communist society he advocated could not be
established by violence, and therefore thought it his duty to dissuade
the workers from violence. Thompson did not expect to persuade the
rich to reform society for the benefit of the poor; he hoped rather to
help the poor to help themselves, which he thought they could do without resorting to force. In general, we may say that, as one decade succeeded another and society became more industrial, the socialists grew
more sharply aware of the hatreds and suspicions dividing the rich
from the poor; the facile optimism of the earliest socialists gave way to
more sober expectations and to more urgent fears. This was especially
true after the July revolution in France and the passage of the first
Reform Bill in England, two events which aroused great hopes among
the poor and led to great disappointments. Class antagonisms had
never seemed deeper, and there was widespread fear of revolution.
Yet the socialists, with rare exceptions, remained social pacifists. They
mostly refused to believe that the violence which threatened society,
and whose causes were perhaps as well understood by them as by any
of their contemporaries, could bring their countries nearer to the social
order which would remove these causes. They did not share the faith
of Marx that the violence produced by the ills of society could purge
society of those ills.

Proudhon did at times come close to arguing that class war and
violence were inevitable, but he never advocated violence. At times
the situation in France seemed to him so tense that he could not see
how violence was to be avoided. Yet his attitude to it was not so very

different from, say, Tocqueville's; he sometimes saw the hatred between classes leading France into an *impasse* out of which there might be no issue except by violence. His sympathies were with the workers, as Tocqueville's were not; he felt a need to defend them when they were most reviled, which was apt to be when they had resorted to violence, as after the June days of 1848. It was not the workers on the barricades who were to blame, he said, so much as the authorities whose indifference to their sufferings had driven them to such courses. But, though he sometimes condoned violence, he never preached it and never foretold it with relish. He never looked forward to the workers *smashing* anything or anybody. The cult of violence of the Blanquists and some of the extremer radicals seemed to him sometimes disgusting and sometimes ridiculous. He abominated the Jacobins of '93 and despised their nineteenth-century imitators.

What explains this early socialist dislike of violence? We might expect it in England, but it was not less marked in France.[1] We cannot, as we have seen, explain it by postulating a simple-minded belief in the efficacy of persuasion by argument. Perhaps the French socialists, reflecting first on the great revolution and afterwards on the revolution of 1830, had noticed that those who did the fighting, who took the risks, did not get the rewards. Perhaps to men of ideas violence rarely seems attractive when it is seen close at hand, when there is more than book-knowledge of it. Perhaps many of the early socialists, precisely because they had fairly well-defined ideas about what they thought needed doing, were afraid that violence would make it less likely than ever that they would be listened to. Perhaps Proudhon and Cabet, born of working-class parents, were afraid that the grievances of their class would be used by revolutionaries of bourgeois origin for their own purposes. Perhaps the cult of violence in intellectual circles varies inversely with experience of freedom or with civic courage, and is therefore less to be expected among the English and the French than among the Germans and the Slavs.

III. HODGSKIN AND THOMPSON AS CRITICS OF CLASSICAL ECONOMICS: FOURIER'S IDEAL SOCIETY

The early socialists contemplated the same economy as Adam Smith or Ricardo. But, whereas the classical economists saw it as a system ensuring that, on the whole, available resources were put to the most productive use, the socialists condemned it as wasteful. These two

---

[1] Indeed, it is *more* marked in France than in England; for the English socialists did not feel the same need to condemn violence since they lived in a country at that time less given to it.

almost contradictory judgements passed on the same system are not to be explained by a difference of opinion about what constitutes productive use. It is not that the economists wanted the total product, measured in money or in some other external way, to be as large as possible, while the socialists had in mind the optimum satisfaction of wants. The economists, just as much as the socialists, thought it desirable that men should so use their energies as to produce with the least effort what was needed to satisfy their wants. They both assumed, as Bentham did, that no man's satisfaction is more valuable than another's unless it is greater. True, the socialists aimed at kinds of equality to which the economists were indifferent, but there was one conception of equality common to them, the conception implicit in Bentham's greatest happiness principle. Moreover, the economists were as convinced as the socialists that, beyond a certain point, every successive addition to a man's income procures him a less than proportionate satisfaction. They both knew that competition brings ruin to the unlucky and the weak, that in a free market economy the adjustment of supply to demand is always imperfect and involves losses. The economists were not really blind to the waste and the suffering caused by the system they described, but they thought it a price worth paying because the advantages of the system outweighed the disadvantages. The socialists believed the contrary. Naturally, believing what they did, the socialists paid greater attention than did the economists to the disadvantages and less attention to the advantages. They did not so much argue with the economists or challenge their assumptions as lay heavy emphasis on what the economists tended to neglect. But there were two early socialists to whom this judgement does not apply: Hodgskin and Thompson.

The early socialists were not moved primarily by the belief that inequality diminishes happiness by preventing available resources being used to produce what satisfies the most wants, nor yet by a pure love of equality, a feeling that every man ought to get a return in proportion to the contribution he makes; they were moved (above all) by the belief that poverty, insecurity and ruthless competition are degrading. Men who become socialists, even though they have a taste for abstract argument, are not moved in the first place by the pure desire that certain abstract principles of justice should be put into practice; they are moved by sympathy with the poor and are perhaps also offended by the indifference and smugness of the fortunate. Even Hodgskin, who attacked some of the assumptions made by the economists, was not arguing with them for the sheer love of argument, he was not merely enjoying an intellectual exercise; he attacked their assumptions because they were used to justify a system which he condemned for the suffering and degradation involved in it. But he did not expatiate on the suffering or seek to describe the degradation; nor was he concerned to show how the system frustrated the individual and prevented his attaining happiness. Others were less reticent; they were copious and explicit when they spoke of the sufferings of the poor and the heartlessness of the rich. But only one of them, Fourier, produced an elaborate theory about the human passions, their frustration in existing society, and the type of community in which they could have free and harmless expression.

1. Hodgskin and Thompson

In *Labour Defended against the Claims of Capital* (1825), Thomas Hodgskin is concerned to do only one thing: to refute the argument of the classical economists that the capitalist performs a useful function and is therefore entitled to his reward.[1] He quotes these words from James Mill's *Elements of Political Economy*: 'The labourer has neither raw materials nor tools. These are provided for him by the capitalist. For making this provision the capitalist of course expects a reward.' Mill gives us to understand that the capitalist not only expects but expects justly; and this is what Hodgskin sets out to disprove.

The economists say that the labourer, in order to work, must live, and cannot live on the product of his own labour before that product is completed and sold. The capitalist provides him with the wherewithal to live while he is producing, and for this indispensable service gets his reward. But, says Hodgskin, the capitalist does not in fact possess ready prepared the commodities needed by the labourer. He possesses only money which he uses to pay the labourer for his labour before the product of that labour is sold. The labourer spends his money on what other workers have produced. Hodgskin is at great pains to show that capitalists do not in fact have a large quantity of food, clothing and so on in store to supply their workers while they are at work, and that, in any case, only a small part of what workers need is produced much in advance of their needing it. By so doing he rather obscures the essential point of his argument, which is this: what the worker needs to keep him alive while he is working is itself the product of labour; and the only reason why he cannot buy it and also get the whole price fetched by what he produces when it is sold is that he has no money unless he sells his labour to the capitalist. If he had the money he could buy what he needed while he worked and then get

---

[1] Though the classical economists took it for granted that the capitalist is *entitled* to his reward, they were in practice more concerned to explain how wealth was produced and distributed than to justify its being so distributed. Explanation passes over into justification more perhaps with M'Culloch and James Mill than with Smith, Ricardo and Malthus: and it is M'Culloch and Mill that Hodgskin quotes.

the full market value of his product; but, having no money, he is obliged to sell his labour and to allow the purchaser of it to sell what that labour produces.

In the language of the classical economists the commodities needed to supply the worker while he worked (or the money to buy them) were known as *circulating capital*, while the machinery and tools he used and the buildings in which he worked (or the money invested in them) were known as *fixed capital*. Hodgskin argues that the capitalist is no more entitled to a reward as a provider of *fixed* than as a provider of *circulating* capital. Fixed capital is itself a product of labour, and is useful only while labour is applied to it (that is to say, as a tool). The capitalist neither produces it nor does the work which makes it useful. For a nation to have fixed capital (and it must have it if it is to put labour to the most productive use) only three things are necessary: knowledge and ingenuity for the inventing of machines, ability to arrange for their construction and profitable use, the skill and labour to use them. These abilities and skills are manifest in labour, in useful work, and are at bottom so many forms of labour. The capitalist does not really provide them; they are provided by the men who actually do these kinds of work, and the capitalist merely purchases their labour. Since men labour in order to produce what satisfies their wants, there is no need for capitalists to purchase labour to ensure that useful work is done: by purchasing labour they merely enrich themselves at the expense of those who labour. And we have seen that Hodgskin does not mean by labour only manual labour; he means also the work involved in ensuring that manual labour is put to the most productive use, the work of the inventor and of the manager. 'No subject of complaint is', he thinks, 'more general or more just than that the inventor of any machine does not reap the benefit of it. . . . Thousands of capitalists have been enriched by inventions of which they were not the authors.'[1] And later he says: 'The labour and skill of the contriver, or of the man who arranges and adapts a whole, are as necessary as the labour and skill of him who executes only a part. . . . But because those who have been masters, planners, contrivers, etc, have in general also been capitalists, and have also had a command over the labour of those who have worked with their hands, their labour has been paid as much too high as common labour has been under paid.'[2] In other words, to direct the labour of others to make it more productive is useful work entitled to a reward, but a man need not be a capitalist in order to do it. The capitalist does not owe his high income to his doing this work; he owes it to his ability to purchase labour and to sell what it produces. Because wealth is distributed as it is, those who do the planning and contriving are

---

[1] *Labour Defended*, London, 1922, Labour Publishing Co., Ltd. edition. pp. 63-4.
[2] Ibid., pp. 88-9.

mostly capitalists; they therefore do some useful work but their incomes are far greater than what their work entitles them to.

In the last pages of his short book Hodgskin foretells that the workers, as they gain in knowledge, will examine closely 'the foundations of the social edifice', and will dig them up and not restore them 'unless justice demands their preservation'.[1] He is certain that 'till the triumph of labour be complete . . . till man shall be held more in honour than the clod he treads on, or the machine he guides – there cannot, and there ought not to be, either peace on earth or good will among men.'[2]

We have here as vigorous an account (and a more concise one) of exploitation as we can find in the writings of Marx; we have the argument that where the capitalist flourishes, capital (the clod and the machine) is more valued than the man who produces or works it; and we have the prophecy that, until labour gets its full reward, there cannot be true social peace. We have here by no means all, but at least some, of the bare bones of Marxism.

Thompson's purpose, in his *Inquiry concerning the Distribution of Wealth*, is also to contest the claims made, openly or by implication, by the economists in favour of the capitalists. But, as a disciple of Bentham who accepts the greatest happiness principle, he is disturbed by the master's argument that, where security and equality conflict, the second must be sacrificed to the first. Bentham had allowed that, once a man has enough to live on, each successive increment of wealth brings him a diminishing return in happiness, and had therefore admitted that, *ceteris paribus*, the more equal the distribution of wealth the greater men's happiness. But he had then gone on to argue that there was another principle involved, even more important than this one: men suffer more for being deprived of what they reckon on having than they are pleased by getting what they do not expect. If men are to be happy they must have security: they must be able to reckon on getting what law and convention have led them to expect and to believe they are entitled to. Equality is good but security is better (i.e., more conducive to happiness), and therefore, when the two conflict (as they often do), it is security which is to be preferred.

Thompson might well have called in question the relative importance attributed by Bentham to these two principles. Did Bentham really mean to be taken literally? Did he really mean that, *whenever* security and equality are in conflict, there is more to be gained than lost by sacrificing the second principle to the first? Presumably not, for we cannot suppose him to have been so unrealistic as to have held that no increase in equality, however great, if it deprives anyone of what he expects and believes he is entitled to, can add to happiness

[1] Ibid., p. 102.
[2] Ibid., pp. 104-5.

more than the deprivation takes away from it. Did he mean, then, that an increase in equality, if it diminishes security, *usually* affords less happiness to those who benefit by it than unhappiness to those who lose by it? Though this is not absurd on the face of it, it is also not obvious. To make the assertion without producing arguments in support of it is not enough. No doubt, when two men are more or less equal in wealth, the chances are that, if we deprive one of them of £100 which we give to the other, we cause more pain than pleasure. But, if equality is a valid principle at all (and Bentham admitted that it is), it follows that, the greater the inequality of wealth between two persons, the smaller the chance that, if we take something from the richer of the two to give it to the poorer, we are causing more pain than pleasure, and the greater the chance that we are doing the opposite. Did Bentham believe that in the England or the Europe of his day (for these were the only parts of the world with which he was at all familiar) inequalities of wealth were not yet great enough to make it likely that, if the rich were taxed heavily for the benefit of the poor, the poor would gain in happiness more than the rich lost? If he did believe it, it was presumably a matter of faith, for he certainly produced no reasons to support his belief. Bentham, the great champion of calculation and measurement to decide social issues, was sometimes extraordinarily self-confident in his judgements, speaking as if a vast experience enabled him to take the measure of things without putting himself to the trouble of actually measuring them, like a shrewd old farmer who can tell at a glance which of two almost identical bullocks is the heavier with no need to use the scales.

But Thompson did not attack Bentham on these lines. He did not say that it is absurd to put it forward as a general rule that to preserve security is more important than to increase equality (or the other way about), since the relative importance of the two varies with the degree of inequality. Nor did he say that equality is more important than security. He tried rather to argue that the worker does not have security unless he gets the whole product of his labour. The worker feels that he is entitled to this whole product or to its equivalent, and feels deprived of what is justly his when he does not get it. Moreover, the closer he is to getting it, the stronger his incentive to work.

The problem then is to reconcile the labourer's right to the whole product of his labour (which Thompson calls his *security*, using that word in a sense which is similar to, and yet not quite the same as, the sense in which Bentham used it) with the principle of equality, the principle that the more equal the distribution of wealth the greater the total happiness. His solution is to put forward two rules: the first, that what is not a product of human labour ought to be distributed equally, and the second, that every departure from the rule, *secure to the labourer the value of his whole product*, ought to be in favour of equality. Thus Thompson surmounts the difficulty created for him by Bentham's assertion that security is to be preferred to equality when the two conflict, not by denying the assertion, but by defining *security* in a way which greatly reduces the divergence between the two principles.

The objection to this sort of argument is that it involves an unusual, and perhaps improper, use of words. Unless the worker expects and feels entitled to the whole product of his labour, it is a misuse of language to say that he is *secure* only if he gets it. As the word is ordinarily used by social and political theorists, a man is *secure* when he can enjoy his established rights, legal and conventional. By saying that the worker is secure only if he gets the whole product of his labour, Thompson implies that he expects to get it or at least feels entitled to it. But this is unlikely in a community where for generations workers have received less than the whole product of their labour and are brought up to respect established rights of property. True, if the matter were put to them, they might agree that, in a community very different from their own and ideally superior to it, they would receive the whole product of their labour; they might be persuaded that, if there were more justice in the world, they would work less and get more. It is perhaps not difficult to convince the poor that, in strict justice, they are entitled to more than actually comes their way. But then they ordinarily do not expect strict justice; they only dream of it. Such dreams, delicious though they may be, do not produce expectations whose disappointment causes a deep sense of grievance. The poor are not insecure because they get less than they would get if a justice other than they are used to were done to them, attractive though they may find that justice when it is brought to their notice; they are insecure only when they cannot rely on getting what they expect to get because it is what they are entitled to according to notions of justice which are widely accepted in practice or which seem to them practicable in the world as it is.

Against the claim made on behalf of the capitalist that he performs a service which entitles him to the reward he gets, Thompson argues that this is only one, and the less reasonable, of two alternative claims. It has been held that the capitalist should get the whole difference between what is produced by workers using the capital he provides and what they would be able to produce without it; but it can also be held that he should get only an allowance for the depreciation of his capital and as much more as would enable him to live as comfortably as the workers. The first alternative leads to great inequality while the second leads, if not to equality, to something not far removed from it, and is therefore the better of the two.

The economists, who prefer the first alternative, mistakenly believe that profits and interest depend on the amount of capital accumulated by the community. If capital remained in the hands which produced it, the price that a man could get for putting his capital at another man's disposal would be small; it is only because those who own capital are few, while those who need it are many, that its owners can get so high a price for the use of it. The concentration of capital in a few hands ensures that workers get much less than the whole product of their labour; it reduces their incentive to work and so prevents the community from becoming as wealthy as it would otherwise be. It also ensures that the wealth which is produced gives less happiness than it might, for that is the usual effect of inequality.

In 1827 Thompson published a reply to Hodgskin's *Labour Defended*, calling it *Labour Rewarded*.[1] He attacked Hodgskin for wanting to make the economy even more competitive by merely getting rid of the exactions of landlords and capitalists.[2] Competition leads to periodic crises, and in any case can never be really free unless no one at the outset of his career has greater wealth or knowledge, greater freedom of action, or greater access to means of production than anyone else. It is possible to go a considerable way towards ensuring that competitors start with equal advantages but it is never possible to go the whole way. Moreover, competition leads to over-exertion, which endangers health and prevents mental improvement. If men are to continue using machinery on a large scale (and they ought to do it since it vastly increases production and therefore the power to satisfy wants), it is impossible to assess exactly each man's contribution to the common product and the reward to which he is entitled.

Therefore, says Thompson, instead of competition there should be co-operation, and all who contribute should receive the same reward. Otherwise – since all who work willingly expect equal treatment – by giving larger rewards to the meritorious, we undermine security. In a co-operative community the workers provide a ready market for one another; they produce only what they need. There is no waste from the failure of supply to meet demand. Thompson advocated the setting up of small communities, which should increase in size gradually until

---

1 Or, to give it its full title, *Labour Rewarded – the Claims of Capital and Labour Conciliated, or How to Secure to Labour the Whole Product of its Exertions.*

2 It is sometimes said that Hodgskin was not a socialist because he did not advocate co-operative production or any sort of public or communal control of production. Certainly, by Durkheim's criterion (see his *Le Socialisme*) Hodgskin was not a socialist. But, then, it has also been said that Saint-Simon was not a socialist because he did not condemn unearned incomes. The word *socialist* has been used in several different ways. If we are not to use it in a way which obliges us to deny that a Hodgskin or a Saint-Simon (or, for that matter, a Proudhon or a Fourier) is a socialist, we ought to allow that any man is a socialist who advocates *either* public or communal control of production for the benefit of the poor, *or* the abolition of types of property which enable some men to live on the labour of others.

they consist of two thousand persons. A community of more than two thousand is too large to manage its affairs democratically and efficiently, whereas, if it is appreciably smaller, it cannot be self-sufficing and prosperous, providing its members with an ample living. Thompson expected the workers to finance these communities out of their own savings and looked for support to the trade unions. Like Hodgskin, he had little faith in the propertied classes and believed that the labouring poor could improve their wretched condition only by their own exertions.

2. *Fourier*

'My theory', Fourier tells us, 'aims at using the censured passions [*les passions réprouvées*] as nature gives them and without changing them in any way. That is all there is to it, the whole secret of passionate attraction. There is no questioning whether God was right in giving such and such passions to human beings; the associative order [*l'ordre sociétaire*, or the social order in which men are true partners, the name that Fourier gives to the type of community he favours] uses them without changing them at all and as God has given them.'[1] Fourier delights to attack the *moralists*, meaning presumably not everyone who offers advice to men about how they should live (for he does that himself) but those who teach the sort of morality which makes a virtue of restraining the passions. The morality of the moralists whom he condemns impels man to be at war with himself; it rests on the assumption that God does not know how to fashion men's souls wisely but needs a Plato or a Seneca to improve the work of his hands. The 'moralists' have taught man that he must get the better of his nature, as God made it; that he must tame it. But this, Fourier tells us, is quite to mistake the matter. Man must not repress his nature but must create the sort of community where it can have free play. The natural passions, which have harmful effects in society as it is today, will find full and harmless scope in communities of about 1,600 persons, properly organized. Fourier claims to have discovered the key to that proper organization, and offers it to mankind.

Fourier the psychologist, the interpreter of the passions, in some ways recalls Hobbes; there is the same love of definition, enumeration, and order, and the same unspoken conviction that he has taken the full measure of mankind. Man, we are told, has five sensitive passions; they are the five senses, and they tend to luxury. Perhaps it would be better to say that the object of many desires is to gratify the senses,

[1] *Théorie de l'unité Universelle*, 2nd edition, Vol. IV, p. 157, quoted by Gide in *Fourier, Pages Choisies* 1932 edition, pp. 27-8. I am responsible for the translation from the French.

and that these desires can be roughly classified according to the sense or senses they aim at gratifying. Fourier insists against the 'moralists' that these five passions (or, as we might prefer to say, these sensuous desires) ought to be satisfied as much as possible; he approves of luxury provided it does not lead to boredom or disgust. Man has also four affective passions which make him sociable: friendliness, love, ambition and parental feeling.[1] And he has three distributive passions, the *cabalistic* or passion for intrigue, the *composite* or desire for satisfactions which are of more than one type (for example, a desire for an experience which satisfies both the senses and the intellect, like a good dinner in good company), and the *butterfly* or passion for variety. It is above all the distributive passions which have been misunderstood and called vices; they are the pre-eminently worldly passions; and the 'moralists' have castigated them as impediments to virtue. They are passions denounced under such names as vanity, deviousness, hypocrisy, triviality and inconstancy. They are also the passions which have produced most of the refinements of art and social life. Besides these twelve passions, there is another, a thirteenth, which is unlucky in at least one respect, for Fourier could find only ugly names for it; he called it *harmonisme* or *unitéisme* and described it as the natural inclination which a man has to reconcile his own happiness with other people's. Presumably, man does not seek this reconcilation deliberately; it is rather that he is inclined to get happiness from what gives happiness to others, that he tends to put a higher value on shared than on solitary pleasures. Fourier's problem is to find a form of association in which these passions are not repressed but are given a free course and yet serve to hold the association together.

Society, as at present constituted, is both repressive and wasteful. Parents, in order to prepare their children for life in society, feel bound to restrain their passions, and the children secretly rebel against parental authority. Thus neither parents nor children feel for one another as they should feel; their love is spoilt by resentment and fear, and they get as much pain as pleasure from each other's society. Production cannot but be disorderly because it must respond, in large measure, to the speculations of middlemen who levy tribute on producer and consumer alike and who by their manoeuvres create monopolies and cause bankruptcies. Sismondi has admitted that consumption is 'upside down' because effective demand is determined by the whims of the unproductive and not the needs of producers. There are

[1] Fourier uses the word *paternité* to denote the fourth affective passion. Clearly, he has not in mind fatherhood, the condition of being a father, nor the sexual desire which causes a man to become a father; he means presumably some passion which is satisfied in paternity. And, since he uses the word *man* in the sense of *human being*, he means a passion which is also satisfied by maternity.

other absurdities: as man's power to create wealth increases, the rich grow richer while the poor remain in their poverty and are less secure than they used to be; the rich accumulate possessions which add nothing to their happiness while the poor are consumed with envy. Waste is enormous because there are idlers, because there is inefficiency, and because much is produced which is not wanted or does not satisfy.[1]

The remedy for these ills is the *phalanx*, a community of from 1,000 to 1,600 members differing in age, fortune, experience and character. In this community all work is voluntary, and workers are put into groups according to the work they do, a group being formed for every different kind of work. Groups doing similar work are arranged in series, each group taking its place in the series between the two groups whose work is most like its own. Fourier supposes that workers will join a group because they are attracted by the kind of work it does, and supposes also that there will be considerable rivalries between contiguous groups in a series. Every worker will want to join several groups and to work in each for only a short time. In this way the community will benefit from a wide division of labour and from the incentive to work which springs from emulation, while the worker will find an outlet for several talents and will do work which gives him pleasure. Fourier expects that there will be at least fifty to sixty series in a phalanx, and probably many more. It may well be that there will be more groups than workers, so that every worker will belong to many groups and each series will therefore work for only short periods. The system aims at making the best use of the three distributive passions: the butterfly passion for variety, the composite passion for blended or multiple satisfactions, and the cabalistic passion for intrigue. These are reprobate passions in actual society, repressed and harmful, but in the phalanx they are respectable and useful. How the passion for variety is given a wide field needs no explaining; and it is almost as easy to see how the other two are provided for. The worker in the group gets the satisfactions that come from competition as well as those that come from co-operation, for his group is striving to do better than those closest to it in the series. He helps to decide how the group will work

---

[1] Fourier reckons up the waste thus: three-quarters of the housework done by women in the towns and half done in the country would not need doing in a rationally organized community; nor would three-quarters of the work done by domestic servants, all the work done by the armed forces, by customs officers, and by 'sophists' (i.e., lawyers), nine-tenths of the work done by merchants, two-thirds of that done by transport workers, and half of that done by manufacturers, taking into account the shoddiness of what they make. There is also the waste involved in unemployment, in the idleness of the rich, of prisoners, and of the preventably sick, in crime, begging and prostitution, and in the uselessness of the studies and games of children. In the eyes of the reckoner it is a formidable reckoning because he sets it up against the phalanx, the hive of industry, full of healthy, happy and busy workers.

and also takes part in the work; he is both manager and worker. Every different kind of work which he chooses to do offers him a different blend of pleasures. Since every group is the rival of other groups, there is constant scheming to do better, there is room for the arts of persuasion and manoeuvre, and the passion for intrigue is satisfied.

The distributive passions are not satisfied only in the work done by the groups arranged in series; they are satisfied also in other ways, in the loosening of the ties which bind men and women to one another and to their children, in the very different and less restrictive ties resulting from a widening of the circle of intimacy. So, too, the sensitive and affective passions are satisfied in the working groups as well as outside them. Yet it is mostly to social activities outside the groups that Fourier looks to give a head to the sensitive and affective passions, whereas it is to these activities and to the groups equally that he looks to set free the distributive passions. The passion for variety is satisfied by the absence of restrictive family ties as much as by the freedom to do many different kinds of work, and the passion for multiple satisfactions as much by common meals and other forms of social intercourse as by work which is both co-operative and competitive. Only the passion for intrigue is perhaps better satisfied in the working groups than outside them.

The members of the phalanx are to live in one large building, the *phalanstery*, where they take their meals and leisure together, though they also have separate apartments to which they can retire when they feel the need for privacy. Fourier derived great pleasure from describing the life of the phalanstery, the excellence and delicacy of the food, the comforts of the building, the variety of the entertainment, the warmth and politeness of social intercourse, and the doing away with many unpleasant forms of housework. It is the vision of a bachelor with a taste for good living, a tenderness for women, and charity towards children but with a strong dislike for the intimacies and stuffiness of family life. The small family, he thinks, stifles its members; there may be affection between them but they are also held together by bonds which they find irksome and cannot undo. The family is not what Fourier understands by *an harmonious group*; for a group is *harmonious* when the passion which in fact holds it together is also the tonic or *apparent* passion (*passion d'étalage*), the one it exhibits to the world. The family, as we know it, is supposed to be held together by love, much of its behaviour (especially the front it puts to the world) is inspired by the need to give evidence of love, and yet it is in reality held together more by material needs and social conventions than by love. The family is, as Fourier puts it, *a subversive group*, a group where the real and the tonic passions are different. In the phalanx all groups are harmonious; the passions that hold them together are the passions exhibited by the outward behaviour of their members.

The phalanx must be recruited from all classes, and no one must be called upon to make a great sacrifice upon entering it. If the rich do not enter it, its resources will be meagre and it will have less to offer its members. The rich must enter voluntarily, hoping to live the better for doing so, and they must not be deprived of their wealth; it must be treated as an investment which they have made in the phalanx. They will, says Fourier, get a better return on their money in the phalanx than they could get outside it. Of the annual wealth produced by the phalanx and distributed to its members, capital should get four-twelfths, talent three-twelfths, and labour five-twelfths or less than half. But Fourier's concern for the rich is not quite as great as might appear. The return on capital is to diminish with each successive thousand francs invested, and the workers who come into the phalanx without capital are encouraged to save, so that soon all the workers are likely to be capitalists as well, getting a proportionately much larger return on their investments than the rich.[1] And, of course, capital is to be managed, not by the individual investor, but by the community through its appointed agents.

Once the phalanx is a going concern and its members are used to the work and the leisure it provides, the rich will not want to spend their money on themselves; they will spend it rather on the community as a whole or on some part of it with which they are closely connected. The life of the phalanx will be such that differences of income will not there have the significance which they now have. The rich will work as much as the poor, and the poor will be able to save and invest. Who will resent the wealth of a man whose capital is ten times greater but who lives more or less as other men do and is a close collaborator with them? Fourier's purpose is neither to preserve the wealthy in their riches nor to dispossess them; it is rather to draw them into a community where their wealth will be useful but will cease to divide them from the poor, where there will still be inequality (though much less than before) but where inequality will have no harmful effects. In the phalanx everyone will have adequate food, clothes and lodging, even though he does not work; but the spirit of the

---

[1] It may seem that, if the return on each successive amount invested is to diminish, the rich man with a large sum to invest can hardly get a better return in the phalanx than outside it. True, Fourier believed that productivity in the phalanx would be immensely greater, so that, if holders of capital received one-third of the distributed product, the return that any man would get on the first amounts invested would be several times greater than he could expect to get outside. Even so, the really wealthy man could hardly expect to get a better return on his capital in the phalanx, and must probably get a much worse one, especially as Fourier supposed that the return would diminish steeply with every thousand francs invested and never envisaged a rate of interest of more than 50 or 60 per cent, even on the first shares. Perhaps the 'rich' men he had in mind were merely solid well-to-do bourgeois and not men with hundreds of thousands of francs to invest.

E

community will be such, the work it offers so attractive, that no one will be idle unless he is incapable of work. Where most work is unpleasant or unsatisfying, where most men work only because they need money, to offer men even a bare living regardless of the work they do is to encourage idleness, it is to make the lazy parasites on the industrious; but in the phalanx work, even though it is not always easy, is always attractive. In the phalanx the rich will reject the notion, now so widely accepted, that many must be poor if some are to be rich; this notion (which Fourier calls, rather oddly, the 'political principle' of the civilization he abominates, meaning presumably that it is there taken for granted and not that it serves as a guide to policy) will give way to another, that the poor must enjoy a degree of affluence if the rich are to be happy. Even donkeys will be better lodged and cared for in Harmony (which is one of the names that Fourier gives to the social order he approves of) than the peasants now are in France.[1]

Man is by nature good but society has corrupted him. What proves better the vagueness of this maxim than that it serves to express Fourier's doctrine as much as Rousseau's? For the two doctrines are very different. If we look at Rousseau's description of the education of Émile, we see that the boy is faced one after another by problems which need energy, and often also courage, as well as intelligence, to solve; he learns, not without difficulty, that he cannot have all that he wants, that he must control his desires, that he must become his own master. Though Rousseau sometimes speaks as if Émile were never thwarted by human beings, but only by his physical environment, this is not at all borne out by the facts as Rousseau describes them. The boy has to learn to live with others, to moderate his demands on them, to do without what he could not get except by making them subservient to his wishes, which he is too weak to do. He must learn self-discipline, not only that others may have peace, but that he should be capable of freedom. The tutor does not remove all obstacles, except those which nature imposes, out of the boy's way; he does not create a condition in which the boy can give play to all his passions without harm to himself or to others. He does not insulate him from society; he merely sees to it that society does not present him with problems which he is too weak and immature to solve. Society both stimulates and represses. The function of education, as Rousseau describes it, is to

---

[1] Fourier was fond of animals. We are told that it is a rule in Harmony that whoever ill-treats an animal is himself more animal than the creature he ill-treats. As we are not told what are the practical effects of this rule, we must suppose that it is not so much a rule as a sentiment. It is an odd sentiment in a community of animal lovers. Is it also the rule in Harmony, where there is so much tenderness for all man's present victims, that whoever ill-treats a woman is more woman than she is?

ensure that the child, by his own efforts, is able to come to terms with society in such a way that his need for autonomy and self-respect is satisfied. Though this need is itself a product of social intercourse, the pressures of society on the individual, especially while he is still a child and immature, may make him incapable of satisfying it. The aim of the tutor is to preserve the child from these harmful pressures until he is strong enough to resist them. But he does not acquire this strength in isolation from society; he acquires it by solving social problems which are within his powers, by exerting himself, by becoming his own censor. The tutor tries, as far as possible, to ensure that the child learns from experience; he does not demand unquestioning obedience; he seeks to avoid situations in which the child yields to adults merely because he fears their power. But he does not preserve the child from having to take account of the wishes of others. Repression is inevitable in any society, even the most perfect; and the best that we can do is so to educate the young that they can find freedom and happiness in a self-discipline compatible with social harmony. This, I believe, is the essential doctrine of Rousseau in *Emile*.

But it is not the doctrine of Fourier, who usually speaks as if in the phalanx there were no need at all for self-discipline, as if nobody, whether child or adult, would ever want to do anything incompatible with social harmony. True, he does not always speak in this way; he does, when he describes the process whereby children educate one another, acknowledge that a child learns to behave partly by being rejected by other children and altering its ways in order to be accepted by them. He does sometimes admit, indirectly, that in every society education involves repression. Yet the whole bias of his doctrine is to suggest the opposite. He does not say, as Rousseau does, that, though the passions we are born with are neither good nor bad, we must ensure that society, which in any case will profoundly modify them, does not pervert them, and that we can do this only by creating a social environment which enables the child to become, largely by its own efforts, a reasonable adult; he is not even much interested in the process whereby a child becomes a grown man or woman, and seems almost to take it for granted that human passions are little affected by the social environment, so that all that matters is that they should have free play. He speaks almost as if the passions were like water, whose flow can be stopped but whose nature is not changed by the stopping. Man is cramped in society as it now is, and therefore must have room to stretch himself. This is not at all the doctrine of Rousseau and takes far less notice of the facts.

Several of the other socialists favoured easy divorce but none of them attacked the close family of the western type with the ardour of Fourier. He did not want it broken up immediately, and even criticized Owen for being in too great a hurry to make divorce easy.

The close family is part of the established system, and it is a mistake to undermine it while that system lasts. *Phanerogamic morals* (or, in plain English, free love) are suited only to Harmony, to the phalanx after its members have worked and played themselves free of the restrictive conventions of civilized society. Fourier, who found Owen impatient and superficial, prided himself on his prudence and judiciousness; he disliked rival theorists but had no wish to shock the well-to-do and the respectable.

The close family cannot be defended against some of Fourier's strictures upon it. There is often a pretence of love where no real love is felt, especially between persons bound to each other by ties which, for one reason or another, they cannot bring themselves to break; and the tyrannies of the possessive are the most unbearable of all. The worst cruelties, the deepest betrayals, the most elaborate and degrading insincerities are reserved for the family circle. There is nothing nastier, when it is nasty, than family life. We can admit this, and yet defend what Fourier attacks. Every close tie is apt to make demands on us which are excessive, and yet we feel the need for such ties. The passions for whose sake Fourier (a bachelor) would destroy the family are perhaps products of family life. The sort of love upon which he set so high a value might not exist in a society where there were no enduring bonds between men and women. Even the capacity for the friendships which for some men (especially bachelors) take the place of love, a capacity acquired in childhood, may develop in the intimate family circle. Fourier supposed that in the phalanx men's passions would be deeper as well as more varied; that men would live more intensely. It never occurred to him that the capacity to feel strongly is acquired in the closest and most demanding of human communities, in the hothouse which is the family; nor yet that the looser ties, which to him were the most precious, might lose their savour if the closer ties, which he feared, were abolished.

IV. THEIR ATTITUDE TO RELIGION, NATIONALISM AND WAR

The *philosophes* in France and the Utilitarians in England were, for the most part, hostile or indifferent to Christianity; some of them were atheists and others deists, and the few whose devotion to Christ it would be uncharitable to question (since they were in Holy Orders) gave little outward evidence of faith. But the early socialists, with two important exceptions, were not hostile to organized religion, and several of them were friendly to Christianity. They were not orthodox Christians, they did not accept whole-heartedly any of the established creeds. Indeed, we may question whether, strictly speaking, they were

Christians, for they may not have believed in the divinity of Christ or even in a personal God. But they spoke sympathetically of religion in general and of Christianity in particular, dissociating themselves from the philosophers who had attacked them. They also sometimes put themselves forward as spokesmen of God. 'Listen,' says the Innovator [whose opinions are those of Saint-Simon] to the Conservative, 'listen to the voice of God speaking to you through my mouth; become good Christians once again.'[1] 'At the sight of this enchantment [Fourier is speaking of the social order he has invented and delights in] . . . we shall witness a frenzy of enthusiasm for God, the author of so beneficial an order;'[2] and in several places he introduces what he recommends with the words 'God has willed'. But we are not so much concerned with the personal faiths of the early socialists or how close they stood (in their own eyes) to God, as with their attitude to religion. They did not think of it as the 'opium of the people', and wanted rather to reform than to abolish it.

Nearly all the early socialists were indifferent to one of the strongest sentiments of their age, nationalism. This indifference is not peculiar to them among the social and political theorists of their time; it is as marked in the Utilitarians. But Saint-Simon and Proudhon were more than indifferent; they were strongly hostile to it, and their arguments are worth noticing. Saint-Simon, educated before the French Revolution, was used to thinking of Europe as a cultural whole and looked upon nationalism as a relic of the past. It was unsuited to the times, he thought, and he even persuaded himself that it was already giving way to more generous and more appropriate sentiments. Proudhon, born some forty years later, believed as strongly that nationalism was out of place but saw it as a growing menace.

1. The Abuse and Use of Religion

The two socialists conspicuously hostile to religion were Owen and Proudhon. About Owen's attitude to it little need be said. It was very much like an attitude common in educated circles in the eighteenth century in both England and France, though more aggressive in France than in England because the Catholic Church had long been more intolerant and formidable than the Church of England. Even in the decades before the French Revolution it had still been more dangerous (and also more exciting) to attack the Established Church in France than in England. Men like to think themselves braver than

---

[1] *Le Nouveau Christianisme*, Vol. 23, of *Oeuvres de Saint-Simon et d'Enfantin*, p. 192.
[2] *Le Nouveau Monde Industriel*, p. 287.

they are, and find it exhilarating to take small risks boldly, especially when they can take them in good company.

Owen believed what the eighteenth-century rationalists had taught: that men, while they were still too ignorant to explain the world rationally, had taken to religion, but were now growing out of it – a process which men of good will and good understanding must want to hasten. This belief alone might not have sufficed to move Owen to attack religion. He had another and more pressing motive for doing so. The Churches taught that man is responsible for his own actions, and can justly be blamed and punished for the harm he does. It was this doctrine that Owen believed to be the most pernicious of errors. It had caused men to devote their energies to detecting and punishing crime and to neglect what really matters, which is to remove its causes. Not until they are persuaded that character is a product of environment will they cease punishing the individual and set about reforming society, will they take the course which is the only sure road to happiness. But, once they are persuaded, they will act upon this truth, for such is their nature. And so to Owen it seemed that the Churches were teaching a doctrine which prevented men taking his salutary advice.[1]

It is often difficult to make out just what it is that Proudhon disliked about what he attacked. Did he object to religion because its teachings are false? He seems to have shared Condorcet's belief that religion thrived while men were ignorant but that there is now no place for it.

---

[1] Owen was a poor tactician. It should have occurred to him that nobody denies that character is deeply affected by environment. Since his object was to persuade his contemporaries to change the environment which, in his opinion, produced crime and misery, he was ill advised to raise the issue he did raise. He had no need to attack the Churches for teaching that men are responsible for their actions and ought to be punished for the evil they do; he would have done better to enlist their support in his endeavours to change the social environment in order to reduce the temptations which move men to do evil. The Churches were not committed by their creeds to leaving the environment unchanged. Those who hold to the doctrine of responsibility which Owen rejected are not logically committed to resisting social reform, and it is not at all obvious that they are psychologically disposed to resist it. By offending the Churches Owen did more harm than good to his own cause.

The truth is that Owen was so much excited by his doctrine that men are not responsible for what they do (of which he sometimes spoke as if he were the discoverer of it) that he could not help attacking whoever denied it. He attacked first, and then justified his attack by putting forward mistaken opinions about the practical consequences of denying his doctrine. Moreover, his arguments in support of this doctrine are so weak and ambiguous as to create the impression that he has raised an issue beyond his intellectual powers. Men who have been successful in business – and in this they resemble politicians – when they engage in controversy of this kind sometimes give the impression of great arrogance, because they have strong convictions and yet are blind to the weaknesses of the position they take up. Though their arrogance, being simple-minded, rarely gives offence, its absurdity causes them to be dismissed as cranks.

Yet he did not agree with Condorcet that religion, though inevitable in the past, had been harmful even then; he said that religion had been useful in the past, though he did not make it clear just how it had been useful. Perhaps he believed that its threats and promises had helped to induce men to behave well while they were still too little enlightened to see that good behaviour was in their own enduring interest. Perhaps he believed that while organized force was still necessary to maintain social discipline, religion provided supplementary sanctions. Perhaps he believed that, at a time when men were still too ignorant to know how to remove the social causes of their wretchedness, it was good that they should have religion to comfort them.

Whatever his views about the past, he saw no need for religion in the present. Religion is now worse than useless, it is harmful. It is an obstacle to progress because it turns men's minds away from reforming society, now that it is at last in their power to do so. It attributes all the virtues proper to man to a God without whom man is nothing. It thus weakens man's self-confidence, his sense of his own dignity; it puts him in perpetual tutelage. Perhaps in the past, while his understanding and powers were small, it was good that he should create for himself an image of benevolent omnipotence and take shelter under it. But now he must dare to see himself without a master anywhere, he must trust in his own powers, he must strive to realize justice here and now and not look for it in an imaginary world beyond death. Man cannot reach maturity in the shadow of a God fashioned by his own hopes and fears. Proudhon is not concerned to prove that religion is false; he is content to hint at its origins and to condemn it for the harm it now does. He condemns it for a reason almost opposite to Owen's; he accuses man of taking refuge in God to escape his worldly responsibilities, which are the only true ones.

Much the most interesting of the early socialists, when he speaks of religion, is Saint-Simon. He tells us that every society needs a system of beliefs which not only explain the world but also determine the goals of human endeavour. Otherwise men will have no firm principles to guide them; they will be morally at sea and therefore disturbed and unhappy. In the Middle Ages there was such a system: theology purported to explain the world, all other studies being subordinate to it, and it also provided a morality acceptable to men at that stage of social evolution. The theology and the morality were intimately related to one another, so that whoever accepted the first found it reasonable to accept the second. If the world were as the theologians described it, it was the part of wisdom to do what the moralists prescribed. Saint-Simon agreed with such Catholic writers as Maistre and Bonald, who condemned the moral anarchy of their age, contrasting it unfavourably with the Middle Ages.

But he thought it impossible and undesirable to restore the hold upon men of religion as the Middle Ages had known it. The progress of science has destroyed many of the beliefs on which that religion rested; it is therefore beyond anyone's power to revive it. And if it could be revived, it would have to be to the detriment of the positive sciences to which men owe opportunities of happiness unknown to any previous age – though they are opportunities still largely untaken. What is needed is not a return to a system of beliefs suited to a different type of society but an advance to a new system suited to a new society. The positive sciences – the sciences which study the facts and produce theories to explain them which are subject to verification – have made progress enough to debilitate the old religion beyond hope of revival; but they have not yet advanced to the point where they can do for society all that religion once did. There is still one large gap in men's knowledge; they know much more about the world external to them than about themselves and the communities they form. Before science can take the place of religion, this gap must be filled; there must emerge a science of man in society, a science which Saint-Simon called *social physiology* and to which his one-time disciple, Comte, later gave the name of *sociology*. Saint-Simon believed that he had himself laid the foundations of this new science.

When the circle of the sciences is completed, when man has learnt to use the same methods in studying himself as he already uses in studying the world external to himself, there will arise a philosophy entirely in harmony with science.[1] This philosophy will not purport to give men knowledge of a reality lying behind the phenomena studied by the scientist; it will merely explain how the aspects of reality studied separately by the special sciences form a single universe. It will be the science of sciences, not as directing the others what they should do, but as putting together into a whole what they produce, which must, as they produce it, be fragmentary. Philosophy will therefore be a kind of compendium of the sciences, though it will call for intellectual gifts as rare as any possessed by the special scientists. It is to philosophy thus conceived that Saint-Simon looks to do for industrial society what theology did for feudal society: to provide it with a cosmology intimately connected with a morality suitable to the

---

[1] Saint-Simon did not suppose that mankind were on the verge of producing, in every sphere, scientific theories which could not be improved upon. He looked forward to indefinite scientific progress. The circle of the sciences would be *completed* when men used scientific methods in every field of enquiry; its completion would not therefore mean that there would be no further progress. Yet Saint-Simon did not foresee the sort of revolution in science we have lived through in our century: he supposed that the principles discovered by Newton would be accepted always, and that progress would take the form of building upon principles such as these and not of discarding them for others. His conception of scientific progress was in important ways different from ours.

age. He even proposed that the Institut de France should prepare a catechism to be taught in all elementary schools. That body was, he thought, a congregation of the finest intellects, many of them learned in the sciences, and therefore the most competent to devise a moral code suited to a society dominated by industry and science.

Later, in the last years of his life, Saint-Simon seems to have changed his mind considerably, though perhaps without himself noticing the extent to which he had done so. Durkheim[1] suggests that Saint-Simon began by believing that men, though predominantly self-regarding, can become enlightened enough to follow their own advantage without harming one another. In other words, he believed in a natural harmony of interests: it is the long-term interest of every man that he should accept rules which, while they prevent his doing harm to others, also prevent their doing harm to him. Men are unhappy, not because they are egoists, but because they are unenlightened egoists. It is possible to discover rules which are in the long-term interest of them all, and to persuade them to accept these rules. But the rules must be suited to the type of society in which men live, and must be inculcated by methods likely to be effective. Saint-Simon therefore long believed that some such body as the Institut de France could decide both upon the rules and upon the methods. It was a task for which intellectuals, learned and dispassionate, were eminently fitted. But later he changed his mind, experience having taught him that the obstacle to progress is as much egoism as ignorance. It is not enough to enlighten the selfish; it is also necessary to combat their selfishness.

To combat selfishness we must do more than enlighten men about themselves and teach them how best to reconcile their interests with other people's; we must strengthen sentiments in them which are not made strong merely by extending their knowledge. We must teach them to love one another. But we cannot teach them to love one another by showing that otherwise they will be unhappy, for it is of the nature of love that, though it brings happiness, men cannot be brought to feel it by being persuaded that without it they will not be happy. And so – all this according to Durkheim – Saint-Simon, though without admitting it to himself, lost faith in the ability of a philosophy derived from science to provide a morality suited to industral society; he lost faith in the wisdom of intellectuals and scientists and turned back to the morality of the gospels. He did not, however, turn back to Christian theology; he did not believe in the divinity of Christ, nor even perhaps that God is a person. He cared only for Christian morals, and saw no logical connection between them and Christian theology. He remained what he had perhaps always been, a pantheist with vague beliefs about a divinity immanent in all things.

[1] See his book, *Le Socialisme*.

Now this, though Saint-Simon might not know it, was to abandon the doctrine that every moral code goes along with a philosophy, or general theory about the universe, appropriate to it. The Christian moral code appeared in the world centuries before even the first beginnings of the industrial society in which alone (according to Saint-Simon) it could be applied fully. When Jesus taught, civilization was still in its infancy and society was divided into masters and slaves; it was not yet possible for men to organize society in the spirit of the doctrine of love which He preached to them.[1] He sowed a seed which could not ripen into a full harvest in nearly two thousand years. Both Catholics and Protestants have neglected the core of His teaching. Men have made progress in all the sciences except the most important of all, which is the science of morals. And Saint-Simon makes it clear that progress in this science does not consist in finding better principles than those taught by Jesus; it consists only in discovering how to apply His principles. Nor does Saint-Simon say that in all the generations since Christ taught, no one has understood His moral teachings and tried to live up to them; he does not say that men have possessed the letter of those teachings for centuries without ever having understood their spirit. He says only that the social order was an obstacle in the way of men's receiving them and acting upon them. While that order lasted it was difficult but not impossible for them to understand Christian doctrine fully, and difficult also to act upon it when they understood it. But, presumably, these difficulties did not arise because men lacked the knowledge which science provides; they arose for two quite different reasons. Men were still deeply influenced by the moral values of a society divided into masters and slaves, so that, even when they were sincere Christians, they often did not aim at what sincere Christians should aim at. They made mistaken decisions about what they ought to strive for. And, even when they did not make mistakes of this kind, but wanted what they ought to have wanted, it was difficult for them to achieve it.

If this is so, then the connection between science and the morality of which Saint-Simon approved is not what he, in his earlier writings, supposed it to be. The knowledge which comes with science adds nothing to man's understanding of this morality, which is, indeed, an *understanding* different in kind from scientific knowledge or opinion; a man could *understand*, could acknowledge and inwardly digest this morality, could possess it in the spirit as well as in the letter, and yet have little or no science. He could be as scientifically ignorant as the most ignorant of the apostles. The connection between science and this morality is merely that the progress of science is one of the causes of the disintegration of the old social order whose values and behaviour

---

[1] So Saint-Simon tells us in *Le Nouveau Christianisme*.

stood in the way of men's receiving Christ's teaching in the spirit of the teacher and acting upon it. This is the revised doctrine of *Le Nouveau Christianisme*; or perhaps we should say (to avoid attributing to Saint-Simon opinions which he never put into words), it is the doctrine about the connection between science and morality implicit in *Le Nouveau Christianisme*. But we have to admit that Saint-Simon probably never saw the implication; there is no evidence that he was aware how far he had broken away in *Le Nouveau Christianisme* from his earlier teachings.

Saint-Simon was right in believing that mediaeval theology and cosmology were closely bound up with the moral values of mediaeval society. He was mistaken in supposing that the cosmology and ethics of the Middle Ages formed a system of mutually consistent beliefs, but he was right in holding that they deeply influenced each other. But then, as he himself insisted, the mediaeval explanation of the world was not *positive*; it was not scientific. It pretended to a knowledge not got from experience; it put forward hypotheses incapable of verification. The function of mediaeval cosmology was partly to strengthen the hold upon men of the values asserted by mediaeval ethics. The contrary was also true: mediaeval moral values were made to square with the mediaeval conception of a universe created and controlled by a God more wrapped up in man than in any other of His creatures.

But a philosophy which is merely a compendium or summary of the special sciences[1] cannot stand to any system of values as mediaeval cosmology stood to mediaeval ethics. Such a philosophy is morally neutral. No doubt, someone who accepts it will be inclined to reject (in large part, if not completely) a cosmology of the mediaeval type; and his rejection of it will incline him also to reject many of the values of mediaeval society. The man who will take for true only what the sciences vouch for is likely to have moral values different from those of the man who believes in a divinely ruled universe and a life after death. But the effect of science on morals is entirely negative; it merely destroys or weakens beliefs which incline men to accept certain values. It does not itself incline them to accept other values. This is because it consists of beliefs different in kind from those contained in the cosmologies it undermines. No doubt, there are some values common to all societies and without which no society could endure. If an unscientific cosmology which serves to support them along with other values is destroyed, they will survive its destruction, even though they

[1] This is a different conception of philosophy from that of some (perhaps many) contemporary philosophers who disparage or neglect theology and metaphysics. They do not look upon philosophy as the summary of the special sciences but as the explanation of what is involved in experiencing, knowing, reasoning, making moral judgements, etc. The philosopher in this sense is concerned with scientific method but not with explaining what the sciences, between them, make of the universe.

are temporarily shaken by it. These are values indestructible by science or by philosophy as understood either by Saint-Simon or by some present-day philosophers. But they are not values supported by science or by philosophy thus understood as mediaeval morals (including these values) were supported by mediaeval cosmology. The experience which, apart from unscientific cosmology, inclines men to accept these universal and indispensable values is not science or philosophy in the special senses of Saint-Simon and of some philosophers of our time; it is an experience common to the illiterate peasant and the most gifted scientist or philosopher. Though the social scientist may enlighten us about that experience, the knowledge he provides will still not stand to those values as theology did to morals in the Middle Ages.

Saint-Simon wanted too much: he wanted to reject religion on intellectual grounds and to get from science the assurance and comfort which religion gives to those who accept it. And when he found he could not get it, when he was moved to write *Le Nouveau Christianisme,* he refused to admit his disappointment; he continued to speak of the old theology as unacceptable because it conflicted with science and of science as the cause of progress. But he no longer looked to science or to a philosophy derived from science or explanatory of it to support morals. Nor did he confine himself to repeating the moral teachings of Jesus and showing how they could be followed in industrial society; he resorted, as his disciples did after him, to a verbose and cloudy pantheism, as if he wanted to tap all the emotions connected with the old religions without committing himself to any of their explicit doctrines.

2. Fraternity

Seeing that hostility to the Church and to Christianity was so much more conspicuous in the eighteenth century in France than in England, it is surprising to find the early French socialists so friendly to religion, if not to the Catholic Church.[1] There was more religiosity among them than among the early English socialists. The German radicals who came to Paris preferred Proudhon to the other French socialists because he stood out among them as an enemy of religion. These radicals came from a country where most of their kind were against religion, and

---

[1] The disciples of Saint-Simon, though they rejected Catholic dogma and criticized the Church for making a virtue of asceticism, were in one respect closer than any of the other socialists to Catholicism. They wanted to organize a Spiritual Power, an intellectual élite, whose pronouncements on matters of theory and morals should be final. They criticized liberty of conscience as leading to intellectual and moral anarchy.

the attachment to religion of the French socialists seemed to them old-fashioned and out of keeping with 'advanced' views about the organization of society. Many of the French socialists, despite their hostility to the established hierarchy, temporal and ecclesiastical, clung to the Christianity of the gospels, as the Anabaptists had done in Germany in Luther's time; they clung to it for all the world as if Voltaire and the Encyclopaedists had never been heard of. And this to some of the young German radicals in Paris seemed, after the great flood of the French Revolution, positively antediluvian.

There is, of course, no logical incompatibility between socialism and Christianity. Christianity, in itself, is neither radical nor conservative. To the extent that it turns men's thoughts to another world, or inclines them to believe that their relations to God are more important than their relations to other men, it may weaken their motives for wanting to change this world. St Paul preached obedience to the established powers, and the Churches have often taught men that they ought to be content with their earthly lot; because, no matter what it is, they can obey God's law and receive His reward. Yet Christian morals can be understood as much in a radical as in a conservative sense. Many Christians have held that it is possible to follow the teachings of Christ without attempting in any way to change the established order, while others have believed that that order must be changed if men are to live as Christ taught them to do. The second position is logically just as sound as the first. Certainly, it is not less sound than the first merely because it has been less often adopted; or less often until quite recent times. Nor is Christian theology in any way incompatible with socialism. The religiosity of the French socialists, if it seemed out of keeping with their socialism, must have seemed so only because for historical reasons radicalism was associated in the eyes of many with hostility to the Christian faith.

I suspect that the French socialists were attracted to Christianity mainly for two reasons, both of them connected with the great revolution. For they were disappointed in that revolution. It had proclaimed three principles, liberty, equality, and fraternity, but had taken little notice of the third. It had removed many barriers and privileges; it had established a kind of equality of opportunity. It had created a society in which it was easier than it had been for the able and the energetic to make successful careers. It could, of course, be criticized for not having gone far enough in that direction, for not having ensured that the child of poor parents has as much chance to make good as the child of rich ones, for not taking the principle of equality of opportunity to its logical conclusion. And it was criticized for this reason by the socialists. They argued that, to the extent that competition is inevitable or is good for society, justice requires that all who have to complete should have the same advantages. Since some are born abler and stronger than others, they cannot have the same natural advantages, but society ought to aim at eliminating all other inequalities. If competition there must be, let it be fair.

But the faith of the early socialists in competition, no matter how fair, was limited. They believed in more than equality of opportunity, and were concerned to do more than insist that the avowed supporters of that principle, proclaimed by the French Revolution, should be true to it. They believed also in another kind of equality. A competitive society, even though it does everything that can be done to ensure that competition is fair, inevitably raises some persons above others; and every society is to some extent competitive. But it must not exalt the competitive spirit, which is essentially selfish even when it makes for the common good; or otherwise the successful will despise those who fail, who will in turn envy them. The other kind of equality, the kind which takes no account of success or failure, is fraternity. It is equality between members of the same family or community, of whom each feels that the others belong to it as fully as he does himself; it is like the equality of Christians in the sight of God. It is the equality which justifies inequality, making it tolerable, enabling one man to say of another, *Let him be raised above me because he has more to give to the community to which we both belong.* The revolution, so it seemed to many of the French socialists, far from strengthening this kind of equality, had weakened it.

The French socialists also disliked the great revolution for its violence and the passions which it aroused, passions at least as strong as those which caused it. They believed that these passions had prevented the revolution from achieving as much as it otherwise might have done. They were therefore attracted to a religion which both condemned violence and preached doctrines which seemed to them to justify the great changes they wished to make. What was later to be called the ' opium of the people ' seemed to them a fence against passions which, if not controlled, might make it easier for the ambitious to use popular grievances to help them get power. The French socialists had seen this happen in their own country.

3. Dislike of Nationalism

One of the many ways in which Saint-Simon differed from the rationalist philosophers of the eighteenth century was in preferring the Middle Ages to antiquity. Condorcet, though he believed that progress was now inevitable because the forces making for it were stronger than all the obstacles in their way, did not hold that every age had been superior to the age before it; the course of events from the fourth to the eleventh century, from the decline of Rome to the domination of the West by the Church, did not look to him like progress. He saw no great advantage to mankind from the triumph of Christianity. But Saint-Simon claimed to see one: Christianity had taught men to transcend the narrow loyalties of the Greeks and Romans. It had superimposed humanity or philanthropy on the many patriotisms of the ancient world.[1] Christendom in the eleventh and twelfth centuries was a single community in a way in which the Roman Empire had not been; its unity did not consist in its all being subject to one prince or even in its having traditions and practices marking it off from the rest of the world. It consisted in the feelings that Christians had for one another as sharers of one faith. The patriotism of the old Greek or Roman had been inferior, not as being a sentimental attachment to the country of one's birth, but as excluding wider loyalties. What Saint-Simon objected to in the Roman was that he made service to his country the supreme duty of man.[2]

Saint-Simon believed that the spread of industry was making the nations more than ever dependent on one another. Classes were coming to have more in common than nations. The industrial class in France had less to divide it from the same class in England than from the feudal nobility in its own country. Indeed, the industrial class had interests transcending national barriers as no class before it had had. The barons of mediaeval England might share many of the attitudes and prejudices of the barons of mediaeval France. To the outsider contemplating them both, they may seem very much alike. But this similarity did not prevent their often making wars upon one another. The new dominant class were not merely like one another from country to country; they had interests which drew them together. They were the class destined, according to Saint-Simon, to create an international order which would bring peace to the world. As we have seen already, Saint-Simon's 'industrial class' included all productive workers, manual and administrative; it included men of business and

---

[1] Saint-Simon did not consider the claim that the Stoics had done this several centuries before the Christians; he did not know how much both Christian theology and Christian ethics owe to the Greeks.

[2] It might be objected that Christians have in practice been as exclusive and as uncharitable to outsiders as ever Roman patriots were. Christians have sometimes taught that who does not share their faith will suffer everlasting punishment. Perhaps it was in part because Christians taught this while Stoics did not that Diderot, Condorcet and others preferred antiquity to the Middle Ages. Yet Saint-Simon was not as simple-minded as this comment might make him appear. He made much of what seemed to him good about Christianity because Condorcet and Diderot had passed it over and also because he believed that it would survive what was bad. The appeal of Christianity was not confined to the sophisticated; it was altogether more exciting and wider than the appeal of Stoicism. Saint-Simon was attracted by all that is warm and generous in a religion which requires the giver of charity to respect the taker of it, and condemns compassion when it is mixed with contempt.

captains of industry as 'the natural leaders' of that class. Saint-Simon made for both capitalists and proletarians the claim which Marx was to make for the proletarians alone: that their class interests, to the extent that they are aware of them, move them to oppose war.

This claim is not so much false as misleading. But I shall not contest it, for I could not do so without looking carefully into the concept of 'a class interest', a task better left until I come to examine the Marxian theory, which makes much greater use of it. It is perhaps enough for the moment to say that capitalists probably stand to lose as much by war as proletarians do, if we estimate their gains and losses in terms of the preferences usually attributed to them. They are supposed to want to increase their wealth without their right to do what they please with it being diminished, just as proletarians are supposed to want a better standard of living, greater security, and perhaps also a larger say in the running of the businesses which employ them. There is no evidence that war is a greater obstacle to proletarians getting what they want than to capitalists doing so. But the feudal nobles, having quite different preferences, wanted what could not be obtained without war: they wanted danger and glory, they wanted to assert themselves in a society where they could best do it by making war. It would be wide of the mark to say that they sought to enrich their country, or even themselves, by making war, but it is true that they could not get what, as a class, they most wanted unless they made war. They were so placed socially that their ambition found its largest scope in war.

Saint-Simon disliked the scheme proposed by the Abbé de Saint-Pierre in 1713 in his treatise on *Perpetual Peace*. Saint-Pierre advised the sovereign princes of Europe to set up a permanent congress of plenipotentiaries, pledging themselves to accept the decisions of this body. The scheme seemed as unrealistic to Saint-Simon as it had done to Rousseau, and for much the same reasons. The governments of Europe had been each other's rivals for centuries; they were deeply suspicious of one another; and their policies sprang from these suspicions as well as from ambitions which they were unlikely to abandon. Only when the nations had acquired governments of a different type, governments pursuing different ends from those they now pursued, would it be possible to set up a real international authority, a body able to make important decisions and to carry them out. Saint-Simon believed that governments, constituted as they were in his day, were moved by ambitions surviving from an earlier type of society. These ambitions were both dangerous and absurd in an industrial age, and would disappear as soon as industrial society acquired the kind of government (or rather administration) appropriate to it. Therefore Saint-Simon was hopeful. True, nothing good could be expected from governments of the sort that Europe still had, but these governments had survived beyond their time and something much better would

soon take their place. When the last traces of the feudal order disappeared, there would be no more war, for the industrial class is by
nature pacific just as the feudal class is by nature warlike.[1]

Proudhon was both less hopeful of the future and less scornful of
the past than Saint-Simon. He did not look upon war as the profession
of a class surviving from a decrepit social order about to disappear completely; he did not believe that the manual workers (who were included
by Saint-Simon in the industrial class) were any more devoted to peace
than other classes. The people, he said, admire the strong and the
ruthless. And Proudhon, though himself a pacifist, came at times
close to sharing this admiration. The popular attitude to war seemed to
him neither absurd nor evil. The military virtues, courage, discipline,
devotion to duty, self-sacrifice (virtues which are military not because
soldiers always possess them but because they make a nation formidable in war) rightly inspire respect. Success in war has in the past often
been an effect of moral superiority. Proudhon, who admired courage
in all its forms and who was also a man of the people, did not disparage
it in the form best understood by the class he sprang from. Just as
individuals who are self-confident and high-spirited are often combative, so too are communities, and self-confidence is good in both
individuals and communities.

If then Proudhon condemned war, it was not because he believed it
to be inherently evil or irrational. He condemned it because he
believed that, in modern conditions, it is not only more destructive than
ever before but also more brutal and more degrading. It has always
been both good and bad: it has encouraged some virtues and set loose
some vices. As communities grow larger and instruments of war more
formidable, war gives less scope to the virtues and more to the vices.
The combativeness natural to vigorous persons and communities persists and must be given an outlet other than war. But so long as the
State, as we know it, endures, there will be danger of war. There will be
lasting peace between the nations only when the enormous concentration of power, which is the modern State, has been dissolved. In this
connection, as in every other, Proudhon was suspicious of the vast

[1] Saint-Simon was not quite as consistent as I have made him appear. He said
that ' the feudal class ', dominant in the Middle Ages, was warlike, but he
also spoke admiringly of the cosmo-political ' character of mediaeval society,
and even suggested that wars in the Middle Ages had been fewer and less
' important '. But why had wars been less ' important '? Presumably, because
resources were smaller and authority less centralized, so that it was impossible to put large armies into the field. If resources were larger in later
centuries, this was surely because of the expansion of industry, and if these
resources could be more readily mobilized for war, it was because the State
had grown strong at the expense of the feudal class. Saint-Simon's thesis, that
industrial society is essentially pacific, clearly needs to be stated much more
carefully than he stated it, if it is to be even plausible.

organization which enables a few ambitious men to manipulate the masses. The danger of war, now that war has become terrible and degrading, does not spring from the combativeness natural to man; it springs from the political order which allows this combativeness to be exploited by a narrow ruling group. There is no social class conspicuously less warlike than the others. Peace will not come when some other class dominates society in the place of the now dominant class; it will come only when the apparatus of power which makes modern war possible shall have ceased to exist.

Proudhon was closer to the truth than Saint-Simon when he spoke of the causes of war, but his suggested remedy is too improbable to leave room for hope. The apparatus of power which he condemned is unlikely to disappear. Undoubtedly, it is a condition of war as we know it; if it did not exist, the kind of war which he feared (and which we have so much greater cause to fear than he had) would be impossible. But there is no comfort in this truth: for not only is it unlikely that the State will disappear, it is also, given what most people nowadays aspire to, undesirable. The State is a condition of the material prosperity which must exist if everyone is to have the opportunities which not only socialists but men of other persuasions now agree that he should have. We speak of the right of every man and woman 'to realize his or her potentialities'. We may be hard to put it to to give a precise meaning to these words; but, whatever we understand by them, we mostly agree that they refer to opportunities still out of reach of most people, by reason of their poverty or ignorance. Prosperity greater than the world has known in the past, though not a sufficient, is a necessary condition of everyone's having these opportunities. This, at least, is a belief widely shared, and to which Proudhon subscribed. He wanted the prosperity which everyone sharing this belief thinks desirable; he wanted the prosperity but not the concentration of very great power in a very few hands, without which it is impossible. 'Be rid of the State and you will be rid of many evils, including war', is apt to appear useless advice to persons convinced that they have much to hope for from the State and who yet passionately desire peace.[1]

Proudhon did not share in French sympathy for Polish and Italian nationalism; for it seemed to him that those most eager to create large

---

[1] Proudhon also believed that war is an effect of the unequal distribution of wealth, whether between nations or inside them. Poor nations make war to get wealth, if their poverty does not weaken them to such an extent that they have no hope of success; and the wealthy classes in a nation sometimes provoke wars, either from cupidity and ambition or to distract the poor from their wretchedness. There is nothing new about these arguments, which are perhaps not worth refuting. Even if it were true that war has often been an effect of these kinds of inequality, it would not follow that with greater equality there would be less danger of war, for other causes of war might then operate more strongly.

nation-states cared too little for the autonomy of smaller groups and the freedom of individuals. He saw how illiberal nationalism was or might soon become. He was a man of many loyalties. Far from disparaging patriotism, he thought well of it. But he was suspicious of the strident nationalism which swallows up all narrower loyalties, and which strengthens the State at the expense of associations closer to the individual or more sensitive to his needs.

He was alive to the dangers of what he disliked but not to its causes or advantages. Why was it that wider loyalties were gaining strength at the expense of narrower ones? Could the Poles or the Italians, as individuals, get the freedom which Proudhon thought desirable while as nations they remained under foreign rule? Could they shake off that rule unless they were united by devotion to a larger community? Nationalism is dangerous to freedom, and yet national independence is often a condition of it. To Proudhon, belonging to a nation long united and too formidable to be ruled by foreigners, nationalism was distasteful. What he valued most seemed to him threatened by it. He was perhaps too insular to imagine how what was distasteful to himself could be attractive to a Pole or an Italian no less devoted to individual freedom than he was. He was a shrewd but a one-sided critic.

*　　*　　*

The early socialists are not to be reckoned among the most profound or subtle or many-sided or lucid of social theorists. With two conspicuous exceptions, Saint-Simon and Proudhon, they had narrow views; and Saint-Simon was careless and diffuse while Proudhon was obscure and elusive. It cannot be said of them, as it can of Rousseau, Hegel and Marx, that their writings, for all their defects, are worth close and repeated study, because there is so much in them. And they also lack the rigour and clarity of the English Utilitarians. Judged by the standards we should apply to Rousseau, Hegel or Marx, they are men of small talents. Not that their theories are more open to criticism than those of these so much more gifted men; they are merely less comprehensive and less profound.

Nevertheless, taken collectively, the early socialists are intellectually rich. They are also important. In the field of social theory, it is they who, with Rousseau and Hegel, take us from the eighteenth to the nineteenth century. Like Rousseau, they put forward an ideal of equality which could not be realized unless society were transformed, like Rousseau and Hegel they see the individual, as a purposive and moral being, as the product of his social environment, and like Hegel they see him involved in a social process leading eventually to his emancipation. Most of the ideas that go to make up the social theory of Marx and Engels are already present, somewhere or other, in their works. The extent to which they anticipate Marx is obscured by the Marxian vocabulary, which owes more to Hegel than to them. There are, for example, remarkable similarities between Saint-Simon's account of social evolution in the West since the Middle Ages and Marx's account. There are also remarkable differences: Saint-Simon attributes less importance than does Marx to changes in methods of production and more to the progress of science, and he sees no deep cleavage of interest between capitalists and proletarians. But where Marx differs from Saint-Simon, he often agrees with another of the early socialists. He is the heir of them all, and also, of course, more than the heir. He elaborated upon the ideas he took over from them, he saw connections which escaped their notice, he took more than they did into account. It has been claimed for him, and not untruly, that he saw deeper than they did, which means not so much that he went further than they went in the directions they took as that he saw what they saw as they did not see it, for each of them saw only a part of it, while he came closer to seeing the whole. He was more versatile, more intense, more imaginative than they were. Repeatedly he reminds us of them, and yet, when we stop to take his measure, he stands out clearly above them all, as Shakespeare does above the other Elizabethan dramatists. He absorbs and transcends them.

The early socialists, judged by the highest standards, were men of small talents but generous impulses. They have been, above all other social theorists, the interpreters of the aspirations and fears of mankind in the industrial age. It would perhaps be unjust to say that they have contributed less to enlarging our understanding of society than to formulating our social aspirations, for, as I have said already, taken collectively, they were prolific of good ideas. But certainly, if we take them individually and compare them with Marx, they have contributed less to our understanding and more to our hopes and fears. Marx called them *petits bourgeois*. And yet they were not, in their habits, moral standards and personal ambitions, noticeably more bourgeois, *petits* or otherwise, than he was. They were not, any more than he was, preaching doctrines likely to attract the lesser *bourgeoisie*. Nevertheless, Marx's judgement upon them is not entirely untrue; they probably did sympathize more than he did with some aspirations of the 'small man', the craftsman, the shopkeeper and the peasant. They sympathized with his desire to raise his standard of living, his craving for equality, his love of independence, his mistrust of the middle-man, his fear of organized power. But these feelings seemed to them as strong in the proletarian as in the man of small means. They were the spokesmen for all in society who were weak and hard put to it to defend their interests against the strong who owed their strength either to wealth and privilege or to their position in some powerful organization. Certainly, their sympathy for the proletarian, for the man with nothing to sell but his labour, was not less than Marx's. Indeed, it may well have been greater. When they contemplated the situations of the proletarian and the small man struggling to maintain a precarious independence, they saw much that was common to them. They looked steadily at what Marx was inclined to neglect, because they had no wish to draw the proletariat away from other classes.

They were, as Marx never was, advocates for the small man.[1] Hence their deep suspicion of the State, their dislike of bureaucracy, their preference for small communities where there is little or no difference of status. No doubt, Marx too predicted the eventual disappearance of the State; and yet he gave little thought to it. It was something that was to happen after the revolution, and the best of his mind was given to explaining how the revolution would come and to hastening its coming. He merely foretold that men would be equal and free in the future, and did not stop to consider what their condition would be like when they were so.

The early socialists attended carefully to what he neglected; they never lost sight of the goal which made the journey worth taking, it was never beyond their horizon. The world, since their time, has become even more complicated, with even greater concentrations of power than they knew, and so their fears are more than ever our fears. And we still, in the West, share their aspirations. We want the poor to live more abundantly, we want equality of opportunity, we want security and independence. Though we have abandoned all hope that the State will grow weaker or disappear, we seek to make it our servant rather than our master. The merely rich or 'well-born' or highly educated are much less important than they were; we are all small men today, unless we are big men by virtue of some office we hold in the State or in some large organization in close contact with the State. We are all, in some respects, *petits bourgeois*; we share some of the fears and some of the aspirations of the early socialists. Their solutions may not tempt us or may seem to us impossible, but the motives and sympathies which inspired them are still ours. In some ways they are closer to us than is Marx, in spite of the vast influence he has had and still has.

By temperament the early socialists were more sanguine, more charitable, and less resentful than Marx. This is true even of Saint-Simon, the least *petit bourgeois* of them. They were much more reluctant than Marx was to use force and much more afraid of the consequences of using it. They hardly spoke of the *masses* who figure so largely in Marx's thought, and their political vocabulary, compared with his, is conspicuously unmilitary.

[1] This, of course, is not equally true of all of them, and is least true of Saint-Simon.

They failed to reconcile their aspirations with one another. They wanted life made easier and more comfortable for the poor, and therefore (though with some exceptions) welcomed industrialism. Yet they often closed their eyes to the obvious, and would not see that the growth of industry, by making society more intricate and its parts more tightly knit, made centralized bureaucracy inevitable. They wanted the benefits of industrialism without accepting the hierarchy and bureaucracy inseparable from it. They therefore neglected matters of capital importance to persons who care, as they did, for equality and freedom as well as material well-being. They did not ask themselves just what kinds of equality and freedom are desirable, and how far they can be achieved in an industrial society where there must be large-scale administration if there is to be the efficient and smooth production on which prosperity and security depend.

Industrialism and bureaucracy are necessary, if not sufficient, conditions of some kinds of equality and freedom, and are incompatible with others. What we need to discover is what these kinds and the others are. Unfortunately, when we raise this question, we get no help from the early socialists. Not even from Saint-Simon, though he roundly condemned the doctrine of the rights of man and the political democracy it was used to justify. He wanted administration by experts, who could not (so he thought) exercise their authority for the common good if they were responsible to the people, and he also wanted equality of opportunity. He never asked himself what equality of opportunity will amount to in communities where every man's capacities and needs are determined by a self-recruiting *élite*.

The inadequacy of the political thinking of the early socialists is striking. It leaps to the eye as the poverty of Marx's political thought does not. Marx attacked bureaucracy and the State as fiercely as they did, but, since he never seriously attempted to describe the kind of society in which bureaucracy and the State would disappear, his writings do not bring home to us the full absurdity of the dream of an industrial society without bureaucracy and without the inequalities of power inseparable from it. Our attention is not drawn to the weakest part of his political thought, his theory of the State; it is drawn rather to the stronger part, to his beliefs about how classes struggle for power and what the working class should do to get power. Marx understood politics as none of the early socialists did. Not that he made – or would have made had he had the chance – a conspicuously successful politician, but he was a profound observer of political events. He was, like Machiavelli, a frustrated politician, and frustrated as much by temperament as by lack of opportunity. Such men are sometimes born politicians; not born to get power, not born to success, but born to a deeper knowledge of how power and success are to be had.

Chapter 3

THE SOCIAL AND POLITICAL PHILOSOPHY OF HEGEL

I

As everyone interested in Hegel knows, his social and political theory forms part of a general philosophy that is elaborate and difficult, a philosophy that is metaphysical in the sense that it offers to explain not so much how things happen in the world as why the world is necessarily as it is. I am not, as a student of theories about society and government, interested in the Hegelian metaphysic for its own sake. It may be that its essence is beyond me, and I do not think I greatly mind if it is so. But I have to take notice of it – though only in broad outline and in the most superficial way – for two reasons.

Firstly, because persons interested in Hegel's political theory have taken a brief look at his metaphysical system and have misinterpreted it. This, in itself, would not matter to us, except that their misinterpretations have caused them to misunderstand what Hegel says about society and the state. For example, Hegel calls the state *divine*, and also says that it is a *substance* and that citizens are its *accidents*. It is easy, if the sense of these words is misunderstood, to draw false inferences from them about Hegel's theory of the State.

Secondly, because we must do more than avoid certain common errors about Hegelian metaphysics if we are to do justice to his social and political theory. In expounding that theory Hegel uses concepts which belong to his metaphysical system. For example, he calls the State *Objective Spirit*, and he calls Spirit a *concrete universal*. To understand what Hegel is saying about the State when he calls it a spirit, we have to understand what he means by a *concrete universal*. But this notion is the central notion of his metaphysics.

It may seem that I have brought myself to an *impasse*; for I have admitted that the essence of Hegelian metaphysics may be beyond me, and I have said that, if we are to understand his theory of the State, we have to know how he uses the notion which is central to his metaphysics. My purpose is to expound and criticize the social and political theory of Hegel. Have I not as good as confessed that that purpose is beyond my power? Am I not stopped short at the very beginning of my enterprise?

I do not think so. The impasse, I hope, is more apparent than real. I suspect that the notion of the concrete universal, if we try to take it literally, is unintelligible; that it is a conflation of ideas which, taken together, do not really make sense. At the same time, I believe that the notion, if we take it metaphorically, does make sense; or, rather, I believe that it contains several notions which, if they are so taken, make sense. Hegel, if I may so put it, says to us, ' I mean by the concrete universal *this* and *that* and *the other*, and I mean it all literally'. Let us suppose that he defines it as A, B, C, D, and E, all to be taken literally. My contention is that, though this combination, taken literally, makes no sense, several of its constituents, taken together and metaphorically, do make sense. Sometimes it may be A & B together that make sense, sometimes C & E, and sometimes B & E. I see the fundamental concept of the Hegelian philosophy as a family of concepts which are not quite what they are made out to be but which are (most of them) highly effective in various combinations, each combination always going under the family name.

It is not the business of a political theorist to attempt a complete exposition or to offer a satisfactory criticism of a metaphysical system, even when that system is closely connected with a political theory which interests him. He need go no further, in his exposition and criticism, than what seems to him far enough to make the best sense he is able to make of the political theory. Therefore his exposition is unlikely to seem adequate to anyone interested in the metaphysical system for its own sake. And his criticism is intended to be only superficial. His criticism, indeed, is not so much criticism as a putting of his own cards on the table. He does not say: ' This and that part of the system is unacceptable for these reasons, which ought, in my opinion, to convince anyone who considers the matter closely'; he says rather, ' I can make nothing of this or that part of the system, but I think that his political theory makes sense even without it.' The political theorist, criticizing a metaphysical system, does not attempt to argue an elaborate and careful case, meeting all objections to it which he can think of and which seem important to him. He merely takes up a stand, and has done as much as can be reasonably expected of him if he makes it plain just what that stand is.

This exposition and criticism, therefore, superficial though they are, are also necessary, because they give notice how we intend to deal with the social and political theory of Hegel. As we have seen already, Hegel calls the State Objective Spirit, and says that Spirit is a concrete universal. I shall reject as false or unintelligible much that Hegel says about the concrete universal. The rejection will not be criticism meant to satisfy the logician or metaphysician, for I neither regard myself as competent to make such a criticism, nor do I think it the duty of a social and political theorist to attempt it; but it will, I hope, help me to explain what I think is true or important or suggestive in what Hegel has to say about society and the State.

Hegel was, I believe, a profound social and political theorist, and also a profound psychologist. Since I find his metaphysics unacceptable, I have to show what it is that is profound in his social and political theory, even when it is divorced from his metaphysics. Unfortunately, Hegel did not produce a metaphysical system, using concepts appropriate to it, and then produce a social and political theory, using other concepts which his readers could understand without reference to his metaphysics. He used, as I have said, metaphysical concepts to expound his views about man in society and about the State. Therefore anyone interested in those views, but who cannot accept the metaphysics, must learn to translate what Hegel says in his peculiar and metaphysical language about man, society and the State into more ordinary speech. If he refers to the metaphysical system, either to expound or criticize it, he does so primarily to make it plain how he proposes to make the translation.

If we treat Hegel's metaphysical language as largely metaphorical, we can, I believe, see that he uses it to say many important and true things not said by others before him, or not said nearly so well. No doubt, the convinced Hegelian will protest that this method is wretchedly inadequate. He might perhaps be moved to put his protest in such words as these: ' What you say makes no sense unless it is taken metaphorically makes excellent sense when taken literally, and that is how Hegel invites us to take it. Your exposition of Hegel's political and social theory necessarily misses a great part of the truth – indeed the essential part.'

This is a criticism to which the political theorist who takes the line that I propose to take with Hegel is necessarily exposed, and which, as a mere political theorist, he cannot meet – at least not to the satisfaction of the critic. For to meet it he would have to do more than say that he could not accept the Hegelian metaphysical system for such and such reasons; he would have to prove that it is untenable. And I have already said that I cannot do this, and that it is not even my business, as a social and political theorist, to attempt it. I must therefore admit that my account of Hegel's social and political theory may be seriously inadequate for the reason put forward by the hypothetical critic. I do not believe that it is; I believe that its inadequacies, whatever they are, are due to other causes, but this I cannot prove. A notion like that of the concrete universal may be unintelligible to someone either because, though it has a sense, he cannot get it or because it has no sense. But he cannot be sure that it has no sense unless he can prove that it has none. I wish I could say that whatever in Hegel's philosophy is unintelligible to me is so for the second reason. Unfortunately, I cannot say it. I can say only that the arguments of the critics of

Hegel's metaphysics seem to me more convincing than the arguments of his defenders, to the extent that I have understood them.

Even if it were true that an account of Hegel's social and political theory which assumes that the central concept (taken literally) of his philosophy is unintelligible must be inadequate, it would not follow that it must also distort his meaning. It might still be a fair account of part of his theory, and that part might be important. It is my hope that even Hegelians may say that my account of it, though it falls far short of the whole doctrine, is a fair enough interpretation, as far as it goes.

In reading the works of contemporary sociologists and political scientists, especially the more theoretical among them, I have often been struck by how much they have in common with Hegel. They have, I believe, as much in common with him as with Marx; and yet they are much less aware of their community with Hegel. His metaphysics and his vocabulary bother them; they make little or nothing of him, and are easily tempted to dismiss him as a purveyor of nonsense. Nothing could induce them to take his metaphysics seriously. If they were disposed to try to make sense of his social and political theory, they would, in all probability, discount his metaphysical beliefs. They would seek an answer to this question: What does that theory amount to divorced from these beliefs? But that is precisely the answer that I am seeking. Even if it is true that whoever rejects the Hegelian metaphysics misses the essence of his theory of the State and of man's progress in society, the fact remains that it is those parts of the theory which still make sense when the metaphysical system is rejected that are important in contemporary social and political thought.

Croce once put the question, What is living and what is dead in the philosophy of Hegel? I believe that what is living still amounts to a great deal, but that we cannot see clearly what it is until we have extricated it from the clutches of what is dead.

I. HEGELIAN METAPHYSICS

A. *Puzzles and Solutions*

Hegel reaches his doctrine about what reality essentially is by examining critically the attempts made before him to explain it; that is, by examining critically the philosophies prior to his own. As he sees it, these philosophies were all, in one way or another, faced by two kinds of puzzles, epistemological and logical, which they failed to solve, or to solve completely, and which he thinks are solved only by his philosophy, which asserts that reality is essentially spiritual, or the activity of Mind or Spirit whereby it produces a coherent world and comes to full knowledge of itself and full satisfaction in the process of coming to know that world as its own product. I shall say more later about his conception of the world as essentially spiritual, but first I want to consider the puzzles which he believes that philosophies prior to his own had not completely solved.

I. EPISTEMOLOGICAL PUZZLES

Philosophers have reflected about the nature of knowledge, distinguishing the knowing self or the act of knowing from the object known. In the course of this reflection they have been caught up in all kinds of puzzles about what is independent of the mind and what is not. The same object appears different to different observers, and yet it is only one object and not as many as there are observers of it. We distinguish between changes in how an object appears to us and changes that happen to it. We distinguish between our dreams and our waking experience, calling only the first illusory. Ordinarily, we are not puzzled by such things, but when we reflect on the nature of our experience, we are puzzled. How do we distinguish between knowledge and illusion, between reality and appearance? None of the answers to this question given by philosophy in the past is entirely satisfactory, though each, according to Hegel, has an element of truth about it, some of the answers being much nearer the truth than others. If we take philosophers who come only a little time before Hegel, we find Hume reducing all experience to mere clusters and sequences of impressions and their faint copies in memory, or we find Kant saying that space and time are forms of intuition (or ways in which what is given in sensation appears to the mind) and that concepts such as substance and cause are imposed by the mind on what it senses. Hume's theory allows nothing for the mind's activity; it treats mind as passive. Or rather, it neglects it altogether, for mind, Hegel tells us, is essentially active, and anyone who fails to notice this really leaves mind out of account. Kant makes a false distinction between things as they appear to us and things as they are in themselves, making the absurd assertion that we can know that there are things-in-themselves, quite independent of our minds, but that we can know nothing more about them than that they exist. Yet there is an element of truth in both their theories; Hume is right in holding that there is nothing outside the range of experience, and Kant is right in holding that the mind creates the world which it knows.

If we are to get over these difficulties we must, Hegel tells us, realize that knowing or thinking and its object are but two sides of a single experience, separable in thought but not in fact, and that knowledge is active and not passive.

II. LOGICAL PUZZLES

Philosophers, in explaining the world, have used certain basic concepts or categories, such as *being, substance, quality, change, cause* and *effect, finite* and *infinite*. These concepts were not, of course, invented by philosophers in order to explain the world; they were already present in ordinary speech, sometimes implicitly and sometimes explicitly. Philosophers have merely examined them, refined upon them, and explained them. Hegel does not question the utility of these concepts or suggest that, as ordinarily used, they involve the user in obscurity or contradiction. He says only that, if they are examined critically, it is seen that they are contradictory in themselves.

Let me take an example to illustrate his meaning. Hegel thinks that the notion of being, critically examined, proves to be self-contradictory. For if we say of anything that it has only being, we attribute nothing to it, for mere being, without any other properties, is nothing. Thus the concept of being is seen to contain within itself the concept of nothing, which is its opposite, and it is therefore a self-contradictory concept. Hegel is even prepared to say that the two concepts, being and nothing, are identical, and also that they pass into one another. But the passing of these two concepts into one another gives us a third concept, which is that of *becoming*. We have here three concepts *dialectically* related to one another; the concept of being, the *thesis*, which passes into its opposite or *antithesis*, the concept of nothing, and the concept of becoming which contains them both and is their *synthesis*. It is equally true, says Hegel, that the concepts of being and nothing are different and that they are identical; we cannot help but distinguish between them, and yet we also cannot help, if we take either in pure abstraction, seeing that it is the same as the other. We have two concepts which we cannot deny are both identical and different, and we cannot see how they can be both until we pass to the concept of becoming, or of coming to be and ceasing to be. What is coming to be both is not and is, what is ceasing to be both is and is not, and so, in the concept of becoming, being and nothing are reconciled; that is to say, they are both necessarily contained in it, because it is unthinkable without them.

If we take the concept of *becoming* in pure abstraction, we see that it too contains its opposite, and is therefore self-contradictory, and then again that both it and its contradictory opposite are necessarily contained in some other concept; and so the process goes on until we eventually reach a concept which is not self-contradictory and which Hegel calls the Absolute Idea. Thus, for Hegel, the concepts in terms of which we describe and explain our experience form a hierarchy whose highest member contains all the others within itself. Therefore, the peculiarity, if I may so put it, of this hierarchy is that its highest member is the hierarchy, for it contains all the members below it. It alone is fully self-consistent, whereas the concepts contained in it, if they are considered in abstraction from it, are not self-consistent.

So far, we have been considering only concepts and not the reality to which they apply. Now, what is real cannot be self-contradictory; it must therefore realize the Absolute Idea, which alone is completely self-consistent. But only Mind or Spirit realizes the Absolute Idea; so that it follows that reality must be spiritual. The puzzles and contradictions, from which we cannot escape when we consider what is involved in our having knowledge and when we analyse the concepts which we necessarily use to describe the world, can be resolved only if we think of the world in a certain way: if we think of it as Mind or Spirit rising progressively to a full knowledge of itself.

The philosophies prior to his own interest Hegel for two reasons. They interest him because, by reflecting on their inadequacies, he can make his way to the true philosophy. But they also interest him as stages in the process whereby Spirit comes to full knowledge of itself. He thinks of them as necessary stages; and so, in his opinion, the study of the history of thought is an important part of the study of what reality essentially is.

Spirit, says Hegel, is essentially active; it is what it does. It is revealed only in its actions, and exists only as so revealed; it is by action and by reflecting on its actions that it constructs for itself coherent knowledge of a world and in the same process acquires self-knowledge. But we have seen that, for Hegel, knowledge and its object are but two sides of a single experience, so that Spirit, as it creates for itself a coherent knowledge of a world, creates the object of that knowledge, which is the world. Since Spirit is active and is revealed only in action, Hegel speaks of it as self-creating; and since it comes to know itself in the process of knowing a world (that is, in the process of acquiring a coherent experience), he speaks of it as discovering itself in the world, or as positing a world in which it comes to full knowledge of itself as it comes to know that it has posited the world.

The process whereby Spirit comes to full self-knowledge is dialectical. Spirit is active in producing for itself a coherent knowledge of a world, but it does not at first know that it has produced it; it therefore takes the world as something outside itself, contrasting itself, as Spirit, to nature as the opposite of Spirit. Then, as it reflects on its experience, it comes to know that nature, which it took to be external to itself, is its own product. As Hegel often puts it, Spirit negates itself in a world which it takes to be external to itself, and then negates that negation when it comes to know the world as a projection of Spirit. In other words, it comes to know itself as what necessarily produces a world and cannot attain self-knowledge except by so doing.

Spirit necessarily acquires self-knowledge in a plurality of finite minds; of minds like yours and mine, of minds in the ordinary sense as understood by anyone ignorant of the Hegelian philosophy. Spirit is revealed to itself, necessarily, in a plurality of selves because Spirit involves self-consciousness, and a self becomes self-conscious by distinguishing itself from other selves. And, of course, it cannot distinguish itself from other selves unless it distinguishes itself from a world external to itself. Spirit is not conceived of by Hegel, as God is by most theologians, as a mind separate from ordinary minds and differing from them chiefly in being omniscient and omnipotent.

There are, in the ordinary sense of mind (the sense in which Smith and Robinson have minds) only finite minds. Spirit is revealed to itself only through finite minds; it is self-conscious only through their consciousness of it. Yet it is greater than any of the finite minds in which it comes to know itself. For, though each finite mind also acquires self-consciousness in the process of acquiring coherent knowledge of a world, this knowledge is not its sole product. Knowledge involves the use of concepts logically related to one another; in other words, it involves the use of a language, and a language is not the product of this or that finite mind but of many such minds related to one another. And the relations are not external, like the spatial relations between material objects; they involve communication. The knowledge through which any finite mind acquires self-consciousness and consciousness of an external world is the product of a community of minds.

Therefore, when Hegel says that Spirit reveals itself by producing a world and comes to full knowledge of itself as it comes to recognize the world as its own product, we must not suppose that he is talking about a process which happens separately in each finite mind. He is not saying that each of us reveals himself in producing a world, and exists only as so revealed; he is saying that Spirit which reveals itself in producing a world comes to know itself only in our knowledge of it. He is not a solipsist or a subjectivist; though Spirit is the whole of reality and is manifest, at higher levels, in a plurality of finite minds through which it obtains self-knowledge, each of these finite minds is only an infinitesimally small part of reality. Spirit, as Hegel puts it, is a concrete universal; it is a process whose nature is revealed through everything which is a part of it, and the end or goal of the process is a self-knowledge achieved in a plurality of finite minds. Therefore, if I have understood Hegel aright, only a part of the process which is Spirit is revealed in finite minds and in the forms of their communal life. But this part is the highest, for the end or goal of the process is self-knowledge, which is attained only in the knowledge of finite minds. The process which is reality is said by Hegel to be timeless, and so we have the paradox of a timeless process whose goal is a self-knowledge achieved only in the knowledge of finite minds whose experience is necessarily temporal.

Hegel, though he conceives of the whole process which is reality as spiritual, also uses the word Spirit more narrowly to refer to the higher stages of the process, the stages revealed in finite minds. So we find Hegel treating all reality as spiritual, and also contrasting nature with Spirit, saying that Spirit arises out of nature and is a higher stage of the process in which they are both involved. If we think of Spirit as all reality, then nature is its product; if we think of it as the higher stages of the process which reality is, then Spirit emerges out of nature. And here we come upon another paradox, which, for the moment, I will mention only, without commenting on it. The process is dialectical; it involves contradiction and the resolution of contradiction, repeated over and over again, until a final stage is reached which involves no further contradiction. The process is spoken of as if it were both logical and teleological; as if the lower stages implied the higher ones, and also as if they produced them in order that the process should achieve its goal. This goal is the full self-knowledge of Spirit, and all the stages that lead up to it, since they imply it, are said to be explicit in it, and it is said to be implicit in them. And so, just as the Absolute Idea, the only fully consistent concept, contains all the other concepts in it, so the highest stage in the process of Spirit, the Absolute Spirit, contains all the lower stages. That a complex idea should be made up of simpler ones is readily intelligible, but it does seem odd to speak of a process whose ultimate stage contains all the stages leading up to it.

The concepts contained in the Absolute Idea are, we have seen, abstract and self-contradictory when considered apart from the whole which contains them. As it is with the Absolute Idea, so it is with Absolute Spirit; whatever is contained in it, whatever it is the culmination of, is said to be abstract and self-contradictory when considered apart from it. To understand anything which is involved in the process, we must understand the process as a whole. Even to understand the end of the process, its culmination, we must understand the whole process, for the end of Spirit is that it should know itself. To understand what it is to be a finite self we must understand what it is to be a member of a community, for a finite self is what it is only in a community of selves; and to understand what a community is we must see it in relation to the whole process whereby Spirit attains self-knowledge. As revealed in the thoughts, purposes and feelings of finite selves, Spirit is, in the Hegelian parlance, subjective; as revealed in the forms of communal life, especially the State, it is objective.

B. Why Hegel's Solutions are Unacceptable

I. SPIRIT AND NATURE

The mere student of social and political theory, as he attempts to take stock of Hegel's account of what reality essentially is, and why it must be so, finds himself torn between two emotions, admiration and suspicion. There is a boldness and a magnificence about it which are impressive. It is a high-sounding account, it is philosophy in the grand manner. But does it really solve the difficulties it claims to solve? Does it provide us with ideas which really help to make the world, and especially the social world, more intelligible?

Hegel, by his doctrine that knowledge and its object are essentially one (meaning, apparently, not that they cannot be distinguished, but that they are inseparable aspects of a single experience) seems to create as many problems as he solves. Unless we can legitimately speak of things being as we know them to be quite independently of our knowing them, how can we distinguish between truth and error? We can, of course, resort to a coherence theory of truth, saying that an opinion is true if it is compatible with those of our opinions which form a consistent or coherent body of opinions, a systematic whole which we treat as knowledge. But, in that case, it follows that an opinion which is compatible with the coherent system of our opinions at one time but not at another can first be true and then become false. It remains true while it fits in with the system, but, if the system changes (which it must do as the experience of mankind is enlarged), it may become false. I find it impossible to accept this; I would rather say, as most men do, that what was believed to be true on the best evidence then to be had has since been shown to be false. It seems to me that the Hegelian philosophy requires us to hold that this is merely another way of saying that what was true has become false, which it clearly is not.

Moreover, if knowledge and its object are one, in the Hegelian sense, it surely follows that where there is no knowledge there is nothing. For, though we are told that Spirit is not to be confused with the finite minds in and through which it attains self-knowledge, we are also told that it reaches the level of self-consciousness only in them, and that only where there is self-consciousness can there be knowledge and thought. It would therefore seem that, where there are no finite minds, there is nothing.

But Hegel, though he seems committed to this conclusion, in fact avoids it. We have seen that he sometimes speaks as if nature were a projection of Spirit, and at other times says that Spirit emerges out of nature. As we have also seen, when he speaks in the second way, which he does the more frequently, he uses the word Spirit in a narrower sense. But it is in this narrower sense that Spirit involves self-consciousness and knowledge. Therefore, in the ordinary sense of mind, there could be a mindless world, a world without knowledge or thought or even feeling in it. It is true that Hegel says that Spirit, in this narrower and more usual sense, arises *necessarily* out of nature, and is higher than nature. Nature exists for the sake of Spirit; nature implies Spirit; Spirit is the *truth* of nature. Hegel says all these things, and I do not pretend to know what he means by the last of them, which is the oddest. Presumably, to say that Spirit is the *truth* of nature does not imply that, unless there is a mind to know it, there is no nature; it must surely be only another way of saying that nature exists for the sake of Spirit, or else it must mean that nature is not fully intelligible except as giving rise to Spirit. But all this does not allow us to escape the conclusion that there could be a mindless universe. No doubt, if nature necessarily gives rise to Spirit, the universe could not remain mindless for ever, but it would have to be mindless before Spirit and self-consciousness and knowledge arose in it. But how can this be, if, as Hegel says, thought and its object are *essentially* one? For Hegel, when he asserts the identity of thought and its object, does not mean merely that whatever is real is thinkable or knowable; he means that whatever is real is actually an object of thought. Or, rather, he means that whatever is real is both thought and its object.

If we want, as Hegel and his disciples do, to hold on to both these assertions, that thought and its object are essentially one, and that Spirit (in the narrower sense which involves the existence of finite minds which think and have knowledge) emerges out of nature, we are driven to speak as if there could be thought even with no minds to do the thinking. But to speak in this way is surely to speak nonsense. This, it seems to me, is the sort of paradox to which philosophers are driven when they have got themselves into a difficulty they cannot get out of.

I must also confess that I can attach no meaning to the assertion that Spirit arises *necessarily* out of nature. Hegel intends to convey by it something more than that the universe was once mindless, and that minds later emerged in it, not by chance, but from causes which would appear sufficient to us if we knew them; he intends to convey something deeper and altogether more difficult to grasp. Nature, he says, *implies* Spirit. When he says this, Hegel is perfectly well aware that the causes to which science points to account for an event do not imply it. He is not saying that nature is the cause of Spirit; he is saying that it is inconceivable that there should be a universe in which Spirit (which is essentially reason and will) does not arise. The process which is reality, and which includes the emergence of Spirit out of nature, is a *necessary* process; it is inconceivable that it should be otherwise

F

than it is. For this process is the realization of the Absolute Idea, the only self-consistent concept. Reality, which is self-consistent, must therefore be a case of this concept, and it must be the only case, for the concept is of a Whole that is all-inclusive, a process which culminates in Spirit knowing itself.

II. THE DEDUCTION OF THE CATEGORIES

Hegel's deduction of the categories would appear to attribute to concepts contradictions which arise only when the concepts are misused or when mistaken theories are put forward about their use.

To consider the example we took before, the assertion that something has only being. This is a meaningless assertion; it purports to say something and in fact says nothing. But that does not make *being* and *nothing* identical concepts. If we say that X has only being, we speak improperly; we speak as if there were something to which we were attributing being, whereas in fact there is nothing. If I were to say that X is only red (that is, has no property other than redness), I should be speaking nonsense, for nothing can have only this one property; but it would not follow from my nonsense that red and not-red are identical concepts. That being is not a property, while redness is, makes no difference to the argument; for Hegel speaks of being as if it were a property.[1] Thus – or so it seems to me – we have, at the very start of the *Logic*, a piece of false reasoning: that to predicate only being of something is to predicate nothing of it. The truth is, rather, that to predicate only being of something is to predicate being of nothing; but from this it clearly does not follow that to predicate being is to predicate nothing.

This is not the only kind of false reasoning to be found in Hegel's *Logic*, in his attempt to show that all our basic concepts involve one another and are free of contradiction only if we see them as a hierarchy whose highest member contains all the rest. His reasoning varies with the nature of the concepts which he wants to prove are both different and identical. For example, he does not use the same type of argument to prove that the finite and the infinite are identical as he does to show that being and nothing are so. Most people suppose that finite and infinite are mutually exclusive terms. But, says Hegel, those who think this fail ' to note the simple circumstance that the infinite is thereby only one of two, and is reduced to the particular, to which

---

[1] The Idealists think it important to distinguish between *being* and *existence*. Universals, they say, do not exist except in particulars; but they can be thought of apart from particulars. When we speak of whiteness, without speaking of any white thing, we are speaking of something which does not exist; yet we are not speaking of nothing. Thus whiteness has being.

the finite forms the other particular'.[1] Stace, who quotes this passage from Wallace's translation of Hegel's *Logic*, comments on it thus: 'The infinite, according to this view, is limited by the finite, and is therefore itself finite.' If I have understood this strange argument, it amounts, in effect, to this: *Whatever is finite is not infinite, and so the concept of infinity is confined only to what is not finite. But to be confined is to be finite, and so the infinite is finite.* In other words, because the term *unlimited* is limited in its application, *limited* and *unlimited* are equivalent terms. Hegel then goes on to deduce, from these two concepts, which are different and identical, a third concept in which this contradiction is reconciled. The finite and the infinite limit one another, and yet are identical. But if A is identical with B and is also limited by it, we can say that it is *self-limited*. The self-limited is the truly infinite.

I give these two examples to illustrate why I think that the attempt to show that our basic concepts form a hierarchy whose highest member is alone free of contradiction fails. I take the first example because it is the most frequently taken by exponents of Hegel's philosophy, and the second because the concept of the self-limited or truly infinite is one that Hegel applies to Spirit. Reason and Will, which are aspects of Spirit, are self-limiting. Reason determines the limits of its own competence, and the will is self-determined whenever a deliberate choice is made. But this is mere playing with words; for the concept of self-determination, as applied to reason and will, is not a combination of the concepts of finite and infinite, as Hegel interprets them when he offers to show that they are both different and identical. Finite and infinite are concepts which apply to things that can be measured or quantified, and it does not make sense to say of such things that they are self-limiting. No finite space is self-limited; it is only limited by what is external to it. In the sense in which a quantity or series can be finite or infinite, it means nothing to say that it is self-limited; and it also means nothing to say that it is self-determined.

No doubt it does make sense to speak of the self-determined or the self-limited, when the self we have in mind is a self-conscious and rational being. But, in that case, the word limited is used in a different sense from the sense in which a space or a series is limited. If we take this second sense to be the literal one, then the other sense is metaphorical. We have here a line of reasoning which is by no means rare in Hegel; we are first invited to believe that two concepts which are mutually exclusive are also identical, and then we are offered a third concept which is said to contain them both and to 'reconcile' them.

---

[1] Looking at Hegel's argument as Wallace translates it, I did not trust myself to select the passage that gives the gist of it, and so I thought it best to allow a professed Hegelian to select it for me. This, as Stace sees it, is the clue to Hegel's meaning.

They are 'reconciled' in the third concept, presumably, because, though it contains them both and they contradict one another, it is nevertheless intelligible. If, however, we look more closely at what Hegel says, we see that the argument showing that the two concepts are identical is fallacious, and that the third concept does not really contain them, and can only be passed off as doing so because there is a verbal similarity between them. The connection between self-limitation, in the sense in which the term can be applied to the activities of a self-conscious and rational being, and the limited and unlimited, as applied to what can be measured, is not logical but etymological.

The concept of the truly infinite or self-limited is of great importance in the philosophy of Hegel, for with it we pass from the concepts applying only to nature to those which apply to Spirit as well. According to Hegel, it is the concepts which apply only to nature, to the material world, which are the more 'abstract' and the more obviously 'self-contradictory'. As we pass from them to the concepts which apply to Spirit and not to nature, we pass, so Hegel tells us, from the more to the less abstract, from the more to the less self-contradictory, till we reach the Absolute Idea, the only fully consistent concept. And so we get, unless I am mistaken, this strange result, that the less abstract concepts which apply to the higher levels of existence, the levels of rational endeavour, being nearer to self-consistency, apply to what is in itself more real than what the more abstract concepts alone apply to. Thus Spirit, in the narrower sense, as consciousness, reason and will emerging from nature, is more real than nature. It is in the concepts which apply to it, but not to nature considered apart from it, that the contradictions involved in the concepts which do apply to nature are resolved. The concepts which apply to nature imply the concepts which apply to *Spirit*. Therefore nature implies Spirit, and exists for the sake of Spirit. Hegel sometimes speaks as if nature existed in order to be known and used by Spirit, as if the material world were unintelligible except as being destined to be so known and used.

I must confess that none of this makes sense to me. I should have thought that concepts which are self-contradictory apply to nothing. But the Hegelian philosophy appears to rest on the contrary assumption, that self-contradictory concepts do apply to certain aspects of reality, which are therefore, taken in themselves, less rational and less real than other aspects, not being fully intelligible apart from them and existing for their sake.

Spirit, says Hegel, is a concrete universal. He calls it *concrete* to distinguish it from the *abstract* universal, from the concept which applies to any one of many instances. The abstract concept of circularity is fully realized in every instance of it, and there need be only one instance for it to be fully realized. But Spirit is not realized in each of its actions as an abstract concept is realized in every instance of it. Spirit is realized in the totality of its actions. It is revealed in its actions and exists only as so revealed. But it is not a mere collection of actions; for the actions that reveal it exhibit a character which it can know. Thus, if we consider Spirit in relation to the actions which reveal it, we see that it stands to them differently from the way in which an abstract universal stands to its particulars or a material whole to its parts. Hegel speaks of it as a universal which particularizes itself, or as a concept involved in a process of revealing or making explicit what it is potentially. Thus, he says in *The Philosophy of Right*, which is the most elaborate exposition of his theory of the State, that it is his purpose to reveal the development of will from concept to Idea. He offers to show how from the bare concept of will it follows that will can only be realized or made actual in the State, in a community of rational beings who conscientiously accept the rules they are required to obey. This, clearly, is to use the words 'realized' or 'made actual' in a special Hegelian sense.

There are three ordinary uses of the word *realized* which are relevant here. We speak of a concept being realized whenever anything exists to which it can be applied. Realization, in this sense, does not involve growth or development or endeavour. We also speak of realizing an ideal. Whenever a person imagines a state of affairs which he thinks desirable and then succeeds in bringing it about, he realizes an ideal. This second sense involves the notion of endeavour. We also sometimes speak of growth or development as a process whereby a thing realizes its potentialities, as when we say that a seed is realized in the mature plant. Hegel's concrete universal would appear to be a running together of these three quite different senses of realization.

It is also more than that. Realization in the third sense, which is growth or development, is treated by Hegel as if it were a necessary process. There is here a running together of the notions of development and implication. The seed does not merely grow into the mature plant, it implies it.

Again, the concrete universal is not merely the sum of its particulars; it is not merely the whole of which they are the parts, it is a whole contained in each of its parts. The finite self is one example of a concrete universal; it is not, we are told, the mere subject of its actions, the 'I' to which they are all referred, for it is present in each of them in some deeper sense than that. A man's character is revealed both in the totality of his actions, and in each of them; for it is not a bare subject that acts, but a man with a definite character. A community of selves is another example of a concrete universal; and again its character is revealed both in the pattern of life of the whole community and in each of its members; for each of them is what he is as a member of the community. The community is *reflected* in each of its members.

Hegelians say that the concrete universal is a rich notion. No doubt it is; there is a great deal put into it. But if we take it literally, it does not make sense. A concept does not develop; it has no potentialities to be realized. It can either be applied or it cannot; and its application adds nothing to it. It makes no sense to speak of it as particularizing itself, as if it were the cause of its own instances and revealed its essential nature the more fully, the more varied the instances it produced. A concept does not stand to its instances as a seed does to the mature organism that grows out of it. Nor can we say that the earlier stages in a process, whether it be a natural growth or a psychological or social development, imply the stages that follow it. If we describe the earlier stages, as they are in themselves, without regard to what comes after them, we cannot infer the later stages; we can infer them only if we know the process as a whole; and that is knowledge which we get from experience. From the fullest possible account of the actual properties of an acorn we cannot infer that it will grow into an oak. Hegel seems both to admit and to deny this. He admits that if we knew only the earlier stages of a process, we would not be able to predict the later ones; but he also insists that, when we do know the whole process, we can see that it is necessary. This I find unacceptable. No doubt, if we do know the whole process, we can define its early stages by reference to the later ones; we can put into our definitions potential as well as actual properties. Having done that, we can speak as if the early stages implied the later ones; but the implication is in our definitions and not in the facts.

It does, I concede, make sense to speak of the self as revealed in the whole course of its actions, and it also makes sense to say that the self is present in each of its actions. And Hegel is right in contending that when we speak of the self in this way or use the pronoun 'I' we are doing something different from, or at least something in addition to, referring to a bare subject of conscious feelings, thoughts and actions. This is clear enough in the first case. Nobody supposes that the self revealed in the course of a man's life is the bare subject of all his experiences; for he would need to have only one self-conscious experience for that self to be revealed, he would need to be able to say 'I' only once in his life. The self revealed in the course of a man's life is his character, which is something complex and yet peculiar to himself; whereas the bare subject, considered apart from its experiences, is, like any other bare subject, a mere abstraction.

But the self revealed in the course of a man's life is not the self present in each of his actions. When we say that a man's self is present in each of his actions, we are not, I think, speaking of his character. True, his actions are influenced by his character, though even then they are influenced, not by his character as revealed during the whole course of his life, but by his character as it was when he acted. Nevertheless, when we say that the self is present in each of its actions, we do not mean that a man's every action reveals his character, even though only in part. Nor do we mean that all his actions have a common subject. And yet, when we speak in this way, we do refer to something peculiar to creatures which, like man, are self-conscious. As Hegel saw, the experiences and actions of such a creature differ in kind from all other events known to us. Since man is, in fact, the only self-conscious creature, the only creature capable of saying 'I' known to us, we can say that human experience is unique. Man, being a self-conscious creature, is alone capable of passing false and true judgements on the situations he contemplates and in which he acts; he alone is capable of deliberation and choice. When he says to himself 'I see this' or 'I desire this' or 'I choose this', he is doing more than just stating a fact; which is, for instance, all that he is doing when he says 'the door is open'. He is, when he so speaks or thinks, being himself. According to Hegel, it is the peculiarity of the self that it does not exist unless it is self-conscious; and in being self-conscious it is necessarily active. Mere sensation may be passive, but any experience which involves self-consciousness is always active; it involves thinking. In one sense of the word action, only a self can be active; and when it is active, in the peculiar sense in which it alone can be, it is present to itself in the action (in mere thinking, or in consciously desiring, or in making a choice), and it exists only in being so present. This is, I think, what Hegel means when he says that the self 'posits itself'. All its actions involve self-consciousness, and it is not self-conscious except in action, and it is a self in being self-conscious. Therefore when I use the word 'I' I am not merely speaking or thinking about myself; I am not becoming aware of a self which existed, or could exist, apart from my awareness of it; I am being myself. I am exhibiting what it is to be a self.

Hegel was right in believing that a self-conscious creature has a character in a sense peculiar to creatures of its kind, and right also in believing that the statements whereby it expresses its self-consciousness are more than merely descriptive. A self-conscious creature develops in ways in which it could not develop if it were not self-conscious. Hegel used his notion of the concrete universal to express these beliefs. Unfortunately, that notion is more misleading than helpful; it suggests so much that is unacceptable that what is both true and important is apt to be lost to the view.

So also, in considering the relation of a community to its members, Hegel has important things to say which are easily overlooked if we allow ourselves to be too much put off by the words he uses to say them. Though it makes no sense to speak of a whole which is contained in each of its parts, or to speak of it as implicit in them, or of them as explicit in it, it does make sense, if we speak metaphorically, to say that a community is *reflected* in each of its members. Not only because men become rational and moral persons in the process of making their own a language and norms of behaviour which are communal and not merely personal, but also because a human community differs in important respects from other communities, its members being aware that they belong to it.

Hegel's notion of the concrete universal enables him to speak as if mind, a class-concept, were itself a mind, as if it were present in finite selves as the finite self is present in its experiences. It enables him to speak of it as if it were itself active and conscious and self-conscious and yet to insist that it is so only in and through finite selves. To anyone to whom the notion of the concrete universal is unintelligible (as it is to me) this looks like an attempt by Hegel to have his cake and eat it. He can deny that there is any self-conscious and rational mind apart from finite minds, and he can also speak of a mind or spirit which is infinite. He can say that Mind or Spirit is essentially infinite and also that it is its nature to be revealed in a plurality of finite minds and to exist only as so revealed. The notion of an infinite mind active and conscious only in finite minds is one that I can make no sense of; and yet, as I hope to show, Hegel uses this notion to say a great deal that makes excellent sense about man and society. In my opinion, we can get at this sense only if we treat the notion as a bundle of metaphors, of which Hegel makes use now of one and now of another, as serves his purpose.

If I pass on now to other topics, it is not because I feel I have done justice to Hegelian metaphysics, either in exposition or criticism; it is because I hope that I have said enough to make it clear what method I shall use in interpreting his social and political theory.

I shall begin by discussing Hegel's account of the development of Spirit as revealed in the intellectual and social evolution of mankind, and then I shall go on to consider his theory of the State.

II. THE PROGRESS OF SPIRIT-(A)

By the progress of Spirit I mean the process whereby, as Hegel puts it, Spirit comes to know itself fully and to be satisfied, or as we should prefer to say, the process whereby mankind come to understand themselves and the world they live in and attain the contentment of full maturity in so doing. This process is described in *The Phenomenology of Spirit* and in the *Lectures on the Philosophy of History*. Certain aspects of it are also described in the *Lectures on the History of Philosophy*, but we, as social and political theorists, are interested in the account in broad outline, and that we can find sufficiently in the *Phenomenology* and in the *Philosophy of History*.

In the *Phenomenology*, Hegel explains how Spirit appears to itself at each stage in its evolution towards complete self-knowledge and satisfaction, or, as we should put it, how men see themselves and the world at each stage. He also claims to show how these stages are necessary parts of a single process. Hegel claims to see the process as a whole, to understand the significance of each stage as the men involved in it could not understand it; or, to use his language, he sees Spirit as it actually is at each stage and also as it appears to itself; he sees it as it is *in* itself and as it is *for* itself. Only at the end of the process, when Spirit attains complete self-knowledge and satisfaction, is it *for* itself what it is *in* itself; or, in other words, does it appear to itself as it really is.

Hegel begins by describing what knowledge is, how it consists of sensation, perception, and understanding. He is not, at this stage, explaining a process of intellectual and social evolution; he is merely explaining what goes to make up knowledge, properly so called. Knowledge is always, as he sees it, architectonic; it involves having a more or less coherent picture of a world. Even the child, as soon as it learns to think and to use a systematic language, is conscious of itself as living in a world in which it distinguishes itself from what is external to it.

Hegel then goes on to describe a temporal process: how one way of thinking about man and the world gives way to another. He links up, often in the most ingenious way, these pictures of the world, these *Weltanschauungen*, with moral attitudes and forms of art and religion. Much of Hegel's argument is specious; he wants to make everything fit into his scheme, and sometimes resorts to the oddest devices to achieve his object. The poverty of his argument, when it is poor, is often hidden by the obscurity of his style. Hegel has sometimes been accused of being a charlatan: he is so confident, so all-knowing, and at times so tricky and so thin, that he annoys or disgusts the reader. It is difficult to believe that so acute and ingenious a mind could have been taken in by some of his arguments. More perhaps than any other philosopher of his calibre, he gives the impression of being intellectually dishonest. His are not the lapses of a slow or a tired mind; he makes great claims for his philosophy, and claims that are unprecedented. For it is in his philosophy that Spirit attains full self-knowledge. We may expect, but we do not excuse, shoddiness in those who give us to understand that they have solved the riddle of the universe.

Yet Hegel's enterprise is not, take it as a whole, shoddy and trivial; it is exciting and bold, and even magnificent. He sees a process whereby man, by getting to know the world and to master it, gains self-knowledge and self-mastery; he sees man, before he has achieved this knowledge and mastery, as a stranger in a social world which, though he does not know it, is the product of his own actions; he sees him

F*

transforming himself as he transforms his environment; he sees him learning gradually to be at home in the world.

This process, on its intellectual side, takes two forms: it is revealed in the attitudes of mind of the individual, in personal philosophies of life, and it is also revealed in the myths and dogmas of religion. A personal philosophy can be shared by many people, and indeed usually is so; it is not personal as being exclusive to the person who holds it but only as being how he sees the world and himself in it. It is the conscious stand he takes, though he may have motives for taking it (as Hegel clearly saw) of which he is unconscious. It is his faith, in the broad sense of that word. No doubt, it is connected with the myths and dogmas of his community, but it is different from them. Faith is personal, whereas religion, in this conception of it, is communal; religion consists of dogmas which the individual may not understand, or to which he may pay only lip-service. Religion, Hegel tells us, expresses a community's attitude to itself, though not explicitly; it is a manifestation of Spirit different in kind from a personal philosophy. In the *Phenomenology*, Hegel discusses both these forms in which Spirit reveals itself.

Hegel believes that the progress of Spirit towards self-knowledge is necessary, every stage in it following logically from the one before it. Being necessary, it can be explained abstractly without reference to actual societies and historical events. This is what Hegel undertakes to do in the *Phenomenology*. When he happens to refer to historical events, he does so only to illustrate a point. The facts of history provide only footnotes to the theme of the *Phenomenology*. Of course, since the process is necessary, it is in fact revealed in World History, but it can be explained, so Hegel believes, without reference to what has actually happened. Spirit first takes one form and then another, and we can see, if we know what Spirit essentially is, that it must be so. No doubt, since the process to be explained is the progress of Spirit towards complete self-knowledge, the process cannot be explained until it has in fact reached its goal; it cannot be explained until the course of World History is complete. The events recorded by the historian, the events in and through which Spirit attains complete self-knowledge, must have happened before there can be a philosopher capable of explaining what Spirit essentially is (or, which for Hegel is the same thing, how Spirit attains self-knowledge); but the philosopher can make his explanation without referring to those events. For example, Spirit passes necessarily through the stages which we call Stoicism and Christianity, but the philosopher can explain these stages without mentioning Zeno or Christ or Greece or Palestine. He can even – and here philosophy and modesty join hands – explain how Spirit attains complete self-knowledge without mentioning Hegel. As we read the *Phenomenology*, the actual societies and events and philosophies which correspond to what Hegel is describing come readily to mind; and this, he would no doubt say, is as it ought to be. For though it is not implied in the nature of Spirit that Zeno or Socrates or Christ or Luther had to do what they did, it is implied that there had to be the attitudes of mind which they expressed. In the *Phenomenology of Spirit* we have the intellectual history of mankind given to us without proper names.

In the *Lectures on the Philosophy of History* we have the same history given to us with proper names. We are not told merely what Spirit had necessarily to accomplish through finite minds and communities of such minds; we are given the names of the finite minds and the communities actually involved. This, however, is not the only difference between the two works. *The Philosophy of History* takes much larger account of institutions than does the *Phenomenology*, which is almost exclusively devoted to attitudes of mind and doctrines. *The Philosophy of History* also has much more to say about doctrines and social forms peculiar to the Orient or seldom found in Europe. In that respect it is broader in scope. The *Phenomenology* was completed in 1807 when Napoleon, whom Hegel greatly admired, was at the height of his power, whereas the *Lectures on the Philosophy of History* were delivered several years after Napoleon's fall. Hegel, from being an admirer of the conqueror of his country, had by then become a German patriot. Though the central theme of both works is the same, the ascent of Spirit to full self-knowledge, there are many differences between them; the earlier work is a mixture of epistemology and of an abstract philosophy of progress, while the second tells us nothing about the nature of knowledge and is an account of how progress actually happened. Again, in the *Philosophy of History* Hegel is much less concerned than in the *Phenomenology* to explain how each stage appeared to the finite minds involved in it; he tells us rather what each stage was *in* itself and is *for* us, who, viewing it through his eyes, see it for what it was, an inevitable phase of a necessary process.

We have the *Phenomenology* in the form that Hegel himself gave to it, whereas we have the *Philosophy of History* only in the form in which it was put together by an editor from notes taken by persons who attended his lectures. The *Phenomenology* is the more impressive work of the two, and I shall devote more attention to it than to the *Philosophy of History*. I shall try to explain its general argument, and then offer some criticisms of it. I shall not consider in the same way the general argument of the *Philosophy of History*; I shall confine myself to drawing attention to how it differs from the argument of the *Phenomenology*.

I. The General Argument of the Phenomenology of Spirit

THE PROCESS OF SPIRIT AS REVEALED IN PERSONAL ATTITUDES AND PHILOSOPHIES

1. Experience and Knowledge

Hegel begins by explaining what is involved in experience and knowledge. At the lowest level of consciousness, that of bare sensation, the subject does not distinguish between itself and what it senses. It is not, at that level, properly a self, because it is not self-conscious. At a higher level, the subject distinguishes between its sensations, and also between them and itself. It is at this level that it is self-conscious, that it is a self, for, in order to be a self, a subject must be self-conscious. As a self-conscious being, it can organize its sensations into a coherent experience, into a vision of a coherent world. As Hegel puts it, in his peculiar way, the self finds itself, as reason, reflected in a rational world. A rational world means, here, a coherent and intelligible world.

I find the details of Hegel's account of what constitutes knowledge difficult to follow. He appears to begin by saying that the self must be self-conscious before it can organize its sensations into a coherent world, and then later to speak as if it became self-conscious in the process of becoming rational, in the process of organizing its sensations. No doubt, he believed that there are different levels of self-consciousness. But the details of his account, though modern psychology and epistemology might question many of them, need not detain us. We are concerned only with the broad outline. Hegel sees the self as constructing, out of its sensations, the world in which it lives. At the lowest level, where there is no distinction made between the subject of consciousness, between the sensor and the sensed, there is as yet no coherent experience; it is the self which constructs out of its sensations a coherent world within which it distinguishes between itself and what is external to it. The concepts which it uses to make sense of its sensations are not themselves given in sensation; they are applied to its sensations by the self. But these concepts are not the products of any one self; they form a system of concepts used *by a community of selves*. They are the products of many finite minds in communication with one another; and they are produced, not by one generation, but by many. They form a public language which every finite mind must learn if it is to become fully self-conscious and rational. The world as it appears to men, as they understand it and form purposes inside it which they strive to realize, corresponds to the language they use to build up a coherent picture of it.

Merely to see himself as existing in a world, man does not need to be a philosopher. He must use a system of concepts to construct a world (or, as those of us who are not Hegelians prefer to say, to construct a picture of the world); but he need not reflect upon the concepts he uses. He need not know what a concept is or how he uses concepts. He uses them without analysing them, and without thinking of himself as constructing a coherent picture of the world by means of them. He takes the world for granted.

So, too, man can change his concepts without reflecting upon how he has come to do so, and often even without knowing that he has done so. Hegel shows how, for example, at one stage of their development, men use (among others) the concept of substance to construct their picture of the world, and how, at a later stage, as in Newtonian science, they come to use the concept of force. They think of force as something independent of themselves which causes things to behave as they do; and they do not know it for what it in fact is, a concept invented by themselves to help them explain that behaviour in a way more satisfying to them. The Newtonian physicist thinks of himself as discovering force and not as inventing it, but he is mistaken.

There is a good deal about the nature of scientific knowledge and scientific progress in the *Phenomenology*, especially in the earlier parts of it. I dare say that Hegel was in some respects in advance of his time, and in other respects superficial or even perverse. I deal with this part of his theory only cursorily, for it is not of special interest to the student of his social and political theory; and I deal with it at all only because it explains what Hegel means when he asserts that Spirit, active in a plurality of finite minds, constructs a coherent world and becomes self-conscious and rational in the process of doing so. It constructs the world without knowing *how* it has done so, or even *that* it has done so, and so treats the world as something independent of itself. But eventually, so Hegel tells us, it necessarily discovers that the world which it begins by taking as independent of itself is its own product. It recognizes that the world is rational (or intelligible) because it is the product of reason; it recognizes itself in the world (as Hegel puts it) and so is at home in the world and is satisfied.

2. The Need for Recognition

We have seen that, for Hegel, only a self-conscious being can have knowledge, properly so called, for knowledge has for its object, not sensations, but facts, and facts are referred to in judgements which involve the use of a variety of concepts forming a system of concepts or a language. Self-consciousness and consciousness of a coherent world go necessarily together. Yet the self is not most sharply present to itself in mere knowledge, in contemplation of a world. It is most sharply present to itself as a subject of conscious desire. It can have desires without knowing that it has them, just as it can have sensations without knowing that it has them. But it cannot know that it has desires and express this knowledge without using the word 'I'. Though it cannot have knowledge unless it is in fact self-conscious, it can express its knowledge (when that knowledge is not self-knowledge), without referring to itself, without being sharply present to itself, without using the word 'I'. It is above all as a conscious subject of desire that the self is intensely self-conscious.

Hegel does not, of course, think of the self as *first* becoming self-conscious as a subject of knowledge and then afterwards becoming more intensely self-conscious as a conscious subject of desire. Desire, as much as sensation, is prior to self-consciousness and knowledge; the lower animals have desires as well as sensations and yet are not self-conscious and do not have knowledge. The self that rises to self-consciousness and knowledge is essentially active, and it would not be active unless it had desires. As it strives, at first blindly, to satisfy its desires, it becomes gradually aware of its environment; it comes gradually to acquire knowledge and self-knowledge. Thus the self becomes conscious of itself as a subject of desire in the same process as it becomes a self-conscious subject of knowledge. Nevertheless, it is, thinks Hegel, as a conscious subject of desire that the self is most sharply present to itself, and from this circumstance he draws some important conclusions.

The self, as it comes to see itself as having an environment external to itself, distinguishes itself from more than merely natural objects; it also distinguishes itself from other selves. It becomes self-conscious in the process of learning to distinguish itself from an external world which contains both natural objects and other beings like itself.

It is the peculiarity of a self-conscious being that all its desires are not natural appetites; for it has, apart from such appetites, a desire to be *recognized* by other beings like itself. The lower animals are without this desire; they have no sense of their own dignity or worth. They have no need to assert themselves, no need for acceptance or recognition, because they have no self-consciousness. This desire for recognition Hegel calls *spiritual* because he thinks of it as a desire which goes along with self-consciousness, which he takes to be the essence of Spirit. It is the first among man's desires which is specifically human; it marks him off from the other animals.

At first, man wants to be recognized by others without according to them the recognition which he demands from them. He wants to be alone recognized. This necessarily brings him into conflict with other men, for they too make the same demand on him. It almost seems that we have here a Hegelian version of Hobbes' war of all against all. But there is a difference. The conflict arises, neither from competition to satisfy natural appetites nor from a desire for power as a means to their better satisfaction; it arises from a desire different in kind from the natural appetites and unconnected with them.

If all were equally resolute in demanding recognition from the others and in refusing it to them, the conflict would end with the death of all, or with the death of all but one; and that man would have failed of his purpose, for there would be no one left to recognize him. But not all men are equally resolute; they all risk death for the sake of recognition, an action possible only to self-conscious creatures. Some, however, are less steadfast than others, and from fear of death recognize the others without being recognized by them. Some become slaves and some masters.

Hegel speaks of this conflict both as if it were an effect of man's self-consciousness and a means to it, both as if men engage in the conflict because they are self-conscious and as if the conflict made them so. There is here an apparent contradiction, but it is apparent only. There are, for Hegel, as indeed there are in fact, different levels of self-consciousness. Or perhaps it would be better to say that the word *self-conscious* is used in different senses. As Hegel does not distinguish carefully between these senses, it is sometimes difficult to get his meaning; but in this case it is not too difficult. I take it that to demand recognition from others involves insisting on deference from them. It may involve more than this, but it involves at least this. It also involves, to use Kantian language, insisting on being treated by them as an end-in-oneself. To refuse recognition involves refusing deference; it also involves, in Kantian language, refusing to treat others as ends-in-themselves. No doubt, the man who demands recognition is not able to use Kantian language and perhaps has no words to express his desire. He may merely demand services from others, but if he does, he demands them, not because he needs them, but because he needs to be important to others and to show that he is so by imposing his will on them. He is then like a child who insists on being the centre of attention. If the child is asked whether it wants to be the centre of attention, it may not even understand the question; and yet that is what it wants. And it wants it because it is a self-conscious creature.

Man has a sense of his own dignity or worth; he has it even though he is not able to express it in words. But his sense of this dignity or worth is insecure unless he is recognized by others as being what he takes himself to be. His self-importance depends on his being important to others, or on his being treated by them as if he were important to them. He would not insist that his dignity be recognized unless he had some sense of it. Hegel speaks of men's need to 'bring their certainty of themselves, the certainty of being for themselves, to the level of objective truth', and to do this 'they must enter into this struggle'.[1] This, if we take it literally, means that man has a need to validate or verify his belief that he exists through conflict with other men. And this, certainly, is part of what Hegel means. But, presumably, he also means more than this. By the 'certainty of being for oneself' he cannot, I think, mean mere self-consciousness; he must mean by it what philosophers of the Kantian School are getting at when they speak of man's being an end for himself. He means what I have deliberately put in more familiar (but not therefore more precise) language by calling it man's sense of his own worth. A self-conscious being needs assurance both that it exists and that it has value, and it is through a conflict of wills with other self-conscious beings that it gains this assurance. This, I take it, is what Hegel means, because this is what makes the best sense of this part of his argument. For he says, in the sentence which follows the one from which I have just quoted, that 'it is solely by risking life that freedom is obtained; only thus is it tried and proved that the essential nature of self-consciousness is not bare existence.' As we shall see, man is free because he is, in a sense not yet explained but to be explained later, 'his own end'.

Hegel, for all his insistence that Spirit makes its own world, and makes itself in doing so, lays heavy stress on the distinction between the subjective and the objective, or, as we might put it, between the private and the public. We have seen that it is not each separate self that builds up its own private world; it is a community of selves that builds up a public world by using a common system of concepts, a common language. So, too, though it is supremely important to the individual self how he thinks and feels about himself, he cannot hold firmly to what he thinks and feels unless he is recognized by others as being what he appears to himself to be.

3. Master and Slave

With Hegel's doctrine of the master and the slave, we come to the part of his *Phenomenology* which is of peculiar interest to the social and political theorist; and that part is in fact the major part. My interpretation of it owes a great deal to Kojève's *Introduction à la Lecture de Hegel*; it also owes something, though less, to Jean Hyppolite's *Genèse et Structure de la Phénoménologie de l'Esprit de Hegel*. I have sometimes found Hyppolite's commentary more difficult to follow than the text it seeks to explain, though at other times I have found it illuminating.[2] My criticisms of the *Phenomenology* are mostly my own.

---

[1] *The Phenomenology of Mind*, p. 232.

[2] But, since my German is too poor to enable me to follow so difficult a text, I have relied mostly on Hyppolite's translation of the *Phenomenology*, which I prefer to the English translation by Baillie.

The slave, in working for the master, works on nature. He transforms it; or, to use Hegel's own expression, he *negates* it. In the process of transforming what he works on, he transforms himself. He is a worker, and therefore feels the need to make the most efficient use of his labour and his materials. As a worker, he gradually increases his understanding of nature and of himself; he acquires self-discipline. Though he has put himself in the power of his master, he inevitably, through his work, extends his own power. He gets power over nature and over himself. But the master does not acquire the same understanding of nature or the same power over it, nor does he learn discipline. He does not even get, from his recognition by the slave, the satisfaction that he seeks, because it is not the recognition of an inferior but of an equal which is truly satisfying. If I despise the man who recognizes my worth, his recognition of it does not give me the assurance which I seek.

The master is in an *impasse*. He cannot give to the slave the recognition which he has demanded and obtained from him. For he has subjugated the slave and is served by him. The slave is the living proof of his worth, of his superiority, and is therefore indispensable to him; and yet he cannot find the satisfaction he needs, the full assurance of his own dignity, in his recognition by the slave. Also, his condition, morally and intellectually, remains unchanged; he is the master of the slave. He is so from the moment that the slave recognizes him without insisting on being recognized in return, and his aim is merely to continue his mastery. He does not acquire knowledge and self-discipline in a struggle to master nature. He does not contrive and work to satisfy his appetites; he merely forces another man to work for him.

The slave is not in an *impasse*; he is transformed by his work and by what that work involves; his condition, morally and intellectually, changes as a result of what he does. He acquires knowledge, power over nature, and self-discipline. Only fear keeps him docile; if he can overcome this fear, he can cease to be a slave. He does not need his master as his master needs him. He will come eventually to demand for himself the recognition which he gives to the master. His servile condition, though it does not satisfy him, is not such as to prevent his doing anything to improve it. He is not both attached to his servility and dissatisfied with it as the master is to his mastery. When he comes, at last, to demand recognition for himself, he does not refuse it to others. The recognition of his demand does not involve putting others in a situation which cannot satisfy them and which they must in time strive to change. Therefore the future is with the slave. It is his destiny to create the community in which everyone accords recognition to everyone else, the community in which Spirit attains its end and achieves satisfaction.

This 'dialectic' of the master and the slave has been greatly admired.

It has much in common with the Marxian account of the class struggle. Of course, the essence of the domination of man by man is explained differently by Hegel. The life and death conflict for mere recognition, for the satisfaction of a spiritual need, would no doubt seem to Marx sheer fantasy. But the assertion that the future belongs to the oppressed is altogether in the spirit of Marxian philosophy, and so too are the reasons given for the assertion. The slave is a producer, and in the course of production acquires the qualities, intellectual and moral, the knowledge, the skill and the self-discipline, which he needs to enable him to put an end to his servile condition. The slave evolves while the master remains unchanged. It is the slave, not the master, who comes to understand the limitations of his condition, who decides to put an end to it, and who carries out his decision. The community where everyone recognizes everyone, the community of equals, is his creation. All this that Hegel says of the slave Marx says of the proletarian, though Hegel, as we shall see, has a very different conception of equality.[1]

4. Stoicism and Scepticism

The slave is dissatisfied with his servitude. For he, too, like his master, once strove for recognition, and abandoned his claim only from fear of death. But the desire for recognition does not disappear in the condition of slavery. It is a desire natural to every self-conscious creature, and the slave is such a creature. His work is educative; it forms his character. This education, though (as we have seen) it changes him, does not cause him to find satisfaction in his servitude; it does not weaken his desire for recognition. He comes eventually to differ from the master in being willing to recognize others; and this willingness proceeds from his seeing the justice of according to them what he seeks for himself, and not from fear.

Thus the self-conscious self is not satisfied either in servitude or in mastery. It is essentially free; it strives for independence, or (to use a Hegelian expression) it seeks assurance that it exists *for* itself. That the slave is dependent is obvious; and the master is dependent on the services of the slave and gets from him a recognition which does not satisfy.

It is at this point that there arises a form of self-consciousness, or (as I should prefer to say) an attitude of mind, of which Hegel says that it 'has been called Stoicism, in so far as it has appeared as a pheno-menon conscious of itself'[2] in human history. It is an attitude which

---

[1] Professor Berlin suggests that, in interpreting this part of the *Phenomenology*, I have read too much of Marx and of Kojève into Hegel. Certainly here, as in several other places, I owe much to Kojève.

[2] *Phenomenology*, Baillie's translation, p. 244.

he says is *negative* towards the relation of master and slave. As Hegel puts it, the master does not 'find his truth' through the slave, and the slave does not 'find his truth' in the will of the master. We can put this another way by saying that both master and slave have a conception of what man, as a self-conscious rational being, essentially is, a conception realized neither in mastery nor in servitude. Man is essentially free. I take this to mean that man, being self-conscious and rational, necessarily aspires to freedom, and is not satisfied until he gets it.

But the Stoic does not stop at the belief that man is essentially free in the sense that he necessarily aspires to freedom; he also believes that man, if he only but knew it, always is (or always can be) free, no matter what his social condition. Mereby by virtue of being self-conscious and rational, man is free, or can obtain freedom, whether he is master or slave.

This belief arises out of the master's and the slave's dissatisfaction with mastery and servitude. They are both dissatisfied, and yet they yearn for satisfaction and delude themselves into believing that they already have it, or that they can obtain it without ceasing to be master and slave. This belief involves a pretence, a withdrawal from the realities of life; it is a form of escapism. The Stoic conception of freedom Hegel calls 'abstract', whereas true freedom, he says, is concrete. We achieve freedom, not by withdrawing from life, but in life; not by affecting to despise the world but by getting satisfaction in it. The wisdom and the virtue of the Stoic soon wear thin; they do not stand the test of experience; they prove in the end to be wearisome.

Scepticism is a more extreme form of what is, at bottom, the same attitude of mind; it is even more sharply negative. The scepticism here in question is not, of course, the scepticism of the English empiricists. English empiricism is essentially a theory of knowledge. As we find it in Hume, it involves no rejection of the world, no withdrawal from life, no pretending that nothing really matters. The scepticism that Hegel has in mind is that of the Greeks, the kind which asserts that nothing is good or evil, that nothing is certain, and nothing worth striving for. It takes the world for mere show and illusion. It is a state of mind, an attitude to life, which, like Stoicism, is rooted in dissatisfaction; it is an even more extreme attempt to find freedom by rejecting the world. And, again like Stoicism, it does not satisfy. For the man who says that everything is illusion and that nothing matters must, in practice, behave as if it were not so. He says that life is worthless and meaningless. If he does not destroy himself (and he seldom does that), he must continue to live, which involves his acting as if life were not worthless and meaningless. He gives the lie to his creed merely by continuing to live, by having desires and seeking to satisfy them.

Though Hegel speaks of Stoicism as an attitude of mind common to master and slave, and of Scepticism as an extreme form of Stoicism, Kojève, in his book (which is much more a commentary on the *Phenomenology* than an account of Hegel's philosophy taken as a whole), treats them both as forms of servile consciousness. Kojève is apt to be too free in his interpretations. I feel a considerable sympathy with him. Hegel's philosophy is like a ploughed field water-logged, which it is safer and quicker to walk through on stilts, taking long strides, for fear of getting stuck in the mud. Or, to change the metaphor, it is more palatable taken in large doses than small. Hegel takes a large and free view of the facts, and the interpreter is tempted to do the same with Hegelian theory. Kojève seems at times to ignore the details of Hegel's argument or to adjust them to suit his own lucid and masterly, indeed masterful, interpretation of it.

According to Kojève, the master, though not fully satisfied, is free; or he is, at least, freer than the slave. There is, in his case, no disparity that he is aware of between what he aspires to be and what he is; he fought for recognition and has achieved it. The slave also fought for it, and did not achieve it. It is therefore the slave rather than the master who makes an ideal of liberty. But the slave cannot be free unless he fights and risks his life for freedom, and this he is not yet ready to do. The doctrine that man, being essentially free, possesses the dignity proper to his kind, no matter what his social condition, is the doctrine of the slave who aspires to freedom though he dare not yet fight for it. He persuades himself that he already has it; he retreats from the world into himself. But this attitude cannot satisfy; it comes to birth in order to justify not fighting for recognition, for freedom. It discourages action; it seeks refuge in speech and theorizing. But Spirit, to be satisfied, must find itself in this world; or, as we might put it, man achieves satisfaction, and freedom also, by creating a social world acceptable to himself, and not by seeking escape from it.

It was certainly Hegel's belief that all doctrines which preach withdrawal from the world or indifference to it are due to man's seeking to attain an ideal which is not yet clear to him and which he fails to attain. Man's progress is a search for freedom, but in the early stages of that search he does not know exactly what he wants. He gropes his way towards it, and comes to have a clearer idea of it as he comes closer to getting it. He does not fully understand what he aspires to until he has achieved it. In the course of his progress towards freedom, not finding what he seeks and having only a dim understanding of what it is, he is again and again afflicted by despair and by hope; he takes up attitudes of mind and produces doctrines which either keep alive his aspirations or reconcile him to his lot, or which do both the one and the other. Stoicism is an aspiration to freedom and also an attempt to reconcile man to his condition, which is not yet free; and so too is

Scepticism. Freedom, as imagined by the Stoic and Sceptic, is inadequate, and the reconciliation is illusory. Stoicism and Scepticism are both creeds of man who has not yet achieved freedom. To that extent Kojève is right in his interpretation of Hegel. But Hegel does not, I believe, think of them as creeds of the slave rather than the master. They are creeds of the unfree who are confusedly aware of their condition and wish to shut their eyes to it. The master is, in some ways, freer than the slave, but in other ways he is not; he too is dissatisfied and unfree, and needs to delude himself.

5. The Unhappy Consciousness

Stoicism and Scepticism are, as we have seen, creeds of unsatisfied man, of man not yet at home in the world. But there is a human condition more poignant even than the ones expressed by these creeds. Hegel calls it the *unhappy consciousness*. The Stoic and the Sceptic both delude themselves that they are free in this world. The Stoic believes that, provided he is rational and self-disciplined, provided he has learnt to rise above his social condition, he has achieved all that man can achieve. The Sceptic says that the world is meaningless and illusory and yet continues to live in it, behaving as if what he said were not true; but he is not aware of his inconsistency. Both the Stoic and the Sceptic imagine that they have come to terms with life; they do not admit that, in this world, they are unfree. But the unhappy consciousness does admit this; it recognizes that it is not free. It is consciously wretched in this world. Hegel also calls it the 'alienated soul', and speaks of it as being a stranger to itself. It is a stranger to itself, presumably, because it is the essence of Spirit to produce a world and to come eventually to recognize that world as its product. Consciousness and its object are, Hegel tells us, inseparable; consciousness by the use of concepts constructs out of its immediate content (the merely sensed) a coherent world. It is a rational consciousness only in so far as it does so. It reveals itself as reason in constructing a rational (that is to say, coherent or intelligible) world. If, then, it sees itself as a stranger in this world, which it does when it is an unhappy consciousness, it is estranged from that in which it is revealed as a rational consciousness; it is estranged from itself.

The self-estranged Spirit seeks the satisfaction which it cannot get in this world in another; it imagines an after-life. It projects itself into another, an imaginary world, in which are satisfied the aspirations which are not satisfied in this world. We have seen that man necessarily seeks recognition, that every self-conscious being needs to have its worth admitted by other such things. And so in the next world, the imaginary world, the worth of every man is recognized by God. Man asserts his sense of his own dignity, a sense which is frustrated in this world, by supposing himself infinitely precious to a Being infinitely greater than himself. In his image of another world he expresses both a deep sense of his own unworthiness and a sense of his worth. He feels unworthy because of his condition in this world, where he is diminished in his own eyes. But he does not therefore puff himself up into something much greater than he feels himself to be; he sees himself, rather, as the beloved of a Being infinitely more worthy than himself. This Being he conceives of as essentially like himself. Into his notion of God man puts his sense of what Spirit is. And we have seen that, for Hegel, Spirit (though in itself infinite) is revealed in and through finite minds. Therefore, in worshipping God man expresses his sense of the worth of the Spirit which is in him. This does not mean that man, without knowing it, worships himself. For man is finite, while Spirit is infinite. It means that man, without knowing it, worships what is revealed in creatures like himself and gives them their worth; he worships what still has to be fully revealed, what has not yet become fully actual.

The unhappy consciousness is clearly the Christian consciousness, though Hegel, in the *Phenomenology*, does not call it so. Christianity, for Hegel, is the religion of individualism; it is the religion which, above all others, asserts the intrinsic worth of the individual. In the Hegelian sense of recognition, the Christian recognizes everyone. The master demanded recognition from the slave and refused it to him, and became a master because he was given what he asked for; the slave began by behaving as the master did, and became a slave only because fear drove him to give what he was asked for without insisting on it in return; whereas the Christian voluntarily gives to all men what he asks for himself. But in Christianity the equal worth of all men is recognized only in another world. It is therefore recognized inadequately. To be recognized adequately, it must be recognized for everyone by everyone in this world, which is the real world.

The unhappy consciousness is a necessary phase in the evolution of Spirit. The self must be thrown back upon itself, it must feel isolated in its environment, detached from it and oppressed by it, if it is to become deeply self-conscious. An intense self-awareness, which necessarily takes the form of self-estrangement, must precede the full attainment of freedom. In order to be free, man must consciously 'find himself' in the world; his acceptance of it must not be merely habitual. He is not free unless his acceptance of it is rational; he is not free until he knows what it is to act conscientiously and finds it possible to do so in the world. What Hegel calls 'the moment of subjectivity' must be developed in him to the full; he must have an intense self-awareness. He must first feel himself to be a stranger in the world before he can become fully at home in it; he must have a profound sense of his own unworthiness before he can come fully to appreciate the dignity of man. The Christian alone with God is alone with what he obscurely feels to be the Spirit within him, though he does not yet know it for such. Intent on his relations with God, man is also intent upon himself, for he has no privacy from a God who reads his innermost thoughts. The Christian feels himself close to God and yet remote from Him, supremely important to God and yet liable to be rejected by Him. This ambivalent attitude to God expresses man's intense self-awareness and anxiety about himself, and his sense of his own worth and his unworthiness.

6. Spirit in Immediacy

The three attitudes of mind which we have considered – Stoicism, Scepticism, and the Unhappy Consciousness – are all symptoms of man's dissatisfaction with the world and with himself. If we look at history, we see that they all three come with the decay of the ancient city-state. Hegel, of course, using his abstract method, does not speak directly of the city-state or of its best-known example, the Greek *polis*. He speaks of Spirit existing ' in its immediacy'. But clearly he has in mind a community of the type of the *polis*, and I shall therefore refer to it, for convenience sake, by that name. In this type of community, the social order, or, as Hegel would put it, the ethical order or objective Spirit, is accepted by man, not critically, not after reflection, but as a matter of course. Morality is custom. There are two spheres of custom; there are the customs of the city and the customs of the family, or human and divine law. These two spheres are complementary, the customs of the city having their roots in the customs of the family. These two spheres may, to some extent or in some circumstances, clash, but men do not admit this or take it consciously into account.

The *polis* is a compact community; the citizens are the city. In the *polis* there is no contrasting the State with the individual, and no asserting of individual liberty against the State. In so far as the value of the individual is recognized, it is so within the family, in the honours paid to the dead. I do not quite follow Hegel's argument at this point, but he means, perhaps, that when we honour the dead we do not benefit either ourselves or them, and we need not express gratitude or love. Grief and gratitude and love we may or may not feel or express, and yet we bury the dead with ceremony, and thus bear witness to our sense of the dignity of man.

Hegel uses Greek tragedy to illustrate how the two spheres of custom, the two laws, human and divine, clash. Antigone defies Creon; divine law requires that she should bury her brother, though Creon has forbidden his burial. She is certain that she is right, just as Creon is certain that he is. There is no conflict, either within her mind or within his, between two laws, and no conflict between passion and duty. The conflict is between Antigone and Creon. Neither of them is faced with a moral problem, neither of them has to make a morally difficult choice. The situation is tragic because Antigone, by her narrowness, brings her fate upon herself. By the only law which she recognizes, she does no wrong. Neither she nor Creon acts conscientiously, as we today understand conscientious action; she does what family custom, or divine law, requires of her, and he acts by another law. Her fate is terrible and yet necessary; it serves to bring out the narrowness, the inadequacy, of the law which she accepts. Though Antigone sees herself as the victim of fate, and learns nothing, and is not shaken in her convictions, whoever contemplates her predicament and Creon's, whoever understands them both, has already passed beyond her and him. Sophocles may not see her predicament as we now see it, but he already sees it as Antigone could not see it. In looking at her predicament through the eyes of Sophocles, we can see how her morality differs from ours, and also how reflection on her fate prepares the way for our morality.

7. The Soulless Community

The compact community, where morality is custom and where there is no contrasting the individual with the State, the community in which Spirit is revealed 'in its immediacy' gives way to what Hegel calls *the soulless community*, where the free man (i.e. the man who is not a slave) ceases to be a citizen and becomes a subject. He is not reduced to servitude; his status is embodied in his personal rights, and above all in his rights of property. In this type of community, law becomes elaborate and precise, and there develops a science of jurisprudence. It matters greatly that personal rights should be carefully defined and adequately secured. But, politically, the free man is no longer a master; he takes no effective part in government, and has no share in a general will. He is a private person, who looks upon the State as set in authority over him, necessary to his well-being but out of the reach of his influence. He is neither citizen nor slave; he is something between the two. He even ceases to fight for the State, which is defended by mercenaries. The example of the soulless community which Hegel has in mind is clearly the Roman Empire, for he speaks of it as dominated by a 'master of the world'.

The private person, the possessor of personal rights, is not, in the same sense as the slave, a worker. He is personally free and therefore does not work for a master. Nor does he work for the community. His work is not service; he exerts himself for himself and his family, and his business is above all to maintain and to enlarge his property. It is in the 'soulless community' that Stoicism and Scepticism flourish.

8. The World of Culture

The soulless community, the world of universal monarchy, of elaborate private rights, of Stoicism and Scepticism, is succeeded by what Hegel calls the *world of culture*. It is the world of *Spirit in self-estrangement*; or, in other words, though Hegel avoids referring to actual societies and events, it is the Christian world or Western Europe from the establishment of Christianity and the fall of the Roman Empire until the French Revolution. Together, the 'soulless community' and 'the world of culture' cover all the phases in the evolution of Spirit from the phase in which it exists in immediacy to the phases in which it finds itself *in* the world and attains self-knowledge and satisfaction. In the world of Spirit in its immediacy, Spirit is not yet self-estranged; it is not, of course, fully satisfied, for that it can be only when it has attained a self-knowledge which is still far off. But it is not consciously dissatisfied, and has no need to seek to reconcile itself to its lot in such attitudes and beliefs as Stoicism, Scepticism and Christianity. In the compact community of citizens, the ethos of the master predominates, and yet the worth of the individual, merely in virtue of his humanity, is not recognized. It is not recognized, not only because there are slaves as well as masters, but also because the masters are concerned with status and privilege and with the affairs of the community, and have no conception of freedom of conscience. The Greek idea of freedom is, in Hegel's opinion, inferior to the idea that gradually emerges in the world of culture and is eventually realized in the community where everyone is recognized by everyone.

9. Forms of Individualism

Spirit, estranged from the world and from itself, does not merely seek the satisfaction denied to it in this world by imagining another; it also seeks satisfaction in this world. Hegel describes how it does so, and also how, in the process, it comes gradually nearer to what it seeks and at last finds. It does not find it merely by chance; it does not make one unsuccessful attempt after another until at last it succeeds. It is transformed and educated by its efforts; it seeks satisfaction and does not find it, and reflects on its experience, and grows wiser. In *In Memoriam* Tennyson speaks of our 'rising on stepping stones of our dead selves to higher things', and this comes close to how Hegel conceives of the progress of Spirit. Not that he thinks of man as being always, in each later phase, better than in the phase before it; he thinks of him, rather, as gaining in depth and understanding, so that, though he may sometimes be more wretched and evil, he is always more mature and more completely a man. To illustrate my point from drama, as Hegel loved to do, Hamlet is not a better man than the Oedipus of Sophocles, but he is a moral agent in a deeper sense.

Hegel discusses three attempts of Spirit to find satisfaction in the world, and explains why each of them fails of its object. They might be called three types of individualism.

The first is the pursuit of pleasure. The individual seeks pleasure and judges the community and its laws as they help or impede the pursuit of pleasure. But the pursuit of one pleasure after another cannot satisfy him, because each separate pleasure is momentary and a self-conscious being can find satisfaction only in what is enduring. I am not sure that I have taken the point of Hegel's argument, and so I shall not go into the details of it. Part of his meaning, perhaps, is this: a self-conscious and rational being can be satisfied only by a way or pattern of life which seems to it worth while. It needs, if it is to get happiness, not repeated success in achieving one disconnected end after another, but the sense of a life well lived or the feeling that it is making progress towards some goal which it makes persistent and rational efforts to attain. This is a common criticism of the pursuit of pleasure, and though Hegel uses uncommon language, he does not, any more than Burke did, avoid or despise common or received opinions. They often contain, he thinks, much wisdom. So I continue to hope that this criticism, which I find intelligible, is, if not the whole, then a part, of what Hegel means. He says that the pursuit of pleasure involves contradiction, meaning thereby, no doubt, that the man who makes pleasure his end in life seeks satisfaction where it is not to be had. He means perhaps more than this, but at least this also.

The second form of individualism might be called romantic; Hegel calls it *the law of the heart*. It is the doctrine that man is naturally good. Let him follow the dictates of his heart, and all will be well with him. Man is natural and society is artificial. This second form is also self-contradictory, though it is so (as Hegel does not trouble to notice) in a different and more literal sense than the first. The man who takes up this doctrine is presumably not speaking only about himself. If his heart-felt sentiments are right, so presumably are other people's. But the sentiments of one man are not always shared by other men. So each man condemns the sentiments of other men when they conflict with his own, irrationally refusing to their sentiments the validity he claims for his own. The believer in this doctrine is inevitably driven to self-contradiction or absurdity; he begins by saying, 'Let every man act upon his heartfelt sentiments, for they are good', and he ends either by denying that the heart-felt sentiments of others which do not square with his own are good, or by insisting that they are not really what those who express them say they are – that they do not really come from the heart.

The third form of individualism Hegel calls *the virtuous conscious-*

ness. It condemns conventional standards. The virtuous man claims knowledge of a moral truth superior to 'the way of the world'. But this truth is an abstract ideal; it is expressed in the form of general principles whose practical implications are not yet known by the persons who assert the principles. The ideal they cherish may be impossible; it can be tested only when people try to live up to it. Or it may be that the ideal is already to a great extent realized, though the persons who uphold it, owing to their ignorance of what is involved in the practical application of it, do not see that it is. Hegel's point, if I have understood it, might be put briefly in this way: an ideal which is used to condemn current practice is necessarily understood very imperfectly by those who proclaim it. It purports to put forward rules of conduct which differ greatly from accepted rules. But to understand rules of conduct we must know how they apply to concrete situations. If, for example, we proclaim the equality of all men, how is our proclamation to be understood? Presumably we are not saying that no man must have any right which every other man does not also have, for in every society there is a wide diversity of functions, and men doing different work must have different rights. Our proclamation acquires a precise content only when the attempt is made to put it into practice. We see then what it amounts to. We elaborate and qualify it in ways we could not foresee when first we made it. While we use it merely to condemn established ways, having only the vaguest notions of what it involves in practice, our condemnation is blind; we use a criterion which we scarcely understand. Here, too, as Hegel sees it, we are involved in contradiction. We put forward an ideal for all men to live up to, but we do know how far or in what way it can be realized, nor even to what extent it is realized. When we come to understand it more fully, we are apt to find either that it is unrealizable or that it is much nearer being realized than we thought.

10. The Base and the Noble Consciousness

In the world of Spirit self-estranged, in the world of culture, as in the soulless community, man looks upon the State as alien to himself. He is expected to obey the State, but as a mere subject and not a citizen. He does not take thought for the State, he merely takes into account what the State requires of him when he takes thought for himself. He is, as a member of the State, passive; he is active in his private life. In this type of community the pursuit of wealth is important.

There are some who willingly acknowledge the State power and seek satisfaction by accumulating wealth, while others are suspicious of the State and indifferent to riches, and are even inwardly in revolt against them. In these last is manifest what Hegel calls the *base consciousness* in contrast with the *noble consciousness* of those who accept the State and who seek and respect wealth. Noble and base do not, in this connexion, express approval or disapproval; when Hegel uses them he has in mind what he takes to be the typical attitudes of the privileged and the unprivileged orders in the West before the French Revolution.

In the world of culture the State emerges and gathers strength as the nobles gradually abandon some of their rights. Presumably the rights here in question are rights of private jurisdiction and private war. Hegel calls them the 'natural being' of 'the noble consciousness', which suggests that it was by virtue of them that the nobles were noble before they began to decline from their nobility. But their nobility is a social status, it consists of their rights; and the rights they must surrender before there can be an effective State power are rights of private jurisdiction and war. Eventually the nobles abandon more than these rights to the bearer of the State power, the monarch; they do more even than avow themselves ready to die for him. They become courtiers, and by their flattery raise the monarch high above themselves. They behave outwardly as if the great purpose of their lives were to serve and honour him. But this surrender of themselves to the monarch is more apparent than real. The class who flatter and serve the monarch, who abase themselves before him as the embodiment of the State, really own the State; the public service is their property; the State is a form of their wealth.

Here, too, the keen eye of Hegel discerns a contradiction. The established social order rests on the distinction between the noble and the base. But when the nobles give up honour for riches, and the service of the State becomes for them principally a means to wealth, this distinction loses its point. Those whose position allows them to do so pursue wealth and power, but get no real satisfaction from doing so. They become arrogant and superficial, while the unprivileged or the base grow angry and cynical.

It is not the noble and the wealthy who see the situation for what it is: it is rather those among the base who stand closest to them, who are on the periphery of their closed circle, the poor clients and the hangers-on. Hegel finds in Diderot's *Le Neveu de Rameau* the model of the cynical rogue who has taken the full measure of the world and of himself, and who yet, in a sense, rises above the corruption in which he is involved because he understands it and is frank about it. Jean Hyppolite, in his commentary on the *Phenomenology*, sees in Hegel's interpretation of Rameau's nephew an account of what is perhaps 'a pre-revolutionary state of the soul'.[1] The social and psychological condition of man which is treated cynically by Rameau's nephew is the source of anguish in Rousseau and of indignation in Robespierre.

[1] Jean Hyppolite, *Genèse et Structure de la Phénoménologie de l'Esprit de Hegel*, p. 401.

Some take refuge from this condition in faith; but others seek to find a remedy for man in this world. Man's condition, they say, is due to his failure to see himself and the world as they really are. Man must be delivered from the irrational; he must learn that there is nothing mysterious, nothing miraculous, nothing unintelligible. He is a rational being, and everything is in principle capable of being rationally explained.

11. Rationalist Philosophy

There is therefore necessarily a conflict between those who put their trust in faith and those who put it in the intellect; between those who accept a revealed truth and rationalist philosophers. Hegel approves of rationalist philosophy for insisting that everything is intelligible, that the world is coherent and unmysterious, and that man can find complete satisfaction in it. The philosophers reduce God to a mere first cause, so that the conception of the divine no longer contains man's obscure sense of the Spirit in himself, of what he is capable of, of what must eventually be manifest in him. Perhaps without knowing it, they make God irrelevant to man; they deprive Him of humanity, making Him indifferent to man and man indifferent to Him.

Yet their contempt for revealed religion is rooted in ignorance. They do not understand its significance for man; they dismiss it as superstitious nonsense because they take it literally. They do not know that religion (and especially Christianity, which Hegel takes to be the highest form of religion) expresses, though not explicitly but in *Vorstellung*, man's sense of what Spirit essentially is. *Vorstellung*, in this context, is usually translated *representation*; so that Hegel presumably means that religious doctrines stand for truths which they do not express literally. If we are to make explicit the truths they stand for, we must take them metaphorically, we must translate them. The faithful, of course, do not take them metaphorically; they take them for literally true. And yet, since they do not (as the philosophers do) reject them as absurd, they must in some sense apprehend the truths contained in them. They must understand more than they are capable of putting literally. Both the faithful and the philosophers say that they take religious doctrines literally, the first to accept them and the second to reject them. But the faithful, since they do not reject them, since they find them significant, must read more into them than they literally say, and yet this more is more than they are capable of explaining. Therefore, those who have faith know, in a sense, more than they are aware of knowing, and the philosophers, in rejecting the dogmas which they accept, miss this knowledge.

The world of culture is the world of Spirit 'in self-estrangement'. But with rationalist philosophy, we are on the threshold of the world in which Spirit finds itself, in which self-estrangement ends. Rationalist philosophy, the philosophy of the Enlightenment, is utilitarian; it asserts that the world must be adapted to man's needs. In itself it is no more than a theory, but it is a theory which encourages action. It stimulates man's first deliberate and comprehensive effort to refashion society to suit himself.

12. Revolution

We are now at the phase in the evolution of Spirit which Hegel calls *absolute freedom and terror.* For Spirit, in the form of absolute freedom, 'the world is. . . absolutely its own will, and this will is universal will'; it is 'concretely embodied universal will, the will of all individuals as such', so that 'what appears as done by the whole is at once and consciously the deed of every single individual'.[1] Hegel describes this phase, as he does every other, in the most abstract terms, but clearly his description is inspired by the French Revolution. Therefore I shall speak of this phase, as I have done of several of the others, more concretely than Hegel does, but without, I hope, being false to his meaning. I shall call it the revolutionary phase.

In this phase of his development man, as never before, claims that the world shall be as he wants it; he puts himself forward as the maker or re-maker of society. As Jean Hyppolite puts it, 'Man is thus like a God and creator who finds himself entire in the work of his hands, and that work is the terrestrial city.'[2] The revolutionary possesses adequately the notion of freedom. Freedom is not, for him, mere absence of constraint; it must be realized in a community which gives effect to a universal will. This will is not what *I* want for myself or what *you* want for yourself or what *he* wants for himself; it is what *we* want for ourselves. It is not merely what is common to our wills; for even if we were entirely self-regarding creatures, we should have some ends in common, because our interests would still sometimes coincide. It is what each of us consciously wills because we have a sense of belonging to a community which is precious to us as being the context which gives meaning and purpose to our lives. It is Rousseau's general will, which is not a harmony of selfish wills nor yet a will in which the individual sacrifices his interests to the public good.

But Spirit, in the form of absolute freedom, is still not the realization of freedom. Hegel speaks of the 'undivided substance of freedom' putting itself 'on the throne of the world, without any power being able to offer effectual resistance'; and he says that 'in this absolute freedom all social ranks or classes, which are the component spiritual

---

[1] *The Phenomenology of Mind,* Baillie's translation, pp. 600 and 601.
[2] J. Hyppolite, *Genèse et Structure,* p. 440.

factors into which the whole is differentiated, are effaced and an-
nulled'.[1] Translating Hegel's argument into more concrete terms, we
might say that the revolutionary, the man who insists that the social
order shall give effect to the universal will, though he has an adequate
conception of freedom, fails to realize it because he seeks to do so by
abolishing all hierarchy. Freedom is in fact realized in an elaborate
social structure which allows of a great diversity of functions; but the
revolutionary, though he rightly believes that freedom consists in the
realization of a universal will, does not see that it cannot be realized
except in a society whose structure necessarily involves hierarchy. Jean
Hyppolite, commenting on Hegel's argument, says that, for Hegel,
'the French Revolution failed . . . not because its principle was false,
but because it sought to realize it *immediately*. . . . It is this immediacy which is here . . . an error.'[2] Now, the immediate, in the
sense in which Hegel uses the term, is the simple and undifferentiated,
or what appears to be so to the unphilosophical mind.

Hegel's highly abstract argument suggests that the revolutionary
sees in a stable, hierarchical social structure an obstacle to the universal
will. He speaks as if the revolutionary believed that there is no freedom except where men can do, at any time, what they please with
that structure, or even as if he believed that freedom were incompatible
with any such structure. The claim that the universal will may do
what it pleases with the social order is destructive of that order, and
yet the universal will is made effective, and liberty achieved, only
within a stable order. There is here, according to Hegel, a contradiction.
He sees in the Terror an effort of the universal will to destroy all
obstacles in its way. The nation, as the embodiment of the universal
will, claims to suppress every particular will opposed to it. Thus it is
that the assertion of absolute liberty leads to death.

We must remember that Hegel, in this part of the *Phenomenology*,
does not refer by name to the French Revolution, though he very
clearly has it in mind. He discusses what he takes to be a necessary
stage in the evolution of Spirit. He does not say that, when certain
things happen, they spring from such and such causes; he says that
they must happen. Spirit cannot attain its end, mankind cannot
achieve freedom, except by this process, whose every phase is implied
by all the others.

13. *The Moral Will*

The contradiction involved in Spirit in the form of absolute freedom seeking immediate realization (or, as we might put it, in the

[1] *Phenomenology*, p. 601.
[2] J. Hyppolite, op. cit. pp. 440-1.

revolutionary spirit) is that the universal will negates particular wills although it is itself manifest only in particular wills. There cannot be freedom except where there is harmony between the universal will and the particular wills required to conform to it. Spirit, reflecting on its experience in the revolutionary phase, rises to a higher level where the negation of the particular by the universal will is no longer a process whereby some people, in the name of the universal will, coerce and even destroy others. At this level the universal will is *internalized* as a moral will. The claim that the universal will shall govern the particular wills of individuals becomes the claim that, inside the individual, the moral will shall govern particular inclinations. The claim of the individual to take part in realizing the universal will of his community gives way to the claim of the individual to live according to moral standards which he freely accepts. This is the passage from the revolutionary ethic to morality as men like Kant conceived of it.

This morality is far indeed from the morality of Antigone. Antigone had no moral will, as Kant understood it; she had no conception of duties incumbent on her as a rational being. She felt no need to justify, either to others or to herself, the principles of her conduct. She was merely *fated* to do her duty; she did what she had to do, what she was impelled to do by a force which seemed to her external to herself; she did what the gods required of her. In Kant's moral theory (and we are here concerned with an attitude which Kant elaborated and made explicit rather than with opinions peculiar to him), the moral will, the will to do one's duty, is contrasted with the natural impulses, which have to be surmounted for duty's sake. Freedom and nature are opposed, and man achieves freedom by mastering his nature.

This attitude of mind, which Kant elaborated into a systematic philosophy, Hegel finds self-contradictory and sterile. It is, he admits, necessarily involved in the progress of Spirit, and it emerges at a late (and therefore high) stage of that progress. But though Hegel claims to do full justice to it, he is also strongly critical of it. His debt to Kant is great, and yet clearly he thinks that he has gone beyond Kant. Hegel stands to Kant rather as Aristotle does to Plato; he does not deny his greatness, but is perhaps less fully aware of what he owes to him than where he differs from him. He puts him in a high place, but puts him there severely.[1]

Hegel's criticism of this attitude of mind can be put briefly thus: If morality consists in our doing our duty in spite of our inclinations,

---

[1] Though Hegel, in this part of the *Phenomenology*, is not concerned with Kant but with an attitude of mind which others have shared with Kant, he gives the impression that he is arguing against Kant without mentioning him by name.

if it is a struggle against our nature, then, if the struggle were successful, nature would be suppressed in us, and we should cease to be
moral; and yet the object of the struggle is this suppression. I mention this argument because both Hegel and his commentators seem to
think it important. But, having mentioned it, I hasten to add that I do
not see the force of it. If we could suppress nature in us, we should
have what Kant calls a holy will to distinguish it from a moral will. We
should no longer have inclinations standing in the way of our doing
our duty, and we should therefore cease to be moral. But Kant, as far
as I know, does not think this outcome undesirable; he merely thinks
it impossible. To say, as he does, that we must do our duty for duty's
sake is not to say that we should struggle against our inclinations
merely for the sake of struggling against them.

Hegel puts forward another and a better argument against the
the Kantian type of ethic. Duty for duty's sake is, he says, an empty
notion. We cannot deduce from the notion of duty what we ought to
do; nor can we consult our inclinations to discover our duties, for our
duty is to resist them. If we ought to obey rules for their own sake, then
it does not matter what the rules are, provided they are compatible with
one another, provided they form a coherent system. But if that is so,
then any set of mutually compatible rules is as good as any other. We
have no criterion for choosing one set rather than another, unless we
depart from our principle that we must do our duty for duty's sake.
To avoid this absurdity, those who adhere to this principle are driven
to postulate an external legislator, a God who lays duties upon mankind. Though they say that the moral law is rational, their criterion
for deciding what that law commands is purely formal, so that any
set of mutually consistent principles would conform to it. To give
content to the law they must either tacitly abandon their criterion or
must appeal to the will of God. But the appeal to God contradicts the
very notion of the moral will, because the essence of that will is that
it is free. According to this notion, in doing our duty we conform to
principles which we accept because we are convinced that they are
rational; we do not bow to a will external to our own.

Hegel would agree with Hume that before an action can become a
duty there must be a reason for doing it other than a sense of its being
a duty. This, I take it, does not mean that a man can never do a duty
for duty's sake; it means only that there must be something about the
type of action which he does for duty's sake which explains how it
came to be considered a duty; something about it other than the sense
that it is a duty.

14. Spirit Satisfied

It is not in the ideal of duty for duty's sake that man finds satisfaction.

G

He finds it only where the principles which he is convinced are right are recognized to be so by others.

A man who acts conscientiously expects that the principle of his action will be recognized by others. But he may find that it is not. He cannot insist on this recognition, and yet he feels that his convictions must, in the last resort, guide his own actions. He cannot hang back from action waiting for other people to agree with him. He must act, and it is in the light of experience that his conviction is tested. A morality which is both generally recognized and conscientiously accepted emerges as a result of action. We test our moral convictions not so much by discussing them as by acting upon them; in no other way can we bring our convictions into harmony with one another and with the convictions of others. Hegel condemns what he calls *the beautiful soul* so anxious that its actions shall be from the highest motives that it dare not act.

As moral beings we are both active and self-critical, and we cannot be fully moral unless we are both. When we act, our action often falls short of our profession; we are mistaken about the motives of our action, which are not what we make them out to be. We discover our mistake by seeing how our action appears to others, and also to ourselves when we look back upon it.

There must be both action and judgement. The man who is merely judicial is apt to be hard-hearted. The mere judge cuts himself off from his fellows; he claims to express the shared values which hold men together, and yet, by his purely condemnatory attitude to wrongdoers, he makes outcasts of them and weakens the bonds of society. We must have judgement between men but also forgiveness. The judge who forgives identifies himself with the wrong-doer, just as the wrong-doer who accepts punishment as his due identifies himself with the judge.

Man is free when he is at home in the world, when what society requires of him is what he conscientiously wants to do. It is by action and by reflecting on his actions that man learns to adjust his convictions to his situation in the world, and so to be at home in the world. He cannot learn except by being active. By his strivings man creates a social order, and in the process transforms himself. Striving consciously for a variety of ends which differ at different stages of his spiritual and social evolution, he is involved in a necessary process which he comes to understand only when he has reached the end of it, although it has consisted, all along, of his own activities. When he comes to understand this process, he sees that the social order and the attitudes of mind making for freedom are products of his own activity; he sees this and is satisfied.

Or, in the Hegelian idiom, Spirit is satisfied when it is manifest in a community of selves who conscientiously desire what the community requires of them, which they can come to do only after the process of social, moral and intellectual evolution described in the *Pheno-menology*. Spirit is satisfied when it knows the process which it is, which it can do only in the knowledge of finite minds.

At this point of Hegel's explanation, we are impelled to put several questions. Is it enough, if Spirit is to have complete self-knowledge, that that knowledge should be revealed in only a few, or even in only one, finite mind? Is it enough, if Spirit is to be satisfied, to the extent that its satisfaction depends on self-knowledge, that Hegel should have written the *Phenomenology*? Or must all finite minds know what Hegel knows? Hegel gives no clue to the answer to this question. Kojève speaks as if it followed from Hegel's philosophy that Spirit must have the knowledge contained in that philosophy in order to have self-knowledge. But even if we grant this conclusion, as I think we must, my questions are still unanswered. Though we grant that the know-ledge, in all essentials, is contained in Hegel's philosophy, we can still pertinently ask: Must all finite minds understand and accept this philosophy, if Spirit is to have complete self-knowledge? Kojève takes it for granted that, in Hegel's opinion, Spirit attained complete self-knowledge as soon as he had produced his *Phenomenology*. I am in-clined to agree with Kojève, though less because the conclusion seems to follow from the general argument of that book than because of the impression of Hegel produced by a study of his philosophy.

We may also ask: Can Spirit attain self-knowledge, even though only in one finite mind, before it is manifest in a community of selves who conscientiously desire what the community requires of them? Kojève takes it for granted that it cannot; and it seems to me, this time, that his conclusion does follow from Hegel's philosophy. For how can Spirit attain self-knowledge before the completion of the process which Spirit is? And, clearly, the process is not complete until Spirit is manifest in such a community. Must we then conclude that the Europe dominated by Napoleon was such a community? For it was in that Europe that Hegel wrote the *Phenomenology*. According to Ko-jève the highest manifestation of Spirit is Napoleon-revealed-by-Hegel. Perhaps it would be better to say, it is the community dominated by Napoleon and explained by Hegel. Kojève puts and answers questions that Hegel failed to put. Indeed, writing the *Phenomenology* in such abstract terms, he did not need to put them. I shall return to them again later.

THE PROCESS OF SPIRIT AS REVEALED IN RELIGION

1. Hegel's Idea of Religion

So far we have been considering Spirit as it is revealed in the attitudes of mind and activities of individuals. For example, we have not considered Christianity as a body of doctrines and practices; we have considered only the predicament of the typical Christian, his needs, anxieties, and aspirations. So, too, we have not considered the institutions of the community in which the noble and the base consciousness flourish but only the ambitions and the moods which constitute those attitudes.

But Hegel also has a theory about religions, as bodies of doctrine, apart from the moods and aspirations of their adherents. Religion is, he thinks, a way in which Spirit expresses its awareness of what it essentially is. Spirit is revealed in communities of finite selves, and the religion of a community expresses its sense of what it is in itself, as a manifestation of Spirit. The doctrines which make up the religion are, of course, lodged in finite minds, but they form, none the less, a system of beliefs which may not be present, entire, in any one finite mind. The system can be considered apart from the needs and hopes of the faithful. Just as a symphony played by an orchestra, though it exists as music only when it is played, has a significance apart from the feelings about it of the members of the orchestra, so a body of doctrine, though it is nothing apart from the finite minds in which it is lodged, has a significance beyond what they feel about it.

Religion, as a system of beliefs, is a manifestation of Spirit to itself which anticipates the full self-knowledge it achieves in the Hegelian philosophy. Religious doctrines do not describe Spirit literally as it is; they describe it in *Vorstellung*. In other words, what they describe is Spirit as it appears to those who have not yet found words adequate to what they have in mind. Hegel distinguishes three main types of religion, natural, aesthetic and revealed, and discusses the sorts of community in which they flourish.

2. *Natural Religion*

Natural religion flourishes where men have not yet acquired a sense of belonging to a rationally organized community, where they are creatures of custom and have no conception of an ethical order or body of rules and practices which form a more or less coherent system. They are not citizens, nor have they attained the 'subjectivity', the heightened self-consciousness, of men in the world of culture and self-estrangement. They are not political, as the Greeks were, nor do they reject the world in the manner of the Christians. They have, indeed, no conscious attitude to the social order, they merely have attitudes which make them part of that order. They have gone almost no way towards producing a science of nature. Yet they are not beasts but men; they are rational beings capable of systematic speech and are therefore aware of themselves as living in a world. Being rational they are not altogether uncritical; but they are not consciously critical. They are not investigators and have no standards of criticism. Hegel speaks of them as lacking self-confidence. He does not mean that they are diffident in their dealings with one another; he means only that they have not yet acquired a strong faith in man's capacity to understand the natural world and to use it for his own purposes. He speaks of them as partly ' submerged' in nature. That is why their religion is pantheistic; they deify nature or those aspects of it which most impress them. They make gods of plants or animals, of the sun and the stars, and even of light. Their religion is not to be confused with fetishism or magic. Men who practise magic merely guard themselves against, or else try to use, powers, noxious or salutary, attributed to natural objects, whereas men who have natural religion express, in their attitude to nature or to certain aspects of it, their sense of what Spirit essentially is. They express their sense that Spirit is what gives life or meaning to all things, or what governs all things. They attribute to what they worship in nature qualities which, though they may not know it (not yet having learned to distinguish Spirit from nature), are spiritual.

3. Aesthetic Religion

Aesthetic religion is the religion of peoples who are political and not yet estranged from the world. They have confidence in man's capacity to understand and dominate his natural environment; they are not half ' submerged' in nature. They therefore deify man. Their gods are men rather more than life-size; they are immortal heroes just as their heroes are mortal gods. They are on familiar terms with their gods; they respect but do not stand in awe of them.

Later, in the *Encyclopaedia*, Hegel distinguished between art and religion as ways in which Spirit is aware of itself, or, as he put it, ' is reflected into itself'. Art, according to this later view, is intuitive, and expresses what it intuits in the form of symbols. The artist sees in some aspect of nature or man the Spirit manifest in it, and he puts what he sees into his work. He thinks in symbols, which he need not be able to interpret. If it should happen that an artist can explain his work, it is not as an artist that he does it, but as a critic or philosopher. The artist can give his message, and the spectator or auditor can take it in, without either of them being able to put it into words. The art of an age or people expresses in symbols how Spirit appears to that age or people. Art, Hegel tells us, is Spirit revealed in immediacy; that is to say, it is understood, at that level of understanding which is artistic appreciation, without needing to be explained. This does not mean, of course, that appreciation cannot be cultivated, that there is no such thing as an educated taste, nor yet that appreciation is instantaneous and does not grow with time; it means only that a work of art can be fully appreciated without being explained.

How then does religion, as a form in which Spirit is aware of itself, differ from art? In art Spirit is revealed sensuously and symbolically, whereas in religion it is manifest in the form of doctrines and myths. But art can be verbal and narrative as well as plastic and musical; it can also make statements. How then does art, when it is verbal and narrative, differ, as a way in which Spirit is manifest, from religion? For Hegel has told us that religion, like art, does not reveal Spirit literally as it is.

Religion differs from narrative art in making assertions which purport to be true and of the utmost importance. Religion is authoritative and didactic as art is not. Though, as Hegel tells us, religion reveals the essence of reality only in *Vorstellung*, only figuratively, its priests, the guardians of its doctrines and myths, believe that what they teach is literally true, and that it is a truth necessary to men. Without it men cannot 'fulfil their destiny', or cannot live as men should live. Religion purports to reveal the 'meaning of life'; it purports to teach men why they are in the world. The teachers of religion aim deliberately at deepening our understanding of the world and at improving the quality of our lives. They are apt to speak of men who reject the truth they offer as 'lost' or 'spiritually dead'. But art, though it is in fact a manifestation of Spirit, has no such conscious aim; even when it is verbal, it is not primarily didactic. If it deepens our understanding of the world, it does so unconsciously. Art is a form of self-expression, and Spirit is manifest in it because it is manifest in the finite selves who, through their art, express themselves. Religion, as distinct from faith; religion as a body of doctrines and myths, authoritative and didactic, is not a form of self-expression.

In the *Phenomenology* Hegel is much less concerned to distinguish religion and art, as manifestations of Spirit, than he was to be later; yet the distinction is there already, implicitly. Why, then, does he call one of his three types of religion *aesthetic*? Presumably not because, where religion is natural or revealed, there is no religious art. When he calls a religion *aesthetic*, he is, I suppose, contrasting it with revealed and not with natural religion. Revealed religion is much more doctrinal than aesthetic religion, which puts what it teaches more in the form of myths than of doctrines. And myth is much closer to art than is doctrine.

Where there is a revealed religion, myth expresses nothing essential about Spirit which is not also expressed doctrinally; whereas, where religion is aesthetic, this does not hold. When he spoke of aesthetic religion, Hegel had in mind mostly the religion of the Greeks, which was less doctrinal than mythological. Where religion is 'aesthetic', there is little systematic theology, and the community's conception of Spirit is revealed in myths about the gods rather than in the form of doctrine. Though the beliefs embodied in these myths make up a more or less coherent system, they are not abstracted from the myths and put forward as doctrines. Or, if some of them are, others are not, so that there is more in the myths than in the doctrines; and piety consists more in accepting the myths than in adhering to the doctrines. No doubt, where there is revealed religion, there are myths also, but there are no essential truths contained in the myths which are not contained in the doctrines.

If this is what makes religion aesthetic, then what Hegel calls natural religion is no less aesthetic than the religion of the Greeks. If Hegel had been as much concerned to make a sharp distinction between Greek and Oriental as he was to make one between Greek and revealed religion, he might have called religions of the Greek type anthropomorphic rather than aesthetic. The term *aesthetic*, used in this connection, does not, I think, point to the distinction that really matters. Hegel would have done better to call his three types of religion natural, anthropomorphic, and dogmatic rather than natural, aesthetic, and revealed.

4. Revealed Religion

Revealed or dogmatic religion is the religion of communities where Spirit is self-estranged. Judaism and Christianity are examples of this type of religion. The Jews imagined a God from whom man is almost entirely separate, a God who is a master rather than a father, an angry and exacting God rather than a God of love. Since man's conception of God is his conception of what Spirit essentially is, and since Spirit exists in finite selves, men, when they magine a masterful and angry God, express their sense of not being what they aspire to be, or (to speak metaphorically) of not being themselves. In Christianity, too, man imagines himself separate from God, from the Spirit which is in him; but he also imagines himself reconciled with God. God the Father represents the Spirit which is in man, though man does not know it, the Spirit to which man aspires and which he feels is out of reach; God the Son represents man's sense that what he aspires to is nevertheless within his reach and must be realized in him; God the Holy Ghost represents man's sense that Spirit is revealed in a plurality of finite selves. In the doctrine that the Holy Ghost is present in the community of the faithful is implicit the truth that the Spirit which is the essence of man is fully realized in a community whose members are perfectly at home inside it and are satisfied. In Hegel's opinion, the Christian conception of the Holy Ghost and of the Church are theological versions of the Hegelian concept of the concrete universal; they contain implicitly a truth which the Hegelian philosophy makes explicit. Though the coming of Christ, which is the reconciliation of man with God, represents the sense of the finite self that it is united

with the Spirit, Christ must die in the flesh, if men are to see this
truth more clearly; if they are to move from the less adequate idea
that God has taken human form to the more adequate idea that God
is present in a community of finite selves who attain what they aspire
to as members of it. Christianity is, in Hegel's opinion, the highest
religion; it expresses, at a certain level of expression, the whole truth
about the essential nature of Spirit. It reveals that truth as fully as it
can be revealed short of being made explicit in philosophy.

5. Hegel's Religion

It has been both asserted and denied that Hegel was an atheist. His
detractors seldom go far enough into his philosophy to raise the question, which seems to have interested only his admirers. My impression
is that the atheists among them have wanted to claim him for one of
themselves, but that most of the believers, more cautiously, have been
concerned to show that it cannot be proved that he was an atheist.
Some twenty years ago I was rebuked by a bishop for venturing to
say that, strictly speaking, Unitarians are not Christians, and I am now
much more careful than I used to be about expressing opinions on
such matters. I do not know whether or not Hegel was an atheist, and
I shall confine myself to making the statements that follow.

Hegel did not admit that he was an atheist, nor yet that he was not
a Christian. He thought of himself, not as denying Christianity, but
as making explicit the truths contained in it, as saying literally what
it says figuratively. He thought it inevitable that, as soon as men
began to speculate about themselves and their world, religion and
philosophy should both arise, being intimately connected and yet
different in kind. Religion expresses what a community senses about
reality but does not put into words which are true when taken literally;
whereas philosophy consists of theories put forward by individuals
whose purpose is to explain the world as it is and who deliberately
challenge criticism. There is progress in both philosophy and religion.
But philosophy, unlike religion, is scientific, in the broad sense that it
seeks to prove what it asserts, inviting doubt in the hope of overcoming
it; it puts questions and argues for some answers rather than others.
It offers what it takes to be a literal explanation. As one philosophy
succeeds another, the explanation becomes gradually more adequate.
Religion, too, makes progress; for though it does not give a literal, but
a figurative, account of reality, and asserts rather than explains, it does
increase in adequacy until it says in its own way all that there is to
say. In Christianity, it is fully adequate; it says all that there is to say
about the essential nature of Spirit, leaving nothing unsaid, though it
says it only figuratively. It is not until philosophy becomes, with Hegel,
a comprehensive and fully explicit account of reality, that it puts into

words to be taken literally the entire truth implicit in Christianity.

This might seem to imply that the Hegelian philosophy supersedes Christianity. But Hegel never says that it does; he claims no more for it than that it supersedes the incomplete philosophies of the past. Yet he believes that Spirit attains complete self-knowledge only in philosophy, which implies that philosophy is superior to religion. It implies it because the end of the whole process, which Spirit is, is this complete self-knowledge.

B. The Argument of the Phenomenology Examined

THE DEFECTS OF THE ARGUMENT

1. A Process Unique and Necessary

I have already rejected as unacceptable two Hegelian conceptions: that of a Mind or Spirit which is revealed in a plurality of finite selves and exists only as so revealed, and that of a process of development whose every phase implies all its other phases. To speak of Spirit as self-conscious only in the consciousness of it of finite selves is to use words to which it is impossible to attach a meaning; the concrete universal is unthinkable, and is merely a putting together of notions which do not make sense when thus combined. I shall add no more to what I have said already to explain why I reject it.

However, I should like, at this stage, to elaborate on what I said earlier about a logically necessary process of development. I have argued that such a process comes to appear logically necessary only if we include among the properties of each phase its relations with later and earlier phases. If we take into account only its inherent properties, we cannot infer from what it is either what came before it or what will come after it. We must know the process before we can know what phases belong to it, and we learn what the process is only from experience. If we define the process as A succeeded by B succeeded by C succeeded by D, then the process implies each of its phases only because it is defined as consisting of them. A, B, C and D do not imply one another unless they are defined as phases of the process, which only experience teaches us that they are. Only experience teaches us that As develop into Ds. But Hegel's theory is not about As that develop into Ds; it is not about a process of which there are many examples. It is about something unique; it is about Spirit, which he says is such that it must develop in a certain way.

No doubt, some of the properties which Hegel attributes to Spirit are included in others. For example, the ability to discriminate is included in the ability to make a deliberate choice. It is possible to have the first property without the second, but not the second without the first. Thus, even when we are considering a unique course of development, we can say that some properties are logically prior to others. But this does not mean that, if the properties which are prior are acquired, the others must be so too; it means only that, unless they are acquired, the others cannot be. Otherwise, only experience can be our guide. It may teach us that one property is in fact always acquired before another, that a always comes before β.

But experience is no help to us when we are dealing with a process which is unique; or it can help us only to the extent to which the process, or some part of it, is like some other process; that is to say, only in those respects in which the process is not unique.

Hegel has built up his account of a unique and necessary process by a variety of devices which ought not to be used as he uses them. He has seen that some properties are logically prior to others, in the sense already explained, and he has seen also that, very often, where we find the first properties, we also find, sooner or later, the second. He has then simply concluded that where we find the first properties we must find the second; that the first properties logically require the second, just as the second logically require the first. Nothing can have β without having a, for a is included in β; and whatever has a usually acquires β. This moves Hegel to conclude that what has a *must* acquire β, in the same sense of *must* as that in which what has β *must* have a.

Hegel sees that man has acquired a certain conception of freedom, and he sees also that certain other conceptions are logically prior to this conception. Man has in fact acquired this conception of freedom, and must have acquired certain other conceptions before he could acquire this one. Hegel therefore feels entitled to speak as if there were here a necessary course of intellectual and moral development, as if it followed that because there could not be freedom (as he defines it) unless there were conscientious defiance of established conventions, there had to be freedom if there was this defiance. Indeed, he goes even further; he sees that man has acquired particular conceptions under given social conditions. He sees a connection between the social and the intellectual, and also a logical priority of some conceptions to others, as well as a temporal one; and so he includes social changes along with intellectual developments in the same necessary process.

Though Hegel is quite well aware that temporal and logical priority are not the same thing, he does not distinguish between them when it serves his purpose not to do so. He sees that some properties are included in others which come after them; they are logically as well as temporally prior to their successors. He also sees that, as a matter of fact, some properties usually come before others, and whenever his argument requires it and he can plausibly do so, he speaks as if, being temporally prior, they were also prior logically. For example, our modern conception of freedom may plausibly be held to include the Greek idea of the citizen who has a say in the affairs of his community, the Roman idea of the legal person as a subject of precisely defined rights, and the Christian idea of the individual. If this is true, as Hegel says it is, then we have here at least three ideas included in our notion of freedom, three ideas logically and temporally prior to it. But Hegel has noticed that the Greek idea of the citizen came in time before the Roman idea of the legal person, and so he speaks as if the first idea were logically prior to the second, though it clearly is not.

If we know that A has developed into X (say, that primitive man, self-conscious and potentially rational, has developed into the West European as Hegel conceived of him), and if we know how X differs from A, we know what properties A must acquire in order to become X. But this knowledge does not tell us in what order these properties are to be acquired, or which (if any) are logically prior to others. Nor can we conclude from it that A, being what it is, must develop into X. Man has, in fact, developed into other things besides the West European. From the properties which make up the humanity of man, the properties included in our definition of him, we cannot infer that he will develop in one way rather than another. But Hegel thinks that we can, for he believes that wherever we have the type of change which is called growth or development, what is temporally prior is also logically prior. He is wrong on two counts: biological growth is not a 'logical' process, and the intellectual and social development of man differs in kind from biological growth.

Hegel says that the process cannot be seen to be necessary until it is completed. I find this assertion puzzling. No doubt, if the process is thought of as culminating in the emergence of a creature capable of understanding it, then the process must be complete before it can be understood. If, for the moment, we suppose that there is no intelligence superior to man's, we rightly conclude that man had to evolve out of the ape before it could be understood how man could evolve out of the ape; but we cannot conclude that there had to be a process of evolution from ape to man. Hegel is, I think, saying more than that the process, which he calls necessary, must produce an intelligence capable of understanding it before it can be understood; he is also saying that it must be complete in order to be intelligible. From this it would follow that, even if there could exist, independently of the process, a being capable of understanding it, that being could not understand it unless it were complete. The process is necessary and yet is unintelligible until it is complete. This is, I believe, Hegel's position, and it seems to me untenable.

2. *Hegel Begs the Question*

Having made up his mind that the process is logically necessary, Hegel sometimes uses the oddest arguments to show how one phase of it leads necessarily to the next. Let me give an example. Why should the type of community which Hegel calls an embodiment of Spirit in its immediacy ever pass away and something different take its place? Hegel admits that in this type of community men are happy; he does not find in it the phenomenon which he calls self-estrangement. Why then should this type of community ever be superseded? The only reason that Hegel gives is that Spirit, at that stage of its development, is deficient in what he calls *subjectivity*. If it is to become fully developed, it must be self-estranged and must afterwards 'find itself' in a coherent world order which it recognizes as its own product.

But this reason is not properly a reason at all. It amounts to saying that something must develop merely in order to acquire a property which it lacks. And what is meant by its lacking a property? No more than its not having it? If that is all that is meant, the argument is absurd. No doubt, if something is to acquire a property it does not have, it must change; but its not having it is not a reason for its changing. Is the lack here in question a felt want? Who, then, feels it? Not the members of the community, for they as yet have no inkling of what it is they lack. To explain why this type of community gives way to another, we must show what there is about it which causes it to do so. But this Hegel does not do. And even if he did it, it would not serve his purpose; for it would be a causal explanation, and a cause does not imply its effect.

Hegel is caught in a dilemma which he does not see, and which, if he did see it, he could not resolve. He speaks of a process which he says is necessary, and then, to explain what it is and how it is necessary, he gives an account of it, phase by phase. But when he comes to show how one phase leads necessarily to the next, he is often incapable of doing more than show how it falls short of its successor and what must come after it to make up the deficiency. He does not see that it only makes sense to say that the next phase has to make up for what is deficient in the phase before if it is assumed that the process is necessary. Or, if he can point to something about the phase which causes it to give way to its successor, he feels himself obliged to speak of that something as if it explained how the phase is logically prior to its successor; but again he can do this, with a show of plausibility, only because he has already taken it for granted that the process is necessary. He offers to show that the process is necessary by showing how each phase of it leads inevitably to the next, and then (although he does not know it) his explanation of how any phase leads inevitably to the next assumes that the process is necessary.

3. Hegel's Irrelevance

Again, because he has made up his mind that the process is logically necessary, Hegel feels the need to include in it whatever he cannot afford to ignore, whether or not it fits into the process. He is a European writing for Europeans, and so, although his account does not refer to actual events, European or otherwise, it finds a place for all the more important types of community, philosophy, attitude of mind, and religion of which Europe provides examples. Nothing important is left out because it is assumed that it *must* have made its contribution to the final result. But this final result is not the state of affairs in Europe in Hegel's time as the most learned and impartial historians might describe it. It is not that, but the actualization of freedom, understood in a certain way. It is no doubt true that all the important phenomena, social and intellectual, then recorded in European history had contributed to make Europe what it was when Hegel wrote the *Phenomenology*, but it is not true that they all contributed to the actualization of what Hegel understood by freedom.

Is it necessary, in order that freedom should be made actual, that the compact community of the type of the Greek *polis* should be superseded by what Hegel calls the 'soulless community' with 'a lord of the world' to govern it? Is it necessary that this 'soulless community' should give way to the feudal system, and that that system should in its turn give way to absolute monarchies of the type known to Europe in the seventeenth and eighteenth centuries? Even if we allow that what Hegel calls 'self-estrangement' and 'the unhappy consciousness' are necessary to the realization of freedom, does it follow that Stoicism and Scepticism are so too?

If we took the Hegelian conception of freedom, which is admittedly complex, and broke it down into the simpler ideas contained in it, we should no doubt find that some of them are logically prior to others. They are all logically prior to the conception of freedom, and there are also no doubt some logical priorities among them. We could then put these ideas into a logical order, and argue that, unless they appeared simultaneously (which we might think most improbable), they must have appeared in a temporal order corresponding to the logical one. But the logical order would not be quite what Hegel had in mind, for though we might, for example, be able to say that A and B, unless they came at the same time as C, must have come before it, there might be no reason why A should have come before B rather than after it. We could also, no doubt, by studying history, discover a good deal about the social conditions that favour the appearance of these ideas. We could build up an account of a course of social and intellectual development culminating in the emergence of freedom. We could then say that such and such conceptions had to appear in roughly a certain order, and under certain conditions. But our account, to be plausible, would differ considerably from Hegel's. It would leave out, on the ground that it is irrelevant, much that he put in.

We might perhaps claim for our imaginary account that it described a *necessary* course of development, but that course would be necessary in a different sense from Hegel's. It would include what experience had taught us about how the ideas that make up our conception of freedom and also the practices that realize that conception emerged. We should then not say that freedom thus conceived had to be realized; we should say only that, if it was to be realized, certain things had to happen. And we should not speak of logical necessity, otherwise than to insist that, where one conception includes another, it could not have emerged before it. We should make a very modest claim compared with the one that Hegel made.

4. Self-Consciousness and Contradiction

In his attempt to show how the evolution of Spirit is necessary, Hegel constantly reminds us that Spirit is self-conscious. Indeed, that of which the development is traced in the *Phenomenology* is called self-consciousness much more often than Spirit, the word Spirit being applied more to the later phases of the process. Self-consciousness, at any point in its development except the last, is involved in contradiction; but, precisely because it is self-conscious, it becomes aware that it is so involved, and then surmounts the contradiction. Or, as we might put it, men take up an attitude which involves contradiction, but, precisely because they are self-conscious and self-critical, they eventually come to see the contradiction and to abandon the attitude, taking up another. The development, which is a progress or movement from the lower to the higher, is necessary because the beings involved in it are self-conscious. Though they are not aware of the process as a whole until it is near completion, every phase of it is reflected in their minds. The reflection may be mistaken; they may not see themselves and their situation as they really are, but they are, being self-conscious, inevitably also self-critical. Their mistakes and defects are eventually brought home to them, and once this has happened, they are no longer quite the same creatures they were before. Because man is a self-conscious being, he is transformed by his own activities.

It is true that a self-conscious creature is affected by its own activities in ways in which an un-self-conscious creature is not. It is also true that its attitudes often change because it has come to believe that they are, in some sense, inadequate or defective. They often change for this reason, but not necessarily. Because man is self-conscious, it does not follow that he must discover the contradictions involved in any attitude he takes up; it follows only that he may.

Moreover, what Hegel calls contradictions are not, for the most part, literally contradictions; they do not involve logical inconsistency. Hegel, in the *Phenomenology*, is not so much concerned with systematic theories as with what might be called, in the popular sense, philosophies of life. He is not so much concerned to point out false reasonings as to show that certain attitudes of mind are produced by needs of which men are not conscious, or of which they are only half-conscious, and that the attitudes, for one reason or another, do not satisfy the needs that produce them. This is, indeed, what makes the *Phenomenology*, despite its pretentious metaphysics and obscure style, a fascinating and a profound book. What Hegel calls contradictions are mostly no more than attempts to get satisfaction in ways that do not give it. But it does not follow that, because man is self-conscious, he must discover that these ways do not bring satisfaction, especially when he does not even understand the needs that he is groping to satisfy.

Let us consider, for a moment, what Hegel says about the Unhappy Consciousness. Men desire recognition in this world but they do not get it, and so they imagine another world where they do get it from a God to whom they attribute the essential qualities of man. They need recognition in order to be satisfied, but while they seek that recognition in another world, not being able to get it in this, they are not satisfied. The contradiction consists in their seeking recognition where it is not to be found.

For my part, I do not see that, even in this peculiar sense of contradiction, there is contradiction here, and I do not see why, if there is one, man, as a self-conscious being, must eventually resolve it. I do not see why the situation should be unsatisfying, or why, even if it were unsatisfying, it should not last indefinitely. Even if we allow that men imagine another world to compensate themselves for the recognition they do not get in this one, it does not follow that the compensation is not satisfying. Hegel, at least, produces no good reason for thinking so; he merely takes it for granted that because man first wants recognition in this world, which alone is real, he can be satisfied only if he gets it in this world; he cannot be satisfied by the mere belief that he has it, or will have it, in a world which he has imagined but which does not exist. But recognition is not like food, which must be real before it can satisfy; it may be enough that a man believes he has it for him to find satisfaction in it.[1] Provided he has no doubts, why should he not be satisfied? Hegel does not do what he might have done; he does not attempt to show that belief in an after-life is apt to be too weak

---

[1] If I believe that I am recognized by a Being who does not exist and whom I do not expect to meet in this life, and if my belief in an after-life is mistaken, then I need never be disillusioned.

to enable a man to find in the hope of what he will get in it adequate compensation for what he lacks in this life.

And why, even if hope of an after-life cannot satisfy man, should he come to know this and to seek satisfaction where alone he can get it? Hegel does not suppose that man, knowing what he wants in this world and not being able to get it, deliberately imagines another world and seeks compensation in it; he does not suppose that man is a deliberate escapist. He does not offer us any so crude an explanation of how man comes to believe in an after-life. Though man is dissatisfied in this life, he does not understand what makes him so; his faith is a remedy for a condition of which he is only dimly aware. The very notion of an unhappy consciousness supposes that man does not yet understand his own nature, that there is more to him than he himself knows. He is not yet, as Hegel puts it, *for* himself what he is *in* himself. Man is a self-conscious creature. Indeed he is; but his being so does not of itself make it necessary that he should overcome a condition whose roots, though they lie in him, are not known to him. Freud would agree that repression and sublimation are processes which occur in man because he is self-conscious and rational, because he has a need for what Hegel calls 'recognition' and therefore seeks satisfaction in ways peculiar to his kind. Being self-conscious and rational, he needs to justify himself to himself. Man alone is capable of self-knowledge, and therefore man alone feels the need to hide from himself. The sub-conscious in man is not the part of him which he shares with the lower animals; it is what it is, not in spite of his being self-conscious and rational, but largely because he is so. His mental ills, even those of which he is not conscious, are the ills of a self-conscious creature; they are the ills of a creature who, in Hegel's sense of the word, is spiritual, acquiring self-consciousness in the process of building up for itself a coherent picture of a world in which it strives to satisfy desires peculiar to its kind. Only a self-conscious creature could suffer from such ills and could find a remedy for them; but it does not follow, merely because it is self-conscious, that it must find it.

5. Rationalism and Revolution

Hegel often confuses what is required by his theory with what is required by the facts. For instance, he says that the rationalist philosophers explain the world and show that it is rational (or, as we should say, that it is completely intelligible), but that Spirit needs to do more than explain the world; it needs to transform it. Not for a moment does he suggest that it is the philosophers who feel the need to transform the world, and are not content merely to explain it. It is Spirit that is still unsatisfied, and not the rationalist philosophers; and therefore, in order that Spirit should be satisfied, there must be revolutionary zeal as well as critical philosophy. Spirit is manifest in both philosophy and revolution; it is both theoretical and active. It follows, therefore, from the nature of Spirit that there must be both rationalist philosophy and revolution. The philosophers need not be revolutionaries, but there must come to be revolutionaries after there have been philosophers, because it is in the nature of Spirit that there should be. Hegel's explanation is no explanation at all. He ought to show us how men, when they succeed in explaining the world, come inevitably to want to transform it; he ought to show us how rationalist philosophy and revolution are connected in human minds, for it is in such minds that Spirit is manifest. Instead of that, he merely tells us that there must be both rationalist philosophers and revolutionaries, because Spirit is active as well as theoretical. We might as well say: Love and jealousy go necessarily together, and therefore, since John is in love, James is jealous.

Hegel's theory requires him to hold that men come to have a new attitude to (or philosophy of) life, because they have failed to find satisfaction in an old one. For example, as Hegel might put it, Spirit seeks satisfaction in Stoicism, discovers contradictions in it, and therefore passes on to something else. It does not occur to him that an old philosophy may come to seem unsatisfying because a new one has begun to take its place. As he sees it, there must be something wrong with the old philosophy which causes it to lose its hold on men and allows a new philosophy to supplant it. But this is by no means always so. There may be all kinds of reasons, other than anything inherently unsatisfying about it, which cause a philosophy of life to be supplanted. External conditions may change, and men may acquire ambitions which they did not have before; or they may have ideals imposed upon them which are unsuited to them and which they come to discard. A philosophy of life is not a scientific theory which is abandoned or modified because it is seen not to fit the facts. Nor does it lose its hold on men because it is logically inconsistent. The contradictions which Hegel claims to see in the philosophies he discusses are not, though he pretends otherwise, for the most part, logical inconsistencies; they are much more often failures to satisfy. Stoicism, he tells us, leads to boredom, and the systematic pursuit of pleasure defeats its own end. But is this so, always? And when it is so, what makes it so?

Stoicism is not boring to the man who is by temperament suited to it. Nor is the systematic pursuit of pleasure always self-defeating. We do not all come to terms with life in the same way. Hegel takes no account of the possibility that there may be several perennial philosophies, which take different forms in different ages, but which remain essentially the same from age to age, each of them attractive to only some people. There are Stoics now, as there were in the ancient world. Their explicit beliefs may be considerably different, but their attitude to life is at bottom the same. There are also sceptics and hedonists and believers in an after-life; their beliefs, too, have changed with the times, but the philosophies that come nearest to satisfying them have remained true to type. Hegel's theory requires him to hold that one type of philosophy gives way to another until at last there is left a single philosophy which is completely satisfying, and also that a philosophy is supplanted only because it has been found to be inherently unsatisfying. Both these opinions seem to me mistaken.

6. Master and Slave

One of the most admired parts of the *Phenomenology* is the dialectic of the master and slave. It has caught the imagination of several of Hegel's critics, and they have made much of it. Kojève, in particular, has expounded it with extraordinary force and lucidity. Hegel, in this dialectic, points to certain quite fundamental aspects of human and social experience. I hope to make clear what they are, confessing that I would not have seen, as clearly as I do now, how Hegel conceived of them, if I had read only his *Phenomenology* and not also Kojève's commentary on it. Yet I believe that there are, in this part of Hegel's argument, important defects which Kojève has not seen, or at least has not seen to be important, for he has not troubled to mention them.

Man's desire for recognition, his longing to seem valuable in his own eyes and to have others admit his value, leads to a conflict which Kojève, interpreting Hegel, calls a conflict of pure prestige. Man cannot be certain of his value unless others admit it, and he requires of them what he will not, except from fear of death, accord to them. As a result of this conflict some become masters and others slaves.

I should not quarrel with Hegel for insisting that the desire for recognition is the pre-eminently human desire, that it is strong and persistent only in self-conscious and rational beings, that with them it takes forms unknown in other creatures, and that they become more fully self-conscious and develop their reasoning powers largely in the process of seeking to satisfy it. I should agree with him that conflicts of pure prestige are enormously important in human life, which owes its specifically human character much more to them than to conflicts for what satisfies the appetites which man shares with the other animals.

But what Hegel forgets – and I am surprised that a family man should forget it – is that the human being first engages in conflicts of pure prestige in the nursery. It is there, and not on the battlefield, that man wins his first victories and sustains his first defeats. And by the nursery I do not mean the room set aside for children in the homes of the well-to-do; I mean the relations in which children, in the process of becoming self-conscious and rational, stand to one another and to adults in the family circle. It is true that, to begin with, a child cannot distinguish between itself and its environment, and that when it comes to make this distinction, it comes also to distinguish between itself and other selves. It is true also that, as it becomes aware of other selves, it behaves towards them as if they existed only to satisfy its appetites. It does not at first require recognition; it merely has appetites, and gives vent to them until they are satisfied; it then gradually comes to be aware, as it acquires self-consciousness, that its appetites are satisfied by others. When it gets this awareness, it tries to make others do what it wants; it does so, at first, in order that they should satisfy its appetites, and then, later, also to show its power over them. But the persons whom the child seeks to make subservient to itself are much more powerful than it is; and they soon create in it, usually without aiming to do so, a lively sense of its dependence on them. Even the most self-willed and spoilt child is often frustrated; it has it often brought home to it that its power is limited. Being aware of its dependence on others, it seeks to please them. It acquires self-esteem in the process of endeavouring to be the sort of person they approve of. Thus, though it may be true that, almost as soon as it can distinguish other people from itself, it seeks to make them subservient to its wishes, and also that it needs recognition in order to have self-respect, or a secure sense of its own worth, there can be no question of its enslaving others. It gains recognition by obedience.

I should have thought that the need to dominate and the need for recognition are distinct, and that the first precedes the second. The child wishes everything to happen the way it wants; when it becomes aware of other people besides itself, it wishes them to satisfy its desires as soon as it gives vent to them. No doubt, it soon acquires an appetite for power; it asks for what it does not really want, merely for the sake of asking and getting. But an appetite for power, at this stage, consists merely of the need to express wishes for the pleasure of having them gratified. The child with this appetite may not be in the least concerned about what other people think and feel towards it; it may, as yet, have no need for recognition. I suspect that the need for recognition comes with frustration and a sense of dependence; the child needs to placate adults, and is therefore interested, not just in getting them to do what it wants, but in their feelings towards itself. It wants to be important to them, and this desire soon becomes the most persistent and absorbing of all. It is, as Hegel implied, the predominantly human and educative desire. It is abnormally strong in man because he is self-conscious and rational, and it also serves to deepen his self-consciousness and to develop his reasoning powers. But it is a desire born of a sense of dependence and a need to placate; and when it first appears in the human being, it makes him docile rather than aggressive. A child seeks recognition from grown-ups rather than from other children, and from children older than itself rather than from younger ones, and is apt to be docile towards them provided it can earn their recognition by docility. This docility, of course, is not slavishness; the child is not seeking to make itself a mere instrument of their wills, but is seeking their approval by conforming to what it believes are their standards.

Mastery and slavery are facts that have to be explained; they have their social and psychological causes. They may even mark a usual phase in the social and intellectual development of mankind. Slavery, in one form or another, has existed in many, and perhaps even in most, human societies. John Stuart Mill, who was, much more than Hegel, a thorough liberal, conceded that slavery, or at least a high degree of dependence of some men upon others, might be necessary to produce habits of regular and hard work, and might therefore have been beneficial to mankind. I would not deny this. It may be so. It may be true that slavery could hardly have been avoided and that the world is now a better place, even by standards acceptable to the liberal, than it would have been had there never been slavery. I am not concerned to deny this. I deny only that Hegel, in his dialectic of the master and the slave, has shown that mastery and slavery are necessarily involved in the process whereby man becomes a deeply self-conscious creature with a lively and urgent sense of his own dignity, the sort of creature for whom freedom can be a supreme value.

7. Slavery and Progress

In an argument which has found admirers, Hegel contends that, whereas the slave is progressive, the master is not. This is so, he thinks, partly because the master is in an *impasse*, being unable to get real satisfaction from his recognition by the slave, whom he cannot recognize without forfeiting his mastery, which he will not do voluntarily; and partly because the slave is a worker, and through his work attains understanding of, and power over, both nature and himself, as the master does not.

The first of these reasons holds only if there is only one master, or if, where there is more than one, they do not form a community. But clearly there is more than one master, and there is also a community of masters, as Hegel tacitly admits. He speaks of a community which is concrete Spirit in immediacy, whose members are citizens. This is the type of community of which the Greek *polis* is an example. In it there are both masters and slaves, and presumably the masters recognize one another, or otherwise the community would not subsist. Now, according to Hegel, the recognition accorded to the master by the slave is not fully satisfying because the master does not recognize the slave. He is recognized by an inferior, by a person worthless in his eyes, and therefore is not satisfied. This implies that the recognition of an equal is satisfying; so that, if there are several masters and they recognize one another, they are all satisfied. Hegel's argument is merely that a man's sense of his own worth is secure if that worth is recognized by others, and that the recognition is fully satisfying only if it comes from persons whose worth he in turn recognizes. His argument is not that recognition is not fully satisfying to anyone who gets it unless everyone recognizes everyone else. Therefore, provided there is a community of equals who recognize one another, that recognition is fully satisfying to them, no matter how many slaves there may be. This is what follows from what Hegel says about recognition and about the reasons which makes servile recognition unsatisfying. His argument that servile recognition cannot satisfy the master rests therefore on the tacit (and absurd) assumption that there is only one master or that, if there is more than one, they do not recognize one another. Unfortunately, Hegel's style encourages this kind of false reasoning. He is interested in the master and the slave as types, and so he speaks of the lordly and the servile consciousness, or of *the* master and *the* slave, as if there were only one of each.

Hegel's other reason for holding that the slave is progressive while the master is not is historically more important. It asserts a doctrine of which Marx was to make great use: that it is the oppressed rather than the oppressor who makes progress because he is enlightened and disciplined by work.

But it is not true that only the servile and the oppressed work; the free and the oppressors do so as well. Slavery and oppression are possible only in a community, and wherever there is a community there is some form of government or management. This too is work, and it is work as disciplined and as educative as any done by slaves or serfs or hired labourers. How are we to distinguish between work and activity which is not work? Work, presumably, is regular and obligatory. If these are the properties which distinguish work from other kinds of activity, then government and management are as much entitled as anything else to be called work. Even if we say that work is essentially service, we cannot deny that the ruler and the manager also serve. They are not free to do as they please; they carry out obligations; they do what is required or expected of them, and there are sanctions to ensure that they do it. Even in the economic sphere, they have as much interest as the servile and the oppressed in raising production; they study nature and themselves just as closely, and are just as inventive. If they are less progressive, it cannot be because they are not disciplined and enlightened by the work they do. On the contrary, they are, much more than the servile and the oppressed, the intellectual and reflective class.

I am not, in saying this, trying to suggest that there is really no such thing as oppression or exploitation; I am not saying that so-called oppressors or exploiters serve the oppressed and exploited just as much as they are served by them. Admittedly, the oppressors, when they serve, serve only their own class, and the rewards of their labour are incomparably greater than the rewards of the oppressed, because they dominate the community. Nor am I denying that they have much more leisure than the oppressed. Though I suspect that the hardest workers are usually to be found among them, because their work is more absorbing and more rewarding than menial labour, I concede that many of them do little or no work. But to concede this is not to admit that their work is less disciplined and educative than the work of the servile and subordinate.

If the slave is progressive, at least potentially, in some respect in which the master is not, he is not so because he is a worker and is transformed morally and intellectually by his work; he is so because it is much more obviously his interest than the master's that all men, and not only some, should be free. Once you allow that freedom is good and that all men can have it, you must conclude that, if some men, owing to their position in society, are more disposed than others to demand universal freedom, they are, in at least one respect, the more progressive. But this has nothing to do with the effects upon them of their work.

8. An Odd Account of Revolution

Hegel's account of absolute freedom and terror, or revolution (though he does not use that word), is awkward and obscure; it is an unsuccessful attempt to make the course of events square with his theory. He says that for Spirit, in the phase of absolute freedom, 'the world is . . . absolutely its own will, and this will is universal will'.[1] In other words, the revolutionary believes that the world ought to be as men wish it to be; that society exists for men, who have the right to mould it to their will. And the will here in question is the will common to them all, the universal will. The revolutionary sees freedom as the realization of this will, and to that extent is right; but he seeks to realize it by abolishing all social ranks and classes; he seeks to realize it *immediately*, as Jean Hyppolite puts it in trying to explain Hegel's meaning. It is there that the revolutionary is mistaken, and his mistake leads to terror. And all this, so Hegel would have us believe, is necessary; it is a necessary phase in the evolution of Spirit.

We may ask, what is involved in trying to realize the universal will *immediately*? We have seen that, in Hegelian parlance, the *immediate* is the simple and the undifferentiated, or what appears to be so to the

[1] *The Phenomenology of Mind*, p. 600

unphilosophical mind. The revolutionary has an adequate conception of freedom and therefore understands that it is not mere absence of constraint; he understands that freedom is realized only when the universal will is made effective in a social order. This being so, it follows that the attempt to realize the universal will *immediately* is an attempt to realize it in a simple and undifferentiated social order, a community without social ranks and classes. It is this attempt, apparently, which leads to terror.

The point of this argument escapes me. Hegel admits that the revolutionary has an adequate conception of freedom, that he sees it as the universal will realized in a social order. The universal will is, indeed, his object; his supreme desire is to see that will embodied in the laws and institutions of society. The revolutionary presumably does not deny that in society there is a considerable diversity of functions, that every society has a definable structure; he merely wants to ensure that that structure accords with the universal will – or, as we might put it, with principles of justice which he believes all men would accept if they considered them impartially and saw their practical implications. In believing this he may be simple-minded; there may be no such principles. But that is irrelevant here; and, in any case, his belief is not one that Hegel would reject. No matter how simple-minded the revolutionary, he does not want to do without a social structure, and therefore does not want to do without a hierarchy. He wants to transform the social structure and the hierarchy to accord with his conception of justice. He does not want to abolish *all* social ranks. He may perhaps say that that is what he wants, but if he says it, he is using the term *social ranks* in a narrow sense to refer to the kind of hierarchy he dislikes – as, for example, to hereditary classes. But this is not the sense of *social ranks* required to make sense of Hegel's argument. A society without hereditary classes is not simple and undifferentiated; it may be – and indeed, unless it is small and simple, it must be – elaborate in structure. It must be hierarchical, and must have social ranks. An attempt to abolish hereditary classes or unearned privileges is not an attempt to abolish *all* social ranks, *all* hierarchy; it is not an attempt to make society simple and undifferentiated. But Hegel says that, when Spirit takes the form of absolute freedom, there is an attempt to abolish *all* ranks, *all* hierarchy.

Now, an attempt to abolish all ranks and all hierarchy, if it is made in any but the smallest and simplest societies (and it is not them but countries like France that Hegel has in mind at this stage of his argument), is tantamount to an attempt to abolish organized society. How then can Spirit, at this stage of its evolution, have an adequate conception of freedom? Or, as we should prefer to say, how can man have it? The adequacy of the conception consists in freedom's being acknowledged to be a universal will realized in a social order. The claim of the revolutionary is that society shall conform to the universal will. He can have no adequate conception of freedom unless he understands that there must be a structure of authority to hold society together, unless he understands that there must be hierarchy, even though neither wealth nor rank is inherited.

Hegel cannot condemn the revolutionary for wishing to change society; for, if he has an adequate conception of freedom which he sees is not yet realized, he must wish to change society in order to realize it. Hegel could condemn him, as Burke does, for acting in haste and ignorance; but that condemnation would have nothing to do with the necessary evolution of Spirit. He could also condemn him for attempting what is both impossible and undesirable: for trying to ensure that the momentary will of the people, no matter what it is, always prevails. He might have argued that this attempt is self-defeating; he might have said that trying to give immediate effect to the will of the majority must lead to chaos and then to oppression and terror, so that, eventually, it is not the will of the majority, but that of a ruthless minority, which prevails. If Hegel had put forward this argument, he would have been more convincing, for it may be that the institutions most likely to ensure that the people get what gives them enduring satisfaction will often prevent their getting what, at the moment, they happen to be clamouring for.

Indeed, I do not wish to deny that Hegel may have meant to say this as well. Reading his highly abstract argument, it is often difficult to see just what he does mean to say. He may also have meant to say that every citizen can be free, accepting the social order as being in harmony with his enduring will, where there is no democracy; and even that democracy prevents the full realization of freedom.

It may have been Hegel's intention to use these two more plausible arguments as well. I do not exclude that possibility. But the argument he makes the most of is that the revolutionary wants to achieve freedom by abolishing all social ranks. This argument is either out of place or else does not square with Hegel's admission that, at this stage of the evolution of Spirit, men have an adequate conception of freedom.

Nor is it clear why the attempt to abolish all ranks should lead to terror. Hegel's argument amounts to no more than this: revolution, or the attempt to realize universal freedom *immediately* (in the Hegelian sense of immediate), is necessarily destructive, and therefore the sole achievement of universal freedom is death. And this death he calls, coming down suddenly from the heights of abstraction to homely language, 'the most cold-blooded and meaningless death of all, with no more significance to it than cleaving a head of cabbage or swallowing a draught of water'.[1] But in what does the destructiveness of

---

[1] *The Phenomenology of Mind*, p. 605.

revolution consist? Apparently, in the attempt to achieve universal freedom by abolishing all social ranks. Now, the abolition of social ranks is the destruction of institutions; it is not the killing of men. Hegel's argument seems therefore to be that the destruction of these particular institutions leads necessarily to killing. It may be so, but it is not self-evident. Yet Hegel has nothing more to say about it than this. He does not offer to show how the attempt to destroy these institutions leads to killing; he moves directly from this destructiveness to death, as if the first logically implied the second. It is only because he puts his argument in such abstract terms that its absurdity escapes notice.

The abolition of all ranks is clearly impossible. For the attempt to abolish them is made by an organized power, and organization involves hierarchy. It is also impossible to ensure that the momentary will of the people always prevails. Thus, we have here one aim which Hegel clearly (though mistakenly) attributes to the revolutionary, and another which can be attributed to him and whose attribution is more plausible; and both are aims at the impossible. Can we say, then, that Hegel believed that revolution leads inevitably to killing because it aims at the impossible? He may have believed it. Yet this belief, if it is merely asserted and not argued, carries no conviction; for it is by no means obvious that merely aiming at the impossible leads to killing. But there is here a possible line of argument that does make sense, and Hegel may have had it in mind without putting it into words. People who have power and who try to achieve the impossible, believing it to be possible and also important, are quickly frustrated, and made angry and suspicious; they suspect treachery and ill-will and take easily to extreme measures. They look upon themselves as spokesmen for the community, or as guardians of its enduring interests, and so, when they find things going seriously wrong, are apt to blame others rather than themselves and feel justified in punishing them. When, after centuries of accepting society for what it is, men seek to transform it, they easily lose control of the course of events they have set in motion, and in their bewilderment and panic resort to violence. But this argument, even if Hegel had it in mind, has nothing to do with the development of Spirit as he imagined it.

9. Hegel and Napoleon

As we have seen, it seems to follow from Hegel's philosophy being possible that the process whereby Spirit achieves self-knowledge is complete, for that self-knowledge is knowledge of the process which is Spirit and is revealed in finite minds. Hegel is such a mind and this knowledge is revealed in his philosophy, and therefore (unless we assume that it must be revealed in all finite minds) the existence of that philosophy proves that the process which is Spirit is complete. But Spirit is both Reason and Will; it is fully actual and satisfied when it attains complete self-knowledge, and when it is manifest in a community of selves who conscientiously desire what the community requires of them. It would appear, too, that Spirit cannot attain full self-knowledge unless it is manifest in such a community, for the process must be complete before it can be fully known, and Spirit is as much Will as Reason.

It would seem, then, that the Europe in which Hegel wrote the *Phenomenology*, the Europe dominated by Napoleon, must be the community whose members conscientiously desire what is required of them, the community which is completely free. But this is surely an odd conclusion to a philosophy which makes the realization of freedom its central theme. Hegel admired Napoleon as perhaps only a German is capable of admiring a conqueror of his own country, as Goethe admired him, and Beethoven too before the First Consul turned Emperor. Napoleon was never admired by intellectuals in France as he was in Germany. The Napoleon that Goethe and Hegel admired, without perhaps seeing him for what he was, was much more than a soldier; he was, they thought, the heir of the revolution. In the place of terror he put order, and he knew how to make men secure in the possession of the rights granted to them by the revolution. He extended to the territories he conquered the civil liberties which the revolution brought to Frenchmen. It was still possible, in 1807, to think of Napoleon as a liberator rather than an oppressor. Hegel shared an admiration which was still respectable, and which it would be absurd to call abject or servile. It would be more than unjust; it would be stupid to speak of Hegel as if he were a crude worshipper of power or a quisling. Yet it is odd that a man who could speak of freedom as he did, making so much of the claim to be allowed to live conscientiously, should have implied that freedom was achieved in the Europe of his day.

According to Kojève, Hegel saw in Napoleon the fully satisfied man, the man who knew what he had to do and how to do it, the man completely at home in the world. He saw him as the instrument of the universal will, the legislator whose laws are entirely acceptable. Since Napoleon is not mentioned by name in the *Phenomenology*, not even as Antigone is to illustrate a point, we must suppose that the opinions about Napoleon attributed to Hegel by Kojève are opinions to which Kojève thinks that Hegel is committed by his philosophy. If the attribution is just – and perhaps it is – it serves to show that Hegel's ideas about how freedom is realized were as inadequate as those of the revolutionaries.

THE MERITS OF THE ARGUMENT

I shall speak more briefly of the merits than of the defects of Hegel's argument, not because the merits are smaller, but because they are more easily explained. The mere exposition of an argument as rich and varied as that of the *Phenomenology* brings to lights its merits. What Hegel says abstractly and obscurely can be put more concretely and lucidly, so that often no more is needed to establish the value of what he says than to translate it into plain English.

1. The Self and its Environment

If we take such Hegelian expressions as 'negation', 'self-development', 'self-estrangement', and 'the self finding itself in what is external to itself' metaphorically, it is often possible to make excellent sense of what Hegel says; and this sense, as I said before, is at least part of what he means, though it may still (if we are to believe his admirers) fall far short of his whole meaning. For example, Hegel speaks of the self as *negating* what is external to itself when it acts upon it or consumes it. When a man eats something he is said to negate it, and so also when he changes its character to make it useful. If we take 'negating' to mean 'transforming something for a purpose', we do not take it literally but metaphorically; and yet we take it to mean part of what Hegel meant by it. And this is also true, if by 'self-development' we understand man's developing his potentialities by his actions; and by 'self-estrangement' his feeling frustrated in society and having a sense of his own unworthiness; and by the 'self finding itself in what is external to itself', his coming to understand himself in relation to his environment and finding satisfaction thereby. These are not the only meanings of these expressions, even when we take them metaphorically; and therefore, if we are to do justice to Hegel's argument, we must not always translate them the same way. I take these particular examples by way of illustration, though I think they give us the most important meanings of the expressions they translate – or, to speak more cautiously, the most important meanings which the non-Hegelian can accept.

If we interpret these expressions in these ways, we find in the *Phenomenology* an elaborate and suggestive account of how man acquires self-knowledge and self-discipline in the process of reacting to, acting upon, and acquiring knowledge of, an environment which he distinguishes from himself and in which he seeks satisfaction. It is by acting in an environment and by acquiring a systematic understanding of it that man becomes a rational and purposeful creature, with a conception of a coherent world and of himself as a person distinct from other persons.

2. The World and Language

It is true that this systematic understanding, this capacity to create a coherent picture of a world, depends on the creation of a language, which is the work, not of each man separately, but of many men able to communicate with one another. Language is the product of a community, and every man uses it to acquire knowledge both of an external world and of himself in that world. Man becomes self-conscious, rational, purposeful, and moral as a member of a community.

3. Recognition and Self-esteem

It is true also that man is much more than a creature of appetites which he seeks to satisfy. He desires to have value in his own eyes, he needs to have some conception of himself which he finds satisfying. To be assured of his value, he needs to have it recognized by others. He needs self-respect and cannot have it unless he is respected by others. Admittedly, some men are much stronger than others, and are much less dependent on the good opinion of their neighbours, but this is a strength which they acquire by education, in the process of adapting themselves to a form of communal life. It is an independence which grows out of dependence. A man's self-esteem, no matter how invulnerable, rests on his acceptance of certain values, which he either gets from others by example or precept, or which he evolves for himself in reaction to how others treat him. Moreover, no man's self-esteem is anywhere near being invulnerable; even when he is indifferent to the opinions of most men, there are nearly always some whose opinions he values. There are always some circles in which he could not bear to be despised. Hegel was right in treating the need for recognition as the pre-eminently human need, and also as the pre-eminently educative need in the sense that a man's character is formed largely by what he does in his endeavour to satisfy it. It is the need of a self-conscious and rational creature able to see himself as living in a coherent world with other creatures like himself.

4. Man, the Producer and Product of Society

Every social order is a product of human activities which differ in kind from the activities of other animals because men are self-conscious and are capable of speech and communication, and therefore of relations, practical and emotional, of which other animals are not capable. Society is, as Hegel saw, the unintended product of specifically human actions; of actions that are purposeful and involve reasoning. Yet, though man has, in this sense, produced society by his activities, he need not know how he has done it, nor even that he has done it. He may feel 'estranged' from society; he may be incapable of acquiring inside it the self-esteem and recognition which he seeks. This phenomenon of estrangement or *Entfremdung* is, psychologically and socially, of the greatest importance. Hegel was the first to give it a name and to try to explain it. We can, I think, see the idea of estrangement already present in the social theory of Rousseau, but it is there, as it were, under the surface and is never brought into the full light of day. There is nothing like a systematic attempt at explaining it. It is not an idea lightly touched upon by Rousseau; he seems to be again and again on the point of making it explicit and yet never quite succeeds in doing so. He is absorbed by it and yet does not see it for what it is. It is Hegel who makes it explicit and gives it a central place in his theory of man and society.

5. *The Role of the Unconscious*

In the *Phenomenology* Hegel distinguishes, in many connections, between Spirit as it appears to itself at a certain stage of its evolution and as it really is at that stage; he distinguishes between self-conscious mind as it *is for itself* and as it is *in itself*. It is *in itself* what it is *for us*: we being the author of the *Phenomenology* and those of his readers capable of understanding him. This distinction between the *for itself* and the *in itself*, if it is applied to the mind, sometimes comes very close to the distinction made by modern psychology between the conscious and the subconscious. Much more than any social theorist before him, Hegel is aware that what man knows about himself is, or may be, only a small part of what there is to know. Everything that goes on in our minds is discoverable, but not therefore discovered; and the process of discovery is long and painful. This is a conclusion to which the *Phenomenology* points as clearly as any contemporary work on psychology.

6. *The Concept of Freedom*

There is a great and important difference between the Greek and the modern conceptions of freedom, which Hegel, if he was not the first to notice it, was the first to emphasize and explain. That difference is, as he said it was, connected with the notion of conscience. In all communities law and custom are disobeyed, but there is a difference between disobedience and rejection. It is one thing to disobey the law when moved by passion or appetite, and quite another to condemn it as unjust. The man who disobeys conscientiously deliberately prefers a higher law to the law which he is required to obey. Condemnation of positive law and custom takes, to begin with, the form of an appeal to the commands of God against the commands of men, and then later

becomes an appeal to a law of reason, a law supposedly discoverable by
considering what sort of creature man is and what rules of conduct are
incumbent upon a creature of his kind. Even if we believe (as Hegel
did not) that no rules of conduct derive logically from man's being
the sort of creature he is, we can still agree that man, until he has conceived of rules superior to positive law and custom, and has sought
to justify them by an appeal to something more than the mere will
of God, is incapable of the idea of freedom as we now have it.

7. Freedom and Law

Where men have this conception of freedom, they cannot in fact be
free except in a society where what is required of them accords with
what they think is right or good. Law and custom must not stand in
the way of their living what they think is a worth-while life. If men are
to be free, there must be, as a sociologist might put it, harmony
between subjective values and imposed norms. And the sociologist
would agree with Hegel that subjective values, even where they do not
square with imposed norms, are always deeply influenced by them; or,
in other words, that a man's conception of what is desirable largely
depends on the standards to which, at one time or another, he has
been required to conform. Only social creatures can be socially maladjusted; by which I do not mean merely that they must be in society
before they can be maladjusted (as a man must wear shoes before he
can feel uncomfortable in them), but that they must have values,
which can only be acquired in society, before they can have the needs
and aspirations which society frustrates. To be consciously unfree and
to aspire to freedom, a creature must be self-conscious and must be
able to make value-judgments. Therefore only a social and moral
creature can be consciously unfree and can desire freedom; and it can
only have freedom when what it finds desirable is compatible with
what it is required to do.

8. The Social Rôle

No doubt, it is a mistake to call a community a mind or Spirit. Yet
those who make this mistake often do so, I suspect, because they have
noticed a fact about communities which many fail to notice and which
they think supremely important. A community's being a community
depends on more than how its members behave; it depends also on
how they feel and think about it. A human community is not adequately described as a number of persons related to one another in
certain ways, or among whom a certain pattern of behaviour prevails.
The members of a human community are aware of themselves as being
members of it; they are aware also of the relations in which they stand

to one another. A human mother does not merely bear children and
nurse and protect them; she also knows that she is a mother, and in
knowing this is aware of herself as a member of a family. The
peculiarity of social relations is that they involve awareness of what
they are. This awareness is not, of course, the kind of knowledge that
the sociologist aims at; but it is conscious acceptance of a social role.
A human mother behaves like a human mother because she knows
that she is one. Thus, we can say that truly social relations, which
exist only between human beings, are what they are because the beings
involved in them acknowledge that they are so involved; and there is
a sense, therefore, in which a human community is what it is only
because it is, as Hegelians would put it, 'reflected' in the minds of its
members.

9. The Concept of Ideology

Hegel's conception of systems of beliefs (or, as we should now say,
ideologies) whose function is to reconcile men to their social condition
or to compensate them for it, systems which would not exist if men
were not dissatisfied with that condition, is admirable. It enables him to
give a much more plausible explanation of religion than the eighteenth-century philosophers gave. They explained religion as a product
of curiosity combined with ignorance or as arising from the need to
appease irrational fear. Hegel explains it as expressing, figuratively,
the aspirations of frustrated men. Of course, this is not the whole of
his explanation. He insists that religious beliefs are essentially, even
though not literally, true; which is to claim more for them than that
they express the aspirations of the dissatisfied. But this is, historically,
the more important part of his explanation; the part which Feuerbach
accepted and developed, and which Marx took over from Feuerbach.

When I say that this conception of ideology is admirable, I do not
mean that it gives us the whole truth about religion. I am sure that
it does not. But it is a conception which can be applied to much more
than religious beliefs; it is a good idea, a fruitful hypothesis. Moreover,
this conception, as we find it in Hegel, is free of several of the defects
which spoil the Marxian theory of ideology. There is no suggestion
in Hegel that the function of ideology is primarily to support class
interests, or that it is to be dismissed as fantasy because it serves to
reconcile the dissatisfied to their condition. Yet Hegel agrees with
Marx that it is only because men cannot find happiness in this world
that they imagine another and aspire to it.

Those who have faith, in perhaps a deeper sense than Hegel had
it, would not deny that faith helps to reconcile man to his worldly
condition; they would not deny that unhappiness often brings a man
to faith, and that faith makes him less unhappy. And they mostly

would not claim that the articles of their faith are to be taken quite literally. They would be inclined to admit that some of these articles say more than, to the literal-minded, they appear to say. But they would deny that man has faith *only* because he is dissatisfied in this world; they would assert that man, even if he got in this world all the satisfaction he could get, would still need faith.

10. The Idea of Progress

Progress, as Hegel conceives of it, is an altogether richer idea than we find in any social theorist before him. The idea of progress, as we find it in Condorcet, is simpler, shallower, and less suggestive. Hegel's account of it is more impressive both in its central theme and in its details. I have no wish to praise mere size and complexity. It is astonishing how much Hegel knew or guessed at. In criticizing so vast and so pretentious a theory, and a theory vulnerable on so many different grounds, it is easy to lose sight of what makes it admirable: the grandeur of its conception and the originality and subtlety of many of its arguments. A vast theory is almost certain to have many faults, and sometimes has few virtues. But Hegel's theory abounds in virtues as in faults. Unfortunately, men are not builders with ideas as they are with bricks and stones; any vast and elaborate intellectual structure which they put up is almost bound to be shoddy. So it is with the *Phenomenology of Spirit*; many of its deductions are plays on words, and others are trivial or silly. In England, and more particularly in Oxford, we are not trained to make the best of such a thinker as Hegel. We are easily put off by his arrogance and his obscurity, and we are disgusted by the poverty or (as it sometimes seems to us) the dishonesty of his arguments. His faults strike us first and blind us to his virtues. Among philosophers interested in man as a moral and social creature, there have been not a few more lucid, more self-critical, and more rigorous than Hegel, but has there been another as imaginative since Plato?

III. WORLD HISTORY

Hegel's *Philosophy of History* is much simpler and easier to read than his *Phenomenology of Spirit*. It is not an account, in the abstract, of how Spirit progresses to complete self-knowledge; it deals with historical events and actual societies. Thus it deals with what is already familiar to us. It purports to explain these events and societies as manifestations of Spirit, and often uses abstract language when speaking of Spirit, but we can always, if we are at a loss to understand that language, turn to what Hegel says about the Greeks or the Romans or the Germans in the hope of getting his meaning. His arguments in the abstract and his versions of actual events throw light upon one another. Moreover, the form of the *Lectures on the Philosophy of History,* as the title indicates, is more popular; Hegel was concerned to make himself understood by an audience which was not necessarily familiar with his philosophy. The version which we have of the *Lectures* is not even directly from the pen of Hegel and was never revised by him. It was put together after his death mostly from notes taken down by those who listened to him. Hence a certain carelessness in the arguments, and also many gaps. The *Philosophy of History,* though much more readable, is also, when closely studied, much less impressive than either *The Phenomenology of Spirit* or *The Philosophy of Right* – the other two works of special interest to the social and political theorist.

Though the *Phenomenology* is not, properly speaking, a philosophy of history, because it makes no open reference to historical events, it is, as we have seen, largely inspired by historical events, and by actual philosophies, religions and forms of communal life, as they appeared to Hegel. Therefore, if I were to expound the general argument of the *Lectures on the Philosophy of History,* I should inevitably be repeating much that I have already said in discussing the *Phenomenology.* I shall therefore confine myself to matters not treated of in the *Phenomenology* or only lightly touched upon, and which seem to me to raise issues worth discussing. Hegel was a considerably older man when he gave the *Lectures on the Philosophy of History,* and the state of Europe was then very different from what it had been when, at the height of Napoleon's power, he wrote the *Phenomenology.*

The Philosophy of History, if we compare it with the *Phenomenology,* makes it clear how heavily, in his account of progress, Hegel relies on European experience. It also emphasizes the importance of great men, the special qualities and destiny of the Germanic peoples, the superiority of Protestantism over Catholicism, and the defects of liberalism. It reveals, much more obviously than the *Phenomenology,* how selective Hegel's method is: how he takes notice only of what suits his purpose, or else how, where he cannot ignore what does not suit it, he twists it to make it suitable. There is no process of social transformation described in the *Philosophy of History*; we are told how a number of societies are manifestations of different phases of Spirit; how they form different stages in the evolution of mankind. But it is not explained how one type of society gives way to another.

H

1. Hegel's European Bias

We have seen that the *Phenomenology* is an account of progress in the abstract, purporting to show how the self-conscious mind moves necessarily through certain phases until it attains complete self-knowledge and satisfaction. Though the account is abstract, we soon notice, if we consider these phases, that there are historical events and forms corresponding to them. But we perhaps do not notice that the events and forms are nearly all European. Only when he discusses the Unhappy Consciousness[1] and natural religion[2] does Hegel appear to have non-European examples in mind. We know from his earlier writings that he thought of Judaism as an example of self-estranged Spirit, so that the Unhappy Consciousness is Jewish as well as Christian; and it is clear that what Hegel calls natural religion (which is not to be confused with natural religion as philosophers and theologians conceived of it in the seventeenth and eighteenth centuries)[3] is more Asian and Egyptian than European. And yet, though it is almost entirely on European experience that the *Phenomenology* rests, this fact is not brought home to us because the whole argument is so abstract. We are told that natural religion is inferior to aesthetic religion, but we are not told that natural religion is Asiatic and Egyptian while aesthetic religion is Greek. We are told that a certain type of religion is the highest of all, but we are not told that that type is Christianity, and so it is not brought home to us that the highest type of religion flourishes in Europe.

The *Philosophy of History* takes much larger account of non-European experience than the *Phenomenology* does, but, precisely because it makes open reference to actual societies, forms of art, religions and philosophies, it drives home how entirely European are the institutions and attitudes of mind which Hegel believes are necessarily the highest. Spirit attains self-knowledge and satisfaction in Europe. The essence of reality is Mind or Spirit, moving necessarily towards self-knowledge, freedom and satisfaction, which it attains in the civilization that Hegel belongs to. Though Hegel is often ingenious in the distinctions he makes between one oriental culture or religion and another, he treats them all as inferior to Greek civilization. He discusses four worlds or civilizations, the Oriental, the Greek, the Roman, and the German; and though it may be open to question whether he considers the third superior to the second, it is abundantly clear that he regards

---

[1] *The Phenomenology*, Ch. IV, B.III.
[2] Ibid., Ch. VII, A.
[3] They meant by natural religion beliefs about God attested by reason alone and not by revelation, whereas Hegel meant by it the attribution of divine or spiritual qualities to animals or the sun or stars or other natural phenomena.

the first as the lowest and the fourth as the highest. It is the lowest because it is the furthest removed from the realization of freedom, defined as the concordance of the conscientious and rational will of the individual with the laws and customs of his community. In other words, it is the lowest because the furthest from realizing a European ideal. But Hegel cannot admit that it is the lowest merely from the European point of view; he cannot allow that this European ideal is one of several, of which none is intrinsically superior to the others. For that would be to admit that the European ideal is parochial or provincial; whereas he thinks he has proved that it follows from the very nature of mind that it is the highest ideal. But to anyone who cannot accept this proof, the *Philosophy of History* necessarily wears a provincial look; it sets up the standard of one part of mankind to judge all mankind.

It was no novelty, in Hegel's day, for Europeans to treat non-European ways and ideals as inferior to their own. Montesquieu, so much praised for his breadth of mind and freedom from prejudice, was not less convinced than Hegel of European superiority. But Montesquieu merely took that superiority for granted. He never sought to prove that European ideals were the best; he was content to find in climate and geography obstacles in the way of other peoples attaining those ideals or even coming to conceive of them. Indeed, he made excuses for them; he explained why through no fault of their own they could not be like the Europeans. His was the plain, unmetaphysical arrogance of the Frenchman or the Englishman.

2. *World Historical Individuals*

In the *Philosophy of History*, Hegel speaks of World Historical Individuals who are, if I may so put it, chosen vessels of the Spirit. By their actions they help to change accepted institutions and ways of thought; they help to establish new forms which reveal Spirit at a higher level. Hegel sometimes speaks of these great men as if they had a deeper insight than their contemporaries into 'the needs of their times', while at other times he suggests that they need not have this insight but may act from selfish or wicked motives, or be short-sighted. They may fail to achieve what they set out to achieve, and yet, by their actions, though neither they nor their contemporaries know it, they contribute to the progress of Spirit. Hegel speaks of Reason working through them; he speaks of *the cunning of Reason*, which uses men for purposes they know nothing of. Though the chosen vessels of the Spirit are not always worthy vessels, they serve their turn.

What are we to make of all this? What is involved in having a deeper insight into 'the needs of the time'? This is not, I think, an empty phrase; some men do have a deeper insight than others into the needs of their time. Some, like Socrates, see further than was seen before them into human nature or into the condition of man in society, and propose remedies for human ills. They are the wisest men of all, they have the deepest insight. Others, like Luther, without perhaps seeing much further than their neighbours into man and his social predicament, make claims never made before, or never at so opportune a moment. They too are wise, though in a lesser degree; they too can plausibly be said to have a deeper insight into the needs of their times, for they have judgement enough to see that the claims they make will receive wide support. They have a sense of what is troubling men and what claims will find a response.

Men can have this wisdom or deeper insight, in the higher as much as in the lower degree, without in the least seeing how their wisdom contributes to the realization of freedom. If, then, we believe that freedom, as Hegel conceived of it, is desirable, and that their wisdom has in fact contributed to its achievement, we call them agents of progress. Yet, when we do so, we give them a title they never aspired to, and which perhaps would have been meaningless to them; for they did not understand, as we do, the historical significance of their wisdom. Indeed, if the Hegelian philosophy is true, it follows that men, until they come near to Hegel's time, cannot understand the historical significance of what they do; for freedom (and whatever comes with it) is fully intelligible only when it is on the point of being achieved. The further men are from its achievement, then (no matter how wise they may be) the less they can understand it. The course of history, which Hegel says is a progress towards freedom, cannot be seen to be so by those involved in it until the process is near to completion.

What of the men who are no wiser than their own generation, who see no further into human nature or the social condition than other men, but who are, nevertheless, called great men? Though they act from ambition and even from worse motives, they too can be agents of progress. Without knowing that they do so, they may set going processes which in fact contribute to the achievement of freedom. Indeed, they may contribute more to it than the men of deeper insight. What is Hegel's attitude to them? They are, he admits, justly condemned by the standards of their time. But this much could also be said of the wise men. By the standards of their time they too are justly condemned, and not the less justly because they have seen a need to change those standards.

Hegel admits that the merely ambitious are justly condemned, and yet seeks also to justify them without troubling to distinguish between them and the truly wise. Now, it does, I think, make sense to say that Socrates, though justly condemned by the standards of his time, was nevertheless justified, because he acted by different standards which those who say he was justified believe to be higher. They do not blame the men who condemned him, but they say that Socrates was right to conform to standards which he believed to be higher and they also say that they share his belief. But the merely ambitious do not conform to standards which both they and Hegel (who seeks to justify them) believe to be higher. Their actions are bad by the standards of their own day and by Hegel's standards, and they have no standards of their own which they sincerely believe to be higher than the standards that condemn them. It makes no sense to say of them that they are justified. Even in the community which is truly free, in Hegel's sense of freedom, such actions as theirs are condemned. Of Socrates it could be said that he asserted principles which a later age accepted though his own age rejected them; and this, to the believer in progress, is a justification of Socrates. But Socrates is justified, not because by his actions he helped (though he did not know it) bring about something good, but because his actions were right by standards which were already his and which those who justify him accept.

If great men who are ambitious or wicked can be justified merely because the unforeseen consequences of their actions are good, then so too can little men. If thousands of petty criminals by their crimes produce unintended good, they are as much justified as the great criminal. This is a conclusion we cannot avoid if we accept justification in the peculiar sense of Hegel. Yet I feel sure that Hegel would never have accepted it. He aspired to greatness and sympathized with the great, even in their crimes. He took it for granted that all important change, especially change for the good, is due to the initiative of great men, or rather (and this for him comes to the same thing) of men who have made a great name for themselves; it did not occur to him that it may just as often be due to the actions of large numbers of little men with no great man among them to move them to action.[1]

3. The German World

By the German world Hegel means the civilization which emerged in the West after the spread of Christianity and the invasions of the Roman Empire by the barbarians. Thus the German world includes Italy, Spain and France. The peoples belonging to it are of mixed origin, as Hegel well knew, and it might therefore seem that there is no

---

[1] Professor Berlin suggests that I have not allowed enough for Hegel's idea of great men as artists who ' understand the material they work in ', the situation they dominate and affect, though they may not be able to describe it. Having genius, they are better instruments of Reason than are masses of lesser men.

racial or national pride behind his use of the word German in this context. Perhaps he calls the fourth of his civilizations *German* merely because it resulted from the invasion of the Roman Empire by German tribes; perhaps he uses the word merely to refer to a type of society or culture. He could hardly call it Christian, for the Slavs are not less Christian than the West Europeans, and yet do not belong to this fourth civilization; and he may not have wanted to call it simply Western because the Roman Empire, his third civilization, was also in large part western.

I would not deny that this is one reason why Hegel speaks of a German world. But it is not the only reason. He also attributes to the Germans a special quality, which he calls *Gemüth*, and which he clearly thinks of as an inborn quality of the German people, the *Volk*, and not as a quality acquired by men who belong to a certain kind of civilization, no matter what their racial origin. *Gemüth* or heart is, in his eyes, a racial characteristic. Again, he speaks of the 'time-honoured sincerity' of the Germans. He says that they need Christianity to discipline them but also suggests that they are somehow destined by their inborn qualities to raise Christianity to its highest level. Protestantism is, he thinks, German, and is also a higher form of Christianity than Catholicism.

Within the German World Hegel distinguishes the pure German peoples (the Germans, the Scandinavians, the Dutch, and the English) from the Romanic peoples (the French, the Italians, and the Spaniards), and claims for them that, having achieved in Protestantism a deeper sense of freedom than the Romanic peoples, they do not need to make a revolution of the kind made by the French in 1789.

Hegel has been criticized for his nationalism and racialism, in my opinion too harshly. Nationalism takes with him a comparatively harmless form, and if other writers later twisted his doctrines to suit their purposes, he is not to blame. But we ought to notice that the considerable traces of nationalism and racialism to be found in Hegel's writings are in no way logically connected with his philosophy. The notion of Spirit making itself actual in world history does not entail that pure peoples are any better adapted than mixed peoples to achieving higher forms of Spirit. For the purposes of Hegel's theory, the *Volk*, whether it constitutes one or several political communities, does not need to be pure. Hegel admits that the ancient Greeks, whom he greatly admires, were of mixed origins, and yet he treats them as one people. If the Greeks did not attain the highest levels of Spirit, this was due to their place in history, coming before the Germans, and not to their mixed origins. Not until he comes to consider the German World does Hegel feel the need to prefer pure peoples to mixed ones. It was a need still unexpressed (and perhaps unfelt) when Napoleon was at the height of his power and Hegel was writing the *Phenomenology*;

it comes to the fore only with the German revolt against Napoleon and the defeat of the French. As a show of feeling it is neither un-natural nor contemptible; it is merely out of place in a philosophy of history of the Hegelian kind.

It seems never to have occurred to Hegel that the German-speaking peoples were as much Catholic as Protestant, and that the Catholics among them were not less German than the others. Indeed, it is in the most stoutly Protestant parts of Germany, in Saxony, Brandenburg, Pomerania and East Prussia, that the admixture of Slav blood is the greatest. It is also odd to call the English a pure German people, seeing how much they are Celtic as well as German by racial origins; and the Welsh and the Scots are even more so, and yet are more fiercely Protestant than the English.

4. Hegel's Protestant Bias

I would not quarrel with Hegel for preferring Protestantism to Catholi-cism. That is his own affair. But some of the grounds of this preference seem to me mistaken.

It is the special merit of Luther, Hegel tells us, that he first clearly put forward the claim to freedom implicit in the notion of conscience, the claim that a man must be inwardly convinced of the rightness and truth of the rules and doctrines he accepts. The priesthood of all believers is, he thinks, a doctrine of freedom, and it is clearly Protestant rather than Catholic. Since Spirit in its maturity is free, Protestantism is a higher form of Spirit than Catholicism; it put the honest convic-tion of the believer in the place of external authority.

To this argument there are two objections. In the first place, Luther did not understand the full implications of his own doctrine, because in practice he denied anyone's right to read into Holy Scripture what he (Luther) said was not there. He allowed some room for honest differences of opinion but took it upon himself to set the limits to that room. Secondly, the Catholic Church also expects its adherents to be honestly convinced of its authority; it puts a value on inward convic-tion and not on mere obedience and outward conformity from no matter what motive. It offers reasons for accepting its authority. If it is true that it matters what men believe, and not merely that their beliefs should be sincere; if it is true (as Luther did not deny) that there is a truth necessary to salvation, then it is reasonable to suppose that God established an authority on earth to ensure that this truth was brought to men.

The first of these objections is less important than the second. Hegel was very willing to admit that the full implications of an epoch-making doctrine are not understood by the persons who first put it forward.

It is true that Luther would not in practice, in spite of his proclaiming the priesthood of all believers, agree that no one must be molested for the way in which he interprets Holy Scripture, and that he rejected, even more harshly, the plea that anyone has the right to deny the Scriptures as untrue or irrelevant. Yet the claim, that every Christian (that is, everyone who honestly believes that the Scriptures reveal the Will of God) is entitled to interpret the Scriptures, was epoch-making and did, in the long run, make for freedom.

The second objection is more serious. In practice, Catholic priests may often be content with mere obedience and outward conformity among their flock; but as much could be said of Protestant pastors. Catholics do not hold that anyone who is received into their Church, no matter what his motive, will be saved provided he is obedient; they hold, as much as Protestants do, that only sincere belief is acceptable to God. If Hegel had been more anxious to be fair as between Protestantism and Catholicism, he might have noticed that, though the doctrine of the priesthood of all believers has the seeds of freedom in it, the Protestant doctrine of grace (whether Lutheran or Calvinist) is more illiberal than the Catholic. The doctrine that a man must deserve grace in order to get it is nearer being Catholic than Protestant. The orthodox Lutheran (not to speak of the Calvinist), if we compare him with the Catholic, is much nearer believing that whether a Christian has the faith necessary to salvation depends entirely on whether he receives the grace of God and not on how he exercises his freedom of choice.

Hegel considered both the separation of Church and State and the division, within the Church, of priests from laymen as necessary stages in the evolution of Spirit. If certain feelings and ideas which men have about themselves are to reach full maturity, there must be a Church separate from the State. The Christian idea of man is deeper and richer, more adequate to the reality, than the Greek or Roman idea, and it needed a Church in order to reach full expression. The separation of the Church from the State serves to preserve and to deepen aspirations which, in the society where there is that separation, cannot yet be realized. The division of the Church into priests and laymen is a mark that men, though they have acknowledged their duty to realize these aspirations (an acknowledgement expressed in the form of a desire to serve God), are still too weak and ignorant to realize them. The aspirations are there, kept alive and enriched by the Church, but there is still lacking the disciplined will and the mature understanding needed to make them come true. In the vision of heaven the Church preserves ideals which mankind are destined to achieve in this world. As Spirit progresses, or (and this for Hegel is the same thing) as its capacity to seek and find satisfaction in this world increases, both these divisions, that of the Church from the State and that of priests from laymen, become less marked. The State achieves the possible while the Church aspires towards the ideal, and as the ideal becomes possible the separation of Church and State loses its importance. In Protestant countries the separation of Church and State and the division between priests and laymen are of less account than in Catholic countries, and this, for Hegel, is a mark of Protestant superiority.

Hegel says that in the Catholic Church the priest is a mediator between the layman and God, and he even speaks as if he believed that the lay Catholic does not venture to communicate directly with God but only indirectly through the priest. Did he really believe that Catholic priests discourage prayer? Or that lay Catholics pray only to the saints and not to God? Hegel knew that the Lutheran pastor, when he administers the sacraments or gives spiritual guidance, endeavours to bring the faithful closer to God and not to stand as a screen between them. Why then should he suppose that the Catholic priest acts with a different intention? In all this I see much prejudice and little reason.

Except for the doctrine of the priesthood of all believers, I see nothing about Protestantism, in either its Lutheran or Calvinist form, which accords better than Catholicism does with Hegel's conception of freedom.[1] The Protestant doctrine of grace, especially in its Calvinist form, accords with it less well; and what could be less Hegelian in spirit than Luther's doctrine of justification by faith? No one more than Hegel believed that a man is justified by his works, that it matters more what he does than what he claims, however sincerely, to believe. It is indeed a Hegelian principle that the real quality of a man's faith is revealed only in his works.

5. His Dislike of Democracy

Hegel regarded himself as the philosopher of freedom. The world, he said, is essentially Spirit, and Spirit is essentially free. Yet he was not attracted to liberalism or to democracy. Why was this so?

Freedom, as he conceived it, is realized in a community where what law and custom prescribe accords with the dictates of the individual conscience; or, in other words, where the individual can live as he sincerely believes that he ought to live. Now, this conception of freedom is very much the same as Rousseau's; it is implicit in the doctrine of the general will. Rousseau believed that freedom can be realized only in a community all of whose members take part in making the law. Hegel disagreed with him, but the grounds of his disagreement are not made altogether clear.

[1] No doubt, some of the sects preached doctrines more libertarian than either Lutheranism or Calvinism, but Hegel says nothing of them.

That a democratic society *may not* realize freedom, in Hegel's sense
of it, is obvious; and yet it may be that freedom in his sense can
be realized fully only in a democracy. Hegel considers the first possibility and not the second; he sees the dangers of democracy but not
its opportunities. In the *Philosophy of History* he does not so much
argue against democracy as exhibit his distaste for it. He says that
the 'abstract' French doctrine of the rights of man is too 'individualistic', treating men too much as atoms. He objects to what he calls
'the atomistic principle, which insists on the sway of individual wills,
maintaining that all government should emanate from their express
power, and have their express sanction'. Liberalism (by which he
means partiality for the abstract doctrine of the rights of man) has, he
thinks, a special appeal in Catholic countries, where it is a weapon
against the Church, but elsewhere it is going 'bankrupt'.

This line of criticism, which is common to Hegel and Burke, seems
to me irrelevant. What is the point of calling the doctrine of the rights
of man 'abstract' and 'atomistic'? Any doctrine which attributes
rights to individuals is, in a quite obvious sense, 'atomistic'; it is a
doctrine about individuals, about the 'atoms' which compose the
social whole, and not about groups or communities or institutions. To
call it atomistic or individualistic, in this sense, is merely to define it;
it is not to make a criticism of it. The doctrine that all sane adults
should have the vote is no more 'atomistic' than the doctrine that
nobody with less than £1,000 a year should have it. It is also no more
and no less abstract, for it makes a claim for individuals considered
apart from the actual situations in which they are placed.

Hegel's criticism of the doctrine of the rights of man ceases to be
pointless only if it is interpreted as meaning that those who assert
the doctrine are unaware of the difficulties in the way of putting it
into effect, or else do not see that the rights they claim for all men
would, if all men had them, prevent their getting the freedom they
strive for or ought to strive for or will come eventually to desire. But,
as a matter of fact, many liberals were well aware of these difficulties,
and differed from Hegel only in believing that they could be surmounted. There is nothing atomistic or abstract about this belief; it
may be mistaken or it may not. Hegel produces no arguments to
show that it is mistaken. A liberal or a democrat might accept the
Hegelian conception of freedom (and even the metaphysics associated
with it) and might then insist that freedom, thus conceived, cannot
be achieved unless the rights of man are made good.

He might insist with a good show of reason. Freedom, as Hegel conceives of it, is not habitual obedience to law and custom; it is a conscientious and critical acceptance of them. It could plausibly be
argued, as Rousseau tried to argue, that this kind of acceptance is
possible only in a democracy. Hegel produces no arguments that

could be used to prove Rousseau wrong; at least, he produces none in the *Philosophy of History*. Hegel's condemnation of democracy rests on the same line of false reasoning as Burke's. The democrats assert that democracy is a condition of freedom. Burke and Hegel reply that where there is democracy, freedom is faced with peculiar and great dangers. Their reply, as a warning to democrats, is timely; but as a condemnation of democracy it is pointless unless it is shown that the dangers are insurmountable.

6. Stagnation and Progress

We have seen that, in Hegel's opinion, progress is necessary: Spirit is essentially active, and moves necessarily from phase to phase until it reaches full self-knowledge and satisfaction. Why, then, we may ask, should some peoples (e.g., the Oriental peoples) be unprogressive? Why should they be confined to expressing Spirit only in its less developed forms? They are not late-comers on the stage of history. On the contrary, they are the first peoples to be civilized. The march of progress, as Hegel imagines it, is a kind of relay race, with some peoples taking up where others have left off. The idea that it is one may perhaps be true, or partly true, but it certainly does not accord with Hegel's belief that progress is a necessary and dialectical process.

The various forms, psychological, social, and ideological, in which Spirit is manifest, develop – so Hegel would have us believe – contradictions of which Spirit eventually becomes conscious and therefore surmounts, thus moving inevitably from phase to phase. These forms and contradictions, and the consciousness of them, exist only in and through finite rational minds; or, in other words, in and through men. We should therefore expect every people to move necessarily from one phase of Spirit to another. We should expect a people to progress as long as it continues in existence; for while it exists it is involved in the life of the Spirit, which is necessarily progressive. We should not expect it to go so far and no further. We should not expect it to stagnate.

And why, if it does stagnate, should some other people carry on from the point where it left off? Each phase, we are told, develops out of the phase before it, and we are also told that each phase is manifest in the life of a community of rational beings. How, then, if one phase is manifest in one community can the next phase be manifest in another, which has not even passed through the earlier phase? Or, if we concede that this is possible, how can we say that one phase develops necessarily out of another? Let us suppose that men, if they reach a certain pitch of anger, necessarily resort to violence. That being so, if James reaches that pitch of anger, it is he who is necessarily violent, and not John.

It might be said, in defence of Hegel, that one people or community can assimilate the experience of another. It might be said that the Romans assimilated the experience of the Greeks and even (though less plausibly) that the 'Germans' assimilated the experience of the Greeks and the Romans. But it can hardly be said that the Greeks assimilated the experience of the Oriental peoples, who all, so Hegel tells us, manifest phases of Spirit prior to the Greek phase. No doubt, the Greeks were stimulated by their contacts with the Egyptians and with the peoples of Asia Minor; but it is a far cry from this kind of stimulation to the assimilation needed to save Hegel's theory. The Greeks never absorbed the cultures of the East, and Hegel does not even pretend that they did. The Oriental peoples lived through certain phases of Spirit, and the ancient Greeks lived through certain other and higher phases. It was necessary that the lower Oriental phases should come first, and that the higher Greek phases should emerge out of them, but it was apparently not necessary that the Greeks should absorb the cultures of the Orient; it was enough that they should be stimulated by them. This I find unacceptable. I do not doubt for a moment that there are unexplained mysteries in the real world. But there ought to be none in the world as Hegel explains it; for it is his belief that the world, which is the progress of Spirit, is not only intelligible in principle but is also in fact understood – by Hegel and by those who understand him.

Whatever our idea of progress, we can always find some peoples who cease to make progress, who stagnate. We may also, if we study the available facts carefully, be able to discover the causes of the stagnation. We may do this even if we accept Hegel's idea of freedom, and therefore believe that anything makes for progress which helps to achieve that idea. There must be reasons why the Oriental peoples ceased to make what Hegel called progress; but these reasons, if we could discover them, would be evidence against the truth of Hegel's philosophy of history, for they would show how a certain phase of Spirit failed to give rise to the phase which, according to Hegel, necessarily comes after it. Again, there must be reasons why the Greeks reached what in the Hegelian scale is a higher phase of Spirit than the Orientals without needing to assimilate Oriental culture, and these reasons, too, if we could find them, would be evidence against Hegel's theory.

Hegel's philosophy of history differs in one important respect from Marx's. There is, Hegel tells us, a necessary course of development of Spirit. He describes this course, abstractly and without open reference to particular events, in the *Phenomenology of Spirit*. In the *Philosophy of History*, he gives concrete examples of Spirit in various phases of its progress; he discusses these phases in what he believes to be their logical and necessary order. But even in the *Philosophy of History* he makes not the least attempt to show how a society in one of these phases passes into the next; he never describes a process of *social transformation*. All that he does is give us a series of tableaux; and this is as true when he is speaking of European as of Oriental civilizations. He presents the Greek world to us as a manifestation of Spirit at one level, and he shows what was still lacking to Spirit at that level. He then presents the Roman world to us, showing how it differed from the Greek. Finally, he presents to us the German world, explaining it as the fullest and deepest manifestation of Spirit. It is true that he shows us (or at least attempts to show us) that the German world has absorbed and transcended the Greek and Roman worlds. But he never attempts to show how the Greek world was transformed into the Roman world, or how the ancient world was transformed into the modern. Spirit necessarily attains full self-knowledge and satisfaction, and in order to attain them must pass through certain phases. First there is one phase, and then the next, and then the next, and so on to the full flowering of Spirit. We are told that it must be so, because such is the nature of Spirit, and the world is not intelligible unless it is Spirit, and the world is intelligible and therefore is Spirit. Yet there is nothing about any phase, as Hegel describes it, which explains why the next *must* come after it; we only know that it must because the full maturity of Spirit, which is inevitable, requires that it should. But this explanation is absurd, for unless each phase leads necessarily to the next, the full maturity of Spirit is not inevitable.

Whatever the shortcomings of Marx's philosophy of history, he at least does not confine himself to presenting us with a series of tableaux, each an image of something higher than the one before it. He describes a process of social transformation, and tries to explain how it happens, how one phase of it gives way to the next.

Chapter 4

THE SOCIAL AND POLITICAL PHILOSOPHY OF HEGEL

II

IV. HEGEL'S THEORY OF THE STATE

A. *General Observations*

1. Why Man Needs Freedom

Spirit, Hegel tells us, is made actual in communities of finite rational minds. As we have seen already, it does not follow from this that Spirit is a mind in the same sense as Socrates or Luther was one. Yet what does follow from it is, for reasons which I tried to give earlier, unacceptable; it entails taking literally what only makes sense when taken metaphorically. The State, says Hegel, is the highest type of community in which Spirit is made actual, and Spirit is made actual necessarily. Spirit is essentially free.

If we take all this metaphorically, forgoing resolutely (or with reluctance) the deeper wisdom which it may contain for those who find it possible to take it literally, what can we make of it? We must, I think, interpret Hegel's meaning thus: Since man is a rational and self-conscious creature capable of deliberate choice, he puts a supreme value on freedom, which he can get only in the State. This is not the whole Hegelian doctrine of the State, even when that doctrine is taken metaphorically, but it is fundamental to it. Put thus succinctly, it is not self-explanatory; it calls for elucidation and elaboration.

2. Society an Unintended Product of Human Action

Hegel also says that the State is *objective will*, and he calls freedom, which is realized in the State, *the will that wills itself*. These expressions could mislead us into believing that Hegel thought that man has created the State in order to get or to preserve freedom. But, as we have seen in studying the *Phenomenology*, this is not so. Hegel believes that man does not even fully understand freedom until the process which brings it about is almost complete. According to Hegel, it is only as members of a community, as creatures belonging to a moral and political order, that men come to conceive of freedom and to desire it. Though he speaks of Spirit creating the world in which it is made actual, and also speaks of it as existing only in and through finite minds, he does not think of these finite minds as deliberately creating the world. On the contrary, the world, in so far as it is produced by finite minds, is the *unintended* product of their activities.

We are not, for the moment, interested in the world but in society, which is only a part of the world. We may then say that, in Hegel's opinion, society is the unintended product of men's activities. If men had not the potentialities they do have, there could be no society, but equally, if it were not for society, men would not realize their potentialities. By their activities they produce their social environment, and, in the process of doing so, they transform themselves, becoming rational and purposeful creatures capable of deliberately pursuing, within a social order, what they have come to believe is desirable. That Hegel calls this process logical makes no difference here; for by calling it so he does not mean to imply that men have deliberately produced society in order to get what they want.

The contemporary sociologist, while rejecting or ignoring Hegelian metaphysics and the claim that social evolution is a logically necessary process, might accept Hegel's account of how man produces society and what society does for him. He might agree that primitive society is the undeliberate, unforeseen, and not-understood product of human activities, and that men acquire, in the process of being formed by society, the purposes and the knowledge, theoretical and practical, which make rational and moral creatures of them. It is only then that men, educated in society, can form projects to change society.

The sociologist's main objection to Hegel might be that he speaks too often of the State where he ought to speak of society. It is not the same thing to say that man becomes rational, moral and freedom-loving in the State as to say that he becomes so in society. Hegel's doctrine of the State is open to serious criticism. But it is not open to the criticism that he looks upon the State as a product of human will, or that he thinks of it as existing to provide for needs or appetites which men could have outside society.

3. Morality and Freedom

Hegel, as we have seen, makes much of man's self-consciousness and of his rationality. These two qualities are, he thinks, closely connected; only a creature capable of abstraction and comparison, capable of using concepts, can distinguish between itself and what is external to itself, including other selves. It can also distinguish between itself as a subject of thoughts and desires and the thoughts and desires of which it is a subject. Because it is conscious of itself as a subject of desires, it is led inevitably to seek an end which is more than the satisfaction of one desire after another. For it soon discovers that all its desires cannot be satisfied, and that some must be sacrificed to others. It learns to think ahead, to compare its desires, to consider the chances of satisfying them and the consequences of attempting to satisfy them. Nor can the self stop at establishing a system of preferences among its desires; for it is aware that there are other beings besides itself whose needs and actions it must take into account. It must adapt itself to other selves; it must adapt itself to a community of selves. If this adaptation took the form of mere prudence, with everyone trying to get for himself whatever he could safely or conveniently get, every man would think of other men as standing in the way of his getting more. Man can be fully satisfied, completely free, in a community only when what he wants is compatible with what other people want. But this, in practice, involves more than just learning to do without what he cannot get; it involves more than just putting up with rules which restrict his actions for the sake of others and their actions for his sake; it involves more than the sense of getting as good terms from others as he can in the circumstances reasonably expect to get. It involves accepting the rules inwardly, it involves desiring the public good and the moral order for their own sakes. The man who respects the rules with nothing in view other than his own advantage acts, as Hobbes said, reasonably. But reasonable though he may be, he is not truly satisfied; for he gets, not *all* that he wants, but as much as he can safely and conveniently have. If he could get everything that he wanted, he would be better satisfied, or he imagines that he would be; he reconciles himself to what he can get only because he cannot reasonably expect to get more.

But if he accepts the rules inwardly, if he desires justice, if he wants to be a good neighbour and a good citizen, then he may be fully satisfied. For then he is not reasonable and just merely for the sake of satisfying as many as possible of his desires; he actually desires to be reasonable and just. He seeks satisfaction in a way of life which is capable of giving complete satisfaction. In practice it may be difficult to get this satisfaction, but in principle it is possible. A community of completely selfish persons, no matter how reasonable they were, could not be fully satisfied; but a community of moral persons, provided they were reasonable, could be. Now, for Hegel, to be fully satisfied is the mark of freedom. Man is fully satisfied when he knows what he wants, endeavours rationally to obtain it, and succeeds. But man cannot be free in society unless he desires to be just and his conception of justice accords with the established order; and again, he cannot be free unless he desires justice as much as ends private to himself, and unless those ends accord with his notion of justice. Yet again, man cannot be free outside society, for it is in society that he acquires purposes which he can rationally pursue; and it is also in society that he comes to conceive of freedom and to desire it.

Hegel says, in the *Philosophy of Right*, 'if we hear it said that the definition of freedom is the ability to do what we please, such an idea can only be taken to reveal an utter immaturity of thought, for it contains not even an inkling of right, ethical life, and so forth';[1] and he also says that 'it is only as thinking intelligence that the will is genuinely a will and free'.[2] Freedom is the ability to do what we deliberately choose to do, and is conceivable only to creatures who live in a moral order. And they cannot attain freedom until that order is one that seems good to them, desirable for its own sake and not only as a means to their private ends.

4. Morality and Rationality

Actually, Hegel is not content to say that man, if he is to get full satisfaction, cannot stop at establishing an order of preferences among his desires; he says also that it is only as a moral person that he can establish such an order rationally. To the extent that man is moved only by impulses and appetites, he has what Hegel calls an arbitrary will. We are told that 'the contradiction which the arbitrary will is, appears as a dialectic of impulses and inclinations; each of them is in the way of every other – the satisfaction of one is unavoidably . . . sacrificed to the satisfaction of another. An impulse has no measuring rod in itself, and so this determination of its . . . sacrifice is the contingent decision of the arbitrary will.'[3] In other words, it is not a rational decision. Only after a man has become a moral being, after he has acquired some values, can he rationally prefer some of his impulses to others.

Hegel therefore thinks himself entitled to conclude that only a rational (which is for him also a moral) will is free. The arbitrary will, wanting incompatible things, is necessarily frustrated time and again. The rational will, which does not seek the satisfaction of one impulse after another but seeks rather to live up to a self-consistent set of standards, need not be frustrated. It will be free if its standards accord with the laws and conventions of society. But a rational will does not emerge in the privacy of an individual mind unconnected with other minds; it is the product of a life lived in society. There is therefore for Hegel (as there was for Plato and Rousseau) always a close connection between the rationality of the individual will and the rationality of the social and political order. The individual can have a coherent and

[1] *Philosophy of Right*, translated by T. M. Knox, p. 27, para 15.
[2] Ibid., p. 30, para 31.
[3] Ibid., p. 28, §17.

viable system of ambitions and principles only where social and political conditions are favourable.

Bentham would not have been much impressed by Hegel's criticism of the arbitrary will. We can imagine him putting this question to Hegel: 'What is the point of your assertion that an impulse has no measuring rod in itself? Do you mean that a man cannot know that one of his impulses is stronger than another or that he cannot weigh the consequences of indulging them and then decide to indulge one rather than the other on the ground that, in the long run, he will get greater satisfaction by doing so? But we know from experience that a man can do this. If, then, he does it, he acts rationally.'

No doubt, Bentham is right. It is often possible to prefer one impulse to another on this ground, and such a preference would be rational, as that word is ordinarily understood. Hegel does not deny that this kind of preference is possible. He admits that the arbitrary will 'may proceed either by using intelligence to calculate which impulse will give most satisfaction or else in accordance with any other optional consideration'.[1] He does not make it clear how far he thinks it possible to choose between impulses by making calculations of this kind, and he also speaks of these choices, where they can be made, as acts of 'the arbitrary will'. Whether he really means to deny that they are rational choices, even though he admits that they are intelligent, I do not know. This part of his argument is by no means clear. But, despite its obscurity, it looks very much as if Hegel were denying that we can establish a hierarchy among our impulses merely by calculating how much satisfaction they are likely to bring; that he is denying one of the assumptions on which the Utilitarian philosophy rests, the assumption that we can, by considering the pleasures and pains likely to result from indulging our impulses, formulate rules enabling us always to choose rationally between them.

If this is part of what Hegel means when he contrasts the arbitrary with the rational will (and I do not see how it can be denied that it is), it would seem that he is right and that Bentham is wrong. More often than not, if to maximize pleasure and to minimize pain are our sole objects, we have no rational ground for preferring one impulse or appetite to another because, more often than not, we could not make the calculations needed to achieve our object, even if we were omniscient. Hegel, though he puts his point obscurely, is (if I have not misunderstood him) nearer being right than Bentham; it is as a creature who accepts certain norms which cannot be derived from a comparison of the satisfactions to be obtained from indulging his desires that man acquires a rational order of preferences among those desires. It is nearer the truth to say, with Hegel and the other Idealists, that man has a rational order of preferences because he has moral principles than to

[1] Ibid., p. 28, §17.

say, with Bentham and the Utilitarians, that it is because he has such a rational order that he acquires moral principles. The Utilitarians might agree with Hegel that it is in society that man comes to have moral principles, and perhaps also that it is as a creature having a rational order of preferences that man comes to desire freedom, but they necessarily part company with him when he says that the will which is not moral is arbitrary, and that the arbitrary will is not free; for if he is right in saying so, Utilitarianism cannot stand.

I have said that Hegel is nearer being right than Bentham. Yet he is not entirely right. When he says that only the rational and moral will is free, he means to assert more than is acceptable. If by a moral creature we mean a creature capable of deliberate choice and of making value-judgements, we can say that only a creature who is moral in this sense conceives of freedom and desires it. This, very probably, was part of what Hegel was saying; but he was also saying more, and more than is true. He was also saying that man is free only when he desires and is able to do what he ought to do. He was implying that a wicked man is not free; which is to imply more than that only a creature who is moral in the sense defined above conceives of freedom and desires it.

No doubt, if man is to have freedom, as Hegel understands it, if he is to be able to live up to his own principles, those principles must be consistent with one another and also viable or practicable. It is irrational to adhere to principles which are not consistent with one another, and irrational also to seek to apply them where, though they are mutually consistent, they cannot in fact be applied. Therefore, we may say that, if man is fully to achieve freedom, he must have a rational will. Unless he has it, he will be frustrated both by his own actions and other people's. But it does not follow, when a man does act in a way which is inconsistent with his own principles, that that particular action is not free. The action itself may be free though it has consequences frustrating to the doer of it. Insofar as we do not live merely from hand to mouth, insofar as we have principles and wish to be true to them, we cannot live as we want to live unless we have what Hegel calls a rational will; and if we cannot live as we want to, we are not free. This makes good enough sense, but we must not make false inferences from it; we must not speak as if, because man by his own action can diminish his freedom, the action whereby he diminishes it is not free.

We must make distinctions which Hegel and the Idealists do not make; we must distinguish what constitutes a free action from what makes freedom desirable or attainable. Unless men had values by reference to which they could prefer some of their appetites or impulses to others, they could have no enduring ambitions and aspirations, and unless they had them, they would not care for freedom as they do.

These values emerge in social intercourse and are not utilitarian; they are not accepted because men have estimated (however roughly) the satisfactions to be derived from indulging their various impulses. And a man who has come to value freedom cannot fully attain it unless his ambitions are compatible with one another, which they will not be unless he has what Hegel calls a rational will and that will accords with what he calls the universal will. We may accept all this, and yet deny that a man does not act freely when he acts wickedly or when the principle from which he acts does not form part of a coherent set of principles.

We may also insist that though it is as a creature engaged in social intercourse that man becomes moral, his principles may be perfectly consistent with one another and yet be inconsistent with established laws and conventions, with the universal will. He will then not be free, for he will be required to conform to rules which he does not accept. Yet he may be entirely rational. No doubt, it would be irrational of him to seek to apply his own principles regardless of the consequences, to behave as if the social order were already what he thinks it ought to be. But it would not be irrational of him to seek to reform that order.

Hegel, presumably, does not believe that the laws and conventions of a community always form a consistent and viable system, for he admits that some communities are higher (and therefore more rational) than others. He even admits that a man who challenges authority (e.g. Socrates) may be more rational than the authority he challenges. But he does seem to take it for granted that the individual's will cannot be fully rational except where there is a fully rational universal will. That is to say, though he does not hold that the individual, to be fully rational, must conform to law and convention, no matter what they are, he does assume that there must be a self-consistent and viable legal and moral system if the individual is to be fully rational. I can see no reason why this should be so.

Hegel also takes it for granted that there is constant progress towards full rationality and towards harmony between the rational will of the individual and the universal will. He does not allow that there could be several legal and moral systems, several universal wills, very different from one another, and yet each as self-consistent and viable as any of the others; nor does he allow that there could be widely different types of individual will, all of them equally rational. For example, he does not allow that the universal will manifest in the Greek city-state or the moral will of the citizen in such a state could be as fully rational as the universal will manifest in the modern state or the moral will of the modern citizen. He cannot allow it without undermining his conception of World History as the necessary progress of Spirit towards complete self-knowledge and rationality. But, though he cannot allow it, it may well be true.

5. Rationality and Law

According to Hegel, there is always a close connection between the individual's rational will (his principles and aspirations insofar as they form a coherent and viable system) and the universal will, the laws and conventions of his community. These laws and conventions are the fruits of the experience of many generations of men who have sought to achieve their purposes and who have had to adjust those purposes to one another, to the purposes of other men, and to the means at their disposal. The individual acquires a rational will in the process of learning to take his place in a social order; or, in other words, he acquires it by partaking in the life of a community having a universal will or system of laws and conventions which give it its distinctive character. Since Hegel conceives of a very close connection between the individual's rational will and the social order within which he acquires that will, he finds it easy to say of a man's rational will that it is the universal will manifest in him. And his metaphysical system, his conception of reality as universal Spirit or Mind manifest, at its higher levels, in the rational activities of communities of finite selves, seems to him to justify this manner of speaking.

Now, if we reject the Hegelian metaphysic, we have to say that this way of speaking, taken literally, does not make sense. We have to deny the identity of the universal will, embodied in law and convention, with the rational will of the individual. But we can take what Hegel says metaphorically, and it then becomes a theory about the conditions, psychological, social, and moral, of desiring freedom and attaining it. This theory may not be wholly true; but whatever the measure of truth in it, it is intelligible and ingenious. It is a theory worth study and deserving respect. Moreover, it is not a theory read into Hegel's words and one which it was never his intention to assert. It was his intention to assert it. That it was also his intention to assert more than this does not make it any the less his intention to assert this as well. When we take Hegel metaphorically and refuse to take him literally, we do not part company with him, while pretending not to do so. We are still dealing with Hegelian theory, though with only a part of it; and if we concentrate on this part to the neglect of the other, it is because the other part means nothing to us.

Hegel says that will is *essentially* free, and that his purpose, in *The Philosophy of Right*, is to show how the concept of will is necessarily realized in a community of free persons. His purpose is to explain what he calls 'the proper immanent development' of the will from concept to Idea; the Idea of a concept being that in which it is most fully realized. Hegel believes that it follows logically from the concept of will that it must be realized in communities of free persons. If we take this quite literally, we can hardly make sense of it. The concept of will is presumably the concept of deliberate choice, which involves the use of reason. It would seem that wherever there are creatures making deliberate choices, the concept of will is *realized*. What is the realization of a concept except its application to actual things or events? It is realized whenever there is anything real to which it applies. The concept of will is as much, as completely, realized in a prison as in a community of free persons. We must therefore suppose that Hegel is using the term *realized* in some different sense. The concept of will is not realized, in his sense of realization, wherever there is a genuine instance of deliberate choice; it is realized only when creatures capable of deliberate choice constitute a community of free persons. But realization, understood in this way, is clearly not *necessary*; it does not in the least follow from there being creatures capable of deliberate choice that there must eventually be a community of free persons. Admittedly, only creatures capable of deliberate choice could form such a community or could want to form it; but that does not allow us to say that they must eventually form it or even that they must come to desire it.

This doctrine, that the concept of will is eventually realized in the State, or the community of free persons, is another example of something we have come across before: the deliberate running together of different ideas or sets of ideas. In this case the ideas run together are that of a concept and what it applies to, and that of the less and more developed. It would be misleading to call this a confusion of thought; it is quite deliberate. Professor Knox, explaining Hegel's purpose, says: ' We are tracing the development of the will from concept to Idea. The start of a process of development is abstract in comparison with its end . . . " immediate ", not yet mediated and made explicit in and through the later states; e.g. a man's character is built up in the course of his life, but it was implicit and undeveloped in his childhood.'[1]

We owe it to Hegel and to his disciples to say that this running together of ideas that most people think are best kept apart is not due to a failure to notice that they are different; it is deliberate and is held to be justified by the Hegelian philosophy taken as a whole. Indeed, it is held to be the key to a deeper insight. We may protest that concepts do not develop into anything but either have or do not have instances; we may boggle at calling childhood the concept of manhood, or a child's will more abstract than a man's. We may protest at applying to concepts categories which apply to things. But we must not suppose that the Hegelians do not know what they are doing. To them our protests seem misplaced, if not philistine, due to a failure to understand the essence of their philosophy, which alone gets to the heart of reality. They are the protests of the superficial who cannot help being what they are.

[1] *Philosophy of Right*, p. 37.

But if nature has condemned us to superficiality, what are we to make of Hegel's theory of the State, of his 'tracing the development of will from concept to Idea'? We can find in that theory a number of assertions about the social and psychological conditions of the capacity for deliberate choice; we can also find the doctrine that creatures having this capacity come easily to conceive of freedom and to attach a supreme value to it, though they can attain it only when certain further conditions, social and moral, hold. No doubt, Hegel speaks as if the conditions of deliberate choice, the coming to conceive of freedom and to desire it, the conditions of attaining it were all implicit in (that is, logically deducible from) the capacity for deliberate choice or the will. This we can firmly reject, and yet hold that his beliefs about the conditions of deliberate choice and the conditions of freedom make excellent sense and may be largely true. They are certainly worth close study.

6. The Duty of Obedience

In justice to Hegel we must notice that his theory of the State is not a doctrine of political obligation. As we shall see later, there is a doctrine of political obligation implicit in his theory of the State, and there is also another doctrine, which is not implicit in that theory but which Hegel puts forward tentatively and almost furtively, as if he wanted, without seeming to do so, to persuade people to accept it. There is, as I shall try to show later, an ambiguous and somewhat repulsive doctrine of political obligation in the *Philosophy of Right*, a doctrine more hinted at than openly propounded, a doctrine not even in keeping with the Hegelian conception of the State. Nevertheless, the *Philosophy of Right* is not, and is not meant to be, a doctrine of political obligation. We have Hegel's own word for it when he says that his 'book, containing as it does the science of the State, is to be nothing other than the endeavour to apprehend and portray the State as something inherently rational. . . . The instruction which it may contain cannot consist in teaching the State what it ought to be; it can only show how the State, the ethical universe, is to be understood.'[1] The books aims neither at teaching the State what it ought to be nor the citizen how he ought to behave. It purports to explain what the State is, which of course involves explaining what it is to be a member of the State. That this explanation, as Hegel conceives of it, also involves explaining what it is to be a rational and moral being does not in itself make it a doctrine of political obligation.

Hegel tells us that man is free only as a member of a community whose laws and conventions he can conscientiously accept. This pur-

[1] Ibid., p. 11.

ports to be a statement of fact; it may or may not be true. Whether or not it is true, it does not imply that a man ought always to accept the laws and conventions of his community; it says only that he cannot be free unless he is able to accept them conscientiously. As we have seen already in discussing the *Phenomenology* and the *Philosophy of History*, and as we shall see once more as we discuss the *Philosophy of Right*, Hegel does not believe that freedom is realized in a community whose members accept its laws and conventions merely from habit. To be able to attain freedom they must accept the established legal and moral order conscientiously, which they can do only when they have reached a certain level of intellectual and moral maturity. Conscientious acceptance of law and convention is possible only in what we might call, using words which Hegel did not use but which seem to convey his meaning, a self-critical and sophisticated community. Hegel admired men like Socrates and Luther who defy authority and thereby help to raise mankind to what, in his opinion, is a higher level. It is clear, then, that Hegel did not believe that the individual ought always to accommodate his principles to the laws and conventions of his community. I think we may say that he believed that the individual, more often than not, is perverse or irrational when he defies authority, that he is blinded by prejudice or self-interest, that he is confused or self-contradictory or does not see clearly the consequences of his principles. He probably believed that men in authority are more often right than the rebels who defy them. This is the impression that most of his readers derive from his books, and from none more than the *Philosophy of Right*. Yet he clearly does not believe that rebels are always wrong. Indeed he cannot believe it and reconcile that belief with his philosophy of history. Hegel is a believer in progress; he holds that some states and civilizations are better than others, and that the better ones supersede the less good. He therefore cannot condemn the men who, by their defiance of authority, help to give currency to better principles. His approval of Socrates and Luther is not fortuitous; it fits in admirably with his doctrine of progress and does not conflict with his conception of the State. Logically, he can condemn all disobedience and non-conformity only in the highest type of State, the State which is in the fullest sense a community of free persons.

Even this condemnation does not follow logically merely from what Hegel says about the nature of freedom and the conditions of attaining it. It follows only if it is assumed that freedom, and therefore also the type of community in which freedom is realized, are good. Hegel, of course, makes this assumption. That is why we can say that the *Philosophy of Right*, though its purpose is not to put forward a doctrine of political obligation, does contain such a doctrine implicitly. Once we accept Hegel's philosophy, it follows that, if freedom is the essence of will, if creatures capable of deliberate choice come necessarily to desire freedom and cannot find complete satisfaction until they attain it, freedom is desirable. Therefore the State, as the ethical universe (or, in other words, as a community of rational beings involved in a system of moral relations with one another) in which freedom is realized, is also desirable. But it is desirable only to the extent that freedom is realized in it or its realization is brought nearer by it.

This is the doctrine of political obligation implicit in Hegel's account of freedom and of the State. But, as I said a while ago, there is also put forward equivocally in the *Philosophy of Right* another doctrine of political obligation, which is repulsive to the liberal as this one is not and which is not in keeping with what Hegel says about freedom and the State. I shall discuss this doctrine later. For the moment, my purpose is only to remove a source of misunderstanding which sometimes leads people to suppose that Hegel's conception of the State commits him logically to assert a duty of complete submission to established authority.

B. Aspects and Forms of
Social Life, Considered Generally

1. The Presentation of the Doctrine

Since Hegel's political philosophy is part of a general philosophy which explains reality as essentially Spiritual, and treats Spirit as a process of development which is necessarily dialectical (every phase in the process generating within itself a tension or contradiction which comes eventually to be resolved and whose resolution constitutes a passage to the next phase), it is presented to us in the form of an explanation of two dialectical triads. The first consists of abstract right, morality and ethical life, and the second of the family, civil society and the State. Abstract right and morality constitute the thesis and antithesis of the first triad; they necessarily go together and yet there is a tension or contradiction between them which is resolved only in ethical life. The family and civil society constitute the thesis and antithesis of the second triad, and Hegel also says of them that they are necessary and yet *contradictory* of one another, the contradiction being resolved in the State. Hegel's dialectical scheme implies that the three moments of the first triad are related to one another in much the same way as the three moments of the second. But this, as we shall see, is far from the truth. Hegel's dialectical scheme, applied to society and the State, is quite artificial. The sense in which there is a contradiction between abstract right and morality is quite different from the sense in which there is one between the family and civil society.

2. Abstract Right and Morality

By abstract right Hegel means the claims which a man makes to assert his individuality; for man, as a rational and purposeful creature, is essentially a bearer of rights. Though it is part of Hegel's philosophy that man becomes rational and purposeful only as a member of a social order, as a partaker in what he calls ethical life, he does not, in the section of the *Philosophy of Right* in which he discusses abstract right, speak about the social order. That is because his purpose is not to explain how man comes to make claims, to assert rights, but rather the significance of his doing so. Therefore, it is only at a later stage of the argument that we see how man, as a bearer of rights, is also necessarily a social being; at this stage of it, what Hegel seeks to bring home to us is that man expresses his awareness of himself as a rational and purposeful creature by the assertion of rights.

By morality Hegel means the feelings and intentions of man, not as a mere creature of appetite, but as a bearer of rights and obligations. He includes in morality what he calls conscience, or the claim of the individual to be allowed to act on principles which he is inwardly convinced are right. But conscience is not all that he means by morality, for morality exists in all societies, just as abstract right does, whereas the claim which Hegel has in mind when he speaks of conscience is not (as he admits) made in all societies.

Clearly, abstract right and morality are aspects and not forms of social life; they are involved in social life and cannot exist apart from it. This Hegel never for a moment denies, even though, in the *Philosophy of Right*, he explains the aspects (or, as an Hegelian might put it, *deduces* them from the concept of will) before he explains the whole of which they are aspects. Yet, this manner of proceeding, though it is required by the type of explanation at which Hegel aims (which moves from the more abstract to the more concrete, from the partial to the complete), can be seriously misleading, as I hope to show.

Abstract right and morality are complementary, and there cannot be the one without the other. Men who have rational purposes and moral sentiments are creatures who make and recognize claims; they are social creatures forming communities, and where there is a community there are more than just uniformities or patterns of behaviour. There are rules which those who conform to them or reject them are aware of and which they choose to obey or to disobey. The making of claims, the assertion of rights, and the moral sentiments are of the essence of social or ethical life.

So far, so good. But Hegel goes further. He is not content, after he has explained abstract right and morality, to show how they are complementary, how they are but two aspects of social life and are inconceivable outside it. He also treats them as contradictory opposites in a dialectical triad. They not only go necessarily together but they are also necessarily *contradictory*. But *contradictory* in just what sense?

The Hegelian concept of *contradiction* is extraordinarily loose. In Hegel's political philosophy, as in his philosophy generally, it is applied to concepts, to states of mind, to distinct but inseparable aspects of a whole, and to different forms of life. Hegel always speaks as if he were using the word *contradiction* in what is, at bottom, the same sense; and indeed his doctrine that reality is a logically necessary dialectical process requires that he should so use it. But, though Hegel strives to create the illusion that he uses the word consistently in the same sense, and no doubt deceives himself into believing that he does so, the truth is that he uses it in several different senses. When he says that two concepts contradict one another, he often means that, considered in a certain way (which he thinks is an inadequate way), they exclude one another logically, in the sense that if one of them applies to something the other cannot do so; and the contradiction is resolved when, considering the two concepts in another way, we see that both can apply to the same thing. But when, in his philosophy of man-in-society, his philosophy of the State, he says that two states of mind or two aspects or two forms of social life contradict one another, he sometimes seems to mean no more than that they can be effectively contrasted with one another, positive statements about the one alternating with negative statements about the other, while at other times he seems to mean that some sort of tension or incompatibility necessarily arises between them.[1] When two things, psychological or social, are contradictory in the first of these senses, the contradiction is resolved when they are included in or superseded by something which combines their contrasted characteristics; and when they are contradictory in the second sense, the contradiction is resolved when they are included in or superseded by something in which the tension is relieved or the incompatibility removed. The two things said to be contradictory are also said to imply or entail one another; which sometimes seems to mean that they are inseparable aspects of a whole apart from which they could not exist, and at other times that they are stages in a process which Hegel regards as being, for some reason or other, necessary.

It is easy to see the sense in which abstract right and morality are supposed to imply one another. But in what sense is there a *contradiction* between them? No doubt, abstract right and morality, as Hegel describes them, can be effectively contrasted with one another. Yet this is not all that Hegel has in mind when he calls them contradictory.

---

[1] These two are not the only senses of *contradiction* when it is applied to states of mind or to aspects or forms of social life, but they are, I believe, the most important.

He also means to assert that a serious tension or incompatibility necessarily arises between them.

Abstract right and morality can, of course, be incompatible, and they often are so. It often happens that moral sentiments are out of keeping with the system of rights. But are they incompatible necessarily? In primitive and static societies, rights and obligations are usually very much in keeping with moral sentiments. No doubt, even in primitive societies, rights are, infringed; men's passions move them to steal or in some other way to violate right. But there is – as Hegel knew – a great difference between violating right and challenging it in principle. In all societies rights are violated but they are not in all societies called in question. Men do not, in all societies, acquire *moral* sentiments which move them to challenge recognized rights. Only in sophisticated, self-critical and dynamic societies are rights widely challenged on moral grounds; only in them is there a conflict between abstract right and morality of which men become conscious.[1]

It may be that there is never complete harmony between recognized rights and moral sentiments; it may be that even the most seemingly static society is never quite as static as it seems, and that there is always some adjustment of right to morality or of morality to right, though it goes unnoticed. But Hegel, when he treats them as necessarily contradictory, has more in mind than this; he is suggesting that they must become so seriously incompatible that men become aware that they are so and challenge established right on moral grounds. He is suggesting much more than is true.

And yet he is also saying something which is both true and important, though he does not say it clearly. He is saying that, unless established right and morality come into so sharp a conflict that men notice it and are disturbed by it, a certain idea of freedom (which in his eyes is the most precious) does not emerge. This is the idea of freedom as moral autonomy. Only where men have come to challenge on principle, and not merely to violate, established right does the claim arise that what a man is required to do shall not be contrary to what he is convinced is right. This is the claim which Hegel calls the claim of conscience. Since he also says that freedom is realized where what men are required to do is in keeping with what conscience dictates, it follows that, before there can be freedom in the sense of moral autonomy, established right and moral sentiments must first come into a conflict sharp enough to disturb men so deeply that they

---

[1] Even in these societies, many more rights are accepted than challenged; even in a quickly changing social environment, men ordinarily approve of much more than they disapprove of. The illusion to the contrary arises because disapproval is so much more self-conscious and vocal than approval, so much more noticeable. If right and morality were more incompatible than compatible, society could hardly hold together.

challenge established right, and that afterwards harmony must be restored. This we may accept. But then we accept only a part of what Hegel says. We accept only that, *if* there is to be a certain kind of freedom, right and morality must first come into conflict and then be 'reconciled'; we do not accept that there must be this conflict and this reconciliation.

What Hegel understands by conscience is only a part of what he calls morality, though it is the part he attends to most. Believing, as he does, that the realization of freedom is necessary, he is committed to the assertion that the conflict which is a condition of its being realized is also necessary. And yet he makes admissions which undermine this assertion, though he does not see that they do so. For example, he admits that men can respect right even though they do not make the claim which he thinks is of the essence of conscience. They must, of course, have sufficient motives for respecting established right, and some of these motives will be, in the broad sense of the word, moral sentiments. In all societies men are moved by shame or a desire to be approved by their neighbours or a sense of honour, and all these can be called moral sentiments. But a man moved by any or all of them is not moved by conscience as Hegel understands it. That Hegel is aware of this is proved by his account, in the *Philosophy of History*, of other than European societies. In these societies (as he describes them) the claim of conscience, the claim that a man be not required to do what he is convinced is wrong or to leave undone what he is convinced is right, is not made and the idea of freedom as moral autonomy does not arise. Hegel does not say that in these societies established right and moral sentiments are always in perfect harmony, he does not deny that they are ever in conflict. Perhaps he would admit that they sometimes are; but, if they are, the conflict apparently does not give rise to the peculiar claim of conscience and to the highest conception of freedom.

Abstract right and morality, when they do conflict, can only be reconciled in ethical or communal life. Thus ethical life is their *synthesis*, not only in the sense that they are inseparable aspects of it, but also in the sense that it is the sphere in which the tension between them is resolved. It is also, presumably, the sphere in which the tension arises, though Hegel does not trouble to say so because his attempt to explain man in society dialectically does not require that he should say it. The synthesis is neither logically nor temporally posterior to the elements whose contradiction is resolved in it, for they are merely parts of the whole which it is and have no being outside it.

3. Family and Civil Society

The three 'moments' of the dialectical triad we have been examining are inseparable, two of them, abstract right and morality, being aspects of the third, ethical life. Abstract right and morality can be in conflict, and must be so if men are to rise to the idea of freedom as moral autonomy, and the conflict must be resolved if this freedom is to be achieved, for it can be achieved only in a community where what men require of one another (the claims they make) accord with their deepest conviction about what is right.

The three moments of the second triad (the family, civil society, and the State) are not related to one another in the same way as are the three moments of the first. Where there is right of any kind, there is also some kind of morality, and the two are mere aspects of social life. But it is not true that, where there is any community of the family type, there is always some form of civil society, and that neither family nor civil society is ever found outside the State. The type of family which is found together with civil society is by no means the only type, and if it is *negated* by civil society it is so in a different way from the way in which morality, in the form of conscience, *negates* abstract right. Civil society does not challenge the family, there is no conflict or tension between them which needs to be resolved in the State; or, if there is, Hegel does not explain what it is. He says merely that civil society arises from the 'break-up' of the family, and this, presumably, is the sense in which it *negates* the family. And this sense, as we shall see in a moment, really makes no sense.

I do not deny that what Hegel understands by *civil society* has arisen from the break-up of a certain type of family; but I do deny that it was necessary that it should arise, and also that the type of family out of which it in fact arose is the type that Hegel has in mind in the *Philosophy of Right*. The type of family whose dissolution in fact brings civil society into existence has often endured for centuries without showing any sign of dissolving into civil society. No doubt, there are causes for that dissolution wherever it occurs, but there is nothing about that type of family requiring that it should dissolve into civil society. The dissolution, when it happens, is only contingent in the Hegelian sense of that word; it has its sufficient causes but those causes are not inherent in the structure which dissolves. The family whose dissolution gives rise to civil society is the extended family or clan, the kinship group; and it can endure, as I have said, for centuries without dissolving into civil society. There is nothing about it which requires that it should dissolve and give way to civil society. When it does disintegrate, it is not because it is so constructed that there naturally emerges from it a form of life which supersedes it, as the butterfly emerges from the chrysalis; it disintegrates as a result of foreign invasion or penetration or from some other cause which is no part of the form of life which it is.

Civil society, as Hegel conceives of it, may be roughly defined as a community of producers of the kind described by the classical econo-mists together with the public services needed to maintain order in-side it. Clearly, there have been many societies which were not civil in this particular sense, tribal societies with the family, in one shape or another, as the only important type of community. Where communal life is tribal, there is neither civil society nor State as Hegel describes them. Civil society and the State emerge as the tribe and the clan disintegrate. We may therefore say that civil society *negates* one type of family. But it stands to that type of family in a quite different rela-tion from that in which morality stands to abstract right. Far from being complementary, far from being inseparable in fact, this type of family and civil society are mutually exclusive. As civil society emerges, the tribe and the clan disappear. Where morality is in conflict with abstract right, harmony may be restored between them, for they both survive the conflict. In their case, the *negation* can be *negated*. But it cannot be so in the case of the family and civil society, if the family we have in mind is the type whose disintegration coincides with the emergence of civil society.

When civil society does emerge – and it need not do so – one type of family gives way to another; the extended family gives way to the small family familiar to us in many parts of the world. It is, of course, this small family that Hegel has in mind in the *Philosophy of Right*; it is the family typical of commercial and industrial societies having inside them a structure of authority of the kind we refer to when we speak of the State. It is this family of which he says that civil society arises from its breaking up.

But it makes no sense to say this. The father of the small family, the breadwinner, is a member of civil society; and when his children become old enough to leave the home, when they are capable of playing an independent part in civil society, when they become mem-bers of it, they usually found families of their own. The small family comes into being when a man and a woman marry and have children, and it breaks up when the children leave home and the parents even-tually die. Small families are continually dissolving and other small families are taking their place. From the break-up of these small families other such families arise. This is the truth of the matter. What is not true is that civil society arises from their breaking up. It is there all the time; it is the social environment in which families of this type are born and have their being and cease to be. Where we find civil society, we must also expect to find the type of family which alone Hegel is concerned to explain *philosophically*. Though the two are not complementary aspects of a whole, as abstract right and morality are, though it is conceivable that they could exist apart from one another, the fact is that in practice they are found together. But in just what sense is civil society the *negation* of the family which Hegel describes?

No doubt, civil society and the family can be contrasted with one another. They can be shown to be in some respects opposite. In civil society rights and obligations are precisely laid down, formal contracts are made, and disputes are settled by supposedly impartial persons bound by fixed rules, whereas in the family they are not. In civil society most services are paid for, and in the family they are not. In the family there is great forbearance and little respect for privacy; in civil society there is little forbearance and great respect for privacy. And so we might go on for a long time, contrasting the one form of communal life with the other. In many ways civil society is the antithesis of family life; we can make many true statements about it which would be false if we made them about the family. Indeed, it may be that civil society differs more from the small family which thrives along with it than from the extended family which disintegrates with its appearance; for husbands and wives and parents and children in the small family are perhaps more intimately and less formally bound to one another than are the members of the extended family, so that the ties between them are in even greater contrast with the ties between members of civil society. Nevertheless, civil society does not arise from the break-up of the small family, and there is no tension or conflict between them which is eased or settled in the State.[1]

If we use the word *family* in a wider sense than Hegel uses it in the *Philosophy of Right*, we can say that the family, in the shape of the clan and the tribe, comes temporally before civil society, and even that civil society comes before the State. Thus we have here a time sequence which we do not have with abstract right, morality and ethical life, since the first two cannot exist apart from one another and are merely aspects of the third. But with the appearance of civil society, the type of family out of which it emerges gives way to another type and it would be nearer the truth to say of this other type that it arises out of civil society than that civil society arises out of it. Civil society comes in time before the small family. As Marx and Engels (and others before them) have insisted, the small family, as we know it in the West, is in part at least a product of capitalism. It might even be argued that it is also in part a product of the State, for it could hardly exist except where there were forms of inheritance and contract not to be found in tribal societies and which require for their enforcement a type of authority which is not tribal but political.

Order in civil society cannot be maintained by the same methods as in the tribe; there is a need felt for a quite different structure of authority, and when this need is met we have what is called the State.

---

[1] A man's family obligations can (and often do) conflict with his obligations as a member of civil society, and when they do, the State can sometimes intervene to resolve the conflict. But this is not what Hegel has in mind when he speaks of the State as the synthesis of the family and civil society.

A community of producers and consumers of the kind described by the classical economists cannot long subsist where there is no State. Thus, though civil society precedes the State historically, it does so by only a small interval. Civil society and the State, as forms of ethical or communal life, are closely connected to one another and also to the only type of family which Hegel is concerned with. But these connections, close though they are, differ greatly from the connections between abstract right, morality and ethical life generally.

Hegel's method not only conceals these differences; it also inclines him to say what is false or to suggest it. It inclines him to say that civil society arises from the dissolution of the kind of family which he has in mind, whereas in fact it arises from the dissolution of quite another kind; it also inclines him to suggest that the sort of conflict between morality and abstract right required to produce the idea of freedom as moral autonomy must take place, whereas in fact it need not do so.

4. Hegel's Sophistry and Perceptiveness

But we must be just to Hegel. Let us admit that his attempt to explain the State *dialectically* as a synthesis of two *contradictory* forms of ethical or communal life is a failure; let us admit that he does not prove what he sets out to prove, which is that freedom is necessary because it is implicit in the very concept of will, and therefore cannot but be realized in communities of rational and purposeful creatures; let us admit, too, that he forces the facts, psychological and social, into a mould in which they do not fit. Yet it is astonishing how much, despite his Procrustean method, he takes into account, how perceptive and ingenious he is. Though he sometimes (and indeed often) selects for notice the trivial or the irrelevant because it helps him to make a show of explaining matters *dialectically*, he seldom neglects what is truly important. This Bismarck of philosophy is adept at papering over the cracks, but he is also a social and political theorist of genius, and not all his word-play and tricks of argument can hide his genius. I venture to compare him with a musical (or other) critic using a ponderous vocabulary and style not suited to his subject. Unfortunately, being as insensitive to language as he is sensitive to music, he revels in his vocabulary, and his readers, if they are to learn anything from him, must suffer at his hands. He punishes as he enlightens, but there is no denying his deep understanding of music; he cannot help saying much that is admirable about it though he speaks pretentiously.

I propose to discuss in turn the two triads into which Hegel forces the social facts which interest him. I shall discuss the first very shortly, and the second at greater length; and when I discuss the second, I shall attend much more to the State than to the family or civil society.

I

C. Abstract Right, Morality, Ethical Life

1. Property and Contract

To discover how Hegel conceives of abstract right, we cannot do better than look at what he says about property. 'The rationale of property is to be found', he says, 'not in the satisfaction of needs, but in the supersession of the pure subjectivity of personality. In his property a person exists for the first time as reason.'[1] Hegel does not mean to deny that property helps to satisfy needs, and he is not concerned to explain its origins. He is not trying to answer such questions as *How does property arise?* or *Why do men desire property?*; he is trying to explain how property enables men to live in the way in which rational beings need to live if they are to be satisfied. As a rational being seeking to order his life systematically man needs property. But man does not first choose how he shall live and then set about acquiring property in order to be able to live as he has chosen. It is in the process of acquiring rights, in the process of coming to think of himself and to be recognized by others as being a subject of rights, that man comes to conceive of a way of life as possible and desirable for himself. Both the desire and the ability to lead a purposeful and rational life arise from man's being a possessor of rights, from his having a status, a definite place, in a stable community. We have already seen how, for Hegel, man acquires self-knowledge and self-mastery, and a sense that he is a distinct person in a community of persons, in the process of learning to understand and to control an environment. Part of this process is the acquisition of property, of things set aside for his own use in an ordered life and acknowledged by others to be his. Even inside the family, the child insists on his rights of property; he does so not merely to satisfy his animal needs but to assert himself as a person among other persons in a community.

We can respect someone's property simply by not interfering with his use of it and by not using it ourselves. This is a tacit recognition of his rights. The recognition becomes more explicit when property is exchanged and contracts are made. It is chiefly in the process of dealing in property with others that men come to have explicit and precise titles to what they have acquired for their use.

2. Crime and Punishment

Where there are rights, they may be infringed. The infringement of a right is a wrong. When the wrong is unintentional, when the doer of an

[1] *Philosophy of Right.* Addition pp. 235-6.

action does not know that his action violates a right, he commits a civil offence; when he knowingly makes a false pretence of right, he commits a fraud; when he deliberately violates a right, he commits a crime. Hegel tells us that wrong *negates* right, and is in turn *negated* when the offender makes compensation or the swindler or criminal is punished. Punishment, he says, is 'the negation of a negation', for it negates a fraud or a crime which itself has negated a right. His dialectical philosophy moves him to speak in this way, which seems odd to us; but we need not cavil at it.

Hegel also speaks of the *will negating itself* when a man commits a fraud or a crime. This too is a way of speaking suggested by his need to fit everything into a dialectical pattern. But, this time, we must take exception to it because it contradicts what he himself says about the universal will. No doubt, Hegel's metaphysic enables him to treat Spirit (and therefore Will as an aspect of Spirit) as something greater than finite minds, even though it exists (at its higher levels) only as manifest in their activities. Will, in this larger sense, the universal will, is realized in the community to the extent that its members desire in conscience to behave as established laws and conventions require. Since Will, in this larger sense, exists only as manifest in particular wills, Hegel feels himself entitled to speak of crime and fraud as the will negating itself. The universal will is manifest in particular wills, and it is also particular wills that commit crimes and frauds.

But, even if we do not question Hegel's account of how the universal will is related to particular wills, we can question his right to speak in this way. Will in the larger sense, the rational or universal will realized in the community of conscientious citizens, exists in the criminal only in so far as his actions are in conformity with it. Those of his actions that go against it are by definition not manifestations of the universal will. Thus, though they may *negate* it, in the sense of being in conflict with it, we cannot logically say that, when they happen, the will negates itself. The universal will cannot negate itself, because the acts of will that do negate it are not its own acts. This follows from Hegel's own account of the universal or rational will. If it could negate itself it would not be rational.

Yet even here Hegel has a point worth making. Nobody can do wrong deliberately without knowing what right is. A man can do something which violates right, he can know how his neighbours will describe his action and behave towards him if they are aware that he has done it, he can know what to expect from them and can know that it is unpleasant; he can do and know all this and yet be without a sense of right and wrong. In that case, punishment will be in his eyes merely something unpleasant to be avoided. But if, in spite of his deliberate violation of right, he is capable of feeling as his neighbours do about justice, he will see, not merely that he is liable to suffer for his action, but that he deserves to suffer. If that is his state of mind, then, if he comes to be punished, he will, in a sense, participate in his own condemnation; he will enter into the feelings of those who sit in judgement over him and inflict punishment on him. To do wrong deliberately is more than to do what you know will bring painful consequences upon you if your neighbours know you have done it; it is to act against your own principles. If, when you call an action wrong, you mean more than that it is ordinarily condemned, if you condemn it yourself, then, when you do such an action, you act against your own principles. At the time that you act, your principles may not be present to your mind, but afterwards, as the saying is, the true nature of what you have done is 'brought home to you'. It is brought home to you by the reactions of others, by their punishment of you; but, if it is brought home, you are driven to apply your principles to your own case. The wrong you have done is not brought home to you unless you see your action as others see it. And it is less likely to be brought home to you if they act in anger or for the sake of vengeance than if they seem to you to be acting impartially for the sake of justice. By the manner of their condemnation 'they bring you to yourself'; or, to speak more literally, they place you in a situation which inclines you to pass on yourself the judgement they pass on you.

3. The Claims of Conscience

This brings us to what Hegel calls morality, to our feelings and attitudes towards the standards we are required to conform to and also towards other standards which we may prefer to these. By an attitude I mean something that includes both feelings and opinions. Some of these feelings and attitudes, such as shame, self-respect, and concern for reputation, we may have without ever challenging established laws and conventions. Hegel is less interested in them than in what he calls 'the right of the subjective will that . . . whatever it is to recognize as valid shall be seen by it as good'.[1] He also, a few lines further on, says: 'The right of giving recognition only to what my insight sees as rational is the highest right of the subject.' Until we have asserted this right (and it is in practice asserted by challenging established standards), we are incapable of freedom as Hegel understands it. Merely to assert this right is not, of course, to have freedom; if there is to be freedom the right must be both asserted and made good.

Oedipus killed his father and married his mother without knowing that he was the son of his victim or of his wife, and when he discovered how he was related to them, he was horrified and in his shame put out his own eyes. He was guilty, so he believed, of parricide and of

[1] Ibid., § 132, p. 87.

incest, although he had acted in ignorance. He had in fact killed his
father and slept with his mother, and his ignorance could not alter the
facts; and so, as it seemed to him, he was guilty. We should now say
that his sense of guilt was out of place, because he did not know what
he was doing at the time that he did it; we should say that he was the
victim of circumstances. But that was not how Sophocles felt about it
or the audiences that watched his play. We feel, as the ancient Greeks
apparently did not, that a man is responsible for what he does only if
he understands what he is doing. This notion of responsibility goes
along with the claim we have just discussed; they are both, so Hegel
tells us, involved in our notion of freedom.

'Children', says Hegel, 'have no moral will but leave their parents
to decide things for them. The educated man, however, develops an
inner life and wills that he himself shall be in everything he does.'[1]
Children, we know, are often wilful and decide many things for themselves. Hegel does not mean that children always do what their parents
tell them and never act on their own initiative; he means that they
ordinarily do not challenge their parents' decisions about what is
right and what is wrong. They are wilful and disobedient but they
do not criticize the standards they are required to conform to. But the
educated man (not the learned or the clever but the morally educated
man) does criticize these standards, though not necessarily to reject
them. He is morally educated because he has considered them critically, accepting some and rejecting others on what seem to him to be
rational grounds. His acceptance is not a mere act of the intelligence, as
when a man admits a statement is true after having weighed the evidence for and against it; it is also something more. There may be an
act of will, a decision, involved even in mere intellectual acceptance;
but here there is also something different in kind. Here the man makes
the standards his own, or (to use an expression of the psychologists)
he *internalizes* them. As Hegel puts it, in stranger and more elaborate
language, *he wills that he himself shall be in them.*

The internal standards of one man may not accord with those of
another. If every man is allowed to do what he inwardly believes to be
right, there may in fact be very little freedom; for one man's conscientious action may prevent another's. That every man should be a
law unto himself is an ideal impossible of attainment. But conscience,
says Hegel, is not a man's claim to do what he pleases; it is his claim
to do what he sincerely believes to be right. Now, to say that an action
is right is to say that any man, in a given situation, ought to do it.
When we say that an action is right, we are not, in Hegel's opinion,
expressing or giving vent to our feelings about it; we are putting forward a rule of action which we believe is valid for anyone who finds

[1] Ibid., Addition 68-107, p. 248.

himself in the situation to which the rule applies. As Hegel puts it: ' Conscience is therefore subject to the judgement of its truth or falsity, and when it appeals only to itself for a decision, it is directly at variance with what it wishes to be, namely, the rule for a mode of conduct which is rational, absolutely valid, and universal. For this reason the State cannot give recognition to conscience in its private form as subjective knowing.'[1] We may not wish to put it quite as Hegel does; we may hesitate to speak of the literal truth or falseness of the pronouncements of conscience, which are moral judgements. Yet we ordinarily do believe that it is possible to argue rationally about the validity of moral judgements. This belief is not denied but asserted by the conscientious man. The man who merely says, ' I feel this way about it, and you feel differently, and there's no arguing between us,' is not being conscientious. The conscientious man is not expressing a personal preference; he is asserting a principle which he claims is universally valid.

Let us remember that Hegel is, in his own opinion, primarily concerned to explain the facts. It is, he thinks, a condition of freedom that men should make the claim which he dignifies by the name of conscience; that they should claim to be allowed to act as they honestly believe is right. But, clearly, it is not enough that they should make this claim; they must also be able to realize it. They must *all* be able to realize it, or else some men will be free and others will not; and, in practice, they can realize it only in a community. It follows, therefore, that they can realize it only in a community whose laws and conventions are accepted in conscience by them all. Hegel is not saying that, where a man's principles do not accord with established laws and conventions, he is necessarily wrong. He is not saying that he is right or that he is wrong. He is saying merely that such and such are the conditions of freedom. If the claims of conscience are not even put forward, and laws and conventions are obeyed merely from habit or self-interest or some other motive, there is as yet no freedom. If the conscientious claims of some men conflict with those of others, then not all men can be free; and this is also true if these claims conflict with established laws and conventions. Only when these claims are compatible with one another and do not conflict with established laws and conventions can all men be free. Hegel is not denying that freedom is difficult to achieve, that it cannot be achieved unless men are willing to look critically at the claims which they put forward for conscience sake, that a long process of adjustment is needed before the claims of conscience can be brought into harmony with one another and with established laws and conventions. Far from denying all this, he insists upon it; but he insists also that the process of adjustment which

[1] Ibid., p. 91.

leads eventually to freedom is rational. Only the conscientious man can be free, but he can be free only if his conscience, to use an expression of Hegel's which this time is an expression in ordinary use, is *educated*.

In my desire to do justice to Hegel's account of freedom, I have perhaps created the impression that he was more liberal than he actually was. No doubt, he was inclined to believe that the man who defies authority for conscience sake is much more often wrong than right. His sympathies were much more with authority than with the rebel. But that does not affect his account of freedom, which a man might accept even though his sympathies were different from Hegel's. Hegel was quite willing to admit that the critic of authority may be right. He says that the 'existing world of freedom' (meaning the actual community or form of ethical life) may become 'faithless to the will of better men'[1], and also that, in the age of Socrates, what the world recognized as right and good could not satisfy the will of better men.

D. The Family and Civil Society

1. Hegel's Conception of Communal Life

When he speaks of ethical life, Hegel calls it 'substantial' or 'substance', and says that individuals are its 'accidents'. He is moved to speak in this way by his metaphysical beliefs, and therefore no doubt means to convey much that anyone who rejects those beliefs, or can make nothing of them, cannot accept; he is moved by his doctrine of the concrete universal. Yet Hegel, by this manner of speaking, also means to convey more than this; he also makes assertions which are intelligible even to persons to whom his metaphysical beliefs mean nothing.

Ethical life is communal life, and when Hegel calls it substantial and says that individuals are its accidents, part of what he means is that it is always as a member of a community that man becomes, both in his own eyes and other people's, a moral person. Whatever it is about himself that he values, as well as his capacity to value it, he acquires as a partaker in ethical or communal life. Hegel also means, when he calls ethical life substantial, that it is desirable for its own sake. Men are so made that they cannot realize their capacities except as members of a community; and when they see themselves as members of it, the community is never, in their eyes, merely a means but also an end. Their aspirations are those of social beings, and are achieved when they play whatever part attracts them in society; their

[1] Ibid., § 138, p. 92.

conceptions of themselves are the conceptions of social beings. Society is not the external means of their achieving their aspirations; it is the medium in which they are achieved. As Hegel sees it, it is a condition of men's realizing their capacities that the communities they belong to should seem to them desirable for their own sake. All ambitions, all aspirations, are doubly social; they are possible only to creatures having faculties which are quickened in society, and can be achieved only through activities and enjoyments which have no meaning outside a social context.

All this, suitably qualified, makes admirable sense. I should wish to qualify it in two ways. Though few would take exception to the doctrine that man is destined by his nature for ethical or communal life, if all that were meant by it were that the capacities peculiar to man are developed in him in communal life, many would reject it, if it were taken to mean that man, in order to develop these capacities, must live in the kind of community which Hegel approved of or in any other particular kind. The capacities which interest Hegel, and which most people would agree are essentially human, are reason and deliberate choice. Presumably, even in a community like Auschwitz or Belsen, men reason and make choices. We must therefore suppose that what Hegel means is not that men can reason and make deliberate choices only in a certain type of community but rather that, being rational and capable of deliberate choice, they can lead fully satisfying lives only in that type of community. I see no reason why this should be so. It may be true that men, being rational and deliberate, are fully satisfied only where they have a coherent set of values and find it possible to live up to them. But these conditions may hold just as much in an African tribe as in a liberal society of the Western type. There is no argument from the capacities peculiar to man to any one type of community in which alone a creature having these capacities can be fully satisfied. Thus man might be fully satisfied in a community where freedom, as Hegel understands it, is unknown.

Secondly, it is misleading to speak of the community, as Hegel so often does, as if it were an entity which is active in the same sort of way as a man is. While it makes sense to say that it is as a member of a community that man becomes rational, purposeful, moral and freedom-loving, it is seriously misleading to say that society or the State makes him so. Society or the community or the State, except where we use these words elliptically to mean those who govern or exert the greatest influence on others, is not active; it is merely a sphere of activity, a living together of men. It is true that Hegel often speaks of man as becoming moral in society, and insists that society (or ethical life) exists only in and through indivduals; but he also, and not less often, speaks as if society *made* men moral, as if it had a mind and will of its own and moulded them to that will.

It may be objected that, in making this last criticism, I am being over-precise. To say that society makes man moral is surely only another way of saying that man becomes moral in society. The first way of speaking may be the more accurate, but most people understand the two ways in much the same sense. Do we not all often speak in the second way? Why, then, should we object to Hegel's doing so? I agree that we all often do speak in the second way, and that it would be pedantic to object to Hegel's doing so, if that were all that he did. But it is not all that he does; for he sometimes draws, from this second way of speaking, conclusions, theoretical and practical, which cannot properly be drawn if it is equivalent to the first. Though Hegel is not as illiberal as he is sometimes presented as being, he is illiberal; he does play down the individual. He does sometimes come very close to suggesting that, because society makes us rational and moral, we ought not to challenge established laws and conventions. He also sometimes speaks as if the State stood to the citizen as God the creator stands to His creature man. He insists so much that man owes everything to the communities he belongs to, and above all to the State, that he seems to be suggesting, without wishing to put it into crude words, that he also owes absolute obedience.

M. Grégoire, in his *Etudes Hegéliennes*, in the essay on the divinity of the State, reminds us that Hegel is apt to call anything divine which he regards as a manifestation at a high level of rational Spirit. Thus, he calls the family divine as well as the State. Except for art, religion, and philosophy, the State is, in his system, the highest manifestation of reason; it is a higher manifestation than the family and so is more often called divine. M. Grégoire believes that Hegel also calls the State divine to give force to his repudiation of the contract theory, which makes the State a human device. It is as if he were saying: The contract theorists say that man made the State but I say that man, as a rational and moral creature, is a product of the State. Hegel also disliked the romantic individualism fashionable at the time that he wrote the *Philosophy of Right*. The romantics were proclaiming their right to free themselves from social conventions in order to be more fully themselves, and Hegel was eager to tell them that, without society and the State, they were nothing. He disliked, too, the traditional Christian rejection of this world. The aspirations which the Christian expresses through his belief in another world are to be realized only in this world, in the community of free men, the rational State. For all these reasons, Grégoire tells us, Hegel was impelled to call the State divine. For these reasons, too, no doubt, he spoke with what seems to us an exaggerated respect of other forms of ethical life. This may be true; but not even a philosopher, when he uses such words as *God* and *divine*, can altogether deprive them of their customary associations, either for his readers or himself.

2. *The Family*

Hegel's views about family life are very much in keeping with the upper middle-class conventions of his day, and are less remarkable in themselves than for the vocabulary they are dressed up in and some of the arguments used to support them. Yet this part of the *Philosophy of Right* exhibits, as much perhaps as any other, one of his greatest and least noticed virtues: good sense. Hegel is thought of as the most abstract, the most metaphysical, and the most grandiose of philosophers; he is also – when he comes down to details, as he quite often does – realistic and shrewd. No doubt, he sometimes deals, rather pretentiously, in commonplaces, as when he tells us that marriage, though it involves a contract, is not essentially contractual; or in a mixture of the commonplace and the half-truth, as when he says that the family is 'specifically characterized by love'. But when he says that 'the punishment of children does not aim at justice as such; the aim is more subjective and moral in character, i.e. to deter them from exercising a freedom still in the toils of nature and to lift the universal into their consciences and will',[1] he is not uttering a commonplace but is saying, in a style which is fortunately unique, something well worth translating into plain English. Children are punished less because they deserve punishment than in order to be made moral; they are not only taught by precept and example, they are also taught by the infliction of pain. They are made to suffer not so much because they have done wrong as because they need to have what is right driven home to them. It is not only, nor even mostly, by listening to reason that young children learn to behave; it is much more by being made to suffer when they do not do what they are told.

Hegel would agree with Rousseau that we must not reason too much with children, for, if we do, 'we leave it open to them to decide whether the reasons are weighty or not, and thus we make everything depend on their whim'.[2] This is so, presumably, because young children cannot reason properly, and it does them no good to treat them as if they could do already what they cannot yet do. Though they cannot yet reason, they must be made to act reasonably; they must be made to act as they would act if they were reasonable. They need firm guidance, and will be the more reasonable, when they attain the age of reason, for having had it. The feeling of inferiority and subordination is not bad for children because it is only temporary; it produces in them a longing to grow up and to be accepted by grown-ups as equals. If children are treated as if they were adults when they are still children, this will only prolong their childishness. In spite of his difficult style, Hegel needs only a few sentences to say all this; there are

[1] Ibid., p. 117, § 174.
[2] Ibid., addition III to § 174, p. 265.

psychologists and sociologists today who take many pages to say less.

3. Bentham and Hegel Compared

If Hegel had studied Hume's or Bentham's theory of the State, he would doubtless have said that it falls far short of the truth, taking no account of what the State essentially is. What Bentham or Hume called the State would have seemed to him merely an aspect of civil society. According to Hume or Bentham, government exists only to maintain order, so that citizens can pursue their private ends without getting too much in each other's way. All that matters is that the needs and desires of individuals should be satisfied. Men compete and also co-operate, but whichever they do they care only for their own personal advantage or for that of other individuals for whom, for one reason or another, they happen to be concerned. Bentham in fact believed in universal egoism; or it might be better to say that he often spoke as if that were what he believed without troubling over much about the implications of what he said. But it was not merely this belief that shut his eyes to what Hegel understood by the State; for Hume, who did not believe in universal egoism, was in this respect as blind as Bentham. Bentham and Hume both differ from Hegel in assuming that all ultimate ends are individual or private, in the sense that what men desire for its own sake is always some personal good, their own or someone else's. They assume that the function of all institutions, political no less than economic, is either to satisfy the needs of individuals or else to serve ends which are individual or private in the sense just defined. We may desire the good of another person without hope of benefit to ourselves but we always desire the good of individuals; nothing is desired for its own sake except the good of individuals. Therefore, strictly speaking, the public good is merely a sum of private goods or a means to private good; whatever is good in itself, be it pleasure or happiness or knowledge or virtue or anything else, is always private. John may desire the happiness of James but James' happiness is his alone.

We can make this assumption, not only without assuming that men are always self-regarding, but also without assuming that all institutions have been deliberately contrived to satisfy personal needs and serve private ends; but if we do make it, then what we call the State is only a part of what Hegel calls civil society. No matter what our views about the selfishness of men or the origins of institutions, if we hold that the only function of society and government is to satisfy the needs of individuals and to serve private ends, we do not have what Hegel would allow to be an adequate conception of the State. We have only a conception of civil society; because civil society is the whole system of economic and political relations considered as satisfying individual needs and serving private ends.

4. Civil Society is Educative

Nevertheless, Hegel insists that in civil society we do more than acquire the skills we need in order to collaborate and compete successfully for the satisfaction of personal needs and the attainment of private ends. Life in civil society is educative; it inclines the mind to appreciate the values embodied in the State. In working together to promote private ends we acquire public ends; we begin to value the collaboration for its own sake and not just for what it brings to individuals. Moreover, life in society multiplies our needs; and this, says Hegel, arguing against Rousseau and the ideal of the simple life, is good. The needs we acquire in society bind us to one another and to the community even more firmly than the needs we are born with or acquire merely in the process of becoming physically mature. These needs are, he says, more universal and also, in another sense of the word, more natural. They are more universal, presumably, not in the sense of being more common (for what could be more common than the natural appetites?) but in the sense of being more intimately connected with our principles, with the rules of conduct and standards of excellence we accept, with what Hegel calls the universal will. They are more natural in the special Hegelian sense of being peculiar to creatures of our kind, having the capacities which distinguish us from other animals. They are the needs of rational beings; they are needs born of reason in us, and we become the more rational for having these needs. We would not have the needs if we were not rational, and we perfect our reason in the process of satisfying them. The simple life, to the extent that it leaves some of our faculties undeveloped, is not natural; for it is, according to Hegel, the nature of man to develop his faculties to the full.

It is best, perhaps, not to take sides in this dispute between Hegel and Rousseau, for they both play on words and indulge in paradoxes. Hegel's conclusion, that it is a mistake to aim consciously at the simple life, may be more generally pleasing than Rousseau's, though his arguments are not more impressive.

5. Social Classes

Collaboration and competition for the satisfaction of needs, or the division of labour, give rise to three social classes, the agricultural class, the business class, and the universal class. Now, how a political theorist divides society into classes depends, when it is not determined merely by custom, on the kind of interest he takes in society, on what he wants to explain about it. Hegel made these particular distinctions because the first, between the agricultural and the business class, was traditional, and the second, between the universal class and the other two, suited his theory of the State. Hegel's agricultural class includes all who work on the land or get their incomes from it, no matter how rich or how poor they may be; it includes landowners and peasants and farm labourers. His business class includes all who are engaged in commerce and industry, both employers and employed. The agricultural class is a country class, while the business class is urban. The universal class consists chiefly of magistrates and civil servants; its office is to maintain order and to do justice; it looks after the public or universal interest, and that is why it is called the universal class.

It is interesting to see how these class divisions differ from those made by the classical economists or by Marx. To the classical economists it was also important to distinguish the landowners from the merchants and industrialists, but not more important than to distinguish owners of property from labourers with nothing to sell but their labour; while for Marx the second distinction was the most important of all. Hegel's Prussia was still a 'backward' country, commercially and industrially; the division that mattered most, socially, was between the landowners in the country and the merchants, shopkeepers and craftsmen in the towns. Wage-labourers, rural and urban, were mere dependents of their social superiors; politically they counted for nothing, and the same was true of the peasants. Moreover, Hegel was not an economist. Though he says that these classes arose out of the division of labour, he is not much interested in their economic functions. He is interested rather in their character and temperament, in their attitudes to life and to themselves; and he is interested in them less for what they are intrinsically than for what they contribute to the *ethos* of the society in which, so Hegel hopes to show, freedom is realized. It is a society of the Prussian type. The illiterate classes, the silent classes, with no spokesman of their own in the State, he scarcely notices; he treats them as mere appendages of the classes above them. Though he includes peasants and farm labourers in the agricultural class, the character of that class, as he draws it, is predominantly the character of a class of landowners. So, too, the character of the business class is predominantly the character of a class of independent and enterprising men. Interested, as Hegel is, primarily in the political and intellectual life of a country, it is not surprising that he should almost lose sight of classes which in his day and country were still unimportant, intellectually and politically. The classical economists took notice of these classes because they played distinct parts in the process of production which it was their business to explain, and Marx took notice of them both for that reason and also because he made it his mission in life to define and to fight for their interests.

Neither the classical economists nor Marx were admirers of the Prussian or any other State. The classical economists, like the Utilitarians, many of whose assumptions and prejudices they shared, believed that the only proper function of the State is to maintain order, interfering as little as possible with what private citizens do in pursuit of their interests, while Marx defined the State as an instrument of class oppression. Marx was a Rhinelander who disliked Prussia and was deeply influenced by French and English political and economic theory; Hegel was an admirer of Prussia, the country which, perhaps more than any other in Europe, had been civilized and made strong by the government. Prussia owed much more to her public officials than did either France or England. The kings of Prussia and their officials had made the country strong and prosperous, sometimes even against the wishes of the agricultural and business classes. The Prussian monarchy and bureaucracy were enterprising; they were the great initiators of reforms. No wonder then that Hegel speaks well of what he calls the universal class, the officials who are not gentlemen engaged in public affairs but servants of the State with a tradition of devoted, intelligent and impartial service. In two other of the great monarchies of Europe, in Austria and Russia, the officials were also powerful but were less enterprising and perhaps also less public-spirited than in Prussia. Hegel was the first of the great political philosophers to find a large place for bureaucracy in his theory of the State. He saw the officials, not merely as subordinates, but also as makers of law and policy; he saw them as what they already were in Prussia and were soon to become in every powerful and well-governed State, even the most democratic. But he did not see them as undisputed masters of the State; he did not, as we shall see in a moment, want them out of reach of criticism or out of touch with the people.

6. The Judicial System

With the emergence of civil society there arises a system of positive and precisely defined law with professional courts to interpret and enforce it; it is above all the business class who feel the need for this kind of law. The business class are involved in a wider range of transactions, and are more enterprising, more litigious, more concerned to assert the rights of the individual, and therefore more consciously freedom-loving than the agricultural class. When abstract right becomes positive law, interpreted and enforced by independent courts, it becomes the more conspicuously impartial and universal. The courts are no respecters of persons, for they are concerned only to do justice; and yet, in another sense, they do respect the person, the individual, the bearer of rights and duties, scrupulously.

Hegel, who ordinarily has so much respect for professionals, for the learned and the trained, for men with strong motives for living up to the high standards of their profession, has also a good word to say for the jury system. Juries, he says, judge of the facts in a case and do not interpret the law, and any body of men who have some education and proper guidance are able to do that. When a man is condemned by his peers, the justice of the condemnation is more forcefully brought home to him; he is condemned by men who, in their feelings and opinions, probably stand much closer to him than do judges and lawyers. Moreover, where there are juries, trials must be carried on in a manner intelligible to laymen. Hegel's defence of the jury does not rest on the belief that jurymen are more likely than judges to reach correct decisions about the facts; it attributes no special wisdom or insight to untrained men. Juries do not improve the quality of justice; they merely make it more evident that justice has been done.

7. Corporations

Hegel was neither a socialist nor a champion of private enterprise. He approved of guilds and of other corporate bodies. They give, he thought, a common status and common standards to groups useful to society; they serve to maintain the dignity of their members and to remind them of their obligations. They help the needy among their members without humiliating them. The less the need for private charity, the better; presumably because private charity is good neither for the giver nor the taker of it. If we compare Hegel with the Utilitarians, we find him much less inclined to assume that the poor and the unsuccessful probably deserve their fate.

He believed that the rapid expansion of wealth could, and often did, lead to pauperism, and he thought it the duty of society to look after the poor. He laid that duty, not on the rich individually, but on the government or else on corporations which included both rich and poor. Whether the poor get assistance must not depend on the whim of the rich; they must get it as a matter of right, and yet must also prove that they need it. This is how I interpret Hegel's dislike of private charity, and his praise of corporate bodies because they can help the poor without humiliating them. Hegel also believed that the rapid expansion of wealth produces an 'inner dialectic' of civil society leading to a search for overseas markets.

Some of Hegel's admirers have made much of these beliefs, and have suggested that, even as an economist, he is a precursor of Marx. Does he not say, as Marx does, that the rapid expansion of wealth produces poverty and also floods the domestic market with more goods than it can absorb? Does he not here touch upon what Marx was to call the contradictions of capitalism? No doubt, he does. But he makes these suggestions merely in passing, and without attributing much importance to them. Were they suggested to him by what he had himself observed, or did he pick them up from someone else? I do not know. They are crumbs from his table, which become loaves in the social theory of Marx. They mean much less to him than his belief that government does not exhaust its duty when it protects rights and enforces contracts; it must also protect the weak against the strong, which involves more than giving them merely what they are legally entitled to. It is for society to see that poverty is relieved, and also that children are educated, even against the wishes of their parents.

E. The State

1. What the State Is

I have said that the Utilitarian theory of the State would seem to Hegel to be merely a theory about civil society. How then does Hegel's State differ from civil society? How can we tell the two apart? Have they separate institutions?

Positive law, the courts of justice, the police, and the administrative departments are as much organs of civil society as of the State. To the extent that their function is to reconcile and promote personal or private interests, they are organs of civil society; to the extent that they serve to hold together a community whose members value it for what it is they are organs of the State. Society, conceived as a means to the realization of personal interests, is civil society; whereas, conceived as a legal and moral order in which men acquire these interests and others too, and to which they grow attached for its own sake, it is the State. To conceive of society only in the first way is to conceive of it inadequately. So Hegel tells us.

'The State is actual', we are told, 'only when its members have a feeling of their own self-hood, and it is stable only when public and private ends are identical. It has often been said that the end of the State is the happiness of the citizens. That is perfectly true.'[1] Bentham, if he had read these sentences, might have said, 'This is something with which I can perfectly agree, provided it is suitably interpreted.' But the interpretation which would suit Bentham would not suit Hegel. Not only because, in Hegel's opinion, the happiness in question is not a sum of pleasures, but also, and above all, because it is the happiness of a citizen, of a man whose private ends have no meaning apart from the social context in which they are to be realized. The ends of a citizen, of a member of society and of the State, no matter how private they may be, are the ends of a moral and rational being, and

---

[1] Ibid., Addition 158 to § 265, p. 281.

are not to be understood except in terms of situations and values which are essentially social. These values, which are part of what Hegel means by the *universal will*, are *involved* in private ends. If we explain them, after the manner of Bentham, as if their function were to make easier the attainment of private ends which are perfectly intelligible apart from them, we misunderstand them; we have a false conception of what society is. Public and private ends are not merely closely connected, in the sense that the first must be realized if the second are to be so too (because men will not ordinarily get what they want unless there is justice), nor in the sense that they arise together out of the same experience (because men acquire their values as they acquire their private ends in the mere process of living); they are also involved in one another in the sense that they are not intelligible apart from one another. Men's interests and purposes as distinct from their mere appetites, their ends as moral and rational beings, have no meaning apart from the social relations they stand in and the values they accept. Nor can these relations and values be understood apart from those interests and purposes. This, I believe, is part of what Hegel is saying when he says that private and public ends are identical.

I have already touched on this theme when I was discussing what Hegel understood by civil society, and I now want to go more fully into it in the hope of making clearer what I believe to be the strong and the weak points in Hegel's conception of the State. I think it a mistake to speak, as he does, of the identity of private and public ends, and I also think that he draws some false conclusions from their close connection. Nevertheless, by insisting that they are involved in one another, he points to important truths neglected by the contract theorists and the Utilitarians; truths whose importance he fully recognizes though he never succeeds in putting them clearly.

By a private end Hegel means, presumably, some such thing as the happiness or dignity or wealth or virtue of an individual; a man's happiness may be desired by himself or by some other man, but in either case is merely a private end, in the sense that it is a state or condition of an individual. By public ends Hegel means, presumably, justice or some form or aspect of the social order or the victory of one's country. Hegel believes, as Bentham does not, that public ends are desired for their own sakes and not only as means to the achievement of private ends. Since he believes this, we can assume, in spite of his saying that public and private ends are identical, that he does not hold, with Bentham, that the public good is merely a sum or collection of private goods or something which is a means to private goods. And here, surely, Hegel is right and Bentham is wrong; it simply is not true that men desire for their own sake only states or conditions of the individual and other things merely as means to such states or conditions.

It is also true (and it is implied by Hegel, if not clearly stated) that social values, which cannot be reduced to sums of private good or means thereto, are so intimately connected with men's private ends that these ends are unintelligible apart from them. The connection is there no matter how selfish a man may be. Let us suppose, for the sake of argument, that Hegel's hero, Napoleon, was entirely selfish; that he never cared for the good of anyone besides himself except as a means to his own good. Napoleon's ambition was to be a great general, an emperor, and to play a unique role in history. The playing of such a role involves living up to standards of excellence which are social; and we cannot say that Napoleon accepted the standards in order to fulfil his ambition because his ambition was precisely to live up to those standards. Napoleon's selfishness did not consist in his accepting the standards as means to his private ends; it consisted in his caring for nobody's private ends but his own. Having private interests or ambitions, as distinct from mere natural appetites, involves accepting values which give to those interests and ambitions their distinctive character. We cannot therefore treat these values, as Bentham does, as if they were accepted because they make easier the attainment of private interests and ambitions.

And yet it is misleading to say, as Hegel does, that private and public ends are identical. Though to accept the values involved in a private ambition is not to accept them as a means to the attainment of that ambition, it is also not to desire them for their own sake. A man cannot have private ends without accepting some values, but he can have private ends without also having public ends; he can accept the values (and the institutions connected with them) without its being his purpose to preserve or enlarge them. They are not the objects of his endeavour, they are not his ends. He still has only private ends, true though it may be that he could not have them unless he accepted certain values and institutions.

Of course, men do have public ends; they strive for the preservation or reform of institutions and values because they find them desirable or undesirable in themselves, quite apart from their consequences for individuals. The contrary belief is not borne out by experience; and if it is widely received, it is so probably because such theories as those of the Utilitarians have supported it. One of the simplest ways of explaining the social order is to treat it as if its function were to make easier the attainment of their own purposes by the individuals involved in it. But, though men do have public as well as private ends, a man need not have the first in order to have the second, and the two are never identical. They are different in kind, however closely they are connected in fact.

Here, too, we must make a distinction which Idealist critics of Utilitarianism usually fail to make. A social order is maintained or altered, not only because men pursue private ends inside it, but also because they are attached to laws and institutions for what they are or might be apart from how they affect private ends. Therefore, in all societies, we must expect to find both public and private ends pursued for their own sake. We must not, when we seek to explain a social order, treat public ends as if their function were to serve private ones; we must remember that, closely connected though they always are, the first are no more means to the second than the second to the first. But it does not follow that, because we find both public and private ends in every society, we must also find them in every man formed by society; that whoever has the second must also have the first.

Though Hegel says that public and private ends are identical, he does not mean to deny that they can and do conflict. He means only that in the fully rational community they would not conflict. Clearly, private ends can conflict with one another and with public ends, and the same is true of public ends. So, too, both private and public ends can conflict with the values not involved in them. All this Hegel readily admits; private and public ends, though always in any society intimately connected, are not always in harmony.

But, though he admits this, he also asserts that eventually, in the community of the rational and the free, in the fully evolved State, there will be complete harmony between them. Indeed, this is part of his meaning when he says that public and private ends are identical. He says that, when they are what they ought to be, they form part of a single fully consistent system of behaviour and belief, and also that they must become what they ought to be. The State is what it ought to be (or, to use Hegel's idiom, becomes *actually* what it is *essentially*) when there is this harmony, and there must eventually be this harmony. It can emerge only out of conflict, and it must emerge.

Here, too, we cannot agree with Hegel; but we must take care to define the limits of our disagreement. Because we refuse to admit that this harmony is necessary, we are not bound to deny that the attainment of freedom, as Hegel understood it and as it is widely understood and cherished today, freedom, as the ability to live in accordance with principles critically examined and deliberately accepted, involves both conflict and reconciliation. Freedom, thus understood, is likely to be greatest where, following upon conflicts social and psychological, conflicts which have both deepened men's understanding of their principles and their devotion to them, harmony has come nearest to being restored. As creatures having aspirations and seeking to realize them, we come to conceive of freedom and to desire it ardently. If we are to achieve freedom, we must neither abandon our efforts to realize what we aspire to nor refuse to alter our aspirations; we must continue to aspire and to endeavour but must also reflect on our efforts and our goals and correct them, changing both ourselves and our environment. We must come to terms with life, neither resigning ourselves to wanting only what we can easily get nor persisting in endeavours beyond our powers. Both the idea of freedom and its realization are fruits of our actions and reflections as rational creatures operating in a social order which powerfully affects us but on which we too impinge. Thus, in a community where freedom is understood as the ability to live in accordance with principles critically examined and deliberately accepted, there is likely to be the more freedom, the greater the harmony between public and private ends. This too is good Hegelian doctrine, and is not a commonplace and is acceptable.

2. *The Three Powers of Government*

Hegel distinguished three powers within the State: the power to determine the universal will, which is the legislative power; the power to settle particular cases in conformity with the universal will, which is the executive power and includes, presumably, the taking of both administrative and judicial decisions; and the power of subjectivity or the 'will with the power of ultimate decision', which he calls sovereignty. It is the sovereign power which expresses the unity of the State.

Hegel is most obscure when he speaks of sovereignty; he does not make it clear what is included in that power, nor why he thinks it is best exercised by an hereditary monarch. Since the executive power is defined as the 'subsuming of cases' under laws, it seems reasonable to exclude from it the making of policy. Must we then include policy-making in the sovereign power? Hegel says that 'there is a distinction between the monarch's decisions and their execution and application, or in general between his decisions and the continued execution and maintenance of past decisions'.[1] This suggests that the making of policy is the business of the monarch, and is therefore part of the sovereign power. But the carrying out of policy often requires legislation. Does sovereignty include the power of initiating laws? Hegel does not say. He says merely that 'in a well-organized monarchy, the objective aspect belongs to the law alone, and the monarch's part is merely to set to the law the subjective "I will"', and he also says, the monarch 'has only to say "yes" and to dot the "i".'[2] If this is so, then the monarch has only to ratify the decisions of others and to symbolize the unity of the State. Are we, then, to conclude that the sovereign power is only formally vested in the monarch and is actually exercised by others in his name? Or should we say that the sovereign power is itself merely formal? The first alternative seems the more

[1] Ibid., § 287, p. 188.
[2] Ibid., Addition 171 to § 280, p. 289.

likely, except that the passage from which I have just quoted is the only one that reduces the monarch to merely saying 'yes' and dotting the 'i'. Elsewhere, it is suggested that the monarch takes an effective, and sometimes even a decisive, part in government. Unfortunately, it is never made clear what that part is.

Hegel tries to fit the three powers of government into his dialectical scheme, but, since he fails to make a clear distinction between the sovereign and the executive powers, this part of his argument is unusually obscure and unconvincing. We are told that the sovereign power stands to the other two as synthesis to thesis and antithesis. Sovereignty is vested in the monarch; he has the last word, he is the reconciler, the restorer of harmony. But, if the executive power is as Hegel describes it, if it is merely administrative and judicial and does not include the making of policy, there is little chance of a serious conflict between it and the legislative power, for it merely 'applies the law to particular cases', without challenging it or demanding that it be changed. It is not the administrator or the judge, it is the maker of policy, who is likely to get involved in disputes with the legislature, should it refuse to make laws needed to implement policy. Hegel, by not including the making of policy in the executive power, suggests that it is a function which pertains to the sovereign power vested in the monarch. If that is so, then we must conclude that the monarch, the sovereign, the reconciler of contradiction, reconciles his own power with the legislative power; we must conclude that he is, in this triad, both synthesis and antithesis. Or if, to avoid this odd conclusion, we say that the sovereign power is merely conciliatory and excludes the making of policy, we contradict Hegel. The attempt to fit the three powers of government, as Hegel defines them, into a dialectical triad fails completely.

Nor is it clear why the sovereign power, no matter what its functions, must be vested in an hereditary monarch. Granted that the State needs a symbol of unity, somebody to 'bear its person' and to speak for it on solemn occasions, why is an hereditary monarch better suited to this purpose than, say, an elected monarch or a president? In the past, for a variety of reasons, hereditary monarchy was the most widespread form of government. The nations have become used to it or have come to expect certain attributes in the head of the State, even where he is not an hereditary monarch, which they never would have expected if hereditary monarchy had not once been the prevalent form. Thus, there are attached even to the American presidency certain attributes which might never have been attached to it had not the founding fathers, as men of British extraction, been familiar with British monarchy. The hereditary monarch, for historical reasons, has been the typical head of the State, and hereditary monarchy has seemed to many peoples over long periods of time the most 'natural' form of government. And even today, when it seems so no longer, the popular image of the head of the State owes a great deal to the traditional role of the hereditary monarch. But all this, though true, is nothing to Hegel's purpose; for it does not establish that, in a general way, an hereditary monarch is better suited to be a symbol of the State's unity than is a president.

If we look at the champions of hereditary monarchy in the sixteenth and seventeenth centuries we find none of them using Hegel's argument in favour of it. They are either believers in the divine right of kings or they use historical or utilitarian arguments. Bodin insists that in France sovereign power has always belonged to the king whose title to the throne is determined by the Salic Law. Hobbes admits that the sovereign need not be a monarch but thinks that there are advantages to his being so and to his succeeding by hereditary right. Pascal's brief arguments in the *Pensées* amount to little more than this: though proofs of competence are required in holders of lesser offices, they are not required in the holder of the supreme office; and this, though it may seem unreasonable, is not so, given the insatiate ambition and vanity of men, for the greater the power attached to an office, the more bitter and dangerous the contests for it, so that a rule which avoids this contest for the supreme office, on which all other offices depend, is in the general interest. No doubt, the effective power of the kings of France in Bodin's time or in Pascal's was no greater than the power of the President of the United States today, but in the France of those days it would not have been possible to elect kings as peacefully as presidents are now elected in the United States. France needed powerful monarchs and also needed to avoid contests for the monarchy, and so there was a strong argument for hereditary succession. But where the head of the State is chiefly a symbol of unity, the argument for hereditary monarchy is much less strong.

3. Representative Assemblies

Though Hegel was no democrat, he believed that there ought to be a legislature representative of the better educated and politically more articulate classes whom he identified with the people. He thought it important that these classes should be represented because in that way the State, as he put it, enters 'the subjective consciousness of the people'. The government and the people must be in close and continuous touch with one another; the people must know what the government intends and the government must know the moods, grievances and aspirations of the people. The Estates of the realm speak for the nation; they are the ears and the eyes of the people focused on the government. They have the right to be heard and the right to be informed, presumably because the government ought not to rule without consulting the people's wishes and cannot rule effectively without some measure of popular understanding. Moreover, it matters to the people that they should be heard; if they are silenced or disregarded, they are apt to become ungovernable.

The Estates, as Hegel puts it, are but one *moment* of the legislature; they are not the whole of it. It is not their business, he thinks, to initiate legislation; they are there not to make proposals so much as to discuss them and either accept them or make objections. Presumably, he thinks that proposals of law will mostly come from the king's ministers, who know the facts. Unlike many of his contemporaries, Hegel recognizes, at least implicitly, the importance of the executive,[1] the maker of policy, even in the legislative sphere. We can say this of him, because, though he does not make a clear distinction between the sovereign and the executive power, he leaves us in no doubt that, in his opinion, the Estates do not ordinarily put forward proposals of law. But would he give to the Estates the right to reject the legislative proposals of the government? Or would he confine their right to making objections and imposing delays, the executive getting its way in the end, if it is determined to do so? There is nothing in the *Philosophy of Right* to indicate how Hegel would have answered these questions, if they had been put to him.

There is nothing undemocratic or illiberal about the belief that the initiative in legislation belongs to the executive rather than to the representative assembly, even where, as in Prussia, the executive is appointed by an hereditary monarch. It is borne out by the experience of all modern states. The liberals and radicals of the early nineteenth century who assumed that it is for popular assemblies to make laws and for governments merely to carry them out were much less realistic than Hegel. But a political theorist cannot be called liberal, even as that term was understood in Hegel's time, if he does not allow that the executive, though appointed by the monarch, ought to be responsible to parliament or to the Estates. If the King's minister's can put their measures through, even though the Estates vote against them, then the government is not responsible to the Estates. It is not a responsible or parliamentary government; and the mark of the early nineteenth-century liberal was that he believed in that kind of government. Though, if we study the text of the *Philosophy of Right*, we cannot say that Hegel unequivocally rejected responsible government, we also cannot say that he unequivocally accepted it.

Hegel's attitude to the Estates is not unlike his attitude to juries. They are the popular element in government just as juries are the popular element in the administration of justice. He makes several claims in their favour, but they are all modest claims. The Estates are indispens-

[1] Using this word now as it is ordinarily used in England and not as Hegel sometimes uses it in the *Philosophy of Right*.

able to really good government, but they must not be allowed to do more than they can do well, which is not very much. They are a link between the people and the professionals. Government explains its intentions to the people through the Estates, and so gains the people's confidence, without which it cannot govern efficiently. The need to make legal arguments intelligible to juries brings the law down to the level of the ordinary citizen, convincing him that justice is indeed being done. Government must remain close to the people, must react quickly to their needs, must take account of their feelings and prejudices; but it need not, in the sense of the radicals, carry out their will.

Hegel insists that the universal will, of which he speaks with so much respect, is not to be confused with the momentary will of the people. Though much that he says about the universal will reminds us of what Rousseau says about the general will,[1] there is this great difference between them: Rousseau's general will emerges in a popular assembly debating under certain ideal conditions, whereas Hegel's universal or rational will is not the product of an assembly. Hegel does not deny that the Estates help to formulate the universal will. That they do follows, indeed, from their being a part of the legislature. But their contribution to its formulation is modest, and there is no reason to suppose that when the Estates differ from the government they are the more likely to be right.

Hegel wanted the Estates to represent classes and corporations rather than masses of individual citizens. He was against territorial constituencies. There should be an hereditary upper chamber representing the agricultural class, and a chamber elected by corporations representing the business class. Clearly, he thought that the nobles, the great landlords, could be trusted to speak for all who worked and lived on the land. He was against an extended franchise, even among the business class; it would lead, he thought, to indifference and to the formation of caucuses. He wanted a small but independent electorate; he did not want the voters manipulated by party agents. Nor did he want the Estates reduced to silence or overawed by the government; he wanted their power limited but freely exercised within those limits.

In all this, except that he cared less for responsible government (and I admit that the exception is important), he was not more illiberal than Burke and the old Whigs. In some ways, indeed, he was more liberal than they were. He was much more concerned than they were that government should be clean, and he disliked incompetent amateurs not subject to control. He had a good word to say for juries, but none for justices of the peace ignorant of the law and intent on defending

[1] Hegel's criticism of Rousseau's general will (*Philosophy of Right*, § 258, p. 157) is quite unfair; actually his *universal will* is much closer to Rousseau's *general will* than he cares to admit, though Rousseau's conception, unlike his, is democratic.

the privileges of their class. He condemned the purchase of commissions in the Army and the sale of offices in the State. He was a severe critic of practices long defended by both Tories and Whigs in England but nowadays condemned in all civilized States. He had, I am sorry to say, a keener eye for the abuses than the merits of the English system of government; he was a less generous and perhaps a less candid critic of the English than was Montesquieu. But the fact remains that what he denounced as abuses are now admitted to have been so by most English historians. I will not say that *History* has proved Hegel right, for that would be too Hegelian a sentiment for my taste; I will say only that, if we accept certain moral and political principles which most Englishmen now do accept, we have to conclude that he was right.

4. Freedom of Speech

Hegel was a believer in freedom of speech. Where there are Estates meeting regularly to speak for the nation, there is likely to be well-informed and responsible criticism. And where there is informed and responsible criticism, it is safe to allow great freedom of speech, for the responsible critics will show up the irresponsible. It is not possible to have responsible criticism without also having irresponsible criticism, and it is therefore wise to ensure that you do not get the second kind without the first. The longer the public are offered both kinds, the better they are able to discriminate between them and the more impressed they are by the first kind. Do not be too anxious to silence fools and adventurers or you will silence useful critics as well, but rather give what opportunities you can to the intelligent and the responsible.

Hegel laid three limits on freedom of speech; he said that there must be no libel, no incitement to rebellion, and no 'contemptuous caricature' of the government. The first two are today still regarded as offences in all countries acknowledged to be liberal, and the third could be prosecuted in Hegel's time even in Britain. Hegel favoured religious freedom and the separation of Church and State, saying that it is not for the State to determine what the citizen shall believe. The State can rightfully forbid the propagation of a doctrine only if it is subversive. He advocated civil rights for Jews and the toleration of Quakers who refuse military service on conscientious grounds. I suspect that he cared for the freedom of the individual – though not for the privileges of parliaments, diets and Estates – rather more than did most English Tories, and perhaps even more than the Whigs in the era before the first Reform Bill.

5. Relations Between States

Though Hegel is often obscure and sometimes equivocal when he discusses the internal structure of the State, he says nothing to which his critics have taken strong exception on moral grounds. They have, of course, condemned him for calling the State divine and for saying that the members of the State are its 'accidents', having no value except as belonging to it. As I have tried to show, his critics have misunderstood the significance of these remarks, which are indeed open to criticism though not on the grounds usually chosen. But this 'worship' of the State is not prominent in Hegel's discussion of its structure and the distribution of power inside it. The worst that can be said of this part of his theory is that it exhibits a strong distrust of democracy; and nobody, least of all an honest democrat, need be shocked by that.

Hegel's critics have been shocked more by what he says about relations between States than about the State's constitution. It is here, if anywhere, that he is more than equivocal; that he seems to be putting forward a doctrine which many people would condemn as immoral.

Hegel admits that there are rules which ought to govern relations between States. He does not suggest that they are merely maxims of prudence; he speaks of them as if they were customary and also moral rules. These rules are in fact often, if not usually, disobeyed by States when they think it their interest to disobey and there is no impartial authority to enforce obedience. So far, there is nothing to object to in what Hegel says. He merely asserts that there are moral principles which States ought to conform to, although in fact they often disregard them because there is no power strong enough to ensure respect for them.

But he does not leave the matter there. 'The relation between States is,' he says, 'a relation between autonomous entities which make mutual stipulations but which at the same time are superior to these stipulations.'[1] It is the word *superior* which is here equivocal and perhaps also objectionable. In what sense are States superior to the treaties they make? Are they superior to them merely because, if they choose to break them, they cannot be sued or legally punished? *Superior* is an odd word to choose if that is all you want to say. It suggests more than this; it suggests that it is right for a State to break a treaty if it finds it to its advantage to do so. If this is what Hegel means, he contradicts himself, for he has already said that there are rules which States ought to obey and has included respect for treaties among them. It is absurd to say both that there is a rule which ought to be obeyed and that those to whom it applies are superior to it. If there is

---

[1] Ibid., Addition 191 to § 330, p. 297.

a relevant moral rule, then those to whom it applies have a duty to obey it, and they therefore cannot be superior to it. Unless by *superior* Hegel means, in this context, *not suable or legally punishable*, he is plainly guilty of bad logic and is also putting forward an immoral doctrine. My own impression is that he means more than this and that the charge against him is just; for I find it hard to believe that, if he had wanted to convey no more than that States which break treaties are not legally answerable for what they do, he would have said that they are superior to the treaties they make. He was equivocating; he was saying obliquely what he was reluctant to say outright. He had not the candour of Machiavelli. In this he was not exceptional; there were many people who thought as he did about the relations between States and who were as reluctant as he was to say precisely what they thought.

6. War

According to Hegel, the State is never more sharply present to its members than when it is at war with other States; it is then that their sense of community is strongest. War is good for the moral health of the people. Hegel did not look forward to perpetual peace; he neither expected nor desired it. He has been accused of glorifying war.

This accusation seems to me extravagant and misleading. Even if we grant that Hegel glorified war, the kind of war that he glorified is not the kind that we are nowadays desperately afraid of and wish to avoid at almost any cost. War was much less destructive in Hegel's time than it has since become, and also probably much less demoralizing. War does stimulate some virtues, social as well as military. The Prussians had fought a hard war against Napoleon, a war which had led to domestic reforms and to a burst of patriotism which also had other good effects. It is not surprising that a German who had lived through the war of liberation should have believed that war is good for the moral health of a people. Because we now have so much more reason to fear war, it does not follow that the claims made for it a century and a half ago were altogether false; there was, at that time, a large measure of truth to them. Moreover, to point out, as Hegel does, that war has good effects is not to glorify it; at least not in the sense intended by those who make this accusation against him. Hegel does not advocate continuous or frequent wars, or suggest that war is the noblest activity of man.

F. Observations on Hegel's Theory of the State

1. False Charges Against Hegel

I am conscious that, in discussing his theory of the State, I have defended Hegel from criticism more than I have criticized him. I have not done so because I come closer to sharing his views than those of other political thinkers whom I have been less concerned to defend, but because he has been so much more, and so much more crudely, misrepresented. He has even been treated as an arrogant and pretentious sciolist, a sycophant, a man without originality or penetration, who purveyed the most vicious doctrines under cover of an elaborate but empty metaphysic. No one, not even his worst detractors, have denied him a certain cleverness; they cannot deny that, if he was a charlatan, he was a most successful one, whose victims were not men-in-the-street but men of letters and intellectuals.

That these charges are grossly unjust must, I think, be evident to anyone who has read *The Phenomenology of Spirit*, *The Lectures on the Philosophy of History*, and the *Philosophy of Right* at all attentively. Whatever Hegel's faults as a social and political theorist, it ought not to be said of him that he lacked originality and penetration. To say that is almost like saying that Dante lacked passion, or Shakespeare lacked imagination, or Voltaire lacked wit, or Goethe lacked breadth of mind; it is to deny him the qualities which are most clearly and pre-eminently his own. To refute Hegel's grosser critics, even a summary account of his social and political theory is enough.

There are, however, other charges brought against Hegel which are partly false and partly true. For example, it has been said that he was a believer in the *totalitarian* State. This is an ambiguous and misleading charge. The word *totalitarian* is not to be found in Hegel's writings; his varied and peculiar vocabulary does not include this particular epithet, which belongs to our century. Hegel said that it is only as a member of the State that the individual has value, that he realizes his essence by becoming rational, moral, and free. If to believe this is to believe in the totalitarian State, then Hegel did believe in it. But then this belief, though perhaps mistaken, may be harmless. Harmless, I mean, from the point of view of the liberal; and it is the man who prides himself on his liberalism who is most apt to bring this charge against Hegel. For to say that the individual has value, in this sense, only as a member of the State is *not* to imply that he ought always to obey established laws, nor yet that, even when he ought to obey them, he ought not to criticize them. If we accept this belief, we are not committed to condemning Socrates and Luther, or even the American and French revolutionaries. Hegel's conception of the State commits him only to saying that the individual ought always to obey established laws and conventions when the State is at the highest level of its development; and we have seen that the State, at this level, allows considerable freedom of speech. It is only in the State where freedom is realized that the duty of obedience is absolute. This is all that follows logically from Hegel's account of how man realizes his potentialities and becomes what he is destined to be and ought to be only as a member of the State.

If Hegel had said (or implied) no more than that the duty of obedience is absolute where freedom is fully realized, the liberal would be hard put to it to find fault with him. But, unfortunately, he said more than this; he said enough to suggest that the Prussian State of his day came very close to being a State where freedom was fully realized. This has been denied by M. Eric Weil in his book, *Hegel et l'Etat*, where he quotes several passages from the *Philosophy of Right*, to show that the State there described by Hegel differs considerably from the Prussian State of the 1820s. My impression is that M. Weil makes too much of these passages and partly misinterprets them. I agree with M. Weil that the fully mature State, as Hegel describes it in the *Philosophy of Right*, is not the Prussia of his day, but I suspect that Hegel did not see nearly as great a difference between them as M. Weil supposes.

But this does not seem to me the important point. Whatever the difference between the State described in the *Philosophy of Right* and the Prussian State, both are undemocratic. We can therefore say that, in Hegel's opinion, the State in which freedom is fully realized is not democratic. He does not merely say that it *need* not be democratic; he says that it *must* not be. Now, this is not a conclusion which follows from his conception of the State or from what he says about what the individual owes to the State; it is merely a conclusion he reaches in the account he gives, in the *Philosophy of Right*, of the structure of the State. No doubt, he believes that he has derived this structure logically from his conception of the State as a community of rational and free persons. But the belief is mistaken. Logically, democracy is just as compatible with Hegel's conception of a community of rational and free persons as is the constitutional monarchy described in the *Philosophy of Right*. Indeed, I should go further that that; I should say that Hegel's conception of the State as essentially a community of the rational and the free, though it does not entail that the fully mature State is a democracy, does powerfully suggest it. If Hegel's conception of freedom had been the same as Hobbes' or even Locke's, this might not be so; but in fact it comes much closer to Rousseau's conception and to Kant's. A man is free when he can conscientiously, and not merely from habit, accept the laws and conventions of his community. There are grounds, psychological and sociological, for believing that he is most likely to do this when he has a say in making the laws. There may well be democracy without freedom in this sense; it may even be that democracy generates forces that tend to destroy or diminish freedom. But this is only to say that democracy is not a sufficient condition of freedom; it is not to deny that it may be a necessary condition of it. There are grounds for believing that it is, though Hegel never considered them.

Hegel was against democracy and was also in several ways illiberal. But that does not make him a champion of the totalitarian State in the sense in which liberals today condemn it. Far from believing that one party ought to control the State, he attacked democracy partly because he feared that it might lead to party government, which he took to be the domination of the State by one faction inside it. The universal will, expressed in the law, should emerge, according to Hegel, from the interplay of many forces independent of one another. He wanted the well-to-do and the educated to have much more influence, in proportion to their numbers, than the poor and the ignorant; he wanted professional servants of the State to make policy and not merely to carry it out. Like Burke and like Montesquieu, he wanted a balance of power within the State, with some groups and classes having much more power than others on the ground that, by tradition and education, they were more responsible, less narrow, and more competent. We might call him a Whig, except that he was more critical of parliaments and less mistrustful of public officials than the Whigs were, and also much less willing to have power fall into the hands of persons with nothing to recommend them except birth or riches. He believed much too strongly in what the French revolutionaries called *la carrière ouverte aux talents* to be a Whig. It is true that the cry of 'careers open to talent', as it was raised in Hegel's time, was not equivalent to the call of the socialists for equality of opportunity. The suggestion was not that the system of property should be changed in order to allow the poor and the ignorant to develop their talents, but rather that those who had developed them should not, by reason of their humble birth, be denied the opportunity of using them for the benefit of society and themselves. Yet Hegel did believe in equality of opportunity in a sense in which the Whigs did not.

2. His Excessive Claims for the State

Though Hegel is not a totalitarian, in the bad sense, it cannot be denied that he makes extravagant and false claims for the State. It may be true that man is rational, moral, and free (in Hegel's sense of freedom) only as a member of society, but it is not true that he is so only as a citizen – as a member of the State. Hegel speaks of other forms of ethical (or communal) life besides the State; he speaks of the family and of civil society. Yet he calls the State the highest form.

But in what sense is the State *higher* than other communities? Can we say that it is higher because it includes them? Hegel speaks of the State as that in which the family and civil society, the only other forms of ethical (or communal) life he takes into account in the *Philosophy of Right*, are 'reconciled'; and it would therefore seem that this is at least part of what he means.

If this is what he means, he is clearly wrong. There are many communities which are not included in the State; there are many ways in which citizens of different States are socially related to one another. Even the relations proper to the family and to civil society can and do subsist between members of different States. There are also Churches and many other kinds of associations which transcend the limits of States. Clearly there is no community (unless we treat all mankind as one community) of which it can be said that any community or association having a member in common with it has none outside it. No State includes all the communities and associations to which its citizens belong. Nor can we say that it is only in the communities and associations which fall entire within the limits of the State that man acquires the qualities which, in Hegel's eyes, make him a rational, moral and free being (i.e., a person who has become *actually* what he is *essentially*). It is not here a question of our being concerned with values which Hegel neglects, and our therefore rejecting his doctrine that it is in the State and in communities included in the State that man achieves whatever makes human life valuable. Even if we accept only the values that Hegel accepts, we must reject this doctrine.

The State possesses certain attributes (which I need not define for the purposes of my argument) which other communities and associations do not possess; some of these attributes go by the name of sovereignty. Because the State is sovereign, it can act upon other communities and associations in ways in which they cannot act upon it; and it is widely admitted that it alone should be sovereign. Thus we can say that the State is higher than other communities in a quite usual sense of the word higher; it can control them as they cannot control it. But this sense of higher is not the sense required to justify the claims which Hegel makes on behalf of the State. Because the State possesses these attributes, it does not follow that it does more than other communities and associations to make men rational, moral and free; nor does it follow, merely from these attributes, that a man ought always to put loyalty to the State above other loyalties.

I have argued already that it means nothing to say that the family and civil society are reconciled in the State, and that therefore the State is higher than they are in the way that one moment or aspect of a Hegelian triad is higher than the two others which are 'reconciled' in it. The family and civil society are not contradictory, except in the sense that some statements which are true of the first are false of the second; there is therefore no need for them to be reconciled. If we take the concepts of the family and civil society, as Hegel defines them, they are not self-contradictory or logically inconsistent with one another, and if we take the realities to which these concepts apply, they are not incompatible or antagonistic.

It is true that the State keeps the peace between both individuals and groups; it provides for the settlement of disputes without recourse to violence. In that sense it is conciliatory; but when we think of the State in that way, we have no more exalted a view of it than Bentham had. The State as the conciliator of interests and the guardian of the peace, the State as the Utilitarians defined it, is in Hegel's opinion merely a part of civil society. In the sense in which the State is some-thing more than civil society (a sense which expresses, I admit, im-portant truths neglected by the Utilitarians) it is not a community in which other communities are reconciled; it is rather a community whose members have certain feelings towards it. It is, as far as its institutions go, much the same community as civil society; it differs from it mostly in the spirit that informs it. If, when Hegel distinguishes the State from civil society, we suppose him to be saying that there is something about a community, and especially about a political com-munity, which is altogether missed by such explanations as the Utili-tarians give, we may well agree with him. but this something has really nothing to do with the reconciling of a contradiction between the family and civil society. Moreover, this something is not peculiar to the State, nor always more marked in it than in other communities, nor confined to communities included in it.

3. Why No World-State?

In the *Philosophy of History* and in the *Philosophy of Right,* Hegel takes it for granted that for Mind or Spirit to be made fully actual, there is no need for a world-state; he takes it for granted that the nation-state or the system of such states is the highest manifestation of Objective Spirit. This does not, in my opinion, square with his con-ception of Spirit. Spirit, he tells us, is essentially one. Spirit, in the form of rational self-knowledge, is fully and explicitly made actual in a single, coherent, all-embracing philosophy. This philosophy may develop out of many incomplete and partly inconsistent philosophies but must itself be fully consistent and complete. Why, then, should Spirit, in the form of rational will, not be made fully actual in a single community whose laws can be conscientiously obeyed by all its mem-bers? The universal will necessarily finds expression in the laws and conventions of a community of finite minds. If Spirit is essentially one, there can be only one universal will and therefore only one fully rational and free community. No doubt, that community will include other communities and associations inside it, just as the nation-state does. Hegel admits that the universal will, in so far as it is manifest in the nation-state, is not realized as fully as it might be while the individuals and associations inside the State are in conflict with one another, or rather, while the differences that arise between them cannot be resolved by methods which they all accept as rational and just. How, then, can the universal will, in so far as it is manifest in a system of states, be fully realized while those states resort to war with one another because there are no methods for settling disputes between them which they all accept as rational and just? But if there were such methods and they were effective, there would be a world-state. It seems to follow from Hegel's conception of Mind or Spirit that the fully rational and free community must be a world-state.

4. Success and Justification

Though Hegel is logically committed only to saying that the laws of the fully developed, or completely rational and free, State are always to be obeyed, he does sometimes create the impression that the laws of any state ought always to be obeyed, except by great men or, as he puts it, by World-Historical Individuals. I have already criticized this strange doctrine, and I must not now repeat what I said before. But there is another criticism often made against Hegel and made justly.

For all his talk of conscience and freedom, he was impressed by power and even by the ruthless use of it. If he had not been, he would not have spoken as he did of History justifying those who succeed, even when they act from evil motives. It is one thing to say that good sometimes comes of evil, and quite another to say that the evil is justified even when the doer of it never intended the good. And, as we have seen, it is only the great criminal whose crimes are justified.

Hegel's position here is by no means the same as Machiavelli's. Machiavelli neither condemned nor justified the great criminal; he merely argued that great crimes have sometimes to be committed if power is to be achieved or the State to be saved or enlarged. He despised the man who refrains from crime only because he lacks the courage to commit it, because he lets ' I dare not ' wait upon ' I would '. But he never said that the great criminal is justified; he never sought to elevate him morally. He spoke only of men; he did not speak of larger than human purposes working through men and justifying their wickedness when that wickedness contributes to those purposes. Nothing so logically absurd and morally perverse as the doctrine of justification by unintended good consequences is to be found in his writings. He admired courage, firmness of purpose and intelligence,

K

but he did not revere power, as Hegel did. He was not ignoble, he was not vulgar in that particular way.

I have been concerned only with Hegel's doctrine, and have felt bound to insist that, taken as a whole, it does not have some of the implications which his detractors have read into passages taken out of context. But I would not deny that there is an unpleasant tone about the writings of a man who appears to have believed that the Universal Mind had attained full self-knowledge in his philosophy. His manner is against him; it suggests a colossal arrogance. And we do well to mistrust the arrogant, especially when they speak of freedom.

Chapter 5

MARXISM

I

I SHALL discuss only the social theory of Marx and Engels, saying nothing about their philosophical materialism and their account of how we get knowledge. I shall limit myself in this way for a number of reasons, of which the most important (and perhaps the only one worth mentioning) is that it is doubtful whether we need to understand these aspects of their philosophy in order to understand their social theory. I do not deny that philosophical materialists may be disposed to hold some views about society and social change rather than others; I do not deny that there have been and still are certain connections between theories about matter and mind and the nature of knowledge and theories about society and the State. The intellectual history of mankind does not consist of streams which flow without touching one another, it is one broad river; and how men look at one part of life is deeply influenced by how they have learnt to look at others. Much the same fashions affect, from time to time, all or most branches of study. I would not deny anything so obvious, so well attested by history.

I deny only that certain theories, because they are often found together, or because they are intimately connected as parts of the intellectual life of one man or group of men, therefore stand or fall together or are unintelligible if they are studied apart from one another. Whatever the proper analysis of matter and mind, of physical and mental events, and of the relations between them, I do not see how it can affect the question of whether or not a particular theory about society is true. The social theorist, when he speaks of physical and mental events, speaks of them as all men do, and to understand him we do not need to know what his views are (if, indeed, he has any) about matter and mind. Marx and Engels have been called materialists and economic determinists, and economic determinism has also been called a form of materialism. But economic determinism is not a theory about physical and mental events or a theory of knowledge; it is a theory about how certain forms of social activity – all of them, even those which work on matter for the satisfying of basic needs, 'mental' as well as 'physical' – are related to one another. Economic determinism might still be true even if Marx's views about matter and mind were false or so obscure as to be unintelligible; and

269

if economic determinism is itself obscure, it is not so because it rests on some other obscure theory but on its own account.

Marx's theory of knowledge, which I have never understood, has sometimes been called a form of pragmatism and sometimes a form of naïve realism. Perhaps it is one or the other, perhaps it is not. This is a question which neither interests the social theorist nor inhibits him as an interpreter and critic of Marxian social theory. Admittedly, Marx has something (though not much) to say about science, which he treats as genuine in contrast to spurious knowledge, and also about how science, as an activity of man in society, is related to man's other social activities. But we need not enquire into what he understood by knowledge to discover how he thought science was related to these other activities; because, when he spoke of these relations, he spoke of science as we all do. A pragmatist or a naïve realist (assuming, for the moment, that Marx was the one or the other) might have views altogether different from Marx's about the relations between science and, say, economic production, and yet say nothing inconsistent with pragmatism or naïve realism.

Marx's philosophical materialism and his theory of knowledge have never, I believe, been taken seriously except by people who have been attracted to his social theory; they are meagre and enigmatic, and are less often masticated than swallowed whole as adjuncts to the main course. They are sometimes discussed by persons who are not Marxists, though scarcely ever for their own sake, but rather for the sake of completeness. There is, after all, a literal and obvious sense in which no account of Marxism is complete unless it discusses all aspects of the thought of Marx and Engels, and explains why they thought their materialism and their theory of knowledge were logically connected with their social theory. But, unless this logical connection is there, we do not need to look into their materialism and theory of knowledge in order to understand their social theory. I take it for granted that the connection is not there; it seems to me so obvious as not to be worth an argument. If I were enquiring into how Marx and Engels came by the ideas which constitute their social theory, I should think it my duty to look into these other sides of their thought; for it may be that their materialism and their conception of what constitutes knowledge disposed them to hold certain views about society. But I am not enquiring into the genesis of their social theory; I am concerned only to explain what it is, and to consider how far the ideas it contains help us to understand social facts better than we otherwise would.

The social theory of Marx and Engels is incomparably more interesting than the other parts of their thought; it is studied for its own sake, and those who reject it also learn from it. Students of philosophy scarcely ever mention Marx except when they are actually studying his philosophy, whereas students of society often mention him, and even more often use his ideas, when they are studying society and not his theories about it. The study of Marxism as a social theory is therefore more than intellectual history; it is a study of ideas which, either in the form he gave them or else modified, are still widely used. In studying Marxist social theory we add considerably to our understanding of how men think about society; in criticizing it, we help to make clear our own views about society.

To forestall criticism, there is one point I would like to make to justify my neglect of Marx's philosophical materialism. It does sometimes happen that a theorist uses, in order to explain man in society, conceptions taken over from his logic or metaphysics or theory of knowledge in such a way that we cannot be certain how he uses these conceptions in his social theory unless we study these other aspects of his thought. For instance, we need to know something of Hegel's logic and his metaphysics to understand how he uses certain very abstract concepts, in senses peculiar to himself, to construct his theory of the State. We cannot understand his social and political theory unless we do this, and it is well worth doing because that theory is one of the greatest of its kind. Yet I believe that everything that is important and really intelligible which Hegel says about society and government (and there is a great deal of it) can be said without using his peculiar concepts; I believe that it can all be translated into more ordinary language, language which can be understood by anyone who knows nothing of Hegel's logic and metaphysics, without anything valuable being lost. But, of course, the translation has to be made, and in order to make it, we have to understand, in some sense of understanding, both the languages in question. It may be that Hegel's critics are right, that some of his concepts are empty or perverse;[1] but even if they are, they do form, together with his other concepts, a coherent system. There are rules for the use of Hegel's concepts, even though some of the concepts are empty; both the sense and the nonsense in Hegel are systematic, and we can learn to talk nonsense according to Hegel's rules. That is to say, faced by certain of Hegel's concepts, which he in fact goes to considerable trouble to explain, we can either accept or reject them; and if we reject them as empty or perverse, we must conclude that there is an element of nonsense in the doctrines which contain them. And yet, since Hegel is a systematic thinker who puts his

---

[1] I say *perverse*, rather than *self-contradictory*, because they involve the *deliberate* putting together of what, to Hegel's critics, seem clearly incompatible ideas. Hegel is often as well aware as his critics of what he is doing. He admits that, taken in one way, they are incompatible, but insists that, taken in another, more profound or more adequate, way, they are not. As he sees it, those who, because they cannot follow him, accuse him of nonsense, are blind; while they in their turn say that they are not blind because they know the meanings of the words used by Hegel and see that it makes nonsense to use them as he does.

cards on the table, telling us how he intends to use them, we can learn to discriminate between what to us appears the sense and the nonsense in this theories, and we can then put the sense into our own words. And, since it is not in his *Philosophy of Right* nor even in the *Phenomenology of Spirit* but elsewhere, that Hegel puts his cards on the table and makes clear his intentions, we have to look at his logic (which is a form of metaphysics) in order to understand what he says about society and government; in order to extricate the sense from what we cannot help calling (though with all respect) the nonsense in the *Phenomenology* and the *Philosophy of Right*. Once we have done this, we have done all we can do to make Hegel's social theory as fully intelligible as it can be made, and we are then able to explain the theory to the man who knows nothing of his general philosophy as well as to the man who knows a great deal. To learn how Hegel uses his peculiar vocabulary, we must go to his logic and metaphysics; but I believe that, once this is done, we can say all that is valuable in his social and political theory without using that vocabulary.

We cannot say as much for Marx and Engels. They are not systematic thinkers as Hegel was; they nowhere clearly explain their ideas and intentions. And to the extent that they are systematic and lucid, they are much more so in their social theory than anywhere else. Their philosophy, as far as I can see, throws little light on their social theory; it gives us no insight into how they use ideas peculiar to themselves to explain society and government. If we are to get any such insight, we must get it from the social theory itself.

I shall also say almost nothing of Marxian economics, though my motives for this neglect are different from my motives for neglecting Marxian philosophy. Marx was as much, as elaborately, as systematically, and no doubt as lucidly an economist as he was a social and political theorist. He was not a very coherent or clear or precise thinker in any field; but I dare say he possessed these qualities in as ample measure when he discussed the production and distribution of wealth as when he discussed the social order more generally or the functions of government within that order. Indeed, since economics (thanks to the work of the classical economists) was already, in Marx's day, as it still is now, a more developed field of study using more precise ideas than sociology, it is probable that Marx's account of how the capitalist economy functions is nearer being coherent and lucid than historical materialism, which is his account of how society changes and how different forms of social activity are related to one another. It is probably more coherent and lucid, but also less original and suggestive. Marx is held in much greater esteem by sociologists than by economists – except, of course, when the economists happen to be Marxists. Marx's reputation as an economist has fluctuated considerably among economists who were not Marxists; and some academic economists in

the West have even tried, perhaps successfully, to enhance that reputation. Attempts have even been made to see in Marx anticipations of
Keynes, and these attempts have also been contested.

If I were to discuss Marxian economics, I could at best hope to do
no more than reproduce what other people have said; and I shall
refrain from doing that. It is the Marxian account of society and of
social change and the Marxian theory of the State that I shall discuss,
for they are still of absorbing interest to the social and political theorist.
I have already written a book about them, but I hope that I shall not
repeat in other words what I said there. Since writing it, I have read
several books about Marxism, and two in particular, which have
caused me to change my mind about some things, and to want to put
my views about others differently. These two books are the second and
much enlarged edition of M. Bober's *Karl Marx's Interpretation of
History*, and H. B. Acton's *The Illusion of the Epoch*. My book was
published a year before Acton's, but I greatly regret I did not read
Bober's book before I wrote mine. At the time, I wanted to make up
my own mind about Marxian social theory undistracted by the
opinions of others, and I thought it better to risk making my own
mistakes rather than to repeat other people's. I now think that was
unwise. These are two excellent books from which I have learnt a great
deal.

I shall present my appraisal and criticism of Marxian social theory
in the form of answers to four questions. What, according to Marx and
Engels, is the *basic* determinant of social change, and in what sense is
it *basic*? What did they understand by social classes and class struggles,
and why did they say that class interests are irreconcilable? What did
they understand by 'ideology', and how did they conceive of its function in society? What did they think is the function of the State in
societies divided into classes, and what did they predict would disappear
in the classless society? Each of these is not a single question so much
as a group of questions so closely related to one another that they can
hardly be treated apart. The questions are meant to draw attention to
those aspects of Marxian theory which are still most in need of
elucidation (or perhaps the better word is *disentanglement*) and most
worth elucidating. Marxism has been so often and so severely handled
by critics that most people are willing to admit that the theory, taken
as a whole, is unacceptable. It is, they say, unacceptable, and then they
quickly go on to add that there is a great deal to be said for it. There is
much wider agreement that the theory is both defective and valuable
than about the respects in which it is so. There are still critics of
Marxism who are misled by the theory they criticize. My aim is to be
as precise as I can be, and I hope that I shall not also be tedious.

I. WHAT, ACCORDING TO MARX AND ENGELS, IS THE BASIC DETERMINANT OF SOCIAL CHANGE, AND IN WHAT RESPECT IS IT BASIC?

1. Foundation and Superstructure

Let me begin by quoting once again some often-quoted sentences from the Preface to Marx's *Contribution to the Critique of Political Economy*. 'In the social production which men carry on they enter into definite relations that are indispensable and independent of their will; these relations of production correspond to a definite stage of the development of the material forces of production. The totality of these relations of production constitutes the economic structure of society – the real foundation on which legal and political superstructures arise and to which definite forms of social consciousness correspond.' This short passage is part of what Marx called 'the general conclusion' which he reached in his study of economics, and which, once reached, 'continued to serve as the guiding thread' in his studies, presumably not only of economics, but of society generally. In it he seems to be making several distinctions: between production and the relations men enter into in production, between these relations and the laws and political institutions arising from them, and between these laws and institutions and what he calls the forms of social consciousness corresponding to them. We have first production, then relations of production, then laws and political institutions, and lastly forms of consciousness: these four things co-exist, and yet there is an order of dependence asserted among them. It is production which brings men into these indispensable and unwilled relations; it is out of these relations that law and government arise; and it is to law and government that forms of social consciousness correspond. As we shall soon see, there are all kinds of difficulties to this formulation: there are difficulties about what is to be understood by the four things distinguished from one another, and also about the nature of the relations asserted between them. I want, nevertheless, to draw attention to the actual words used by Marx, or, rather, by his English translators. Though some of these words, in this context, have an indefinite meaning, there is a limit to the plausible interpretations which can be put on them.

There has been controversy between critics of Marxism as to whether the theory makes the technique of production or the economic structure in a broader sense the basic factor determining the general character of social life. Professors Acton and Bober prefer the first alternative; Professor Hook in *Towards an Understanding of Karl*

Marx prefers the second. The passage I have quoted seems to settle the matter in favour of Professor Hook; for Marx there distinguishes production from the relations of production, which he calls the 'economic structure' of society and the 'real foundation' on which law and government and forms of social consciousness all depend. But the matter cannot be settled that easily. For the passage, studied more closely, favours Bober and Acton rather than Hook. Though it is true that Marx calls the 'economic structure' the real foundation of social life, it is equally true that he says that that structure consists of relations into which men enter, whether they like it or not, because they are engaged in production. If the economic structure is basic in relation to law, government, and forms of consciousness, is not production basic in relation to the economic structure? We have here four aspects of social life distinguished by Marx which we can, for brevity's sake, call A, B, C and D. Acton and Bober say that A is basic, while Hook insists that it is B. The passage I have quoted, read superficially, seems to favour Hook. But even if we could not, as in fact we can,[1] find other passages in Marx and Engels to support Acton and Bober, we may wonder whether the point at issue is worth an argument. Does it matter whether we call A or B *basic* in relation to C and D, given that B arises, as Marx says it does, out of A? Moreover, though Marx, in this particular passage, distinguishes what he calls the 'forces of production' (i.e., the materials, tools and methods involved in production') from 'the relations of production' arising out of them, and calls these relations the 'economic structure' of society, his usual practice is to include the forces of production in the 'economic structure'.

Nothing is gained by treating the economic structure or relations of production, rather than production itself, as basic, unless it is assumed that that structure is to a considerable extent independent of production, that there are other things besides production making it what it is. This Professor Hook sees clearly, for he says: 'The social relations of production . . . cannot therefore be regarded as the automatic reflection of technology. On the contrary, the development of technology is itself often dependent upon the system of social relationships

---

[1] For instance, there are these well-known passages: 'In acquiring new productive forces, men change their mode of production, and in changing their mode of production, their manner of gaining their living, they change all their social relations. The windmill gives you society with the feudal lord; the steam-mill society with the industrial capitalist.' Marx, *The Poverty of Philosophy*, p. 119 – 'The bourgeoisie cannot exist without constantly revolutionizing the instruments of production, and thereby the relations of production, and with them the whole relations of society.' *The Communist Manifesto* – 'As individuals express their life, so they are. What they are, therefore, coincides with their production, with what they produce and with how they produce it. What individuals are, therefore, depends on the material conditions of their production.' Marx & Engels, *The German Ideology*.

in which it is found.'[1] This is how we have to interpret Marx if we want to make his position stronger by insisting that it is the economic structure rather than the actual process or technique of production which is basic; and, as I have said already, we can find evidence in the writings of Marx and Engels to support this interpretation.

As there is evidence to support both this interpretation and the other, how are we to settle the matter? Should we say that, where there is a conflict of evidence, we should accept the interpretation which makes the better sense? Professor Hook's interpretation makes the theory more plausible, and there is evidence in favour of it as well as in favour of the interpretation which makes the theory unplausible. Is that not reason enough for preferring it? Ought we not, in justice and charity, to give Marx and Engels the benefit of the doubt?

I shall answer the last question by saying that there is no doubt here to give them the benefit of. The evidence does not make it uncertain what position Marx and Engels took; for there is good evidence that they sometimes took one position and sometimes the other. We can be reasonably certain that they sometimes treated the economic structure of society as *basic* and at other times the process of production, and that they sometimes spoke as if the structure were entirely determined by the process and at other times as if it were not.

Professor Hook's version of it may make the theory more plausible; it may seem to accord better with the facts than the version of professors Bober and Acton. I do not myself believe, for reasons which I hope to make clear later, that Professor Hook's version does accord very well with the facts; but I do admit that, at a first glance, it seems to do so better than the other version. It is an apparently better version, not as being more in keeping with the text, but as being *apparently* more in keeping with the facts. If we ignore the facts and take account only of the text, we may say that, whereas the Bober-Acton version is more in keeping with what Marx and Engels tell us about the basic pattern of social change, Hook's version accords better with their explanations of actual social transformations – as, for example, the decay of feudalism and the rise of capitalism. In other words, their own accounts of major social revolutions do not accord with their formulations of the basic pattern of social change.

Yet it is because they have their own peculiar conception of social change that they use some of the expressions most characteristic of them. Why, for example, should they speak of 'relations of *production*' unless they believe that these relations, which they call the real foundation of the legal and political system and of the moral order, are determined by the character of production, by the natural resources at men's disposal and the tools and methods they use to produce what satisfies their needs?

[1] S. Hook, *Towards an Understanding of Karl Marx*, p. 126.

If, then, I am right, the Marxian terminology suggests one version (which I have called the Bober-Acton version) of what Marx and Engels thought was the ultimate determinant of social change, while their explanations of the rise of capitalism and of other great social transformations suggest another version (which I have called the Hook version). This is one reason among others why their theory is so confused and confusing.

I have said that Hook's version, if we do not examine it too closely, is the more plausible of the two in the sense that it seems to be more realistic, to come nearer to fitting the facts. But if we accept it, there is no longer any point in calling the Marxian theory, as both Marx and Engels call it, *materialist*. Not, of course, because Hook's version takes the theory further away from *philosophical materialism*, which is irrelevant when we are discussing a social theory, but because it plays down the importance of actual production. If the Marxian social theory is *materialist*, it is so because it asserts that it is how men produce what satisfies their needs which determines the general character of the moral, political, and legal order in which they live. Hook's version, if we accept it, deprives Marxian social theory of the right to be called *materialist* in the only sense of that word which makes sense when it is applied to a social theory. If the relations of production, the so-called foundations of the social order, are determined by other things as well as by the character of production, those other things can only be morality, law and government or what Marx and Engels call the 'forms of social consciousness'; they must belong to what the two masters call the superstructure of society in contrast with the *material* basis. Thus, Hook's version, in spite of the evidence in its favour, does, if I may use the expression, knock the bottom out of Marxian social theory in a way that the Bober-Acton version does not; it makes it a theory radically different from what its authors intended it to be.

2. *The Sense of the Distinction*

What could be meant by calling one part of social life fundamental or basic in relation to the rest? If we choose to call production basic, what exactly is the point of doing so?

Clearly, if there is to be social life at all, the species engaged in that life, which in the case that interests us is the species *man*, must survive. Man survives by producing what satisfies his hunger, his thirst, his need for shelter. If men are to be able to engage in other activities besides the production of what they need to keep alive they must at least engage in that production. In this obvious sense, production is basic. No one would wish to deny it. But Marx and Engels were concerned to say more than this; they were concerned to do more than utter a truism. They wanted to say that the *character* of production determines in general the character of social life. It is true that they said other things not compatible with this, things which have moved Professor Hook and others to offer what seemed to them more reasonable versions of Marxian theory; but it cannot be denied that they often did say this, and thought it important to say it. They also sometimes spoke as if this followed from production's being basic in the sense which nobody would wish to deny; as if it followed that, because men must engage in production if they are to be able to do other things, the character of production determines the character of their other activities. But the conclusion clearly does not follow.

Production is *basic* in relation to social life generally in the sense that it makes it possible. It is also *basic* in another sense, if not to all other aspects of social life, then to some of the most important; it is basic in relation to them in the sense that it creates the need for them. For example, wherever there is production in society, there is a need for some rules of property. Or again, given a division of labour on a large enough scale, there is a need for organized government. And doubtless there are other things, which are not themselves parts or aspects of the productive process, for which a need arises because there is production, or because there is one type of it rather than another. But, though we admit that wherever there is production there is a need for some rules of property, we need not hold that the type of production determines what these rules are; nor need we, if we grant that a division of labour beyond a certain scale creates a need for government, go on to say that the form of government is determined by the form of that division of labour. To avoid confusion of thought, let us distinguish between *requiring* and *determining*. I shall say that one thing *requires* another, when, given any form of the one, there is a need for *some* form of the other, and that one thing *determines* another, when, given a particular form of the one, there arises a particular form of the other.

The degree of particularity does not much matter. Several governments differing considerably from one another can all be reckoned governments of the same form or type; and the same holds for systems of property and modes of production. If, for example, we want to say that the mode of production *determines* the system of property, we do not have to show that every change in productive technique, no matter how small, produces a change in the system of property; but we do have to do *more* than show that wherever there is *any* production in society there is a need for *some* rules of property. The least we must do is distinguish between several modes of production and several systems of property, and show how each of these modes creates a need for one of the systems. We must do at least this, and we

must also take care not to include in what we call the determining
factor anything which belongs properly to what we say is determined
by it.

3. Relations of Production

Marx says that production (or, as he often puts it, the 'forces of production') determines the relations of production; and presumably he
includes in what he understands by production (or the 'forces of
production') the resources, tools, and methods which men use to produce whatever they do produce. I have spoken elsewhere[1] of how difficult it is to establish what exactly Marx and Engels mean by 'relations
of production'; they seem to have alternately in mind two different
types of relations without ever making a clear distinction between
them. Sometimes they seem to be referring to relations involved in
actual production, to forms of co-operation in production, and sometimes to relations which arise because production creates a need for
them. An example of the first kind of relation would be the relation
of a foreman to the men whose work he directs; an example of the
second kind would be the relation of the owner of a piece of land to
anyone required to respect his title to it.

Professor Acton distinguishes three types of relations which might
be called 'relations of production': those involved in the actual use of
particular tools and techniques, those which are needed to make
production go smoothly (which he calls paratechnological), and those
which arise when commodities are produced for exchange.[2] As an
example of the first kind, he gives the relations in which the crew of
a ship stand to one another because they co-operate as they do to sail
that particular kind of ship; as an example of the second kind, he gives
the tacit agreement that land which has been dug shall not be
trampled; and, though he gives no example of the third kind, presumably because he thinks it superfluous to do so, I suppose that we can
take for an example the relation of debtor to creditor. To this threefold
distinction I prefer the simpler distinction which I said that Marx
and Engels never make, though it is suggested by the way in which
they use the expression 'relations of production': the distinction
between relations involved in actual production and relations which
arise because production creates a need for them. The first kind of
relations I had already clearly in mind before I read Professor Acton's
book, saying that they exist wherever there is a division of labour, and
change more or less as methods of production change;[3] but my

[1] In my *German Marxism and Russian Communism*, Chap. 2.
[2] Acton, *The Illusion of the Epoch*, pp. 159ff.
[3] *Plamenatz*, op. cit., pp. 23-4.

conception of the second kind is the clearer for my having reflected on Acton's three-fold distinction. My second kind is merely his second and third kinds put together; and they are put together because there is, in my opinion, no need to distinguish them in order to explain and criticize this part of Marxian theory. The important distinction to bear in mind, if we are to see where that theory is defective, is between relations actually involved in production and relations for which the need arises because there is production; distinctions between kinds of relations not involved in production but arising out of it are, for this purpose, irrelevant.

Marx says of relations of production that, though they are determined in the first place by the character of production, they do not change to keep pace with changes in the character of production. He says that these relations 'from forms of development' of the productive forces turn into 'their fetters'; or, in other words, that, from being relations for which the need arises because production has a particular character, they become obstacles to efficient production because the character of production has changed. He also says that property relations are the legal expression of relations of production.[1] It would seem therefore that relations of production, as Marx understands them, are relations for which the need arises because there is production and not relations actually involved in production; it would seem that it is relations of our second kind and not our first which best qualify to be 'forms of development' of and 'fetters' on productive forces, and to have said of them that relations of property are their 'legal expression'. The relations involved in production must change as production changes, and therefore can hardly become fetters upon it, and moreover property relations are not their legal expression.

If, however, we treat our second kind of relations as being what Marx calls relations of production, we are involved in other difficulties, not less serious. Why say of them that property relations are their legal expression, implying that they can be distinguished from them? Why not just call them property relations, and have done with it? Except when they are defining them, Marx and Engels nearly always speak of relations of production as if they were the same as relations of property. Why, then, do they sometimes feel the need to use expressions which suggest, if they do not actually say, that there is a difference between these two sets of relations, one set being the legal expression

---

[1] In my *German Marxism and Russian Communism*, I said that, since relations of property are called the *legal expression* of relations of production, these two sets of relations cannot be identical, and I went on to say that, if they are not identical, it is impossible to discover what relations of production are. To serve Marx's purpose they must be more than relations involved in production, and yet, if they are not relations of property, what can they be? I now think that I was taking Marx too literally in refusing to treat relations of property and relations of production as being the same.

of the other? Presumably because they want to exclude law from what they call the economic structure of society, and therefore feel the need to suggest that relations of production can be defined without bringing the notion of law into the definition. 'The totality of these relations of production constitutes the economic structure of society – the real foundation on which legal and political superstructures arise.' Law belongs to the 'superstructure' while these relations belong to the 'foundation'.

Unfortunately, it is quite impossible to define these relations except in terms of the claims which men make upon one another and recognize – except in terms of admitted rights and obligations. Where there are such rights and obligations, there are accepted rules of conduct, rules which require and forbid and are supported by sanctions; there are, in the broad sense of the word, laws. But it may be that, by taking law in some other quite usual but narrower sense, we could so define relations of production that this narrower sense of law was not brought into the definition. Thus, making a distinction between law and mere custom, we could point to primitive societies and say of them that they have customs but no laws. In these societies without law there would of course be relations of production and relations of property, though it would not be permissible to call the second kind the 'legal expression' of the first.

I shall consider this expedient again later, when I discuss not only Marxism but any theory which seeks to explain morality, custom, and law as determined by something in society more *basic* than they are. For the moment, it is enough to say that this expedient, even if permissible, would amount to a revision and not an interpretation of Marxian theory. There is no reason to believe that Marx and Engels would have admitted that in a primitive society without law as distinct from custom and morality, and without political government as distinct from paternal or patriarchal rule, there would be no 'legal expression', as they put it, of the relations of production.

If we identify relations of production with relations of property (as I think we must if they are to have any identity at all), it becomes easy to see that they are not determined by what is produced and how it is produced. Given any one form of production, widely different systems of property are compatible with it. Some, no doubt, are excluded; the property relations of a tribal society are not compatible with industrial production as we know it today. But the variety of systems of property compatible with any one form of production is so great that it makes no sense to speak of forms of production *determining* systems of property. We can only make what we say look sensible by tacitly including the system of property in our notion of the form of production, and then saying that the form determines the system. We think we are making a statement of the form 'A determines B', which makes sense whether or not it is true, whereas what we are really saying (though we do not know it) is that 'A plus B determines B', which does not make sense. Thus, we say that capitalist production determines capitalist relations of property, without stopping to consider whether we can explain what it is about that type of production which makes it specifically capitalist except in terms of the relations of property which we say are determined by it.

Moreover, it is easy to see that the system of property often has a great influence on the form of production. Let us take a simple example. Where there is agriculture, there is property in land. Though the need for this kind of property arises from the cultivation of the land, the actual rules of property can vary considerably. Two communities using much the same methods when first they take to agriculture may have different rules about the inheritance of property in land; in the one, the custom may be primogeniture, all the father's land passing to his eldest son, and in the other, it may require the equal division of the father's land between all his sons. There will soon be many more large estates in the first community than in the second, enabling it to develop new methods which cannot be used in the other community. Marx, when he says that relations of production can act as fetters on productive forces, admits that the system of property can affect production. But the way he puts it does not do justice to the facts. The system of property is not merely a negative influence; it is also positive. It does more than put obstacles in the way of what is already there; it also creates opportunities. Much larger opportunities, even, than are suggested by the example I have just given. One system of property as compared with another, by allowing a greater concentration of wealth in a few hands, may lead to quicker progress in the sciences and a more rapid improvement in productive techniques. The system of property determines the pattern of effective demand, which in turn has a great influence on what is produced and how it is produced.

These, it might be said, are obvious points. Are we to believe that Marx and Engels did not see them? I am not suggesting anything of the kind. If we look, for example, at Marx's account of the rise of capitalism, we find him admitting readily enough that property relations have a powerful influence on productive methods. A considerable part of the first volume of *Capital* is taken up with explaining how the decay of feudal relations of production made possible the development of new productive methods. There is no question there of the methods of production peculiar to capitalism being born in the womb of feudal society and then gradually transforming it into a capitalist society as feudal relations of property, now become fetters on these methods, give way to other relations more in harmony with them. As Marx describes the transformation, capitalist methods of production could emerge only because feudal relations of property were already giving way to others. There were no limbs to break the fetters until the fetters were broken.

Both Marx and Engels are often ready to admit the obvious. Their fault is much less that they turn a blind eye to it than that they do not see its implications for their basic theory. If the relations of production or property owe their character only in part to the form of production, if they in turn can profoundly affect production, and if they cannot be defined without using moral or normative concepts, what is the point of calling them relations of *production*? And what is the point of calling them the real foundation of law and government, and of all forms of social consciousness? Since they owe their character only in part to the form of production, may they not owe it equally to the other sides of social life? In what sense, then, are they the real foundation of these other sides?

4. *Fundamental and Derivative*

So far I have been discussing only the Marxian distinction between an economic foundation and a non-economic superstructure of society; and I should now like to broaden my argument to cover, not only Marxian theory, but every attempt to distinguish, among the larger aspects of social life, between a fundamental causal factor and what is derivative from it. No doubt, if we take a small enough part of social life, we can easily show that it is derivative, in the sense that it is much more affected by the rest of social life, or even by some other part of it, than it affects it. If we take something like fashion in dress, we can show that it greatly depends on certain other things which it hardly influences. But if we take larger sides of social life, like religion or science or government, it is no longer plausible to treat any of them as fundamental or derivative in relation to the others.

To get our bearings in this matter, we need to keep firm hold of a distinction usually ignored by Marxists and by other writers who put forward theories like theirs; we need to distinguish between forms of social behaviour (or kinds of social activity) and characteristics or features of social life which are not forms of behaviour. Of these features the most important, for our purpose, are rules of conduct. Production, government, art and science are kinds of social activity or forms of behaviour. Law and morality are not; they are features of social life, involved in all kinds of *social* activity. Or, at least, if law, in some narrower sense, is not involved in all kinds of social activity, morality and custom most certainly are. All properly social relations are moral and customary; they cannot be adequately defined unless we bring normative concepts into the definitions, unless we refer to rules of

conduct which the persons who stand in those relations recognize and
are required to conform to.

Going along with these rights and obligations, there are mental
attitudes which it would be misleading to call feelings because they
involve thought as well as emotion. The relation of a mother to a
child is properly a social relation, not because the mother gives birth
to the child or feels affection for it or desires to protect it, but because
she recognizes that she has obligations towards it. And the mother
becomes a mother in the eyes of her child, not when the child learns
that she gave birth to it, but when it comes to make certain claims
upon her and to recognize (though not necessarily in so many words)
certain obligations to her. It knows her for its mother when it comes
to understand that she plays a certain unique part in its life, when it is
aware of itself as a person standing in a special relation to her; though,
of course, it need not be able to define that relation. Creatures having
this kind of awareness feel differently towards one another because they
have it; the love of human parents for their children, and of their
children for them, differs profoundly from the natural affections of
other animals.

Human beings feel about one another as they do because they
become self-conscious and conscious of other selves (as other animals
do not); and this they become in the process of learning to see themselves in moral and customary (and therefore social) relations to one
another. Even the most private relation, the one which seems the
exclusive concern of the persons involved in it, is, in this sense, a moral
and a social relation. Even a clandestine love-affair in which there is
no question of marriage usually imposes obligations on the man and
the woman who have it, though it may matter to no one but themselves what they do. The lover and his mistress have more or less
definite ideas about what each has the right to expect from the other;
they are not creatures of mere desire or habit, they see themselves as
standing in a certain relation to one another, as having parts to play
because they are in that relation. How they think of the relation is
not mere private fantasy; it derives from ideals accepted by others
besides themselves, from ideals which they have taken over much more
than they have made them. Even being in love consists of more than
having certain feelings towards another person; it consists also in making or hoping to be allowed to make certain claims on that person, and
in admitting or hoping to be allowed to admit certain obligations. The
quality of the feeling involved is closely bound up with these claims
and obligations.

Since claims and duties and mental attitudes are involved in all
social relations, in every side of social life, no matter how primitive,
since they are part of what we mean when we call a human activity
social, we cannot take any side of social life and say that it determines,

even *in the last resort*, whatever that may mean[1], men's moral and customary relations and their attitudes towards one another. We can, of course, say that certain things are necessary conditions of social life. We can say that, if human beings were able (as some animals are) to look after themselves without help from the time they were born, they might never have come into customary and moral relations with one another. We can say that, if human children did not need to be protected and fed by their parents for many years, there might be no family life and therefore none of the social relations and affections involved in that life. We can say that, if men had not co-operated to produce and exchange goods and services, they might never have been drawn into such broad communities and into so many and such varied social relations. We may feel the need to insist more strongly on these points, converting *might* into *would*, when we come across someone saying that man is a social merely because he is a rational animal. True, we may say, unless he had natural capacities, including reason, which other animals lack, he could never be a moral and social creature; but that is only part of the truth, because these capacities are developed in him by life in society. Unless he had had certain biological needs and had co-operated with other men in order to satisfy them, he would not have developed his powers of reasoning and have become a social and a moral creature.

But to say these things is to imply absolutely nothing about the relative importance of different forms of social activity as influences upon one another. The biological needs peculiar to man are satisfied by many forms of family life, which in their turn give birth to other needs, which are social and moral and not biological. Therefore the biological needs do not determine what form of family life there shall be; they merely create a need for some form of it. Co-operative production and exchange, in some form or other, are found in all societies, but the form they take in any society cannot be defined without reference to the social relations they involve. We cannot pass from such statements as 'unless men had biological needs peculiar to their kind, there would be no families' or 'unless men co-operated to produce and exchange goods and services, there would be no communities larger than families' to conclusions like 'how men satisfy their biological needs determines moral relations inside the family' or 'how men co-operate to produce and exchange goods and services determines social relations inside the community'. We cannot do it because how men satisfy their needs and how they co-operate cannot be adequately defined without bringing these relations into the definition.

I have argued that any theory which postulates a fundamental causal factor to explain social change is mistaken. But that does not forbid

---

[1] It is usually a saving phrase to which the user attaches no definite meaning.

our making any kind of distinction between the fundamental and the derivative; it forbids only the kind of distinction made by Marx, which commits the maker to holding that what is fundamental determines the character of what is derivative.

We can usefully make a quite different kind of distinction between the fundamental and the derivative. This distinction is worth discussing, not only for its own sake, but also because, though neither Marx nor Engels makes it explicit, it is implicit in much that they say. I suspect that Marxism has been more effective than it would otherwise have been because its votaries have confused this implicit and useful distinction with the explicit and unrealistic one. They are apt to read the first into the second whenever this helps to make better sense of an argument advanced by Marx or Engels.

To elucidate the implicit and useful distinction, I must first make certain other distinctions between rules of conduct. Speaking broadly, we may say that rules of conduct are moral or customary or legal.[1] A rule may fall into all three of these broad categories, or into any two, or into one only. When we call a rule moral, without ourselves wanting to commend the behaviour it prescribes, we mean that people recognize (though they may not always carry out) the obligations it lays upon them, whether or not there are sanctions attached to the rule. In calling the rule moral we have in mind the attitude towards it of the people who have to decide whether or not to obey it. Thus we, as students of society, may call it moral even though we ourselves disapprove of it. When we call a rule customary, we have in mind, not people's attitude towards it, but the fact that they usually conform to it, whether from habit or self-interest, or because there are sanctions attached to it, so that whoever is deemed to have broken it is liable to suffer from how other people behave to him because they believe he has broken it. There are customary rules with no sanctions attached to them and towards which people do not have the attitude which would make moral rules of them. There are therefore some rules which are not obligatory in either sense: which people do not feel obliged to obey and which are not required to obey. They too are involved in social relations; but not more than the others. Though many rules do not impose obligations, it is still true that every enduring relation between men, every relation which we call social, does involve rules which do impose them.

In primitive societies, customary rules supported by sanctions, though quite often disobeyed, may never be challenged on the ground that

---

[1] This is only one possible classification among several. It is not meant to be exhaustive: it does not include rules which are invented for a specific purpose (e.g., a game) and with no sanction attached to them other than that refusal to obey them frustrates the purpose for which they are invented. But it does include nearly all rules in which the social scientist is interested.

they conflict with higher or better rules, so that the distinction which seems so important in more sophisticated societies, between what the community exacts and what morality requires, may never be made. Morality and obligatory custom may there exactly coincide. Also in such societies there may be no law, unless we define law so widely as to include any rule which imposes obligations or confers rights. But if we define law as a rule of conduct declared or applied by legislatures and courts of law, then we can say that there are societies having only customary and moral rules and no laws. We can also show that custom and morality are prior to law in this narrower sense of law.

I said that Marx and Engels did not use this distinction between custom and law to support their theory. They also quite explicitly put morality into what they called the 'superstructure' of society resting on a 'real foundation' consisting of social relations. Moreover, they spoke as if they did not know that there are rights and obligations, moral or customary or both, involved in all social relations. They were not as explicit about custom as about morality; they did not put it resolutely into the superstructure.[1] But though, when we call a rule customary, we are not also saying that it is moral, we have seen that most rules held to be moral are also customary, and that the most important customary rules, those holding the family or some larger community together, are also moral. Therefore, if we put morality into the superstructure, it hardly makes sense not to put custom there as well; or, if we put custom into the foundation, we cannot reasonably keep morality out of it.

But may we not put law, as distinct from custom and morality, into the superstructure? Or, better still perhaps, may we not put law there together with the customary and moral rules which arise in society when it comes to have law? Could we not, in this way, distinguish between custom and morality which are prior to law and custom and morality which are not? If we can show that law emerges to satisfy some need which custom and morality existing before there was law did not satisfy, we can then perhaps go on to show that the custom and morality which come along with law satisfy that same need. Though Marx and Engels never did this, it may still be worth doing; it may be a revision of their theory which helps to make better sense of it, and which is also in keeping with much that they said.

This, at a first glance, is an attractive suggestion. Marx and Engels often speak as if the function of law were primarily to maintain what they call the 'class structure' of society, enabling some classes to exploit others. But, clearly, if we understand by law any rule supported by sanctions, we have to reject this account of law. For, unless there are already some rules supported by sanctions, and in particular,

[1] Ordinarily, Marx and Engels did not distinguish between morality and custom any more than between custom and law.

rules of property, we cannot explain how society ever comes to be divided into classes. It is only if we distinguish between custom and law, in a narrower sense of law, that we can hope to show how, in a society without law, customary rules of property and inheritance operate to divide men into classes, and how, as a result of this division, there arises a need for rules of a different kind, rules connected with the emergence of specifically political institutions, and therefore declared and enforced in ways not known before. Though Marx and Engels did not in fact offer this explanation, they did say that society becomes political as a result of being divided into classes. We could even, I think, by appropriate selection, gather all the elements that go to make up this explanation from their writings. So that, although it is not their explanation, it is not altogether foreign to them.

Again, though Marx and Engels often speak as if all morality were class morality, they do not always do so. They admit, for example, that there have been and still are classless tribal societies, and they never dream of denying the obvious, that these societies too have their moral codes. They predict a classless society in the future, which they say is to have the highest morality of all. They also sometimes admit that all systems of morality, class and classless, have some features in common. Can we not say, then, that even in societies divided into classes there is a large part of morality which is not class morality and which therefore does not belong to the superstructure? Only in this way can we avoid the patent contradiction between these two positions: that all morality is class morality, and that men must stand in social (and therefore also moral) relations to one another before they can come to be divided into classes.

When society becomes political, what were once mere customs may become laws. Also, customs which were originally in the common interest may come to be laws which are in the interest only of the rich. For example, customary rules of inheritance and other rules of property, which to begin with were generally acceptable, may have led in time to such great inequalities and exalted some people so much above the others, that the rules would eventually have ceased to be accepted by the great majority were it not that they had become laws; were it not that there had emerged new methods of enforcing obedience to them and of persuading the majority that they ought to obey them. The minority could not for long have been secure in their privileges unless new sanctions had replaced the old, unless organized government had arisen to protect property, unless much that used to be mere custom had become law, unless an important part of morality had become class morality.

This does not mean that all law must be class law. Many old customs will continue to be in the general interest, even after society has divided into classes and government has emerged, and the new sanctions will also operate to uphold them. There will also be new laws made in the common interest. It will come to be thought the business of government and the courts to declare and enforce the important rules, whether they are in the common interest or only in the interest of the privileged. For what is in the common interest is also in the interest of the privileged, who are part of the community. It will come naturally to them, being the rulers of the community, not to distinguish their own peculiar interest from the common interest, but to run the two together. Therefore, not even all law will be class law. Yet it may still be true that, historically, the emergence of law, as distinct from custom, is a mark that society is becoming divided into classes; that the methods of declaring and enforcing law (which make it law as distinct from mere custom) arise along with the division of society into classes.

It may be that, in some such way as this, we could make a cleaner distinction than ever Marx and Engels made between two sides of social life, one of which we might call, quite plausibly, *fundamental* in relation to the other. But, if we make the distinction along these lines, we abandon economic determinism; because we treat as fundamental all sides of social life which existed before the division of society into classes. Morality and custom we refuse to treat as derivative. Society is the matrix in which classes are born, and whatever was social before there were classes can be treated as prior to what develops in society when distinct classes appear inside it. As we shall see later, we cannot even treat what Marx understood by *ideology* as belonging entire to the derivative side. But we can make a distinction which is not altogether remote from Marx's purpose, seeing that he, too, often spoke of what he put into the 'superstructure' as if its essential function were to serve class interests.[1] To call what must exist before there can be classes fundamental or basic in relation to what emerges when they appear is, I think, an allowable use of these words. And this distinction is better than Marx's because it enables us, as his does not, to decide what to call basic and what derivative. It provides us with a criterion which we can use, even though, in practice, owing to our ignorance of the facts, it may often be difficult to decide whether some form of social behaviour or some feature of social life is or is not basic.

But basic in this sense is not basic in the orthodox and explicit Marxian sense. It does not imply that the basis determines what is derivative from it; that the forms and features of social behaviour which must exist before classes can arise determine the forms and

---

[1] Though, of course, he could not do so consistently. Some of the things he and Engels put in the superstructure are so obviously present in tribal societies, which they admitted are classless, that, when they had these societies in mind, they could not treat these things as if that were their essential function.

features which emerge with them or after they have arisen. It does not deny that what is derivative, after it has arisen, can affect what is basic just as it is affected by it, nor yet that what is derivative can change drastically without being moved to do so by what is basic. It does not imply that we can in any society, class or classless, sort out men's social activities into two groups in such a way that, as the one changes, so does the other. Though it allows us to call co-operative production and exchange basic forms of social behaviour and morality a basic feature of it, it does not allow us to say that government and law, which are derivative, do not change to any great extent except in response to changes in them, or do not affect them as deeply as they are affected by them. Basic or fundamental, in this sense, means only primary and universal. Morality and custom are, for example, fundamental in relation to law because they must exist before there can be law, and because they are common to all societies while law is not; they are not fundamental in the sense that, where there is law, they determine its character while it does not determine theirs.

5. Science as a Social Factor

In the Preface to his *Contribution to the Critique of Political Economy*, Marx distinguishes, among the things belonging to the superstructure, law and government from the forms of social consciousness corresponding to them. These forms of consciousness he calls ideological, and I shall consider later, and at some length, what he and Engels understand by ideology. At the moment I want to discuss only what they have to say about science. Though sometimes, no doubt incautiously, they come close to suggesting that science, too, is a form of ideology, they usually treat it as something quite different. Science is clearly not law or government, and so, if it is not a form of social consciousness corresponding to them, it must belong to the foundation and not the superstructure. As it is not, equally clearly, a relation of production or property, it must be part of the process of production, part of what Marx calls the 'forces of production'. In the Marxian scheme of things social, there is nothing else that it can be; and so we find Marx, in the first volume of *Capital*, speaking of 'modern industry, which makes science a productive force distinct from labour and presses it into the service of capital'.

Some commentators friendly to Marx, arguing that it is unreasonable to include science among the forces of production, have denied that he did anything so unreasonable. No doubt, there are some passages in Marx, and in Engels too, which could be used to support this contention. But a bandying of quotations to and fro cannot settle the matter one way or the other. The important question is not, how many quotations are there in favour of this interpretation or the other? It is rather, which interpretation is most in keeping with the theory? And there is no doubt about the answer to this question. In the Marxian scheme of things, there is no place for science except among the forces of production.

But it only makes sense to treat science as an inherent part of the process of production if men engage in science primarily to solve practical problems. Medicine is studied primarily to cure illness. The labours of a doctor are as much productive as those of a miner; and it is not absurd, though it may be unusual, to speak of the labours, say, of Sir Alexander Fleming as part of the productive process, since he undertook his researches in order to find a cure for disease. That he enjoyed his work and cared little for financial gain is nothing to the point; there are unskilled labourers of whom we can say as much.

But most science is not practical; it is undertaken to solve not practical but theoretical problems; it aims at nothing more than know-ledge. It may later be put to practical use; but it need not be. Often centuries pass before any practical use is made of a scientific discovery, and the use was not intended or foreseen by the discoverer. Science can make great progress, as it did in the ancient world, and yet affect productive techniques very little. Pure science is, of course, in one sense, a productive activity; it aims at knowledge, and when it is suc-cessful, when its hypotheses pass the tests they are put to, it can be said to have produced what it aims at. But then, in this obvious sense, all human activities which have a purpose are productive if they achieve their purpose.

It might be argued that the findings of pure science, while they are not applied, have no important social consequences; that it is not until they are used to improve, or at least to change, productive tech-niques that they have such consequences. It may be said that society was very little affected by Greek science, because that science, for all the progress it made, was not applied to industry and agriculture, or was so only to a small extent. But this argument is unacceptable unless we reduce it to a tautology by defining an important social consequence as one which results from a change in productive technique. The pro-gress of Greek science, affecting production very little, affected Greek philosophy, and through that philosophy, Greek ethics and Greek religion very considerably. As people's understanding of the world changes, so too do their conceptions of themselves, of how they ought to live, of what they are destined for. These conceptions may not them-selves be scientific, they may not follow logically from any conclusions the natural sciences reach, but they are, nevertheless, deeply influenced by science. Theology is not science, as we ordinarily use the word and as Marx used it, nor is metaphysics, nor is ethics (understood as a doc-trine about how men should behave and not merely as an explanation of what they are doing when they pass moral judgements or how they come to make them). Science teaches men nothing about God; yet how they conceive of God does depend considerably upon what science teaches them about the world. The theology of a scientific age differs from the theology of an unscientific age; and so too do its ethics and metaphysics.

Not only does science affect these other forms of intellectual activity, which Marx would call ideological, but they also affect science. Scientific progress is sometimes slowed down, and at other times quickened, by theology and metaphysics. The mental discipline and curiosity stimulated in one field of study may be diverted to another. The universities of Europe, founded principally for the study of theology and law, contributed powerfully to creating the intellectual climate in which modern science was born.

Even if we leave aside pure science and its social consequences, science is not related to practice in the simple way needed to make plausible Marx's conception of it. Science creates practical problems just as fast as it solves them. Just as knowledge may be sought (or, if it is already available, used) to solve a practical problem, so a problem may arise out of an increase of knowledge. Because men have knowledge which they did not have before, because their conception of the world is different, they see opportunities where they used not to see them. They come to want things they used not to want because they had not even imagined them. Marx and his disciples speak as if science were socially important only because it helps men satisfy their needs by teaching them how to make or contrive what will satisfy them, forgetting that science creates needs as much as it satisfies them.

Considered in themselves, the pursuit of knowledge and the production of what satisfies material needs are different activities. True, they affect one another greatly; but they are also greatly affected by other things. It is odd, therefore, to lump them together as 'forces of production'. Marx and Engels do this only because their theory requires them to do it. They want to divide social activities into two main kinds, the economic and the rest, saying that the first kind determines the second. Science, they know, has had an immense influence on social change. They therefore cannot relegate it to the superstructure; they have to put it into the foundation, which means, in effect, that they have to treat it as a part of the productive process, since it very clearly is not a relation of production, no matter how we interpret that difficult phrase. They have to do this whenever they are directly faced with the question: Where does science fit into our division of society into a *basis* and a *superstructure*? When they are not faced with the question, they ordinarily do not treat science as a part of production but as something different from it. Like the sensible fellows they are, they prefer to talk sense except when their theory impels them to do otherwise.

II. WHAT DID MARX AND ENGELS UNDERSTAND BY CLASS, CLASS CONFLICT, CLASS INTERESTS?

A. Class and Class Conflicts

I. MARXIAN CLASSES

There are few social theorists who, having defined the terms they use, go on to use them consistently in the senses they have defined. Marx and Engels, as we should expect, use the word 'class' in several different senses; but there is also a special Marxian sense of the word. In this special sense, two men do not belong to different classes because they do different kinds of work, nor even because they get widely different incomes. Salaried managers and manual workers do not belong to different classes merely because managers direct the work of others and manual workers work with their hands. In a classless society, if it were industrial, there would still be a need for managers, and if their salaries were then no greater than those of ordinary workers, it would be, presumably, because they were no longer working for private capitalists but for the community.

The class a man belongs to, in the special Marxian sense of class, depends on whether or not he owns property and on the type of property he owns. The proletarian does not own natural resources or instruments of production, but he does own his own labour; he has the right to sell his labour[1] to others and to withhold it from them; he has even the right to work for himself though he cannot exercise it because he lacks the tools and natural resources he needs. The capitalist owns natural resources and instruments of production, which enable him to appropriate a large part of the product of other people's work; his income, as a capitalist, is not a payment for work done. The slave does not own even his own labour; for there is someone else, his master, who has the right to decide when he shall work and what he shall do. The serf differs from the slave and the proletarian; unlike the slave he is part-owner of his own labour, being obliged to work for his lord only at some periods, and he can even be said to have, unlike the proletarian, (though Marx does not trouble to make this point) a limited right of

---

[1] Marx says that what he sells is his *labour-power*; but, for our purposes (since we are not concerned with Marxian economic theory), we can ignore Marx's distinction between *labour* and *labour-power*.

property in land. The lord cannot deprive him of his land, even though he can divest himself of his rights over the serf in favour of some other person. The yeoman farmer or free peasant owns his own land and his labour; he has no rights of property in other people's labour, and lacks the means to hire much labour. The artisan is in the same case as the peasant, except that he owns a workshop instead of a farm. Tenants can be treated as a sub-class of the class of persons whose property they rent: if they rent a workshop or a farm to work in or on it themselves, they are a variety of artisan or peasant; if they hire labour to work on the property they rent, they are a variety of capitalist farmers or manufacturers or merchants.

The principle of this classification is clear enough, even though at times it may be difficult to decide to what class a man belongs. The yeoman or free peasant, if he hires any labour, is to that extent a capitalist farmer; but if he hires only a little, and most of the work on his land is done by himself and his family, we should still call him a yeoman or peasant rather than a capitalist farmer. So, too, the rights of the serf in his own labour and in the plot of land he cultivates to feed his family may be so diminished that we are at a loss whether to call him a serf or a slave. But the principle of the classification is none the less clear.

Professor Bober says that Marx and Engels distinguish classes primarily in terms of the property they *own* and the extent of their personal freedom. I do not quarrel with that; though I think that, using the word property in the broad sense in which Marx and Engels often use it, we can define personal freedom as having certain rights of property in one's own person or labour. The slave who has no right to marry or to cohabit except as his master directs cannot dispose of himself as a free man can. So, too, the serf who may not move from his village without his lord's permission can be said to lack certain rights over himself. If the serf is attached to the soil, it is chiefly in order that his lord should not lose his property in the serf's labour; if the slave may not create or refuse to create a family as he pleases, it is chiefly to ensure that his master has the supply of labour he wants. It is with the labour of his slaves or serfs, more than with anything else about them, that the master or the lord is concerned; and labour (or labour-power) is treated by Marx and Engels as a form of property, which may be owned, in whole or in part, by the labourer or by somebody else. To define classes in terms of the property they own is therefore quite in keeping with Marxian theory.

II. CLASS INEQUALITY

Marx and Engels (and their disciples after them) speak as if, where there are classes in the Marxian sense of class, they must be unequal;

and also, as if, where there are no classes in their sense of the word, there can be no deep and self-perpetuating social inequalities. Again, they take it for granted that where there are classes, in their sense, there is necessarily exploitation of class by class. Now, none of these conclusions can be taken for granted. It is important to notice this, because many Marxian arguments are conclusive only if they can be taken for granted. The society divided into classes is, for Marxists, necessarily a society where there are deep and self-perpetuating social inequalities and exploitation, and the classless society (i.e., the society without classes in the Marxian sense of class) necessarily has neither inequality nor exploitation.

In any society, even the kind that Marxists would call classless, there is diversity of function, and there are differences in the rights and obligations which people have. Women have in all societies rights and obligations which men do not have; they have them no matter how strong the belief in the equality of the sexes. If only because the role of the mother in the having and rearing of children cannot be the same as that of the father, mothers have by custom and law duties and rights which fathers do not have. The greater the diversity of functions and the wider the variety of men's rights and obligations, the more different their positions in society.

It is only when the persons who occupy certain positions in society (that is to say, who have certain rights and obligations marking them off from other people) are held to be *superior* to others, not on account of personal qualities, but in virtue of the positions they occupy, that there is social inequality. They receive outward respect; which need not mean that they are liked or admired or even respected, but only that people behave to them in a certain way because of their social position. This outward respect is not attached to certain positions merely by chance; it is attached to them, in the first place, largely because the holders of these positions have much more than ordinary power, because their recognized social function is to control, to protect, and to advise,[1] or because their work is held to be in some other way especially useful to the community. This outward respect is also a source as well as an effect of power.

Superiority can long survive the causes that gave birth to it. A function which was once useful may become useless or even harmful, and yet the persons who perform it may retain the rights attached to it and receive the outward respect. They may have as much or more power than the early holders of their positions, but their exercise of it may now stand in the way of most people's realizing their aspirations, and in that sense may be against the common interest. Or they may

---

[1] Because, in other words, their power is authority; because they owe it, not primarily to their personal qualities, but to their social position.

have lost much of their power and yet continue to receive the old marks of outward respect.

In a tribal society where there are no slaves, in a society all of whose members are kinsmen, in a society without classes in the Marxian sense of class, there can clearly be great social inequalities. Some men, in virtue of their position in society, can have much greater power than others and can receive much greater outward respect. Their power is not a mere capacity to get other people to do what they want, a capacity which a man may owe entirely to his personal qualities or to momentary circumstances; they owe it to their position in society, to the rights and duties which make it the position it is. Their power is a form of authority. Because of it they receive outward respect and are held superior to other people. Moreover, their position may be hereditary; and it may entitle them or enable them to get many things that are withheld from ordinary tribesmen. All this is possible in a community of kinsmen, where there are no classes in the Marxian sense. No doubt, there may be classes in some other sense of that word, but that is here irrelevant.

Let us now consider the second conclusion of the Marxists, that, where there are classes in the Marxian sense, they must be unequal. We have seen that, in all societies, there is more than mere diversity of function, mere difference in rights and obligations; there is also social inequality, there are social superiors and social inferiors. But this is as true of societies which are classless, in the Marxian sense, as of those which have classes. It does not follow that, where there are social superiors and social inferiors in a society divided into classes, some classes are socially superior to others. It may often be so, but it need not be so always.

Of course, if we define differences of class in terms of social superiority and inferiority, it follows that where there are social superiors and inferiors, there are unequal classes. But if we take the Marxian sense of class, it by no means follows.

In the Marxian sense of class, peasants who own their land and artisans who own their workshops belong to a different class from landless labourers and factory workers; but they need not be socially superior or inferior to them. They may be but need not be. A poor peasant is not socially superior to a landless labourer; he may be, even in his own eyes, socially inferior to the skilled men employed on a large estate. Rich and poor peasants belong to the same class, which is different from the class of well-paid but landless workers; but rich peasants may be socially superior to poor ones and the social equals of well-paid workers. People whose incomes consist mostly of rent or interest belong, in the Marxian scheme, to a different class from people whose incomes consist mostly of wages or salaries; but they need not be, and often are not, socially superior to them. Indeed, they are sometimes socially inferior, as many owners of slum property are to professional men. There can clearly be differences of class without social inequality; that is, if we take the Marxian sense of class.

But very often, when we speak of differences of class, we have in mind differences of income or power and not the various types of property that men own, and, since differences of income or power usually carry with them differences in outward respect, it is often true that, when two persons are said to belong to different classes, in this sense of class which is not the Marxian sense, it is implied that one is socially superior to the other. And this is perhaps still the most frequent use of the word class. Therefore difference of class, as ordinarily understood, often implies social inequality. This was even more so in Marx's time than now, and he was therefore disposed to take it for granted that what was true of class in a more usual sense of the word was also true in his special sense.[1] But whether it is so or not depends on whether or not differences in the types of property that men own correspond to differences in wealth and power. Though in some societies the correspondence is much closer than in others, in no society is it nearly as close as Marx and Engels supposed it was.

Just as there may be Marxian classes which are *not* unequal, so there may be two classes (in the Marxian sense) which are unequal though neither is exploited. The feudal nobles belonged to a higher class than the merchants and master craftsmen of the mediaeval towns, but they did not exploit them. There is exploitation, as Marx and Engels understand it, when some people get less than the value of what they produce because others appropriate the difference. If one man produces something which is worth one pound, or if his labour adds one pound to its value, and he gets only fifteen shillings, someone else getting the difference, he is exploited. There are difficulties to this notion of exploitation, some of which I shall have to discuss even though I have decided to let Marxian economics alone. I shall refer to them later in another connection. At the moment, I want merely to make the point that one class can be socially inferior to another without being exploited by it, or indeed by any other class; and by exploitation I mean here what Marx meant by it – the appropriation of surplus value.

It would not be difficult to quote passages from Marx or Engels to show that they admitted, at least indirectly, the three points I have

---

[1] He did not think that he was giving a new sense to the word *class*; he supposed that he was giving the sense in which the word was ordinarily used. As a matter of fact the word was quite often used more or less in the sense which he and Engels stressed. It was also and even more often used in the sense which implied social inequality. These two senses were not clearly distinguished from one another, and there were also other senses. It is not to be wondered at that Marx and Engels should have been confused by these different senses.

made. They did not always speak of tribal societies as if there were no social inequalities inside them; they did not speak as if peasants, no matter how poor, were socially superior to proletarians; they did not say that the feudal nobles exploited the mediaeval burghers, nor did they deny that they were socially superior to them. In this matter, as in so many others, we do not find them denying the obvious so much as ignoring its significance for their own theory.

III. TYPES OF CLASSES

Marx and Engels do not confine themselves to using the word class in the sense which I have called Marxian; they also quite often use it in other senses. It would be sheer pedantry to object to their doing so, provided the context makes clear the sense they are using.

For example, they often apply the term *bourgeois* both to capitalists who own instruments of production and to what are called the professional classes, though these classes, like the proletarians, sell their labour. Of course, they charge more for it, and usually do not sell it by the week or the day or the hour, but by longer periods of time, or else by the piece or the visit, and not to one purchaser but to many, as the need arises.

Again, Marx and Engels do not always include the great landowners among the bourgeois, although their rights of property in their estates are essentially the same as the rights of factory-owners. The terms *bourgeois* and *capitalist*, as Marx and Engels use them, are by no means always equivalent, just as they are not so in ordinary speech. The French word *bourgeois*, when it does not just mean a town-dweller, has largely a cultural significance; it refers to anyone who lives in a certain way, though to live in that way he needs a larger income than the manual worker used to get until quite recently. It also often has this cultural significance for Marx and Engels.

We can discern, in the writings of Marx and Engels, two main types of social classification, which, for convenience' sake, I shall call *primary* and *secondary*. The primary classification is in terms of property rights, and gives us such major classes as slave-owners, feudal lords, capitalists, slaves, serfs, yeomen, and proletarians; and also sub-classes of these major classes, as, for example, factory workers and country labourers, both of them proletarians, or industrialists, merchants, bankers, and non-feudal landowners, all of them capitalists.

The secondary classification is into what I shall call *principal* and *subsidiary* classes. A principal class is a protagonist in the class struggle; in pursuing its class interests it either transforms society or is an obstacle in the way of progress. Its interests are decisive in determining the character of the class struggle. A principal class is always a major class or a sub-class thereof. A subsidiary class is not a protagonist in

the class struggle; it may in fact take a prominent part in that struggle
but its interests are not decisive in determining its character. In the
eyes of Marx and Engels, the professional classes are subsidiary to the
capitalists. Since they get paid for their services, they are clearly not
capitalists. Nor are they exactly proletarians, even when they have
nothing to sell but their services; for normally they do not produce
what the buyer of their services aims to sell at a profit. They are *sui
generis*. Certainly, neither Marx nor Engels ever calls them proletarians, though in their time professional men still made a living by
selling their labour mostly to the substantial propertied classes. It was
the capitalists, and not the wage-earners or the peasants, who hired
stewards, managers, and lawyers, and who sent their children to schools
and universities. Only the most poorly paid of professional men sold
their services to the workers and peasants. The professional classes,
sharing the culture and accepting the standards of the propertied
classes, mostly followed their lead politically. Or perhaps it would be
better to say that their political attitudes were largely determined by
the interests of the propertied classes. In fact, as Marx knew and
admitted, the actual rulers of a capitalist country are as much recruited
from the professional as from the propertied classes. Yet he insisted
that the political behaviour of these rulers is determined primarily
by the interests of the propertied classes.

   Marx and Engels also treat village labourers and even peasants who
own their land as subsidiary classes. Hired labourers on the land are
proletarians, but they are not destined to play a decisive part in the
class struggle. When they come to know their true class interests, they
will become the allies of the urban proletariat, but the lead in the
struggle against the capitalists belongs to the urban workers and not
to them. Again, Marx and Engels often call the peasants *petits-bour-
geois*, not meaning to suggest thereby that they are capitalists in a
small way, but that their interests are often in harmony with those
of the capitalists. They are not protagonists in the class struggle; they
are subsidiary allies of classes much more active, politically, than they
are.

   A subsidiary class may, but need not, belong to the same major
class as the class to which it is subsidiary. Thus, if we consider the
examples just taken, the village labourers belong to the same major
class as the urban workers to whom they are subsidiary, but the same
is not true of professional men or of peasants. Indeed, the peasants,
though they usually follow the lead of the capitalists, may not always
do so; they may sometimes side with the proletariat. Both Marx and
Engels admit that they sometimes have done so. Thus the peasants
can be subsidiary to either of the two classes engaged as principals in
the class conflict; they can even be divided in their allegiance, some
taking one side and some another. Though Marx and Engels make

much less of these possibilities than Lenin was to do after them, they
do admit them.

Neither Marx nor Engels speaks, as I have done, of major and sub-
classes or of principal and subsidiary classes. I have invented these
terms to help explain and criticize their views about the class struggle.
I do not say that every group which they call a class falls into one or
other of the categories I have defined. They often use the word *class*
loosely, as we all do. Nevertheless, if we are to see clearly the merits and
the defects of their theory, we must make explicit certain distinctions
which are only implicit in their writings.

IV. CLASS STRUCTURE AND MODE OF PRODUCTION

Sometimes, when they speak of the epochs into which they divide history, Marx and Engels refer to the tools and sources of power which
which they suppose are characteristic of them. Thus we have such
statements as the one often quoted from Marx's *Poverty of Philosophy*:
'The windmill will give you a society with the feudal lord, the steam
mill a society with the industrial capitalist.' But, though we are
repeatedly told, as for example in the first volume of *Capital*, that 'it
is not the articles made, but how they are made, and with what
instruments, that enables us to distinguish economic epochs', it is not
after these instruments, but after the systems of property supposed to
be peculiar to them or after the classes supposed to dominate them,
that epochs are named. Thus Marx and Engels speak, not of the
steam-and-coal or factory epoch, but of the capitalist or bourgeois
epoch; they speak not of the windmill or workshop or strip-agriculture
epoch but of the feudal epoch, having sometimes in mind the system
of property in land and sometimes the dominant social class. By
antiquity, they seem to mean all the societies on the shores of the
Mediterranean until the fall of the Roman Empire. Though in this
case the name does not indicate it, it is the division of these societies
into masters and slaves which seems to them distinctive of the epoch;
they say almost nothing of the tools and techniques peculiar to it. They
do not seem to have enquired whether, in all or most ancient societies,
the relation between masters and slaves was really the most important,
whether most people belonged to the one class or the other, or whether
there was a marked tendency for these two classes to increase in size
and importance compared with others.

As Professor Bober and other critics of Marxism have pointed out,
neither Marx nor Engels made any attempt to show that slavery and
serfdom arose out of or are connected with different methods or
techniques of production. And indeed there is very little evidence that
they did so arise and much evidence that they did not. Bober, I think,
exaggerates when he says that in Antiquity and in the Middle Ages

methods of production were very much the same. If by these methods
we mean only tools and sources of power used, this is largely true. If,
however, we include in them, as surely we ought, the way in which
production was organized, we must admit that the mediaeval manor
operated in many ways differently from, say, the Roman latifundium,
even though much the same tools were used. Where you have serfs
you cannot have agriculture organized as it can be where you have
slaves. But this difference in methods of production is an effect rather
than a cause of a difference in social relations.

It is therefore, in practice, much more in terms of the class-structure
than of the mode of production that Marx and Engels distinguish
between different historical epochs and different types of society. They
would no doubt say that it does not much matter which criterion you
use, since class structure is determined by the mode of production. But
this, as we have seen, is not true, and only wears the appearance of
truth if we include in the mode of production the social relationships
which are supposed to be determined by it; if we include in it not only
(as we reasonably may) forms of co-operation actually involved in
production, but also kinship and property relations. The distinction
between the ancient and the feudal worlds, as types of society and not
just as periods of history, makes sense (if it makes sense at all) only in
terms of the moral and legal and political relations between men, or of
the division of social classes arising out of these relations, and not in
terms of the mode of production.

V. CLASS CONFLICT AND SOCIAL EVOLUTION

Marx and Engels say that 'the history of all hitherto existing society
is the history of class struggles'. By this they mean much more than
that in all societies there have been classes and conflicts between
classes; they mean that the political struggles of the past have been
very predominantly class struggles. They believe that the transformation of society, of the system of property (or social 'relations of production') and the superstructure resting upon it, results from class
conflict. The established social relations or system of property, together
with the superstructure, are defended by the privileged classes, whose
privileges depend on their maintenance, and are challenged by other
classes as they come to find that their interests are incompatible with
them. Thus the feudal system was undermined, partly because the serfs
fled from their lords' estates or otherwise evaded or reduced their
obligations to them, and partly because the mediaeval burghers, as
they grew in number and in wealth, added to their privileges and
strengthened the monarchy against the feudal nobles. The process was
gradual, but it was, none the less, a social and a political revolution;
it was a social revolution because it transformed the relations between

classes, and a political revolution because it transformed the system of government. Or, to speak more accurately, in transforming the relations between classes, it altered their nature, making new classes out of the old. The serfs, in getting rid of their peculiar obligations, ceased to be serfs and became free peasants or tenant farmers or village-labourers when they did not go to the towns, and when they did go, sometimes became capitalists or (and much more often) proletarians; while the craftsmen and merchants of the guilds became capitalists or sank into the proletariat.

Although, when the requirements of their own theory are present to their minds, Marx and Engels affect to see, underlying this social transformation and causing it, a change in the mode of production, their actual account of it (if we examine it closely) suggests that it was more often the social transformation which made possible the change in mode of production. Nevertheless, it may still be true that important social and political changes, changes on such a scale that they deserve to be called *revolutions,* are usually effects of a struggle between classes. Clearly, the two assertions, that changes in the class-structure are determined by changes in the mode of production, and that social and political revolutions are effects of class conflict, by no means stand or fall together. The second might be true even if the first were false. For my part, I believe that the second assertion comes nearer to being true than the first, though there are two large qualifications I should wish to make. Society can be transformed, socially and politically, by wars and conquests which are not themselves forms or effects of class conflict. Secondly, the classes whose conflicts bring about these trans-formations need not be (though in the past they often have been) classes in the Marxian sense of class; they need not be social groups having different kinds of property-rights.

We cannot explain the social and political transformation of Western Europe resulting from the fall of the Roman Empire as an effect of class conflicts. There were no class conflicts weakening some classes and strengthening others in Western society to explain how it ceased to be what it was in Roman times and became what it was in the Middle Ages. Western society was transformed by the conquest of the Roman Empire by the barbarians and by the spread of Christ-ianity, and neither of these events can plausibly be taken to be bound up with the conflict of some classes with others. The German tribes pressed more strongly against the Roman frontiers because they were pushed forward by the movement of other tribes behind them; they were not urged westwards and southwards by any class conflicts inside them, for they were not, in the Marxian sense, class societies. The Roman Empire was growing poorer and losing population for a long time before it collapsed, but there is no evidence that this decay was due to class conflicts. Indeed, class conflicts had been much fiercer while Rome was creating her empire than when that empire was in process of decay. Moreover, even if the aggression of the barbarians and the decay of Rome had each been the effect of class conflicts in two separate societies, it still would not be true that the invasion of the West by the barbarians was itself a class conflict and that the type of society emerging from that invasion could be said to embody the gains made by some classes at the expense of others in conflict with them. What is true of Western Europe as it passed from Roman imperialism to mediaeval feudalism is equally true of Asia and Africa transformed by European penetration or conquest, and indeed of all great social and political revolutions brought about by foreign invasion and domination. Military conquest and other milder forms of invasion have been, historically, very important causes of social and political revolution. We can often, though by no means always, find class conflicts among their major causes; but they are not themselves class conflicts, even when they are partly caused by them. We cannot treat the social and political transformations resulting from them as advances and retreats in a struggle between classes.

Nor can we treat the conflicts between classes having different property-rights as historically more important than conflicts between groups which are not classes in this sense of class. Conflicts between what we would call, using the terms we devised to help explain this part of Marxian theory, sub-classes of the same major class, or between one subsidiary class and another, or which involve social groups which are classes in some other sense are just as important. The groups supporting Parliament and those supporting the King in the English Civil War were nearly all capitalist in the Marxian sense, for their property rights, whether in land or other things, were already more capitalist than feudal. The professional classes in France, especially the lawyers, played as large a part as any other group in strengthening the old French monarchy and later in making the French Revolution. In doing first one and then the other, they were promoting group interests which were often not in keeping with the interests of the capitalists. Again, wherever there is a vast apparatus of government, State officials are an important group, whose behaviour is often decisive in bringing about social and political transformations. The officials may be recruited from the humbler or from the upper classes, but in either case they acquire professional interests distinct from the interests of the classes they come from. The higher officials in eighteenth-century Russia and Prussia were largely recruited from a class of nobles who still, if we take into account their property-rights, were feudal rather than capitalist landowners. Can we plausibly treat State officials in Russia and Prussia as a class subsidiary to the feudal class? As a class which emerged primarily to satisfy the demand of the feudal nobility for certain services? Or as a class whose social function was to defend feudal interests? The higher State officials, though largely recruited from the feudal class, were not, as State officials, a sub-class of that class; they were not, as servants of the State, a variety of feudal land-owners, as, say, farm labourers are one variety of proletarians and factory workers another. Their interests as State officials were not a variety of the interests of the feudal nobility. These men were both State officials and feudal nobles. The group interests and aspirations which they acquired in the service of the State were as powerful motives for their behaviour as the interests they shared with the rest of the class they were born into.

There is a line of false reasoning which it is very easy to get into when we are discussing social groups and their group interests. We can divide society into groups in many different ways; we can make, so to speak, many different social maps of it. We can classify people according to their property-rights, or the size of their incomes, or their religion, or their political rights, or in some other way. If, for some reason or other, we decide that one of these divisions, one of these maps, is more important than the others, calling it fundamental or primary, we fall easily into the way of treating the group interests of any group on a secondary map as if they formed part of the group interests of a group on the primary map, whenever most (or perhaps only the most prominent) of the members of the first group also belong to the second. For example, if we decide with the Marxists that the division into classes according to property-rights is the one that really matters, and we find that most seventeenth-century Protestants, or the most prominent among them, were capitalists, we easily fall into the way of treating their interests as Protestants as if they were part of their interests as capitalists. Or if we find that the higher clergy who dominated the Church in the Middle Ages held fiefs as the lay nobles did, we are apt to treat the interest of the Church as if it were a variety of feudal interest. Or if we find that higher officials in Tsarist Russia were mostly recruited from the landowning class, we treat their interests as officials as somehow derived from their interests as land-owners. We are not hard put to it to find them using their official position to promote the interests of landowners; we may even find them consistently preferring the interests of that class to those of other classes and groups outside the State administration. Their group interests as officials, or even their ambitions for the State they serve, we tend to forget, or to treat as unimportant, because officials are not what we understand by a class; and we have already made up our minds that only class interests matter 'in the long run'.

We tend also to forget that even a group which is not hereditary may last through many generations and have enduring interests, and also enduring ambitions for the State or other community they con-trol – ambitions which it is misleading to treat as merely the *interests* of that group even if they are much stronger within that group than outside it. For example, in the countries they dominate, Communist parties have ambitions for those countries which, though they are often not shared by the people generally, cannot be treated as mere interests of the party. They are ambitions of the party for the country and not just for the party. The attempt to realize these ambitions constitutes one of the greatest social and political revolutions the world has ever known. The ambitions of the party are supposed by the party to serve the interests of the manual working-classes. But this may be only the opinion of the party. What the party is doing may be understood and approved by only a very small proportion of the classes in whose name it is being done; which does not in the least prevent its being a revolution of tremendous importance.

VI. THE MARXIAN MODEL OF REVOLUTION

The social and political revolution which transformed the feudal into the capitalist system was, as Marx and Engels describe it, a class conflict very different from the class conflict which they believed would eventually put communism in the place of capitalism. The feudal nobility and the rising bourgeoisie, though their class interests conflicted, never stood to one another in the same relation as, according to Marx and Engels, the capitalists stand to the proletariat. The feudal nobility never exploited the mediaeval burghers as the capitalists exploit the proletariat; they exploited the serfs but not the merchants and crafts-men in the towns. The towns got their charters from the feudal lords, temporal and spiritual, whose interest it was to grant them, just as it was the interest of the townsfolk to receive them. As the towns grew larger and richer, they acquired the right to be represented in pro-vincial or national assemblies; the burghers became an estate of the realm. Then (not always but often) they supported the monarch in his efforts to gain power at the expense of the feudal nobility. They also, by creating a predominantly money economy, helped to lighten or to break (though without intending to do so) the ties that bound the serfs to their lords. Without aiming at doing so, they helped to dissolve the manorial system.

The change-over from feudalism to capitalism was slow, and its significance was not understood by the classes involved in it. Sometimes the position of the feudal nobles was undermined by the activities of the burghers without the burghers knowing that it was so; and some-times the burghers, by supporting the monarchy or by their explicit demands, consciously challenged the privileges of the nobility. Yet their actions, even when they knew them to be hostile to the nobles, were usually not thought of by them as a challenge to the established order. Not really until the end of the eighteenth century do we find them aiming at political revolution. But by that time the social revolution had largely happened; the old property-relations had largely given way to new ones. The French Revolution removed only the last vestiges of serfdom, the remaining privileges of the nobility; it was aimed as much against a bureaucratic but inefficient monarchy, which the rising middle class had in the past helped to make strong, as against the nobles; it was directed as much against a system disliked by all classes as against any class. The bourgeois in France, like the classes represented in the English Long Parliament over a century before, wanted a large share of political power at the expense of a monarchy which they had themselves until recently supported; if they were more consciously revolutionary than the Long Parliament, it was because they could not plausibly pass off their demands as traditional rights.

The class conflict of the future which is to put an end to capitalism and replace it by communism, is (as Marx and Engels imagine it) very different from this. It is a struggle of the exploited against their exploiters; and it is much more conscious, deliberate and sustained. The workers, even before they take political action, are directly engaged against the capitalists; they form trade unions to better their wages and conditions of work, they take strike action. As the workers see that there is a limit to the concessions they can extort from their employers by direct action, they come gradually to understand that they must themselves get political power and use it to change the social system, the relations of property, under which they are exploited. They therefore come to aim consciously at transforming the social system; they become, as the burghers never were, a consciously revolutionary class. They do not, as the bourgeois did in England and France, claim political power when the social revolution is largely over; and they cannot, as the English Parliamentarians did, put forward revolutionary political claims without admitting (even to themselves) that they are revolutionary. They make a political revolution not to complete but to begin a social revolution, and both as political and social revolutionaries they know what they are doing; they understand its historical significance.

There are only two conflicts between major classes, conflicts which transform society so deeply that the transformation is a passing from one historical epoch into another, of which Marx and Engels speak in sufficient detail to make a comparison between their accounts worth while. Comparing these two accounts we see how very different are the class conflicts they describe. I do not say this in criticism of Marx and Engels. If we hold that all great social and political transformations arise out of class conflicts, we are not bound to offer only one model of a class conflict. There is no reason why one major class conflict should not differ from another as greatly as the Hundred Years War differs from Hitler's War. Rather than criticism, I should utter a warning.

As Marx and Engels were much more interested in the struggle of the proletariat than of any earlier revolutionary class, a struggle in their time confined to Europe, their ways of thinking and speaking about class conflicts and revolution generally are very deeply marked by their conception of one particular struggle. This is still largely true of their disciples. When they speak of revolution and class conflict, they still have in mind the sort of action which Marx and Engels believed that the proletariat in the West were taking or must take to destroy capitalism. They still often take what the founders of Marxism believed was happening or was soon to happen in Europe as *the* model of revolution and class conflict; which means that the terms they use to describe these kinds of events apply without distortion much less widely than they suppose.

VII. CLASS CONSCIOUSNESS

Marx and Engels often use the term ' class-consciousness'. The French peasants, Marx tells us in the *Eighteenth Brumaire of Louis Bonaparte*, are not a *class-conscious* class. They have a way of life, a culture, and interests which mark them off from other classes, but their similar interests beget no unity; they do not work together to promote their interests, they have no organizations of their own to take political action on their behalf. They are, no doubt, aware of themselves as a class different from other classes; they think of themselves and refer to themselves as peasants. They have class-consciousness in the same sense as people have national consciousness. But they have not what Marx understands by class-consciousness because they do not act together to further their interests.

The bourgeois have class-consciousness; they work together to further their interests. They do not merely know what they want as individuals; they do not merely have personal ambitions. They have demands which they make in common; they know what they want done on their behalf as a class, or, if all of them do not know, they have leaders who do know, and whose leadership they accept. They are organized to make collective demands, and could not even decide what demands to make unless they were organized. To act as a group, to be able to formulate collective aims and to pursue them, a class must be organized. Any class, to be actively engaged in a conflict with other classes, must be class-conscious in this sense.

There is also, I think, another sense which Marx and Engels give to the term *class-consciousness*; and in this sense of it, no class other than the proletariat need be fully class-conscious in order to make successfully the social and political revolution which they are destined to make. The bourgeois had to organize to promote their class interests before they could by their action gradually transform society; but they

L*

did not need to understand the historical significance of what they were doing. They did not have to see themselves as transformers of society in order to transform it. It was never necessary to their playing their part in history that they should consciously undertake the destruction of one social and political system and its replacement by another. But the proletariat, in order to accomplish their historic task, must understand its significance as a whole; for they are to be the *architects* of a new society as the bourgeois before them never were. They are to be revolutionaries in a deeper sense. They do not unwittingly change the system as they pursue their class interests; they see that it is their interest to change the system, and do not change it until they see that it is their interest.

I confess that I have never understood why this should be so. Of course, the study of history and the social studies, which hardly existed while feudalism was giving way to capitalism, were flourishing in the nineteenth century, and it was therefore much more likely that a group active in that century should entertain theories about its place in society and in history. These theories might have more or less of fantasy about them, but their power to influence action would presumably not depend on their truth. The very notions of a course of social development and of a transformation of society were unknown in Western Europe when the bourgeois embarked on the activities which helped eventually to bring feudalism to an end. They had to work in the dark because the light, because the serious study of history and society, came only when their task was almost done. The proletariat, starting upon their task with the light, can aim deliberately at the transformation of society. But this explains only why the proletariat *can* do deliberately what the bourgeois in their time did undeliberately; it does not explain why they *need* to understand their historic rôle in order to accomplish it. Yet Marx and Engels tell us in the *Manifesto*, that the communists are ' the most advanced and resolute section of the working-class parties of every country, that section which pushes forward all the others . . . they have over the great mass of the proletariat the advantage of clearly understanding the line of march, the conditions, and the ultimate general results of the proletarian movement.'[1] It is clear from the context that Marx and Engels look upon this understanding as a condition of successful proletarian revolution; for the communists must not keep it to themselves but must impart it to the class whose advanced section they are.

A class cannot be revolutionary unless it is class-conscious; but it can be revolutionary and class-conscious in one or both of two senses. It can be class-conscious merely in the sense that it is organized to pursue its interests, and revolutionary merely in the sense that, as it pursues

[1] *The Communist Manifesto,* London, 1948 edition, p. 142.

its interests, it in fact transforms society; or it can be class-conscious also in the sense that it understands its historic rôle, and revolutionary also in the sense that it deliberately sets about accomplishing it. The bourgeois were revolutionary and class-conscious almost entirely in the first sense; the proletariat are or will be so in both senses.

The transformation of feudal into capitalist society was a long process; it was certainly not smooth but it was long. Political power did not pass directly from the feudal nobility to the bourgeoisie; there was no simple taking over the government of society by one class from another. The bourgeois at first supported the monarch against the nobles; they grew in numbers, wealth, and influence under the wing of a more or less absolute monarchy which cannot (Marx admits it) be fairly described as a political instrument of their class. They did not, as a class, begin to govern until long after the feudal nobility had lost most of its power. But the transformation of capitalist into socialist society, as Marx and Engels conceive of it, is to be very much more rapid. Control of the State is to pass quickly from the bourgeois to the proletarians. The building up of the revolutionary potential of the proletariat takes a considerable time; the workers acquire political experience in the course of a prolonged struggle against the dominant class; there are many assaults before the political hold of that class on society is loosened. But as soon as it is loosened, it is quickly lost. Not necessarily all at once, but within a short period of time. For the proletariat, ripeness is all. They must strike again and again, not so much to capture the citadel piece by piece, as to learn how to strike the blow which, when their hour comes, will deliver the citadel into their hands. Their political revolution will be a rapid and direct taking of power from the defeated class enemy, as the bourgeois revolution was not.

Marx and Engels had, I think, two reasons for believing this. They saw that, as man's knowledge and his control over nature grow, the speed of social change quickens. Very reasonably, therefore, they expected the social revolution of the future to take much less time than the transition from feudalism to capitalism. But this alone does not suffice to explain why the political revolution of the proletariat, their taking over of the State power, should differ so much from the taking over of that power by the bourgeoisie. Here we must look for another explanation, and presumably it is this. The State power, the machinery of class oppression, controlled by the bourgeois is incomparably stronger than anything that the feudal nobles disposed of. The bourgeois are therefore better placed to defend their class interests intelligently and stubbornly. They also have up against them a revolutionary class whose interests are more and more clearly incompatible with their own. They too are affected by the study of history and society. Just as their class enemies are more self-consciously revolutionary than any revolutionary class before them, so they too are more self-consciously a conservative class, a class defending a threatened social system, than any conservative class before them. Hence the special character of the political struggle between the bourgeois and the proletarians, making it probable that the proletarian capture of the State, when once it begins, will be rapid and complete. Though blood was often shed during the struggle of the bourgeois for power, there was no rapid unseating of a still completely dominant class, even during the great French Revolution; for the French nobles did not rule France before 1789 and had already lost many of their privileges.

The proletariat are a revolutionary class in a special sense, and the proletarian revolution has a character all its own. But this does not mean that the proletarian revolution must involve the shedding of much blood, or indeed of any blood at all. Logically, violence, the shedding of blood, is no essential part of revolution as Marx and Engels conceived of it. True, they thought there would be violence when the proletariat took over power, in most countries if not in all. They even at times, I suspect, took pleasure in the thought that there would be. They were not very gentle persons; nor did they believe, as certain other socialists and communists of their day did, that violence is wrong or that it corrupts those who use it. But all this takes nothing away from the point I am making: revolution, as Marx and Engels conceived of it, does not necessarily involve violence. A class may be consciously revolutionary, may aim deliberately at transforming the social and political system, and yet may be able to achieve its purpose without violence; just as it may not be consciously revolutionary (or indeed revolutionary at all) and yet may, in the pursuit of its interests, be very willing to use violence. No doubt, Marx and Engels believed that the proletariat, in the process of learning to take effective political action, would take many hard knocks from the police and the armed forces; but they did not exclude the possibility that, at least in England and the United States, the actual taking over of power by the working-class might be peaceful. Not that they thought that the bourgeois, moved by a sense of justice, would willingly hand over power to the workers, but they did for a time think it possible that they might in some countries, when the challenge came, surrender power to their class enemies without resorting to violence. Battles and even wars between nations can be lost and won almost without the shedding of blood. So why not also conflicts between classes? 'Force is the midwife of every new society.' It is true that Marx said that. But what of it? Force also decides the issue of every military encounter including the one at Yorktown, where the wise and humane Cornwallis surrendered to the Americans without a fight.

B. *Class Interests, Irreconcilable Class Interests, and Exploitation*

Marx often says that the interests of certain classes are irreconcilable, that it is simple-minded to believe that they can be reconciled by an appeal to justice, and that therefore a conflict of interests of this kind can end only when one (or both) of the parties to it ceases to exist. When one class exploits another, the interests of the two classes are irreconcilable, and the conflict of interests cannot end while both classes remain in existence. Two classes can also have irreconcilable interests though neither exploits the other. The interests of the rising bourgeoisie were irreconcilable with those of the feudal nobles, even though the bourgeois were not exploited by the nobles. The two classes were never reconciled. The conflict between them ended only with the disappearance of the feudal nobility. This did not necessarily involve the ruin of particular families; the descendants of many feudal lords became capitalist landowners. They even intermarried with the newly rich, at first taking their well-supplied daughters, and afterwards, as they grew bolder, giving them their own daughters in return. Still, though many feudal families survived, they ceased to be feudal; their class, as a class in the Marxian sense, disappeared. Or, to say the same thing in other words, the character of their class changed so profoundly that it ceased to be a feudal nobility, though the descendants of that nobility retained a social prestige on account of their descent.

What do Marx and Engels mean when they say that class interests are *irreconcilable*? What do they understand by *exploitation*? These two questions must be answered separately, for, as we have seen, there can be irreconcilable class interests even where there is no exploitation.

I. RECONCILING INTERESTS

Let us first see how we ordinarily speak of the reconciling of interests. John wants one thing and James wants another, and it looks as if both of them cannot get what they want. But, fortunately, means are discovered of giving them both what they want. Their interests are reconciled. This is the simplest case of all, where the reconciling of interests is merely the contriving that everyone gets what he wants. By simplest I mean the most easily explained; because the actual contriving, even when it succeeds, is often difficult.

It may, however, prove impossible to reconcile interests in this way. John wants several things and James wants several others, and there is no way of ensuring that they both get what they want. Their interests are incompatible in the sense that, if John gets all he wants,

James cannot get all he wants; and the contrary is also true. Nonetheless, a settlement is reached between John and James giving each of them part of what he wants, and the settlement seems just to both of them. Their interests are reconciled; for though they may not be satisfied with what they get, they are satisfied that justice has been done between them. But suppose that James has been bullied into accepting a settlement which he thinks unjust. He then says (unless fear stops his mouth) that his interest has been sacrificed to John's. Though a settlement has been reached, interests have not been reconciled.

Though James has in fact been bullied, it may yet be that he and John have much the same standards of justice. This may be so, even if John has taken part in bullying James. In that case we can say that their interests, though they have not been reconciled, are in principle reconcilable, in the sense that, given the facts of the situation, there is a settlement which, by the standards of both parties to the dispute, is a just settlement. John may have so difficult a character that he refuses to accept this settlement; there may be no arguing with him because he refuses to listen to reason. It is in fact impossible to get him to accept what, by his own standards of justice, the standards he would apply impartially in a case in which he was not himself involved, is a just settlement. And yet we should say that his interests and James' are in principle reconcilable. They would be irreconcilable in principle only if there were no settlement which could be reached which would be just by standards common to both of them.

But standards of justice are not unchanging any more than are the demands men make upon one another. John and James have irreconcilable interests only as long as their demands are incompatible with one another and they have no common and relevant standards enabling them to reach a just settlement. If either their demands or their standards change, their interests may cease to be irreconcilable. And it is a matter of observed fact that people's standards and interests do change, and that they change in the process which adjusts demands to one another.

To get our bearings in this matter, we must distinguish between desires and interests; for as soon as we make this distinction we see that interests and standards are not related to one another as Marx believed they were. A child, before it has become a moral person, makes demands on the persons who look after it, demands as yet untouched by any idea of justice. But it soon discovers that there are limits to what other people will do, and that it must make concessions to them if it is to get what it asks of them. It must abate its demands to suit them, if its demands are to be met. As it learns that this adjustment, this moderating of demand, is required of everyone, and not only of itself, it comes to accept it, not only as expedient, but as just. It acquires notions of justice; it no longer demands whatever it desires but only what it feels entitled to. Indeed, its standards affect even its desires; it ceases not only to demand, but often even to desire, what it feels it is not entitled to. And because the child has some standards, because it is willing to take account of the claims of others, it can be reasoned with, it can be persuaded, and it can be trusted as it could not be before it acquired them.

The child, having acquired standards, does not retain them unchanged throughout its life. As a moral and rational person, it is more than a mere subject of appetites; it has a 'place' in society and is aware that it has one, it has more or less settled preferences and ambitions. It has what most men (and Marx) understand by *interests*. And the closer it is to being an adult, the more this is true. But the standards of even an adult change. In pursuing its interests, it makes demands which others refuse to meet. If the demands are refused because the standards of the person who makes them differ from those of the persons upon whom he makes them, it is, for the time being, impossible to reach a settlement which seems just to all the parties to it. Yet, eventually, such a settlement may be reached, because the parties to it have both abated their demands and modified their notions of what justice requires. If some of them have done only the first, the settlement will not seem just to them; it will seem just only if there has been a change in their ideas about what they are entitled to.

No doubt, grown-up persons do not change their standards easily; they are much more set in their beliefs and habits than children are. They are strongly wedded to their principles, and press their demands all the more obstinately because they find them just. Nevertheless, they do change their standards, as well as moderate their demands, though they often do so painfully and slowly, and often also without themselves being aware that they do so. As Hegel, whose writings Marx studied (not always to good purpose) understood, it is because men are self-conscious and self-critical creatures active in a social environment that they acquire standards of justice and other values, which are not unchanging, precisely because they are the standards and values of self-critical creatures whose need of one another is as deep as their need to assert themselves.

If this is true of individuals and their interests and standards, why should we suppose that it is not true also of classes and other groups? Since every large community consists of many smaller ones, and also of many classes and other groups, and since all these groups and communities are differently placed from one another, it is only to be expected that, at any particular time, there will be group interests and group standards which are incompatible. Therefore, at any one time, there will be irreconcilable interests in the large community, both between individuals and between groups. Men coming from different parts of the large community or belonging to different classes and groups inside it may be involved in disputes with one another and have no common and relevant standards enabling them to reach a just settlement, even when they agree about the facts. Their interests will then be irreconcilable. The same may happen with organized groups. They too may be involved in disputes of this kind, and therefore have irreconcilable interests. But, the more frequent these disputes, the stronger will be the need felt for standards making it possible to reach just settlements.

Since group and class interests are always changing and there are always new groups and classes arising, there will always be *some* irreconcilable group and class interests, just as there will always be some irreconcilable individual interests. But they will remain irreconcilable only as long as the classes or groups or individuals whose interests they are persist in their demands and do not change their standards. When we say that interests are irreconcilable, in this sense, we say nothing about the chances that a just settlement will be made. We make only a hypothetical statement. We say, if these people persist in making these demands and standing by these notions of what is just, they can never reach a settlement acceptable to them all; *we do not predict that they will persist.*

But Marx and Engels, when they call the interests of certain classes irreconcilable, say more than this; they say that these classes, having incompatible interests and standards of justice, have no hope of reconciling their interests. Their interests arise out of the social relations they stand in; they are determined by how these classes are situated in society. Given the social situation of a class, its class interests are also given, and to the extent that it is aware of these interests, its standards are determined by them. It may, if it is an exploited class, be conditioned into accepting the standards of the class that exploits it, but these standards are none the less incompatible with its interests. As it comes to know these interests, it acquires the standards appropriate to them; it acquires the class morality which corresponds to its 'true' class interests. What a class is, its social situation, determines its class interests, which in turn, to the extent that the class is aware of them, determine its class standards. Therefore, if it knows its interests and they are incompatible with those of another class, the two classes are irreconcilable and must remain so.

This, presumably, does not mean that Marx and Engels deny that classes having irreconcilable interests do not also have common interests. Though they sometimes, perhaps inadvertently, speak as if they believed that, say, capitalists and proletarians have no common interests, this is not a point to be pressed against them, for their argument that no genuine compromise between the two classes is possible does not depend logically on their denying that they have common interests. Moreover, Marx and Engels do sometimes admit that there are or may be interests common to all sections of a community divided into classes.

Nevertheless, the doctrine that there are irreconcilable class interests, *in the form they give to it*, rests on mistaken opinions about how interests and standards are related to one another. If we take a man's interest to be, not his passing desires and demands, but the demands he makes (or which it would be reasonable for him to make) to preserve or improve his position in society, we can agree with Marx that what those demands are depends largely on his position in society. But we should insist against Marx that it also depends largely on his standards, on the moral and other values which he accepts. It is as a social and a moral creature that he has interests. And what is true of the individual is true also of the group or class. The interests of a group or class are either the interests common to its members (which may be common to them even though they do not know that they are so and have to make the discovery before they become aware of themselves as a group having group interests), or they are the reasonable demands made on their behalf by spokesmen whose right to speak for them they recognize. No doubt, group interests differ in some ways from individual interests, but they do not differ from them in the respect needed to lend substance to Marx's doctrine that class interests are irreconcilable. For they too are interests which cannot be defined without reference to the standards supposed to be determined by them.

Therefore, though Marx was right to distinguish interests from mere desires and passing demands and to treat them as arising out of the social situation of the persons whose interests they are, he was wrong in assuming that they are prior to morality. What gives them a relative stability is that they are the select and persistent demands of creatures having a sense of values. He was wrong also in supposing that, where class interests diverge, there is not a need felt to reconcile them strong enough to cause both class interests and class values to change. Just as the still amoral child in learning to moderate its demands becomes a thoughtful and a moral person having not merely appetites but interests, and just as grown men having divergent interests, learn to reconcile them, even (if need be) by modifying, consciously or unconsciously, their moral standards, so too do classes and other groups continually modify both their interests and their values. The process of adjustment, with groups as with individuals, is unending, is both conscious and unconscious, and is often painful and sometimes violent. But it is as much a process of adjusting values to values as interests to interests, because the two are involved in one another. Interests are irreconcilable only while the values involved in them remain unchanged; but they do not so remain. This is a less exciting conclusion than Marx's, no doubt; it is also nearer the truth.

II. 'OBJECTIVE' CLASS INTEREST

Marx and Engels speak of *objective* class interests, and of classes knowing and not knowing their interests. They therefore imply a distinction between the actual ambitions of a class, their interests as they or their trusted leaders would describe them, and their objective or true interests. Here we have, not a distinction between mere appetite or impulse and what is properly an interest, but between what people conceive their interest to be and what it really is. This distinction, too, has its difficulties, and we must examine them.

We make this same distinction when we speak of individuals. Someone wants something, but, we say, his true interest is that he should not have it. He is not moved by a momentary impulse or appetite; he has a settled purpose, an ambition. Yet we say that it is not his true interest that it should be satisfied. When we say this we are not passing a moral judgement on his ambition; we are not saying that he would be a better person if he did not have it. We are implying, rather, that if he gets what he wants he will be disappointed. If he gets what he wants, he will find he does not like it, or that he gets other things besides which he dislikes. He will be less contented with his lot for having it. So, too, we can say that a man's true interest is to have something which he does not want or even refuses. In saying this about him, we may take into account only what sort of man he now is, assuming that his character and situation remain more or less unchanged. Or we may also take into account the sort of man we think he will become and his probable future situation. We may say: it is not his true interest to have this, because, though it will satisfy him for the time being, he will find as he grows older that he would rather be without it and cannot get rid of it, or must suffer if he tries to do so. This is the sort of thing that parents say when they suppose themselves to know better than their children what is good for them.

We pass these judgements on groups and classes as well as on individuals. But when we pass them on groups and classes, taking into account, not only their present characters and situations, but also what we think they are likely to become in the future, they are far more hazardous than when we pass them on individuals. All men and all women, unless they die young, pass through the same phases of life: childhood, adolescence, maturity and old age. Each phase has needs and attitudes peculiar to itself. When, therefore, we say to a child, 'this may suit you now, but it won't suit you when you grow up', we may be talking excellent sense; and so, too, when we make a prediction about the old age of some man or woman in the prime of life. In more or less stable societies there is a variety of clearly defined occupations; there are typical careers, typical opportunities; there are ladders of promotion. Everyone's choice of occupations is limited, and, his occupation once chosen, there are limits to what he can do or become. If we know a boy's temperament and abilities, and the situation of his family, we can reasonably say that it is his true interest (though he may not know it) to choose one occupation rather than another; and of a man who has already chosen his occupation, we can say that his true interest, seeing that he is the sort of man he is, is this rather than that.

The same kind of judgement made of a group or class or nation is much more likely to be no better than a guess. Groups and classes do not have a normal span of life, passing through the same phases during the course of it. They do not have typical careers. There are not large numbers of them in similar situations with similar ambitions and with much the same prospects for the future. Judging by what has happened to other soldiers or coalminers or farmers, we can often make reasonable predictions about how this soldier or coalminer or farmer will be placed later on in life if he persists in trying to get what he now wants, saying that he would be better off 'in the long run' (which in any case is not long) if he aimed at something else. But, judging by what has happened to other groups, and even to similar groups in other countries or in former ages, we cannot, with anything like the same chance of being right, predict the remoter consequences to this or that group of its persisting in one course or embarking on another. And when it is about classes, in the Marxian sense of class, that we make our predictions, we are even worse placed than when we make them about smaller and more homogeneous groups. Sometimes, no doubt, in a stable society, we can make more or less reasonable predictions for a few decades ahead. But what are a few decades in the life of a class?

An individual has a normal span of life, and often also a fairly stable environment. If the environment is not stable, judgements, his own or other people's, about the remoter consequences to him of his persisting in his present course are apt to be worthless. It is then almost impossible to discover his true interest, unless we take into account no more than a few months or even weeks ahead. In the summer of 1917 it was far more difficult to make reasonable judgements about the true interests of Russians than of Englishmen. But a class has not only no normal or predictable life-span; its social environment, even in a slowly changing society, is not stable. A class endures much longer than an individual, and the longer it endures, the more society changes.

It is odd to speak of the interests of classes over long periods of time for yet another reason. A class does not have identity in the same sense as an individual has it. If you tell a young man that he will be better off in middle and old age for changing his present intentions, he has, if he believes your reasons are good, a strong motive for changing them. You may hope to persuade him that it is his true interest to aim at something different from what he is now aiming at. But in what sense could it be the true interest of the proletarians of one generation to work for a revolution which is not to happen until after they are dead? They may be better off for not working for revolution even though the workers who come after them stand to lose by their indifference. If they are unwilling to make sacrifices for their successors, and yet are forced to make them, can we say that they are working for their own true interests? Surely, it makes better sense to say that they are being forced to sacrifice their own interests to those of future generations? Are they, then, working for the true interests of their class? But they belong to that class no less than their successors do, and what makes for their happiness is as much part of the true interest of the class as what makes for the happiness of their successors. Even if they are willing to make sacrifices for those who come after, it is only their true interest to do so, if they are happier or find life better worth living for doing so.

The interests of a class are merely the interests common to its members; they are whatever satisfies the demands made by its members, or made on their behalf by their acknowledged spokesmen. Its true or objective interests are whatever makes for their enduring satisfaction, whatever satisfies their ambitions without stimulating in them ambitions which cannot be satisfied. If the class we have in mind, like the Marxian classes, lasts many generations, what are the interests common to its members? The situation of the class changes from generation to generation, and so do its members, *and* the interests common to them, *and* what makes for their enduring satisfaction, their sense of well-being. What, then, are the true or objective interests of the class? John at seventy is the same person as John at seven. It makes sense to say that, given his character, his situation, and his prospects, this rather than that was or is or will be his true interest; that, had he aimed at it, or were he to do so now or in the future, he would have been or would be the happier for it. But it hardly makes sense to speak of a class in this way, except for relatively short periods of time, while its situation and its members do not greatly change.[1]

III. EXPLOITATION

The Marxian conception of exploitation is open to serious criticism on the ground that it treats only some kinds of useful work as creating

---

[1] Of a corporate body whose functions are precisely defined, we can say that its true interest is whatever enables it to carry out those functions efficiently. But then its functions are defined without regard to the ambitions or happiness of its members. A class is not a corporate body. A profession may be so. In that case, we must distinguish between its true interest in the sense of what makes for its efficiency, and its true interest in the sense of what makes for the enduring happiness of its members.

value. There are functions which Marx and Engels do not deny are useful, and even necessary, but which they will not treat as productive labour, as creating value. For example, the maintenance of order. Unless order is maintained, production cannot go on smoothly; and it is illogical to treat only the work directly involved in production as productive if there are also other kinds of work which are conditions of efficient production. Exploitation, as Marx defines it, is the appropriation of surplus-value, the taking away from those who produce value of part of the value they produce; and exploitation is not theft because it is legal. Those engaged in non-productive (but not therefore useless) work are paid, so Marx would have us believe, out of the surplus-value appropriated from productive workers. They live on surplus-value just as much as people who do no work at all.

It is true that Marx and Engels predict the disappearance of the State, but this, as we shall see later, does not involve the disappearance of all the functions now carried out by the State, but only of some. Therefore many functions which are not productive labour, as Marx defines it, will survive into the classless society, presumably because they are useful. It is odd to deny that useful, and even indispensable, services are forms of labour that create value.

Marx and Engels admit that the State is necessary in class societies, where its function is to keep the peace between classes whose interests are irreconcilable. They admit that peace is necessary to production, and that, in class societies, there must be a State to keep the peace. There appears to be here a contradiction in Marxian theory. The State is called oppressive, though its function is admitted to be necessary at a certain stage of social development. It would be absurd, Marx tells us, to try to set up a classless and stateless society where conditions do not allow it. The conditions that do allow it are high productivity and a high level of education in all sections of the community. Capitalism, as it develops, helps to create these two conditions. In that sense, it is progressive. But capitalist production could not go on unless the social order were maintained, which, in a class society, it cannot be except by the State. The State is therefore more than an unavoidable evil; it is a condition of progress. How then can it be merely oppressive? How can we deny that those who carry out its functions are engaged in labour which creates value? True, they produce not goods but services; but services can have value as well as goods. Are indispensable services without value now because in the future they will be dispensed with? We might as well say that the services of a nurse are now without value because the child she looks after will not need them when it is older and more mature. The labour theory of value and the doctrine of exploitation derived from it rest on the paradox that not all services indispensable to society are labour which creates value.

A social system might give rise to activities which are unavoidable and yet harmful, activities not necessary to the proper functioning of the system or to its evolution towards something better. There might be, in this sense, some unavoidable but quite useless and even harmful activities. The persons engaged in them, since they consume the produce of other people's labour without doing anything useful themselves, might be called exploiters. They would be no less exploiters than the bone idle. Or a social system might give rise to activities which are necessary to its functioning and its evolution towards something better but which will disappear when that something better comes into the world. To call these last activities oppressive and the persons who carry them on exploiters is to misuse language.

The Marxian theory of exploitation lays so much stress on particular rights of property (e.g. the rights peculiar to capitalists) which make possible the appropriation of surplus-value that Marxists ordinarily deny that there can be exploitation where these rights do not exist; and since these rights are used to distinguish classes from one another, they also deny that there can be exploitation in a classless society. Thus, today, Marxists, if they wish to establish that there is no exploitation in the Soviet Union, set about showing that there are no classes there. Exploitation, thus conceived, is both too wide and too narrow a concept. Sometimes it requires us to treat as exploiters people whose services are indispensable, and at other times inhibits us from treating as exploiters people who compel others to contribute to purposes they do not share but who do not, in the Marxian sense of class, belong to a different class from their victims.

There is, I believe, another important sense in which Marx and his disciples speak of exploitation. This sense has nothing to do with the appropriation of surplus-value. It is a sense which Marx does not define or distinguish from the other.

Professor Acton says that *exploitation* is a moral term. He means, presumably, not merely that it is often used to condemn the activity it refers to, but that it is always so used. I believe that he is mistaken, and that it is important, if we are to do justice to Marx, to realize that exploitation is not always a moral term.

No doubt, Marx condemned exploitation, both in the sense which involves appropriation of surplus-value and in other senses. But it is possible to apply a word to an activity usually condemned or praised without using the word to condemn or praise it. I usually condemn murder; but it does not follow that, when I say 'Yusupov murdered Rasputin', I am condemning Yusupov. I may be saying no more than that Yusupov killed Rasputin illegally, which is merely a statement of fact. The word *murder* is often used to condemn a killing and often to describe it; but surely, though the word has these two uses, we are not bound to make the first use whenever we make the second. The context reveals our purpose; and only when it does not do so need we take the precaution of saying 'illegal killing' instead of 'murder'.

Exploitation is a word like murder; it is often, but not always, a moral term. It refers to an activity which is against the law or which contravenes standards which men accept or might accept. But we can apply the term to an activity without ourselves accepting those standards; and even if we do accept them, we can apply the term without ourselves invoking the standards. We may be speaking of someone in a society different from our own, and even of an activity which in our society is thought good, and we may call it exploitation, meaning that the activity is of a type which in that society is usually condemned; and we may also condemn it ourselves (because we prefer the other society to our own) without revealing that we do so by calling it exploitation.

We may also believe – and this, I think, brings us to the important sense of the word exploitation, which Marx sometimes used without defining it – that there are some things which all men would think desirable if they understood what sort of creature man is and what he is capable of. We may hold, as Hegel and others have done, that in a particular community men have the values and ambitions they do have only because their understanding is limited. If they understood themselves and the world more fully, they would have different values, and would be the happier for having them. We may find that certain activities which people engage in for their own advantage prevent other people getting this fuller understanding and thus acquiring the values which come with it. We may then call these activities *exploitation*, even though they are not condemned by either exploiters or exploited, who are equally ignorant of their consequences. For example, we may say that, in some societies, women are exploited, even though they are not dissatisfied with their lot. We need not be saying that by our standards they are badly treated, nor need we imply that our standards are better than theirs. We may be saying no more than this: by standards which they would accept if they understood human nature and human capacities better than they do, they are being badly treated. This, on the face of it, is not a moral judgement; it does not imply that the standards which come with a fuller understanding are higher than the standards they supersede. But, of course, if the judgement is not to be a moral judgement, the fuller understanding must not be what is sometimes called a deeper moral insight; it must be no more than a deeper understanding of the facts and the possibilities, social and psychological. It must be an understanding which can be expressed without making any moral judgement. We then say only that, when men come to have this understanding, they are disposed to accept these values, and to be satisfied in so doing because their circumstances are then such that they both desire to realize these values and are able to do so. There is attained a harmony of desires, resources and values.

Marx believed that men's values change as their understanding of themselves and their environment grows, and also that eventually they will have values and resources enabling them to lead far more fully satisfying lives than ever before. He may have been mistaken in the latter part of his belief. For the moment, I am not concerned to argue that he was or was not. I want only to say that the assertion of this belief is not in itself a value judgement; it is merely a prediction which may be true or false. No doubt, if Marx had not been a moralist, if he had not himself accepted the values which he ascribed to the future communist society, he would not have made this prediction. It is the prediction of a moralist but it is not a moral judgement.

Of course, I willingly concede that Marx and Engels did often speak as if the values that come with this understanding were higher than the ones they supersede, and also that they often used the word *exploitation* to condemn the activity they applied it to. Nevertheless, they were concerned to do more than just say that the values of the classless society are the highest; they also implied, firstly, that they are values which men in fact prefer to all others when they understand themselves and their environment, and secondly, that they are values in which alone men find enduring satisfaction.[1] If, then, some men use other men in ways which make it more difficult for them to get this understanding and these values, they are exploiting them; they are helping to prevent their getting what they may as yet have no idea of, and therefore do not desire, but would prefer to their present condition if only they knew about it. If this is exploitation – and it is, I think, what Marx *sometimes* meant by the word – then we do not use it as a moral term.

This is not, surely, an unusual use of it. It is often part of what we mean when we say that children or other more or less ignorant persons are being exploited. Admittedly, it is not often the whole but only part of our meaning, the other part being a moral judgement. That is to say, even when we speak of children and ignorant persons being exploited, we ordinarily use the word to condemn as well as to describe an activity. Nevertheless, it is not merely a moral term, and we can use it, if we take the trouble to make our purpose plain, to describe without condemning.

---

[1] Marx and Engels imply this when they speak of the morality of the future classless society as if it were somehow more human than the morality of their day, and also when they speak of *alienation*; of which more later.

III. WHAT DID MARX AND ENGELS MEAN BY IDEOLOGY? HOW DID THEY CONCEIVE OF ITS FUNCTION IN SOCIETY?

Sometimes, when a commentator sets about explaining a theory, he makes it out to be simpler and neater than it is in order to make better sense of it. It is a temptation sometimes difficult to resist; it appeals to the love of order if not to charity in him. Several critics of Marxism have succumbed to it. Among the social activities and features of social life which Marx puts into the *superstructure*, which he distinguishes from the economic *substructure* of society, are law and government and also what he calls the social forms of consciousness. Marx says of these forms of consciousness that they are *ideological*. It might seem, then, that he distinguishes, within the superstructure, between what is ideological and what is not.

No doubt, it would be better if he had done what some of his critics assume he has done; for then one important part of his theory would be clearer and sounder than it is. But, unfortunately, the matter is not as simple as that.

Marxian Uses of the Word 'Ideology'

There are at least three different senses in which Marx and Engels use the word *ideology*, though they do not distinguish between them.

Sometimes, when they speak of *ideology*, they seem to have in mind the entire system of ideas which men use to describe the world and to express their feelings and purposes. This sense is to the fore when Marx and Engels are most self-consciously materialists, when they are concerned to show how men come to have ideas at all. This, perhaps the most obscure sense of the three, is also the least interesting to the social and political theorist. Though not exactly taken from Hegel, it is an adaptation of an idea central to his philosophy. Hegel had spoken of Spirit, of the Real, as essentially active and as coming to know itself through its activities. Spirit is what it does, and by doing acquires self-knowledge. Marx speaks of man as essentially practical, and as coming to understand himself and the world through what he does to satisfy his needs. Men are active in a natural environment which they adapt to their needs, and by their actions they create a social environment which deeply affects them. They learn to think, they acquire a coherent picture of the world and of themselves in it, as they strive to satisfy their needs. But Marx and Engels are not content merely to say that men learn to think in the process of acting to satisfy their needs. They go further than this; they say that how men conceive of the world and themselves is determined by their needs and what they do to satisfy them; by *social production*. They speak as if this conclusion followed, granted that men learn to think in the process of satisfying their needs.

Yet they do not deny that all social activities, not excluding production, involve the use of ideas. Thus, they seem to be saying that certain activities, which are basic in relation to all others, determine men's ideas, and yet to be willing to admit, at least tacitly, that even these basic activities involve the use of ideas. All social activities are rational, in the sense that they involve the use of ideas, and yet some, the ones that are basic, determine what ideas men use. If this is a position that Marx and Engels take up – and it has been argued, not unplausibly, that they do – then it is, so it seems to me, untenable. Even if we allow that men acquire language and the use of concepts as they co-operate to satisfy their needs, it does not follow that we can treat this co-operation, this social production, as a factor which determines what concepts they have and how they use them.

So far, we have been considering only one Marxian sense of the term *ideology*, and that the least important to the social and political theorist. There are two other senses, a wider and a narrower. The wider treats as ideology all theories and doctrines which are not scientific, and also all normative concepts. It marks a retreat from the extreme position which I said was untenable; its use is a tacit recognition that the ideas used to describe the world, whether at the level of ordinary common sense or at the level of science, are not determined by what men do to satisfy their needs, even though they are the ideas of creatures who would never have sought to understand the world had they not had needs to satisfy.

The narrower sense treats as ideology, not all normative concepts, but only those which serve the interests of some class or group, and also all theories and doctrines which are not scientific. This sense is prominent when Marx or Engels is trying to explain the behaviour of social classes.

Critics of Marxism who take it for granted that Marx and Engels make a clear distinction, within the superstructure, between law and government, on the one hand, and what they call 'the social forms of consciousness', on the other, imply that it is in what I have called the narrower sense that the two masters ordinarily use the term *ideology*. Indeed, these critics sometimes imply that they use it in an even narrower sense, to refer only to theories and doctrines which are not scientific. But this is not true. Marx and Engels often use the term in ways which suggest that all normative concepts are ideological, and they seldom use it in ways which suggest that none is so. When, for example, they speak of law and morality as part of the 'ideological superstructure', they clearly imply that all important normative concepts are ideological; they are speaking, not just of theories about law and morality, but of legal and moral rules and of the concepts they contain.

For example, in the Preface to *A Contribution to the Critique of Political Economy*, Marx, having spoken of a conflict between the *forces* and the *relations* of production, invites us to distinguish between the 'material transformation of the economic conditions of production' resulting from this conflict and the 'legal, political, religious, aesthetic and philosophical – in short *ideological* – forms in which man becomes conscious of this conflict and fights it out.' This passage, no doubt, is multiply obscure; it casts shadow upon shadow. Marx seems to be saying both that there are two types of conflict and that there is only one: that there is conflict within the economic substructure giving rise to conflicts within the superstructure, and also that the conflicts within the superstructure are merely ways of being aware of, and carrying on, the conflicts within the substructure. But, fortunately, there is no need, for our present purpose, to try to dispel the manifold obscurities of this often-quoted and therefore familiar statement. For the statement, highly obscure though it is, does at least plainly suggest two things: that there is nothing ideological about the activities which belong to the economic *substructure,* and that the entire *superstructure* is ideological. In this statement, therefore, we see Marx using the word ideological in the wider of the two senses of which the social and political theorist need take notice.

I have said that Marx and Engels were sometimes moved by their *materialism* to speak as if all ideas were determined by social activities prior to them, as if how men think about the world and speak about it to one another were determined by how they co-operate to produce what satisfies their needs; and I have said also that they could not abide by this position, that they had to admit, at least by implication, that all social activities, not excluding production, involve the use of ideas. Yet their materialism, though it did not prevent their admitting what was too obvious to be denied, did move them to use the word *ideology* in as wide a sense as possible. They felt that their materialism required them to treat *all* ideas as determined by activities more fundamental than they are, activities whose function is to satisfy needs. They could not in practice, without patent absurdity, do what their materialism seemed to them to require, but they went as far as they could towards doing it.

I now want to show, if I can, that their bias towards including as much as possible under the head of *ideology* drives them to include more than is consistent either with what they suggest is the primary social function of ideology or with the most striking characteristic they ascribe to it. If not always, certainly very often, they speak as if the function of ideology were to promote or challenge the interests of social classes or groups, and especially of dominant and revolutionary classes.

And they say of ideology that it is *false consciousness* or illusion. I shall argue that not everything which serves this function is false consciousness, and that not everything which is false consciousness serves this function. In the Marxian doctrine of ideology we have a medley of ideas not properly sorted out. It is an extraordinarily confused doctrine, and yet also important and suggestive.

I have said that Marx and Engels use the term *ideology* in too wide a sense for their own purposes, and also that they use it in two senses interesting to the social theorist. Evidently, it is the wider of these two which is the less suited to their purposes; but the narrower is also not well suited to them. It, too, is too wide, for it cannot always be said of it that it refers to false consciousness or to what serves or challenges class or other group interests. Nevertheless, it is this narrower sense which is the more important and suggestive. There are, buried in the morass of the Marxian doctrine of ideology, ideas well worth extracting for their usefulness as tools of explanation.

But before I attempt this extraction, let me give examples to show how easily Marx and Engels could pass from one sense of ideology to another without being aware that they had done so. Though they pass from one to the other unconsciously, they do not do so at random but as serves the need of the argument. They create confusion and exploit it unwittingly, as social theorists so often do.

My examples come from *The German Ideology*. In one place we read:

> Conceiving, thinking, the mental intercourse of men, appear at this stage as the direct efflux of their material behaviour. The same applies to mental production as expressed in the language of the politics, laws, morality, religion, metaphysics of a people. Men are the producers of their conceptions, ideas etc. – real active men, as they are conditioned by a definite development of their productive forces and of the intercourse corresponding to these, up to its furthest forms. Consciousness can never be anything else than conscious existence, and the existence of men is their actual life-process. If in all ideology men and their circumstances appear upside down as in a *camera obscura*, this phenomenon arises just as much from their historical life-process as the inversion of objects on the retina does from their physical life-process[1]

In this passage there is an oscillation between at least two senses of *ideology*: the sense which includes all ideas used in mental intercourse, the widest sense of all; and the sense which includes only normative concepts and theories and doctrines which are not scientific. This

[1] *The German Ideology*, New York, 1947, R. Pascal edit., p. 14.

second sense is suggested by the singling out of the language of *politics, laws, morality, religion* and *metaphysics*, for these languages do not include all ideas but only those involved in the activities relegated to the *superstructure*; and perhaps also by the assertion that *in all ideology men and their circumstances appear upside down*, for presumably they do not appear so in science or in the 'mental intercourse' actually involved in production. This often-quoted passage is not obscure in any ordinary degree, nor is it an empty darkness; it is the darkness of the womb concealing what is already alive but still only half-formed.

In another place we read:

> The individuals composing the ruling class possess among other things consciousness and therefore think. In so far therefore as they rule as a class . . . [they] rule also as thinkers, as producers of ideas. Consequently their ideas are the ruling ideas of the age. For instance, in an age and in a country where royal power, aristocracy, and the bourgeoisie are contending for domination, and where therefore domination is shared, the doctrine of the separation of powers is the dominant idea and is enunciated as an eternal law.[1]

Here the ideas referred to do not include all normative concepts; they include only concepts and doctrines which favour the interests of a class.

2. Moral and Legal Concepts

Marx calls ideology *false consciousness*, and he also calls it *illusion*. I take it that these two expressions have, for him, the same meaning. Now, it makes no sense to treat legal and moral concepts, concepts used to invoke rules of conduct and to make value judgements, as illusory. We may have illusions about them; we may believe that, when we use them, we are doing something different from what we really are doing. Let us suppose, for the sake of argument, that when we use these concepts we are merely invoking rules of conduct or giving vent to our feelings about types of behaviour. Then, if we believe that we are doing more, if we believe that we are describing men's motives or their actions, if we believe that we are referring to qualities inherent in their motives or actions, we are under an illusion. But merely to use the concepts to invoke rules and give vent to feelings is not to be under an illusion. Even if we do not know that that is what we are doing, even if we cannot correctly describe it, we are under no illusion. Any more than M. Jourdain, when he told Nicole to bring him his slippers, was

[1] Op. cit., p. 39.

under an illusion because he did not know that he was speaking prose.

It may be that the effectiveness of rules and moral judgements depends largely on men's being under some sort of illusion about them. It may be that if they did not believe that the judgements referred to qualities inherent in human actions and states of mind, or that the rules followed from the essential nature of man, or were commands of God, or were accepted by all men everywhere, or were adaptations to circumstance of natural or divine or universal law, they would be less moved by the judgements and less disposed to obey the rules. It may be that in all societies men have had, and have needed, some such illusions. I think it probable that Marx and Engels believed that it was so. If they were right, and if ideology is false consciousness or illusion, we can say that there have been ideologies attached to all moral and legal and political systems. Most of these ideologies have not been explicit or elaborate or precise theories and doctrines; more often than not they have been vague though powerful beliefs varying considerably from person to person. Thus, there can be ideology even in the most primitive, the least articulate and sophisticated, the least dogmatic society. But, though it is important to notice these accretions to morality, law, and government, it is no less important to notice that the concepts actually involved in the making of moral judgements, in the invoking of rules of conduct, and in the forms of social intercourse which constitute government are different in kind from them. It makes no sense to call these concepts 'ideological', if ideology is false consciousness or illusion. There is here an important distinction which Marx and Engels failed to make.

Also, it makes no sense to treat these concepts as 'reflections' or 'reflexes' (whatever that may mean) of social relations, no matter how basic the relations are supposed to be; for there are always moral concepts, if not legal ones also, involved in the very having of social relations. They are of the essence of all important forms of social intercourse.

There is another reason, apart from their being used in normative statements which those who make them mistakenly believe to be statements of fact, which disposed Marx to treat moral and legal concepts as ideological. He believed that the function of ideology, of false consciousness, is usually, if not always, to support or to challenge the position or pretensions of some class or other. Ideology, for him and for Engels, is above all class ideology. Now, rules of conduct and moral judgements do sometimes serve to support or challenge the position or pretensions of a class; they can do so just as much as theories and doctrines can, just as much as theology or ethics or social and political theory. Although there must be rules and values which do not serve this purpose (because all social relations involve rules and values, and society is therefore always a moral order, and classes can arise in it only because it is one), yet there are also rules and values which do serve it.

Marx saw that there are rules and values which support class interests; but, unfortunately, he too often lost sight of the fact that there must be others which do not serve this purpose if there are to be communities within which classes can arise. He was therefore sometimes tempted to speak as if concepts involved in rules and value judgements, concepts which are normative but which those who use them are apt to think are descriptive, were illusions serving to support (or challenge) class interests. It came easily to him to treat moral and legal concepts as ideological in a double sense: as serving class interests and as being forms of false consciousness or illusion.

3. Ideology as False Consciousness

If ideology is false consciousness, moral and legal concepts used merely to invoke rules and to make value judgements cannot be called ideological. What then can be plausibly so called? Presumably, such things as theology, metaphysics, ethics, social and political theory. I am not saying that they always are forms of illusion but only that they may be. They may be, they sometimes have been, fantasies whose purveyors have put them forward as true accounts of some aspect or other of reality. It makes sense to say of them that they are forms of false consciousness or illusion. The assertion may not always be true, but at least it is not absurd, as it is to say that moral and legal concepts are so.

When Marx calls such theories and doctrines *false consciousness*, he does not mean that they are sometimes mistaken. Scientists too make mistakes and sometimes very big ones. Yet science is not ideology. What, then, is the difference between them?

The scientist confines himself to explaining the facts of experience; his explanations, his hypotheses, can be tested by an appeal to the facts. As new facts are discovered, or come to be taken into consideration because they are seen to be relevant, old explanations are discarded and others thought to be more adequate take their place. Disputes between scientists can be settled; scientists use, to test their hypotheses and to establish what the facts are, methods which rest on assumptions which they all make. The ideologist, though he claims (and usually sincerely believes) that he is explaining some aspect of the real world, does not confine himself to accounting for the facts; he does not test his hypotheses by an appeal to facts. The primary function of ideology, according to Marx, is not to explain the world but to support interests. The important question to ask about an ideology is not, *Is it true?*, or, *Does it accord with the facts?* It is rather, *Who benefits from it?* We can also usefully ask: *How did it arise?* The answer to this second question often throws light on the first, and the answer to the first on the second. An ideology is a more or less fantastic theory which promotes beliefs which are to the interest of some class or other. This is what Marx and Engels often seem to be saying, though, as we shall see, not always.

'The ideas of the ruling class', we are told, 'are in every age the ruling ideas,' for it is the ruling class who 'regulate the production and distribution of the ideas of their age'.[1] When the position of the ruling class comes to be challenged by another class, there arises a revolutionary ideology; there arise theories and doctrines serving the interest of the revolutionary class. All these ideologies, conservative and revolutionary, put forward the interest of a class as the common interest; they do not openly justify the existing order or challenge it on behalf of a particular class, they justify or challenge it ostensibly for the common good. The function of ideology is to induce as many people as possible to do what it is the interest of some class that they should do; and clearly it cannot carry out this function unless that interest is put forward as the common interest. Yet the makers and purveyors of ideology are not hypocrites; they do not consciously present class interests as the common interest. They are usually sincere in their belief that what they are arguing for is in the common interest.

I have put Marx's position briefly but I hope not unfairly. There is, I think, a considerable measure of truth in it. Many theories, especially theories about man and society, about God and God's purposes for man, and about the universe as a whole tending towards some end, have been largely speculative; or, as some people would put it, have been fantasies. And many of these fantasies have served the interests of some class or other. But there are two observations that I would make: that theories which do not rest on illusion can serve class interests as well as theories which do, and secondly, that theories which are speculative or fantastic, when they do serve interests, do not always, or even usually, serve class interests.

4. Ideology and Class Interests

To establish my first point, let me take social theory as an example. A social theory may seek to explain how society functions, or how it ought to function, or both the one and the other. If it seeks to explain how society functions, it may take serious account of the facts. No doubt, being a social theory, it is likely to be confused and to contain grave errors. It is likely to be confused because of the looseness of the terms used to describe social phenomena, and it is likely to contain grave errors owing to the difficulty of getting at all the relevant facts

[1] *The German Ideology*, p. 39.

and assessing their importance. However impartial the social theorist may be, however eager to discover the truth, however cautious and modest, he is apt to lose his way and commit blunders as the physicist or biologist is not. He has to cope with difficulties which no longer worry the natural scientist. Yet he may be, by temperament, as much an impartial seeker after knowledge as any natural scientist, and he may be very much aware of the difficulties peculiar to his branch of study. If that is so, then his confusions and errors, manifold though they are, cannot properly be called fantasies or false consciousness; any more than the confusions and errors of the natural scientist. They may be bigger mistakes, but still they are only mistakes.

Now, a theory produced by such a theorist might quite easily serve the interests of some class or section of the community, and there might be no good reason for believing that it served them only because of the confusions and errors it contained. Truth is often as useful as error, even to the most self-centred persons or groups. Let us suppose that Marxism is a theory of this kind: an honest, intelligent, impartial attempt to explain the facts of social life by two men conscious of the shortcomings of all social theories before their own and determined to do their utmost to avoid them, and let us suppose also that Marxism happens to favour the interests of the manual working class. We can suppose further, though merely for the sake of argument, that Marxism never pleads for that class nor against any other class. The theory, on this supposition, favours the interests of the manual workers only in the sense that it predicts their victory in a struggle against another class, and so encourages the future victors and discourages their opponents. The theory may become popular precisely because it does this; it may owe its popularity much less to people's being impressed by its intelligence, honesty, and impartiality than to their liking what it predicts. In that case, what makes it popular is that it favours the interests of the working class, and not its intrinsic qualities as a social theory. Does that make it ideology? If so, ideology is not necessarily false consciousness. If this is ideology, then a theory or doctrine, no matter how scientific, is ideological whenever it gains currency primarily because it serves interests.

Marx and Engels believed (much of the time, if not all of it) that their social theory aimed primarily at explaining how society functions and develops, including (among other things) how classes and class interests arise. Perhaps they were mistaken about their theory; it may have been less scientific, even in intention, than they honestly believed it was. But, granted that they were not mistaken, it still remains true that their theory, even if it does not seek to justify claims made by or on behalf of the working class, does predispose people who accept the theory to accept these claims and to work for their realization. It may not commit them logically to doing so. There is nothing illogical about

M

accepting the truth of Marxism and fighting hard against the proletariat, striving to put off the evil day for as long as possible. There are
perhaps some men in the world who will fight the harder against something for being told that its victory is inevitable. But the great majority
of mankind are not like that.

Marx and Engels did not deny that their theory was favourable to
the interests of the working class; they even gloried in the belief that it
was so. Yet they did not call it a class ideology, presumably on the
ground that it was a serious attempt to explain the facts. Ideology, as
they conceived of it, has two essential properties: it is false consciousness or illusion, and it gains currency because it serves interests, especially class interests.[1]

If Marx and Engels had been concerned merely to give notice how
they intended to use the term *ideology*, there would be no point in
quarrelling with them. But in fact they wanted to do more than this.
They often spoke about ideology in such a way as to suggest that any
theory which gains currency because it serves interests is false consciousness, containing a large element of fantasy. The suggestion is
false. Admittedly, they expected their own theory, which they believed
was scientific and not fantastic, to gain currency because it was in line
with the interests of the proletariat. But their hopes for their own
theory are not in keeping with their account of ideology.

It is also important to notice that even a theory which explains what
society ought to be like, a theory which is frankly Utopian, need not
be a form of false consciousness or illusion. Indeed, if the theory is
frankly Utopian, if the maker of it is perfectly aware that he is describing an ideal, it cannot be a form of false consciousness. It may be
fantasy but it is not illusion.

The fantasy may, of course, be unrealistic. It need not be but it may
be. The maker of it may have illusions about human nature or about
the course of history or about God's purposes for man, and his fantasy
may be related causally to his illusions. It may be true that, unless he
had held these false beliefs, he would never have been moved to construct that particular fantasy. It may be that, misled by these beliefs, he
is convinced that his ideal will be realized or could be realized, when
in fact it will not be or could not be. But he need have no such false
beliefs; he may know that his ideal is unrealizable, or he may have
good grounds for believing that it could be realized.

We must distinguish, as Marx fails to do, between theories and
doctrines which contain false beliefs, and theories and doctrines which
rest on false beliefs. To illustrate my meaning, let me take the doctrine

---

[1] Marxists nowadays will often admit that Marxism is a class ideology. Yet they
still insist that it is scientific. Thus (though they may not know it) they use the
word ideology in a different sense from Marx's; a theory is ideological, in their
sense, if only it gains currency because it serves interests.

of the rights of man as it was put forward in the eighteenth century. In so far as this doctrine does no more than make certain claims on behalf of all mankind, there is nothing illusory about it; it merely asserts that all men have certain rights, which is a way of saying how they ought to be treated and what they ought to be allowed to do. The illusion, if it exists, is not in putting forward the claims; it is in the statements made to support them. These statements may be about human nature, or about what has to be done to make good the claims, or about something else; and they may be false. Or they may be so vague that it is impossible to discover whether they are false or true. And yet the claims may be accepted largely because the statements used to support them are accepted. Certainly, there were many illusions connected with the eighteenth-century assertion of the rights of man. Yet to call that assertion a form of false consciousness does not really make sense.

As a matter of fact, Marx himself believed in the doctrine of the rights of man. If he had been asked whether men ought to enjoy these rights, or whether they would eventually come to enjoy them, he would have said that they ought and would. He did not always reject even the assertions about human nature used to support these rights; he sometimes spoke as if he believed that men, by reason of their humanity, ought to have these rights. He merely thought that, society being what it was in the eighteenth and nineteenth centuries, only the property-owning classes could in fact enjoy the rights. These classes, though often willing to concede that all men should enjoy the rights, were determined to preserve a system of property which, in Marx's opinion, made it impossible for most men to enjoy them. As he saw it, they falsely believed that these rights could be enjoyed by all classes in a class society, whereas the truth was that they could be enjoyed by all men only in a classless society.

5. Class Ideology and Religion

Marx was concerned with religion as a psychological and social phenomenon before he took to economics or thought of history as a succession of conflicts between classes. He read Feuerbach's *Essence of Christianity* and was deeply excited by it. In that book Feuerbach argues that religion is a fantasy which compensates man for his sense of his own inadequacy, his sense that he is in fact greatly inferior to what he might be. Into his notion of God man projects his idea of what he aspires to and cannot yet attain; he creates God in his own image, or rather in the image of himself as he unconsciously desires to be. His life to come in the company and love of God is the dream in which he seeks the satisfactions still denied him in the world. The idea of God expresses man's sense of his own worth, of the worth of his fully realized self. As his understanding and his opportunities increase, as he comes nearer to being able to live the sort of life which seems to him worthy of his kind, man will give up seeking in fantasy the satisfactions which he will at last be able to get in the real world. The need for religion will pass away. Man will come into full possession of his humanity and will dispense with the illusion of God. Religion is a product of man's immaturity, of his not yet having learnt to live in ways satisfying to himself.

This idea of religion Feuerbach took from Hegel. Where Hegel speaks of Spirit, Feuerbach speaks of man. Reality, for Hegel, is Spirit, and Spirit is essentially active; it is an activity which culminates in complete self-knowledge and satisfaction, it is a process of self-realization. But before Spirit is fully self-realized, before it has attained self-knowledge, it feels itself a stranger in the world as it actually is, even though that world is merely a projection of itself, and it seeks compensation for this sense of self-estrangement in the idea of another world in which it is fully at home and satisfied. And Spirit, for Hegel, at its higher levels, at the levels at which it is self-conscious, is manifest in the activities of finite rational selves, of men, and in the communities formed by them. Thus, if we eliminate the notion of Spirit and speak only of finite selves, of men, we pass easily from the conception of Hegel to that of Feuerbach.[1] Man aspires to full self-realization, to the full exercise of his capacities, which is possible to him only when he has attained self-knowledge and knowledge of the world, when he has come, morally and intellectually, to maturity; and in the meantime, while he is not yet what he aspires to be, while he is frustrated and unsatisfied, he projects his sense of what he has it in him to become and to enjoy into the ideas of God and of an after-life.

This was the account of religion which first excited Marx. But, whereas Feuerbach was concerned primarily with the psychological state of the believer, Marx soon came to take an interest in the social conditions of belief. Religion is the fantasy of man afflicted by the sense of his own inadequacy and will disappear when he is no longer afflicted. But why is he so afflicted? He is so because he lives in a social environment which does not allow him to realize his potentialities. He is the victim of circumstances which, though they are effects of human activities, he cannot control. He is the victim of forces which he has himself produced, though he does not know how he has done so. He

---

[1] While Feuerbach treated religion as sheer fantasy, Hegel did not do so. He said that religion expresses the truth about the world figuratively, while philosophy does so literally; he spoke of Christianity as the highest form of religion, and of his own philosophy as saying literally what Christianity says figuratively. There is no question but that Feuerbach was an atheist, but with Hegel the matter is not so simple.

engages in production to satisfy his wants, but the system of production is such that he is impelled into courses which do not satisfy him. Only when man ceases to be the victim of the productive system and the money economy brought into being by his efforts to satisfy his needs will he be able to live a fully satisfying life. Only then will he cease to be a frustrated, a deprived creature, and have no need to resort to fantasy.

Religion, thus explained, is false consciousness, it is ideology. But it is not obvious that it is class ideology. And yet both Marx and Engels sometimes spoke of religion as if it were class ideology. What had they in mind when they did so?

Though Marx and Engels, in their views about religion, were more deeply influenced by Feuerbach and Hegel than by anyone else, these were not the only influences working upon them. There were older ideas about religion which also, no doubt, affected their thinking.

Ever since political theorists had taken to considering religion as a social phenomenon, they had noticed certain things about it. They had noticed that its beliefs and ceremonies serve to strengthen the ties which hold communities together. They strengthen these ties because religious beliefs provide men with powerful motives for carrying out obligations necessary to the social order, and because religious ceremonies express and magnify feelings which attach men to one another and to the community.

They had also noticed that religion allays men's fears, especially the fear of death, and comforts them when they suffer. And in this idea of religion as a comforter, we can see one of the roots of the conception common to Feuerbach and Marx. The believer takes comfort in religion and also knows that he does so. As he sees it, religion is comforting because it is true. But to the sceptic contemplating the situation of the believer, religion is comforting to the believer because he believes it is true, whether or not it is so. It is, in the eyes of the sceptic, a consoling fantasy; and the idea that it is, or may be, so is, of course, much older than Feuerbach. Feuerbach, inspired by Hegel, adds to this idea two others: the idea of a process of moral and intellectual evolution which first creates the need for such fantasies and then later dispels the need, and the idea that these fantasies express man's sense of his own inadequacy and his largely unconscious aspirations for himself.

The rationalists of the eighteenth century had spoken of religion as if it were a kind of substitute for knowledge. Men are full of curiosity even when they are still ignorant, and therefore put questions which they lack the knowledge to answer. They therefore invent the answers and easily persuade themselves that they are true; for they do not yet know how to test the answers, how to distinguish truth from fantasy. Mind, like nature, abhors a vacuum; where knowledge is out of its reach, it makes do with something which is not knowledge, but which it takes for such. It makes do with theology. But as men acquire knowledge, and above all as they learn to distinguish between true and false knowledge, between what is clearly demonstrated or well attested by the facts and mere fantasy, they come to be satisfied only with knowledge and put fantasy away. It is the opposite of Gresham's law that operates here: it is not bad money that drives good money out of circulation but good money that drives out bad.

True, the more knowledge accumulates, the smaller the proportion of it that any one man can acquire. Even the most learned man will know only a small part of what is to be known, and all men will be more keenly aware of the extent of their ignorance. But more and more of them will be imbued with the scientific spirit, and will know what it is to have true as distinct from counterfeit knowledge. Religions and other fantasies are taken for true not so much because every man's ignorance is great (which it always must be) as because most men do not know how to distinguish genuine from spurious knowledge. Thus it is that the progress of the sciences undermines the old religions. Perhaps the best eighteenth-century account of how this progress loosens the hold of religion is to be found in Condorcet's *Sketch for an Historical Picture of the Progress of the Human Mind*.

It is a theme repeated by Saint-Simon and linked by him with an account of how in the course of social evolution one class supersedes another. In the Middle Ages society was dominated by a feudal class, a class of warriors, and by a Church which preached a body of doctrine well suited to hold together a society of unequals in an unscientific age. But now a new class, the producers of wealth, are coming to dominate society, and their rise to dominance coincides with the disintegration of the old theology and the substitution for it of science, of genuine knowledge. Though Saint-Simon does not call religion *the opium of the people*, he does say that theology flourishes while men are still incapable of explaining the world and themselves scientifically and that it holds together a society in which an unproductive ruling class live off the labour of others. Of the early socialists none had a greater influence on Marx than Saint-Simon.

In the eighteenth century sceptics who felt that they could themselves do without religion often thought it a good thing for the poor and the ignorant, partly because it helped to keep them obedient to the laws and partly because it consoled them in their sufferings. They believed, most of them, that inequality was inevitable, and they conceded that its being so was more obvious to the rich than to the poor. That the social order was in the interest of all classes might be true, but unfortunately it was a truth not equally apparent to all classes; and therefore it was good that the classes least able to appreciate this truth should find in religion a guide and a consoler. So thought the sceptics who were also conservatives. They too did not call religion the opium of the people; but they agreed with Marx and Engels about its effect on the workers and differed from them only in approving the social order which they condemned.

Though the Marxian account of religion owes more to Feuerbach and Hegel than to anyone else, it also bears the mark of other doctrines and attitudes. Neither Hegel nor Feuerbach treats religion as class ideology, and if we want to discover the beginnings of this conception of it, we must turn to French rather than to German thinkers.

If we take religion in the broadest sense, we can hardly call it class ideology. For there have been, and indeed still are, primitive tribal communities without classes in the Marxian sense of class; and these communities are not without religion. But it may be that Marx and Engels, when they speak of religion as if it were a form of class ideology, do not have in mind the kind of religion which flourishes in very simple communities. It may be that they have in mind, not fetishism and magic, but religion which is properly theological, which explains the world as created or governed by a God or a hierarchy of gods. Such a religion is dogmatic and systematic; it embodied a more or less coherent conception of the world, a *Weltanschauung*. This is the kind of religion of which it can most plausibly be said that it is the religion of alienated man, the religion in which he expresses his sense of what he might be and is not, his aspirations and his sense of present inadequacy.

In the Marxian attitude to religion we can discern two elements. The first and the simpler is no more German than it is French or Italian or English; it is the belief that religion flourishes because men are ignorant and will die away as knowledge accumulates, as science destroys illusion. This belief figures more prominently in the writings of Engels than in those of Marx. The second and the less simple is German, coming from Feuerbach and from Hegel; it is the doctrine that religion is the fantasy of alienated man, the fantasy in which man, unable to live a full and satisfying life, seeks compensation for his incapacity. This doctrine, though there is more to it than the age-old belief that religion consoles men for the frustrations and sufferings of this life, has clear affinities with that belief.

Neither of these doctrines – that religion is the child of ignorance and curiosity and that it is a fantasy of alienated man – in itself implies that religion is class ideology. Yet both doctrines are compatible with the belief that it is so. For religion, on either of these views, can be held to be a cement holding society together; and if society is divided into classes, some of which exploit others, it is a cement which helps to make this exploitation possible. For religion to be class ideology, it is not necessary that only the exploited should believe it, that it should be propagated among them by unbelievers to keep them docile. All classes may accept it, and yet, if it serves to hold together a society in which class exploits class, and tends to disappear as the conditions, social and cultural, of the classless society come into being, it is class ideology, as Marx and Engels understood that term.

Marx and Engels did not believe that the mere progress of science would destroy religion; they believed that the root cause of religion, the alienation of man or his incapacity to live a full and satisfying life, would disappear only in the classless society, the society without exploitation, the society in which men would cease to be the victims of their environment and would become its masters. And yet they too saw a close connection between the progress of science and the decay of religion. Progress in the natural sciences had helped to bring into existence the industrial system which had created the proletariat, and progress in the social sciences will eventually ensure the proletariat's becoming the pre-eminently class-conscious class, the class fully aware of its historic rôle, which is to bring to an end the exploitation of class by class, the system which makes alienation possible. Moreover, though Marx and Engels did not believe that the mere progress of science would destroy religion, they did share the belief, already prominent in the eighteenth century, that science and religion are incompatible.

Today, even when we are not believers, it seems less clear to us than it did to sceptics of the eighteenth and nineteenth centuries that science and religion are incompatible. Condorcet and Saint-Simon took it for granted that dogmatic theology is a substitute for science, that it is a premature attempt to answer questions which men are still unable to answer, though they do not recognize their incapacity. Therefore, as they learn how to answer these questions, how to distinguish true from false answers, they discard the false answers; they discard theology and take to science.

It is true that the questions which science and religion claim to answer have something in common: they are not questions about the use of words or concepts, and the answers to them purport to give us information about the world. Nevertheless, science does not claim to answer the same questions as religion. Science seeks to explain only how things happen in the world. It does not pretend to answer such questions as, Is there an Intelligent Being in control of the world? To what end are we in the world? Like theology, it aims at a systematic explanation of the world, but it is explanation of a different kind. Science does not take the place of theology; it does not do more adequately what theology claims to do. The view that it does, prominent in the writings of Condorcet and Saint-Simon and still discernible in those of Engels and even of Marx, is clearly false.

But the sceptics who proclaimed the incompatibility of science and theology held other beliefs less simple than the one I have just discussed. They also believed that, as knowledge accumulates, men come to understand that some questions which theology claims to answer are not properly questions at all, being unintelligible, and that others are unanswerable. The progress of knowledge, as conceived by Condorcet, consists largely in learning how to put genuine questions and how to find answers to them. It is, I think, implicit in his conception of progress that all intelligible questions can be answered, just as it is in the conception of Marx and Engels. But this does not mean that Condorcet and Marx had any very clear ideas about the criteria to be used to decide whether a question is intelligible or answerable. For this is a matter which has received a great deal of attention since their time.

Perhaps many philosophers and scientists would today agree that there are questions about the world which are intelligible, involving no misuse of language or confusion of thought, and which science cannot answer. The answers to these questions, though not amenable to the tests which scientists use, are not mere value judgements but are also statements about the world, statements which are true or false, though science cannot show them to be the one or the other. And these questions, which science cannot answer, are still supremely important to persons who understand science and its methods as well as anyone does. Today there are many people without religion willing to admit all this, but Marx and Engels would probably not have done so. Religion, in their eyes, is ideology or 'false consciousness', and therefore incompatible with science.

Beliefs can be incompatible either logically or psychologically. They are logically incompatible when, if some are true, others must be false; and they are psychologically incompatible when men who accept some of them are disposed to reject others. Clearly, beliefs can be incompatible in one of these senses without being so in the other. Those who, like Engels and Marx, take it for granted that science undermines religion do not trouble to distinguish between these two senses.

Theologians have certainly made some assertions which must be false if the findings of science are true. And clearly, it would be unreasonable to accept these findings on all occasions when they are relevant except when they conflict with theology. But theology has made other assertions which are intelligible and also untouched and untouchable by science. The logician has not shown that they are empty or confused, and the scientist has not, and indeed cannot, show that the world, as he explains it, is such that they cannot be true.

If these assertions are not logically incompatible with science, are they so psychologically? Is it true that the more people accept the findings of science, the more they are inclined to reject these assertions? Does the spread of science incline men to reject all assertions about the world which are not verifiable, even though they are logically compatible with the findings of science? Marx and Engels, like so many other rationalists of their day, seem to have taken it for granted that it does.

M*

But it is not immediately obvious why it should do so. If it is true that theology claims to answer questions of a type which science does not put, it is not clear why men should be inclined to reject the answers on the ground that they cannot be tested as the hypotheses of the scientist can. It is surely not unreasonable to accept unscientific answers to important questions of a type which science does not put and cannot answer. Nor is it unreasonable to *put* such questions merely because science cannot answer them. If the questions are important, if they matter greatly to the persons who put them, they will accept unscientific answers to them.

Can we then say that the questions which theology purports to answer cease to be important to men as science progresses? Marx and Engels apparently believed that they do, and this for two reasons. They took it for granted, as sceptics so often do, that men, as they become imbued with the scientific spirit, come to be indifferent to theology. Believing, as they did, that questions about the world which science cannot answer are either empty or unanswerable, it seemed to them that men who have come to understand what science is all about must soon lose the taste for them. They took for granted what had seemed obvious to the materialists of the eighteenth century. They took it for granted that science and religion are incompatible, without making it clear in quite what sense they are so.

But they also, as we have seen, had another and a more plausible reason for believing that men lose interest in religion as science progresses. They do so, not because science and religion are incompatible, but because religion is a need of alienated man and the social evolution which involves scientific progress brings this alienation to an end. Thus, it is not the mere spread of science which destroys religion; it is rather the transformation of society, a transformation closely connected with the progress of the sciences, natural and social.

Logically, we can accept this second reason even if we concede more than Marx and Engels were willing to do; even if we concede that religion provides intelligible answers to important questions which science does not put, answers which science cannot show to be false. If we accept this second reason, we do not have to attack religion on the ground that all, or even most, of its doctrines are logically absurd or inconsistent with science; we can confine ourselves to saying that men will come to do without religion because the questions it claims to answer will eventually cease to be important to them. The need for religion will disappear.

This account of religion goes deeper than the eighteenth-century conception of it as the product of ignorance and curiosity which disappears with the mere spread of science. It is not open to the same objections.

But there are objections to it. Even if we do not (for the moment) question Marx's conception of what religion essentially is, even if we allow that it is a response to a need rooted in man's sense of his own inadequacy, why should we suppose that the need will be weaker in the future than in the past? Why should we suppose that this sense of inadequacy and the need for a compensating fantasy will disappear in the classless society in which all men are educated and enjoy a high standard of living, material and cultural?

The sort of religion which Marx has in mind when he speaks of it as the fantasy of alienated man is not the animism and magic of the simplest societies; it includes a dogmatic theology and flourishes in relatively sophisticated societies. Such evidence as we have suggests that, in societies of this kind, dogmatic theology has often (though not always) been the religion of the privileged and the educated, of those enjoying the widest opportunities. We must not allow ourselves to be deceived by appearances. It is easy to make a misleading contrast between ages of faith and ages of scepticism. In the Middle Ages, most people who were called, or who called themselves, Christians were ignorant and illiterate; and it is improbable that many of them understood what the religion they adhered to was about. They were church-goers and partakers in ceremonies rather than persons having definite beliefs. We ought surely to say of them, as of illiterate peasants in the Balkans and the southern parts of Italy as late as our own century, that they did not challenge the doctrines of the Church, and not that they accepted them. Where orthodoxy is unchallenged nothing more is required of most people than outward conformity, and orthodoxy is never less challenged than when the vast majority are illiterate, or almost so, and are incapable of either accepting or rejecting the doctrines which are orthodox. Do we really know that true believers were a larger proportion of the population of Christendom in the thirteenth century than they are now? That the authority of the Church was less challenged then than it is now is not in itself enough to show that they were. The religion of the illiterate, of the oppressed, of the deprived, is in practice often very different from the religion officially established, even in so-called ages of faith. And yet it is established religion, elaborate and sophisticated, which seems to answer to Feuerbach's and Marx's conception of it rather than the practices and beliefs of the ignorant and the oppressed, which often retain about them much of the spirit of primitive religion, of animism and magic.

No doubt, theocentric religion, as distinct from animism and magic, flourishes in relatively complex societies; and nearly all such societies have so far been class societies, in the Marxian sense of class. They have also been literate and sophisticated societies; that is to say, there have been literate and sophisticated classes in them, even though most people remained illiterate. In societies of this kind the sense of deprivation among men, the sense that they are not what they aspire to be, the sense of frustration and inadequacy, may be much greater than in primitive societies. In them the ideas of all classes about what is desirable, what is worthy of a creature like man, are deeply influenced by the values and the opportunities of the privileged. Thus the unprivileged are apt to feel deprived because the opportunities of the privileged are denied to them; and it may well be that, sometimes, when they see that they can do nothing to improve their lot, they become resigned to it and seek compensation in some image of the world which religion presents to them. The spread of Methodism in England during the industrial revolution has been explained in these terms, and there are, no doubt, other examples. But if we look at the records, we see the spread of Methodism described as the bringing of Christianity to classes which until then had been only nominally Christian. These were classes rapidly becoming more literate, classes becoming more sophisticated, morally and intellectually, than their ancestors had been, and therefore able to get from such a religion as Christianity what, according to Feuerbach, it is the function of religion to provide. This, I suspect, was not the condition of serfs in the Middle Ages, just as it was not the condition of most peasants in eastern and southern Europe in quite recent times.

Theological religion, the type presented to us by Feuerbach and Marx as the religion of alienated man, is the religion of the sophisticated. It has been most fully accepted by the educated and the privileged. I would not deny that it has also been, genuinely and not merely nominally, the religion of the unprivileged, especially at times when the unprivileged have been gaining in sophistication. Among the unprivileged, it has served sometimes to reconcile them to their lot and sometimes to justify revolt.

At this point, it may be objected that to call religion the fantasy of alienated man is not to imply that it is the fantasy of the unprivileged rather than the privileged. This is certainly true. Though Marx speaks of exploitation and oppression in class societies, and of the degradation of the worker under capitalism, he does not say that only the exploited are alienated. It is man, and not just the exploited worker, who is alienated, who is frustrated and incapable of realizing his potentialities, who is the victim of his social environment.

To this objection, there are two answers. The first, and the less important, is that Marx, though he speaks of alienated man and not just of the alienated worker, also sometimes speaks as if the exploited were more alienated, further from self-realization, more the victims of environment, than the wealthy and the privileged. The second answer is that, if we take all men in a class society to be alienated, it is difficult to be clear just what alienation is.

Alienated man is man who has not realized his potentialities. But what are we to understand by his potentialities, seeing that there are so many things that man can become? What men aspire to depends on the values they accept, which vary from age to age and society to society. In all class societies there are some values accepted by all classes and others which are peculiar to this or that class; and, presumably, by the values common to the whole society, it is the privileged classes who are best able to live well. They are the least deprived classes. If this were not so, they would not be held by the other classes to be privileged but merely to be different. If the idea of the full or the satisfying life, the life worthy of such a creature as man, differs according to the values generally accepted in a society, it would seem that, in class societies, it is the privileged who have the largest opportunity to live up to the idea. We can then say that, if the other classes had the same opportunities (that is to say, if society were classless), there would be less deprivation, less alienation. But in saying this, we tacitly make an assumption which may be false; we assume that the values generally accepted, the values by reference to which men construct their idea of a full and satisfying life, will not have changed as a result of society's becoming classless.

On the other hand, if we construct our idea of the full life in some other way, we still cannot conclude that, when society becomes classless, men will be able to lead full and satisfying lives. We can, of course (as Rousseau did), so define our idea of the full (or good) life that society's being classless is a condition of its being realized; but we still have to show that in a classless society men would in fact accept this idea. Nor can we, as Marx and Engels do, without making it clear what a full and satisfying life is, simply take it for granted that in the classless society men will be able to live up to their idea of it. We cannot take it for granted that in the classless society man will not be alienated.

I would not deny that the sort of religion which is a cosmology, which ascribes to man a place in the world, can serve to compensate him for a sense that he does not live a worth-while life, for frustrations deeply felt and whose causes are not understood though they lie in the social environment. Nor would I deny that these causes, when they come to be understood, can be removed. But I suspect that the frustrations which arise because the social order is such that man cannot live what seems to him a worth-while life are only some among the causes of religion. And by religion I mean what Feuerbach and Marx meant by it; I mean a cosmology which presents the world to man as a theatre in which are unfolded purposes larger than his own. Religion, thus understood, is not less, but perhaps even more, attractive to those who enjoy most fully the opportunities which a complex and highly cultured society has to offer than to the socially deprived.

According to Feuerbach and even Hegel, religion springs from man's need to feel 'at home' in the world. I would not quarrel with this opinion, which only repeats in rather different words what some of the most deeply religious men have said. The fear of insignificance, of purposelessness, is one of the most terrible to which sophisticated man is liable. But is it a fear which arises in men because they cannot live satisfying lives in society as they find it? Is it a fear that would cease to plague them in a society offering to all men the opportunities which only the most favoured now enjoy? Is it not as true that men are unsatisfied because they have this fear as that they have it because they are unsatisfied? No doubt, the need for a religion which is a cosmology is a need of sophisticated man, and not all sophisticated men feel this need. But what reason is there for believing that, as society grows wealthier and more equalitarian, as it makes more abundant provision, culturally as well as materially, for all its members, this need will disappear?

If you want to understand what religion is, even though you are moved only by curiosity, it is not wise to pay exclusive attention to writers whose purpose is to show that it is a passing need. Marx was too much impressed by the arguments of Feuerbach and the materialist philosophers of the eighteenth century. If he had paid more attention to religious writers, if he had tried in imagination to put himself into the state of mind of a Luther or a Pascal, he might have remained a staunch atheist and yet have understood better than he did what it is that makes men turn to religion.

6. The Theory Tidied Up

To extract from the writings of Marx and Engels a clear, coherent, and useful conception of ideology, a conception which helps to explain important aspects of social life, we have to eliminate what makes for confusion and what is inconsistent with the facts. If we do this, we are left with this residue: a theory or opinion which purports to describe some aspect of reality, or a moral or legal rule, or a concept used to express such a rule or to encourage obedience to it, is *ideological* when its function is to maintain or challenge some part of the social order, or (as Marx might have put it) of the system of social relations; and a theory or opinion is *ideological* also when it serves to allay fears and create hopes. A descriptive theory or opinion may be fantasy or 'false consciousness' or it may not be; but what makes it *ideological* is that it is widely accepted, not primarily because there is good evidence of its truth, but because it serves to maintain or challenge the social order, or to allay fears and create hopes. And a moral or legal rule, though neither it nor the concepts used to express it or to encourage obedience to it can be false consciousness, is *ideological* in relation to some part of the social order provided it is not included in that part and serves to maintain or challenge it.

I have already insisted that moral and legal rules (and therefore also moral and legal concepts) are part of the very stuff of social relations; that to stand in a social relation to someone involves recognizing that you ought or are required to conform to certain rules in your behaviour towards him. Every form of social intercourse involves accepting some rules and using some normative concepts, and it therefore makes no sense to say that these rules and concepts are determined by the nature of the intercourse; they are an integral part of it. But we can distinguish rules and concepts *involved* in the having of certain relations from rules and concepts *serving to strengthen or undermine* those relations. For example, co-operation is possible even among people who have no *esprit-de-corps*, who feel no loyalty to the group they belong to, who, for one reason or another, merely conform to the rules involved in the co-operation, approving conformity and condemning non-conformity. But out of this co-operation there may (and there usually does) arise a group loyalty expressed in rules and concepts not involved in the actual co-operation but helping to strengthen it. These secondary rules and concepts we could call ideological. Marx called them so, and we may take issue with him, not for giving them that name, but for failing to distinguish them from the primary rules and concepts which are an integral part of the co-operation.

The practice of these secondary rules is itself a form of social intercourse, but it is intercourse different from the intercourse it helps to maintain. Provided it serves to strengthen the primary intercourse and not to undermine it, it can be called, in the parlance of Marx, a *superstructure* upon it. In every army, and in many other types of social organization, there are practices whose function is to make subordinates more readily obedient to their superiors; there are also practices, which Marxists are more prone to ignore, making superiors more attentive to the needs of their subordinates. These practices are distinct from the proper work of the organization; they are not part of it but serve only to make it smoother. The rules which these practices embody and the concepts used to express the rules and to encourage conformity to them are therefore ideological in relation to the work, but are not ideological in relation to the practices serving to make the work go smoothly.

Ideology, thus defined, is a really important aspect of social life. There are theories and opinions by which men set great store and which they take for true because they feel the need to do so, and these theories and opinions have a large influence on their behaviour. But this type of ideology is not always, nor even usually, class ideology. There is no reason to believe that, even in societies divided into classes, class ideologies are the most important. They are, no doubt, characteristic of class societies; and if we want to distinguish one kind of class society from another we can point, among other things, to differences in their class ideologies. But *characteristic* and *most important* are not equivalent terms; we may not conclude that class ideologies, because they are peculiar to class societies, are, even in these societies, more important than others.

Nor must we imply, as Marx does, that the only function of ideology is to support or challenge the social order, the system of social relations. Religion can, and often does, strengthen men's motives for doing what they are required to do; it can be, and often is, a set of beliefs helping to preserve the social order. It can also help to undermine it. If the social order favours some classes more than others and religion serves to maintain that order, it can be treated as a form of class ideology. But it is always more than that. It is more than class ideology, and more even than an ideology preserving the social order for the benefit of all classes. It serves another function besides strengthening (or weakening) men's motives for doing what their neighbours require of them; it also allays fear and creates hope in them. This fear and this hope are the fear and the hope of rational creatures whose reason has developed in society. The need which religion satisfies is, in this sense, a social need; it is the need of a rational and moral creatures that life should seem worth living; it is, as Hegel saw, the need of a self-conscious creature, aware of its mortality and fearful of solitude, to feel at home in the world. That all men do not turn to religion to satisfy this need is no proof that it is not an important function of religion to satisfy it.

Nor must we, as Marx and Engels do, call morality and the law ideological. We must distinguish between the moral and legal rules and concepts actually involved in the social relations we have in mind, and the rules and concepts which serve to strengthen or undermine those relations; we must call only the second, and not the first, *ideological*.

Marx and Engels also set too wide a gulf between science and ideology. They were too much inclined to believe that theories and opinions which gain currency primarily because people feel the need to take them for true are false or fantastic. Even if we agree with them that most social and political theories prior to their own, to the extent that they aimed at explaining the facts, were further from the truth and took less notice of what they purported to explain than their own theory, we may set this down chiefly to greater ignorance. If the makers of these theories had been better informed, or had known better how to use what information they had, they might have produced theories equally attractive to upholders or challengers of the social order and also much nearer the truth. The more people know the facts and the better they understand how to use them to test the truth of explanations, the more carefully social and political theorists must construct their theories if they are to gain currency.

Theology and metaphysics, since they claim to transcend experience, need take much less notice of the facts. In spite of their close connection, historically, with social and political theory, they are intrinsically different from it. Taken in themselves, they rarely serve either to preserve or to challenge the existing social order; they only seem to do so when a show is made of deriving social and political conclusions from them. I doubt whether Christian theology favours one type of social order more than another; I doubt, for example, whether the democracy and liberalism we adhere to today are any more in keeping with Christianity than the feudal order of the Middle Ages. We like to make a show of deriving our political principles from our religious beliefs; and yet persons who agree in their religion but disagree in their politics make equally plausible attempts to show how the second follows logically from the first. But social and political theory, being necessarily much more concerned than is theology with what happens in this world, is also closer to being scientific. I suspect that, among the theories that Marx would call ideological because they serve group interests, those which are nearer to being scientific are also nearer to being class ideologies.

7. Ideology as a 'Reflection' of Something Else

Marx says that ideology *reflects* social relations or conditions, and also that it *reflects* class interests. I have already argued that some forms of ideology, with religion the most important of them, do very much more than serve class interests or support or challenge the social order; I have argued that Marx neglects their more important for their less important functions. Nevertheless, there are ideologies which support or challenge the social order, and there are also class ideologies. I want therefore to consider in what sense, and to what extent, ideologies serving these purposes *reflect* social conditions or class interests. Let me take the first point first. What can be meant by saying that an ideology *reflects* social conditions?

When people who work or live together acquire a sense of community and group loyalties, the rules and attitudes which embody this sense and these loyalties, together with the beliefs which sustain them, can be said to arise out of their working and living together. They serve to make the collaboration and the living together easier, and their character varies, more or less, according to how men collaborate and how they live together. When we say that an ideology *reflects* social conditions we mean presumably that it helps to support them, that it would not arise unless a need were felt for this support, and that what it is is largely determined by the nature of its function. But, if this is what is involved in an ideology's *reflecting* social conditions, how can we say that a revolutionary ideology reflects them?

Some concrete examples may serve to illustrate my meaning. Marriage is one of the most important of social relations, and differs greatly in different societies. If we take any form of marriage, we can distinguish between the rules and attitudes inherent in it, making it the kind of marriage it is, and the ideology which builds up around it, owing its existence and its character to it. In so far as the aspirations of the men and women bound together by this kind of marriage are affected by this ideology, they are aspirations in keeping with the marriage, and are satisfied in this kind of union, provided it is a normal union of its kind. The Bantu woman who is married after the fashion of her tribe, and whose attitude to what is required of her as a wife is in line with what is thought and felt about marriage in her tribe, will presumably be satisfied with her marriage; or, if she is not, it will be for some other reason than because it is that kind of marriage.

Let us now take another example. To the extent that a slave's attitude to his servile condition arises out of that condition, being in harmony with ways of thinking and feeling which build up around it, he is satisfied with it. But if he wants to be free, his aspiration to freedom must come of his having ideas incompatible with his condition. No doubt, he would not want to *become* free unless he were a slave. But a free man also puts a value on freedom; if he does not want to *become* free, he wants to *remain* free. The slave's wanting freedom does not spring from an attitude to servility which arises from his being a slave; it springs from an attitude to servility which he acquires by adopting for himself the ideals of the free man. It is paradoxical to say that a revolutionary ideology *reflects* the social conditions which it aims at destroying. If we admit this paradox, we must, I think, concede that both an ideology and its opposite can reflect the same social conditions. Let us suppose that the slave's beliefs and values make him contented with his servility, that he knows his station and is happy in it, that he has an ideology in keeping with his station. We can hardly refuse to say that this ideology reflects his social condition. If, then, we go on to say that the beliefs and values which make him loathe his condition also reflect it, we are bound to conclude that two opposing ideologies reflect the same condition. No doubt, a master and a slave can have different beliefs and values arising out of the social relations between them; but that is because their social conditions differ, because the master is not related to the slave as the slave is to the master. The master and the slave, though each of them is content with his condition, will have different ideologies *reflecting* their different conditions, but neither ideology, if it reflects its possessor's social condition, will be revolutionary.

It is also paradoxical to say that the ideology of a revolutionary class reflects the interests of the class. How can people having a given social status come to have interests incompatible with that status unless they acquire an ideology which is also incompatible with it? So long as what they strive for is in keeping with their status, they seek for nothing which is to be had only by destroying that status. As a matter of fact, no class has an ideology entirely in keeping with its status; even a ruling class is never completely conservative and contented, for it too has aspirations, and therefore also interests, which cannot be satisfied while existing social relations remain unchanged. But it has an advantage denied to the other classes; it can change the social order to suit its interests much more easily than they can. It feels the need to do this precisely because no class ideology, not even the ideology of the ruling class, merely reflects the social condition of the class whose ideology it is.

We cannot say that the feminism of the early nineteenth century *reflected* the interests of women at that time. For generations before the rise of feminism, women had accepted a social status in many ways different from, and in some ways inferior to, the status of the other sex. While they accepted that status, they had interests and ideologies in keeping with it. If their interests, their ambitions and aspirations, changed it was largely because they acquired ideas which women before them did not (except rarely) have.

Instead of saying, as Marx does, that class ideologies reflect class interests, we should say rather that the interests and ideology of a class, to the extent that they are in keeping with its social condition, reflect that condition, and that the interests of a class, to the extent that they are not in keeping with its social condition, are affected by an ideology which does not reflect that condition. This conclusion, though it does not square with what Marx says about how class ideologies, class interests, and social conditions are connected with one another, is entirely in keeping with what he says about the political rôle of ideology.[1] A class, he tells us, becomes class-conscious in the process of learning what its interests are and what it must do to promote them; and says also that, as it becomes class-conscious, it elaborates its ideology. True, even a class which is not class-conscious has some kind of class ideology; it has prejudices and values peculiar to itself. But, as it becomes class-conscious, it acquires opinions about its position in society and what needs to be done to preserve or change that position; it acquires a more elaborate and sophisticated ideology. It acquires this ideology as it comes to recognize its interests and learns to work

---

[1] We have here yet another example of something we have already come across several times in the writings of Marx and Engels; the generalizations they make about how certain aspects of social life are connected are contradicted by their accounts of actual processes in which these aspects are involved.

for them and becomes a political force to be reckoned with. Learning to recognize its interests and acquiring a sophisticated ideology and becoming politically formidable are all, for Marx, parts of the same process. If we look at this process, even as Marx imagines it, we see that ideology affects interests and social conditions just as it is affected by them. We see that Marx's own account of what classes do politically, especially when they are revolutionary classes, gives the lie to the famous sentence so often quoted: 'It is not the consciousness of men that determines their being but, on the contrary, their social being determines their consciousness.' 'Consciousness' or ideology has a profound effect on social being, on the most important social relations. Indeed, if it were not so, there would be no point to the class conflicts and revolutions in which Marx believed so strongly. If it were really true that class ideologies only *reflect* class interests and do not also powerfully affect them, Marx would not be nearly as important a figure in world history as he actually is.

Chapter 6

MARXISM

II

IV. WHAT DID MARX AND ENGELS THINK IS THE FUNCTION OF THE STATE IN SOCIETIES DIVIDED INTO CLASSES, AND WHAT DID THEY PREDICT WOULD DISAPPEAR IN THE CLASSLESS SOCIETY?

A. The State and Social Classes

1. THREE VIEWS ABOUT THE STATE

There are three assertions about the State characteristic of Marxism: that the State arises when society divides into classes, that the State is an instrument of class rule, and that when society becomes classless there will be no need for a State. Marxists, and Marx and Engels also, sometimes speak as if these three assertions stood and fell together. We shall see that they do not.

Though Engels tells us that in tribal societies there is no need for a State, he does not deny that in such societies there is a need for authority. In the tribe, as in the State, there are persons admitted to have a right to give orders and to interpret rules, and there are also customary rules which impose obligations or confer rights – that is to say, there are, in the broad sense of the word, laws. Those who have authority inside the tribe owe it, not merely to personal qualities giving them an exceptional influence over their fellows, but to status, to the position they occupy in the tribe. They are not leaders whose authority rests on mere strength of character; they are rulers who come by their authority in traditional ways. In saying that there is no State in tribal societies Engels does not mean to deny that there is in them a structure of authority resting on customary rules. Sometimes he even speaks of the rudiments of State power in tribal societies. In saying that there is no State in such societies, he means, I take it, that in them the business of declaring the rules and enforcing them is not recognized as a special function. Society is not yet clearly divided into rulers and ruled. The authority of the chiefs is quasi-paternal; it is clear who has it, but it is not clearly defined. Exercising authority is only a part of what the chiefs do; the extent of their authority varies with the circumstances, and there is almost no hierarchy of rulers. Authority is exercised as the need is felt for it.

When the State appears, the business of declaring what the rules are and applying them becomes the whole-time activity of some persons; it becomes, more and more clearly, a separate function, a political function, and elaborate procedures are evolved for carrying it out. There arises an organized hierarchy to carry on the government; there are superiors and subordinates, and there are more or less definite rules limiting their competence. The sanctions that maintain social discipline are no longer the same: in place of the rebukes of elder or chief, the pressure of public opinion, the fear of magic, there are courts of law using a settled procedure to establish responsibility and to impose penalties or remedies. The political function, as it becomes a distinct and elaborate activity, also becomes coercive; the breaker of an important rule is no longer exposed to private vengeance or to the mere displeasure of his community; his offence is investigated and he is liable to fines, imprisonments, whippings, or even death at the hands of a public executioner. This, I take it, is what Engels, like most other political theorists, has in mind when he speaks of the emergence of the State.

Both in *Anti-Dühring* and in *The Origins of the Family, Private Property, and the State,* Engels says that the need for the State arises as the division of labour increases and society divides into classes. In tribal societies the division of labour is still relatively simple; it does not divide society into classes, and the maintenance of social discipline, the seeing to it that people carry out their customary obligations and that disputes between them are settled peacefully or in a way that does as little harm as possible to the community, is still too simple a business to require that it should be the whole-time occupation of a hierarchy of persons clearly marked off from the rest of the community as its rulers. The need for the State arises from the increasing size of the community and from the extended division of labour inside it.

That the need for the State arises in this way is not to be disputed. It is what Plato said at the dawn of political theory, and what has often been repeated since. But it is important to notice that the increasing division of labour does not of itself divide society into classes; at least, not unless we so define or use the word *class* that differences of occupation are differences of class. And this, as we have seen, is not how Marx and Engels define or use it. Though tinkers and tailors have different occupations, they do not therefore belong to different classes, in the Marxian sense of class. The increasing division of labour, making the clan or tribe no longer self-sufficient, breaks up the old social order. As the clan or tribe disintegrates into many smaller independent families, communal ownership of land and cattle gives way to private ownership, and the father of each small family becomes the only possessor of the land cultivated and the animals used by his family.

Whether we regard the break-up of the clan or tribe as the cause or the effect of this change in the system of property, or as partly the one and partly the other, does not matter when we are considering the emergence of the State. Nor does it matter that property in workshops and tools increases in importance with the greater division of labour.

The point to bear in mind is that all this could conceivably happen without society being divided into classes, in the Marxian sense of class. Instead of the extended family or clan enjoying common rights over large pieces of land, we might have the fathers of small families enjoying private rights over smaller pieces of land, and we might have artisans and traders owning other kinds of property than land or cattle. We might have all this, without masters or slaves, without feudal lords or serfs, without capitalists or proletarians. We might have a society as classless, in the Marxian sense of class, as the tribal society. And yet the task of maintaining discipline inside it would be quite different. The need for forms of authority different from those which sufficed to keep the peace and to enforce obligations in tribal society would still be there. We should then have a classless society giving birth to the State.

No doubt, with the break-up of the tribe and the emergence of a new system of property, classes in the Marxian sense soon arise. I am not concerned to deny it. I say only that, even if they did not arise, there would still be a need for forms of authority which tribal society could do without; there would still be a need for the State. In a boarding school children are kept in order by different methods from those found sufficient inside the family. It may be that children who are sent to boarding schools become more troublesome for being sent there; but even if they did not, they would have to be under a form of discipline different from that of the home. The whole-time occupation of their masters is to teach them and keep them in order, and their relations with their masters are different from their relations with their parents. This must be so, no matter what happens to the children as a result of their being sent to such schools; it must be so even if they become quieter and more amenable to reason.

The larger the community and the more diverse and specialized the occupations inside it, the more elaborate and precise the rules needed to control the behaviour of its members. There must be forms of contract unknown to tribal society which have to be interpreted and enforced. There is room for many more and far more varied disputes, and therefore a need for more regular and more elaborate procedures for settling them. It is not just a question of finding other people to do what the chiefs and elders did in tribal society; there is a need for authority of a different kind, and therefore for different relations between those in authority and the persons subject to them. Of course, Engels does not deny this, he insists upon it; but he does not see that the need would be there even if there were no classes in the Marxian sense. He sees the need arise and the classes, and therefore takes it for granted that the classes create the need.

The truth is that Engels, when he says that the division of society into classes makes the State necessary, is not using the word *class* in the same sense as when he speaks of class exploitation or calls feudal lords or capitalists a class. He is treating as separate classes groups whose interests diverge because their occupations differ, and is saying that their interests cannot be reconciled by the methods open to the old tribal authorities, so that a new structure of authority, the State, emerges. He calls the interests of these groups irreconcilable, presumably because they cannot be reconciled by the old methods, and then goes on to say that it is the function of the State to keep the peace between groups having irreconcilable interests. He does not trouble to ask himself what is meant by calling the interests irreconcilable if the State is able to keep the peace between the groups having the interests. There is here, surely, an odd line of reasoning: an increased division of labour gives rise to groups with divergent interests leading to disputes which cannot be settled by the old methods, and therefore the groups are called *irreconcilable*; there then emerge new methods of settling disputes used by a new type of authority, the State, whose function is therefore said to be to keep the peace between irreconcilable groups. But why, if the peace can be kept between the groups by these new methods, should it be said of them that they are *irreconcilable*?

Engels speaks of the groups as separate classes. But in what sense are they classes? Even in tribal societies there are different occupations; the division of labour in them may be rudimentary but still it exists. And in all societies, tribal or otherwise, persons with different occupations have interests which often diverge. Engels admits that there are no classes in tribal societies. It would seem therefore that persons having different occupations and divergent interests do not, for those reasons alone, belong to separate classes. Do they, then, belong to separate classes because disputes between them can no longer be settled by the old methods? Or, rather, because the disputes can only be settled where there is a structure of authority of the kind we call a State? If we say this, then we do not use the word *class* to refer to groups which are distinct from one another because they have different property rights. Two groups are then separate classes, not because their interests diverge or their social positions differ, but because disputes between them (or, rather, between persons belonging to them), can only be settled by a certain type of authority.[1] But if this

---

[1] Engels does not distinguish disputes between individuals which need a new type of authority to settle them because the individuals belong to groups having divergent interests from disputes between these groups. He probably has in mind both kinds of disputes.

is so, it is by no means obvious that where private property in the means of production is abolished, society is made classless and the need for the State disappears; it is by no means obvious that, where this type of property ceases to exist, there is no need for the State to settle disputes.

Engels, having first explained how an increased division of labour produces groups whose divergent interests lead to disputes which can only be settled by the State, then goes on to show how out of these groups there emerges, in course of time, a society whose members have different property rights. Of course, as soon as this happens, we have a society divided into classes, in the specifically Marxian sense of class. And, no doubt, these classes, as much as the groups out of which they arise, are involved in disputes which cannot be settled by the old tribal methods. Thus, because the process which first produced groups whose disputes could not be settled in the old ways later produced classes, in the Marxian sense of class, Engels slips easily into the way of calling these groups *classes*. He does not notice that he is using the word *class* alternately to refer to two quite different things: to groups having divergent interests arising directly out of the division of labour, interests which cannot be reconciled by the old tribal authorities, and to groups whose property rights differ and who therefore have divergent interests for quite other reasons. There are here at least two movements of thought which are logically unsound but which easily escape notice: the movement from interests which cannot be reconciled in the old ways to interests which somehow remain irreconcilable even though new ways are found of settling the disputes they lead to, and the movement from groups arising directly from the division of labour to classes in the Marxian sense.

As the extended family disintegrates, as land and cattle and other forms of property are divided at a father's death between his children or his sons, so that each becomes the separate owner of what passes to him, as the division of labour expands and the use of money becomes general, it is much easier for some persons than for others to grow rich, acquiring more property than they can cultivate or use profitably. While they grow rich, others fall into debt and lose their property, and are obliged to hire themselves out as labourers or even to sell their liberty. Given a fast expanding division of labour and new systems of property and inheritance, society, as Engels saw, is soon divided into classes, in the Marxian sense of class. Keeping the peace in society may then be even more difficult, and make more urgent the need for strong government. Engels was impressed by the quarrels between rich and poor, between creditors and debtors, in Athens and in Rome. He saw struggles between classes almost destroying these two States; he saw compromises reached between the classes when Solon reorganized the Athenian state and when the office of tribune was instituted at Rome. Though he was candid enough to admit that these compromises set limits to the oppression of the poor by the rich, he yet insisted on seeing in them evidence that the function of the State is to keep the peace between irreconcilable classes. No doubt, where there are classes and they are in conflict, it is the business of the State to keep the peace between them. And it may be that conflicts between classes in the Marxian sense are apt to be more bitter than most other conflicts. All this we can admit without also admitting that to keep the peace between classes is ever the sole or often the most important business of the State.

We can also admit that the form of the State often depends considerably, though never entirely, on how society is divided into classes. The class structure in turn depends partly on the division of labour and partly on the system of property. Given the division of labour, several different systems of property are possible, and therefore also several different forms of class-structure. Though the need for the State arises in the first place from an extended division of labour, the way the State is organized depends only in part on the extent of that division; it also depends on the class-structure, and no doubt on other things as well. Engels mistakenly supposes that to say that the need for the State arises from an extended division of labour which eventually gives rise to classes is equivalent to saying that it arises from the division of society into classes, and that therefore how the State is organized depends *primarily* on the class structure. And yet, though this extreme position is mistaken, it is certainly true that the form of the State is often deeply affected by the class-structure. Thus we have here an important truth, and we owe our firmer grasp of it mostly to Engels and to Marx. Others before them had said that the rich use the State to oppress the poor, but they were the first to insist strongly that how the State is organized depends largely on how society is divided into classes. They exaggerated the dependence, no doubt, but they put forward an hypothesis which is plausible and has proved fruitful. They brought into prominence a matter neglected before their time.

II. THE STATE AND 'IRRECONCILABLE' CLASSES

Very sensibly, Engels admits that the persons who carry on the tasks of government, as those tasks come to be more clearly marked off from others, can (and usually do) become a distinct class. They use their political power to acquire forms of property which put them in a class apart from other classes. Engels does not say that these forms of property are acquired only by the use of political power. They can also be acquired in other ways. But he does admit that the use of political power is one of the important ways of acquiring them. Those who get power usually accumulate wealth the more quickly for having got it.

This wealth, acquired by those who have political power and also by others, makes the possessors of it not only a distinct, but an exploiting, class. They have more land than they can cultivate themselves; they employ labour. They also acquire, in various ways, rights of property in other people's labour; they acquire slaves or serfs. Therefore the exploitation of class by class arises, at least in great part, as a consequence of the emergence of the State. It is sensible of Engels to admit this because there is much evidence that it is so. But the admission, as we shall see, is not consistent with other things that he says about the State.

Not only do those who wield political power use it to acquire wealth which puts them into what Marx and Engels call an exploiting class; they also make it easier for others who have no political power to acquire wealth enough to become exploiters. One of the important ways in which the rich get their wealth in primitive societies where the State has recently emerged is by acquiring the properties and even the persons of debtors. Another way, also important, is by making slaves of prisoners captured in war. The importance of both these methods is acknowledged by Engels. But a man is no richer for what is owed to him unless his debtors, when they prove unwilling, are coerced into paying their debts. If they are required to surrender everything that is theirs, including the free disposal of their labour, the chances are that they will be unwilling. Prisoners captured in war, if they are to be enslaved, must be distributed among the victors and kept properly subservient. All this, Engels admits, is scarcely possible, or at least cannot go far, where there is no authority strong enough to enforce it. The emergence of the State is therefore a condition of society's becoming divided into unequal classes, some exploiting others. It may not be a condition of the extended division of labour which first breaks up tribal society, nor yet of the rules of property and inheritance which first supersede the tribal rules; but it is a condition of these things leading eventually to the division of society into unequal classes, exploiting and exploited.

If all this is admitted – and I think it is admitted by Engels either in *Anti-Dühring* or in *The Origins of the Family, Private Property, and the State* – what can we make of the famous sentence in *The Communist Manifesto* that 'political power . . . is merely the organized power of one class for oppressing another'? This sentence suggests that the State arises as a result of the division of society into unequal classes. Yet Marx and Engels are ready to admit that there cannot be class oppression, at least on any considerable scale, unless there is a State. Where there is no apparatus of power controlled by one class to the detriment of others there cannot be much class oppression. Yet nearly always – except when Engels is actually describing how, in his opinion, the State arises – they speak as if the division of society into unequal classes happened independently of the emergence of the State. This does not imply that these two processes, the appearance of unequal classes and the appearance of the State, do not overlap, but it does suggest that the first is the cause of the second, and not the other way about. It suggests what Engels implicitly denies when he describes in detail the origins of the State. That description, obscure though it often is, attributes the division of society into unequal classes in large part to the emergence of the State. True, it does not suggest that the rise of the State is the sufficient cause of class inequality, but it does suggest that it is a necessary condition. Here, as in other parts of their social theory, we find that what Marx and Engels say about the connections between two social processes does not accord with their actual descriptions of those processes. They tell us that one process determines another, and then, when they come to describe one or other of the processes, they admit (though more by implication than in so many words) that each has a powerful influence on the other.

Though Engels says that the State arises to keep the peace between classes whose interests are irreconcilable, he does not trouble to explain why they should be irreconcilable. The expanded division of labour which breaks up the old tribal society is presumably in the general interest; and so too, at least to begin with, are the rules of property and inheritance which replace the old tribal rules. Certainly, Engels says nothing to suggest the opposite. These rules may not be the only ones compatible with the increased division of labour, but they are compatible with it. Only after the division of labour and the new rules have been in operation for some time does society become divided into classes in the Marxian sense of class. This happens for a variety of reasons: because families differ in size and some men get much more by inheritance than others, because debtors forfeit their properties and even their persons to their creditors, because some people work harder or are abler or more lucky than others. Not until there are classes can there be *irreconcilable* class interests; and the rise of the State is, as we have seen, as much a cause as an effect of the emergence of classes.

It may be that, when tribal society breaks up, disputes are less easily settled than they used to be. It may be that the new methods evolved for their settlement do not reconcile the parties to the disputes as well as the old tribal authorities did. Within the kinship group, the authority of the chief is almost paternal; his business is as much to restore amity as to adjudicate claims or punish wrong-doers. He wants to change people's attitudes towards one another, restoring good feeling between them. The judge or arbiter in the State is perhaps not a restorer of amity in the same way; he is a maker of judicial decisions, a settler of claims, a meter-out of punishment. When he settles a dispute, the parties to it may or may not find the settlement just. If they do not, they may still accept it because they cannot safely do otherwise or because they recognize in general the need for courts of law. Accepting the decision from such motives as these, the parties to the dispute are not fully reconciled.

It may be that it is much more usual for men to feel this way about professional judges in a political society than about chiefs or patriarchs in a tribal society; and it may be that this is one reason among others why force or the threat of it has to be used to back up judicial decisions more often than to back up the decisions of tribal chieftains. Fear of the consequences of disobedience may be a more frequent motive for obedience in the State than in the tribe, and respect for the wisdom and good will of the arbiter a more frequent motive in the tribe than in the State. If this is so, then parties to disputes are less easily reconciled in the State because the social relations between them are different. Perhaps Engels had this also in mind. He may have confused a greater intransigence, a lesser docility, between disputing parties whose social relations are no longer those of the tribe with a clash of irreconcilable interests between classes. He may also have believed that, when society divides into classes, parties to disputes are even less easily reconciled, so that it is more than ever necessary to use force and the threat of force for the settlement of disputes.

Therefore, even though we disagree with Engels that the State arises to keep the peace between *irreconcilable* classes, we may still agree with him that it arises to settle disputes less easily settled than they used to be because the parties to them are no longer socially related as they were. We may agree also that the settlement of disputes in the State often does not reconcile the parties to them, and that the causes which produce the State help to divide society into unequal classes, thus making it yet more difficult to settle disputes and to reconcile the parties to them.[1]

There is also another possibility; it does sometimes happen that, as class divisions deepen, the settlement of disputes becomes easier, even though the parties to them are less often reconciled. The privileged classes may be so powerful that the others quickly accept the settlements forced on them. They may think quick submission less dangerous than resistance; they may even, from prudence or timidity, refrain from making claims which they are legally entitled to make. Not long ago, in most parts of Africa and some parts of the United States, disputes between white and coloured persons were often settled more

---

[1] By the settlement of a dispute I mean the reaching of a decision which puts an end to it, and by the reconciliation of the parties I mean their accepting the decision as just.

quickly than disputes between white persons; but this is no evidence that the parties to the disputes were reconciled.

It could also happen, where the *ideology* of the privileged class is accepted by all classes, that parties to disputes are reconciled almost as easily as disputes are settled. If the socially inferior classes accept their position, if they are resigned to it, if they think it the work of Fate or Providence, it makes no sense to say that their class interests are irreconcilable with those of their exploiters; unless we can make the distinction that Marx and Engels wanted to make between actual aspirations and *true* interests, which I think we cannot make for the reasons already discussed.

But, though I say that it *could* happen that, in a society divided into unequal classes, parties to disputes were reconciled almost as easily as disputes were settled, I think it most unlikely. I very much doubt whether, where class divisions are deep, the poor and the powerless do accept the class ideologies of the rich and the powerful. They may not reject them consciously; they may not even know what they are. They may put up with the system without understanding it and without producing theories to condemn it; but I suspect that very often, in their disputes with their 'betters', they feel themselves to be victims of injustice.

Marx and Engels sometimes weaken their own case unnecessarily. They are much too ready to concede that ideas which suit the special interests of the privileged classes are accepted by the whole of society. 'The ideas of the ruling class are, in every age, the ruling ideas. . . . The class which has the means of material production at its disposal has control at the same time over the means of mental production, so that . . . the ideas of those who lack the means of production are, in general, subject to it.'[1] This is not true, or is so only in part. No doubt, where the privileged classes are firmly entrenched, the ideas and theories serving to strengthen their position are much the most important; and even when not produced by the privileged, flourish and are respectable because they serve their interests. They are taught in the schools and are printed in books. They loom the largest in men's conscious minds; they are the most paraded and the most discussed. Therefore, we can say that, in a stable society divided into unequal classes, most *theories* which are class ideology favour the ruling or privileged classes, if only because it requires trained minds and a large expenditure of mental energy to construct such theories. A stable society with unequal classes is stable only while the ascendancy of the privileged is not seriously challenged. Thus, it is true almost by definition that the prevailing ideology of a stable society which is also a class society is the ideology of the ruling classes.

[1] *The German Ideology*, p. 39.

But not to challenge the ascendancy of a privileged class is by no means the same thing as to accept its ideology. In societies where there are deep divisions, whether between classes in the Marxian sense or between races or religious groups, the ideology of the ruling class or race or group may have very little influence on the thinking of their 'inferiors'. This is only the more likely when the 'inferiors' are poor and illiterate. As often as not, the ideology of the ruling class or group serves much more to hold that class or group together and to justify the social order in the minds of those who benefit from it than to reconcile the subject classes or groups to it by persuading them that the social order is just. The ruling ideology in Ireland in the early part of the eighteenth century was that of the Protestant and privileged minority, and it was probably not shared to any but a small extent by the Catholic majority. Yet Ireland, at that time, was nearer than she had been in the seventeenth century, and than she was to be in the nineteenth, to being a stable society divided into unequal classes.

It does not always, nor even often, happen that, where some classes dominate others which accept their inferior position, the thinking of the inferior classes is moulded by the ideology of their superiors. No doubt, where classes are very unequal, the intellectual life of the com-munity is confined to the superior classes; but that life consists of much more than class ideology, so that, if other classes come later to share in it, it is not the class ideology of their superiors which they imbibe so much as a cultural inheritance which is classless even though hitherto confined to only some classes. Marx and Engels were too much inclined to speak as if the socially inferior classes, until they acquire a revolutionary ideology to challenge the ideology of the socially superior, accept the ideas which it suits those who are set above them should be in their heads. There is plentiful evidence that this has not always, nor even usually, been so, at least in Europe.[1] We have evidence that the serfs often resented the grievous burdens placed on them, which they could hardly have done if their ideas of justice had been moulded by the ideas of their masters. And yet, most of the time, they had nothing worth calling an ideology of their own to set against the dominant ideology; they had no ideas and no principles coherent enough to draw them togther to resist their masters or to reform the social order. They could not do battle on the intellectual front and, with rare exceptions, felt no need to produce a theory to justify the resentment they felt. And yet they often felt resentment, and often saw themselves as the victims of their superiors or of circumstances.

Marx and Engels were intellectuals, and were prone to a mistake often made by intellectuals; they took it for granted that persons not

[1] And in Asia and Africa, where European rule has been widespread and the influence of European ideas immense, no ideology favourable to that rule has been successfully purveyed to the subject peoples.

equipped by education to challenge the ideas of those who dominate
society mostly accept them or at least do not condemn their masters.
If they had looked more closely and with greater sympathy at the
peasants, whom they despised for their ignorance and boorishness,
they might have seen how wide of the mark they were.[1]

I am not now going back on what I said before; I am not arguing
that there are, after all, classes with *irreconcilable* interests in the sense
which I denied earlier. I am saying only that, if the poor and unprivileged feel oppressed, as they often do, it is because, even when
they are not class-conscious and revolutionary in the Marxian sense,
even when they do not challenge the established order, their ideas of
what is right and just are much less affected by the class ideology of
their social superiors than Marx supposed.

It may even be that the unprivileged have beliefs favourable to the
interests of the privileged but which do not come to them from the
privileged and which are compatible with a deep hatred for them. The
unprivileged may believe that the social order is unchangeable; they
may accept it from mere habit or because it has never occured to them
that there is anything they can do to improve their lot. This belief
that society is unchanging and unchangeable is ordinarily an effect
of habit and illusion; men take for granted what they are accustomed
to, and therefore have no idea either that it changes or that it can be
changed. There is always some change from generation to generation
in all societies, even the most primitive or the most stagnant, but it may
not be noticed because it is slow and there are no records kept of the
past, or because such as are kept are too meagre to destroy the illusion
that there is no change. This illusion, shared by all classes, favours the
interests of the privileged; and yet it is not class ideology. It arises
because society changes slowly and imperceptibly; it arises as readily
in classless societies as in those divided into classes; it is not an
illusion produced, deliberately or unconsciously, in the unprivileged by
the privileged, nor does it arise to consolidate the position of the
privileged. The socially inferior may hate the classes above them, they
may have notions of justice moving them to condemn the behaviour
of those classes, they may be almost untouched by whatever, in the
ideas of their superiors, can be plausibly treated as class ideology; they

[1] In a society where there are great inequalities, the 'lower orders', when they
speak to their 'betters', often speak as if they shared their beliefs, and yet
speak quite differently among themselves. Their 'betters', if they catch them
at it, condemn their hypocrisy, but to the 'lower orders' this hypocrisy is a
necessary precaution of the weak in their dealings with the strong. The
socially weak are apt to imitate the socially strong when actually in their
presence, sometimes from the desire to placate, or deceive and sometimes
from a sense of their own inadequacy. No doubt, the imitation also springs at
times from a conviction that the manners and beliefs of their superiors are
the best.

may be all this, and still be long-suffering and make a virtue of their patience. They may be resigned to their fate.

Or, if they are not exactly resigned to it, they may lack the ideas which would give them social cohesion and make them politically formidable. In that case, they put up with their lot indefinitely, not because they have been touched by the ideology of their masters, nor because they do not hate and condemn them, but because they do not know how to set about putting an end to the oppression they suffer from. Perhaps the serfs felt like this in the Middle Ages in the West, or in Russia in the seventeenth and eighteenth centuries. Occasionally they rose in revolt but they did not know how to change their social condition, and most of the time they merely put up with it as they did with their natural environment. Did religion make them more docile than they would have been without it? Who can tell? But, for my part, I doubt it. What did Christianity mean to the mediaeval or the Russian serf? How much of it did he imbibe? How differently did he understand it from his master? How much was his Christianity mixed up with pagan beliefs?

It may be that Christianity has served as much to make the oppressed rebellious as to make them docile. That the promise of a life after death reconciles the humble to their lot in this life is by no means obvious. Nor is it obvious that, when they are told that all men are equal in the sight of a God who is in Heaven, they are the more willing to be treated as inferiors in this world by their fellow-men. We know that the privileged classes, when the classes beneath them become restive, use Christianity to try to calm them and make them more docile, but this is no proof that Christianity usually has the effects they hope for.[1]

III. INSTRUMENT OR CONDITION OF CLASS DOMINATION?

Though Marx and Engels often speak of the State as an organ or instrument of class rule, they by no means do so always, even when they are speaking of long-established States in class societies. Almost as often they speak as if the State, merely by helping to maintain the social order, makes the exploitation of class by class possible. But this is to say only that the State is *a condition of class exploitation* and not that it is *an instrument of class rule*. Yet Marx and Engels treat these two quite different assertions as if they were the same. In this they

---

[1] There is good evidence that the spread of Methodism in England during the industrial revolution helped to dissuade the poor from resorting to violence to alleviate their miseries, but we must not generalize from one example. Besides, in the long run, Methodism may have added to the discipline and effectiveness of the poor in their struggle for greater equality.

N

are followed by more than their disciples; they are followed even by some of their critics.

If we are to see the weak and the strong points of the Marxian theory of the State, it really is important to notice that the two assertions are not the same. It is important as much in order to do justice to Marx and Engels as for any other reason. For, though neither of these assertions is true, one is much nearer being true than the other. It is nearer the truth to say that the State is a condition of class exploitation. But the Marxian doctrine about the eventual disappearance of the State rests on the second of these assertions and not on the first; it rests on the one which is the furthest from the truth. If, then, we treat the two assertions as equivalent, we treat evidence which bears out the first as if it also bore out the second, and we are disposed to accept the doctrine which rests on the second. We are disposed to treat evidence which goes to show that the State is a condition of class exploitation as if it supported the conclusion that in a classless society there is no need for the State. Or else, if we find the conclusion too extravagant to be accepted, we question the evidence on which it is supposed to rest; we are then too apt to deny that the State is a condition of class exploitation.

To call the State an instrument of class rule is to suggest that, if there were no unequal classes, with the superior among them needing to use force to maintain the social conditions of their superiority, there would be no State. The system of property being what it is, society is divided into exploiting and exploited classes, and the State is used by the exploiting classes to maintain the conditions of exploitaton. There is no need to deny that the State also keeps the peace; but the implication is that it would not be needed to keep it, if there were no exploitation of class by class. This is what the founders of Marxism and their disciples mean to suggest when they call the State an instrument of class rule.

But, as we have seen already, Engels – though he does not know it – gives us a description of the rise of the State which does not square with its being an instrument of class rule. He says that it arises to keep the peace between irreconcilable classes without troubling to notice that the classes which emerge with the division of labour that breaks up tribal society are not classes in the Marxian sense of the word. They are groups owning different sorts of things, but they do not have different property rights in the sense needed to make them different classes, in the Marxian sense of class. Farmers own land, cattle and agricultural implements; wheelwrights own workshops and the tools of their trade, which differ from those of the smiths and the potters. But these differences in the kinds of things that are owned are not enough to divide society into separate classes. It is not until later, when more and more people have forfeited to others their property in their means of production, and even in their own labour, that classes, in the proper Marxian sense, arise; which they can hardly do except where there is a State to enforce the rules whose enforcement enables them to arise. It is only after classes have arisen within the legal order protected by the State that some of them, the exploiting classes, can get control of the State and use it to protect their interests more effectively than it could do when it merely enforced the rules enabling them to rise superior to the rest of society; it is only then that the State can become an instrument of class rule. In order to become an instrument of class rule it must first be a condition of class exploitation.

I have tried to explain how Engels' account of the rise of the State gives the lie to the assertion that the State is merely an instrument of class rule. How could what seems obvious to us not be so to him? How was it that he did not see the significance of his own account of the origins of the State? I think he failed to see it partly because he failed to distinguish between two different senses of the term *a system of property*; in one sense it refers to rules of property and in the other to the distribution of property. He failed to distinguish between the rules, customary or legal, governing the use of things and their transference and the way in which things that are owned are distributed among their possessors. Two countries might have much the same rules of property, and yet property might be much more evenly distributed in one country than the other. We have seen, in considering Engels' account of the rise of the State, how the rules of property which superseded the old tribal rules were, when they first arose, in the common interest, and how in the course of time they led, for a variety of reasons, to a very unequal distribution of property, enabling a few people to live luxuriously on the labour of others who lived miserably. There was no need to change the rules to get the inequality; all that was needed was that the rules should go on being enforced even after they had ceased to be in the common interest. If there had been no State, the division of society into unequal classes might never have gone as far as it did, because the poor might have refused to pay their debts when they found that, by paying them, they would be left without property. Rules which began by being generally convenient might have ceased to be obeyed when they ceased to be convenient except to a part of society. But, fortunately for that part, fortunately for the rich, the State was there to enforce the rules. It was there to serve their interest, though it arose in the first place, not for their benefit, but to enforce rules which could not be enforced by the old tribal authorities, rules which affected a much wider area of transactions; that is to say, transactions more varied in kind and involving a much larger number of persons more remotely related to one another.

Since Engels and Marx, and also their disciples and critics, use such expressions as *relations of property* and *system of property* to mean indiscriminately the rules governing the use and transference of things and the way these things are in fact distributed, they fail to make a distinction which needs to be made if we are to see clearly how different these two assertions are: that the State is the *condition* of the exploitation of class by class, and that the State is an *instrument* of class oppression. If the State is the condition of the exploitation of class by class, then it does not follow that where there is a State there must be class exploitation. It is only if the State is defined as an instrument of class rule that it follows that, where there are no unequal classes and no class exploitation, there is no State.

Of course, it might be true that most States, at one time or another, have been instruments of class rule; that they have been controlled by exploiting classes. It might even be true that most States, more often than not, have been instruments of this kind. If Marx and Engels, in calling the State an instrument of class rule, had meant to say no more than this, we might be content to let the statement pass, leaving it to the historians to contest it if they felt so inclined. But that is not what they meant by it; for they drew from it the conclusion that, if there were no class oppression, no exploitation of class by class, there would be no need for the State. Now, clearly, even if it were true that most States most of the time have been controlled by oppressing classes, it would not follow that, if there were no class oppression, there would be need for the State.

In *The Origins of the Family, Private Property, and the State* Engels says that the State arises to keep the peace between classes having irreconcilable interests. But we have seen that the classes which exist when the State arises are not classes in the Marxian sense of class; they are merely groups engaged in different occupations and having divergent interests. Therefore, if Engels is right, it follows that there can be irreconcilable interests even where there are as yet no classes in the sense in which he uses the word class when he calls the State an instrument of class rule or a condition of class exploitation. The division of labour breaks up the old tribal society and creates groups with irreconcilable interests; then the State arises to keep the peace between these groups; then, within the social order maintained by the State, there emerge classes in the proper Marxian sense; and gradually the exploiting classes gain control of the State and shape it to suit their peculiar needs. I put this forward as a revised version of Engels' account of the origins of the State. I call it a revised version precisely because it adds nothing substantial to the original; it merely refrains from drawing from Engels' account the conclusions which Engels drew, and does so on the ground that they do not follow from it. If what Engels says about the origins of the State is true, it follows that the State is *not* an instrument of class rule in the sense which requires that where there are no classes there is no State; and it also follows that the State is a condition of class exploitation.

4. *States not Controlled by any Class*

Though Marx and Engels speak of the State as an instrument of class rule, they are willing to admit that there have been States not controlled by any class. I have in mind here something more than Engels' saying that the State first arose to keep the peace between irreconcilable[1] groups which he calls classes although they are not so in the specifically Marxian sense; I have also in mind what Marx says in such pamphlets as *Class Struggles in France* and *The Eighteenth Brumaire of Louis Bonaparte*, where he admits that the old French monarchy of before 1789 was not controlled by any class. If the French monarchy was not so controlled, then presumably most of the other absolute monarchies in Europe were not so either, for they, like the French monarchy, ruled over societies where the feudal nobles were fast losing ground and the middle class were still too weak to take over the State. The First and Second Empires in France were also not States controlled by either the decayed nobility or the rising bourgeoisie. It is the parliamentary form which Marx treats as *par excellence* the bourgeois form of government; and that form has been the exception rather than the rule in the West since what Marxists call *capitalism* began to replace the productive system prevailing in the Middle Ages.

How is it that the Marxists, who so confidently speak of the State as an instrument of class rule, are so ready to admit that this or that State is not controlled by any class? I suggest that their readiness is due to a mistaken belief that the State's being a condition of class exploitation is equivalent to its being an instrument of class rule. If this equivalence is taken for granted, it comes much easier to say that the State is an instrument of class rule and at the same time to admit freely, whenever the facts warrant the admission, that the French or some other State is not in fact controlled by a class. For, clearly, the State could be a condition of class exploitation without being controlled by a class; it could maintain a legal system enabling one class to exploit another without actually being in the hands of the exploiting

[1] I argued earlier that there are no *irreconcilable* interests in the sense imagined by Marx and Engels. I am not now retreating from that position; for that sense, I tried to show, rests on a false theory about how interests are related to values. But I also said that there might be conflicts which could not be settled in a way that seemed just to the parties to them while they retained their notions of justice unchanged. Conflicts *irreconcilable* in this weaker-than-Marxian sense can arise between classes and also between groups that are not classes.

class or of their agents. This mixture of candour and paradox is typical of Marxism. It is also useful; it enables the Marxist to stick to his assertion in spite of the evidence against it. Indeed, it enables him to do better than this; it enables him to use the evidence against his assertion as if it were in favour of it.

It might be objected, in favour of Marxism, that this criticism is of small importance and scarcely worth making. No doubt, if the exploiting class or classes do not control the State, it is not literally true that the State is an instrument of their rule. But if those who control the State, whoever they may be, maintain a legal system which allows some classes to exploit others, it is surely not seriously misleading to call the State an instrument of the exploiting classes. Those who rule may not be their agents, but they maintain a system favourable to them, and so in practice act pretty much as they would do if they were their agents.

This objection is not sound. Admittedly, if those who rule, though they are not agents of the exploiting classes, maintain a legal system favourable to those classes, they act pretty much as they would do if they were their agents. But, since in fact they are not their agents, there is no good reason for believing that they will continue to maintain the legal system favourable to the exploiting classes if, for any reason, it should happen to become their interest to change it for the benefit of other classes. Perhaps Marx and Engels believed that this was most unlikely to happen; perhaps they believed that, in a society divided into classes, those who govern, even when they are not agents of any class, always have interests more in line with the interests of the exploiting classes than with those of the exploited; perhaps they believed that, since the form of government varies with the class structure, it follows that, however little the rulers may be directly controlled by the exploiting classes, they will always find it their interest to maintain the legal system favourable to those classes. If they held these beliefs – and they often spoke as if they did hold them – they were mistaken.

Even where they admit that the State is not controlled by any class, Marx and Engels still insist that the form of the State depends largely on the situation of the classes inside it. The old French monarchy and the First and Second Empires were not States controlled by the exploiting classes. Neither the nobles nor the bourgeois actually ruled France. Yet the Bonapartist type of absolute monarchy differed from the Bourbon because, as a result of the French Revolution, the relative position of different classes had changed. The old nobility had been greatly weakened, the peasants had rid themselves of their remaining 'feudal' obligations, the bourgeois were richer and more influential than they had been. The two Napoleons relied, much more heavily than the Bourbons had done, on the loyalty of the peasants and of the lower middle class. They respected the property rights of the capitalists, thus maintaining the conditions of exploitation from which the bourgeois profited; they kept the urban workers down. A Bonaparte on the throne was security against the re-establishment of the old order, which had kept the rich bourgeois socially inferior to the nobles and had put restraints on their money-making enterprises. But the Bonapartes also used the loyalty of other classes to make themselves politically independent of the bourgeois. Like the Bourbons, they played class off against class; though the game in their day was different. The devices used by those who have power to keep it varies with the way in which society is divided into classes, with the sorts of classes there are and with their relative size and importance. Thus, even where the State is not controlled by any class, even where it is not literally an instrument of class rule but only a condition of class exploitation, the structure of the State depends largely on the class structure.

This is perceptive and true, but it is only part of the truth, and a small part, if we use the word *class* in the Marxian sense. The structure of the State depends also on other things besides the class structure thus understood; it depends on whether or not the country is industrialized, on whether the people are mostly illiterate, on whether the rulers enjoy the people's support or can rely on their acquiescence. Marx, no doubt, would say that these other factors are closely connected with the class structure. When a country becomes industrialized, it acquires (he thought) a capitalist and a proletarian class. We cannot blame him, writing at the time he did, for thinking so. But we can now see that it need not be so. Industrialization can be brought to a country by its government, even where there are no capitalists, as it was in Russia. Although industrialization, when it comes, must transform the social order, it can do so without creating capitalists and proletarians. The Soviet Union is, in the Marxian sense of class, a classless society. It may well be divided into groups whose interests, if they were free to push them openly, would prove just as near being irreconcilable as the interests of classes in Western Europe in Marx's time. It may, in some other sense of *class* which is just as usual and important as the Marxian sense, be divided into classes as jealous of one another as any in the West. The enormous power wielded, often most ruthlessly, by the government in the Soviet Union suggests that the State is as much needed there as anywhere to keep the peace between groups with divergent interests. Nevertheless, the Soviet Union, in the specifically Marxian sense of class, is a classless society, or is much nearer being one than any western country. It is therefore misleading to say that the form of the State *depends* on the *class* structure; it is much better to say that it *varies* with the *social* structure.

Marxists might say that the two statements come to much the same thing. They do not. When we speak of the social structure we refer to the division of society into groups, whether or not they are classes in the Marxian or any other sense; and when we say *varies* instead of *depends*, we allow that the form of the State and the policies of its rulers may powerfully affect the social structure, as they clearly have done in Russia and elsewhere.

Neither Marx nor Engels denies that the rulers of the State, whether or not they are the agents of a class, have their own group interests which differ considerably from the interests of all classes. They also admit that organized bodies like the Army and the Church, which are not classes in their sense of the word, have their own corporate interests. We should expect to find that, in a class society, the officers of the Army, the higher clergy, and senior State officials are mostly recruited from the privileged classes. We should expect to find them favouring those classes against others. Yet they also have their own professional interests, and they are powerful in the State. They are powerful in it even when the State is controlled by a class; and are only the more powerful when it is not. I take the Church and the Army for examples because they were important in Europe in Marx's day; but they are not the only examples.

If we allow, as I think we must, and as both Marx and Engels sometimes do, that in the State there can be powerful bodies with interests peculiar to themselves, bodies which are not mere class organizations even when their leaders come mostly from the same classes, we must also allow that the interests of these bodies may clash with the interests of the classes whence their leaders come. Now, if this is so, why should it never be the interest of these bodies to side with the unprivileged against the privileged classes, or at least to pursue policies which in the long run strengthen the unprivileged classes? Why, as the relative strengths of the classes change, should not these groups find it their interest to support the classes that are growing stronger against the classes that are growing weaker? Why should we suppose that these bodies, when they have to choose between their corporate interests and the interests of the classes from which their leaders are mostly recruited, will ordinarily choose to sacrifice their corporate interests? Marx and Engels make an assumption which is by no means obviously true: that class interests always, or nearly always, take precedence over the interests of bodies or groups which are not classes. Of course, while the senior ranks in these bodies are recruited mostly from the upper classes, they will favour the interests of those classes against other class interests, provided their corporate interests do not move them to do otherwise. But if their corporate interests do so move them, why should we assume that they will sacrifice them to their class interests? And why should we assume that these two types of interest will never diverge so widely as to move the body to do what undermines the position of the class?

Marx and Engels believed that, as the machinery of government grows more massive, as more and more people take a full-time part in one capacity or another in the business of government, the State acquires, as they put it, a certain 'independence of society'. The persons who exercise political authority, as they grow in number and in power, come to think of themselves as raised above the rest of society. This is only another way of saying that government, as it grows bigger and more active, becomes more bureaucratic. The larger and more active a group becomes, the greater its social importance, and the more its group interests count as against other interests. This is as true of those who take part in government as of any other group; and perhaps even more true. Therefore, the mere increase in the size of the government machine creates an enormously powerful group, which is not a class, and which, precisely because it is so powerful, is unlikely to be controlled by any class. This is, I think, what Marx and Engels admit when they speak of the State rising above society and becoming a parasite upon it.

But they admit this without seeing the implications of what they are saying. If the State can do this, it may become its interest to put an end to the exploitation of class by class. And yet it may still deserve to be called a parasite, for it may be as oppressive as any class ever was. Yet it may be impartial as between the classes; it may be the sole oppressor. It may care no more for one class than another, and yet be as little public-spirited as any class government; it may be as ready to sacrifice any interest, even the public interest, to its own. An entirely selfish bureaucracy could be so placed that it was its interest to deal impartially with all classes and groups subject to it except when their interests conflicted with its own; which of course they often would do.[1]

It is a pity that Marx, who was one of the shrewdest of political observers, did not see more clearly the light that some of his own observations throw on his theory of the State. *The Eighteenth Brumaire of Louis Bonaparte*, though spoilt by violence and diffuseness, is essentially right in many of its judgements. Louis Napoleon was an adventurer surrounded by others of his kind; he owed his success largely to the support of the lower middle class, envious of their social superiors and contemptuous of the workers, and also to people whose class allegiance was uncertain, the *déclassés*. No one at that time understood better than Marx a phenomenon which, in its later and much grosser form, has come to be known as fascism. Far be it from me to suggest that Bonapartism was ever as cruel and unprincipled a movement as fascism has been in our day. In political nastiness we have outdone

---

[1] A government as completely selfish, as completely indifferent to the public interest, as this is doubtless most unlikely; but a government habitually impartial as between the classes subject to it might be as much disposed to selfishness as any class government. That is the point I wish to make.

N*

our ancestors. Nevertheless, Bonapartism and fascism have more than a little in common. Neither is really a class movement; they both play upon the fears and jealousies of all classes, and their leaders are mostly adventurers – persons who, for one reason or another, are *déclassés* and therefore not inhibited by ordinary loyalties. The Fascist Party in Italy and the National Socialist Party in Germany were not class organizations. They got control of the State in order to bend all classes to their will; or rather they got control of it in order to satisfy ambitions which could not be satisfied except by the sacrifice of class interests. This, of course, was much less true of Bonapartism in Marx's day; Louis Napoleon was kinder to the propertied classes than were Mussolini and Hitler, and also less anxious to flatter and to soothe the industrial workers. This was partly because his ambitions were more modest and his political weapons weaker, and partly because the industrial workers in France were still a small and unorganized class. In Bonapartism we find only the small beginnings of a new kind of illiberal and popular Caesarism which is neither bourgeois nor proletarian.

No one was shrewder than Marx in describing these beginnings, and it is therefore all the more to be regretted than he did not see more clearly their significance for his theory. He saw that classless adventurers could, by playing off the classes against one another, capture the State and use it to promote interests which were not class interests. He also saw, sometimes at least, that modern bureaucratic government, owing to its very size, can rise superior to all social classes. What he did not see is that the modern State, when classless adventurers get control of it, can be used to make society classless, in the Marxian sense of class, without in the least diminishing the oppression of man by man. No doubt, the State could conceivably also be used to reduce oppression, for it might be the interest of those who took over the government to remove class exploitation in the Marxian sense without putting other forms of oppression in its place.

If by a classless society we mean a society where there are no classes in the Marxian sense of class, we have to admit that in such a society there can be just as much oppression as in any class society, and also that there can be groups with interests just as difficult to reconcile as the interests of different classes. The modern State, as it grows larger and more enterprising, reduces the importance of classes, as Marx understood them, and adds to the importance of other groups. This is proved as much by what has been happening in the West in the last hundred years as by the history of the Soviet Union. It is a truth which strikes at the roots of the Marxian theory of the State, though Marx was among the first to get an inkling of it. We can often appeal to Marx against Marx; and when we do so, it is by no means in order to score at his expense. For we appeal to his perspicacity. It is a tribute to him even more than a criticism to say, as I do now, that we learn too much from him to be able to accept some of his most famous doctrines.

B. *The Disappearance of the State*

If we define the State as an instrument of class rule, or if (more cautiously) we say that its essential function is to keep the peace between irreconcilable classes, in the Marxian sense of class, we have to conclude that, if society becomes classless, the State will disappear. But our conclusion is then a mere tautology. We know only that there will be no State, as we have defined it, if there are no classes, as we have defined class. We do not know that, where there are no classes, there will be no parliaments and law-courts, no civil servants, no police, no armed forces. Nor do we know that, where there are no classes as we define class, there will be no groups with interests as difficult to reconcile as class interests.

Now, Marx and Engels were not uttering a tautology when they predicted the disappearance of the State; they really believed that, where there were no classes in their sense of the word, there would be no need for many of the institutions of what we ordinarily understand by the State. I say *many* advisedly and not *all*; for they did not deny that there would always be a need for administration. Wherever there is organization on a large scale, as there must be in every industrial society, there is always the need to allot work and to see that it is done, and also the need to make rules and to see that they are observed. Marx and Engels, like Saint-Simon before them, made a distinction between *government* and *administration*, predicting the disappearance in the classless society of only the first. Though they did not, as I shall try to show, make it clear just what this distinction amounts to, they seem to have included in administration some of the activities usually called governmental. We therefore put, and try to answer, two questions: What is it that they thought would disappear with the disappearance of the State? and what reasons are there for believing that the institutions whose disappearance they predicted are needed only where there are classes?

I. NO MORE ORGANIZED FORCE

The answer to the first question is not easy. Or perhaps I should say that part of the answer is easy and part is not.

The easy part of the answer is *organized force*. In the classless society, it will not be necessary to use force to get people to carry out their obligations. I take it that this does not mean that there never will be disputes about what people's obligations are; I take it that it means that where there are disputes, the parties to them, if they cannot settle them amicably, will always submit them to arbitration and loyally accept the decisions of the arbiters. Men will be so much in agreement about essentials, and will have methods for settling disputes which seem to them so just, that they will readily accept the decisions they are required to accept. If anyone should not accept them in this spirit, the pressure of public opinion will ordinarily be enough to induce him to do so. Crime, the doing deliberately of what is known to be against the rules, will be virtually unknown; or at least so rare that there will be no need to organize the use of force to prevent it. The motives for crime will be less urgent and less frequent, and the criminal will be more easily brought to his senses by the need to regain the good opinion of his neighbours. The assumption is that he lives in a society which is not divided, where men are not one another's victims, where no man is an outcast or an inferior merely in virtue of his position in society. In a society of this kind, crime is much more clearly irrational, much more clearly against the interests of the criminal; it is an aberration, and the criminal, when the mood which led to the crime has passed, sees it as such. He then wants to make amends. He is in a society which seems just to him, he is provided for, he is a man among equals, he is a man who counts; he is not the victim of society, and is therefore not its enemy.

These are the reasons which the anarchists gave, and which the founders of Marxism shared with them. They are part of a stock of ideas common to all the communists of the last century who denounced the State as an instrument of class rule. Marx and Engels were not anarchists in the ordinary sense. They did not want, then and there, to get rid of the State; they wanted the workers to capture and transform it so that they could use it to destroy the social relations and attitudes of mind of bourgeois society. But in another sense they were anarchists: they wanted the workers to use the State to destroy the social conditions which made it necessary to have a State; they shared the belief common among anarchists that class privilege and State power are corrupting.

The defenders of the capitalist system which Marx attacked were sometimes given to expatiating on the dignity of labour. Hard work, they said, is good for men; it gives them self-discipline. Labourers compete with one another for work, and this competition makes for self-reliance. Marx felt only contempt for this line of argument, treating it as a form of hypocrisy. He held that in capitalist society labour is monotonous and degrading. Men are forced to work long hours to earn the necessaries of life; the work they do is not creative, it does not call forth their powers. They work, not for the enjoyment they get from what they do, but only to get a wage. Their labour is a commodity which they sell on the market to the highest bidder; it is not something they do because it absorbs them and gives them a sense of achievement. It takes up most of their waking hours and most of their strength, and yet in itself means nothing to them. They use up their lives and their strength in the effort to keep alive, and have neither time nor energy left over to enjoy life by making an ample and free use of their talents. Their labour, as Marx puts it, is *alienated*; it is a commodity sold to others and not a form of self-expression. And the capitalists, in their competition for profits, also lead unsatisfying lives; they chase the outward marks of success. They are driven to it by the system they are involved in. Both workers and capitalists are slaves of the system in the sense that it impels them to pursue ends which cannot satisfy them; it prevents their living fully human lives. This distortion and crippling of human nature is an inevitable consequence of a system which makes a fetish of production, driving men to behave as if it mattered more that goods should be produced and profits made than human needs satisfied. Crime flourishes under capitalism because of what capitalism does to human nature.

In the classless society of the future the social and psychological causes of crime will disappear, and therefore it will not be necessary to use force to maintain obedience to social rules. Men will be richer than ever they were before; productive techniques will be so efficient that there will be much less time spent on producing the necessaries of life and much more on creative and satisfying activities. There will be plenty for all, due partly to the much greater efficiency of production and partly to men's not wanting things merely to impress their neighbours. There will be neither poverty nor ignorance in the classless society, and there will be leisure to lead a full life. There will be no rebelling against a system of law and morality that cripples human nature; there will be little or nothing to move men to crime. They will obey rules which serve the common interest because they see that the rules in fact do serve it.

The easy part of the answer to the question, What is involved in the disappearance of the State? is *organized force*. The less easy part is, a hierarchy of persons, *separate* from the rest of society, managing its common affairs. This is what Engels tells us comes into existence when the State appears, and it is presumably what is destined to wither away when the State disappears. But what this is is not as easily understood as what organized force is. How must we interpret Engels' meaning? Is he saying that in the classless society there will be no administration other than business management? That there will be no need for any decisions to be made except about the assignment of work and the use of resources? Or is he saying that, though there will also be a need for decisions of other kinds, they will be taken by the workers themselves or by part-time officials whom they appoint? Or, lastly, does he allow that the work of administration will be done by whole-time professionals, insisting only that those who do it will be very closely

responsible to those affected by what they do? I do not believe that the
texts make it possible to decide roundly in favour of any one of these
three interpretations, though I suspect that the first two come closer
than the third to giving us Engels' meaning. I shall consider all three,
including the one which seems to me the least likely, for I am less
interested in weighing the evidence in favour of this or that interpretation of Marxism than in seeing what can be said for and against
such views as Marx and Engels held.[1]

II. NO MORE ALIENATION

But before I consider these three versions of what is involved in the
disappearance of a hierarchy of persons, *separate* from the rest of
society, managing its common affairs, I want to go back for a moment
to the prediction that in the classless society there will be no need to
use organized force to get men to carry out their obligations. Such force
will be unnecessary because there will be no more *alienation*. Society
will no longer produce in us the motives that lead to crime, to the
deliberate flouting of the rules which we are required to obey.

The Marxian doctrine of *alienation* bears a strong likeness to Rousseau's doctrine that society corrupts man. Marx and Rousseau agree
that it is in society that man becomes moral, a maker of claims and a
recognizer of obligations, a rule-prescribing and rule-respecting animal,
and that it is also in society that man acquires the motives impelling
him to break the rules. That, at bottom, is what is wrong with society;
it sets up standards and at the same time produces in men passions
which move them to reject those standards. The remedy for this
condition is a society which so acts upon its members that they
willingly do what is required of them.

Marx's doctrine of *alienation*, like Rousseau's doctrine of social corruption, rests on this assumption: Given men's natural capacities, there
is a form of society whose discipline is pre-eminently acceptable to
them, because in it their environment creates in them the motives
which make them willingly obey the rules needed to hold society
together. This is the just society, the social and moral order in conformity with human nature. In bourgeois society, men acquire values
in which they cannot find satisfaction; they are frustrated, and are
therefore prone to actions which are wrong or illegal according to the

[1] When two or more versions of some doctrine of theirs are put forward, I am
less concerned to argue that one version comes closer to their meaning than
the others, or to explain how they shift from one to another, than to consider
what is to be said for these different versions. There is a good deal of
ambiguity in all social and political theories, and it is less important for my
purpose to decide what their authors can most plausibly be held to have
meant than to consider how much truth there is in the doctrines attributed
to them.

moral rules and laws which embody these values. The morality of bourgeois society is not a truly human morality; it does not allow men to make the most of their natural capacities.

Leaving aside this condemnation of bourgeois society, we may agree that a community can be so organized as to dispose many of its members to break the rules which it requires them to obey. Communities do vary greatly in what, for want of a better word, I shall call cultural solidarity. In some communities people find it easier and more satisfying than in others to live up to the standards expected of them. But the doctrine of *alienation* or *social corruption*, which is sociological and psychological as well as moral, has never, to the best of my knowledge, been put clearly and adequately; it has never been put in a way which is intelligible and which also seems to account for the facts. I suspect that it is a doctrine containing a large measure of truth; though just how large, I do not know.

What evidence is there that *alienation* is peculiar to societies divided into classes, in the Marxian sense of class? Marx seems to have believed that alienation is an effect of poverty and of man's being somehow the victim of his social environment. Man is helpless in bourgeois society; he is pushed by forces he does not understand and cannot control into courses which restrict and stultify. Though some countries are much richer now than they were in Marx's time, they seem to be afflicted as much as ever they were by what Marx calls *alienation*. Crime flourishes even where the extremes of poverty have disappeared. Britain, Russia and the United States are, in the Marxian sense of class, much less class societies today than they were in 1859: the rights of property which distinguish the privileged or 'exploiting' classes have been greatly curtailed, while the workers who have nothing to sell but their labour are much more sure of a market for it and are able to sell it at a better price. No doubt, new kinds of inequality have arisen; but the kinds that go along with class divisions as Marx understood them are much less important than they were. Yet there is little evidence that men feel less helpless, less lost, in society than they used to do, or that they are less driven by passion than they used to be to flout social rules.

Marx was so certain that *alienation* springs from the division of society into classes, from the pursuit of profit, from unrestricted competition, from the treatment of labour as a commodity, that he never stopped to enquire how far it was due to the scale and complexity of industrial society. Men can no longer rely, as their ancestors could, on custom and tradition to guide them; for they live in societies which are swiftly changing as well as immense. Whether the societies they live in are bourgeois or proletarian, men are still apt to lose their social bearings, to feel isolated and rootless, to feel themselves impelled into courses which do not satisfy them. It may be possible to save them from these feelings which (as Marx saw) move them to crime. But it seems that it cannot be done merely by abolishing social classes and exploitation as Marx understood them.

Given a certain definition of class, a society becomes classless as soon as there are no groups inside it falling under the definition. Marx disliked the division of society into classes and he also disliked inequality. Unfortunately, he took it for granted that where there were no classes there would be no inequality. He never asked himself whether society, even though it should become classless, might continue to produce inequalities leading to *alienation*. He disliked capitalism, and took it for granted that, when it disappeared, the harmful effects of competition and the division of labour would disappear also; he never enquired whether they might survive in a socialist society which was also industrial.[1] He believed that *alienation* is in large part a result of using money. The pursuit of profits is the pursuit of money, and under capitalism the measure of a man's success is the amount of money he can make. Money is only a medium of exchange, but the capitalist economy drives men to pursue it as if it were worth having for its own sake. This attack on money is an old theme of the moralists to which Marx adds twists of his own. He is eloquent and ingenious. But to quite what purpose? Will there be no money in the classless society of the future, which is to be as industrial and enterprising as bourgeois society? Is not the use of money, in some form or other, essential in every society where there is a great division of labour? And must there not be such a division wherever modern techniques of production are used? And even should the coming of plenty make the pursuit of money pointless, will not men compete for other things to prove their superiority over one another? How are we to distinguish between the kinds of competition that produce *alienation* and the kinds that produce cultural solidarity? How can we know that the disappearance of classes as Marx defines them will leave us with only the kinds that produce this solidarity, so that organized force is no longer needed to maintain order?

III. MANAGEMENT AND HIERARCHY

Can we suppose, as Marx and Engels seem to do, that in the classless society administration will consist only of business management and the adjudication of disputes?

The classless society is to renounce none of the benefits of large-scale

[1] Some socialists have so defined a socialist society that it is by definition very little competitive. But a classless society where there is no private property in the means of production can be intensely competitive and can induce in those who are outdistanced a sense of failure which is deeply frustrating. The Soviet Union is as fiercely competitive as the United States.

industrial production. It must therefore have a highly complicated economy. What exactly are the workers to take over? Are they to take over each separate factory and enterprise and to run it as they think fit? If they do that, the economy, taken as a whole, will be just as little regulated as it was under capitalism in Marx's day. There will be competition and the risk of economic anarchy. Are the workers to take control of the entire economy? But if they do that, they undertake much more than mere business management.

We must not be the dupes of words. The control of a factory or a farm is essentially different from the control of an entire economy. To call both these activities business management or administration, and to leave it at that, is to mask, or at least to play down, the differences between them. The manager of a business organizes production for the market; the controller of an entire economy plans over-all production for the benefit of all sections of an immense community. If administration is taken to be the sort of thing that the manager of a business does, and if government is taken to be (as it often was in Marx's time) the keeping of order and the settling of disputes, then the running of an entire economy for the benefit of all concerned is neither administration nor government. It is a kind of activity with which we are now familiar but which was much less known in Europe a hundred years ago. This activity – since it is primarily concerned, not with increasing profits and lowering costs, but with reaching goals which are not commensurable, and are not to be understood apart from accepted notions of justice, decency, dignity, and freedom – clearly comes closer to being *political* than *economic*, as those terms were understood long before Marx's day and are still understood in our day; though it may be that in Marx's time the term political, owing largely to the influence of the *laissez-faire* economists, was used more narrowly than either before or since.

But the word we choose to describe this activity does not much matter. What matters is that the activity is vast in scale and many-sided, involving not only hierarchy and desk-work, but the making of decisions different in kind from those made by the manager of a business. It calls for special training, great experience, and, at the upper levels of the hierarchy, uncommon talents. It cannot, as Marx and Engels sometimes imply, be a part-time activity of the workers. It is whole-time work for men who make such work their profession.

Of the three versions of what is involved in the disappearance of a hierarchy of persons, *separate* from the rest of society, managing its common affairs, only the third is at all realistic, though what Marx and Engels say suggests that it is the one they had least often in mind. This version makes *separate from* the rest of society equivalent to *not closely responsible* to it. If we accept this version, then, in the classless society which is also highly industrialized, the management of common affairs, though it is a massive and diverse undertaking and the whole-time occupation of thousands, will be the work of persons closely responsible to the rest of society.

But how is this to be contrived? This is a question never really faced by the founders of Marxism. How, in a large and complicated society, can persons whose whole-time occupation is the management of common affairs be made closely responsible to the people, who can spare only a little time to consider these affairs? How can the great majority, who are inevitably largely ignorant, control the actions of a minority much more knowledgeable than they are?

If we retain Rousseau's model of democracy; if we think in terms of a *will of the people* put into effect by their agents, we cannot solve this problem. As Rousseau saw, his model can apply only to a small and simple community whose citizens themselves constitute the legislature. In an advanced industrial society, where the important decisions, even when they are made by an elected assembly, are made by a body tens of thousands of times less numerous than the people on whose behalf it takes them, there is no *will of the people* as Rousseau understood it. The people do not decide the great issues of policy, and then appoint agents to carry out their decisions; at the best, they merely choose the persons who are to make the decisions, having only the vaguest ideas about what those decisions should be. If we are to speak realistically of representative democracy on a vast scale we must use another model than Rousseau's. We must speak of organized bodies whose function is to define and promote the interests of all important sections of the community, of the freedom to form such bodies, of the need to ensure that they are so organized as to be highly responsive to the demands and feelings of their members, of the need for procedures enabling these bodies to compete fairly for the attention of the government and to reach settlements which seem just to them, of the need to ensure that governments lose power when they lose the people's confidence. We have to ask, as Marx and Engels did not ask: What institutions and what rules of political conduct best serve these needs?

I suspect that Marx and Engels accepted, for the classless society of the future, something not unlike Rousseau's model of democracy. Of course, they did not accept, as he did, the enduring need for organized force, and they did not want a simple society, but they did share his belief that in the community of equals the deciding of important public issues is the part-time occupation of all the members of the community. It is their business to decide in principle what shall be done, though they may appoint agents to execute their will and even to take minor decisions.

I think it probable that Marx and Engels were victims of their own phrases. Having called the State an instrument of class rule, they were disposed to take it for granted that the enormous machinery of the modern State is needed because that State is the most repressive of all or because the task of repression is now more difficult than it used to be. To keep scattered and illiterate serfs in order, there was no need for such massive organs of repression as are now needed to keep down a proletariat congregated in large towns and fast growing in literacy and political intelligence. The modern State is a heavier lid on a pot boiling more furiously than ever.

One after another, the organs of the nineteenth-century State, authoritarian or liberal, are dismissed as serving the interests of the exploiting class. There would not be large armies were it not that the class-structure of bourgeois society makes the bourgeois State aggressive, and were it not also that armies are needed to supplement the police in maintaining domestic order. If it were not for the division of society into classes, there would be no huge departments of State, no courts with professional judges and lawyers, and no assembly elected at long intervals, ostensibly to represent the people, but actually to increase the pressure on the executive of the wealthy and exploiting classes.

It is taken for granted that these organs, because they are often used for the benefit of some classes against others in a society divided into classes, will disappear in a classless society. But why should that be so? Are not some of them needed in any large industrial society? What evidence is there that classless societies are less aggressive than others, and that therefore, in a world consisting only of classless societies, there would be no need for armies? Are the proletariat less inclined to war than other classes? If there is more pacifism in the world today than there was in Marx's time, is this because the workers now have more influence than they had or because war has changed its character and is much more to be feared?

IV. THE PARIS COMMUNE AND THE SOVIETS

Marx admitted that in the modern State power grows at the higher levels at the expense of the lower levels of government. Sometimes he welcomed its doing so. The revolutionary State of the Jacobins was stronger and more centralized than the old French monarchy, and it needed to be in order to destroy the remains of feudalism. Marx derided the German liberals of 1848 for wanting to give Germany a federal constitution. What Germany needed was a strong central government to do for her what the Jacobins had done for France. About the Paris Commune of 1871, which he hailed as the first proletarian government, Marx spoke equivocally: although it wanted to dissolve France into a loose confederation of communes, he defended it by denying that it wanted to do what in fact it did want to do – which was to destroy the power of the centralized State. Marx seems to have believed that the modern State, bourgeois or proletarian, must be strong at the centre to carry out its class purposes: to destroy the vestiges of feudalism and to defend capitalist social relations in the bourgeois State, or to destroy the vestiges of capitalism in the proletarian State.

Marx's defence of the Paris Commune is a defence of proletarian government, of a form of State. We cannot infer from it how he conceived that *administration*, as distinct from *government*, would be organized in a classless society. We know that he thought proletarian government the most popular of all forms of government, and the institutions of the proletarian State the best adapted to serve the interests of the great majority. Proletarian government, if we take the Paris Commune as an example (however imperfect) of it, though democratic, is neither parliamentary nor presidential. The legislative assembly is elected annually, deputies can be recalled if they displease their constituents, and the executive is elected by the assembly. Parliamentary government, in the eyes of Marx and Engels, is essentially bourgeois, and so too is the separation of powers as we find it in the United States.

We cannot know how Marx and Engels imagined that the classless society would be administered. They reveal their minds so little that it would be foolish to attribute definite opinions to them. I shall therefore confine myself to considering the possibilities.

The Communards in Paris, though Marx pretended otherwise, wanted to destroy the power of the central government in France. Many of them were very much influenced by the teachings of Proudhon, who was a kind of anarchist. They believed, as Marx did, that in the society of equals there would be no centralized State and eventually almost no need for the use of force to keep order. They wanted the smallest administrative unit in France, the commune, to be sovereign, being responsible to its members alone for how it managed communal affairs. Matters common to a district larger than the commune were to be settled by delegates chosen by all the communes in the district, and the delegates were to be bound by their instructions; and matters common to a region larger than a district were to be transacted by delegates from all the districts in the region also closely bound by their instructions. This gives us a pyramidal structure rather like the Russian system before the Stalin Constitution; that is, like the Russian system, not as it really was, but as it was supposed to be by its apologists. This Russian system was said by its champions to be more truly democratic than any other then existing; it was alleged in its favour that it made government at every level more closely responsible to the people than any Western parliamentary government. It made all public officials mere agents of the people or of their representatives.

This Russian system, as it was described by its champions, as it was on paper, did not really correspond to the system which Marx insisted that the Communards had wanted to establish in France; but it did correspond rather more closely to the true aspirations of the Communards. In other words, the illusions of its apologists about the Soviet system before the Stalin Constitution came closer to the real aspirations of the Communards than to the aspirations attributed to them by Marx; whereas the Soviet system, as it really was, came closer to being what Marx mistakenly believed the Communards had wanted for France.

Certainly, the Communard Constitution, *as it really was*, was not in the least a suitable model for the proletarian State, as Marx conceived of it; for the rôle assigned to that State by Marx was to use force boldly to establish its authority and to destroy the vestiges of the old order. And nobody was more convinced than Marx that a revolutionary State carrying out such a rôle would need to be highly centralized. Indeed, it was because he was convinced both of this and of the proletarian character of the Paris Commune that he was so strongly impelled to misinterpret the Communard Constitution.

But it may be that Marx, though he would not have accepted the Communard Constitution, as it really was, as a model for a proletarian State, might have thought it well suited, with certain modifications, to serve as a model for the administration of a classless society. I do not say that he would or that he would not; I say only that it is a possibility not excluded by anything that he or Engels says about communist society. The Communard Constitution was a scheme inspired by anarchists as certain as Marx ever was that in the classless society, the society of equals, there would be no need for the State, no need for government as distinct from administration. And Marx, though he differed strongly from the anarchists about how the transition to the classless society was to be made, was yet considerably influenced by their ideas; he looked forward to anarchy, if not as lovingly, at least as confidently as they did, and what hints he gave as to what the society of equals would be like suggest that his image of it did not differ greatly from theirs.

The Communards, many of them disciples of Proudhon, looked upon the French State of their time as an instrument of class rule; they saw and disliked in it all the features which Marx and Engels said were characteristic of the State. They intended, in their projected constitution for France, to abolish the old State and to put in its place an administrative system suited to the needs of a society of equals. The scheme they put up for France to adopt was inspired by just the same doctrine about the State as the one which caused Engels to predict that, with the coming of the classless society, the State would *wither away*.

Now, this scheme can be shown to be unworkable. It can only give the appearance of working when it is controlled by some body which decides beforehand what decisions shall be taken at each level of the pyramid.

The bodies lower down the pyramid are busy, most of the time, discussing their own affairs, which are in many ways different from the affairs of the bodies higher up. The affairs of a village are not the affairs of Normandy or of France. If the persons elected by the lowest bodies to the bodies immediately above them are mere delegates, bound to carry out their instructions, how can the higher bodies reach any decisions? Suppose that each of twelve delegates gets different instructions from the others. How is a decision possible? There can be no decision unless at least seven of the delegates reach agreement, which requires that six of them, if not all seven, agree to something which does not accord with their instructions. Those who vote against the decision can remain true to their instructions only at the cost of being out-voted. But if each delegate is merely told that his electors have certain preferences, and is instructed to vote for whatever proposal has a chance of acceptance and accords best with these preferences, he ceases to be a mere delegate. What proposal is accepted cannot be inferred from the instructions given to the twelve delegates; it depends on the trend of the discussion between them. The supposedly mere delegate becomes in fact a representative.

Moreover, the lowest bodies cannot be sovereign. If the system is to work at all, they must abide loyally by the decisions reached at higher levels, whether they like those decisions or not. In a highly industrial society, the decisions they take must in practice be closely limited by the decisions taken by the bodies above them. Their own decisions are not the most important, and their influence on other decisions is the smaller the higher up the pyramid we go. By the time we get to the top, the instructions given to the delegates chosen by the lowest authorities have little bearing on the decisions actually taken. They are too remote and too irrelevant.

Logically, it is possible for all decisions reached by a higher body to be referred back for approval to the lowest bodies within its region, the supposedly sovereign bodies. But what rule should govern this process? Should each lowest body be bound by a decision reached at a higher level only if it votes in favour of it? This rule alone preserves its sovereignty. But there are many decisions not worth anyone's acting upon unless all whom it concerns are bound by it. Or should the rule be that all the lowest bodies are bound by decisions endorsed by a majority of them? In that case, it is no longer true that each lowest body is sovereign.

Even if the second rule is adopted, the process is absurdly cumbersome. It can be made to appear to work only where all the bodies at the

lowest level are in fact controlled by one party or organized group
ensuring that compatible decisions are taken quickly at the lowest
level, and therefore also at all levels above it. But this remedy takes
the life out of the system, reducing it to make-believe. This is what
happened in Russia with the soviets almost as soon as they were established. The country would have been ungovernable if the soviets at
the lowest level, in the factories and villages, had really been sovereign,
and if the soviets above them had consisted of mere delegates. The
country was saved from chaos because all the soviets at all levels were
controlled by the Bolsheviks, who saw to it that they took the decisions
which the party decided they should take. The chaos that threatened
Russia was ascribed to the illiteracy and political inexperience of the
people. No doubt, they were illiterate and without experience. But
that was not the only cause of confusion and disorder. The system was
unworkable. The pyramid of soviets was not a possible structure of
administration; it could only be a screen to hide the real structure
from view.

Where in an industrial society there are many units and several
different levels of authority, the units at the top (or at the centre) will
be responsible to the people only if they are elected by them. Not
everyone who has authority at the centre need be directly elected, but
those who take the important decisions, the policy-makers, must be so.
The central legislature must be directly elected, if the central government is to be democratic. If the legislature is elected indirectly, at
several removes from the people, there may or may not be chaos but
there cannot be democracy. The more industrial a society, the more
the really important decisions must be taken at the centre. Therefore
if the society is to be democratic, the persons taking these decisions
must be directly responsible to the people. There must be a periodic
and free judgement passed by the people on the central legislature and
executive. This is precisely what the systems called 'bourgeois' by
the Marxists provide for: whether, as in Britain, the same election
produces a legislature and an executive, or whether, as in the United
States, there are separate elections for the two branches.[1]

This does not mean that local autonomies are not worth preserving
or enlarging, that the trend towards centralized administration ought
not to be resisted, that devolution is undesirable. The more active your
lesser authorities within the spheres of their competence, the better for

[1] There are, of course, other models than the British and the American. A
general election need not be a virtual choice of government, as it is in
Britain; it may merely decide that governments are to be taken from one
part of the legislature rather than another. But where the people come to
believe, as they did in France under the Fourth Republic, that how they
vote has little to do with deciding how they are governed, or by whom,
democracy is in danger.

democracy. No matter how industrial, how closely integrated, your society, there are always many decisions which are best not taken at the centre and others which need not be taken there. The democrat will be rightly concerned that decisions which can be taken locally should be so taken. But this does not affect the point at issue. However desirable it may be that local autonomies should be preserved or enlarged, the fact remains that in industrial societies, many, indeed most, of the important decisions must be taken at the centre. Therefore, unless the persons who take them are directly responsible to the people, the society, no matter how impressive its pyramidal structure of administration, has gone only a little way towards being democratic.

Often, in a pre-industrial society, where villages are almost self-supporting and small towns depend for their living on the districts immediately surrounding them, there can be really considerable local autonomies, even though authority at the centre is quite irresponsible. And the local authorities can be democratic, though in fact they have more often been aristocratic or oligarchic. What they are depends on local circumstances rather than on the character of the central government. Thus, there can be autocracy at the centre and aristocracy or even democracy at lower levels of government. But the power of the central government, great though it is on paper, is in fact much smaller than it appears. The central government must in practice respect the rights of the authorities subordinate to it. But, in an industrial society, the power of the central government is necessarily much greater. Therefore, where the central government is not democratic, it is most unlikely that the authorities in fact subordinate to it (whatever their rights on paper) are so. It is not impossible but is unlikely; except where there are good grounds for believing that the central government is intent upon setting up democracy among a backward people and is making a beginning at the lower levels. In that case, we must look at the record of the government and of the party that controls it. We must enquire what they have done to justify the belief that they honestly desire to establish democracy, and know how to set about achieving their purpose.

V. CONFLICTS IN THE CLASSLESS SOCIETY

Marx and Engels were precluded by their own theory about classes and the State from considering the group conflicts that might arise in a society which was classless in their sense of class. They set a fashion which their disciples have followed. They made a number of statements about conflicts between classes, and said that the State is needed because there are these conflicts. They never stopped to enquire whether such conflicts could arise between groups which were not classes in their sense. Wherever they looked they saw only what they wanted to see; they saw only class conflicts. This was so partly because they looked most closely at the societies and epochs which came nearest to bearing out their thesis; they looked at the history of Western Europe from the fifteenth century onward, and at the periods of Greek and Roman history when class conflicts were most bitter. It was so also because, without knowing that they did so, they used the word *class* in other senses than the sense they defined; they spoke of class conflicts when the groups in conflict were not classes in their sense. This is what Engels did when he spoke of classes with irreconcilable interests arising at the break-up of tribal society and the emergence of the State.[1]

Conflicts are difficult to settle for one or both of two reasons: because there is no procedure generally accepted for their settlement, or because the parties to them have widely different conceptions of justice and honour. These two reasons are closely connected: where there is an agreed procedure, there tend to be the same conceptions of justice and honour, and, where these conceptions are the same, there is usually an agreed procedure, or it is easy to set one up where it is lacking. All conceptions of justice and honour need not be the same or closely similar; it is enough that the relevant ones should be so. Two countries with different conceptions of justice and honour in family life do not therefore find it difficult to have pleasant relations with one another.

As far as I can see, there is no reason for believing that in a society without classes, in the Marxian sense of class, these two causes making difficult the settlement of disputes will not operate. No doubt, in a society which is classless in some other sense, they may not operate. We can even define a classless society as one in which there are no groups having widely different conceptions of justice and honour or different ideas about how disputes should be settled. I suspect that Marxists sometimes, perhaps often, when they speak of a classless society, have this also in mind. I should not quarrel with them for using the phrase in this sense; I should quarrel with them only if they took it for granted that a socialist or a communist society must be classless, if this is what classless means.

---

[1] As Engels describes it, the break-up of tribal authority involves a change in the system of property. Common ownership gradually gives way to private property, and this transformation is accompanied by the rise of groups with 'irreconcilable' interests. But, as we have seen already, these groups with 'irreconcilable' interests are not, *to begin with*, different classes in the Marxian sense, though Engels calls them classes; they do not differ in their rights of property, and yet they have 'irreconcilable' interests in the sense of divergent interests leading to disputes which require a new type of authority, the State, to settle them.

C. 'Backward' Societies and Their Political Problems

I. TWO ASSUMPTIONS

When we call a society *backward* we make either or both of two assumptions: that there is a normal course of social evolution or that some social forms are more desirable than others. Logically, if we make one of these assumptions, we need not make the other; and it has often happened that only one has been made. But in the nineteenth century it was usual for radicals to make both, and in this respect Marx and Engels followed the common example.

Their assuming that there is a normal course of social change did not prevent their allowing exceptions. Though they predicted that socialism would come to most countries after a violent revolution, they allowed that in Britain and the United States it might come without violence; and Marx at one time thought it possible that the proletariat might first get power in Germany, though Germany was then more 'backward' than either France or England; and at another time he thought it possible that the revolution bringing socialism might even break out in Russia, which he thought of as the most backward of the great European Powers. But, though Marx and Engels were willing to admit that there might be exceptions, they were never moved to examine critically their assumption that there is a normal course of social change.

I have tried to explain elsewhere what is peculiar about this assumption.[1] A biological organism which grows or has a normal course of change and span of life can be easily identified; it develops in a more or less stable environment, and its growth is not affected by the growth of other organisms. But what is it of which we predicate a normal course of *social* change? Whatever principle we adopt to classify societies, we find few societies belonging to any one type, and we find great differences even among those few. How, then, can we speak of a normal course of change for any one type of society, not to speak of all types? And what is to constitute a single society for this purpose? Can we treat a community like England as a single society? Clearly Marx did not do so. He had in mind, not independent States, but large populations with broadly similar productive methods and social institutions. The society whose evolution is described in *Capital* is not England or France or Germany but Western Europe from the later Middle Ages to the nineteenth century. But what exactly were the confines of this society? Where did it end and other societies begin? To what extent was it one society distinct from others?

[1] In my *German Marxism and Russian Communism*.

If people having similar institutions constitute a society, we can divide mankind into separate societies in more than one way, depending on the institutions we choose to take into account. If we take some into account, France and England are parts of the same society; if we take others, they are separate societies.

And observe that we have here, not only the difficulty of deciding into what class to place a thing, but the further difficulty of locating the thing we want to classify; the difficulty of separating it off from other things. The entomologist may be puzzled as to whether the insect he is examining belongs to one species or another, or even as to whether it is an insect or some other form of life, but at least he knows it as a specimen separate from all others. He can distinguish it from its environment. It is a distinct individual in the animal kingdom. There may be other systems of classification than the one he uses, and if another were used, his specimen would be differently classified. But it would be put entire into a different class.

But a population which is the whole of a society of one type may be only a part of a society of another type, and may contain several societies of a third type. Or again, people living within a given area who at one time belong to the same society because they share certain institutions may at another time belong to different societies because they no longer share them. I must not elaborate on these points, which I have discussed at greater length elsewhere. I repeat them only to show how improbable it is that mankind can be divided into societies following a normal course of change.

When we speak of a normal course of social evolution we use ideas taken from biology to explain social change, and we use them improperly. Perhaps because society consists only of men, we are tempted to apply to it ideas which apply to its constituents; man has a normal course of maturation and senescence, and a normal span of life. We see society as man writ large, as the macrocosm of which he is the microcosm. Sometimes, since man is a contriver, a mechanic, we see society as his product, as the instrument he has devised to attain his ends. But, if we look more deeply, we see that society is not deliberately man-made; we see that, though it is the product of his activities, it is an unintended product. We see also that man is deeply affected by his social environment, and differs greatly from one society to another. And so, forced to admit that society is not made by man, we are tempted to speak of it as if, like man, it grew, as if it followed a normal course of change determined by what it is. Change which touches us so nearly, if it is not contrivance, must be growth. We do not like to admit that it is neither the one nor the other.

It is true that not every normal course of change known to us is biological, consisting either of organic growth and decay or of a course of mental evolution closely connected with organic change. We can speak of a normal course of moral or cultural change, which may differ considerably from society to society, though the individuals subject to it are biologically the same. This course of change is much more difficult to observe and to measure than organic growth, and more difficult even than the psychological change connected with that growth. Yet we can sometimes construct a realistic model of normal cultural or moral development because, in a given social environment, we can find a large number of persons exposed to fairly similar social influences. We can speak plausibly enough, for example, of a normal course of moral or cultural development for an English child born into the professional class or into the manual working class; we can even speak of a normal course of cultural development for the child born in the West or in a Westernized community. The more we know about how social environments differ and about the children born into them, the more we can distinguish what, in a child's moral and cultural development, is common to societies of many types from what is peculiar to one type and therefore normal only inside it.

Here we are considering only individuals. There are many of them in every more or less stable environment, and so, by taking a random sample, we can construct our model of a normal course of change. But we cannot do it as easily with communities; not even where we are able to identify them in their separateness. For communities differ from one another much more than individuals do, and their social environments are much less similar. It is much more difficult to find many communities of much the same type and exposed to much the same external influences, and to show that they have changed in much the same ways. No doubt, there are many towns and villages in Europe and Asia which have existed for centuries as separate and self-conscious units. They are the most easily identified; and they were, until the rise of the nation-state, perhaps the most sharply self-conscious of communities. But we can hardly speak of a normal course of change, even for English villages, so greatly have they differed from one another in size and structure, and so enormous the variety of influences that have touched them. Or if we do speak of it, we are immediately aware that this is merely a device of explanation, and we heap one qualification upon another in the attempt to get closer to the truth. The shorter the period we take and the smaller the area, the more confidently we speak. This, we say, is what was happening to the villages along the Welsh borders in the second half of the fifteenth century. But we would not presume to speak so confidently of a course of change undergone by the villages of England from the fifteenth to the nineteenth centuries. If we cannot speak in this way of the most compact, easily identified, and numerous communities, how can we do so of the loose and shapeless giants whose limits in space and history we are hard put to it to determine? To construct a model of a normal course of change we must have many specimens, easily discerned and closely similar in structure, from which we can take a representative sample.

11. TWO TYPES OF 'NORMAL' EVOLUTION

There are thus two kinds of *normal evolution* which we are apt to call *organic change* or *growth*, though one differs profoundly from the other. How a plant or an animal evolves, from the moment at which it acquires a separate identity, depends on what sort of plant or animal it is. The seed of a rose will not grow into a lily. Provided its physical environment is suitable, the seed, being what it is, will grow into a rose bush. This is the properly organic change. But the cultural development of a child depends on the social influences to which it is exposed in a quite different way from that in which the growth of a plant depends on its physical environment. No doubt, unless the child were, biologically and psychologically, the sort of creature it is, these influences would not affect it as they do. Yet these influences are not conditions of organic growth; we cannot say of them that they must be present to allow of a course of change determined by the structure of what changes. If an English child were exposed to other social influences, it would still develop culturally, but the development would be very different. It is therefore improper to call it organic. And yet we can properly call it normal, where there are many children exposed to much the same social influences. So also, though much more cautiously, we may speak of a normal course of evolution for communities of the same general type exposed over a certain period of time to the same external influences.

Neither Marx nor Engels troubled to distinguish between these two types of a normal course of change. Does that mean that we cannot say whether they had one or other of the two in mind? I do not think so. For, like most of the philosophers and historians of their day who spoke of a course of social evolution in the West, they thought of it as almost untouched by external influences. They spoke as if how society evolves were determined by its structure, by the complex of operations which it is; or, at least, they came closer to this way of speaking than to any other. They took man's nature and his physical environment for granted, and sought the cause of social change in the nature of changing society. We may therefore say that the normal course of social evolution which they had in mind, most of the time if not all of it, was organic.

Yet they could not ignore the fact that societies – even the vast and amorphous societies they had in mind when they spoke of a normal course of social evolution – can deeply affect one another. Though they took almost no notice of external influences on the West, they often insisted that the influence of the West on other parts of the world was profound. They could not shut their eyes to the obvious: that countries poorer and less powerful than the great Western Powers were exposed to their influence, and were therefore, by reason of that exposure, differently placed from the Western countries. Can the course of social change in a 'backward' country deeply influenced by a country more 'advanced' than itself be the same as the course in the country that influences it? Marx and Engels did not exactly address their minds to this question. They may even perhaps have unconsciously turned away from it because of the difficulties it creates for persons committed to such a theory as theirs. But they could not avoid it altogether. When Marx, towards the end of his life, considered the impact on 'backward' Russia of Western techniques and ideas still unknown to the West at the time when it was at roughly the same stage of evolution as Russia then was, he could not deny that Russia's advance towards socialism might be different from that of the West.

But, though we can sometimes notice, in the writings of Marx and Engels, a certain awareness that 'backward' societies deeply affected by 'advanced' ones are placed as the 'advanced' societies never were, they do not appear to have given much thought to the matter or considered its implications for their theory. The 'advanced' societies of the West contain only a minority of mankind. Must we therefore conclude that the social evolution of only a minority is normal? But the West, too, has been deeply influenced in the past by other societies. How, then, in a world in which every society has, at some time or other, been deeply influenced by other societies, can there be a *normal* course of social evolution? Is it the course that a society would follow if it were never influenced by other societies, or never deeply influenced by them? But how can we discover what that course would be?

We have seen that Marxism, like other theories of its kind, makes two assumptions: that there is a normal course of social evolution, and that some social forms are more desirable than others. Thus, one society may be more 'advanced' than another in either or both of two senses: it may be further along the normal course or it may have social forms which are more desirable. Usually, but not always, Marx and his disciples speak as if a society were necessarily more advanced in the second sense when it is more advanced in the first. Serfdom belongs, they think, to a later stage of social evolution than slavery, and is also a milder form of exploitation; and they speak of the proletarian, who belongs to a still later age, as freer than the serf. Since they in fact condemn exploitation and approve of freedom, we can conclude that, by their standards, it is better to be a serf than a slave, and better to be a proletarian than a serf. But they also admit that in tribal societies there is greater equality than in the societies coming

after them, and they sometimes speak as if exploitation must grow
worse as capitalism grows older.[1]

Apart from these two assumptions, there is another which Marx
and the Marxists ordinarily make; they take it for granted that when
an 'advanced' society impinges on a 'backward' one, it hastens its
progress, moving it more quickly along the normal course and bringing
it nearer the desirable goal; or else that, if it deflects it from the normal
course, it does not push it onto another course which takes longer to
reach what is ultimately desirable or which leads away from it. Their
usual assumption is that the progress of 'backward' societies is
quickened by the impact upon them of the more 'advanced', and they
take little account of the possibility that the progress of the more
'advanced' may be retarded. Admittedly, Marx and the Marxists do
not say this in so many words; but it is not, I think, unfair to them to
say that they often take it for granted.

III. THE IMPACT OF 'ADVANCED' OR 'BACKWARD'
SOCIETIES

In only one of his writings does Marx take serious account of the
effects on a 'backward' society of the impact upon it of a more 'advanced' one. In the *Address to the Communist League* he admits
that Germany is more backward than France or England, and yet
expects the German Communists, the members of that league, to take
an active part in the coming revolution, and exhorts them, so far as
they can, to control its course. He sees Germany as a still partly
'feudal' country where the bourgeois have yet to make, or to complete,
the revolution which their class have already made in England and
France. When the bourgeois in those two countries made their revolutions, there was no scope for the sort of activities to which Marx
urged the German Communists in the *Address*. England and France
were not influenced by countries more advanced than themselves. But
the situation in Germany in 1848 was different. Socialist ideas had
penetrated into that country while it was still partly feudal, and had
attracted many of the workers in the towns. Marx believed that
Germany, though she had still to complete her bourgeois revolution,
already had a proletariat capable, if properly led, of acting independently of the bourgeois; whereas in France, during the great revolution,
the workers in Paris had been the tools of the bourgeois. If in Germany
in 1849 the workers need not be such tools, it was presumably because
socialist doctrines and proletarian organizations were already developed
enough to enable them to know their own class interests and to act

---

[1] There is a certain ambiguity here. What comes after may, in itself, be worse
than what went before it, and yet may be more desirable as bringing us
closer to the best, which comes last.

decisively to promote them. Though Marx advised the League and the workers to co-operate with the bourgeois parties to complete what he called *a bourgeois revolution*, that being the unavoidable next step in the advance towards communism, he also told them to mistrust their bourgeois allies, and to harass and scare them into making as many concessions as possible to the workers. He even believed that the Communists and workers, if they used the tactics he advised, might stampede their bourgeois allies into converting the great 'feudal' estates and larger industrial undertakings into public property, thus making easier the eventual passage from a capitalist to a socialist economy.

Though Marx believed that Germany's situation in 1849 was unlike that of France in the 1790s, though he saw her progress towards socialism as different in important respects, he did not see Germany as moving on a widely different course. A bourgeois revolution in which the workers take an independent and decisive part is, of course, different from one in which they do not, and has different and important consequences. Had those to whom Marx gave his advice been able and willing to take it, Germany after her 'bourgeois revolution' would have been different, in important respects, from the France of the first Napoleon and the restored monarchy. But the difference would not have consisted in events happening in Germany which had never happened or never would happen in France; it would have consisted merely in events happening in Germany simultaneously or hard upon one another's heels which in France had been or would be separated by considerable intervals. There would have been a telescoping of events in Germany which would even – so great were Marx's hopes at that time for his own country – have put her in some ways ahead of countries until then in all ways ahead of her. Though socialist ideas and proletarian organizations were more widespread and stronger in France and England than in Germany, the bourgeois were also stronger and more firmly in power; and so 'backward' Germany had in 1849 (in Marx's eyes) an opportunity to take a leap forward which would put her, in some respects, in the van of progress.

There is no trace, in Marx's *Address*, of a fear that the Communist League and the workers, by trying to force the pace towards socialism, might set going a train of events which would lead Germany away from it. Though the passage from capitalism to socialism might be different in Germany from what it would be in England or France, it was still inevitable. Marx could conceive of a society which was part capitalist and part socialist just as he could conceive of one which was part feudal and part capitalist. He could see that 'backward' countries deeply affected by countries more 'advanced' than themselves might have mixed economies and mixed political systems of a kind that the 'advanced' countries had never had. But it never occurred to him

that the countries he called 'backward' might move along courses
quite different from the one he took to be normal because England and
France had already moved some way along it; it never occurred to him
that these 'backward' countries might acquire social and political
systems to which the categories familiar to him did not apply. It never
occurred to him; any more than today it occurs to his Russian disciples that the country they govern is no more socialist than capitalist
in the senses in which those terms were used by Marx.

So, too, it never occurred to him that the 'advanced' countries might
be so deeply affected by their increasingly close ties with the rest of the
world as to develop quite differently from how they would otherwise
have done. He did suggest that the exploitation of colonies and
dependent territories might delay the collapse of capitalism in the
West, but he went no further than this. We can conclude, from his
rather scanty references to the impact of 'advanced' and 'backward'
countries on one another, little more than this: that he was very sure
that the effect of 'advanced' on 'backward' countries was to hasten
their progress and might sometimes even give them an opportunity
of taking a lead, and that he took some notice of the possibility that
the effect of 'backward' on 'advanced' countries might be to retard
their progress. All countries, he thought, must travel what is essentially the same road; their influence upon one another cannot divert
them from it but can only increase or slacken the speed at which they
move along it.

The later German Marxists were not much interested in the effects
of 'advanced' and 'backward' countries upon one another. They
discussed, in much greater detail than either Marx or Engels had done,
what they called the later stages of capitalism; they discussed such
topics as the increasing concentration of capital, international finance,
the failure of the capitalist farmer to displace the peasant on the
Continent as he had done in England, the growth of vast working-
class organizations in the West able to exert a strong pressure on
bourgeois governments. They refined upon the doctrines of the two
masters and sometimes revised them. They were the most learned, the
most thoughtful, the most intellectually fertile of the disciples of
Marx. But only when they discussed imperialism did they turn their
minds to the problem of the relations between 'advanced' and 'backward' countries. They were interested in them only from the point of
view of the 'advanced' countries, confining themselves to little more
than the elaboration of Marx's suggestion that the exploitation by the
West of the rest of the world slowed down the trend towards falling
profits and thus delayed the collapse of Western capitalism.

As might be expected, the Russian Marxists were much more
interested than the Germans in the impact of 'advanced' societies on
'backward' ones. But they, like Marx, assumed that it could serve only

o

to increase the rate of progress in 'backward' countries. Though they criticized the Populists for teaching that Russia might become socialist without ever passing through industrial capitalism as the West knew it, they were, for obvious reasons, eager to see as many signs as possible of quick progress in their own country. They took the fullest advantage of any hint they could find in the writings of Marx to justify their belief that Russia, though backward, was destined to play a major part in the coming triumph of socialism in the world. The doctrine of the 'uninterrupted revolution', as we find it in the writings of Trotsky and Lenin,[1] is merely an application to Russian circumstances of ideas to be found in the earlier pamphlets of Marx, above all in the *Address to the Communist League*.

The Russian Marxists, though sometimes bold, were seldom deep or rigorous thinkers. It would be absurd to say that they were timid in their interpretations of Marxism, that in the realm of doctrine they only followed and never led; for they sometimes drew astonishing conclusions from familiar texts. They were adroit and resourceful. But they were not much concerned with consistency. This is especially true of Lenin and the Bolsheviks. Though they felt, more even perhaps than the German Marxists, the need to be orthodox, to support their policies by copious quotations from Marx and Engels, their concern for orthodoxy was not concern for consistency. The Bolsheviks took from the treasure house of Marxist doctrine whatever they needed to justify what they thought it necessary to do; their skill and audacity were remarkable. What mattered to them was that they should always be able to get support from the same sacred source; it did not matter nearly so much that their various policies should be in keeping with one another or with a self-consistent body of doctrine.

That is why the Bolsheviks or Communists, in spite of the ingenuity and audacity with which they have adapted Marxism to their needs, have never been impelled to think deeply about it, to subject it to rigorous criticism or to revise it drastically to make it more consistent in itself or with the facts. That is why, as social and political theorists, they have been as shallow as they have been bold. It is only the thinker who cares deeply for consistency and adequacy who, when he is bold in action, feels the need to reconcile his policies with the body of doctrine he adheres to. It is not enough for him to quote texts in his own favour; he feels the need to show that the policy he proposes really is in keeping with the doctrine he holds. He is therefore moved to think the doctrine out afresh, to reinterpret it; and if he

---

[1] I do not deny the great historical importance of this doctrine, which I have discussed elsewhere when it seemed relevant to do so; but in this book, which examines doctrines not because they are historically important but because they enlarge our understanding of society and government, I feel no need to discuss it.

cannot, when he has done that, show that the policy is in keeping with the doctrine, he will be impelled either to change the policy or to revise the doctrine, or both together. But if he cares greatly for orthodoxy and little for consistency, he is easily satisfied provided he can find in the sacred texts the quotations he needs. Though he is bold in action and even in thought, producing new doctrines when he needs them with just enough ingenuity to persuade himself that they are in line with the old, he is never moved to reinterpret or to revise the old body of doctrine systematically. Indeed, it would be fatal to him if he did so, for he would undermine the faith on which his energy and courage largely depend.

Thus the Communists, though they have been the Marxists most concerned with applying the doctrine in countries which, in the Marxian scale, are *backward*, have never been moved to reconsider that doctrine in the light of the problems they have faced. They have been too busy getting and using power to think deeply and rigorously about the faith to which they appeal to justify their having it.

IV. THE BOLSHEVIK PREDICAMENT

Marx and Engels believed that the proletarian revolution, though it might start earlier in one country than another, and even perhaps earlier in a less than a more 'advanced' country, would quickly spread to all the great industrial countries, the countries dominating the world economically and politically. They believed that the proletarian revolution would be, or would quickly become, a 'world revolution'. This does not mean that it would affect, either simultaneously or in quick succession, all or even most of the countries of the world; it means only that it would spread so quickly among the most 'advanced' countries as to become irreversible. With the workers firmly in control of the industrially more powerful countries, the forces of reaction elsewhere would be too weak to dislodge them. An isolated and premature[1] attempt at proletarian revolution, like the Paris

---

[1] A revolution which is premature in the sense that, given the situation in which it is made, the revolutionaries can neither succeed in their purpose nor retain power is not necessarily a revolution which ought not to have been attempted. Marx believed (not altogether truly) that the Paris Commune was a proletarian revolution, an attempt by the workers to seize power in Paris and in France, and he also thought it premature because the workers were not strong enough to retain control of Paris, let alone to get control of France. But he did not therefore condemn the attempt. Some defeats, though inevitable at the time, help to bring nearer the ultimate victory; others do not. It is sometimes wise to refuse a fight when you have no chance of victory; and at other times it is unwise, the failure to fight being even more demoralizing than defeat. Though Marx exhorted the workers to prepare carefully for the class war, though he condemned recklessness, though he spoke of *premature* revolution, he never said that it is always a mistake to fight when defeat is certain.

Commune of 1871, might be quickly put down, but a revolution which spread to the whole industrial West would not be at the mercy of forces outside the West. Provided the revolutionaries were strong enough to put down all domestic attempts at counter-revolution, they would be safe in a world where the most powerful countries were controlled by them.

Marx and Engels never considered what would happen if the proletarian revolution did not spread quickly to all or most of the powerful industrial countries; they never contemplated the situation of a country ruled by the industrial workers surrounded by other countries not less powerful ruled by the bourgeois. They therefore never put to themselves the question: What will the workers' State, the dictatorship of the proletariat, be like in a country surrounded, perhaps for decades, by capitalist countries industrially as powerful as itself? Nor did they ask what would happen to the State in such a country if, when it became classless, it was still surrounded by capitalist Powers. If the State is defined as an instrument of class rule, there can be no State where there are no classes. But where a classless society is surrounded by class societies hostile to it, it must be organized for defence, it must be able to wage war on a much larger scale than a mere tribe can wage it. It must have a military organization as formidable as the armies of the States which surround it. It must have some at least of the attributes which are ordinary considered attributes of a State.

The Bolsheviks, before they seized power in Russia and retained it for years, before they had reconciled themselves to the idea that their country might be surrounded by capitalist Powers for a long time to come, had been as indifferent as Marx and Engels to these questions. They too had never contemplated the possibility of a proletarian country isolated for decades in a bourgeois world; or of a classless society obliged to organize its defence against external Powers. They had taken it for granted, as all Marxists had done, that when an industrial society, an 'advanced' society, became classless, there would be no question of its having to wage war against foreign enemies as powerful as itself. Lenin had justified his intention to make what he called a 'proletarian revolution' in backward Russia by arguing that it would set off a world revolution; the example set by Russia would be quickly followed by the Western Powers. The industrially most advanced countries, whose collective power was overwhelming, would soon be proletarian and socialist, and there would be no prolonged isolation of a workers' State in a predominantly bourgeois world. It was only in the years after 1917 that the Bolsheviks, slowly and reluctantly, made some show of facing the problems created for Marxists by the West's remaining obstinately 'capitalist' and 'bourgeois'.

To justify their retaining power they could not indefinitely use the argument which they had used to justify their seizing it. They could

not say that they were touching off in backward Russia a world proletarian revolution which would be successful because it would spread
quickly to the most advanced countries, the countries where the
'objective conditions' of socialism and proletarian rule already existed,
and whose resources were great enough to enable them to help the
workers in more backward countries to create those same conditions.
They could not say that a revolution, which would be premature if it
were confined to Russia, was not premature because it must soon
spread to countries riper for it. They therefore argued that the proletariat, even in a backward country like Russia surrounded by
capitalist countries industrially more advanced, could create a socialist
society.

The argument is a denial of a basic tenet of Marxism, that socialism
can only be established where certain economic and cultural conditions
are present. These conditions are developed under capitalism, and so it
is impossible to set up socialism successfully where capitalism has not
prepared the 'objective conditions' of it. Marx, as we have seen, does
not forbid the proletarians from attacking the bourgeois before the
time is ripe for their final victory; he does not advocate their doing
nothing until the capitalist economy is sufficiently developed to allow
the establishment of socialism. The workers must acquire discipline,
class solidarity, and political experience before they can defeat the
bourgeois and set about creating socialism. He foresees a political
struggle starting long before the time is ripe for final victory, a struggle
in the course of which the workers sustain many defeats, a struggle
which is necessary because it prepares the way for victory. The time
is not ripe for socialism unless the workers are politically mature, no
matter how developed the capitalist economy. But Marx, though he
does not put off the proletarian struggle whose goal is socialism until
the economy is ripe for socialism, does hold that the struggle will not
bring victory until that point is reached; he does not envisage the
workers getting political power in the infancy of capitalism and using
it to establish the economic and cultural conditions of socialism.[1]

Yet this Bolshevik argument, though it denies a principle basic to
Marxism, may well be true. Even if we admit that industrialism and
widespread literacy are conditions not only of socialism but of aspirations to socialism, we need not agree that a country must have an
industrial economy and a literate working class before it can have a
government capable of establishing socialism in it. No doubt, Marx

[1] This statement needs to be qualified. The advice that Marx gives in *The
Address to the Communist League* does suggest that the workers can use
political means to create the economic and cultural conditions of socialism;
he does not actually say this but it is a fair conclusion from what he says.
Nevertheless, the implications of the advice given in the *Address* deny a
doctrine basic to Marxism.

was right in believing that before the rise of industrial society socialism, as he and the other socialists of the nineteenth century understood it, was inconceivable; that before men could have such aspirations and could conceive of ways to achieve them, it was necessary that there should be industrial production on a large scale. We can admit this and yet hold, quite consistently, that a devoted minority can use political methods to create the economic and cultural conditions of socialism where they do not exist. Though we admit that the minority would not have acquired socialist aspirations had there not existed somewhere in the world 'the objective conditions' of socialism, we are not bound to concede that men who get their socialist convictions from abroad cannot deliberately create these 'objective conditions' where they do not exist. Indeed, it might be true – I do not say that it is but only that it might be – that, though aspirations to socialism could only have arisen in an industrial society, once they have arisen, it is easier to achieve them in countries on the threshold of industrialism than in countries which are industrially 'mature'. Or if we grant that socialism can be achieved only in an industrial society, we may hold that it is more easily achieved in a country whose industries are the creation of the State than in a country which has become industrial as Britain or France has done. For where there have never been great industrial enterprises in private hands, certain powerful interests strongly opposed to socialism do not exist.

Of these possibilities Marx took no account. Except on rare occasions and almost inadvertently, his doctrines suggest that a country must be already industrial before socialists can hope to get control of it in order to make it socialist. But this is not to be taken for granted. Though what Marx calls the 'objective conditions' of socialism (conditions as much cultural as economic) are not to be created in a backward country by such methods as the Bolsheviks and their imitators have used, it may be that they could be created by other methods. There are doubtless peculiar and great difficulties facing a government seeking to establish socialism in an economically backward country, but there are other difficulties, different in kind and perhaps as great, facing a government intent upon establishing it in an advanced country. It may be that the difficulties facing the first government are greater than those facing the second; I am inclined to believe that they are, but I am not certain of it. And yet, even if they are greater, it does not follow that the first government cannot succeed in its object.

There is another argument which Marxists have used to show that the attempt to establish socialism in a country isolated in a capitalist world must fail. This argument, unlike the one we have just considered, applies as much when the country striving for socialism is industrially advanced as when it is industrially backward. According to this argument, the governments of the capitalist countries fear the attraction to the classes they exploit of the example of successful socialism; they therefore combine to suppress any government which aims at creating socialism, as soon as it looks as if it might succeed. The class struggle takes the form of hostility between nations, and the nation aspiring to socialism is much weaker than the nations combined against it.

This argument is defective because it is unrealistic. Countries are seldom dominated by classes having well-defined class interests, and it is therefore by no means certain that the governments of the countries called 'capitalist', whose ambitions differ greatly, will want to combine to suppress the dangerous example, or will even agree that it is dangerous. In several, if not most, of the 'capitalist' countries, the workers and socialists are likely to be organized and powerful, and some of their aspirations are likely to be recognized as just by all parties with a hope of forming a government. Socialism will therefore be held by many to be a respectable creed even in the capitalist world. There may well be widespread sympathy in the encircling States for the lone government aspiring to full socialism.

I have no wish to argue in defence of the Bolsheviks, and especially not in defence of the Stalinists. I am not more certain of anything political than that socialism, as Marx and the Marxists understood it before 1917, cannot be established in any country by the methods used by the Bolsheviks. But that has nothing to do with the issue I am now discussing. If we look at the course of events in Russia during the decade before and the decade after the Bolshevik seizure of power, we can see how it came about that the Bolsheviks used the methods they did use. We can see how their party acquired, before 1917, the temper which made it possible for them to resort to such methods, and we can see how, in the situations which arose after 1917, it seemed to them in their own and the country's interest to use them. Perhaps, given the conditions in which they seized power, given the exhaustion and confusion of Russia, they could not have maintained their power except by using methods whose use precludes the creation of a socialist society.[1]

But we must not generalize from the example of Russia. We are not bound to hold that any government aspiring to socialism in an industrially backward and largely illiterate country must either despair of achieving its object or must, in the endeavour to retain power in order to achieve it, be driven to methods which make it impossible of achievement. There very probably are, as Marx said there were, economic and cultural conditions of socialism, and there are also, as

---

[1] It could be argued that, though some of the more brutal methods they used were not needed to maintain their power, others probably were. I think it could also be argued that, long before the October Revolution, the Bolsheviks had become a group unlikely to use methods which could bring socialism to a 'backward' country.

the Bolshevik example teaches us, political methods which must be avoided if socialism, as it was understood by Marxists and by most other socialists before 1917, is to be successfully established in any country, whether it is industrial and literate or not. The temptation to resort to such methods may, perhaps, be greater in a 'backward' country than in an 'advanced' one; but there were causes which need not exist in all 'backward' countries which made them unusually tempting to the Bolsheviks.

The Bolsheviks say, and perhaps believe, that they have achieved socialism in Russia, but they can do this only by shutting their eyes to the immense differences between the system they have established and socialism as it was understood before they seized power. Their example is attractive to other 'backward' peoples, partly because they are impressed by the power of Russia and partly because they are not aware of how far what Russia has become under the Bolsheviks falls short of the ideals proclaimed by Marx. It may be easier to achieve what the Bolsheviks have achieved in Russia than what all Marxists before 1917 understood by socialism and it may be a great temptation to the weaker and poorer nations to try to follow the Russian example now that Russia seems so formidable to the world. I do not deny this. I am concerned to say no more than that socialism, as the world knew it before the Bolshevik revolution, is an ideal which can reasonably be pursued by a resolute, intelligent and humane minority even in a country which is industrially weak and where most people can neither read nor write. Such a minority would do well to study the activities of the Bolsheviks in Russia, not in order to follow their example, but to learn to avoid their mistakes. And they would perhaps have a better right than the Bolsheviks to call themselves Marxists, for, though they too would be attempting what Marx said was impossible, they would at least be striving for what he thought desirable.

D. The Marxian Ideal

The idea of a normal course of social change, allowing us to call some countries more *advanced* than others because they are further along it, must be rejected. It may serve to excite people to move more quickly in the direction desired by the exciter, it may be a useful trick of propaganda; but if we try to use it to explain how society changes, we involve ourselves, as the Marxists and others have done, in spurious or insoluble problems. No community, no matter how large or small, has ever, during the periods when it could be readily distinguished from other communities, been free of external influences, and we cannot know how it would have evolved if it had been free, and no two communities, except for short periods of time, have been exposed to the same external influences. Untenable also is the conception of the State as an instrument of class rule destined to wither away when society becomes 'classless'. It is by using these ideas, and others as defective, that Marxists have been caught up in unprofitable[1] disputes about whether it is possible to establish *socialism* in a *backward* country isolated in a *capitalist* world, or about the survival of the *State* in a country which is *socialist* and *classless* but still has to reckon with the enmity of other countries as powerful as itself. It is not difficult, if we follow these disputes at all closely, to uncover the confusions of thought and the contradictions of the persons engaged in them; persons making use of such loose notions as those I have put into italics.

But let us not allow the defects of Marxian theory, defects which have led to such loud and sterile controversy, to blind us to its merits. Some of these merits I have already tried to explain. Marxism is one of the richest and most suggestive of social theories, one most worth careful scrutiny. It has been exciting in two quite different ways: it has deeply moved the radical dissatisfied with the world as he finds it and in quest of a philosophy to guide his endeavours to change it, and it has stimulated the curiosity and the imagination of the student whose object has been, not to change society or to prevent its changing, but to enlarge our understanding of it.

There is an ideal, common to Hegel and to Marx, which, even if it should prove unacceptable in the forms which they give to it, or should need to be greatly qualified, has had a deep influence on many liberal and radical thinkers. This idea is not peculiar to them, though their versions of it, for all their obscurity and elusiveness, are among the most elaborate and the most suggestive. It is the idea of *perfectibility*, which receives at their hands dimensions unknown in the eighteenth century because Hegel penetrates more deeply into the human mind and Marx into the social processes affecting that mind. Though their versions of this idea may be open to criticism on other grounds, they are hardly touched by most of the criticisms levelled at the Hegelian and Marxian social philosophies. It would be a pity if this idea, so largely and rightly associated with them, were lost in the general condemnation of their systems. It is an idea which deserves to be extracted from those systems and to be considered on its own merits.

It is the idea that men, in the process of coming to understand themselves and their condition as self-conscious creatures aware of themselves as living in a coherent world which can be rationally explained, come in the end to acquire a set of values more *adequate* to their nature and condition than any they had before. This idea, as

---

[1] I mean intellectually unprofitable, for the disputants have often raised these issues as a manoeuvre to get power or to confound rivals. From their point of view, the disputes have sometimes been immensely profitable.

I have now briefly formulated it, cries out for elucidation; but, before I endeavour to make it clearer, I must insist that it is not just another version of the old Stoic and Christian idea of an eternally valid moral law, a law of reason, likened by those who seek to expound it to the axioms of mathematics: a supposedly self-evident law which anyone capable of understanding (and therefore of defining) human nature can see applies to any human being in his dealings with other such beings. Even if we should hold, with Hume and with many contemporary philosophers, that moral rules differ in kind both from statements of fact and from the propositions of mathematics and logic, and even if we agree that an 'ought' cannot be derived logically from an 'is', we need not reject this Hegelian and Marxian idea.

Admittedly, Hegel's views about statements of fact, mathematical axioms and moral rules differ greatly from Hume's, while Marx, even if we suppose that he had (in the privacy of his mind) views definite enough to deserve consideration, never succeeded in communicating them to the world. After all, Marx was not, in the same sense as Hume and Hegel, a philosopher, a systematic critic of the ideas we use to explain the world or to act in it. But this does not touch the point I am making. No matter what we believe to be the correct explanation of moral rules and value judgements, we are not thereby inhibited from agreeing with Marx and Hegel that men gradually acquire rules and values adequate to their nature and social condition only in the process of coming to understand that nature and condition, a process enduring through many generations and modifying its objects. What we come to understand has been altered by the process of our coming to understand it. Rules and values are *adequate* to human nature and the human condition whenever men are so placed, psychologically and socially, that their desires and ambitions are in keeping with one another and with the rules and values they accept, and the means are not lacking to realize them.

Rousseau taught that man's usual condition in society is such that there arise in him passions incompatible with one another and with the rules and values he is taught to accept. He therefore only half accepts them; he is by no means free of their influence, and yet he cannot in practice live by them because of his passions. Both the passions and the values are social products, being what they are because human nature and man's social condition are such and such and not otherwise; they are also human products, effects of man's activity, for society is no more than the living together of men. But they are such that man cannot live a satisfying life, a life in which his passions and his values are in harmony and he has the means to get what he most strongly desires. Rousseau condemned nearly all human societies for precisely this reason, because they make it impossible for man to live a satisfying life, or, as he put it, 'a life according to nature'. He imagined an ideal society free of the defects of actual society. No doubt, he claimed to understand man's nature and his social condition; he would have agreed that without this understanding he could never have imagined the ideal society. But he was very far from believing either that the coming of the ideal was inevitable or that knowledge is the cure for man's ills.

It is here that Hegel and Marx differ from him; they both imagine, each in his own way, a long process of social, intellectual and moral change leading man steadily but inevitably to the condition where he understands himself and the world, which is also the condition where his passions are in harmony with his values and his most cherished ambitions can be realized with the means at his disposal. In this condition man is at long last no longer 'alienated' but is at peace with himself, is 'whole' and morally secure in his 'wholeness', because he is 'at home' in the social world which is both the product and the sphere of his activities.

If we deny – and most critics of Marxism do deny it – that there is any such steady and inevitable process, we are not bound in logic also to deny that there is a set of rules and values, a moral system, which all men would accept if they understood the nature and social condition of man, a system in keeping with the passions and ambitions which would be strongest in them if they and other men had that understanding. We may admit this possibility, even though we are at pains to insist, against the Stoics and against Rousseau, that there is no eternally valid moral law in the sense of a set of moral rules which can be derived logically from a true description of human nature or of the divine purpose for man. We can also hold, quite consistently, both that there is a moral code which men, having reached the condition, social and intellectual, enabling them to conceive of it, can see is the most fully adequate to their nature and condition, *and* that all other moral codes, though each is received while social conditions are propitious to it, are inadequate in the sense that men, in those conditions, acquire passions and ambitions difficult or impossible to satisfy and not in keeping with the moral code they accept. In other words, we can, without logical inconsistency, accept *both* the moral relativism of Marx and his belief that there is a morality more adequate than the others because it is what men are moved to accept when they have come to understand themselves and the world, when they have taken their own measure and have cheerfully assented to it; a morality they are unlikely to abandon because the understanding which brings it in its train also educates their passions and ambitions to conform with it.

There may have been primitive communities where men's passions and values were so much in harmony that there was almost no trace of what Marxists call *alienation*. We should have to say of such communities that in them moral and cultural values were adequate to human nature and man's social condition, as they then were; and, unless we postulated certain absolute values, we should have no ground for treating them as inferior to more sophisticated communities where the same condition holds. But such communities, if ever they existed, no longer do so now, and are not attractive to civilized peoples, especially when they bear in mind what they would have to forgo in order to re-establish them. Or, if they are attractive, they are out of reach; they cannot be deliberately created. Like innocence, once lost they are never to be recovered.

Rousseau and Hegel both suggest that men, when their passions and values are not in keeping with one another, are profoundly unhappy; they are, as the common phrase has it, 'untrue to themselves' or, as Rousseau puts it, 'outside themselves', or as Hegel says, *alienated*. They are in a painful condition possible only to rational creatures, and only reason can find a remedy for it. As Hegel sees it, men, when they reflect on this condition, strongly desire to change it; they strive, at first confusedly but more deliberately and hopefully as their understanding grows, to set themselves and society in order. They make their way slowly to a condition where their passions and values are in harmony with one another, where their ambitions are within their powers, where self-respect is possible, where life, though strenuous, seems worth all the effort it calls for, where men need look for nothing outside themselves and the societies they have created to console them for being alive. Rousseau describes the evil but suggests no practicable remedy for it; Hegel has more to say than Rousseau about its social and historical causes and makes bold to predict an inevitable remedy. Rousseau's pessimism is excessive, being as much an effect of temperament as supported by cogent argument, and Hegel's optimism is no better grounded. But it is, or may be, more useful; it is encouraging and perhaps also, to some extent, a guide to action. Though we do not believe that what Hegel predicts must come true, we may, insofar as we find it good, sharing his idea of freedom, strive to make it come true.

Marx, like Hegel, is an optimist, but, in at least one respect, he is more plausible than Hegel. He foretells great social and political changes before what he thinks desirable can come to be, before there can be a morality adequate to man's nature and his social condition. Man is still *alienated*; he is still so situated, socially and culturally, that he is impelled to strive for what does not satisfy him, that he lives, not as he would live if he knew how, but as the market requires. He may not accept wholeheartedly the values of bourgeois society but, unless he is consciously a revolutionary, he does not reject them either; and if he is revolutionary, he cannot live by the values he accepts, for society will not let him. Man in bourgeois society, as Marx depicts him, is still short of the knowledge and self-knowledge needed to put an end to *alienation*; he has still to make great changes in society and to be himself greatly changed before his condition is such that what he strives for is within his reach and seems to him fully worth while, before he sees himself and his situation as they really are and wants what he can get and what will satisfy him. Though Marx says too little about the society of equals to make it clear just how he conceives of the freedom which is (so he thinks) the condition of men's living truly satisfying lives, he does not find his ideal, as Hegel does, fully realized in the nation-state of his own century. He is, in this, both truer to the ideal which he shares with Hegel and more realistic. For their ideal is also, at bottom, the ideal of Rousseau and Kant: that no man should be the mere instrument of other men, and that all men should be able to live in accordance with principles they inwardly accept. They differ from Rousseau in being altogether free from parochialism and obscurantism, and from Kant in the interest they take in the cultural and social conditions of freedom. Marx is truer, I think, to this ideal than Hegel, not in giving a clearer account of it, not in speaking more profoundly about freedom and equality and how they stand to one another, but in refusing to admit that it could be achieved in the kind of social and political order which satisfied Hegel. There existed in Hegel's time and in Marx's, as there still exists today, a widespread desire for greater freedom and greater equality, a widespread striving after an ideal which was deeply attractive though not clearly defined; and there was also a strong belief that freedom could not be much enlarged unless there were greater equality. Though Hegel spoke more eloquently and even perceptively of freedom than ever Marx did, it is not too much to claim that Marx held the more firmly of the two to the common ideal.

Whether or not this ideal, suitably elaborated, is the morality adequate to man's nature and condition (if, indeed, there is such a morality[1]), it is most improbable that it came anywhere near being realized in Hegel's Europe. In spite of his great hopes for the future, Marx was quite free from complacency; he saw man, even in the society which he considered most advanced, as still very much in the throes of

---

[1] Hegel and Marx both assume that most men would be rational and moral in the right social environment, that the causes of *alienation* are mostly social and will eventually disappear; they do not consider the possibility that there are many men who are born to *alienation*, i.e. who have inherited qualities making it unlikely that they could in any society acquire passions and ambitions in keeping with values they wholeheartedly accept and which society approves or tolerates. But I am not concerned to argue that their ideal is beyond criticism; I want only to say that we can reject their accounts of social evolution, and still accept it or be strongly attracted to it. We can also conclude, quite rationally, that the ideal, though never to be realized completely, is worth striving for.

a social and moral revolution nowhere near completed; he saw him striving to make real an ideal seen only fitfully and confusedly, an ideal about whose social conditions man was still largely ignorant. Perhaps it is a mistake to suppose that revolutions are ever completed, that there is ever a final passing from stormy seas into calm waters, a consummation of human effort. If this is a mistake, then Marx made it no less than Hegel. But at least he could never have brought himself to believe that in the Europe he knew, with its poverty, illiteracy, oppression and war, man had already almost attained the goal he strove for.

Chapter 7

THE BELIEF IN PROGRESS

MAN cannot help but see himself a traveller, and can change his mind only about the road he is taking. He cannot be aware of himself as a person, cannot know that he is alive, without looking back to a past and forward to a future. Whoever can put to himself the question, What am I? will also be tempted to ask, And where am I going? Again, man knows himself as one among others of his kind, as a member of society, as an heir and an ancestor; and so passes easily from seeing himself to seeing his kind as a traveller. From the beginning the philosophical student of politics has been interested in the course of social change. Aristotle imagined the *polis* growing out of the village, and the village growing out of the family; and, since he called man a *political animal*, a creature whose nature it is to create a political community and to realize itself in so doing, he saw the movement from family to *polis* as a movement in a desirable direction, as progress. But he imagined nothing better than the *polis*, and did not ask himself what might come after it to take its place. When he looked to the future, he apparently expected nothing more of it than had happened already. The more hopeful among the ancients, those with the most robust faith in their own civilization, confined their hopes to maintaining in the future what had been achieved in the past; and the less hopeful expected decay. Some believed in a progress whose highest point was reached already, others in a golden age in a remote past, and still others in a perpetual movement repeated over and over again, through the same stages. There will always be men with a future, with a life to live, a journey to make from birth to death, from a beginning to an end; but mankind have reached the end of the journey, or are moving away from a perfection they once knew or are passing ceaselessly through a cycle of change.

In the Middle Ages, both journeys, of the individual and the kind, were conceived differently. There was a destination which the individual might reach, though it was not in this world; for he passed through this world only on his way to something incomparably better or incomparably worse. He could earn his reward or his punishment in this world, but would get his deserts after he had left it. As for the kind, the species, its days also were numbered in this world. It was to endure for a time, and to achieve nothing while it endured; it moved neither forward nor backward, nor in circles. In the mediaeval view of the world, humanity, as distinct from the individuals who composed it, had neither destiny nor history; it merely occupied the space and the time allotted to it by God. There was nothing for mankind to accomplish or to live through and be affected by; no course of change, social and cultural. There were no achievements, no endeavours, no failures to be attributed to mankind: there were only the efforts of men. The mediaeval view of the world was dramatic, but there was no collective actor on the stage; there were innumerable actors, each a soul making its own way to salvation or perdition.

Belief in progress, as the modern world has known it in the last two or three hundred years, was unknown in antiquity and in the Middle Ages. Yet we find, in Aristotle and in others, the idea of a course of change, social and cultural, determined partly by man's nature and partly by his environment, and we find in the Middle Ages the idea of a journey still uncompleted and leading (at least for a happy few) to a condition infinitely better than the present. If we add to these two ideas two more – that man's knowledge and power over nature increase indefinitely, and that this knowledge and power bring worldly happiness – we have the modern belief in progress. My purpose is not to examine how this belief arose (except to the extent that to do so serves to bring out more clearly what it is) nor yet to examine particular examples of it; for some of the best known of them have been examined elsewhere together with the social philosophies which embody them. I shall discuss only three matters: what is involved in the belief in progress; the rôle of the individual in social evolution; and the belief that the expansion of knowledge leads to increasing happiness.

I. WHAT IS INVOLVED IN THE BELIEF IN PROGRESS

1. Before the Age of Science

To believe in progress is to believe that there is or can be movement in a desirable direction. But men find many things desirable, and movement towards one or more of them may mean movement away from the others. In other words, getting more of some things thought desirable may involve getting less of others. Differences of opinion about whether there has been or will be progress may be due to several causes: men do not find the same things desirable, or they have not the same preferences among the things they find desirable, or their estimates differ about the extent to which the things they find desirable are compatible with one another. Some have believed in progress who have not believed that happiness has increased or will do so: they have set a higher value on freedom than on happiness, and have believed that men are freer than they were, even though not happier. Others have believed that happiness cannot be measured while freedom can, and so have thought it reasonable to aim at increasing freedom rather than happiness. Virtue, knowledge, freedom, happiness, justice, and 'self-realization' have all often been held to be desirable in themselves; though some of them have also been held to be valuable only as means to others. The Utilitarians have said that nothing is desirable for its own sake except happiness. Nevertheless, all these things have been held by some people to be intrinsically desirable. Moreover, those who have said that happiness alone is to be desired for its own sake have not always been agreed about what happiness is: some have sought to reduce it to a mere sum of pleasures, but the greater number have spoken of it in ways that suggest that it includes some of the things which they have also said are to be desired only as means to it.

No doubt, it has been widely assumed that the things desired for their own sakes are closely connected. Widely and perhaps not unreasonably. Let us consider for a moment two of these things: virtue and happiness. We have to allow that men, taken individually, are not always the happier the more they are virtuous; and yet we may reasonably argue that the connection between virtue and happiness, though by no means simple, is close. We may argue, with the Utilitarians, that behaviour comes to be thought virtuous because its general tendency is to increase happiness and to decrease unhappiness; or we may argue that men get happiness by getting what they strive for and that their ideas of what is worth striving for are affected by what they see praised or blamed, admired or despised. Whichever of these two explanations we accept, it would seem that virtue and happiness are so connected that they flourish and decay together, if not in each individual, at least over an entire community. So, too, if we take justice and happiness, or 'self-realization' and happiness, or freedom and happiness, we can argue, plausibly, that they are closely connected. The freedom which is precious to man is not mere absence of impediment; it is the opportunity to do what he thinks worth while, and he finds his happiness in doing it. And he 'realizes himself' by becoming what he aspires to be, and what he claims the 'freedom' to become; and his idea of what makes for his happiness depends on his aspirations. We may explain the connections in these ways or in others: there is room here for a wide diversity of opinions. And yet, diverse though these opinions are, they all affirm the closeness of the connections which they explain so differently. The moralists of Greece and Rome, of the Middle Ages, and of our era seem to be agreed in seeing here a closely related family of ideas, even though their descriptions of the family vary widely.

They also agree, for the most part, that knowledge is a means to these desirable things. Man, if he is to be securely free or virtuous or happy, must understand himself and his circumstances; he may, if he is lucky, be happy without this understanding, or without much of it. He may acquire tastes and habits suited to his condition, and his condition may not change. But, if his happiness is to be secure, if he is not to lose it as soon as his circumstances change, he must be adaptable; he must know himself and his limitations and must also know something of the 'world', of the chances and changes to which men are liable. If he has this knowledge, he will be more free, less the victim of change and better able to make decisions and carry them out; and he will also acquire a clearer understanding of the principles on which he acts. If they are good principles, he will be the more virtuous for having them, for he will not conform unthinkingly to convention. From Socrates to Kant, nearly all the great moralists have seen a close connection between knowledge, virtue and happiness or whatever else they have considered desirable for its own sake. Even Rousseau saw it, who deplored the 'progress' made in the arts and sciences.

It was conceded, long before the modern faith in progress was born, that knowledge could make for happiness, or for the greatest good otherwise conceived, and that it could do so in two ways. It could help the individual to attain that good whatever his social condition, and it could guide the ruler in his efforts to improve society. The Stoics set a high value on knowledge mostly for the first reason, and Plato for both the first and the second. So, too, Rousseau valued it for both reasons: Emile, to be capable of virtue and happiness in a corrupt society, had to acquire self-knowledge and had to learn how to live. And society could not be cured of its ills unless these ills were correctly diagnosed and a social and political order suited to man's nature discovered. But Rousseau, though he believed that knowledge is or can be a means to virtue, freedom, and happiness, denied that the accumulation of knowledge tends to make men more virtuous or happier or more free. He denied what philosophers had seldom affirmed before the eighteenth century, though it was then beginning to seem obvious to them. That knowledge is a means to the good was an opinion which nearly all moralists had shared since the time of Socrates: that the accumulation of knowledge increases the good was an opinion hardly worth denying before the eighteenth century, for almost no one held it.

Yet the idea that knowledge accumulates is much older than the eighteenth century. The Greeks, at times, were acutely conscious of having added to the store of knowledge inherited from their ancestors; they were aware that later thinkers had built upon the achievements of their predecessors. The Epicureans believed that there had been progress in knowledge, which they valued for its own sake and also for some of its effects. They welcomed the decline of superstition and also a variety of useful discoveries and institutions. But, if we compare them with the Utilitarians of the eighteenth century, who, like them, were conspicuous hedonists and enemies of superstition and prejudice, we see how much weaker was their belief in a connection between increasing knowledge and increasing happiness. No doubt, any Greek or Roman who was attached to his community, who believed that it was better than what it had grown out of, believed in progress; he believed that there had been progress and also a considerable increase in knowledge. The citizen of the *polis* or the Roman citizen, proud of his condition, no doubt thought himself more favoured than his ancestors, and believed that his advantage rested in large part on greater knowledge. But he did not believe that there would be progress in the future; he did not believe that the condition of his descendants would be better than his own. Or, if he did believe it, it was because he believed that his community was in decay, having declined from some better condition to which it might in the future be restored. The best condition was already achieved, either now or in the past; and the future, though it might offer something better than the present, would offer nothing better than both the present and the past.

Such knowledge as was needed to live the good life existed already; it was not to be added to, it was merely to be imparted. Yet, the Greek or the Roman who saw progress entirely in the past and not in the future, did not do so because he believed that men already knew all that they could or were likely to know. Though he did not share the modern belief that the accumulation of knowledge would go on indefinitely, his lack of faith in future progress was not rooted in a conviction that there would be no further increase in knowledge. He merely took it for granted that any such increase would not add to man's capacity to live well and be happy. The civilized man, the partaker in the life and culture of the *polis*, the citizen of the republic, was better off than the primitive man, having a knowledge which that man lacked. That knowledge had not been acquired separately by each possessor of it; it had been accumulated over the generations. But it was now all that it needed to be; it was an immutable store of wisdom, entire and sufficient. Any man, to be able to live well, must make it his own; and some men might have a better opportunity than others of doing so. Or it might be that some men were unfitted by nature to profit by it. Or the community might be corrupted and not provide the education needed to impart it. For a variety of reasons, the knowledge conducive to the good life might be less or more entirely possessed by the individual, less or more widely spread in the community; and therefore there could be either progress or decay. It was reasonable to try to improve education or to reform the community. But, though there could be progress, it was not progress as the eighteenth century conceived of it; for there could be no surpassing the best already achieved. And progress was held no more probable than decay. As the ancients saw it, the knowledge needed for the good life was, in at least one respect, like the grace of God; it was an unchanging and inexhaustible treasure offered to any man capable of receiving it.

This knowledge was usually spoken of as if it were all of one kind, all knowledge in the same sense, though it consisted partly of factual knowledge, partly of skill, and partly of what is best called wisdom. It was acquired by getting information, by learning how to do things, and by learning to value things at their 'true worth'; or, to use language less out-of-fashion today, by acquiring the preferences needed to lead a satisfying life. It was assumed that these were the same in all societies.

Rousseau's attack on the arts and sciences would have seemed as extravagant to the Greeks and Romans as it did to his contemporaries; they set a high value on knowledge generally, both as a means to other things and in itself, and they did not see the evil effects which he claimed to see. Yet they took for granted what also seemed obvious to him: that the accumulation of knowledge, beyond a certain point, does nothing to increase freedom, virtue or happiness. They put a higher value on knowledge than he did (though he valued it more highly than he sometimes pretended), but at bottom he and they were agreed about how knowledge is connected with other things thought to be desirable.

In the Middle Ages, knowledge was less esteemed both in itself and as a means to the good life than it had been in antiquity. It was also more often condemned as a source of pride. The idea that there had been progress in the past and the preference for a civilized over a primitive life disappeared almost entirely. The faith necessary to salvation was not a knowledge which men had acquired by their own efforts over many generations, an intellectual inheritance which they must make renewed efforts to preserve; it was a gift of God (through the Church) which the humblest and most ignorant were as well placed as any to receive. Also, the sense that knowledge had accumulated in the past and might continue to do so, which had been strong in some circles and periods before Christianity took a large hold, was quite lost. It did not become important again until the Renaissance.

Its renewed importance came long before the modern belief in progress. Machiavelli believed that he lived in a more enlightened age than Italy had known since the fall of the Roman Empire. He believed that knowledge lost or neglected for centuries had been recovered. But he also believed that Italy was decadent; he expected no increase in freedom, virtue or happiness from the recovery of what was lost. Bodin was more impressed even than Machiavelli with the knowledge recovered or acquired in his own age, which he thought fully the equal of any age before it. Nor would he agree that his own age was morally inferior. He believed in progress and decay, both in knowledge and in other things. But he saw no connection between the accumulation of knowledge (which, like the Greeks, he valued for its own sake) and other forms of progress. True, he did not foresee a continuous increase in knowledge; but he also said nothing to suggest that, if he had foreseen it, he would have looked forward to men's becoming indefinitely more virtuous or more happy.

2. *In the Scientific Age*

In his book, *The Idea of Progress*, J. B. Bury claims for Francis Bacon that he was the first great philosopher to preach the doctrine that the accumulation of knowledge is desirable because it puts it in men's power to increase their happiness. The Greeks had valued knowledge primarily for its own sake, whereas Bacon urged men to obtain it so as to use it for their own benefit by increasing their power over nature. He saw knowledge as a means to power, and power as a means to happiness. Also Bacon differed from the Greeks about how knowledge is to be obtained; he advocated, as the Greeks had not done, the use of the experimental method.

This, no doubt, is important; but to point to it, as Bury does, distracts attention from what is common to Bacon and modern believers in progress. Though important experiments had been made before Bacon wrote a word about the experimental method, and though his account of it was not altogether accurate, his advocacy of it encouraged its use and so quickened the increase of knowledge. But to say this is not to explain what Bacon contributed to the idea of progress; it is to explain only what he contributed to the increase of knowledge. Since, for the moment, our concern is with the idea of progress, it is more important to notice how Bacon differs from the Greeks about the kind of knowledge which makes for happiness. In their opinion it consists in self-knowledge, in knowing how to behave, and in what the French call *savoir-vivre*. But the knowledge which Bacon recommends as useful is 'natural philosophy'. The greater men's understanding of the material world and the greater their ability to harness nature to their purposes, the better for them. The Greeks, said Bacon, had excelled in morals and politics, but had not gone far in studying nature as he wanted it studied; and it was on this study, on the natural sciences, that he grounded his hopes for mankind. Bacon, as Bury points out, did not foresee an indefinite extension of knowledge; he believed he was living in the old age of mankind. But he gave clear utterance to a belief which is at the root of the faith in progress; it is a belief in the utility of a kind of knowledge not thought particularly useful by philosophers before his time, the kind that was later denounced as harmful by Rousseau.

Bury is right when he argues that faith in progress rests partly on the belief that knowledge will grow indefinitely, and that this belief was not strong and widespread until men had learned to distinguish knowledge from opinion, until they had acquired clear ideas about how opinions are to be tested to establish whether they are true or false. It was in the seventeenth century that these ideas were acquired; it was then that philosophers turned their minds once again to questions long neglected: What is knowledge? How is it to be increased? Though, no doubt, they learned a great deal from the Greeks, who had put these questions before them, they gave answers different from the old ones. The seventeenth century did more than make scientific discoveries; it discovered science, it made explicit the assumptions on which science rests and defined the methods it uses. Bury sees this as above all the achievement of two men, Bacon and Descartes; he might have added a third, Galileo, who had clearer ideas than Bacon of what is involved in the experimental method. Of course, these men did not say the last words in these matters, but they did say the decisive ones. They produced a solid faith in methods of explanation and discovery which have enormously increased man's power to predict and to control the course of events. Bury rightly sees in the idea of science a necessary, though not a sufficient, condition of the idea of progress; of the idea of progress, not as the ancients sometimes knew it, but as we have come to know it in the last two to three hundred years.

To use the language of Hegel, science first became, in the seventeenth century, *for* itself what it was *in* itself: scientists were aware, as they never had been before, of how their activities, their methods and explanations, differed from those of theologians and other builders of theories. It was also in the seventeenth century that it first came to be widely accepted that knowledge tends to increase steadily, if no calamity occurs to prevent its doing so. It was not forgotten that barbarian invasions had destroyed the Roman world. Yet there were comparisons made between antiquity and contemporary Europe; and it was both widely asserted and widely denied that the moderns had surpassed the ancients. Those who claimed superiority for the moderns rested their claim above all on the recent achievements of science. But even the most ardent champions of the moderns did not yet claim for them that they were more virtuous or more happy than the ancients. They felt themselves superior only because they had more knowledge or (less often and less confidently) because they had gone beyond them in the arts. They made no claim which Rousseau would have been concerned to deny: he did not contest that there had been 'progress' in the sciences and the arts, that knowledge had increased greatly and that artists had extended their powers, giving vivid and delicate expression to a wider range of feelings. He said only that progress in the sciences and the arts had been bought at too high a price in virtue and happiness. In the seventeenth century nobody was much concerned with this price: the belief which Rousseau denied, that progress in the arts and sciences makes for happiness, was as yet seldom asserted.

Not till the next century was it widely believed both that knowledge would increase indefinitely and that happiness would increase with it. It was argued that the invention of printing had diffused knowledge more widely than ever before, and so made it unlikely that a calamity would destroy it, as the barbarians had destroyed the accumulated knowledge of antiquity. Moreover, there probably would be no such calamity, for the European peoples were so much stronger than the others that they could not be conquered by them unless the others acquired the sciences and the skills of Europe. Peoples who had made progress could no longer be conquered by peoples who had not made it, and so the conquest of some peoples by others would no longer destroy what had already been achieved or seriously retard further progress. It was also argued that knowledge stimulates curiosity; that the more widely it is diffused, the more minds there are able and willing to add to it. The more men know and the more men there are who share the knowledge, the faster knowledge accumulates and the less likely that something will happen to slow down the rate of accumulation. There is a natural tendency for knowledge to accumulate, because men are endowed with memory and can keep records and so make a store to which they can add continuously; and the greater that store the more unlikely its destruction. Knowledge, like man its possessor, is most vulnerable in infancy, and becomes the less so the larger it grows. This was the faith of the philosophers of the eighteenth century, of the enlightenment; the faith which finds clear, confident and classic expression in Condorcet's *Sketch for a Historical Picture of the Progress of the Human Mind*. Or, rather, this was part of their faith, the part that Rousseau was not concerned to deny; and the other part was the belief which to him seemed certainly false: that as knowledge increases so too does happiness.

Bury says of the idea of progress before the nineteenth century:

It had waited like a handmaid on the abstractions of Nature and Reason; it had hardly realized an independent life. The time had come for systematic attempts to probe its meaning and definitely to ascertain the direction in which humanity is moving. Kant had said that a Kepler or a Newton was needed to find the law of movement of civilization.[1]

Though Bury's book is excellent in its kind, it is sometimes misleading. The search for a 'law of progress' belongs, he says, to the nineteenth century, and the earliest would-be Keplers were such men as Saint

[1] J. B. Bury, *The Idea of Progress*, Ch. XV, first para.

Simon and Comte. Bury is right in suggesting that the theories of progress of Saint-Simon and Comte differ radically from earlier theories, but he does not (so it seems to me) make it clear just where the difference lies.

What are we to understand by 'a law of progress'? It was often asserted before the nineteenth century – as Bury himself admits – that, given man's natural capacities, his living together with other men, and his physical environment, wealth and knowledge will accumulate if nothing happens to prevent their doing so. It was conceded that in the past the accumulation had not been smooth, and that sometimes, when disaster supervened, what was slowly acquired over the generations was quickly lost. Yet the tendency to accumulate was often asserted. Was not the assertion a putting forward of a law of progress? Was it not an assertion of what would happen, *ceteris paribus*? Was it not as much a *law* as the laws of the classical economists? As we have seen already, the men who, before Saint-Simon and Comte, asserted and explained this tendency also gave their reasons for believing that the causes which had impeded its operation in the past would not do so in the future.

Or are we to understand by 'a law of progress' a law asserting a set course of change, a passage from stage to stage, in a definite order? If that is 'a law of progress', then such a law was asserted (to take account of France alone) by three important writers before Saint-Simon: Fontenelle, Turgot and Condorcet. Fontenelle argued that scientific knowledge, as it accumulates, must do so in a certain order: some discoveries presuppose others, some sciences can come to birth only after others have made considerable progress. True, Fontenelle did not say that progress is inevitable, and spoke only of scientific progress, without affirming or denying that it conduces to progress in other directions. But he clearly implied that, unless something happens to prevent its doing so, knowledge will accumulate, and argued that, if it does accumulate, it must do so in a certain order.

According to Turgot, given man's natural capacities and the nature of the world in which he lives, all societies, as they change, tend to pass through the same stages, though, from a variety of causes peculiar to this or that society, all societies do not pass through these stages at the same speed. Some make progress more quickly than others and some stagnate, and there are also other differences between them due to their different circumstances. But, where there is progress, the order of it is determined in a general way by two factors: by human nature and by what is broadly similar in man's natural environment in all parts of the world. Though Turgot, like Fontenelle, paid special attention to the accumulation of knowledge, he conceived of progress more broadly, as Saint-Simon and Comte were to do after him.

Where Turgot saw only three stages of progress, Condorcet saw ten, which he described in considerable detail. He, too, was interested in more than the accumulation of knowledge, believing that men, as they come to know themselves and their environment better, grow in virtue and happiness. Like Turgot, he saw in the accumulation of knowledge the prime cause of other kinds of progress; but then so too did Saint-Simon and Comte.

How, then, do Saint-Simon and Comte differ from Condorcet and Turgot? In asserting the *necessity* of progress in some sense in which Condorcet and Turgot did not assert it? I doubt it. Do they not all four agree that, given the capacities peculiar to man and what is common to his environment everywhere, mankind will move in a certain direction, unless something happens to prevent their doing so, and will pass from stage to stage in a given order? And, if Saint-Simon and Comte believed that nothing would happen to prevent them, can we not say the same of Turgot and Condorcet? We have seen already that it was widely held, in the eighteenth century, that 'progress' had gained such momentum that what had stopped it in the past could stop it no longer. Mankind had made progress and would almost certainly continue to make it. This was what Turgot and Condorcet believed. Did Saint-Simon and Comte believe more than this? Did even Marx do so? I doubt it. Nineteenth-century believers in progress do not, I suspect, differ from earlier ones in asserting the *necessity* of progress in some sense in which it was not asserted before, though they do assert it more loudly and more often.[1] They differ rather in having a more unquestioning faith in progress, no longer troubling to argue that what had stopped progress in the past would do so no more.

And yet Bury is not wrong in suggesting that the theories of progress of Saint-Simon and Comte differ greatly from those of Turgot and Condorcet. He merely fails to explain the difference. Turgot and Condorcet say only this: It is not mere chance which causes men to make some discoveries before others, for there is a necessary order in the accumulation of knowledge, later achievements presupposing earlier ones. Knowledge is not acquired as pebbles are collected on a beach, as the whim takes the collector. Creatures capable of acquiring a comprehensive understanding of the world (and not just bare facts) and who perforce acquire it little by little must do so in a certain order; they cannot begin anywhere and then go on from there in any direction. There is a natural beginning and an orderly course. If men's capacities and their situation were different, the beginning and the course might also be different; but, given their capacities and situation, they must

---

[1] Hegel and the Hegelians are a special case; for, according to them, it follows from the very nature of Spirit, which is all reality, that it moves inevitably to a consummation. Here we have a properly metaphysical conception of progress. But Saint-Simon and Comte's conception of it was no more metaphysical than Condorcet's.

begin where they do and move forward as they do. If we suppose that the needs and motives which cause them to begin to acquire knowledge do not cease to operate after they have made a beginning, we must conclude that the accumulation of knowledge will continue indefinitely, unless something happens to put a stop to it. And we know from experience that these needs and motives do not cease to operate, for the speed at which knowledge accumulates increases with the amount accumulated. If we suppose further, as both Turgot and Condorcet do, that the increase of knowledge brings other benefits to man, we naturally conclude that it is the source of progress in a larger sense.

But Turgot and Condorcet, though they take it for granted that the increase of knowledge affects other sides of man's life in society, do not assume that all social activities are so closely connected that they all change in a fixed order; they do not assume that there is a fixed course of *integral* social change. Thus, if we make only the assumptions which they make, we are not at a loss to explain either social stagnation or how it is that countries can be very similar in some ways and yet differ greatly in others. The acquisition of knowledge is only one of man's social activities, and it does not determine but merely affects the others. Though there is a tendency for science to make quicker progress the greater the progress it has already made, there may arise *within society itself* obstacles to that progress.[1] It need not be so but it may be. It is true that Condorcet, when he speaks of obstacles to progress, has in mind natural disasters and barbarian invasions as much as internal obstacles, and that of *internal* obstacles he takes account only of the Church. But we are not here discussing his particular beliefs so much as his assumptions and what follows from them. He asserts a law of progress: he says, firstly, that knowledge will increase, provided that nothing happens to prevent its doing so, and secondly that, if it increases, it must do so in a certain order. But he does not assert a law of integral social change.

Now, this is precisely what Saint-Simon and Comte do assert, and so too does Marx. The difference between the earlier and the later writers

[1] Those who, like Saint-Simon, Comte or Marx, assume that there is a fixed order of *integral* social change must hold (if they are to be consistent) that obstacles to progress which arise within a society are merely temporary. Their assumption rules out the possibility of some aspects of social life developing in ways which stop the progress (or set course of change) of the others; whereas Condorcet's assumption does not rule this out. Yet their assumption still allows that an *external* cause (e.g. a natural disaster, or the impact of another society on this one) may put a stop to progress.

I dare say that those who made one or other of these two assumptions did not understand what they were committed to by so doing. Indeed, they seem hardly to have been aware that these are two different assumptions. Some writers (Saint-Simon perhaps?) may even have vacillated between the two. But this makes it only the more important to distinguish between them and to consider their implications.

is not what Bury takes it to be; it does not consist in the later writers saying that progress is *necessary* in some sense in which the earlier ones do not say it. Saint-Simon, Comte and Marx do not hold, with Hegel, that progress is necessary in the sense that it could not conceivably be otherwise; they hold rather, with Condorcet and Turgot, that it will continue if nothing happens to stop it, and they take it for granted that nothing will happen. The later writers differ from the earlier ones in assuming that all aspects of social life are so connected that they pass from stage to stage in a fixed order, though some move forward sooner than others. They make a more complicated and a less plausible assumption. To sustain it they use stranger arguments and take more frequent refuge in ambiguity. It is they, rather than Condorcet and Turgot, who produce a Procrustean bed on which to stretch the facts of history. I have no wish to belittle the difference between them and their eighteenth-century precursors, but only to say that it is not what Bury says it is.

Saint-Simon, Comte and Marx differ from Condorcet and Turgot in yet another way; they speak as if how men behave in society were determined by the social and cultural order. Or, rather, though they do not deny that there are certain natural functions, which men would exercise much as they do now, even if they were subject to no social influences, they speak as if the rest of their behaviour, if it is important, if it is of the kind that the historian or the social theorist takes notice of, were socially determined. There are some things which men would do even if they were not social creatures, even in a hypothetical state of nature, and some of these things are no doubt important since they satisfy biological needs; and there are also forms of behaviour peculiar to this or that person, which are unimportant, except to the person himself and to those close to him. But men have capacities which are developed in society, by social intercourse with other men, and their properly social activities consist in the exercise of these capacities. It is the system of these activities which constitutes the social system, and it is these same activities which determine how the system changes. In other words, the behaviour which brings about social change is itself socially determined.

This doctrine, which is common to Saint-Simon, Comte and Marx, I shall call *social determinism*. Many writers on society and politics have found it attractive, though they have also felt the need to qualify it. It has seemed to them to give proper weight to important truths unknown or neglected before the nineteenth century. Yet the doctrine is more obscure even than most of its critics have noticed, as I shall try to show later. It contains important truths but fails to put them clearly, and in the meantime suggests a good deal that is false. It is a difficult and a slippery doctrine; those who accept it do not know quite what it is that they are accepting, and are apt to abandon it (without noticing that they have done so) when to adhere to it would put them in a false position. It is a doctrine loudly proclaimed to which even its loudest champions are frequently disloyal.

3. Rousseau's Denial

Rousseau denied what Condorcet affirmed; he did not believe in progress. Yet he too, in the *Discourse on the Origins of Inequality Among Men*, described a course of social change. Though he reached conclusions different from Condorcet's, their conceptions of social change were not unlike. He too argued that, men's capacities being what they are, human societies evolve as other animal communities do not. Much less versed than Condorcet in the sciences, he could never have shown how the scientific spirit emerged or how one science prepared the way for another. Yet the course of change which he envisaged was not fortuitous, though he admitted that his description was conjectural; it seemed to him, as it did to Condorcet, that some achievements presuppose others and therefore necessarily come after them. His method also was deductive; he argued to his conclusions largely from two assumptions: that certain capacities are peculiar to man, and that what first brought men together was the need to co-operate for the better satisfaction of their wants.

The account of man's evolution which Condorcet gives in his *Sketch* is more elaborate and perhaps also more lucid than Rousseau's in the second *Discourse*, and he comes much closer than Rousseau to formulating a 'law of change'. Rousseau saw himself merely as a reconstructor of the past, explaining in broad outline what must be presumed to have happened to a creature endowed by nature as man is to bring him to his present condition, whereas Condorcet saw himself more clearly as the discoverer of a fixed course of cultural change. But though, of the two, Condorcet used history the more copiously to illustrate his theme, they were both more concerned to explain what must have happened than to establish what in fact did happen. And if Rousseau never assumed an integral course of social change, or what I have called social determinism, neither did Condorcet. In spite of the great differences between them, in several important respects they are alike. The claim which is implicit in the *Discourse* is made explicit in the *Sketch*: given the capacities peculiar to man and the fact of social intercourse, there are certain developments to be expected if nothing happens to prevent them.[1]

---

[1] Rousseau, less lucid and elaborate than Condorcet, had perhaps a deeper sense of what social intercourse does to man, forming his character and making a moral person of him. Condorcet was mainly concerned with the intellectual achievements of man, and Rousseau with the effects of the social environment on the *psyche* of the individual.

Yet Rousseau denied what Condorcet affirmed; he denied progress. He did not, as we shall see, deny progress in all the senses in which Condorcet affirmed it; but he did deny it in the most important sense. He denied that the increase of knowledge makes eventually for greater happiness. I shall discuss, in the third part of this chapter, the belief affirmed by Condorcet and denied by Rousseau; but before I do that, I want to examine certain objections to the doctrines of an integral course of social change and social determinism.[1]

II. INTEGRAL SOCIAL CHANGE AND THE INDIVIDUAL

I discuss elsewhere certain difficulties about the conception of a set course of integral social change.[2] What is it, exactly, which is said to change? How can there be a set course of change when societies are continually affecting one another? In just what sense of the word is the supposed law of social change a *law*? It is quite unlike any *law* of the natural sciences; it does not say what will happen to anything of a certain kind under such and such circumstances. Nor does it describe a course of change normal to members of a species having many members clearly distinct from one another and from their environment. A law of social change is a pronouncement *sui generis*: it refers to groups of individuals and to relations and attitudes of mind which individuals have as members of groups. These relations and attitudes give to the groups their identity, and the law asserts that they change in a fixed

---

[1] A fear, now very present to us, that the increase of knowledge and of power over nature may lead to the destruction of mankind, was unknown to the eighteenth and nineteenth centuries. The pessimists then predicted, not destruction, but misery and corruption; and they mostly did not trouble to describe in detail the long course of deterioration which they foresaw. Even Rousseau, the arch-pessimist, attempted only a rough outline. It was not the pessimists, not the Rousseaus, but the optimists, the believers in progress in some larger sense than the mere increase in knowledge and wealth, who were tempted to map the future.

There are two forms of pessimism in Rousseau: there is the belief that man is deteriorating morally, becoming feebler and more confused in his passions, and there is the belief that, as society grows more complex, man's problems pile upon him so fast that he cannot keep pace with them. Who holds the first belief is often inclined to hold the second, seeing a connection between the state of society and the decline of man; but the converse is not true. Today, the second belief is probably more widely held than the first: there are many who see no reason for holding that men are feebler than they were but who doubt their ability to remedy the evils and avoid the dangers which their achievements have brought on them. To them, the first belief is sheer prejudice, the product of depression or misanthropy, while the second looks reasonable.

[2] In treating of the social theories of Hegel and Marx.

order. Wherever men stand in social relations to one another, these relations, together with the modes of thought and feeling which 'correspond' to them, will change in this order, so long as there is no breach of continuity; that is to say, so long as each generation can pass on to their successors the wealth, the knowledge, the skills and the values they have acquired either by inheritance or in their own generation. The peculiarity of a statement of this kind, the extent to which it differs from a *law* of the natural sciences (not excluding biology), is masked by the practice of speaking of groups of men socially related to one another and of their *social posterity* (those to whom they pass on what they have acquired) as if they were organisms. Clearly, men are not just externally related to one another; their 'nature' is modified by the relations they stand in to other men, other creatures of their kind. To express their sense that this is so, social theorists have used conceptions taken from biology, which are useful in some ways and misleading in others.

Statements of this kind are shielded from criticism by their very obscurity, and they are obscure because it is uncertain both what they refer to and what they say of it. Indeed, these two uncertainties go naturally together. Where a word is used in several senses, we get the particular sense in which it is being used mostly from knowing what it is being applied to. But, unfortunately, it is by no means easy (perhaps not even possible) to identify a society of the kind said to be involved in a set course of change.

It is sometimes astonishing how little men know what they are about when they speak of social change or social *evolution* in the grand manner of a Comte or a Marx. Marx has been called the *Darwin* of the social sciences. Some who have called him so have meant only that he put forward ideas which, in their own way, have been as revolutionary as those of Darwin; but others have spoken as if they had in mind something more. Presumably, they have known that there were men before Marx who said that there was a set course of social change or evolution. What then have they meant to convey about Marx by calling him the Darwin of the social sciences? Have they meant that his conception of social change, as compared with earlier conceptions, is more like Darwin's idea of evolution? But this is absurd; for the idea of evolution, as we find it in Darwin, makes no sense whatever if we apply it to a course of social change. Neither Marx nor anyone else has ever come near to so applying it. Darwin never spoke of a set course of change, of a normal course of evolution, of a fixed order of stages through which a species must pass unless something extraneous prevents its doing so; he never spoke of the species as if it were an individual, going through a course of change peculiar to its kind; and he spoke not of groups but of species. Evolution, as Darwin conceived of it, differs *toto coelo* from the course of social change as Marx explained it. To the extent that Marx used ideas taken from biology to expound what he meant by social change, they were ideas as old as biology itself, as old as Aristotle.[1] Marx was no more 'Darwinian' than was Condorcet.

But I must not repeat what I have said elsewhere. I shall confine myself to defending such theories as those of Comte and Marx from some of the charges brought against them, and to making one or two criticisms of my own, which come more naturally here than in the chapters dealing with Hegel and Marx.

1. Social Change and Individual Freedom

It is often objected to such theories as Marxism that, if they were true, men would have no freedom of choice; and the objection is made even by persons who accept full determinism, who believe that acts of choice are like other events in the sense that, given the circumstances in which they happen, they must happen. But the truth is that these theories are no more and no less a denial of freedom than determinism itself. If freedom is compatible with the doctrine that acts of choice are just as much caused as other events are, then it is compatible with Marxism. It is important to see why this is so.

Such theories as those of Comte and Marx are theories about what men do, about how they behave; they are not theories about what happens to men no matter what they do. The activities they discuss are peculiarly human in the sense that they involve deliberation and choice. To say that such activities are *socially determined* is no more to deny their peculiarly human character than to say that they are determined in some other way. It may be a false statement, and it might still be false even if determinism, taken generally, were true; but, true or false, it is not a statement about what happens to people no matter what they do. Therefore criticisms of Marx or Comte which imply that their theories commit them to such statements quite miss the mark. I have in mind such criticisms as this: 'It is absurd of Marx to exhort men to action, for he holds that what will happen must happen, whether or not they choose that it shall.' But here, surely, it is not Marx but his critic who is being absurd. Marx does not say that the proletarian revolution will happen, no matter how men choose to act; he says that it will happen because men will choose to act in certain ways. Their choice, he thinks, will be determined; and among its causes there will be exhortations such as his. And the exhortations in

---

[1] Of course, he did not use even these ideas consistently; for, after all, social change is not like organic development, and it is beyond the powers of even the most Germanic system-builder always to speak of something as if it were what it obviously is not.

their turn are determined. Both the decisions of the revolutionaries and the exhortations belong to the course of events which Marxism purports to explain.

When they speak of *deliberation* and *choice*, determinists, whether or not they also believe in a law of social change, mean by these words pretty much what indeterminists mean by them. They do not deny that men take stock of the situations in which they act, that they consider the courses of action open to them, and then decide upon one course in preference to the others. They do not play down the importance of reason and deliberate choice in human affairs; or at least they are not committed by their doctrine to doing so. If the determinist who does not believe in a law of social change is not committed to playing down reason and choice, then neither is the determinist who does. The importance of an event depends on its consequences; and if an event is an action of a kind of which human beings alone are capable, if it involves deliberation and choice, it is none the less important for being determined.

No doubt, Marx and others who believe in a set course of social change often speak carelessly, and they sometimes speak as if it did not matter what men choose to do. They sometimes speak as if 'social forces' were not human activities, and therefore as if there were something which was at once social and different from human behaviour which determined that behaviour. And it may be that this is due to more than carelessness. Marx and others who have thought as he did have not been remarkably lucid; they have put together elaborate and obscure theories and have often been entangled in coils of their own making. They often have not seen precisely what was implied by their own doctrines. There are, no doubt, passages where they speak of men as if they were puppets pulled hither and thither by social forces, laws of social change external to them, as if the course of history did not consist merely of what men do but were a kind of stream into which they are plunged and which carries them along with it until death throws them out of it. But these are aberrations due either to carelessness or to confusion of thought; they do not follow logically from the doctrine that there is a set course of social change. That doctrine is, I think, unacceptable, but not because it commits those who hold it to this kind of absurdity.

Not only social theorists but also natural scientists sometimes speak, carelessly and improperly, as if the laws formulated by them were causally related to the events they apply to; as if the causes of events were not other events but laws. When a physicist or biologist speaks in this way, as if there were something external to events causing them to happen as they do, we are not offended, for it does not matter to us that what is merely physical, what is altogether different from the actions peculiar to us, should be 'subject' to 'forces' external to it. Yet this way of speaking, though it is only sometimes offensive, is always misleading unless it is seen for what it is: as a way of speaking which may sometimes be convenient but must never be taken literally. There are not forces external to events determining their order in the physical world any more than there are in the social world.

We can, of course, often say, without absurdity, that some things will happen to men no matter what they choose to do. We can say, for example, that they'll die. Such events as these are natural and not social, and social theorists are not much interested in them. We can also, without absurdity, make predictions about what men will choose to do; we can say, for example, that seven out of ten persons now between the ages of twenty and thirty and still unmarried will get married within the next ten years. They will not get married unless they choose to do so, and yet the belief that marriage depends on choice does not lessen our confidence in our prediction. Nor does confidence in the prediction weaken our belief that marriage depends on choice.

Though those who say that there is a set course of social change which determines how men act, think and feel are not, except when they are being careless or confused, saying that there are forces external to men causing them to act as they do; though they are aware, in their more lucid moments, that what they refer to as 'social forces' or 'the course of events' consists only of human activities, they are nevertheless, for reasons which I shall discuss later, saying something which, if we consider it carefully, can be seen not to make sense. But, before I go on to discuss these reasons, I want to defend holders of this doctrine from another charge sometimes made against them.

It has seldom been made against them indiscriminately, but more against some than others, and most often against Marx and his disciples. The charge, this time, is not that they speak of 'social forces' external to men moving them to act as they do, but that, by implication, they deny the importance of 'great' men. It is not easy to assess the exact nature of this charge. It would seem absurd to bring it against, say, Hegel or Saint-Simon. For Hegel spoke of 'world historical individuals' and was full of admiration and respect for great men, and Saint-Simon, though his manner was different, was scarcely less so; he made heroes of the great scientists, of Galileo and Newton. Yet Hegel and Saint-Simon also believed that the course of history is necessary; and Hegel believed it in an even stronger sense of necessity than did Marx. How, then, does their position differ from Marx's? In their not believing, as he did, in economic determinism? But this, surely, is not relevant. If he and they are agreed about what, say, Newton achieved, we cannot say that they estimate the importance of his achievement differently merely because they disagree about how such achievements

P

are determined.[1] They all three hold that the opportunities open to great men, be they men of action or men of thought, are determined by the situation, social and cultural, in which they find themselves; they disagree only about how the factors in that situation are related to one another.

To say, as Marxists have done, that if Newton had not discovered what he did someone else would have done so is not to detract from the importance of Newton. For whoever else had done it would have had a mind of Newton's quality, and his achievement would have been no less admirable and important. Marxists need not deny that some men are immensely more gifted than others, and that men as gifted as Newton are wonderfully rare. It is perfectly consistent to hold both that, if Newton had not done what he did, someone else would have done it, and that the history of mankind would be vastly different if there were no geniuses among men. Just as it would be vastly different if men generally had other capacities than they do have, or if men and women were not born in roughly equal numbers. The Marxist need not deny this. He need not say that the course of history would be the same no matter what men were like. Nor need he say that the course of history depends only on capacities common to all human beings. It depends on the bearing of children, and only women, who are not the whole of mankind, can bear them. It depends also on capacities which are incomparably more rare and which we call genius. No doubt, Marxism and other such theories, assume some kind of 'uniformity' in human nature; but they need not assume either that all human beings are born alike or that how they differ is socially and historically unimportant. They assume merely that the important natural differences between human beings remain much the same in degree and extent from generation to generation; they assume that the incidence of genius or talent does not differ greatly from age to age.

There have been Marxists who took it upon themselves to reduce great men to ordinary proportions. Perhaps they believed that historical materialism required them to do so. If this was their belief, they were mistaken. Or perhaps their motive was quite different; perhaps they

---

1 This is not to deny that economic determinism has difficulties peculiar to itself. Marx was (or sometimes passed himself off as being) an economic determinist, holding that men's ideas about the world and themselves are determined by how they produce goods and services to satisfy their needs. Since production is an activity involving the use of ideas and is also deeply affected by science, Marx could not in practice do what he sometimes thought he was doing; he could not explain the course of social change on the assumption that how men think is determined by how they produce what satisfies their needs. But, peculiar though economic determinism is, its peculiarities are irrelevant when we are discussing the Marxist attitude to great men.

were proclaiming a faith in equality without quite knowing what kind of equality they had faith in. That, too, is possible.

2. Of What is Social Change Predicated?

There is another, and more serious, objection than these to such theories as those of Comte and Marx; an objection which I have already touched upon but which I now want to consider from a rather different point of view. When Comte and Marx spoke as if there were a set course of social change, they presumably were not thinking of all mankind as one society; for they found some peoples more advanced, further along the course, than others. Nor did they have in mind either a natural or a 'civil' community (i.e. one involving regular administration); they did not mean a family or class or tribe, nor yet a collection of persons under the same government, however wide or narrow the function of that government. A kinship group has definite limits; and so too has what I have called a 'civil community', using that term because I want to put into the same broad category both States and other associations in which there is a regular control by some persons over others, in which a distinction is made between those who act on behalf of the community and those who do not. What makes a community identical over the years differs not only as between natural and civil communities but also as between different species within each of these two kinds. For example, a civil community may be reckoned to be the same over a long period of time because, throughout this period, its rulers have authority over all persons within a given territory; or because, though its members have moved into another part of the world, it consists of the same natural communities having a common government; or because authority has passed from ruler to ruler by a fixed rule; or because recruitment has continued uninterruptedly. There are many criteria used to establish the identity and continuity of communities, and especially of civil ones. The Church of Rome, the Royal Society, and the French State have existed for a long time, and we use different criteria to decide whom they include and exclude. Yet these criteria, though sometimes far from simple, can be more or less precisely defined.

Comte and Marx (and others of their kind), when they speak of a course of social change, are not speaking of changes of which anything thus easily identifiable is the enduring subject. True, they do not know this; they often speak as if there were societies distinct from one another which must all pass necessarily from stage to stage in the same order if nothing happens to destroy them. Yet they speak improperly, though they do not know it. There is nothing which retains its identity as it changes in the ways they describe; there is only

a course of events. There are men who are born and live and die, and
among whom certain modes of action, thought and feeling endure for
a time and then give way to others. What, then, are we to understand
by a necessary course of social change if we refuse to follow those who
speak as if there were an enduring subject of it?

To say that there is a necessary course of social change is, presumably, to say at least this: Wherever there is social intercourse between
men who are able to pass on to their successors the fruits of their
labour and experience, social modes of behaviour (i.e., those modes
which do not come 'naturally' but are acquired in social intercourse)
will change in a fixed order provided that no extraneous cause inter-
venes to prevent their doing so.

Now, this statement is not analytic; we can establish its truth or
falsity only by appealing to the facts. In order to test it, we should have
to locate in history several quite separate courses of social change,
and see whether and to what extent they were similar. But this we
cannot do. Wherever we look, we cannot find even one region or
one people (let alone several) in which or among whom there has
been a long course of social change unaffected by what went on
elsewhere.

The modes of behaviour here in question are neither natural nor
idiosyncratic; they are not acquired in a process of physical and psychological maturation independently of social intercourse, and they are
not peculiar to this or that person. They are conventional; they are
acquired by the individual as he learns to live with his fellows, as he
becomes aware of himself as a man among men, as he enters into social
relations with them. What, then, causes these modes to change? They
are conventional; there is nothing about them which explains why
they should change. Modes of behaviour have no inherent tendency
to change; they are not organisms. If they do change, it is presumably
because men, for some reason or other, begin to act differently, because
they break with convention, because they deviate from the normal.
What, then, causes them to break with convention? Presumably, it is
not convention itself. Presumably, it is not established modes of
behaviour which themselves produce the behaviour that alters them?
Nor can it be mere 'human nature', the inborn capacities common to
all men or distributed among them in much the same proportions
from generation to generation.

Custom, convention and received opinion may set limits to the kinds
of behaviour which depart from them; we should not expect to find the
innovations of the nineteenth century in the thirteenth. Nonetheless,
established modes of behaviour do not determine what innovations
there shall be; they do not produce what causes them to change. We
cannot, given 'human nature' and the modes of behaviour established
among a body of men (the modes which make of these men a society

having a distinct character or 'structure' of its own), predict the behaviour which will cause those modes to change. But, unless we can do this, how can there be a necessary course of social change?[1]

If we deny social determinism and a set course of social change, we need not deny determinism in general; we need not deny that the behaviour which alters established modes of behaviour has its sufficient causes. We deny only that this behaviour is determined by the very modes which it alters; by the institutions and culture which give to a society its distinctive character. We say no more than that these things, though they deeply affect the behaviour which alters them, do not make it what it is. To speak as if the behaviour which changes the social order were itself the mere effect of that order is absurd, true though it is that this behaviour always occurs in a social context which sets limits to what it can be.

If this argument is contrasted with another, the point of it may become clearer. Bury accuses Comte of failing to grapple with a 'fundamental' question, the question of *contingency*. He speaks of 'the collision' of two 'independent causal chains', meaning by one of them the 'course of history', which Comte and others say is necessary, and by the other any series of events which interferes with that course. For example, Bury says that Napoleon's existence was due to an 'independent causal chain' having nothing to do with 'the course of political events', and then goes on to say that 'the course of history' was profoundly affected by what Napoleon did. This action of Napoleon upon the course of history was contingent in relation to that course; and (so Bury tells us) 'the whole history of man has been modified at every stage by such contingencies'.[2]

This line of argument looks odd because it seems both to affirm and deny that there is a 'course of history' in the sense envisaged by Comte or Marx. Bury speaks as if there would (or might) be a set course of change, were it not that it was continually interfered with by such actions as Napoleon's, actions whose causes are contingent in relation to that course. But it makes no sense to treat the course of history as an 'independent causal chain' with which other such chains are perpetually colliding. True, we can distinguish various kinds of

---

1 Elsewhere in this chapter I speak of a *set* course of social change, and in the last section of the chapter on Marxism I speak of a *normal* course. I use the three words, *set*, *normal*, and *necessary*, in the same sense in this context: to refer to a course which moves from stage to stage in a given order, unless something impinges on it from outside to prevent its doing so. Though most of the theorists asserting such a course did not trouble to qualify their assertion in the way I have done, it is not obvious that they would have refused to qualify it, if invited to do so. In any case, the criticisms made here apply to the assertion whether or not it is qualified in this way.

2 See J. B. Bury. *The Idea of Progress*, Ch. XVI, § 5.

events from one another; and we can give a name to each kind to mark it off from the others, calling one kind *economic*, another *political*, and another *cultural*, and so on. But if events of these different kinds continually impinge upon one another, we cannot treat any one kind as an independent causal chain. No doubt, there are innumerable 'causal chains' which are, over considerable periods of time, independent of one another. What Jones does may not affect Smith nor what Smith does affect Jones for days or weeks on end, and then one of them may impinge on the other. We should then, presumably, have what Bury calls 'two independent causal chains' coming eventually into 'collision'. We need not deny that there are, at any one time, many such 'chains' and also frequent 'collisions'. But there is still no 'course of history', no central causal chain, in relation to which those events of Napoleon's life which are not political or military, which are not to be included in 'the course of history', are contingent. To base an argument against Comte or Marx on a distinction between 'a course of history' and actions which are contingent in relation to it is to build on shifting sand.

But we can distinguish between conventional modes of behaviour and the behaviour which causes these modes to change, and we can see that the modes do not determine (though they set limits to) the behaviour which changes them. Therefore we can see that there can be no set or necessary course of social change.

3. *An Effect of Science and History*

It has been said that belief in a necessary course of social change was a substitute for older beliefs in a Divine Providence or in final causes, beliefs weakened by the intellectual revolution of the seventeenth century, in which Descartes was the chief actor. According to Descartes, the universe is a system in which everything that happens does so according to some unchanging law. There is movement and change in every part of the universe, but the system, as a whole, does not change. The astronomers describe movements which are repeated again and again, the stars and the planets remain physically the same, and in the vegetable and animal kingdoms, though individuals are born and grow and die, the species do not change. So, too, the political theorists described a stable order. Doubtless, they would not have asserted that the social and political order, as they knew it, had been as it was from the beginning; nor would they have denied that it differed considerably from part to part of the world. Nevertheless, when they put together their theories, they took little notice of changes in the past or of present differences.

Later, when the study of history flourished, they could no longer ignore the course of change which had made the present what it was and had made it different from place to place. The historians brought it home to them, as never before, that the social and political order, though it formed a more or less coherent whole and was the product of human activities, was yet not the deliberate creation of man. Men had not decided how it should be, though it was the consequence of what they had done and was fairly well adapted to their needs. How then had it come to be what it was, coherent and useful? It seemed obvious that it could not have become so merely by chance. Burke suggested that God, working through men, had made it what it was, and Hegel put Spirit in the place of God. But what could they do who wanted, without benefit of theology or metaphysics, to explain how society had come to be an elaborate structure adapted to men's needs and attitudes of mind? It seemed to them that they must offer a 'scientific' explanation; and also that no explanation could be properly 'scientific' unless it postulated a 'law of social change'. Thus respect for science inspired an enterprise unknown to any of the authentic sciences: the attempt to formulate a law explaining, not any event of a given kind, but a whole course of events. Yet respect for science alone could not have inspired an enterprise so alien to the scientific spirit. The desire to explain the whole course of history sprang from a need much older than the century which saw the triumph of the scientific spirit: the human need for assurance that man is moving in a definite and desirable direction. It is this same need which has given birth to religion. But, though the need is at bottom the same, these new doctrines meet it differently. Religion gives this assurance conditionally and to each man separately: it assures him that there is a destination which he can reach provided he deserves to reach it. Whereas these doctrines give the assurance unconditionally and to the species. And yet the assurance, to whoever can bring himself to accept it, is worth having, because, though he may not himself reach the promised land, the movement towards it gives dignity and importance to his efforts, which are part of the movement. He strives for the species, seeing it as an enlargement of himself.

III. HAPPINESS AND THE EXPANSION OF KNOWLEDGE

1. Error and Vice

Bacon and the Abbé de Saint-Pierre valued knowledge for its usefulness. They held that men, by extending their knowledge, increase their power over nature and their ability to satisfy their wants, and by satisfying their wants increase their happiness.[1] Bacon had a larger view than Saint-Pierre of the utility of knowledge; he would never have put the inventor of a useful machine higher on the roll of honour than a Newton or a Leibnitz. Yet he, too, set store by knowledge chiefly because it increases man's power over nature; he agreed with Saint-Pierre about the way in which knowledge is useful to man and differed from him only in seeing more clearly how what is not useful immediately may be so in the long run.

Nobody – not even Rousseau – would deny that the expansion of knowledge increases man's power over nature. But Rousseau (and many others) would deny what both Bacon and Saint-Pierre take for granted, that man is the better for increasing this power. As man's power to satisfy his wants increases, those wants change. Why should we believe that his power more than keeps pace with his wants? Why should we even believe that the wants he acquires must be such that he could satisfy them provided his power increased sufficiently? Why should we take it for granted that we are faced here with a problem of the kind to which economists seek a solution; a problem of ensuring that, given men's wants, what is needed to satisfy them is produced as efficiently as possible?

But there are less simple views than these about how knowledge makes for happiness. There is the doctrine that the expansion of knowledge changes man's conception of himself and his environment in ways which make him more capable of happiness, putting him out of reach of what has hitherto led to unhappiness. Hegel is perhaps the boldest and the most exciting exponent of this doctrine. As I have already discussed his theory at considerable length, I shall not return to it here. I shall take other examples of this doctrine; I shall discuss it in the forms given to it by Condorcet and Comte. Not that I am concerned with their theories for their own sake; I consider them only because I want to examine certain assumptions and lines of argument. Assumptions and arguments very like theirs can be found in the writings of Saint-Simon and Marx, and if I choose to examine these particular versions of them, it is only because they are more coherent or are less mixed up with other things. Condorcet and Comte are more systematic than Saint-Simon, and they do not make the excessive demands on the reader made by Hegel and Marx.

Condorcet and Comte were not primarily interested in man's increasing power over nature. They by no means neglected it, but they did not insist upon it. Technological progress was of only secondary

---

[1] This doctrine, in this rather crude form, has been so much and so severely attacked that it no longer appeals to intellectuals; but it is still widely popular. It is implicit in many contemporary arguments which take it for granted that men are the better off for the spread of industry.

importance to them. They were concerned, above all, with how man sees himself and the world he lives in; they were more interested in the nature of science, of man's vision of the world, than in scientific discoveries which have practical effects.

Condorcet believed that vice is grounded in error: not that it is error but that it proceeds from it.[1] And by vice he meant either conduct which is harmful or the motives which ordinarily produce such conduct. Creatures capable of knowledge are liable to error, but are also able to correct their errors. Hence vice is the product of reason and knowledge; or, rather, it is the product of bad reasoning and half-knowledge, and is eliminated as men learn to reason correctly and acquire sounder knowledge. Yet error tends to perpetuate itself for two reasons: because men are attached to their prejudices, to opinions received in childhood, and do not easily discard them even when all the truths needed to destroy them have been discovered; and because, as soon as there is a large store of what is taken for knowledge to be passed on from generation to generation, those whose profession it is to pass it on, the teachers, find it their interest to make a mystery of their supposed knowledge and to use it to get power over the taught. Thus there arises 'organized imposture', which is a powerful cause of unhappiness and an obstacle to progress.[2] But the motives which cause men to seek knowledge continue to operate, and eventually error is dissipated and imposture exposed.

If we consider Condorcet's account of how 'organized imposture' arises, we see that it does not arise from error alone, but from error and the desire for power. And the error consists, not so much in the particular beliefs propagated by the teachers, as in the belief that those who teach are not impostors – a belief which may be confined to the taught or be shared by the teachers also. Before the imposture can be brought to an end, the 'authority' of the impostors must be destroyed, and it cannot be destroyed until men have learnt to distinguish truth from error. Or, to say the same thing differently, it cannot be destroyed until men have learnt what knowledge is; until they have learned what tests to apply to discover whether a belief is true or false. More important therefore, in Condorcet's opinion, than any particular discoveries is the discovery of what constitutes knowledge. Errors will

---

[1] At times Condorcet speaks as if vice were a kind of error, as, for example, when he calls cruelty towards enemies an error. But at other times he speaks as if the two were different, as if vice proceeded from error. As this second is the more plausible doctrine and is as well suited as the first to his theory of progress, I shall assume that it represents what he really believed.

[2] Though from time to time Condorcet admits that the 'impostors' deceive themselves as well as their victims, he usually speaks as if they were deliberate deceivers. The 'imposture' he has chiefly in mind is organized religion. But, even if the deceit were not deliberate, his general argument would remain what it is.

continue to be made, even after this discovery, but those who challenge the errors will be able to do so to good effect.

Condorcet does not explain how exactly vice springs from error. But if we look at the examples he gives, it would seem that ignorance and error do not merely cause men to act harmfully but also affect the motives from which they act. What he calls 'imposture' thrives on ignorance and error, though not on them alone, for it is kept alive by the desire to dominate others. He does not speak as if, were ignorance and error to disappear, this desire would remain as strong as ever and would merely cease to have harmful effects; he speaks as if the desire would evaporate. The kind of domination exercised by impostors over their victims would no longer be possible, and would eventually cease to be desired. Though men might still wish to be important in the eyes of their fellow men, or to be admired by them, this wish would no longer give birth to a lust for power. So, too, envy, jealousy and malice would be greatly weakened, if men understood themselves and the world better than they do. These motives may arise out of passions which are part of man's 'enduring nature', either because he is born with them or acquires them in any social environment; and yet the motives are not the same as the passions from which they arise. A creature incapable of desiring the good opinion of others might also be incapable of envy or malice; but envy and malice are not the same motive as desire for good opinion, though they may be causally related to it. Nor are they distinguishable from it merely by their effects. Men's motives are changed by the situations in which they find themselves and by the opportunities open to them; and these situations and opportunities are in turn changed by how they see themselves and others and the world. Where men see things as they really are, their situations and opportunities produce (or strengthen) virtuous motives in them and not vicious ones. This, I think, is how vice and error, virtue and knowledge, are connected in Condorcet's opinion; for though he does not trouble to explain these connections, this is the explanation most in keeping with what he says.

Comte, though he expresses himself differently, holds what is at bottom much the same opinion. If he does not say, in so many words, that vice is an effect of error, he does suppose that men will become more sociable (that is to say, better able to live happily together) as their understanding is improved. Man, by extending his knowledge, comes to have needs which he can satisfy and learns to adapt the world to his needs. As he acquires a coherent and adequate knowledge of the world, he comes to have needs which are compatible with one another and with the needs of his fellows. The process which is a learning to get what he wants is also a learning to want what he can get; and the process which is a learning what he is and how he is situated is also a learning to be satisfied with his situation. 'Man',

Comte tells us, 'apart from society is a useless, or rather a thoroughly mischievous, abstraction of our psychologists or ideologists which the positive spirit discards. Here at last the full importance of the systematizing power possessed by that spirit comes out. We have already seen how it harmonizes the individual mind; and we now see that it is also the philosophical foundation of human sociability, so far at least as sociability depends on the intellect, and that it depends chiefly . . . upon the intellect is indisputable.'[1] By the positive spirit Comte means the scientific spirit, which is the faith that everything that happens in the world can be explained in terms of laws whose truth is established by an appeal to the facts, by observation and experiment. It is part of that faith that all these laws form a coherent system; and this is what Comte has in mind when he speaks of the 'systematising power' of the 'positive' or scientific spirit. He says of it that it 'harmonises' the individual mind, and also that it is 'the philosophical foundation of human sociability'. He means, presumably, that the knowledge provided by the sciences, being systematic, affects those who acquire it in such a way that they not only see the world as a coherent whole but come to have moral principles and needs which enable them to live together in peace and amity. Comte speaks of the 'intellectual communion' upon which all 'true human association' rests, and says that it must go along with what he calls 'conformity of feeling' and 'convergence of interests'.[2] Though he does not, I think, make it clear precisely how these things are connected, he does say enough to show that, in his opinion, the more systematic and adequate men's understanding of the world, the more they will have the feelings and interests which enable them to form a 'true human association' or, in other words, a harmonious society.

2. Knowledge, Virtue and Happiness

There are two respects in which Condorcet and Comte differ from many present-day philosophers. They take it for granted that there are moral truths which are *true* in the same sense as the discoveries of 'science'; and they do not treat the hypotheses of the natural scientist as propositions different in kind from the axioms and theorems of the mathematician. Condorcet speaks of the discovery of the 'true rights of man' as if it were in the same sense an advance in knowledge as the discoveries of Newton or Galileo, and he also says that these rights 'can all be deduced from the single truth that man is a sentient being,

---

[1] A Comte. *A Preliminary Discourse on the Positive Spirit*, translated by Edward Beesly, p. 42.
[2] Ibid., p. 43.

capable of reasoning and of acquiring moral ideas.'[1] Comte speaks as if ethics were a science in the same sense as physics or biology; and he takes it to be a branch of sociology. He admits that hitherto moralists have not been scientific; they have been untouched by the 'positive spirit'. For that spirit does not direct human curiosity from the beginning, and it does not pervade all branches of study at the same time. Some branches become scientific before others, and the last to do so is the study of man. But Comte predicts that 'irresistible demonstrations . . . confirmed by the immense experience now possessed by mankind, will determine exactly the real influence, direct or indirect, private or public, attaching to each act, each habit, each inclination or feeling. From such demonstrations will follow, as so many corollaries, the general or special rules of conduct most in accordance with the universal order, rules which, consequently, will usually be found also conducive to individual happiness.'[2]

We may reject both these views – that moral principles can be deduced from the capacities peculiar to man or that they can be discovered by seeing what rules of conduct accord with 'the universal order' – and still hold that the expansion of knowledge leads to greater virtue and happiness. It is no argument against the belief in progress that men's tastes and preferences and their moral principles change. For we can still hold that men are the more virtuous the more they live in accordance with their principles, and we can say that they are the happier the more they have the feeling that life, as they live it, is worth living. If then we can show that, the greater men's understanding of the world and themselves, the more likely it is that they will live according to their principles, we can show that the expansion of knowledge leads to greater virtue. Again, if we can show that, the more men live according to their principles, the more they have the feeling that life, as they live it, is worth living, we have established a connection between virtue and happiness.

No doubt, if we put these propositions into the singular, there is evidence in plenty that they are not true. We cannot plausibly say that, the greater any man's understanding of the world and himself, the greater the likelihood that he will live up to his own principles; for it may be that his principles are difficult to live up to because his neighbours are less enlightened than he is. Nor can we say that the more any man lives up to his own principles, the stronger his feeling that life, as he lives it, is worth living; for the attempt to live up to his principles, albeit successful, may exhaust him or cause him to be hated by his neighbours. The virtuous are often reduced to despair, and the intelligent often lack the courage to do what they believe to be

[1] Condorcet, *Sketch for an Historical Picture of the Progress of the Human Mind*, Translated by June Barraclough, 1955, p. 128.
[2] Comte, *A Preliminary Discourse*, p. 110.

right. Yet these propositions, though false in the singular, may be true in the plural. It may be true that the more men in general understand the world, the more likely it is that they will have principles which they can, and will in fact, live up to; and it may also be true that the more men in general live up to their principles, the more widespread and the deeper the feeling among them that life, as they live it, is worth living. It may even be true that men will be the more free, the more they are virtuous. This may be so, even though freedom is not defined as the ability to live up to one's principles; even if it is defined as the ability to indulge one's tastes and preferences. For it may be that the more men live up to their principles, the more likely it is that they will have tastes and preferences which are mutually compatible and can be easily and safely indulged. Thus it may be that knowledge, freedom, virtue and happiness are, as Concorcet believed, so connected with one another, that, if we take society as a whole and not in-dividuals separately, the first brings the other three with it.

The four may not increase *pari passu*; it may be that, from time to time, the increase of knowledge reduces freedom or virtue or happiness. And yet it may be that, in the long run, it increases them. This was the faith of Condorcet, and it could, without absurdity, be shared by someone who denied that moral principles can be deduced from the capacities peculiar to man or can be shown to be 'true' in the manner proposed by Comte.[1] No doubt, whoever shares this faith asserts that at least one of these three things (happiness, virtue or freedom) is desirable for its own sake, but this he can do without claiming that the assertion is true in the same sense as the laws of either the mathe-matician or the natural scientist are so.

3. Reason and Understanding

Condorcet says that 'nature has set no term to the perfection of human faculties'. He has in mind, above all, two capacities, which he does not distinguish from one another: reason and understanding, the ability to make inferences and the ability to explain and predict. We 'reason' (so he implies) better than our ancestors did and also have greater understanding than they had; and as we surpass them, so our descendants will surpass us. But we do not walk or run much better than they did. The expansion of knowledge improves our mental abili-ties as it does not our physical ones. Logic improves our reasoning powers, and science improves our ability to explain and predict; but science does not improve our bodily powers to anything like the same extent. The *perfectibility* of man, as Condorcet conceives of it, is prim-

---

[1] Condorcet set great store by freedom, whereas Comte did not; but this dif-ference between them, important in other connections, is not so in this.

arily intellectual and secondarily moral. Man improves his ability to reason, to explain and to predict, and as he does so, strengthens in himself the preferences, tastes and motives which make for happiness.

But, surely, reason is not susceptible of indefinite improvement in the same sense as understanding is. We can never say of any scientific explanation that it is incapable of improvement; we can only say that, in the present state of our knowledge, it is the best available. But we can say of an argument that it is logically impeccable; that, given its premises, its conclusion necessarily follows. Should we venture to say that the ancient Greeks understood both nature and man less well than we do, we need not imply that the ability to reason was less developed in them than in us. It may have been more developed, even though logic has made progress since their time. For, though our modern logicians may offer us better explanations than we can find in Aristotle of what is involved in reasoning, it does not follow that we reason better than Aristotle and his contemporaries did. This is not to deny that the study of logic improves our reasoning powers; it is to say only that both science and logic can make progress without our reasoning powers being improved. No doubt, these powers can be improved; for, though an argument which is impeccable cannot be bettered, it is possible to ensure that we argue better about more and more things. It is also possible to ensure that, given the knowledge available to us, we more often make reasonable assumptions.

Let us distinguish, rather more carefully than Condorcet troubled to do, between *reason* and *understanding*, between knowing how to use certain methods and being able to give explanations acceptable to anyone who knows how those methods should be used. And let us understand by reason, not only the ability to make correct inferences, but also the ability to make reasonable assumptions; that is to say, the ability to make assumptions which are borne out by the 'available and relevant' facts. This, admittedly, is a rough definition of reason, if only because the words *available* and *relevant* call for further elucidation; but it may be good enough for our purpose, which is merely to examine what Condorcet meant by perfectibility and not to discuss matters better left to the logician. Given this sense of reason, an assumption which is perfectly reasonable at one time, in the sense that it is borne out by such relevant and well-authenticated facts as are available, may not be so at another. Again, an assumption which might be reasonable if more were known than is known, if relevant facts not yet available were available, may be unreasonable at the time it is made. Thus, one man might be nearer being right than another and yet be the less reasonable of the two; he might be so either for the reason just given or because, by making faulty inferences from the same assumptions, he reaches a conclusion later seen to be nearer the truth.

Now, in theory, it is quite possible that, by a certain period, man's reasoning powers should have become perfect; that he should have acquired, as fully as he ever can acquire them, certain skills, that he should have mastered certain methods. This need not mean that logic, understood as the study of these methods, has no further progress to make; it may mean only that what further progress it does make does not improve man's ability to reason correctly. Thus, it may be that logicians will offer better explanations of what is involved in the making and testing of hypotheses than any they have offered so far; if they do, they will improve our understanding of scientific method. But this they may do without in any way increasing the competence of scientists. Scientists may be as fully masters of scientific method as ever they will be. This is not to deny that they may improve their experimental techniques; it is only to suggest that their grasp of the essentials of their method (as distinct from the capacity to explain those essentials, which explanation is the business of the logician and not theirs) is already perfect.

Condorcet spoke, not of perfectedness, but of perfectibility. Yet he also spoke as if, in the seventeenth century, owing largely to the work of Bacon, Galileo and Descartes, science had come to maturity; as if, at that time, men had at last grasped the essentials of certain methods of enquiry and explanation which enabled them to distinguish, as never before, knowledge from mere opinion, and therefore also enabled them to measure progress in knowledge. If he was right, then by the seventeenth century reason was already, in one sense, perfected, even though in later centuries logicians improved their understanding of scientific method and scientists improved their techniques. Thus, though Einstein's theory is an improvement on Newton's, each may be perfectly reasonable, given the facts available when it was produced. To say this is to imply that no improvement in Newton's understanding of logic or scientific method would have made it more reasonable for him, given the facts available to him, to put forward other hypotheses. On the other hand, a theory constructed before science came to maturity might be less reasonable than Newton's, even though the maker of it was as gifted as Newton and made as good a use as could be made of the methods available to him. It might be just as intelligent a theory, just as well constructed, just as perfect in its kind, given those methods, and yet it would be less *reasonable* in the sense of the word implied by Condorcet when he took it for granted than an explanation, to be fully reasonable, must be scientific.

Condorcet sometimes spoke as if explanations constructed by the proper method must endure for ever; as if progress in knowledge consisted in a steady increase in the number of ' truths ' acquired once and for all rather than in the repeated supersession of less by more adequate explanations. He took it for granted that science, as it progressed, would not shake the 'truths' discovered by a Newton but would merely add other truths to them. Yet he did not always speak in this way. For example, he said that 'methods which lead us to discoveries can sometimes be exhausted so that science is somehow forced to stop, unless new methods appear to provide genius with a new instrument, or to facilitate the use of those which, it seemed, could no longer be employed without waste of time and energy'.[1] From the context it would appear that what he had in mind here was not a drastic change in men's ideas about what constitutes knowledge and how it is to be tested, not a change of method of the sort that would interest the logician, but the framing of new hypotheses. An hypothesis, when its implications have been worked out, may be said to be 'exhausted', and further progress may require the framing of a new hypothesis, which can be properly tested only if new instruments and techniques are devised. Science has its technology just as production has; and a technology which changes with time, even though the essentials of the scientific method remain the same.

Therefore, if we understand by the improvement of knowledge, not only the extension of a certain type of explanation more and more widely, but also the substitution of more for less adequate explanations of that type, we do not exactly part company with Condorcet; we merely choose, of two positions which he took up in his book, the one which is the less prominent and the less clearly put. Again, in distinguishing between knowledge thus understood, knowledge which can always be improved upon,[2] and reason, which may be impeccable, we make a distinction which Condorcet did not make but which is implicit in some aspects of his theory of progress.

Once men have mastered the methods of enquiry and explanation which are 'rational', they can apply them more and more widely, more and more successfully. One branch of study after another can become scientific. There is therefore a sense in which reason, the successful use of these methods, can make progress indefinitely; a sense in which reason always has further conquests to make and is never in complete and secure possession of men's minds. In one sense reason, unlike understanding, can be perfect; and yet in another it, too, is always imperfect. Men will always adopt some irrational opinions and put forward some irrational explanations, and what they take for science will never be wholly scientific. And by this I mean, not that new theories will take the place of old ones as men become better acquainted with the relevant facts, but that there will always be current among them theories which are not borne out by such facts as are

[1] *Sketch*, p. 162.
[2] The knowledge here in question, the knowledge susceptible of improvement, is not mere acquaintance with facts, a mere knowing that something is or was the case; it is knowledge of causal connections.

available to them. No matter how great men's ability and willingness to construct rational explanations, it will always be possible to make them greater; and this is the sense in which reason is indefinitely 'perfectible'.

4. Knowledge as a Means to Happiness

In the *Sketch* Condorcet considers the triumph of reason only in the sphere of theory, of general explanation. One branch of study after another becomes scientific, and men come to know nature, society and man more and more as they really are. This increase in knowledge is the progress of science. This is how Condorcet sees it, and Comte also. But how exactly, we may ask, is this progress connected with the increase of happiness? Granted that happiness depends, in some way, on understanding, it is by no means clear how it depends on the kind of understanding which is science. No doubt, there are illusions about himself and his situation which can make a man deeply unhappy. If he is to get happiness, he must be rid of these illusions; he must acquire knowledge which he lacks. But this knowledge is not general, it is not science; it is particular, though it may, of course, involve the use of science.

There are several questions which we must put of which neither Condorcet nor Comte took notice. Granted that there are illusions which make for unhappiness, will men be the less a prey to them the greater the progress of science among them? Are there not also illusions which make for happiness and which science dispels? May it not be true that, as science progresses, illusions making for unhappiness actually increase in number and in strength? Even though science, in itself, is the enemy of all illusions, whatever their effect, it may still happen that scientific progress brings along with it changes which make men more inclined than they were to harbour dangerous illusions. Even though science produces the knowledge which could be used to dispel these illusions, the ability and the will to use that knowledge may be lacking.

Knowledge can be a means to happiness in two ways. Where what men aspire to makes them happy if they get it, knowledge can help them get it; and where they aspire to what does not bring happiness, it can explain to them both what will happen if they persist in trying to achieve what they aspire to and how they come to aspire to it. If what they aspire to brings them happiness, then they may need very little knowledge in order to be happy. They may be living in a simple society, and their understanding of the world and themselves may be small, and yet they may be happy if what they aspire to can be achieved and they know what to do in order to achieve it. They may have illusions and still be happy, even though their aspirations and illusions are closely connected. Provided that what they aspire to is attainable and they know how to attain it, they may be happy. Indeed, they may be happy even if part of what they aspire to is not attainable, and that part the most precious; for they may aspire to a life after death, and there may be no such life. But their aspirations for this world, which they think of as a preparation for the next, may be attainable and satisfying. If they lacked the knowledge to attain what they aspire to in this world, they would be less happy; but they would also be less happy if they lost their illusions.

Clearly, the connections between knowledge, illusion and happiness are less simple than Condorcet supposed. Men may have little knowledge and be happy, or they may have much knowledge and be unhappy. They may have strong illusions and be happy, or they may have no illusions and be unhappy. Or the illusions which make for happiness may be more easily dispelled by science than the illusions which make for unhappiness. For the illusions which make for unhappiness may be much less the sort of theological and metaphysical beliefs which science undermines than the misconceptions about himself and his situation which a man can easily retain in a society where the prestige of science is immense. Science could, of course, help him to get rid of these misconceptions if he applied the findings impartially to his own case, but this he might not be able to do, even if he were himself a scientist.

Still, unhappiness, like everything else, has its causes, which can be discovered. As science progresses, society may change in ways which multiply the causes of unhappiness, but science may discover these causes. As society becomes more complicated and its members more sophisticated, it may be that happiness is both more precarious and more within men's reach. Just as civilization, by herding men together in large towns, may expose them to risks of infection unknown in simpler societies, and may yet contrive to keep them in better health, so it may also add greatly to the risks of unhappiness and yet contrive to make them more happy. The happiness which in simple societies cost so little may require a much greater exercise of will and intelligence, a much larger use of knowledge, in sophisticated societies. For worse and for better, the old innocence (such as it was) has been lost. True though it may be that civilization brings great evils with it, we can only hope to cure those evils by using the knowledge which it also brings.

If Condorcet and Comte had said merely this, it would be easy to agree with them. But they said much more; or, if they did not say it, they implied it. They implied that, as knowledge increases, so too does the likelihood that men will use it to remove the causes of unhappiness.

Nearly all believers in progress have been willing to admit that it brings great evils with it. Even Condorcet admitted that, when know-

ledge begins to accumulate, there arise in society bodies of teachers
who pass on from generation to generation what has been acquired,
bodies whose interest it is that the doctrines they teach should not be
challenged. These bodies arise before men have learned how to test
what passes for knowledge in order to see whether or not it is genuine;
and they therefore teach false doctrines as well as true. They perpetuate error and impede the further advancement of knowledge.
Comte was less inclined than Condorcet to speak harshly of these
bodies. Far from deploring the errors and illusions which flourish when
men make their first attempts to explain the world systematically, he
spoke charitably of their purveyors, because it seemed to him that
men, as soon as their faculties begin to develop, need assurance that the
world is a coherent whole and that there is a way of life proper to
creatures of their kind. They need assurance that the world as a whole,
including their place in it, is understood – if not by themselves, then
at least by teachers and guides whom they trust. They need the
assurance long before it can be well grounded, and therefore the bodies
that create it, though purveyors of error and illusion, perform a useful
task. Yet he too believed that these errors and illusions, the effects of
early progress, eventually become obstacles to further progress. He
believed also that, after the inevitable ruin of these illusions, there
must ensue a period of moral and spiritual anarchy until men can get
from science the assurance which the purveyors of illusion had earlier
given them.

Neither Condorcet nor Comte denied that the increase of knowledge
brings evil with it. But they affirmed or implied that this increase, if it
continues (and they were certain it would continue), must eventually
cure these evils and others also. It never occurred to them that the
knowledge needed to cure these evils might be available and yet not
be used. Man, they thought, desires happiness. Therefore, if he is
unhappy and can discover the causes of his unhappiness and how to
remove them, it is highly probable that he will make use of this knowledge for his own good. Unfortunately, this argument is not as convincing as it looks; but, before we examine it more closely, there is
another matter that needs discussing.

5. Condorcet and Depth Psychology

We have seen that, in Condorcet's opinion, vice, which is the chief cause
of unhappiness, springs from error. But Condorcet did not confuse vice
with error. Properly speaking, it is only our motives and the actions
which proceed from them, and not our beliefs, which can be vicious;
and if we call beliefs vicious, it is because they are inspired by or
encourage vicious motives and actions. The doctrine that vice springs

from error asserts no more than this: that men would not acquire vicious motives unless they had mistaken beliefs. But, in order to be vicious, a man need not be mistaken about the situation in which he contemplates action; nor, in order to be virtuous, need he be free of mistakes about it. Condorcet has been called a 'rationalist', and this doctrine, that vice springs from error or ignorance, has been called a 'rationalist fallacy'. It is therefore well to remember that the doctrine is not quite as simple or simple-minded as it is sometimes made out to be.

To see more clearly both the strength and the weakness of Condorcet's doctrine, let us compare it, for a moment, with what is called depth psychology, which seeks to explain how character is built up out of primitive urges or desires (sometimes called the *libido*), as those urges are transformed and the child learns to control them or contrives to ignore them by thrusting them into the 'unconscious'. Though the depth psychologist is not concerned, as Condorcet sometimes was, to pass moral judgements, though he seldom speaks of vice or virtue, he does attempt to explain how men come to have passions harmful to themselves and to others, passions which most people, including Condorcet, would call vicious. These passions, he says, are acquired in early childhood; and though he does not see them as effects of error, of mistaken judgements, he does see them as arising, at least in part, from a failure to understand. A child's character can be deeply affected by what happens to it before it has learned to think; before it is able to pass judgements, mistaken or otherwise. No doubt, when it is able to pass judgements, it will make mistakes; it will believe what is false and these beliefs will give rise to anxieties and other feelings which are harmful. The psychologist does not neglect or belittle the bad effects on a child of false beliefs, especially of false beliefs about its parents' feelings towards it. But he does allow that its character can be damaged before its intelligence is developed enough to enable it to pass judgements, and therefore to make what Condorcet understood by errors; and he also allows that true beliefs may be damaging to it. Not all children who believe that their parents do not love them or may hurt them are mistaken, and the belief is not the less damaging for being true.

And yet, unless I have misunderstood them, these psychologists do imply that the damage to the child's character is due in large part to a failure in understanding. The child has a painful experience about which it may as yet be incapable of passing any judgement, false or true; or it may pass judgements some of which are false and others true, or all of which are true. But, even if they are all true, they express only a partial understanding of what has happened, an understanding which is insufficient to prevent the misdirection of 'psychic energy', the emergence of harmful passions. And these passions, even when they are not themselves effects of false beliefs, may be fertile sources of error. Fear, jealousy, anger and envy, which move men to hurt themselves and one another, are as much producers as they are products of false beliefs. Thus, if we follow these psychologists, we can deny that the passions ordinarily called vicious always, or even generally, spring from error; and yet also insist that they would not arise in us, or would be much weaker, if we had a better understanding of the situations in which they arise. Had we been able, at the time, to see those situations as they would appear to a perceptive, calm and intelligent adult, they would not have affected us as they did. But we were children, and could not see them as they were. Thus it is that, before we are old enough to understand them, we can have experiences which bewilder and hurt us, and are too painful to recall. We come to be so ashamed or frightened of certain of our passions that we refuse to admit, even to ourselves, that we have them, resorting to false beliefs to help us avoid the shame we should feel if we saw ourselves as we really are or were. From a failure to understand due to ignorance and incapacity, to our faculties not yet being sufficiently developed, there arise in us feelings which inhibit our use of those faculties when they are developed. Because of what happened to us when we were still incapable of understanding, when reason was defective in us, there are now things which we dare not understand even though we are intellectually mature, even though we have learned to think. And because we dare not see ourselves as we really are or were, we construct a false picture of ourselves and our situation as a protection against the truth; we feel the need to assert ourselves, to make ourselves felt in the world, in ways which are harmful, or else we are tempted to withdraw from it, refusing to deal with the problems that face us. We are apt to be either a menace or a burden to others and ourselves.

And the depth psychologist also believes, although not quite in the same way as Condorcet, in the corrective and curative use of knowledge. Though most of us never get rid of the harmful passions produced in us by experiences which we could not understand when we had them, we do, to a greater or lesser extent, learn to keep them under control. We come, more or less, to understand our environment and to have coherent and attainable purposes; we acquire a measure of self-discipline and some capacity to play a part in society which affords us self-respect and the respect of others. This is the corrective use of knowledge. But our harmful passions may be so strong that, when they are upon us, we cannot control them; they may make us incapable of self-discipline, incapable of sustaining a respectable social rôle which can satisfy us. Yet even then we are not without a remedy, for we may be able to weaken these passions by reliving in memory the experiences which produced them. In 'reliving' an experience we see it, for the first time, in perspective; we understand it as we could not do at the time we had it. We put it, as it were, in its proper place. But this we cannot do unaided; we need the help of the psychoanalyst who possesses special knowledge and skills. This is a curative use of knowledge.

The depth psychologist has more elaborate and, no doubt, more profound ideas than any eighteenth-century philosopher about how understanding and passion are connected in the human mind and about the kind of self-knowledge which serves to weaken harmful passion. Condorcet seems to have thought that science alone could weaken them; that it was enough for men to understand the working of the mind, as the psychologist strives to understand it, for them to cease being subject to such passions. It seems not to have occurred to him that a man might have a deep knowledge of psychology without being able to apply this knowledge to himself; that he might even be able to pass shrewd, severe and true judgements on himself and still not know that about himself which a man needs to know if he is to exorcize or weaken his harmful passions. His severity might even serve to protect him from this knowledge; he might castigate himself for faults which are trivial (though he pretends to think otherwise) or which in him are small (though he insists that they are not) to turn his mind away from others which he dare not look at. He might even in some moods, when he can speak of himself as he would of another man, bring himself to admit that he has certain passions, and yet be unable to recognize them when they are actually upon him or have moved him to action.

There is a great deal in recent psychology unthought of or only lightly touched upon by Condorcet. Yet this psychology does suggest that our harmful passions (those which Condorcet would call *vicious*) are often produced in us by something closely akin to error, by a failure to understand; and it does agree with Condorcet that knowledge can cure us of these passions, or at least can greatly weaken them in us. But, we may ask, why should this be so? Why should the light of understanding take life or strength from some of our passions and not from others? Why should our coming to understand what has made us jealous, envious or cruel weaken jealousy, envy or cruelty in us when our coming to understand what has made us affectionate or generous does not weaken our love or generosity? Presumably, because we are social as well as rational creatures, creatures whose happiness depends upon being able to inspire and to feel affection and respect. We aspire to a happiness whose character is determined, not merely by our desires, but by how we see ourselves and the world. To be happy is to be satisfied with a way of life, which only a rational creature can be: that is to say, a creature capable of systematic thought, and therefore of seeing itself as having a life to live. If that creature is also social, its happiness will depend upon how it feels towards others and itself, and how others feel towards it. If, given its capacities and environment, it is to be happy, some of these feelings (which are the feelings of a being that thinks) must be strong and others weak. Therefore such creatures, to be securely happy, need to know more than what to do to satisfy their actual desires; they must, if their desires stand in the way of their happiness, change themselves, which they cannot do effectively unless they know what they are and how they come to be as they are.

The depth psychologist differs conspicuously from Condorcet; he does not treat error or false belief as the sole, or even the prime, cause of harmful feelings, and he sees in these feelings a source of false beliefs peculiarly difficult to eradicate; he has a subtler understanding of what is involved in self-knowledge and considers the curative use of only that one kind of knowledge. Whereas Condorcet can hardly be said to consider self-knowledge at all, for he does not distinguish it from the science of psychology. By man's knowledge of himself he means only scientific knowledge, the apprehension of general propositions about man; he does not mean a particular man's seeing himself as he is or was. He therefore has no conception of the curative use of a self-knowledge which is not psychology, though psychology may be a means to it. The false beliefs which he has in mind when he speaks of the errors from which spring the vices are about the world or society or human nature; they are not false beliefs about unique individuals and particular situations. They are therefore beliefs which are dissipated by the mere dissemination of scientific knowledge. Condorcet does not even seriously enquire whether it is more difficult or more important to dissipate some kinds of error than others. There are many and large differences between Condorcet and the psychologists I speak of, between the rationalists of the century before last and the men of our day who are supposed to have shown how small a part reason plays in human behaviour; and, no doubt, if we follow Condorcet rather than these men, we are apt to cherish much larger hopes of moral improvement and increasing happiness resulting from the progress of science. Nevertheless, there are also important similarities, which we ought to bear in mind, if only to preserve ourselves from some of the criticisms still levelled at the 'shallow' rationalism of the eighteenth century.

Condorcet has almost nothing to say about how the growth and dissemination of knowledge weaken the vicious passions and increase happiness. Believing that vice, which makes for unhappiness, is rooted in error, he takes it for granted that scientific progress, since it dissipates error, strikes at the root of unhappiness. He is therefore much more concerned to show how science progresses and why it is likely to do so indefinitely than to explain how it weakens vice and makes for happiness. But Comte has more to say.

Hitherto, Comte tells us, science has confined itself largely to explaining the physical world; the sciences which have made spectacular progress have been the 'natural' sciences. But already the scientific or positive spirit, the search for uniformities of behaviour rather than teleological and theological explanations, is prominent in the study of man and society. When the positive spirit has triumphed in all branches of study, when what is taken for authentic knowledge (other than mere acquaintance with particular facts) consists only of abstract principles of reasoning and calculation (logic and mathematics) and of empirical laws supported by observation and experiment, then men will understand for the first time what manner of beings they are and the world in which they live. They will know how to organize their lives for happiness; and with the knowledge there will come the will to use it. In a society where the positive spirit prevails, though no man possesses all the knowledge useful to mankind, most men are willing to defer to those whose knowledge is greater than their own. That is to say, where the knowledge needed for happiness is available, there are men able and willing to use it to that end, while those who lack this ability recognize it in those that have it and look for guidance from them.

This, I admit, is not quite what Comte says, but it does, I think, put into words what he implies. For he takes two things for granted: that, when the study of man and society has become positive or scientific, when it has produced 'authentic' knowledge, that knowledge will be used for the common good; and that the knowledge will not be possessed by all men but by an élite to whom other men will defer. And, presumably, this knowledge will not be possessed entire by every member of the élite; it will be knowledge which they have between them. Therefore, there will be deference to superior knowledge both within the élite and from the rest of the community towards the élite. But Comte goes further even than this; he speaks of a need for a spiritual authority, for an organized body to do for the society of the future what the Church attempted in the past, before science began to undermine theology. This body must have all knowledge for its province, making a system of it; its pronouncements must be authoritative. It must be the overseer of society. And Comte does not merely proclaim the need for this spiritual authority; he implies that, as knowledge increases, the need will be felt and met. The progress of science, of positive knowledge, will so affect men that there will arise among them the spiritual authority required to ensure that knowledge is used for their good.

6. The Uses of Science, Natural and Social

Knowledge can be used to dissipate harmful passions in two ways: it can be used to create a social environment unpropitious to these passions, and it can be used to increase the individual's self-control and self-knowledge. For convenience sake, let us call the first use *indirect* and the second *direct*. The second may be either *education* or *therapy*: it may consist in teaching the individual to behave well, or it may consist in improving his physical and mental health. Both Condorcet and Comte had chiefly in mind the indirect use and the direct use which is education. Of therapy, as the psychiatrist now understands it, they, of course, knew nothing. They believed that men, as their knowledge grew, would use that knowledge to create a social order making for virtue and happiness and would so educate the young that they would accept this order. Though this belief was expressed more elaborately and explicitly by Comte than by Condorcet, it was common to them both.

Condorcet and Comte also believed (though this time the belief was stronger in Condorcet than in Comte) that, to cure men of error and prejudice, little more is needed than to bring the truth to their notice. If the truth is brought to them and they do not accept it, this is because, through indolence or inattention or defective intelligence, they have failed to understand it. That a man should resist the truth and fear it, that he should argue himself into rejecting it, even when he has intelligence enough to understand it; that he should attend to it as to an enemy, using his reason to persuade himself that it is not true, even against the weight of the evidence: that he should do this was a possibility that Condorcet never took into account. He admitted that truth might be impeded because some men had an interest that it should be; but he believed that these very men, if they were educated and intelligent, could not attend to the truth and reject it *in foro interno*. If, then, having attended to it, they denied it, they must be impostors. Comte saw rather more deeply than Condorcet into the social causes of false beliefs, and was more willing to allow that these beliefs had been useful while the truth was still undiscovered; but he also was too apt to believe that the soundest arguments convince. The psychological causes of irrational beliefs, of beliefs inconsistent with one another or held against the weight of evidence easily accessible, were less understood (or, at least, less discussed) in their day than they are now.[1]

---

[1] Long before their time, Pascal was aware how strong men's motives might be for fearing the truth and resisting it. He was aware, too, that the ability to reason and irrationality are closely connected in more than the obvious sense that only creatures capable of reasoning are capable of false reasoning. He was aware that truth might be unbearable to such a creature because, being able to think conceptually, it could be an object of thought to itself, and therefore a victim of ambitions and fears unknown to creatures lacking that ability. He understood, as Condorcet and Comte never did, the need for self-deception peculiar to the mind capable of reasoning.

But the optimism of Condorcet and Comte is to be discounted for other reasons than their exaggerating the persuasive power of sound argument. They did not see that the increase of knowledge and the technical progress resulting from it might have social consequences which would prevent men so using their knowledge as to increase happiness. So far, I have attended more to Condorcet than to Comte, but now, if I am to make this point clear, I must attend more to Comte.

Comte emphasized, more strongly even than Condorcet, that in the earlier stages of 'progress' men's understanding of the physical world grows much more rapidly than their understanding of themselves and society. With the increase of knowledge, society grows more elaborate, but the knowledge whose use makes society more elaborate does not enlarge men's understanding of the social order or their power to adapt it to meet their needs. Physics, chemistry and biology make possible the use of methods of production, war and coercion which convert small and simple societies into large ones, but add nothing to men's understanding of themselves and their social environment. It is not until much later that men address themselves to the scientific study of the human mind and social institutions. They want, no doubt, to increase their power over nature the better to satisfy their needs, but they soon acquire a curiosity about the world which moves them to push their enquiries much further than is needed to solve their practical problems. Hence the bold theories, theological and metaphysical, which often change profoundly men's conception of the world without deeply affecting their material way of life. As rational creatures who need to feel that they are living in a tidy and intelligible world, they produce these vast intellectual systems into which they pour such little genuine knowledge as they possess. They create in themselves the illusion that they understand all aspects of reality long before they come anywhere near doing so. Their curiosity about themselves and society and their need to explain them systematically arise as early as their curiosity about the external world. But the ability to explain them *scientifically* comes to them last of all. Precise observation, measurement and experiment are easier in the natural sciences than in psychology and the study of social institutions. Therefore the knowledge which increases men's power over external nature comes to them earlier than the knowledge which increases their power over themselves.

There is more to it than just this. For the use of the first kind of knowledge changes men and their social environment; and, since they still lack the second kind (though believing they have it), it changes them in ways which they do not understand. When society is stable or changes slowly, men need not understand it to be on good terms with themselves and their neighbours. It is enough for them to follow ancestral ways, to do what is expected of them, and to accept the philosophy whose function is to assure them that there is a scheme of things in which they are important. But when society is changing fast, largely as the result of the use of the first kind of knowledge, this type of philosophy can no longer give men the assurance it once gave. Therefore, they are at sea until the study of man and society has also become scientific, until they have acquired the second kind of knowledge. They can then discover what are the conditions of happiness for creatures like themselves, and can set about creating those conditions.

Thus Comte, while he agreed with Condorcet that some sciences necessarily appear long before others, had a much sharper sense that this might be the cause of great suffering. Science deprives men of a faith they can live by long before it provides anything fit to take its place, and in the meantime men are lost and unhappy. The complaint so often heard today that some kinds of knowledge can greatly outrun others, to the detriment of mankind, was one with which Comte, like his one-time mentor Saint-Simon, would certainly have sympathized. Yet he took it for granted that the increase of knowledge must eventually remove whatever evils it has brought with it. The knowledge that comes first without the knowledge that comes after may have consequences that are harmful, but the later knowledge will come in its turn and whatever harm has been done will be undone. If we grant that men desire happiness and can discover its conditions, social and psychological, must we not admit that, having discovered them, they will create them? It seemed obvious to Comte that we must.

7. Knowledge and the Opportunity to Use It

It seemed obvious to him, perhaps, because he did what we all do for convenience sake, because he spoke of mankind as if they were one man; as if all the knowledge acquired by mankind were the possession of one possessor. If a man desires happiness and knows what to do to obtain it, will he not use that knowledge to get what he wants? If it is objected that he may suffer from defects which stand in the way of his using it, the answer is that, *ex hypothesi*, he also knows how to get rid of the defects, to cure himself. Provided that the desire for happiness is not destroyed or greatly weakened in the very process of acquiring the knowledge needed to satisfy it, how can it be doubted that the knowledge, once acquired, will be used?

But this argument is plausible only if it refers to one man having all the knowledge he needs to ensure his own happiness. Even if we grant that a man who strongly desires happiness and knows how to get it will almost certainly use that knowledge to get what he wants, it does not follow that a large number of men, who *between them* have that knowledge, will so use it. They may or they may not. All that needs to be known to make men happy may be known by some member or other of a community, all of whose members strongly desire happiness, and yet there may be little chance of this knowledge being put to good use. Clearly, there is a great difference between two communities, of which one is so organized that the knowledge available inside it is likely to be put to good use and the other is not; and yet the knowledge of how a community should be organized to make the best use of what knowledge is available inside it might be as great and as widespread in the second community as in the first. The increase of knowledge may have profound effects on society without ensuring that it is so organized that good use is made of the knowledge available inside it. Have any people in our time been more learned than the Germans? Has their superiority been less marked in psychology and the social studies than in the natural sciences? What people have had a greater respect for learning? The knowledge useful to the social reformer and the educator has been as abundant and as widespread among them as among any other people. Yet the Germans have never been more dangerous to themselves and their neighbours than during this period of their intellectual pre-eminence.

The increase of knowledge makes possible technical changes which transform the economy and the social structure. Men must, if they are to earn their livings and achieve their ambitions, acquire skills and knowledge unnecessary to their ancestors; they must become literate and learn a great deal from books. There must be, in a complicated industrial society, a wide and varied dissemination of knowledge. Yet the transformation of society may strengthen harmful passions or otherwise create conditions making it unlikely that knowledge will be used for the common good, though it is used abundantly to attain a much greater variety of goals than are known to simple and illiterate communities. The kind of knowledge which to Comte seemed the most valuable of all, the understanding of man and society, the knowledge needed for moral progress (as he conceived of it), for individual happiness and social harmony, may be available, and yet the persons who have it may have neither power nor influence. There may be theoretical knowledge and practical ability in plenty, and yet the two may seldom come together for the common good.

No doubt, in every technically advanced society, knowledge and skill are held in high esteem. Men in high positions are expected, much more than in simpler societies, to be efficient, and efficiency depends on knowledge. Not only children, but adults too, spend long hours acquiring knowledge and skill. And this knowledge and skill are doubtless, in the economist's sense, useful, not only to their possessors but to others as well. For those who acquire them perform services which are marketable, which have a price; and their having a price is a mark of their utility. There is an effective demand for these services; there are persons willing and able to pay for them. But if, like Condorcet or Comte, we have in mind utility in a sense different from the economist's, we cannot conclude that whatever is marketable is useful, let alone that its price is a measure of its utility. Those who attain the highest positions, who make the most successful careers, who acquire the largest shares of power and influence, may owe what they get to proved competence, and not to birth or patronage, and their competence may be rare, requiring a degree of knowledge and skill to which few can aspire, no matter how great their opportunities. But this knowledge and skill, though useful for certain purposes, may not be used for the purposes which, in the eyes of a Condorcet or a Comte, are the most important. The politician, the business man, the civil servant, or the teacher, to rise to the top of his profession, may need rare abilities useful to his party or his business or his profession, or even his country; but his having these abilities is no warrant that he has others needed for the common good.

In short, as society accumulates the products of men's muscles and their brains, it may come to have the knowledge and skill required for moral progress, for movement towards some desirable condition of man and society, as well as the knowledge and skill required for the making of successful careers and the acquisition of power; but, unless the makers of successful careers and the acquirers of power also have the first kind of knowledge and skill, or are able and willing to make use of those who do have them, society will make no progress though it has the means to do so. Knowledge, power and will are closely related to one another, and related in many ways, both in the individual and in society. Unfortunately, they are not so related that we can assume that, as knowledge accumulates, it will be so distributed among men that it comes to those who have the power and the will to use it for the common good. But this is precisely the assumption tacitly made by Condorcet and by Comte, as by so many other believers in progress.

The uses to which men put their knowledge often have harmful consequences which they do not foresee, and which it takes time for them to understand and to learn to avoid. Therefore, it can easily happen that, before they have understood them and discovered remedies, such passions have been aroused that it is unlikely that those who know the remedies will be in a position to apply them. For example, it can easily happen that, as a country grows rapidly industrial, the crowding of people together in enormous towns, the great mobility of labour, mass unemployment, the weakening of family ties, and other causes, will generate such passions that power and influence come easily to the fanatical or the unscrupulous. The 'masses' subject to these passions are not more ignorant or more mistaken than their ancestors. On the contrary, they may well have a larger understanding as well as a greater variety of skills. And yet it is because they have these passions and because their understanding is defective that they can be made use of by the fanatical and the unscrupulous. It requires greater understanding than either they or their leaders possess to find a remedy for their condition. Their ancestors, living in a simpler society and relying on tradition, could make do with less understanding, but *they* need more. Thus, we may say of them that they are victims of the use of one kind of knowledge who can be saved only by the use of another kind. But the evils which knowledge brings may grow faster than the knowledge required for their remedy, or may prevent the effective use of that knowledge when it comes.

Condorcet valued both freedom and happiness, as liberals still do in the West. He even believed that the two go together: not that any man will be the happier the freer he is, no matter what the condition of other men, but that men generally will be the happier the freer they are. The more resolutely men claim for themselves and respect in others the rights of man, the happier they will be; and the greater their knowledge, the greater their attachment to these rights and their capacity to realize them. Condorcet was so much struck by the idea (which is partly true, though it needs to be qualified) that the harmful passions are rooted in error and ignorance, that he failed to notice that the use of knowledge can create conditions which encourage ambitions destructive of freedom and happiness, even where the knowledge needed to remedy those conditions is not lacking. Not lacking but unlikely to be used.

Comte valued happiness more than freedom, and his ideal was a society ruled by an educated and public-spirited élite. He saw that the prestige of science had increased and was increasing, and that the study of man and society was beginning to rely, as never before, on observation. The purveyors of fantasy were losing ground to the discoverers and disseminators of authentic knowledge. He saw, too, that the rôle of the managers, the administrators, the directors of effort on a large scale, was greater than it had ever been, and that the activities of man in society were both more diverse and more tightly connected. It was easier than it had been for a group of men working closely together to control a vast community. Never before had there been such opportunities for the enterprising and competent few. No doubt, Comte was right; but the few most likely to take those opportunities were perhaps not the sort of élite he had in mind.

Neither Condorcet nor Comte saw the real point of Rousseau's indictment of modern society: that the increase of knowledge has social consequences which strengthen the harmful passions. This might be true even though the men best able to discover this knowledge or to master it were less a prey than others to these passions. The scientists and inventors whose achievements make possible a great expansion of trade and industry, the philosophers, artists and poets who help to form men's tastes and their values, might be morally, as well as intellectually, among the best of men, and yet society be the worse for what they do. Sometimes Rousseau spoke as if the corrupters of society, the scientists and artists whose achievements seem so admirable to believers in progress, were themselves the worst corrupted; but he need not have done so, and in his more sober moments did not do so. For example, in the *Letter to d'Alembert* he condemned the theatre without condemning the men who wrote for it or belittling their talents.

Rousseau would probably not have denied that it was largely to the enlightenment, which believers in progress valued so highly, that he owed his own insight into the social evils of his day. He might even have agreed, since he believed that the arts and sciences corrupt society, that only a corrupt society produces the knowledge needed to cure its ills. For he believed himself to possess some part of that knowledge; he did not confine himself to making a diagnosis, but also suggested remedies, though without much hope that they would be taken. What he despaired of was not so much men's acquiring the knowledge to cure social and moral ills as their making use of it for that purpose. *Si jeunesse savait, si vieillesse pouvait!* We have only to amend this to read, *Si innocence savait, si corruption pouvait!* to get the gist of Rousseau's pessimism.

I would not say that his pessimism is better founded than the optimism of Condorcet or Comte. But at least it is not worse founded. And just as we can say of them that their faith in knowledge was not so simple-minded as some have taken it to be, so we can say of him that his attack upon it was not so perverse. Both he in his fears and they in their hopes were extravagant; they all three spoke as if they knew much more about the effects of knowledge than in fact they knew.

It is more reasonable, perhaps, to follow neither him nor them, but to say, in the spirit of Pascal: we blame equally those who are sure of the coming of what they think desirable, and those who despair of it, and the indifferent, and approve only those who hope and who strive for what they hope.

INDEX

INDEX

Abbé de St. Pierre, 122, 433-4
Perpetual Peace, 122
Absolute Freedom, 168-70, 192-5
Absolute Idea, 134-7, 140, 142
Absolute Monarchy, 16, 22, 309, 367
Absolute Spirit, 137
Absolutism, 15-17, 23
Acton, H. B.,
on Marx's theory of social change, 273-280, 320
The Illusion of the Epoch, 273, 279n
Address to the Communist League, by K. Marx, 393, 394, 396, 399n
Administration (*v.* Government), 48-50, 53-4, 72, 81, 373, 375-6, 379, 382, 385
Africa, 303, 359, 361n
Alienation and early socialists, 38-40
in Hegel, 159, 165, 167, 184-5, 197
in Marxism, 322n, 334-43, 375-8, 404-7
Althusius, ix
Anabaptists, 119
Analysis of the Human Mind, by James Mill, 11
Anarchism, 64, 374, 383
Anti-Dühring, by F. Engels, 352, 357
Antigone, 161-2, 170
Appeal of One Half of the Human Race, Women, etc., by Wm. Thompson, 62
Aristocracy, 24, 386
Aristotle, xii, xvii, xxi, 23, 170
on social change, 409-10, 425, 440
Army, 370
Asia, 303, 361n
Athens, 355
Austin, John, 21
Austria, 248

Bacon, Francis, 415, 433-4, 441
Balkans, 341
Bastiat, C. L., 37-8
Bazard, A., 76-8, 83
Exposition of the Doctrine of Saint-Simon, 76
Beethoven, Ludwig van, 196

Bentham, Jeremy,
Fragment on Government, xii, 2, 4n, 15, 17n, 20n, 21, 25
Introduction to the Principles of Morals and Legislation, 4n
Springs of Action, 2
The Theory of Legislation, 8
and Hegel, 220-1, 245-6, 250-1, 266
and Hobbes, 14-21
and Hume, 5-6, 15-16, 35
and Montesquieu, 15-18, 20-1, 35
his theory of morals, xvii, 1-15
on sovereignty, 1, 15-21, 23, 26
on democracy, 1, 21-36, 51
on government: its form, 19-22, 26; its usefulness, 25, 27-8, 32-4; its responsibility, 29-34
on the greatest happiness principle, 1-3, 7-12, 17, 22, 26, 33, 36, 96, 99-100
on equality, 21-8, 99-100
on pleasure, 2-5, 7-12, 32
on rights and duties, xii, 1-7
on sanctions, 2-3, 17, 25-6
his belief in progress, 31, 34, 36, 39, 57
Berlin, Sir I., 156n, 207n
Blanc, Louis, 51, 84-5, 88, 93-4
Blanquists, 93
Bober, M.,
on Marx's theory of change, 273-7, 294, 300
Karl Marx's Interpretation of History, 273
Bodin, Jean, xi, 256
Bolsheviks, 92, 385, 396, 397-402
Bonald, 113
Bonaparte family, 368-9, 371-2.
Louis, 371-2
See also Napoleon
Bonapartism, 64
Bouglé, C., 51
La Sociologie de Proudhon, 51n
Bourbons, 368-9
Bourgeoisie, 92, 126-7, 275n, 298-300, 305-11, 367-8

Bourgeoisie—*cont.*
petite, 64, 92, 126-7
Bourgeois government, 382, 398
Bourgeois revolution, 393-4
Bray, 93
Brotherhood, early socialists on, 118-20
Bureaucracy, 50, 53, 55n, 85, 93, 128,
248, 371
Burke, Edmund, x, xi, 15, 24, 55n, 91,
164, 194, 212-13, 258, 264, 433
Bury, J. B., 415-21, 431-2
The Idea of Progress, 415, 417n, 431n

Cabet, E., 93-4
Calvinism, 210-11
Capital, by K. Marx, 282, 290, 300, 388
Capitalism
and the early socialists, 97-9, 101, 107
rise of, according to Marx, 276-7, 282,
369, 305, 308-9, 311
decay of, according to Marx, 309, 319,
394-5
Capitalists:
a dominant class, 293, 298, 299, 300,
303-5
interests of: 311, 314, 320, 353-4, 375
Catéchisme des Industriels, by A. Comte,
68n, 78, 83
Categories, Hegel on the, 134, 140-6
Catholic Church, 111, 116, 118n
Catholicism, 70, 361
and Protestantism, 203, 208-12
Change, social
Hegel on necessity of: 179-87, 215,
216-17, 222, 419n, 421
Hegel's account of, in *Phenomenology*,
146-202; *in Philosophy of History*,
202-15; *in Philosophy of Right*,
216-68
Change, social
Marx on basis of, 273, 274-93
Marx on process of, 301-5, 319-20, 336,
339, 388-93, 395, 398-9, 402
Saint-Simon on, 42, 68-83, 126
laws of, 42, 71, 73, 77, 418-20, 422-4,
426, 433
See also progress
Christ, 58, 110-11, 115-19, 148-9
Christianity, 22-4, 38, 41, 68, 110-11,
115-19, 121, 160, 161, 163, 167, 174,
177-9, 181, 204, 207, 303, 334, 341-2,
347, 363, 414
Church, 69-70, 76-7, 80-1, 118-19, 304,
336, 341, 370, 414, 420, 450
and State, 210-11, 259

Civil society, 227, 231-5, 240-50, 251,
265-6
Class, 67, 82-4, 90, 246-8, 293-322
conflict, 83, 84, 86, 94, 126, 128, 156,
289-300, 301-7, 333, 350
consciousness, 67, 307-10, 338, 349
exploitation, 54, 63, 97n, 99, 192, 287,
295, 297, 305, 311, 314, 318-22, 354-7,
363-9, 371, 393
inequality, 294-8, 358, 361, 364, 377
interests, 87-8, 122, 201, 289, 299, 301,
303-9, 311-22, 354, 370-2
ideology, 325-33, 337-8, 345-9, 360-1
and the State, 45, 54, 351-73
Classical economists, 38, 56, 67, 86, 95-8,
235, 247-8, 272, 418
Classless society, 288, 293, 295, 319, 338,
341, 343, 351, 353-5, 362, 364, 369,
372, 378-83, 386-7, 398, 403
Class Struggles in France, by K. Marx,
367
Cobbett, William, 85
Code de la Nature, by Morelly, 60
Communes, 69-71, 82
Commune of 1871, Paris, 381-3, 397-8
Communist Manifesto, by K. Marx and
F. Engels, 275n, 308, 357
Communist Party, 77, 305, 308
See also Bolsheviks
Comte, Auguste
Catéchisme des Industriels, 68n, 78, 83
Politique Positive, 68n
*Preliminary Discourse on the Positive
Spirit*, 437n, 438n
organic view of society, 78, 79, 81, 83
theory of change, 418, 419, 429, 431-2
deterministic outlook, 420-5
on knowledge and happiness, 436-9,
443-5, 449-57
Concrete universal, 129-31, 136, 142-6,
177, 179
Condorcet, A. N. de
*Sketch for an Historical Picture of
the Human Mind*, 336, 417, 422,
438n, 442n, 443
theory of change, 120, 202, 417-25
knowledge and process, 39, 112-13,
434-57
religion, 112-13, 121n, 336, 338-9,
435
Conscience, 199, 209, 228, 230-2, 238-41,
267
Consciousness, 151, 152, 159
base and noble, 165-7
class-, 67, 307-10, 338, 349

consciousness—*cont.*
  false, 326-31, 335, 339, 344
  self-, 135-9, 145-54, 184-6, 188-9, 195,
    197-8, 200, 284, 323, 334, 403, 451
  servile and lordly, 191
  social, 274, 277, 283, 290, 323, 350
  virtuous, 164-5
  unhappy, 159-61, 183, 185-6, 204
Consent, xi, 13, 21, 22, 28
Considérant, Victor, 93
Contract, 236, 243-4, 251, 353
Contradiction, Hegel on, 228-31
Copernicus, Nicolas, xiii, 70
Cornwallis, Charles, 310
Covenant, ix
Creon, 161-2
Crime, 236-7, 374-5, 377
Critique of Political Economy, by K.
  Marx, 42n, 274, 290, 325
Croce, Benedetto, 132
Custom, 19, 24, 161, 162, 246, 281, 283,
  286-90, 295, 351, 430

Dante, 262
Darwin, Charles, xii, 424
Darwinism, 424-5
De Cive, by Hobbes, xi
Definition, xi, 103
  persuasive, 6-7
Democracy
  Bentham on, 1, 21-36
  the early socialists on, 48-9, 51, 53n,
    56, 62, 74, 128
  Hegel on, 194, 211-13, 248, 256-8,
    260, 263-4
  Marx on, 347, 380, 385-6
  representative, 27-8, 34-5
Descartes, Rene, 416, 432, 441
Despotism, 20, 22
Determinism
  economic, 82, 269, 270, 276, 289, 427,
    428n
  and freedom, 410-14, 425-9, 439, 456
  cf. social evolution
Dialectic, 134-7, 141-2, 155, 188, 227,
  229, 231, 235, 237, 249, 255
Diderot, Denis, 121n, 166
  Le Neveu de Rameau, 166
Discipline
  self-, 155
  social, 108-9, 113
*Discourse on the Origins of Inequality
  Among Men*, by Rousseau, 422
Division of labour, 52, 56, 59, 105, 246-7,
  278, 352-8, 378

Durkheim, Emile, 59-60, 83, 102n, 115
  Le Socialisme, 102n, 115n
Duty
  Bentham on, 1-6, 17
  Hegel on, 170-1

Early socialists, *see* socialism
Economics, 15, 29, 51, 67, 272-4, 333,
  379
Economic determinism, 82, 269-70, 276,
  289, 427, 428n
Economic structure, 274-7, 281
Economists, classical, 38, 56, 67, 86,
  95-8, 235, 247-8, 272, 418
Education, 28
Egoism, 7, 9-11, 115, 245
*Eighteenth Brumaire of Louis Bona-
  parte*, by K. Marx, 307, 367, 371
Einstein, A., 441
Elements of Political Economy, by
  James Mill, 97
Emile, by J.-J. Rousseau, 109
*Encyclopædia of the Philosophical
  Sciences*, by G. Hegel, 175
Encyclopædists, 24, 38, 57, 59, 61, 119
Enfantin, 61, 65
  Oeuvres de Saint-Simon et d'Enfantin,
    71n, 72n, 73n, 78n
Engels, F., 44, 53, 55, 82, 87-8, 92-3, 234
  Anti-Dühring, 352, 357
  *Origins of the Family, Private Prop-
    erty and the State*, 352, 357, 366
  and K. Marx,
    German Ideology, 275n, 326, 327n,
      330n, 360n
    Communist Manifesto, 275n, 308,
      357
  Political theory of Marx and Engels,
    See Marxism
England, 24, 25, 58, 59, 84-5, 90, 94-5,
  111, 208, 209, 310, 377, 385, 388-9,
  393-5, 400
  English Civil War, 303
  English Socialists, 37, 44, 57, 67, 93,
    118
English Utilitarians, by J. Plamenatz,
  1
Enlightenment, 168
Epicureans, 411
Equality, 21-2, 25, 27-8, 156, 165, 191,
  429
Equality
  natural, 21-4
  of opportunity, 119-20
  and the early socialists, 37, 40-1, 46-7,

Equality—cont.
    49, 53-9, 61, 65, 73-4, 85, 90, 96, 99-
    101, 107, 119-20, 125-8
    and Marx, 288, 294-8, 336, 358, 365,
    378, 382, 383, 401
Essay on Government, by James Mill,
    27, 62
Essence of Christianity, by Ludwig
    Feuerbach, 333
Estates, 256-9
Etudes Hégéliennes, by F. Grégoire, 243
Evolution, 424-5
    social, 301-5, 319-20, 336, 339, 388-93,
    395, 398-9, 402
    See change, progress
Exploitation, 54, 63, 97n, 99, 192, 287,
    295, 297, 305, 311, 314, 318-22, 342,
    354, 356-7, 363-9, 371, 393
Exposition of the Doctrine of Saint-
    Simon, by Bazard, 76

Family, 63-5, 109-10, 285, 352-3, 355, 358
    Hegel on, 162, 188-9, 201, 227, 231-5,
    240-50, 265-6
Fascism, 371-2
Fascist Party, 372
Felicific calculus, 11-12
Feminism, 61-6
Feudalism
    early socialists on: 68-70, 73-4, 81n,
    82, 121-3
    Marx on: 276, 282, 300-9, 347, 353-4,
    358, 381-2
Feuerbach, Ludwig
    Essence of Christianity, 333
    and Marxist view of religion, 201, 333-
    344
First and Second Empires, 367-8
Fleming, Sir Alexander, 291
Fontenelle, Bernard de, 418
Force, the basis of the State, 45-54, 80,
    93, 113
    and Marx, 373-6, 380, 382
Foundation and superstructure
    Marx on, 273-293, 301, 323-5, 345
    and production, 274-6, 279-83, 290,
    300-1
    reason for the distinction, 277-9, 283-
    90
Fourier, 41, 47, 58, 59, 62, 65, 93, 94, 97,
    111
    Théorie de l'Unité Universelle, 103n
    ideal society of, 50, 87, 92, 103-10
    theory of change, 42, 43, 61n, 83n, 91,
    92

Fourth Republic, 385n
Fragment on Government, by Jeremy
    Bentham, 2, 4n, 15, 17, 20n, 21, 25
France, 24, 25, 50, 59, 74, 82, 84, 94-5,
    108, 193, 207-9, 367-8, 372, 381-4,
    388-9, 393-5, 400, 418
French Monarchy, 303-6, 367, 394
French Revolution, 24, 49, 66, 71, 73,
    81, 91, 111, 119, 120, 166, 168, 169,
    262, 264, 303, 306, 310, 368, 393
French Socialists, 37, 44, 57, 67, 93,
    111, 118-20
Freedom
    Bentham on, 18-22, 27, 33-4
    Early socialists on, 37, 47-8, 57-9, 73-4,
    90, 108, 125, 127-8
    Hegel on, 154, 157-63, 168-72, 183-4,
    190-6, 200, 205-27, 230-2, 240, 242,
    244, 253-4, 262-4, 267-8
    Marx on, 294, 348, 379, 392, 406-7
    and law, 47-8, 200, 219, 222-3, 225-6,
    240, 243, 263
    and morality, 217-19, 221-2, 228-32,
    235, 238, 240-1, 263-4
    of thought and speech, 70-1, 259, 263
    and progress, 410-12, 414-15
Freud, Sigmund, 186

Galileo, 70, 416, 427, 437, 441
General Will, 47, 168, 211, 258
Genèse et Structure de la Phénomeno-
    logie de l'Esprit de Hegel, by Jean
    Hyppolite, 154, 166n, 168n, 169n
German Ideology, by K. Marx and F.
    Engels, 275n, 326, 327n, 330n, 360n
German Marxism and Russian Com-
    munism, by J. Plamenatz, 279n,
    280n, 288n
Germans, 196, 203-4, 207-9, 214-15, 454
Germany, 372, 381, 388, 393-4
God, xvi, 3, 13, 62, 66n, 80, 81, 103, 111,
    113, 115, 117, 119-20, 136, 159-61,
    167, 168, 171, 177, 185, 199-200, 210-
    211, 243, 292, 328, 330, 332-4, 337,
    363, 410, 414, 433
Goethe, J. W., 66n, 196, 262
Government, 53, 191, 249, 250, 256-7,
    328, 352, 356, 371, 373, 382
    Bentham on form of, 19-22, 26
    on responsibility of, 29-34
    on usefulness of, 25, 27-8, 32-4
    Early socialists on end of, 48-9, 52-3,
    72
    on form of, 71n, 81
    on Government and war, 122-4

Government—cont.
  Marx on forms of, 274, 278, 281, 288, 302, 323, 368
  on bourgeois, 382, 398
  and proletarian, 381-3
  See also State
Grand National Consolidated Trades Union, 89
Greatest happiness principle, 1-3, 7-12, 17, 22, 26, 33, 36, 96
  an alternative form of, 12, 36
Greece, 121, 148, 157, 161, 163, 411
Greeks, 174, 176-7, 181, 190, 199, 202, 204, 208, 210, 214-15, 239, 291, 412-416, 440
Grégoire, F., 243
  Etudes Hégéliennes, 243
Grotius, Hugo, ix

Happiness, 56-9, 104, 184, 201, 245, 250, 251
  Bentham on, 5-6, 8, 14, 25, 27, 30-2
  and increased knowledge, 410-14, 416-417, 423, 434, 438, 443-57
  and psychology, 445-51
Harmonism, 43
Harmony, 108, 110
Hedonism, 11, 413
Hegel, G. W. F., xi, xiv-xix
  Logic, 140, 141
  Encyclopædia, 175
  Phenomenology of Spirit, 146-51, 154n, 156n, 158, 160, 166, 168n, 169, 170n, 173, 175, 183-5, 188, 192n, 194n, 196-7, 199, 202-4, 208, 214, 216, 226, 262, 272
  History of Philosophy, 146
  Philosophy of History, 146, 149, 202-5, 212-14, 226, 262, 266
  Philosophy of Right, 143, 203, 219, 220n, 223, 224n, 225-8, 231-4, 236n, 238n, 239n, 240, 241n, 243-4, 250n, 254, 257, 258n, 260n, 262-3, 265-6, 272
  on the progress of spirit:
  in the *Phenomenology*, explained, 146-79, defects of 179-96, merits of 196-202
  in the *Philosophy of History*, 202-15
  as theory of the State, 216-68
  his metaphysics, 129-46, 185, 197, 244, 262, 271-2
  and the dialectic, 134-7, 141-2, 155, 188, 227, 229, 231, 235, 237, 249, 255

Hegel, G. W. F.—cont.
  and the concrete universal, 129-31, 136, 142-6, 177, 179
  and the categories, 134, 140-6
  on self-consciousness and self-knowledge, 135-9, 145-56, 160, 173-4, 179, 184-9, 195-8, 200, 217, 222, 236, 266, 313, 346
  on abstract right and morality, 227-41
  on ethical life, 227-8, 234-43, 265
  on the family and civil society, 227, 231-5, 240-50, 265, 266
  on the State, 227, 232, 234-5, 245-6, 250-68
  on experience and knowledge, 150-1
  on the need for recognition, 151-6, 158, 185-6, 188-9, 190-1, 198-9
  on master-slave relation, 153-60, 162-3, 188-92
  on Stoicism and Scepticism, 156-9, 162-3, 183, 187-8
  on individualism, 161-5, 212, 228, 243
  on the unhappy consciousness, 159-161, 183, 185-6, 204
  on the base and noble consciousness, 165-7
  his rationalism, 167-8, 186-7
  on revolution, 166, 168-9, 187, 192-5
  on the Moral Will, 169-71, 222, 239
  on the Satisfied Spirit, 171-3
  on religion, 148, 167, 173-9, 208-11, 334-5, 337, 343
  on natural religion, 174-5
  on aesthetic religion, 175-7
  on revealed religion, 177-8
  his own religion, 173-4, 178-9, 201
  on the process of change, 179-87, 215, 216-17, 222, 274
  on world history, 203-15, 222
  and world historical individuals, 205-7, 427-8
  on the German World, 207-9
  his dislike of democracy, 211-13
  his views on progress, 206-7, 213-15, 416, 419n, 421, 422n, 425, 427, 433-4
  on the will, 222-5, 235-7
  on rational will, 219-23, 237, 260
  on arbitrary will, 219-21
  on universal will, 168-70, 222-3, 237, 246, 251, 254, 258, 264, 267
  on general will, 168, 211
  objective will = state, 216
  on morality and freedom, 217-19, 221-2, 228-32, 235, 238, 240-1, 263-4
  on morality and rationality, 219-22,

Hegel, G. W. F.—cont.
  238-41, 243, 250, 321-2
  on law and rationality, 223-5
  on obligation, 225-7
  on classes, 246-8
  on ideology, 201-2
  on powers of government, 254-6
  on method of government, 256-9
  on international relations and war,
    260-1, 266-7
  his psychology, 38-41, 125, 131, 144,
    150, 166, 199, 213, 223, 225, 239,
    245
  and Marx's Ideal Society, 403-8
Hegel et l'Etat, by E. Weil, 263
Hierarchy, 49, 53-5, 63, 72, 128, 169,
  192-5, 352, 379-81
History of Philosophy, by Hegel, 146
History, ix, xi
  philosophy of, 42, 67, 74, 83-5, 202-
    215, 308
  world history, 148, 202-15
Historical Materialism, 272, 277
  and progress, 410, 422, 426-8, 431-3
  See also change
Hitler, Adolf, 80, 372
Hobbes, Thomas, ix, x, xi, xvii, 39-41,
  103, 153, 218, 256, 263
  and Bentham, 1, 4, 15-23
Hodgskin, Thomas, 58, 67-8, 96-103
  Labour Defended against the Claims
    of Capital, 97, 98n, 99n
Hook, Sidney, 274-8
  Towards an Understanding of Karl
    Marx, 274-5, 276n
Human nature, xvi-xxii, 40-1, 84, 86,
  103-4, 206, 246, 321-2, 333, 342-3,
  375, 404-6, 410, 418, 436, 438
  in Bentham, 5-7, 13-15, 28, 36
Hume, David, xvi, 1, 5, 15, 16, 35, 38, 57,
  133, 157, 171, 245, 404
Hundred Years War, 306
Hyppolite, Jean, 154, 166, 168, 169,
  192
  Genèse et Structure de la Phénoméno-
    logie de l'Esprit de Hegel, 154,
    166n, 168n, 169n

Idealism, xvi, 15, 140n, 220-1, 252
Ideals, 13, 14, 91-2, 143, 165, 284
Ideal society, 46
  of Marx, 402-8
  See Utopianism
Idea of Progress, by J. B. Bury, 415,
  417n, 431n

Idée Générale de la Révolution, by
  Proudhon, 52n
Ideology, xiv, xv, 201-2
  Marx on, 289, 290, 292, 323-50, 360-2
  and class interest, 325-33, 337-8, 345-9,
    360-1
  and moral concepts, 327-9, 344-6
  and science, 336-40
  notion of, assessed, 344-50
Illusion of the Epoch, by H. B. Acton,
  273, 279n
Imperialism, 395
Individualism, 161-5, 212
Individual and group interests, 311-13,
  315-17
Industrial society, 49-50, 57-8, 68, 72,
  74-7, 80, 114, 121
In Memoriam, by Tennyson, 163
Inquiry concerning the Distribution of
  Wealth, by Thompson, 99
Interests,
  class, 87-8, 122, 201, 289, 299, 301, 303-
    322, 354, 370-2
  individual and group, 311-13, 315-17
  objective, 316-18, 360
  reconciliation of, 311-15, 319, 354-9,
    362, 366-7, 369, 373, 387-8
  and ideology, 325-33, 337-8, 345-9,
    360-1
Introduction à la Lecture de Hegel, by
  A. Kojève, 154
Introduction to the Principles of Morals
  and Legislation, by Bentham, 4n
Ireland, 361
Italy, 207, 208, 341, 372, 414

Jacobinism, 64, 95, 381
Jews, 177, 204
Judaism, 177, 204
July Revolution, 94-5
De la Justice dans la Revolution et
  l'Eglise, by Proudhon, 43, 52
Justice, 2, 47, 52, 78, 86, 90, 101, 119,
  218, 244, 249, 311-13, 379, 387, 411

Kant, Immanuel, ix, 133, 170-1, 263, 412,
  417
Karl Marx's Interpretation of History,
  by M. Bober, 273
Kepler, J., 417
Keynes, J. M., 273
Knowledge, 150-1, 269-70, 291-2, 335-6,
  339
  self-, 135-9, 147-52, 173, 179, 186, 222,
    236, 266, 323, 344, 451

knowledge—*cont.*
  and happiness, 410-14, 416-17, 423,
    434-8, 443-57
  and virtue, 437-9, 446, 451
  and progress, 410-20, 423, 433-57
  See also Marx on ideology
Knox, T. M., 224
Kojève, A., 154, 156n, 158, 159, 173, 188,
  196
  Introduction à la Lecture de Hegel,
    154

*Labour Defended against the Claims of
  Capital*, by Thomas Hodgskin, 97,
  98n, 99n
Labour Rewarded, by Wm. Thompson,
  102
Labour Theory of Value, 97
Laissez-faire, 29-30
Language, 198
Law, ix, xi, 8, 16-20, 53, 56, 81, 90, 211-
  212, 222-3, 240, 243, 248-9, 254-5,
  351, 375
  and morality, 16-17
  and rationality, 4, 223-5
  natural, 4, 5, 16-17, 36
  positive, 16-17, 248-50
  international, 260-1
  as superstructure, 274, 277, 281, 283,
    286-90, 295
  and class, 288-9, 301-8, 346
Leibniz, G. W., 434
Legal system, 276, 280, 367-8
Lenin, N., 88, 396, 398
Leroux, P., 93-4
Letter to d'Alembert, by J.-J. Rousseau,
  457
Levellers, 37
Liberalism, 13, 33, 34, 73, 190, 211-12,
  227, 241, 257-9, 262, 264, 347, 456
Liberty, *see* Freedom
Lichtenberger, André
  *Le Socialisme et la Révolution Fran-
    çaise*, 87n
Locke, John, ix, 13-14, 17, 20-2, 35, 37,
  41, 263
Logic, by Hegel, 140-1
Louis XIV, 71
Louis Napoleon, 371-2
Luther, Martin, 69, 119, 149, 206, 209-10,
  216, 226, 262, 344

Mably, Abbé de, 60
McCulloch, 97n
Machiavelli, N., ix, x, xi, xiv, xvii,
  xxi, 128, 261, 267, 414

Maistre, Joseph de, 113
Malthus, T. R., 97n
Mandeville, Bernard, 57
Marriage, 61, 62
Marx, Karl, ix, x, xiv, xviii, xix
  Address to the Communist League,
    393, 394, 396, 399n
  Capital, 282, 290, 300, 388
  Class Struggles in France, 367
  Communist Manifesto with F. Engels,
    275n, 308, 357
  Critique of Political Economy, 42n,
    274, 290, 325
  *Eighteenth Brumaire of Louis Bona-
    parte*, 307, 367, 371
  German Ideology, with F. Engels,
    275n, 326, 327n, 330n, 360n
  Poverty of Philosophy, 275n, 300
  Political theory of, and Engels
    [Marxism]
  compared with early socialists, 37-45,
    54-5, 64, 67, 71, 74, 77, 81-94, 99,
    122, 125-8
  his and their views on history, 42-5,
    67, 71, 74, 81-4, 90, 125
  his attack on their Utopianism, 44-5,
    54-5, 85-94
  compared with Hegel, 42, 132, 156,
    191, 201, 215, 234, 247-50, 271-2,
    313, 331, 334-5, 337, 343, 346,
    403-8
  and the belief in progress, 419-34
  on the basis of social change, 273-93
  his theory of class, 293-322
  his theory of ideology, 289, 290, 292,
    323-50, 360-2
  on the functions and origin of the
    State, 351-73
  on the ultimate disappearance of the
    State, 364, 373-87, 403
  on backward and advanced countries,
    388-402
  on the ideal society, 402-8
  on foundation and superstructure,
    274-7, 281, 287-90, 292, 301, 323-5,
    345
  and the point of the distinction, 277-9,
    283-90
  no class divisions, 288, 293-4, 298-307
  on class inequality, 294-8, 358, 361,
    364, 377
  on class interests, 299-322, 354, 370-2
  on class conflicts, 298-307, 333, 350
  on class consciousness, 307-10, 338,
    349

Marx, Karl—*cont.*
  on objective class interests, 316-18, 360
  and their reconciliation, 311-15, 319, 354-9, 362, 366-9, 373, 387-8
  on class and ideology, 325-33, 337-8, 345-9, 360-1
  on social evolution, 301-5, 319-20, 336, 339, 388-93, 395, 398-9, 402
  on moral and legal concepts, 327-9, 344-6
  on false consciousness, 326-30, 331, 335, 339, 344
  on religion, 325, 327, 333-44, 346, 363
  on science and society, 270, 283, 290-3, 324, 327, 329-31, 336-40, 346
  on the State and class, 351-73
  the variety of his views on the State, 351-6
  on the Paris Commune, 381-6
  and Bolshevism, 397-402
  on production and its basic status, 274-80, 291, 319, 324, 326, 375
  on forces of production, 290-2, 326
  on modes of production, 278-9, 282-3, 300-2
  on relations of production, 274-6, 279-283, 290, 300-1
  on production and property, 278, 280-283, 287, 293-8, 300-1, 303, 306, 320, 352-3, 355-7, 364-6, 377
  on revolution, 302, 305-10, 318, 325, 348-50, 362, 388, 393-9, 408
  on bourgeois revolution, 393-4
  on proletarian revolution, 397-9
Karl Marx's Interpretation of History, by M. Bober, 273
Materialism, 269-71, 277, 323, 325, 344
  of early socialists, 56-61
  historical, 272, 277
  philosophical, 269-71
Metaphysics, 4, 5, 272, 291-2
  Hegelian, 129-46, 185, 197, 244, 262, 271-2
Methodism, 342, 363n
Mill, James, 1, 11, 14, 27-30, 33, 62-3, 97n
  Analysis of Human Mind, 11
  Elements of Political Economy, 97
  Essay on Government, 27, 62
Mill, John Stuart, 190
Monarchy, 24, 70-1, 82, 86, 248, 254, 263
  limited, 15
  absolute, 16, 22, 367
  French, 303-6, 367, 394

Montesquieu, xi, xiv, 15-21, 35, 61, 205, 259, 264
Morality, 40-1, 90, 103, 161-2, 170-1, 180, 277, 281, 285-90, 312, 315, 321-2, 327-8, 346, 375-7, 404-7
  Bentham's view of, 1-15
  and rationality in Hegel, 219-22, 238-241, 243, 250, 321-2
  and freedom in Hegel, 217-19, 221-2, 228-32, 235, 238, 240-1, 263-4
  and society, 47, 60, 63, 117, 146, 198-200, 216-17, 220-2, 232
Moral order, 78-80, 276, 301, 328
More, Sir Thomas, 60
Morelly, 60-1
  La Code de la Nature, 60
Mussolini, B., 372

Napoleon, 149, 173, 195-6, 208-9, 252, 261, 394, 431
Nationalism, 64, 111, 120-5, 208
National Equitable Labour Exchange, 89, 90
National Socialist Party, 372
Nature, law of, 4, 5, 36
Nature, human, xvi-xxii, 5-7, 13-15, 28, 36, 40-1, 84, 86, 103-4, 206, 246, 321-2, 333, 342-3, 375, 404-6, 410, 418, 436, 438
Nature, state of, 39-40, 421
Natural equality, 21-24
Natural rights, 13-14, 21-2, 36, 37
Necessity of change, 179-87, 215-17, 222, 419, 421, 430-1
Neveu de Rameau, Le, by Diderot, 166
New Harmony, 84, 88
Newton, Isaac, xiii, 114n, 417, 427-8, 434, 437, 441-2
New View of Society, A, by Robert Owen, 44n
Non-violence of early socialists, 93-5, 122-4, 127
Nouveau Christianisme, Le, by Saint-Simon, 111n, 116n, 117n, 118
Nouveau Monde Industriel, by Saint-Simon, 111n

Obligation, 2, 16-17, 21, 225-7, 281, 284, 286-7, 295-6, 302, 351, 353, 373
October Revolution, 401n
Oedipus, 238-9
Oeuvres de Saint-Simon et d'Enfantin, 71n, 72n, 73n, 78n
Opportunity, equality of, 119-20

Orbiston, 89
Organisateur, L', by Saint-Simon, 48, 68, 72
Origins of the Family, Private Property and the State, by F. Engels, 352, 357, 366
Owen, Robert, 41, 44-5, 50-1, 58, 60-1, 68, 84-94, 109-13
   A New View of Society, 44n
   Mr. Owen's Plan, 58, 84-5
   Report to the County of Lanark, 84
Oxford, 202

Paine, Thomas, 28
Palestine, 148
Paris Commune, 381-3, 397-8
Parliament, 20, 26, 28, 90, 303
   Long Parliament, 306
Parliamentary governments, 51, 72, 257, 382
Pascal, B., 24, 256, 344, 451n, 457
   Pensées, 24, 256
Passions, Fourier on, 103-6, 109
Pasteur, Louis, xiii
Paul, St., 41, 119
Peasants, 294, 296, 298-9, 302, 307, 362, 368, 395
Pensées, by Pascal, 24, 256
Perfectibility, 439-43
Perpetual Peace, by Abbé de St. Pierre, 122
Petite bourgeoisie, 64, 92, 126-7
Phalanxes (and Phalansteries), 50, 59, 62, 85, 103-10
Phenomenology of Spirit, by Hegel, 146-151, 154n, 156n, 158, 160, 166, 168n, 169, 170n, 173, 175, 183-5, 188, 192n, 194n, 196-7, 199, 202-4, 208, 214, 226, 262, 272
Philosophical Radicals, 25
Philosophy, 114-15, 117-18, 186-7
   practical, xv-xxii, 148, 185, 187
   of history, 42, 67, 74, 83-5, 202-15, 308
   and religion, 178-9
Philosophy of History, by Hegel, 146, 149, 202-5, 212-14, 226, 262, 266
Philosophy of Right, by Hegel, 143, 203, 219, 220n, 223, 224n, 225-8, 231-4, 236n, 238n, 239n, 240n, 241n, 243-4, 250n, 254n, 257, 258n, 260n, 262-3, 265-6, 272
Plamenatz, J. P.
   The English Utilitarians, 1
   German Marxism and Russian Communism, 279n, 280n, 288n

Plato, xvii, xxi, 23, 60, 92n, 170, 202, 219, 352, 412
Pleasure, 2-12, 32, 164, 187-8, 220, 245, 250
Political system, 274, 276, 288
Political theory, 130-1
   and political science, xii-xxi
Politique Positive, by Comte, 68n
Populists, (Narodniki), 396
Positivism, 78, 83, 114, 117, 437-8, 450
Poverty of Philosophy, by K. Marx, 275n, 300
Power, 23, 28, 128, 189, 196, 267-8, 410, 415, 434-5, 454-5
   Marx on, 295-7, 351, 356-7, 369
   supreme, 18-20
Preliminary Discourse on the Positive Spirit, by Comte, 437, 438n
Production, 310, 324, 326, 375
   basic status of, 274-80, 291
   forces of, 290-2, 326
   modes of, 278-9, 282-3, 300-2
   relations of, 274-6, 279-83, 290, 300-1
Progress, belief in
   of Bentham, 31, 34, 36, 39, 57
   of early socialists, 38, 41-5, 55n, 58, 62, 67, 83-5, 120-1
   not shared by Rousseau, 37-41, 56-9, 66, 404-7, 412, 414-17, 422-3, 434, 456-7
   before the age of science, 410-15
   and science, 415-22, 432-3, 437-45, 448-453, 456-7
   and the idea of a law of change, 418-426, 433
   and knowledge, 410-20, 433-57
   and happiness, 410-14, 416-17, 423, 434, 438, 443-57
   and determinism, 421-2, 425-8, 431
   and individual freedom, 410-14, 425-9, 439, 456
   and use of knowledge, 453-7
   Hegel on, 206-7, 213-15, 416, 419n, 421, 422n, 425, 427, 433-4
   material, 31, 34, 36
Proletariat, 45, 83-4, 91n, 92, 122, 126, 156, 293, 297-9, 304-5, 308-10, 314, 318, 332, 353, 369, 381, 392, 399
   proletarian government, 381-3
   proletarian revolution, 297-9
Property, 13, 23, 28, 81, 90, 162, 236
   Marx on, 278, 280-3, 287, 293-8, 300-1, 303, 306, 320, 352-3, 355-7, 364-6, 377

Protestantism, 70-1, 116, 304, 361
  and Catholicism, 203, 208-12
Proudhon, P.-J., 41, 43-5, 51-3, 57, 63-5,
  67, 84-5, 93-4, 102n, 111-13, 118,
  123-5, 383
  Idée Générale de la Revolution, 52n
  *De la Justice dans la Revolution et
    l'Eglise*, 43, 52
Prussia, 247-8, 257, 261, 263, 303
Psychology, 36, 40-1, 67, 321, 333-4
  and Fourier, 103-6
  and Hegel, 131, 144, 150, 166, 199,
    213, 223, 225, 239, 245
  and Condorcet, 445-50
Pufendorf, S., 16-17
Punishment, 2-3, 25-6, 171, 236-7, 244,
  352, 359

Queenswood, 84, 88

Racialism, 207-8
Rationality, 7, 41, 171, 222, 313, 324,
  346, 403, 406
  Hegel on its relation to morality, 219-
    222, 238-41, 243, 250, 321-2
  and law, 223-5
  of man, 157, 159, 164, 167, 186, 214,
    216-22, 227-8, 236, 242, 250
  of the world, 139, 142, 150-1, 186, 188,
    197, 213
Reality, 132-40, 142, 178, 185
Reason, 4, 14, 439-43
  and understanding, 440-1
Reform Bill of 1832, 94, 259
Religion, xiv, 433
  Hegel on, 148, 167, 173-9, 208-11, 334-
    335, 337, 343
  Marx on, xiv, 283, 325, 327, 333-44,
    346, 363
  early socialists on, 75, 110-20
Renaissance, 414
Report to the County of Lanark, by
  Robert Owen, 84
Revolution, 37-8, 66, 91-5
  French, 24, 49, 66, 71, 73, 81, 91, 111,
    119, 120, 166, 168, 169, 262, 264,
    303, 306, 310, 368, 393
  July, 94-5
  October, 401n
  1848, 85, 95
  bourgeois, 393-4
  proletarian, 397-9
  world, 397-8
  Hegel on, 168-9, 186-8, 192-5
  Marx on, 302, 305-10, 318, 325, 348-50,

Revolution—*cont.*
  362, 388, 393-5, 397, 399, 408
Ricardo, David, 86, 95
Rights, 1-7, 181, 228, 230, 236, 281, 284,
  295-6, 351
  natural, 13-14, 21-2, 36, 37
  of man, 1, 3, 21, 78, 128, 212, 333, 410,
    456
Robespierre, M., 166
Roman Empire, 162-3, 207-8, 300, 302,
  414
Romans, 181, 202, 204, 211, 214-15, 413-14,
  416
Romanticism, 164
Rome, 120-1, 303, 355-6, 411
Rousseau, Jean-Jacques, ix, xiv, xv, xvii,
  xix, xxi, 15, 35, 343, 376, 378
  Emile, 109
  *Discourse on the Origins of In-
    equality*, 422
  Letter to d'Alembert, 457
  Social Contract, 15, 48
  disbelief in progress, 37-41, 56-9, 66,
    404-7, 412, 414-17, 422-3, 434, 456-7
  and the early socialists, 37-41, 46n, 47-
    48, 53, 56-9, 66, 92n, 93, 108-9,
    122-5
  and Hegel, 166, 168, 199, 211-13, 219,
    244, 246, 258, 263
Rules of social life, 3, 5-10, 12, 17, 19,
  171, 239-40, 260-1, 283-8, 327-8, 345,
  347, 351, 353, 357-8, 365-6, 375-6,
  404
Ruling class, 327, 330, 349, 360-1, 370
Russia, 35, 77, 92, 248, 303-4, 317, 320,
  363, 369-70, 372, 377, 378n, 382, 385,
  388, 392, 395-9, 401-2

Saint-Simon,
  Le Nouveau Christianisme, 111n,
    116n, 117-18
  Le Nouveau Monde Industriel, 111n
  l'Organisateur, 48, 68, 72
  Du Système Industriel, 78
  Oeuvres de Saint-Simon et d'Enfantin,
    71n, 72n, 73n, 78n
  and Marx, 41-2, 45, 53, 67, 71, 74, 77,
    82-4, 86-8, 90, 92, 122, 125-6, 128,
    336, 338, 373
  his theory of change and progress, 42,
    67-86, 417-21, 427, 434, 453
  on the organization of society, 46n,
    47-50, 57, 60-2, 78-81, 102n
  on nationalism and war, 111, 120-4
  on religion, 111, 113-18

Saint-Simon—*cont.*
  his lack of realism, 85-8, 91
  his feminism, 62
  his non-violence, 93-4
Sanctions, 2-3, 17, 25, 286-7, 352
Scepticism, 157-9
Science,
  and morality, 113, 115-18
  and progress, 415-22, 432, 437-45, 448-
    453, 456-7
  and society, 270, 283, 290-3, 324, 327,
    329-31, 337-8, 340-6
Security, 99-101
Self, 144-5, 150, 152-4
  finite, 143, 146, 151, 172-3, 175, 177,
    179, 195, 213, 216-17, 223, 266,
    334
Self-consciousness and knowledge, 135-9,
  145-54, 184-6, 188-9, 195, 197-8, 200,
  284, 323, 334, 403, 451
Separation of powers, 15-20, 327
Shakespeare, 126, 262
Sismondi, 86, 104
*Sketch for an Historical Picture of the
  Human Mind*, by Condorcet, 336,
  417, 422, 438n, 442n, 443
Slavery, 293-4, 296, 300, 348, 353, 357,
  392
  master-slave relation, 153-63, 188-92
Slavs, 208-9
Smith, Adam, 56-7, 60, 86, 95
Social Contract, by Rousseau, 15, 48
Socialism, 249, 264, 396, 398-403
  and capitalism, 394-5
  in one country, 398-400, 403
Le Socialisme, by E. Durkheim, 102n,
  115n
*Le Socialisme et la Révolution Fran-
  çaise*, by A. Lichtenberger, 87n
Socialists, The early,
  English, 37, 44, 57, 67, 93, 118. *See
    also* Hodgskin, Owen, Thompson
  French, 37, 44, 57, 67, 93, 111, 118-20.
    See also Comte, Fourier, Proudhon,
    Saint-Simon
  and Rousseau, 37-41, 46n, 47-8, 53, 56-
    59, 66, 92n, 93, 108-9, 122, 125
  and Marx, 37-45, 54-5, 64, 67, 71, 74,
    77, 81-94, 99, 122, 125-8
  their interests, 37-66
  their theories of change, 41-5, 67-85,
    126
  their illusions, 83-93
  their attack on the classical econo-
    mists, 95-103

Socialists—*cont.*
  their views on the ideal society, 103-
    110
  on religion, 75, 110-20
  on nationalism, 111, 120-5
  on revolution, 37-8, 66, 91-5
  on equality, 37, 40-1, 46-7, 49, 53-9,
    61, 65, 73-4, 85, 90, 96, 99-101, 107,
    119-20, 125-8
  on fraternity, 118-20
  their hostility to the state, 45-55, 64,
    123-5
  their merits, 125-9
  their belief in non-violence, 93-5, 122-
    124, 127, 310
  their belief in freedom, 37, 47-8, 57-9,
    73-4, 90, 108, 119, 125, 127-8
  their belief in female emancipation,
    61-6
Social theories, 330-2, 346-7
Society,
  ideal, 103-10, 403-8
  phases of, 42-5, 68-9, 74-8, 81, 227,
    231-5, 240-50, 410, 418, 422
  man the 'victim' of, 38-41, 46. *See
    also* alienation
  and morality, 47, 60, 63, 117, 146,
    198, 216-17, 220-2, 232
Sociologie de Proudhon, La, by Bouglé,
  5in
Sociology (social science), x-xii, 87, 114,
  132, 217, 245, 272, 438, 454
  and political theory, xiii-xxi
Socrates, 149, 216, 226, 262, 412
Solon, 355
Sophocles, 162, 164, 239
Sovereignty, 1, 15-21, 23, 26, 254-6, 265
Spain, 207-8
Springs of Action, by Bentham, 2
Spirit, 74, 323, 433
  Hegel on, in *Phenomenology*, 149-202
  Hegel on, in *Philosophy of History*,
    202-15
  Hegel on, in *Philosophy of Right*, 216-
    268
Stace, W. T., 141
Stalin Constitution of 1936, 382-3
Stalinism, 401
State,
  and early socialists, 45-55, 64, 80-1,
    93, 123-5, 127-8
  theory of, in Hegel, 129-31, 162, 216-
    268
  as a form of ethical life, 227, 232, 234-
    235, 245-6, 250-68

State—*cont.*
  Marx on its functions and origins in
    class society, 351-73
  Marx on its disappearance, 364, 373-
    383, 403
  variety of Marx's views on, 351-6
  and Church, 210-11
Stoicism, 157-60, 412
Suffragettes, 65
Surplus value, 297, 319-20
Système Industriel, Du, by Saint-Simon,
    78

Tennyson, Alfred, *In Memoriam*, 163
Theology, 291-2
Théorie de l'Unité Universelle, by
    Fourier, 103n
Theory of Legislation, by Bentham, 8
Thompson, Wm., 50-1, 58, 62-3, 67-8, 84,
    93-4, 96, 99-103
  *Appeal of One Half of the Human
    Race, Women etc.,* 62
  *Inquiry Concerning the Distribution
    of Wealth,* 99
  Labour Rewarded, 102
Tocqueville, Alexis de, 59, 61, 95
Tolpuddle, 89
Tories, 259
Totalitarianism, 262, 264
Towards an Understanding of Marx, by
    S. Hook, 274, 275, 276n
Trades unions, 84, 89-90
Tristan, Flora, 65
Trotsky, L., 396
Turgot, A. R. J., de, 418-21
Tyranny, 22

Under-developed countries and Marx,
    388-402
Unitarians, 178

United States of America, 256, 310, 359,
    377, 378n, 382, 388
Utilitarians, xv, xvi, xxi, 1, 5n, 10-11, 14,
    22, 29, 31-4, 57-9, 61, 110, 125, 220-2,
    250-2, 266, 411-2
Utopianism, 44-5, 54-5, 60, 85-9, 92, 94,
    332

Vice and error, 433-7, 445-6, 448-9, 456
Vindication of the Rights of Women, by
    Mary Wollstonecraft, 65
Violence, hostility of early socialists to,
    93-5, 122-4, 127, 310
Virtue and knowledge, 437-9, 446, 451
Voltaire, F. M. de, 61, 66n, 262

War, 122-4, 261
  and government, 122-4
Weil, Eric,
  Hegel et l'Etat, 263
Whigs, 258-9, 264
Whitehead, A. N., xvii
Will, 222-5, 235-7
  general, 47, 168, 211, 258
  universal, 168-70, 222-3, 237, 246, 251,
    254, 258, 264, 267
  arbitrary, 219-21
  objective = the State, 216
  rational, 219-23, 237, 260
  holy, 171
Wollstonecraft, Mary,
  Vindication of the Rights of Women,
    65
World revolution, 397-8

Yorktown, 310

Zeno (the Stoic), 148-9